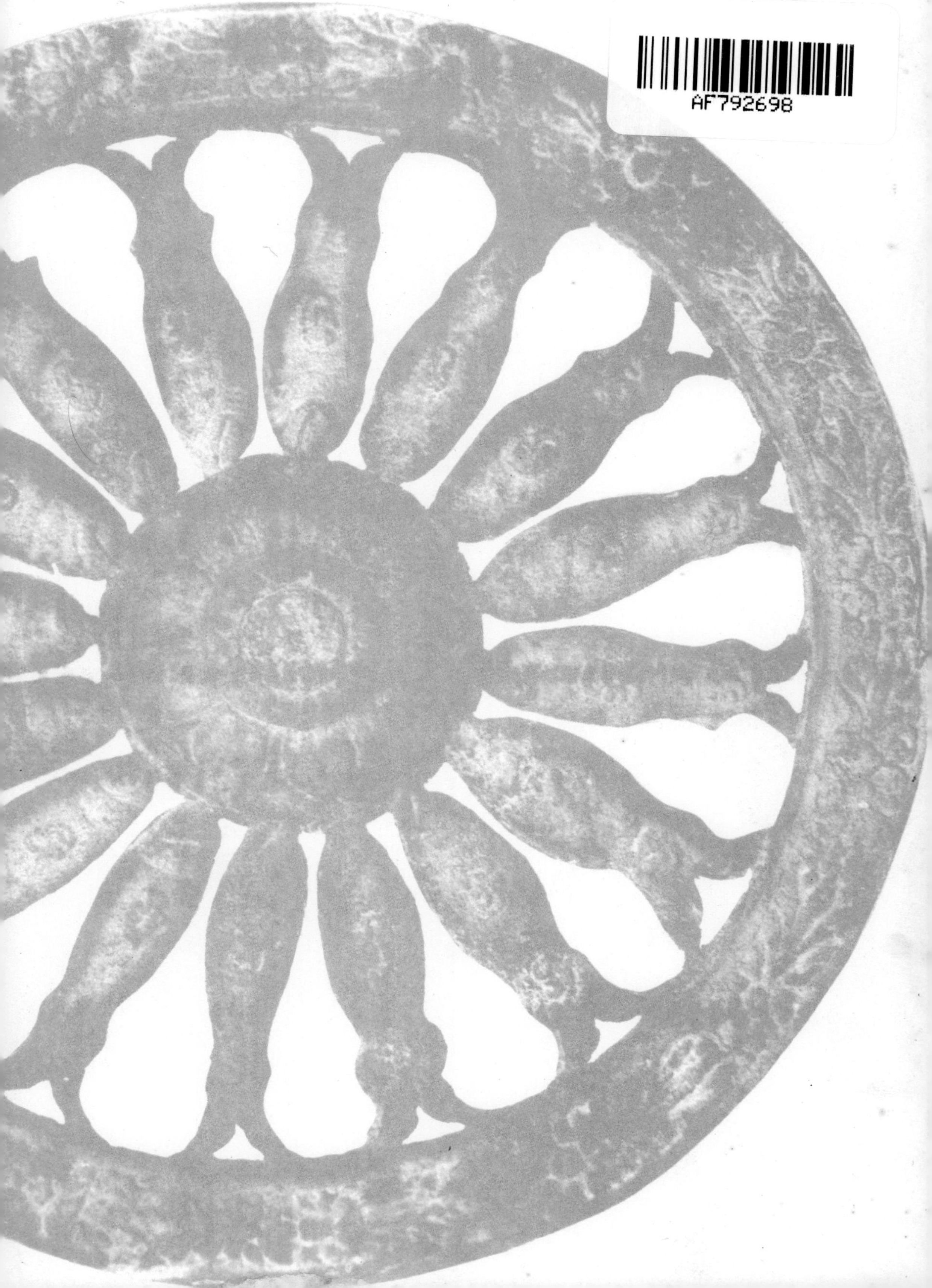

कलातत्त्वकोश
KALĀTATTVAKOŚA

कलातत्त्वकोश

KALĀTATTVAKOŚA

A LEXICON
OF FUNDAMENTAL CONCEPTS
OF THE INDIAN ARTS

कलातत्त्वकोश खण्ड - ५

KALĀTATTVAKOŚA VOL. – V

FORM/SHAPE
ĀKĀRA/ĀKṚTI

KALĀTATTVAKOŚA
VOLUME – V

Editor
Ramesh Chandra Sharma

Associate Editors
Advaitavadini Kaul
Sukumar Chattopadhyay
Narasingha Charan Panda
Pranati Ghosal

INDIRA GANDHI NATIONAL CENTRE FOR THE ARTS
NEW DELHI
and
MOTILAL BANARSIDASS PUBLISHERS PVT. LTD.
DELHI

First Published 2002

Published by
INDIRA GANDHI NATIONAL CENTRE FOR THE ARTS
Central Vista, Janpath, New Delhi - 110001

in association with
MOTILAL BANARSIDASS PUBLISHERS PVT. LTD.
Bungalow Road, Jawahar Nagar, Delhi - 110007

ISBN: 81-208-1917-9 (Vol. V)
ISBN: 81-208-1045-7 (Set)
Price: Rs. 1000/-

Typeset by
The Indira Gandhi National Centre for the Arts,
Varanasi Office: B-1/3, E-7, Lane No. 2,
Ravindrapuri Extension, Varanasi- 221005.

Printed in India
at Shri Jainendra Press
A-45, Naraina Industrial Area Phase-I,
New Delhi-110028

CONTENTS

INTRODUCTION

यां ज्ञात्वा सकलमपास्य कर्मबन्धं
तद्विष्णोः परमपदं प्रयाति लोकः ।
तामेतां त्रिजगति जन्तुजीवभूतां
हृल्लेखां जपत च नित्यमर्चयीत ॥

PrapañcasāraTantra IV.76

The sacred syllable *hṛllekhā*, very essence of all beings of three worlds should always be muttered and worshipped; knowing whom all the enticing fetters of deeds are removed and entire Universe attains Supreme abode of Viṣṇu.

I. General Background

Indian tradition both in theory (*śāstra*) and practice (*prayoga*) evolves from the vision of 'Absolute Reality' that governs the whole universe at all levels and states of existence. The Vedas are revelations from a heightened state of consciousness. Upaniṣads, Brāhmaṇas and Purāṇas unravel the mysteries of the phenomena at various levels of perception. Various systems of thought, including the Buddhist and Jaina emerge. So do the disciplines – Āyurveda, Astronomy, metaphysics, philosophy and the arts. Fundamental conceptions of the cosmos, space, time, body, mind, and self pervade almost all theories and disciplines making each of them interrelated and interdependent just like a *sūtra* (thread) that holds (invisibly) all beads together.

In this framework the wide range of Indian art-forms can never be understood in isolation. For a fuller comprehension of the system of interrelatedness and interpenetration IGNCA identified approximately 250 important terms representing fundamental concepts occurring in various schools and disciplines. This was done after considerable research and deliberations with the scholars. By selecting the groups of terms under particular categories and thereby concentrating upon each category in each volume of the **Kalātattvakośa** while focussing upon their occurrence and significance in the arts, has endeavoured to evolve an important modern device to grasp the essential thought and knowledge system of the Indian tradition.

The criteria of selecting the terms and their grouping in the previous four volumes has been elaborately discussed by the editors of those volumes. The main purpose of the **Kalātattvakośa** is to concentrate on textual traditions principally drawn from Sanskrit, Pali and Prakrit sources. An indepth investigation into the primary sources will and has hopefully already facilitated the reader to learn about the interlocking of different disciplines. The groupings in the first four volumes relate to:

a. pervasive and perennial terms (*vyāpti*);

b. terms relating to notions of space and time (*deśa* and *kāla*);

c. the primal elements (*mahābhūtas*);

d. manifestation of nature (*sṛṣṭivistāra*).

The present volume deals with another cluster – grouped together as: **Form/Shape** – *Ākāra/Ākṛti.* Volume VI will be devoted to symbols. Subsequently another subsidiary series on the subsidiary technical terms specific to the arts will be envisaged.

II. Method and Use

The system followed here in the method and use corresponds almost completely with that introduced in the previous volumes. The same is given as under:

1. The list of terms has been organised thematically by concepts. Groups of related terms are assembled in each volume, and the logic of their arrangement is explained in the introduction. Alphabetical reference is facilitated by the **List of Terms** which gives the complete list of entries for the whole series, mentioning the volume in which an article has already appeared. The **Index** directs the reader to the occurrence of the terms throughout, and also refers him to other significant terms in Sanskrit and English. **Arrow** → refers to an entry, in the same or another volume, where the term in question is treated more extensively.

2. Within a desirable flexibility of structure, the content of an entry generally follows this sequence as under:

Overview
Etymology and Related Terms
Layers of Meaning
Development of the Concept
Manifestation in the Arts
Classification
Process
Conclusion

Quick identification of a section which may interest the reader specifically is thus facilitated.

In some cases where a concept has a distinct meaning in different fields, an article has been divided into two or three parts assigned to different authors.

3. All Sanskrit, Pali and Prakrit quotations are given in Devanāgarī with a full English translation; Sanskrit words or phrases occurring in the running text are transliterated and accompanied by a translation at least once. This is designed to provide access for those having limited knowledge of Sanskrit, and for non-readers of the Devanāgarī script.

4. Text references are abbreviated; full titles appear only in the running text of the entry (in bold face). The **List of Abbreviations** provides the full titles, and the **General Bibliography** notes the text editions and translations used.

5. A **Select Bibliography** is appended to each article; this contains references to secondary literature to which the author refers. These references are not exhaustive but are relevant to tracing further information about the concept.

6. The etymologies, whether traditional or based on modern linguistics, represent the opinion of the author; they have sometimes been edited, and in cases of doubt or difference of opinion the reader is referred to Manfred Mayrhofer, *Etymologisches Wörterbuch des Altindoarishchen*, Heidelberg (Carl Winter) 1986ff.

7. All translations are acknowledged, whether published (see **Bibliography**) or unpublished. If a translator's name is not given, the text has been translated by the author. Where the author has amended a previous translation, this is indicated.

8. The series is illustrated with a minimum number of essential line-drawings of fundamental diagrams, *yantras*. Full photographic illustration of art-historical developments and variations falls outside the purview of these volumes.

III. Concepts of Form/Shape

The present volume is the fifth manifestation of the *vicārāgni* (fire of thoughts) kindled by the earlier seers and continued by later thinkers. This is what has been observed by the Vedic *ṛṣi*: *agniḥ pūrvebhiḥ ṛṣibhirīḍyo nūtanairuta* (ṚV I.1.2).

The earlier four volumes dealt with several terms under the ambits of pervasive terms (*vyāpti*), space and time (*deśa-kāla*), primal elements (*mahābhūta*) and manifestation of nature (*sṛṣṭi-vistāra*).

This volume highlights a number of visual art forms under main heading *Ākāra/Ākṛti*. The form or shape remains the basic element despite its multiple representations and their explanations. The things are recognised by shape and when form is invisible those have to be felt by hint, indication, touch or mind. When a simple line is drawn it takes some shape. Even a line (*rekhā*) is the result of the continuity of a number of dots although this process is some times visible and sometimes invisible. These two aspects, i.e. *rekhā* and *ākāra* give birth to countless forms one after the other: *rūpaṃ rūpaṃ pratirūpo babhūva* (ṚV VI.47.18).

The creation of shapes goes on and we see them as full or in parts. Though, the term *sakala* means entire or having parts and *niṣkala* without parts, they connote the same concept but their usage in different situations offers variety of interpretations.

The form (*ākāra*) becomes more distinct when it is transformed into *arcā, vigraha, mūrti* and *pratimā*. The concept of *ākāra* is also suggested in *bandha-prabandha* compositional form, as without the act of binding no form is possible. The aspect finds much more elaboration when it projects a building or a temple (*prāsāda*). It is, however, interesting to note that our literature and canonical texts unfold multiple layers of meaning of these terms. Much depends on the context and circumstances in which a word has been used. The spirit and message change as per mundane, supermundane, metaphysical, artistic, architectural and musical rendering of the term. As discussed and interpreted by the subject experts of this volume, the study reveals a vast and interesting scope for further studies in the subject.

Acknowledgements

We are greatly indebted to Dr. Kapila Vatsyayan, former Academic Director, IGNCA for planning, supervising and guiding in the preparation of this volume at different stages. Sri M.C. Joshi, ex-Member Secretary also offered useful suggestions from time to time. Prof. N.R. Shetty, present Member Secretary took keen interest and repeatedly reminded for expeditious completion of the volume. Padmabhushan Prof. Vidya Nivasji Misra, Member, Board of Trust and Honorary Adviser, Varanasi Branch, IGNCA was readily available for guidance. Dr. Advaitavadini Kaul, Editor at the Head Quarter in New Delhi was closely associated with the work and its periodical progress.

Sincere thanks are due to all the learned contributors to this volume on *Ākāra/Ākṛti*. Prof. P.K. Agrawala deserves special mention for writing four articles on different aspects, late Prof. Prem Lata Sharma for supplying the materials on music part of *rekhā*, Jñāna Pravāha and Bharat Kalā Bhavan,

B.H.U. for supplying the material of illustrations. The associates in the Varanasi branch particularly, Dr. Sukumar Chattopadhyay, Dr. Narasingha Charan Panda and Dr. Pranati Ghosal laboured hard in going through the text and helping me in various stages of editing and preparing index, etc. Similarly, Sri Gautam Kumar Chatterjee remained busy throughout in carrying out our instructions and feeding them into the computer repeatedly.

Since this volume mainly deals with the terms on visual arts, we recollect a verse from the **Stavacintāmaṇi**(9) (also quoted by Prof. V.N. Misra in his article on *sakala-niṣkala*) on the completion of the work:

निरूपादान सम्भारमभित्तावेव तन्वते ।
जगच्चित्रं नमस्तस्मै कलाश्लाघ्याय शूलिने ॥

We pay our respects to the trident bearer Śiva who excellently paints the Universe even without using canvas, colour box and brush.

Ramesh Chandra Sharma

October, 2001

ABBREVIATIONS

General principles in forming abbreviations, concerning the last part of the title:

Ā	Āgama
Ār	Āraṇyaka
Bh	Bhāṣya
Br	Brāhmaṇa
Ca	Carita
Dh	Dharma (e.g. DhŚ Dharmaśāstra)
G	Gītā
H	Hṛdaya
Ins	Inscription
Kā	Kārikā
K	Kathā
Ko	Kośa
L	Lakṣaṇa
Ms	Manuscript
Nik	Nikāya
P	Paddhati
Pari	Pariśiṣṭa
Prad	Pradīpikā
Pr	Prakaraṇa
Prak	Prakāśa
Prāt	Prātiśākhya
Pur	Purāṇa
R	Ratnākara
Sam	Saṃhitā
Samu	Samuccaya
Saṅg	Saṅgraha
Sā	Sāra
Ś	Śāstra
Śa	Śataka
Sm	Smṛti
Sū	Sūtra
T	Tantra
Ṭī	Ṭīkā
Up	Upaniṣad

Vā	Vārttika
V	Veda
Vim	Vimarśinī
Vi	Vivaraṇa
Vṛ	Vṛtti
Y	Yāmala

Sections of Agamic Texts:

cp	caryāpāda
jk	jñānakhaṇḍa
kp	kriyāpāda
vp	vidyāpāda
yp	yogapāda

Sections of Ayurvedic Texts:

CiSthā	Cikitsā Sthāna
ISthā	Indriya Sthāna
KaSthā	Kalpa Sthāna
NiSthā	Nidāna Sthāna
ŚāSthā	Śārīra Sthāna
SiSthā	Siddhi Sthāna
SūSthā	Sūtra Sthāna
UtT	Uttara Tantra
ViSthā	Vimāna Sthāna

List of commentators/commentaries:

Kṣ	Kṣīrasvāmin
Rāmā	Rāmāśramī

Major Texts

AbhidhKo	Abhidharma Kośa
AbhidhSamu	Abhidharma Samuccaya
AbhŚāk	Abhijñānaśākuntala
Abhil	Abhilaṣitārtha-Cintāmaṇi (also Mānasollāsa of Someśvara)
AbhiBhā	Abhinava Bhāratī
AbhDar	Abhinaya Darpaṇa
Abhis	Abhisamayālaṅkāra

AbhNāṭ	Abhiṣeka Nāṭaka
ĀcD	Ācāra Dinakara
AdhSū	Adhyayana-Sūtra
AghŚP	Aghoraśivācārya Paddhati
AgPur	Agni Purāṇa
AhSam	Ahirbudhnya Saṃhitā
AitĀr	Aitareya Āraṇyaka
AitBr	Aitareya Brāhmaṇa
AitUp	Aitareya Upaniṣad
AjKo	Ajaya Kośa
AjitĀ	Ajitāgama
ĀlP	Ālāpa Paddhati
AmKo	Amara Kośa
Amṛto	Amṛtodaya (Gokulanātha)
AneSaṅg	Anekārtha Saṅgraha
AṅgNik	Aṅguttara Nikāya
AniSam	Aniruddha Saṃhitā
AnnaUp	Annapūrṇopaniṣad
AparPṛ	Aparājita Pṛcchā
ĀpDhSū	Āpastamba Dharma-Sūtra
ĀpGṛhSū	Āpastamba Gṛhya-Sūtra
ĀpŚrSū	Āpastamba Śrauta-Sūtra
ĀpŚulSū	Āpastamba Śulba-Sūtra
ArthŚ	Artha-Śāstra
ArthViSū	Arthaviniścaya-Sūtra
ArthaViSūNib	Arthaviniścayasūtranibandhana (Vīryaśrīdatta)
Ārya	Āryabhaṭīya
ĀryaMŚ	Āryamañjuśrīnāmasaṅgīti (with Amṛtakaṇikānāma... comm.)
ĀśCū	Āścaryacūḍāmaṇi (Śaktibhadra)
AṣṭH	Aṣṭāṅga-Hṛdaya (Vāgbhaṭa-I)
AṣṭSaṅg	Aṣṭāṅga-Saṅgraha (Vāgbhaṭa-II)
AṣṭPrPār	Aṣṭasāhasrikā Prajñā Pāramitā
ĀśvaGṛhSū	Āśvalāyana Gṛhya-Sūtra
ĀśvaŚrSū	Āśvalāyana Śrauta-Sūtra
AV	Atharvaveda (Śaunaka)
AV(P)	Atharvaveda (Paippalāda)
AVPari	Atharvaveda Pariśiṣṭa
AtSam	Atri Saṃhitā
Aṭṭh	Aṭṭhasālinī (on Dhammasaṅgaṇi)
Aucitya	Aucityavicāracarcā (Kṣemendra)
AvaŚa	Avadānaśataka
AvK	Avantisundarī Kathā

ĀNi	Āvassaya Nijjuti (Āvaśyaka Niryukti)
Avim	Avimāraka
BālCa	Bālacarita
BDhSū	Baudhāyana Dharma-Sūtra
BGṛhSū	Baudhāyana Gṛhya-Sūtra
BŚrSū	Baudhāyana Śrauta-Sūtra
BŚulSū	Baudhāyana Śulba-Sūtra
BhG	Bhagavad-Gītā
BhGŚBh	Bhagavad-Gītā Śaṅkara Bhāṣya
BhāgPur	Bhāgavata Purāṇa
BhSi	Bhaktirasāmṛtasindhu (Rūpa Gosvāmin)
BhRas	Bhaktirasāyana (Madhusūdana Sarasvatī)
BhārGṛhSū	Bhāradvāja Gṛhya-Sūtra
BhārSam	Bhāradvāja Saṃhitā
BhārŚrSū	Bhāradvāja Śrauta-Sūtra
BhaBh	Bharata Bhāṣya (Nānyadeva)
BhāCam	Bhārata Campū
BhāT	Bhārgava Tantra
BhāPari	Bhāṣāpariccheda
BhPrak	Bhāva Prakāśana (Śāradātanaya)
BhṛSam	Bhṛgu Saṃhitā
BhuPr	Bhuvana Pradīpa
BoPā	Bodha Pāhuḍa
BoCar	Bodhicaryāvatāra
BoBhū	Bodhisattvabhūmi
BraPur	Brahmāṇḍa Purāṇa
BrPur	Brahma Purāṇa
BrSū	Brahma-Sūtra
BrSūŚBh	Brahma-Sūtra Śaṅkara Bhāṣya
BṛUp	Bṛhadāraṇyaka Upaniṣad
BṛD	Bṛhaddeśī (Mataṅga)
BṛDev	Bṛhaddevatā (Śaunaka)
BṛJā	Bṛhat Jātaka
BṛSaṅg	Bṛhatkathāśloka Saṅgraha
BṛSam	Bṛhat Saṃhitā (Varāhamihira)
BudCa	Buddhacarita
CaRām	Campū Rāmāyaṇa
CāVyā	Cāndra Vyākaraṇa
CarSam	Caraka Saṃhitā
Cāru	Cārudatta
ChāgUp	Chāgaleya Upaniṣad
ChaSū	Chandaḥ-Sūtra

ChUp	Chāndogya Upaniṣad
Chan	Chandomañjarī
CiL	Citra-Łakṣaṇa
Cit	Citsukhī
DakMūSt	Dakṣiṇāmūrtistotra
DaPā	Darśana Pāhuḍa
DBhūSū	Daśabhūmika-Sūtra
DUVṛ	Daśapādī Uṇādi Vṛtti
DaRū	Daśarūpaka
DaSū	Daśavaikālika-Sūtra
Datti	Dattilam (Dattila)
DBhāgPur	Devī Bhāgavata Purāṇa
DPur	Devī Purāṇa
DhPad	Dhammapada
DhSaṅ	Dhammasaṅgaṇi
Dhav	Dhavalā (comm. on ṢaṭĀ) (Vīrasenācārya)
Dhū	Dhūrtaviṭasaṃvāda
DhvĀl	Dhvanyāloka
DhvĀlLoc	Dhvanyāloka-Locana (Abhinavagupta)
DīghNik	Dīgha Nikāya
DīĀ	Dīptāgama
Divyāv	Divyāvadāna
DSaṅg	Dravyasaṅgraha (Nemicandra)
DSaṅgVṛ	Dravyasaṅgraha Vṛtti (Brahma Deva)
DuSapta	Durgā Saptaśatī
Dūta	Dūtaghaṭotkaca
Dūt	Dūtavākya
EpInd	Epigraphica Indica
GāSa	Gāhā Sattasai (Gāthā Saptaśatī)
Gaṇar	Gaṇaratnamahodadhi
GanT	Gandharva Tantra
GarbhUp	Garbhopaniṣad
GarPur	Garuḍa Purāṇa
GauDhSū	Gautama Dharma-Sūtra
GGṛhSū	Gobhila Gṛhya-Sūtra
GomJīv	Gommaṭasāra Jīvakāṇḍa (Nemicandra)
GoBr	Gopatha Brāhmaṇa
GuhyaT	Guhyasamāja Tantra (with Guhyasamāja-Pradīpa ... comm.)
HaiKo	Haima Kośa
HBVil	Haribhaktivilāsa
HarPur	Harivaṃśa Purāṇa
HaCa	Harṣacarita

HyPrad	Haṭhayoga Pradīpikā
HayaPāñc	Hayaśīrṣa Pāñcarātra
HT	Hevajra Tantra
Hit	Hitopadeśa
ĪśGP	Īśānaśivagurudeva Paddhati
ĪśUp	Īśa Upaniṣad
ĪPraKā	Īśvara Pratyabhijñā-Kārikā (Utpaladeva)
ĪPraVim	Īśvara Pratyabhijñā Vimarśinī (Abhinavagupta)
ĪPraVivVim	Īśvara Pratyabhijñā Vivṛti Vimarśinī
ĪśSam	Īśvara Saṃhitā
JaimBr	Jaiminīya Brāhmaṇa
JaimUpBr	Jaiminīya Upaniṣad Brāhmaṇa
Jā	Jātaka
Jāmā	Jātakamālā
JāUp	Jāvālopaniṣad
JaySam	Jayākhya Saṃhitā
JinSam	Jina Saṃhitā
JīvPradṬī	Jīvatattvapradīpikā Ṭīkā (on GomJīv)
Jñān	Jñānārṇava (Śubhacandra)
Kād	Kādambarī
KāCaT	Kālacakra Tantra
KāPur	Kālikā Purāṇa
KāmKVil	Kāma Kalā Vilāsa
KāNīSā	Kāmandakīya Nīti Sāra
KāmSū	Kāma-Sūtra
KāmĀ	Kāmikāgama
KāVṛ	Kāśikā Vṛtti
KāśSam	Kāśyapa Saṃhitā
KāśŚi	Kāśyapa Śilpa
KāVyā	Kātantra Vyākaraṇa
KāṭhSam	Kāṭhaka Saṃhitā
KaṭhUp	Kaṭha Upaniṣad
KātBhāSū	Kātyāyana Bhāṣika-Sūtra
KātŚrSū	Kātyāyana Śrauta-Sūtra
KātŚrSūBh	Kātyāyana Śrauta-Sūtra Bhāṣya (Karka Bhāṣya)
KātŚulSū	Kātyāyana Śulba-Sūtra
KauśSū	Kauśika-Sūtra
KauṣUp	Kauṣītaki Upaniṣad
Kāvyād	Kāvyādarśa
Kāvyāl	Kāvyālaṅkāra (Bhāmaha)
KāvyālSū	Kāvyālaṅkāra-Sūtra (Vāmana)
KāMīm	Kāvya-Mīmāṃsā

KāPrak	Kāvya Prakāśa
KeUp	Kena Upaniṣad
KhGṛhSū	Khādira Gṛhya-Sūtra
KhudNik	Khuddaka Nikāya
Kir	Kirātārjunīya
Kod	Kodaṇḍamaṇḍana
KulT	Kulārṇava Tantra
Kum	Kumārasambhava
KūrPur	Kūrma Purāṇa
Kuva	Kuvalayānanda
LYVās	Laghu Yoga-Vāsiṣṭha (Abhinanda)
LT	Lakṣmī Tantra
Lalitā	Lalitā-Sahasranāma (with Bhāṣya)
LVi	Lalitavistara
LaSū	Laṅkāvatāra-Sūtra
Līlā	Līlāvatī (Bhāskarācārya)
LPur	Liṅga Purāṇa
Lok	Lokavibhāga
MāDhā	Mādhavīyā Dhātuvṛtti
MVy	Madhyamavyāyoga
MāKā	Mādhyamaka-Kārikā
MBh	Mahābhārata
Mahābh	Mahābhāṣya
MNUp	Mahānārāyaṇa Upaniṣad
MNPrak	Mahānaya Prakāśa
MNT	Mahānirvāṇa Tantra
MPur	Mahā Purāṇa
MaMa	Mahārtha Mañjarī
MSSaṅg	Mahāsubhāṣita Saṅgraha (Ed. L. Sternbach)
MVas	Mahāvastu
MaCa	Mahāvīracarita
Mahāv	Mahāvyutpatti
MSūAl	Mahāyāna Sūtrālaṅkāra
MaVim	Mahāyānaviṃśaka
MahāUp	Mahopaniṣad
MaitSam	Maitrāyaṇī Saṃhitā
MaitUp	Maitrāyaṇī Upaniṣad (Maitrī Upaniṣad)
MajNik	Majjhima Nikāya
MālMā	Mālatīmādhava
Māla	Mālavikāgnimitra
MVT	Mālinīvijayottara Tantra
MāMey	Mānameyodaya

MāSā	Mānasāra
MānŚrSū	Mānava Śrauta-Sūtra
MānŚulSū	Mānava Śulba-Sūtra
MāṇḍKā	Māṇḍūkya-Kārikā
MāṇḍUp	Māṇḍūkya Upaniṣad
MMK	Mañjuśrīmūlakalpa
Manu	Manu Smṛti
MarSam	Marīci Saṃhitā (Vaikhānasa Āgama)
MārkPur	Mārkaṇḍeya Purāṇa
MPĀ	Mataṅgapārameśvara Āgama
MatPur	Matsya Purāṇa
Mayam	Mayamata
MedKo	Medinī Kośa
Megh	Meghadūta
MilPañ	Milinda Pañha
MīmNyPrak	Mīmāṃsānyāya Prakāśa (Āpodeva)
MīmSū	Mīmāṃsā-Sūtra (with Śābara Bhāṣya)
MKā	Mokṣa-Kārikā
Mṛcch	Mṛcchakaṭika
MṛgĀ	Mṛgendra Āgama
Mudrā	Mudrārākṣasa
MuktUp	Muktikopaniṣad
Mūl	Mūlācāra (Ācārya Vaṭṭakera)
MūMāKā	Mūla Mādhyamaka-Kārikā
MuṇḍUp	Muṇḍaka Upaniṣad
NādaKā	Nāda-Kārikā (Bhaṭṭa Rāmakaṇṭha)
Nāgā	Nāgānanda
NaiCa	Naiṣadhīyacarita
NāMa	Nānārtha Mañjarī
Ṇāsā	Ṇāṇasāra (Jñānasāra) (Padmasingh Munirāja)
NārBhSū	Nārada Bhakti-Sūtra
NārPur	Nārada Purāṇa
NārSam	Nārada Saṃhitā
NārŚik	Nāradīya Śikṣā
NārŚiŚ	Nārada Śilpa-Śāstra
NN	Nartana Nirṇaya
NLRKo	Nāṭakalakṣaṇaratna Kośa (Sāgaranandin)
NŚ	Nāṭya-Śāstra
Nay	Nayacakra (Mailladhavala)
NT	Netra Tantra
Nigh	Nighaṇṭu
Nir	Nirukta (Yāska)

NīŚa	Nītiśataka
NiṢo	Nityaṣoḍaśikārṇava
NiSā	Niyamasāra (Kundakundācārya)
NṛpūUp	Nṛsiṃhapūrvatāpanīyopaniṣad
NṛKo	Nṛtyaratna Kośa
NṛtRat	Nṛttaratnāvalī (Jayasenāpati)
NyDīp	Nyāyadīpikā (Dharma Bhūṣaṇa)
NyKu	Nyāyakusumāñjali
Nyā	Nyāyamañjarī
NySū	Nyāya-Sūtra
NySūBh	Nyāya-Sūtra Bhāṣya
Pādtāḍ	Pādatāḍitaka
PadMa	Padmānanda Mahākāvya
PPrā	Padma Prābhṛtaka
PPur	Padma Purāṇa
PSam	Pādma Saṃhitā (Pāñcarātra School)
Pañcad	Pañcadaśī
Pañ (P)	Pañcādhyāyī (Pūrvārdha) (Rājamalla)
Pañ (U)	Pañcādhyāyī (Uttarārdha) (Rājamalla)
Pañca	Pañcarātra
PkāSā	Pañcāstikāya Sāra (Kundakundācārya)
Pañc	Pañcatantra
Pā	Pāṇini Aṣṭādhyāyī
PāDhā	Pāṇinīya Dhātupāṭha
PāŚik	Pāṇinīya Śikṣā
PPraṬī	Parama Prakāśa Ṭīkā
ParSā	Paramārthasāra
PPra	Paramātma Prakāśa (Yogīndu Deva)
ParSam	Parameśvara Saṃhitā
PāSū	Pārānanda-Sūtra
PārāŚik	Pārāśara Śikṣā
PārGṛhSū	Pāraskara Gṛhya-Sūtra
PTrī	Parātrīśikā (Tantra)
Paribh	Paribhāṣenduśekhara
PāśuSū	Pāśupata-Sūtra
PauṣSam	Pauṣkara Saṃhitā
PSā	Pavayaṇasāra (Pravacanasāra) (Kundakundācārya)
PiṅgUp	Piṅgalopaniṣad
PraCan	Prabodhacandrodaya
PraPañ	Prakaraṇapañcikā
PramMīm	Pramāṇamīmāṃsā (Hemacandrācārya)
PraRat	Prameya Ratnāvalī (Baladeva Vidyābhūṣaṇa)

PSāT	Prapañcasāra Tantra
PP	Prasannapadā
PrSam	Praśna Saṃhitā
PraUp	Praśna Upaniṣad
PrR	Prasthāna-Ratnākara
PraYau	Pratijñā Yaugandharāyaṇa
PraNāṭ	Pratimā Nāṭaka
PLSSamu	Pratiṣṭhālakṣaṇa-sāra-samuccaya
Prati	Pratiṣṭhātilaka (Nemicandra)
PrH	Pratyabhijñā-Hṛdaya
PravBh	Pravacana Bhāṣya (on SāṃSū) (Vijñānabhikṣu)
PraBr	Pravargya Brāhmaṇa
Pri	Priyadarśikā
Pug	Puggalapaññatti
Rāga	Rāgavibodha (Somanātha)
Ragh	Raghuvaṃśa
RājTar	Rājataraṅgiṇī
RāVā	Rājavārtika (Bhaṭṭa Akalaṅkadeva)
RāmPUp	Rāmapūrvottaratāpinī Upaniṣad
Rām	Rāmāyaṇa
RāmCam	Rāmāyaṇa Campū
RāmUttUp	Rāmottaratāpinī Upaniṣad
RasGa	Rasagaṅgādhara (Jagannātha)
RP	Ratna Parīkṣā (Īśvara Dīkṣit)
RaPa	Ratnatraya-Parīkṣā
Rat	Ratnāvalī
RauĀ	Raurava Āgama
RauUtĀ	Rauravattara Āgama
Rāya	Rāyapasenīya-Sutta
ṚV	Ṛgveda
ṚVPrāt	Ṛgveda Prātiśākhya
Ṛtu	Ṛtusaṃhāra
Rūp	Rūpamaṇḍana (Maṇḍana)
ŚaKal	Śabdakalpadruma
ŚaRa	Śabdaratnāvalī
SaddhPuSū	Saddharma Puṇḍarīka-Sūtra
ṢaḍBr	Ṣaḍviṃśa Brāhmaṇa
SāDar	Sāhitya-Darpaṇa
ŚĀPM	Śaivāgama Paribhāṣāmañjarī
ŚPar	Śaiva Paribhāṣā
Sakala	Sakalādhikāra (Agastya)
SamāRājSū	Samādhirāja-Sūtra

SamSūt	Samarāṅgaṇa-Sūtradhāra (Bhoja)
SV	Sāmaveda
SViBr	Sāmavidhāna Brāhmaṇa
ŚāmPañcā	Śāmba Pañcāśikā
SāṃKā	Sāṃkhya-Kārikā
SāṃSū	Sāṃkhya-Sūtra
Samū	Samūrtārcanādhikaraṇa
SaṃNik	Saṃyutta Nikāya
SanSam	Sanatkumāra Saṃhitā
SDām	Saṅgīta-Dāmodara
SDar	Saṅgīta-Darpaṇa
SMak	Saṅgīta-Makaranda
SRāj	Saṅgītarāja
SR	Saṅgīta-Ratnākara (Śārṅgadeva)
SUpSā	Saṅgītopaniṣat-sāroddhāra
SaṅkSūr	Saṅkalpasūryodaya (Veṅkaṭanātha)
ŚāṅkhĀr	Śāṅkhāyana Āraṇyaka
ŚāṅkhBr	Śāṅkhāyana Brāhmaṇa
ŚāṅkhŚrSū	Śāṅkhāyana Śrauta-Sūtra
ŚāTil	Śāradā-Tilaka
Sark	Sarasvatīkaṇṭhābharaṇa (Alaṅkāra-Śāstra)
SākāT	Sārdhatriśatīkālottara Tantra
SarDSaṅg	Sarvadarśana-Saṅgraha
Sar	Sarvānukramaṇī
SaSi	Sarvārthasiddhi (on TaSū) (Ācārya Pūjyapāda Devanandī)
ŚBr	Śatapatha Brāhmaṇa
ṢaṭĀ	Ṣaṭkhaṇḍāgama (Puṣpadanta & Bhūtabali)
ṢaṭSan	Ṣaṭsandarbha (Śivagosvāmin)
SātSam	Sātvata Saṃhitā
Saun	Saundarananda
SLah	Saundaryalaharī
SeṬī	Sekoddeśaṭīkā
SiKau	Siddhānta Kaumudī
SiddhSaṅg	Siddhāntaleśa-Saṅgraha
SiddhŚir	Siddhānta-Śiromaṇi
ŚikSamu	Śikṣāsamuccaya
ŚiL	Śilpalakṣaṇa
ŚiPrak	Śilpa Prakāśa (Rāmacandra Kaulācāra)
ŚiRa	Śilparatna
ŚiRaKo	Śilparatnakośa (Sthāpaka Nirañjana Mahāpātra)
Śiśu	Śiśupālavadha
ŚDṛ	Śiva Dṛṣṭi

ŚMSt	Śivamahimnastotra
ŚPur	Śiva Purāṇa
ŚSam	Śiva Saṃhitā
ŚSto	Śiva Stotrāvalī
ŚSū	Śiva-Sūtra
ŚSūVā	Śiva-Sūtra Vārttika (Varadācārya)
ŚSūVim	Śiva-Sūtra Vimarśinī (Kṣemarāja)
SkaPur	Skanda Purāṇa
ŚlVā	Ślokavārttika
SP	Somaśambhu Paddhati
SpKā	Spanda-Kārikā
SpNir	Spanda Nirṇaya
ŚrīBh	Śrī Bhāṣya (on Brahma-Sūtra)
ŚHMu	Śrīhasta Muktāvalī
ŚrīkBh	Śrīkaṇṭha Bhāṣya (on Brahma-Sūtra)
ŚrīSam	Śrīpraśna Saṃhitā
ŚTaCi	Śrītattvacintāmaṇi
ŚṛPrak	Śṛṅgāra Prakāśa
ŚNSā	Śukranītisāra
SupĀ	Suprabheda Āgama
SūrSiddh	Sūrya-Siddhānta
SuSam	Suśruta Saṃhitā
SutNip	Sutta Nipāta
SuSū	Suvarṇaprabhāsa-Sūtra
SvT	Svacchanda Tantra
Svap	Svapnavāsavadatta
ŚvUp	Śvetāśvatara Upaniṣad
Syād	Syādvādamañjarī
TĀr	Taittirīya Āraṇyaka
TBr	Taittirīya Brāhmaṇa
TSam	Taittirīya Saṃhitā
TUp	Taittirīya Upaniṣad
TāṇḍMBr	Tāṇḍya Mahābrāhmaṇa (Pañcaviṃśa Brāhmaṇa)
TĀl	Tantrāloka (Abhinavagupta)
TSāSaṅg	Tantrasāra Saṅgraha
TVā	Tantra Vārttika
TSamu	Tantrasamuccaya
TSā	Tantrasāra (Abhinavagupta)
TaBhā	Tarka Bhāṣā
TarkSaṅg	Tarka-Saṅgraha
TaKau	Tattva Kaumudī
TaPrak	Tattva Prakāśa

TaSū	Tattvārthādhigama-Sūtra (Tattvārtha-Sūtra)
TaSā	Tattvārthasāra (Amṛtacandra)
TaVā	Tattvārtha Vārttika
TaSaSū	Tattvasamāsa-Sūtra
TaSaṅg	Tattva-Saṅgraha
TaVai	Tattva Vaiśāradī
Til	Tilakamañjarī
TiPa	Tiloya Paṇṇattī (Vṛṣabhācārya)
Trik	Trikāṇḍaśeṣa
TRa	Tripurārahasya
UbhSā	Ubhayābhisārikā
UjNīl	Ujjvalanīlamaṇi
UṇSū	Uṇādi-Sūtra
Urbh	Urubhaṅga
USū	Uttarādhyayana-Sūtra
UttCa	Uttararāmacarita
VaiKo	Vaijayantī Kośa
VaiĀ	Vaikhānasa Āgama
VaiGṛhSū	Vaikhānasa Gṛhya-Sūtra
VaiŚa	Vairāgyaśataka
VaiśSū	Vaiśeṣika-Sūtra
VaiśSūBh	Vaiśeṣika-Sūtra Bhāṣya
VaitSū	Vaitāna-Sūtra
VaJī	Vakroktijīvita
Vāk	Vākyapadīya
VāPur	Vāmana Purāṇa
VŚrSū	Vārāha Śrauta-Sūtra
VaCa	Varāṅga Carita
VŚ	Vāstu-Śāstra (Viśvakarman)
VSUp	Vāstusūtra Upaniṣad
VVid	Vāstuvidyā (Viśvakarman)
Vasu	Vasudevahiṇḍī
VPur	Vāyu Purāṇa
VedPar	Vedānta-Paribhāṣā
VedSā	Vedānta-Sāra
Veṇī	Veṇī Saṃhāra
Vibh	Vibhaṅga Pāli
ViBhai	Vijñāna Bhairava
Vik	Vikramorvaśīya
VinPiṭ	Vinaya Piṭaka
Vīrmi	Vīramitrodaya
VirPañcā	Virūpākṣa Pañcāśikā

VDhPur	Viṣṇudharmottara Purāṇa
ViPur	Viṣṇu Purāṇa
ViSahasrBh	Viṣṇu-Sahasranāma Bhāṣya
ViSam	Viṣṇu Saṃhitā
ViSm	Viṣṇu Smṛti
ViMag	Visuddhimagga
ViśKo	Viśva Kośa
VSam	Viṣvaksena Saṃhitā
ViśSam	Viśvāmitra Saṃhitā
ViKo	Viśvaprakāśa Kośa
VivR	Vivādaratnākara
ViPSaṅg	Vivaraṇaprameya Saṅgraha
Vicū	Vivekacūḍāmaṇi
VyVive	Vyaktiviveka (Mahimabhaṭṭa)
YājŚik	Yājñavalkya Śikṣā
YājSm	Yājñavalkya Smṛti
YV	Yajurveda (Vājasaneyi Saṃhitā)
YSū	Yoga-Sūtra
YSūBh	Yoga-Sūtra Bhāṣya (Vyāsa)
YVās	Yoga-Vāsiṣṭha
YYāj	Yogi Yājñavalkya
YoH	Yoginī-Hṛdaya
YuDīp	Yuktidīpikā (on Sāṃkhya-Kārikā)

LIST OF TERMS

aṃśa
agni (agni-soma) (Vol. III)
aṅga-aṅgin
adhikaraṇa/ādhāra
adhikāra
adhibhūta-adhidaiva-adhyātma (Vol. IV)
adhiṣṭhāna
anukīrtana/anukṛti/anukaraṇa (Vol. VI)
antaḥkaraṇa (Vol. XIII)
ap/udaka/jala (Vol. III)
abhinaya (Vol. X)
abhiprāya (Vol. IX)
amṛta
arcā (Vol. V)
artha-vācya-lakṣya-vyaṅgya (Vol. XII)
alaṅkāra (Vol. IX)
avatāra
avadhāna (Vol. XIV)
avasthā
avyakta-vyakta-vyaktāvyakta (Vol. VI)
asura
ahaṃkāra (Vol. XIII)
ākāra/ākṛti (Vol. V)
ākāśa (kha, vyoman) (Vol. III)
ākhyāna (Vol. XII)
āgama-nigama
ātman (Vol. I)
ānanda (Vol. XIII)
ābhāsa (Vol. VI)
āyudha/āyudha-puruṣa (Vol. IX)
ālambana/āśraya
āsana (Vol. X)
indriya (Vol. IV)
īśvara
ugra-saumya
ucita/aucitya
utsava (Vol. XV)
uddhata-sukumāra
upacāra (Vol. XV)
upamā
upāya
ṛta-anṛta
ojas
karaṇa-aṅgahāra (Vol. X)
karaṇa/kāraṇa
karuṇā
karman
kalaśa (kumbha, ghaṭa) (Vol. VIII)
kalā (Vol. IX)
kalā-pramāṇa (Vol. IX)
kalpanā
kavi
kāma (Vol. XIII)
kāla (Vol. II)
kāvya (Vol. XII)
kīrtimukha/grāsa (Vol. VIII)
kuṇḍa (Vol. VII)
kuśala/kauśala
koṇa/aśra/vṛtta (Vol. VII)
krama (Vol. II)
kriyā/kṛti
kṣaṇa (Vol. II)
kṣetra (Vol. II)
gandharva-apsaras -yakṣa
garbha/garbha-gṛha (Vol. VII)
gavākṣa (Vol. VIII)
guṇa-doṣa (Vol. IV)
guru/guru-laghu
cakra-paridhi (Vol. II)
catura/cāturya
camatkāra/camatkṛti
cāru/cārutā

cit/caitanya (Vol. XIII)
citi/caitya/stūpa (Vol. VII)
citta (Vol. XIII)
citra (Vol. IX)
citrakara (Vol. IX)
chandas-mātrā (Vol. XII)
chāyā (Vol. VI)
jāti-vyakti
jīva
jñāna-vijñāna (Vol. XIV)
jyotis/tejas/prakāśa (Vol. III)
tattva (Vol. XIV)
tantra
tanmātra
tāla (Vol. II)
triratna (Vol. VIII)
tīrtha (Vol. VII)
darśana (Vol. XIV)
dik/dikpāla
dīkṣā (Vol. XV)
dṛṣṭa-adṛṣṭa (phala) (Vol. XV)
deva/devatā
deśa (Vol. II)
dravya (Vol. IV)
dharma-dharmin
dhātu (Vol. IV)
dhyāna (Vol. XIII)
dhvaja (Vol. VIII)
dhvani (Vol. XII)
nāṭya
nāḍī
nāda (Vol. XII)
nābhi (Vol. II)
nāma(-rūpa) (Vol. XIV)
nāyaka-nāyikā (Vol. XI)
nṛtta/nṛtya
nyāsa (Vol. XV)
paṅkti/avali/mālā (Vol. IX)
patra-racanā (Vol. IX)
pada (Vol. XII)
padma/kamala (Vol. VIII)
pariṇāma
pāda (Vol. VI)
pāpa-puṇya
pīṭha (Vol. VII)
puruṣa (Vol. I)
puruṣārtha
pūjā/upāsanā/saparyā (Vol. XV)
pūrṇa (Vol. II)
pṛthivī/bhūmi/bhūmikā (Vol. III)
prakṛti (Vol. III)
praṇava
pratibhā (Vol. XI)
pratimā-pratikṛti (Vol. V)
pratīka (Vol. VIII)
pratīti/anumiti (Vol. XIII)
pramāṇa
prayoga
pravṛtti-nivṛtti
prasāda
prastāra (Vol. VII)
prāṇa (Vol. I)
prāsāda (Vol. V)
preman/prīti
bandha-prabandha (Vol. V)
bahumukha/bahubhuja (Vol. IX)
bindu (Vol. II)
bimba-pratibimba (Vol. VI)
bīja (Vol. I)
buddhi/dhī/prajñā (Vol. XIII)
brahman (Vol. I)
bhakti (Vol. XIII)
bhagavān
bhāva-vibhāva/anubhāva (Vol. XI)
bhāvanā
bhūta-mahābhūta (Vol. III)
bhoga
makara/mīna (Vol. VIII)
maṅgala (Vol. VIII)
maṇḍapa (Vol. VII)
madhura/mādhurya
manas/mānasika (Vol. XIII)
mantra (Vol. XII)
marman

māna (Vol. II)
mānuṣa
māyā
mārga-mārgin / deśi (Vol. X)
mithuna (Vol. VIII)
mudrā (Vol. X)
mūrti (Vol. V)
mokṣa
yajña (Vol. XV)
yantra/maṇḍala (Vol. VII)
yūpa (Vol. VII)
yoga (Vol. XIII)
yoni (Vol. VII)
raṅga
racanā/ālekhana (Vol. IX)
ratha (Vol. VII)
ram-/ramaṇīya
rasa (Vol. XI)
rāga-anurāga-rāgiṇī (Vol. XI)
ruci
rūpa-pratirūpa (Vol. V)
rekhā (Vol. V)
lakṣaṇa (Vol. I)
latā (Vol. VIII)
laya (Vol. II)
lalita/lālitya
liṅga/cihna/lāñchana (Vol. VI)
līlā/krīḍā (Vol. X)
loka/triloka (Vol. II)
laukika-alaukika
varṇa/mātṛkā/mālinī (Vol. XII)
vastu (Vol. XII)
vākya (Vol. XII)
vāc/vācika (Vol. XII)
vāda-vādin
vādya (ātodya) (Vol. X)
vāyu (Vol. III)
vāsanā/tṛṣṇā (Vol. XIII)
vāstu
vigraha (Vol. V)
vidyā (Vol. XIV)
vidhi/vidhāna
viniyoga (Vol. XV)
vimarśa
viśrānti (virāma)
viśva-viśvarūpa
viṣaya (Vol. XIV)
vṛkṣa (Vol. VIII)
vṛtti-rīti-pravṛtti (Vol. VI)
vedī/vedikā/sthaṇḍila (Vol. VII)
vyakti/abhivyakti
vyāla/īhāmṛga (Vol. VIII)
vrata (Vol. XV)
śakti
śaṅkha (Vol. VIII)
śabda (Vol. XII)
śarīra/kāya (Vol. I)
śānti/śānta (Vol. XIII)
śālabhañjikā (Vol. VIII)
śāstra (Vol. XIV)
śilpa/śilpin (Vol. I)
śuci-aśuci
śuddha-vikṛta-miśra
śubha-aśubha
śūnya/śūnyatā (Vol. II)
śobhā
śraddhā (Vol. XIII)
śrī
śrīvatsa (Vol. VIII)
śruti/veda
saṃskāra/saṃskṛti (Vol. XV)
saṃsthāna/sanniveśa (Vol. VII)
sakala-niṣkala (Vol. V)
saṅketa (Vol. X)
saṅgīta/gāna/gīta (Vol. X)
sat-asat/sattā (Vol. XIII)
sattva/sāttvika
satya
sandhi (Vol. II)
sama-viṣama/samatā (Vol. XIV)
samādhi (Vol. XIII)
sahṛdaya/rasika/bhāvaka (Vol. XI)
sādṛśya-sārūpya (Vol. VI)
sādhanā/tapas (Vol. XV)

LIST OF ILLUSTRATIONS

Bandha-prabandha

Prāsāda

REKHĀ

Overview

Rekhā or *lekhā* (f.), from the verbal root *rikh-* or *likh-*, to scratch, to draw, to engrave, inscribe, write, trace a line, to delineate or outline; means a line, a drawing, outline, sketch, a painting and writing. In writing and especially in the visual arts, in drawing the outlines of a sacrificial altar (*vedi, sthaṇḍila* and *kuṇḍa*), and of a *maṇḍala* or *yantra,* the line is an essential element giving form and outline. Generally, the straight line is implied, and the words for straight *ṛju* and *sarala,* also denote moral qualities of straightforwardness, rightness, simplicity and clarity, the opposite of *vakra,* crooked and distorted. Lines found in nature, such as in stones or trees, and on the human body such as the palm lines, indicate certain properties and are also used for divination. The science of geometry is called *rekhāgaṇita* since it has essentially to do with lines. Devotees of Viṣṇu or Śiva mark their forehead with symbolic lines which are considered auspicious. The line can also mark a border that should not be transgressed, as in Vedic ritual, or the line drawn by Lakṣmaṇa to protect Sītā, popularly known as *lakṣmaṇarekhā* in the **Rāmāyaṇa** of Tulasīdāsa.

Generally, it can be said that no definite form would be possible in nature or art without the line. It is said in the context of painting: *ākārajanikāṃ rekhām...* "The line is the mother of form" (Abhil I.3.161). The art of writing or calligraphy entirely consists of lines, and even a dynamic art-form such as dance can be delineated by lines. Much more so is the line important in the drawing of a groundplan, in the composition and outline of a sculpture and especially in painting. In temple architecture the *rekha* type of North Indian style is characterised by its rising *śikhara* with vertical section lines.

Etymology and Related Words

The term is derived from the verbal root *likh-* (an earlier form *rikh-* is found in the ṚV VI.53.7), meaning to scratch, to tear up (the ground), to draw, engrave, inscribe, write, paint, delineate, etc. (*r* and *l* being interchangeable). Writing, painting and engraving are closely related, since they all depend on the line. *Lekha* (m.) means a stroke, a line, hence writing, a manuscript or any written text or letter. *Lekhana* or *lekhanī* is any instrument for writing or painting, such as a pen, brush or stylus. *Rekhā* and *lekhā* (f.)

then have almost the same meaning of line, scratch, streak, stripe, also a row or series, an outline or sketch, a border-line.

Rekhāgaṇita denotes geometry, and *rekhāṃśa* is a technical term for a degree of longitude. The lines on the forehead and hands of human body are indicators or signs in astrology (cf. Halāyudha Kośa, *s.v.*).

The closest synonym of *rekhā* is →*sūtra*, since lines are normally drawn with the help of a thread. Other synonyms are mostly found in the context of the visual arts: *cheda* means a cut, division, and mostly refers to a diagonal line; *kīla* (or *kīlaka*) literally means a peg or post, and hence a vertical line; →*guṇa* designates a line, being a synonym of *sūtra*, and sometimes *bāhu* is used, literally meaning arm.

The adjectives denoting a straight or curved-crooked line, *ṛju* or *sarala* and *vakra*, are frequently associated with *rekhā*. The straight line is considered to be 'natural' (*sahaja*), and also stands for straightforwardness and honesty of character, whereas the crooked line (*vakra*) represents a crooked character. In poetics, however, *vakra* has an aesthetic meaning, denoting ornamented speech as contrasted to natural or simple speech (cf. VaJī I.21).

Layers of Meaning

Basically, we find two layers of meaning of *rekhā* or *lekhā*: the line physically drawn, engraved or written, and the symbolic line in *yantra* or *maṇḍala*, in sculpture and architecture. There is also a figurative use of the straight or crooked line, as applied to a human character, and as used in poetry and literature. In so far as art has to do with ornamentation, the curved line is essential for beauty in any art-form.

Development of the Concept

Rekhā as such is not found in the Vedic Saṃhitās, but the root *likh-* occurs in the sense of drawing a line. The early meaning of *rikh-*, to scratch, to tear, occurs in the **Ṛgveda** (VI.53.7), where it involves a violent action. The ideas of straightness or crookedness are expressed, as in the well-known marriage hymn of the **Ṛgveda**:

अनृक्षरा ऋजवः सन्तु पन्था येभिः सखायो यन्ति नो वरेयम् ।

ṚV X.85.23ab

Straight in direction be the paths, and thornless, whereon our fellows travel to the wooing. (Tr. R.T.H. Griffith)

In the **Atharvaveda** we find charms for protection against crooked beings (AV IV.6.4, VII.58.4, the term is *vakra*).

The verb *likh-* in the sense of drawing a line assumes importance in a passage of the **Taittirīya Saṃhitā** where, in a sacrificial context, a line is drawn around the sacrificial complex with the help of metres, in order to protect it from evil influences:

> परि लिखति रक्षसामपहत्यै तिसृभिः परि लिखति त्रिवृद्वा अग्निर्यावानेवाग्निः तस्माद्रक्षांस्यप हन्ति ॥ गायत्रिया परि लिखति तेजो वै गायत्री तेजसैवैनं परि गृह्णाति त्रिष्टुभा परि लिखतीन्द्रियं वै त्रिष्टुगिन्द्रियेणैवैनं परि गृह्णात्यनुष्टुभा परि लिखत्यनुष्टुप् सर्वाणि छन्दांसि परिभूः पर्याप्त्यै मध्यतोऽनुष्टुभा वाग्वा अनुष्टुप्तस्मान् मध्यतो वाचा वदामो गायत्रिया प्रथमया परि लिखत्यथानुष्टुभाऽथ त्रिष्टुभा तेजो वै गायत्री । यज्ञोऽनुष्टुगिन्द्रियं त्रिष्टुप् तेजसा चैवेन्द्रियेण चोभयतो यज्ञं परि गृह्णाति ॥
>
> TSam V.1.3.4–5
>
> He (the sacrificer) draws a line around, to smite away the Rākṣasas; with three (verses) he draws a line around. Agni is threefold; verily from the whole extent of Agni he smites away the Rākṣasas; with a *gāyatrī* verse he draws a line around, the *gāyatrī* is brilliance; verily with brilliance he encircles him; with a *triṣṭubh* verse he draws a line around, the *triṣṭubh* is power; verily he encircles him with power; with an *anuṣṭubh* verse he draws a line around, the *anuṣṭubh* envelops all the metres (verily it serves) for complete attainment; with the *anuṣṭubh* in the middle (he draws), the *anuṣṭubh* is speech, therefore from the middle we speak with speech; with the *gāyatrī* first he draws, then with the *anuṣṭubh*, then with the *triṣṭubh*; the *gāyatrī* is brilliance, the *anuṣṭubh* the sacrifice, the *triṣṭubh* power; verily he encircles the sacrifice, with brilliance and power on both sides. (Tr. A.B. Keith)

In the Brāhmaṇas we find it mostly in the context of the construction of the fire altar (*agnicayana*). Here the bricks are marked with straight lines, corresponding to the shape of a bird (*śyenaciti*):

> स सहस्रमृज्वा लिखिता इष्टकाः करोति, सहस्रमित्यालिखिताः... स मध्यमे वितृतीये सहस्रमृज्वालिखिता इष्टका उपदधाति । तद् यानीमानि वयसः प्रत्यञ्चि शीर्ष्ण आपुच्छादृजूनि लोमानि - तानि तत् करोति । अथ सहस्रमित्यालिखिता दक्षिणत उपदधाति । तद् यानीमानि वयसो दक्षिणतो वक्राणि लोमानि - तानि तत् करोति । अथ सहस्रमित्यालिखिता उत्तरत उपदधाति । तद् यानीमानि वयस उत्तरतो वक्राणि लोमानि तानि तत् करोति ।
>
> ŚBr X.2.1.8–11

He makes a thousand bricks marked with straight lines: a thousand marked this way (from left to right), ...

... and on the central part he places the one thousand bricks marked with straight lines: he thereby gives to it those straight plumes of the bird pointing backwards (with their tops, and covering it) from head to tail.

On the right side he then lays down the one thousand (bricks) marked thus (from left to right): he thereby gives to it those curved plumes on the right side of the bird.

On the left side he then lays down the one thousand (bricks) marked thus (from right to left): he thereby gives to it those curved plumes on the left side of the bird. (Tr. J. Eggeling)

The word *rekhā* (or *lekhā*) occurs in the Sūtra literature where detailed rules are laid down for the construction of the altar. Consciously, the phrase *rekhā likhitvā* is used:

यत्र क्व चाग्निम् उपसमाधास्यन् स्यात् तत्र प्राचीरुदीचीश्च तिस्रस्तिस्रो रेखा लिखित्वाऽद्भिरवोक्ष्याऽग्निम् उपसमिन्ध्यात् ।

ĀpDhSū II.1.13

At every (burnt offering), when he wishes to place the fire on the altar (called *sthaṇḍila*), let him draw on that (altar) three lines from west to east and three lines from south to north and sprinkle (the altar) with water, turning the palm of the hand downwards and let him then make the fire burn brightly by adding (fuel). (Tr. G. Bühler)

The first rules of geometry are found in the Śulbasūtras, such as for making a square or circle:

चतुरस्रं चिकीर्षन् यावच्चिकीर्षेत्तावतीं रज्जुमुभयतः पाशां कृत्वा मध्ये लक्षणं करोति । लेखामालिख्य ।

BŚulSū I.22

If you wish to make a square, take a cord of the length which you desire to give to the side of the square, make a tie at both its ends and a mark at its middle; then having drawn the line (i.e. *prācī*, the line pointing to the east and west points). (Tr. G. Thibaut)

समे शङ्कुं निखाय शङ्कुसम्मितया रज्ज्वा मण्डलं परिलिख्य यत्र लेखयोः शङ्क्वग्रच्छाया निपतति तत्र शङ्कू निहन्ति, सा प्राची ।

KātŚulSū I.2

> Set up a gnomon on an even (piece of ground) and by means of a rope equal to the gnomon in length draw a circle (around the gnomon). Drive two pegs on the two lines (i.e. western half of the circle and eastern half of the circle) where the shadow of the tip of the gnomon falls. The (line joining the two pegs is) *prācī* (the east-west transversal of the figure to be drawn). (Tr. S.R. Sarma)

Bricks with straight lines are called *ṛjulekhāḥ* (BŚulSū II.32).

But apart from the geometry involved in the construction of altars, there is also a correspondence between the metres recited at sacrifice and the space-directions:

> ऊर्ध्वो वै प्रथमस्त्र्यहस्तिर्यङ्मध्यमोऽर्वाङुत्तमः । स यदूर्ध्वः प्रथमस्त्र्यहस्तस्माद् अयमग्निरूर्ध्व उद्दीप्यत; ऊर्ध्वा ह्येतस्य दिग्यत्तिर्यङ् मध्यमस्तस्मादयं वायुस्तिर्यङ् पवते तिरश्चीरापो वहन्ति; तिरश्चीह्येतस्य दिग्यदर्वाङुत्तमस्तस्मादसावर्वाङ् तपत्यर्वाङ् वर्षत्यर्वाञ्चि नक्षत्राण्यर्वाची ह्येतस्य दिक्; सम्यञ्चो वा इमे लोकाः सम्यञ्च एते त्र्यहाः ॥
>
> AitBr IV.25
>
> The first three (*soma*) days are ascending; the middle three days are crossed; the last three days are descending. On account of the (metres of the) first three days (*tryaha*) being ascending, the fire blazes up, for the upward region belongs to the fire. On account of the (metres of the) middle three days being crossed, the wind blows across; the wind moves across (the other regions), and the waters flow (also) across; for the region which is across (the others) belongs to the wind. On account of (the metres of) the three last days being descending, that one (the sun) burns downwards (sending his rays down), the rain falls down, (and) the constellations (in heaven) send (their light) down. For the region which goes down belongs to the sun. The three worlds belong together, so do these three *tryahas.* (Tr. M. Haug)

These correspondences between the cosmic elements, the space-directions (*dik*) and the metres will have their impact on later visual art-forms, where for example the diagonal lines in a sculpture panel are linked to the wind (*vāyu*, cf. VSUp II.14).

Another cosmic meaning of *rekhā* is in connection with the rainbow, which consists of lines drawn in the sky by a divine being, hence called *mahendrarekhā.*

> यद्यह्नि वातेषु महेन्द्ररेखा
> महेन्द्रचापः समुदेति रात्रौ ।

तदा भयं पार्थिवमण्डलानां
वदन्ति शास्त्रार्थविदो द्विजेन्द्राः ॥

AVPari 70ga.32.11

Brahmins well-versed in the imports of scriptures declare that if the line of the god Mahendra (i.e. the rainbow) arises in the winds (i.e. in the atmosphere) in the day and the bow of Mahendra (rainbow) arises at night, then there will be great terror in the assemblage of kings. (Tr. R.S. Bhattacharya)

Drawing a line as a device for protection from demonic forces has become famous from the **Rāmāyaṇa** episode, where Lakṣmaṇa wants to protect Sītā by advising her not to cross over the line. This is reflected in Tulasīdāsa's **Rāmacaritamānasa** in the conversation between Mandodarī and Rāvaṇa (VI.36.1-2). In spite of this warning she crosses the line and is abducted by Rāvaṇa.

The implication of *ṛju* as straightness or straightforwardness is a basic moral quality in ancient India. Thus the ideal characteristics of a *brahmacārī* are given in the **Āpastamba Dharma-Sūtra**:

स्वाध्यायधृग् धर्मरुचिस्तपस्व्यृजुर्मृदुस् सिध्यति ब्रह्मचारी ॥

ĀpDhSū I.2.5.11

A religious student who retains what he has learned, who finds pleasure in the fulfilment of the law, who keeps the rules of studentship, who is upright and forgiving attains perfection. (Tr. G. Bühler)

Similarly, the following moral qualities are mentioned in the Upaniṣads:

अथ यत्तपो दानमार्जवमहिंसा सत्यवचनमिति ता अस्य दक्षिणाः ।

ChUp III.17.4

Austerity, alms-giving, uprightness, harmlessness, truthfulness – these are one's gifts for the priests. (Tr. R.E. Hume)

The **Mahābhārata** enlists the qualities of a hero, among which *ārjava*, simplicity or uprightness is mentioned (MBh I.1.181–182). Vāsudeva declares to Bhīṣma:

न ह्यभक्ताय राजेन्द्र भक्तायानृजवे न च ।
दर्शयाम्यहमात्मानं न चादान्ताय भारत ॥

MBh XII.51.11

(Vāsudeva said to Bhīṣma) O foremost of kings, I do not reveal myself unto one, that is not devoted to me, or unto a devotee that is not straight-forward (honest) in his dealing or unto one, o Bhārata, that is not self-restrained. (Tr. K.D. Pandey)

Straightness has thus an intrinsically positive connotation, both physically and morally.

Coming back to the use of *rekhā* in post-Vedic literature, we find the importance of lines in natural phenomena which are often taken as signs and portents. Thus the **Bṛhat Saṃhitā** describes different portents as lines inside the solar disk:

नागरकाणामभ्यन्तरस्थिता यायिनां च बाह्यस्था ।
परिवेषमध्यरेखा विज्ञेयाक्रन्दसाराणाम् ॥
रक्तः श्यामो रूक्षश्च भवति येषां पराजयस्तेषाम् ।
स्निग्धः श्वेतो द्युतिमान् येषां भागो जयस्तेषाम् ॥

BṛSam XXXIV.22–23

The line inside a halo refers to the kings defending a town; one outside it, to the marching kings and the central one, to the two kinds of allies called Ākranda and Āsāra, who come to the rescue of the besieged ones. A line that is blood-red or dark and rough (or impure) denotes defeat to those kings whom it represents, while that which is glossy (clear), white and bright, suggests victory to such kings as are represented by the line. (Tr. M.R. Bhat)

ध्वजचापनिभे युद्धानि भास्करे वेपने च रूक्षे च ।
कृष्णा रेखा सवितरि यदि हन्ति ततो नृपं सचिवः ॥

BṛSam III.32

The Sun appearing like a flag or bow causes wars. The same effect will follow if he is quivering or rough or sharp. If there is a dark streak across the solar disc, the ruling monarch will be killed by his own minister. (Tr. M.R. Bhat)

Natural stones, *śālagrāma* or *liṅga*, are marked with lines which have different significance and are associated with deities:

... त्रिरेखालाञ्छितः ... कूर्मः ... ॥
हयग्रीवोऽङ्कुशाकाररेखः ... ॥
श्यामस्त्रिविक्रमो दक्षरेखः ... ॥

AgPur XLVI.6bc, 7ab, 9cd

The *śālagrāma* stone named Kūrma has three lines on it.The *śālagrāma* stone called Hayagrīva has lines of the form of a goad (*aṅkuśa*) and the stone called Trivikrama is black in colour and has lines on the right side. (Tr. R.S. Bhattacharya)

A *svayambhu liṅga* characterized with lines on it is very significant. These characteristics of a natural *liṅga* should not be rectified.

... वालुकरेखाकलङ्कबिन्दुयुतम् ॥
अथवैकरेखमेतान्युदितान्येव स्वयम्भुलिङ्गानि ।

Mayam XXXIII.89cd–90ab

A self-generated *liṅga* may be made from a stone containing gravel and may have streaks, stains or may have one single engraved line on it (instead of three). (Tr. B. Dagens)

In contrast with this idea it is also said at another place that one should reject the defective gems while installing a →*liṅga*. Discussing the characteristics of gems, the **Mayamata** has marked that in order to make a *liṅga* with precious gems one should immediately reject the gem which has streaks on it (cf. Mayam XXXIII.160).

रेखाबिन्दुकलङ्काढ्या वृद्धा वक्रा च या शिला ॥
सशर्करा विवर्णा च सत्रासायतनस्थिता ।
निःस्वना सदरीभेदा सगर्भा निन्दिता वरैः ॥

Mayam XXXIII.6cd–7

They reject a stone with 'streaks', 'spots' or 'stains' and one that is 'aged' and cross grained; they reject a stone which contains grit or which is of indefinite colour; they reject one with 'cracks' and one found inside a building; they reject one which gives off no sound and one which is alveolar, fissured or 'pregnant'. (Tr. B. Dagens)

रेखाबिन्दुकलङ्काढ्या सा त्याज्या सर्वयत्नतः ।

Mayam XXXIII.16ab

That (stone), which has 'streaks', 'spots', and 'stains' should be abandoned with great care. (Tr. Sadananda)

According to the **Kāraṇāgama** (I.9.63cd–64ab) there are three kinds of streaks which make a stone defective, viz. like a tortoise (*pṛṣṭhapādavadākāra*), like a spider (*sūtrapādavadāyata*), and like sun rays (*sūryaraśmivadākāra*) (quoted in AjitĀ kp footnote under V.33).

However, while making a *liṅga* certain measurement (length and width) of lines is to be engraved on it. This measurement may vary according to the size of the *liṅga*.

आत्तांशे नवभागे भागेन व्यासगम्भीराः ॥
रेखाविकर्कशोक्ता सर्वेषामेव लिङ्गानाम् ।

अर्धयवेनाप्युदिता रेखार्धयवेन पूर्ववद् वृद्धिः ॥
सार्धचतुर्यवतारावनतिः श्रेष्ठ तु लिङ्गे तु ।
मध्यमसूत्रव्यासादर्धततिः पक्षयोस्तु पृथक् ॥
सर्वेषां रेखाणां व्यासावनतिः समा एव ।

Mayam XXXIII.122cd–123ab, 125cd–127ab

The lines (delimiting the frenum) on all types of *liṅga* must be regular; their depth and their width are to be equal to a ninth the fraction (of the Śiva element) chosen as unit. (Otherwise, a depth and width) of half a barley grains are given to the lines (of a one cubit *liṅga*) and a depth and width of four and a half barley grains for the largest *liṅga* are arrived at as above, by adding half a barley grain (per supplementary cubit) for each. The width of the lateral lines is half that of the median lines. All the lines are to have the same depth and width. (Tr. B. Dagens)

Special religious significance is attached to the application of symbolic lines on the forehead of a devotee, such as the three horizontal lines or *tripuṇḍra* for a Śaiva:

तिस्रो रेखा भवन्त्येव स्थानेषु मुनिपुङ्गवाः ।
ललाटादिषु सर्वेषु यथोक्तेषु बुधैर्मुने ॥
भ्रुवोर्मध्यं समारभ्य यावदन्तो भवेद् भ्रुवोः ।
तावत्प्रमाणं सन्धार्यं ललाटे च त्रिपुण्ड्रकम् ॥
मध्यमानामिकाङ्गुल्या मध्ये तु प्रतिलोमतः ।
अङ्गुष्ठेन कृता रेखा त्रिपुण्ड्राख्याऽभिधीयते ॥

ŚPur I.24.84–86

(Sūta said to sages) O leading sages, in the different parts of the body as the forehead, etc. three lines constitute the *tripuṇḍra.*

The *tripuṇḍra* on the forehead extends from the middle of the eyebrows to the tips of the brows on either side.

With the middle and the ring fingers a line drawn in the opposite direction is called *tripuṇḍra.* (Tr. J.L. Shastri)

The Śaiva **Kālāgnirudra Upaniṣad** gives the detailed account of rules as well as the symbolism of marking the *tripuṇḍra* with sacred ash and application of different lines (*rekhā*s).

A line is a mark or a trace (mostly used with *aṅkana, aṅkita,* to mark), hence a symbol of the one who left it. In the **Viṣṇu Purāṇa** it is Kṛṣṇa who leaves the marks of his feet on the path:

ध्वजवज्राङ्कुशाब्जाङ्करेखावन्त्यालि पश्यत ।
पदान्येतानि कृष्णस्य लीलाललितगामिनः ॥

ViPur V.13.32

See here are the marks of Kṛṣṇa's feet, as he has gone alone sportively, and left the impressions of the banner, the thunderbolt, the goad and lotus. (Tr. H.H. Wilson)

One of the important fields where *rekhā* (and the verb *likh-*) is indispensable, is writing, including epigraphy and calligraphy.

There is an interesting discussion in the **Brahma-Sūtras** and their commentaries as to whether the strokes constituting a letter are real, or only the sounds or phonemes thus indicated. Śaṅkara is of the opinion that the lines forming letters are unreal, and he uses this as a simile (*dṛṣṭānta*):

तथाकारादिसत्याक्षरप्रतिपत्तिर्दृष्टा रेखानृताक्षरप्रतिपत्तेः ।

BrSūŚBh II.1.14

We see that the knowledge of the real sound '*a*' etc. is reached by means of the unreal written letters. (Tr. G. Thibaut)

The subcommentaries explain this further. Vācaspatimiśra says that though the lines or strokes are themselves real, their conventional association with letters or phonemes is unreal. And yet, out of this unreality real knowledge is derived (*yadyapi rekhāsvarūpaṃ satyaṃ tathāpi tadyathāsaṃketamasatyaṃ, nahi saṃketayitāraḥ saṃketayantīdṛśena rekhābhedenāyaṃ varṇaḥ pratyetavyo'pi tvīdṛśo rekhābhedo' kāra īdṛśaśca kakāra iti* – Bhāmatī on BrSūŚBh II.1.14). Rāmānuja in his **Śrībhāṣya** argues against this view:

रेखया वर्णप्रतिपत्तावपि नासत्यात् सत्यबुद्धिः, रेखायाः सत्यत्वात् । ननु वर्णात्मना प्रतिपन्ना रेखा वर्णबुद्धिहेतुः । वर्णात्मता त्वसत्या । नैवम् ... रेखाया अविद्यमान वर्णात्मनोपायत्वे च, एकस्यामेव रेखायामविद्यमानसर्ववर्णात्मकत्वस्य सुलभत्वाद् एकरेखादर्शनात् सर्ववर्णप्रतिपत्तिः स्यात् । अथ पिण्डविशेषे देवदत्तादिशब्दसंकेतवत् चक्षुर्ग्राह्य रेखाविशेषे श्रोत्रग्राह्यवर्णविशेषसंकेतवशात् रेखाविशेषो वर्णविशेषबुद्धिहेतुरिति – हन्त तर्हि सत्यादेव सत्यप्रतिपत्तिः, रेखायाः संकेतस्य च सत्यत्वात् ॥

ŚrīBh I.1.1 (p. 87)

Nor can you quote in favour of your view of the real being known through the unreal – the instance of the stroke and the letter. The letter being apprehended through the stroke (i.e. the written character) does not furnish a case of the real being apprehended through the unreal; for the stroke itself is real. – But the stroke causes the idea of the letter only in so far as it is apprehended as 'being a letter and this being a letter' is untrue? – Not so, we rejoin....

... Moreover, if the means were constituted by the stroke in so far as it is not the letter, the apprehension of all letters would result from the sight of one stroke; for one stroke may easily be conceived as not being any letter. – But, in the same way as the word 'Devadatta' conventionally denotes some particular man, so some particular stroke apprehended by the eye may conventionally symbolise some particular letter to be apprehended by the ear, and thus a particular stroke may be the cause of the idea of a particular letter! – Quite so, we reply, but on this explanation the real is known through the real; for both stroke and conventional power of symbolisation are real. (Tr. G. Thibaut)

This discussion is important also since the written word or letter has secondary importance in the Indian tradition as compared to the phoneme or the uttered sound (both being *varṇa* or *akṣara*). Rāmānuja's argument implies that the stroke denoting a letter of the (Sanskrit) alphabet contains as much power as the sound uttered, *rekhā* having the same degree of reality as →*varṇa*. The same applies to the strokes denoting numbers:

यथा चैकापि सती रेखा स्थानान्यत्वेन निविशमानैकदशशतसहस्रादिशब्दप्रत्ययभेदम् अनुभवति ।

BrSūŚBh II.2.17

So, again, one and the same stroke is, according to the place it is connected with, spoken of and conceived as meaning either ten, or hundred or thousand etc. (Tr. G. Thibaut)

The power of the stroke to change a number is equally referred to in the **Vyāsabhāṣya** on **Yoga-Sūtra**:

यथैका रेखा शतस्थाने शतं दशस्थाने दश, एका चैकस्थाने ।

YSūBh III.13

Take for instance, the digit one. When placed in the first column it means unit, in the second column it denotes ten and in the third it stands for hundred. (Tr. H. Aranya)

Though calligraphy as an art has not been discussed much in the Sanskrit texts, it has assumed importance mainly in connection with the writing of *mantras*, more important of Tantric *bījamantras*. As an example we may mention the Siddham script which has been developed in India, which was taken over to Tibet and, by the mediation of Tantric Buddhism, travelled as far as

Japan. In this highly artistic calligraphy on the basis of the Devanāgarī script the drawing of the lines is central.

Rekhā assumes more importance in the context of the Tantras and Āgamas, mainly for drawing the lines of a →*yantra* or *maṇḍala*. Though the term →*sūtra* is often used because of the ritual procedure of 'laying the thread' (*sūtrapātana*), the result is the lines delineating the symbolic diagram. These lines on the one hand have the function of creating a borderline between the inner, sacred space, and the outer, unordered space, which is mostly achieved by the *bhūpura* or the square outer demarcation of a *yantra* with four gates (→*bhū*), mostly drawn with three parallel lines. The inner lines create fields of different shapes which are associated with deities and *bīja mantras*. They constitute an abstraction of highly charged symbolic power, typical of the Tantric worldview. The lines are drawn with powder of different colours, and the shapes symbolise various elements. For instance, we find in the description of a *maṇḍala*:

सुश्वेतानि दलानि स्युर्व्योमरेखा तु वर्तुला ।
बाह्यस्याङ्गुष्ठमानेन श्वेतवर्णा सुशोभना ॥
दलान्तराणि रक्तानि तद्बाह्ये चतुरश्रकम् ।
तथैवाङ्गुलिमानेन सितरेखा तु पीतला ॥

NT XVIII.39–40

The lotus petals (of the *maṇḍala*) should be pure white, and the line of space should be circular, of the measure of a thumb and beautifully white. The other petals are red, and outside (it is enclosed by) a square. In the same way, of the measure of an *aṅgula* a yellow – white line should be drawn.

The **Mālinīvijayottara Tantra** which serves as the basis for Abhinavagupta's **Tantrāloka**, describes the tracing of the *maṇḍala*, as for example:

ततो द्वितीयभागान्ते ब्रह्मणः पार्श्वयोर्द्वयोः ।
द्वे रेखे पूर्वगे नेये भागत्र्यंशशमे बुधैः ॥

MVT IX.12

At the end of the second division, at the two sides of the central line (*brahmasūtra*), the wise should trace two lines towards the east at a distance of a third division.

Abhinavagupta develops this description of the *triśūlābjamaṇḍala* in the **Tantrāloka** (XXXI). There he describes the outer boundary as *bhūrekhā*:

प्राकारं चतुरश्रं तु सभूरेखासमन्वितम् ।

सितरक्तपीतकृष्णै रजोभिः कारयेत्ततः ॥

TĀl XXXI.122cd

Then he should draw the square enclosure with the 'earth-line', with coloured powder in white, red, yellow and black.

The term *guṇarekhā* is also used for an ornamented border-line (TĀl XXXI.37). The drawing of a →*maṇḍala* in general has been indicated by the verb *ālikh-* :

आलिखेन्मण्डलं तत्र चतुरश्रं समन्ततः ।

NT XVIII.30

There one should draw a *maṇḍala* square on all sides.

The same verb is used for tracing the lines of a *maṇḍala* (cf. also NT XVIII.32ab – *tanmadhye cālikhet padmamaṣṭapatraṃ suśobhanam*), and for painting.

The **Jayākhya Saṃhitā** describes the use of *rekhā,* in the sense of line, in arrangement of placing of *brahmaśilā* (*brahmaśilāsthāpana vidhāna*):

कृत्वा नवपदां पूर्वं पद्मं तस्यां पदे पदे ।
विलिख्य रेखया सम्यक् खनेत्सर्वेषु कर्णिकाम् ॥

JaySam XX.297

After marking the *brahmaśilā* with nine squares (*pada*s) one should draw lotuses in each with lines and then in each of the lotuses incise the pericarp beautifully. (Tr. H.N. Chakravarty)

One of the most important and well-known *yantra*s is the *śrīcakra.* The tracing of the lines of this *yantra* is an elaborate ritual, described in various texts. The **Yoginī-Hṛdaya** with Amṛtānanda's commentary describes the beginning of the *nyāsa* of the *śrīcakra* by praising the first line of the square:

चतुरस्राद्यरेखायै नम इत्यादितो न्यसेत् ॥

YoH III.45cd

"Adoration to the first line of the square", starting with this invocation one should start placing (the parts of the *śrīcakra*).

And it continues with similar *mantra*s addressed to the other lines. The fields created by the lines addressed by these →*mantra*s become the abode of various goddesses:

सिद्धीस्तदन्तश्च तनुव्यापकत्वेन सुन्दरि ।
(चतुरस्रमध्यरेखायै नम इत्यपि वल्लभे)
तस्याः स्थानेषु विन्यस्य ब्रह्माण्याद्यास्तदाष्टसु ॥

न्यस्तव्याश्चतुरस्रान्त्यरेखायै नम इत्यपि ।
विन्यसेद् व्यापकत्वेन पूर्वोक्तान्तश्च विग्रहे ॥
तस्याः स्थानेषु दशसु मुद्राणां दशकं न्यसेत् ।
ब्रह्माण्याद्याष्टस्थानान्तस्तासामष्टौ न्यसेत्ततः ॥

YoH III.48, 50–51

O lovely one, all the *siddhis* and inbetween them (I pay obeisance to the middle line of the outer square of the *śrīyantra*) it should be offered in the corner (*vallabha*). They are to be worshipped while conceiving them as forces pervasive of limbs but the spaces between the first line and the middle ones, one should make placement of eight deities beginning with Brahmāṇī and others.

One should make an offering in the ultimate line of the square and also on the body of oneself uttering 'I pay obeisance on the ultimate line of the square' as the pervasive forces (of the bodily elements) similarly done before. In the ten spaces one should make placement of ten *mudrās*. Inside the spaces specified for Brahmāṇī and other deities one should make the placement of(the *mantras* of) Brahmāṇī and others. (Tr. H.N. Chakravarty)

Besides *yantra* and *maṇḍala*, *rekhā* or *lekhā* is also associated with the *bījamantras* ('seed-syllables'), where the power of sound corresponds to the power of the mystic diagram. Thus one of the important Tantric *bījas* denoting the Goddess is termed *hṛllekhā*, lit. 'the heart-line', which stands for the sacred syllable *hrīṃ*. The implication is both that of the stroke of the externally written *mantra*, and of the internal imprint of the *mantra* on the heart. Haramohan Mishra translates the word *hṛllekhā* (f.) as "the luminous streak of the heart of the universe, the essence of all knowledge and existence" (H. Mishra, "*Dimensions of Hṛllekhā*", Abstracts (English) of Xth World Sanskrit Conference, Bangalore, 1997).

Rekhā is also important in the context of Tantric Yoga. The implicit positive association of the straight line becomes evident in the description of the awakening of the *kuṇḍalinī śakti*.

तेन कुण्डलिनी सुप्ता सन्तप्ता संप्रबुध्यते ।
दण्डाहता भुजङ्गीव निश्वस्य ऋजुतां व्रजेत् ॥

HyPrad III.67

By reason of that, the *kuṇḍalinī* which is asleep, feeling the extreme heat, is awakened, just as a serpent struck by a stick hisses and straightens itself. (Tr. S. Iyangar)

For this reason the Śakti is also called *rekhiṇī* (the Goddess of the straight line). Thus we find a quotation from the (otherwise lost) **Tantrasadbhāva** in Kṣemarāja's **Śiva-Sūtra Vimarśinī**:

उत्थिता तु यदा तेन कला सूक्ष्मा तु कुण्डली ।
चतुष्कलमयो बिन्दुः शक्तेरुदरगः प्रभुः ॥
मध्यमन्थनयोगेन ऋजुत्वं जायते प्रिये ।
ज्येष्ठाशक्तिः स्मृता सा तु बिन्दुद्वयसुमध्यगा ॥
बिन्दुना क्षोभमायाता रेखैवामृतकुण्डली ।
रेखिणी नाम सा ज्ञेया उभौ बिन्दू यदन्तगौ ॥

Quoted in ŚSūVim under II.3

When the subtle circular Śakti (*kalā*) is aroused by that creative throb of knowledge, then O dear one, the powerful four-phased *bindu* existing in the womb of Śakti assumes a straight position by the union of the churner (Śiva) and that which is churned (Śakti). The Śakti that passes into the middle of the two *bindus* (viz. of Śiva and Śakti) is known as *Jyeṣṭhā*. Being agitated by that *bindu*, the straight line is known as *amṛta kuṇḍalī*. She is known as *rekhiṇī* (one of straight lines) at the ends of which are the two *bindus*. (Tr. J. Singh)

The bodily posture of the one who practices →*yoga* or meditation should be one where the back or chest, neck and head are in a straight line (mostly *sama* is used, or *ṛju*), as the Yoga texts emphasize (cf. MaitUp VI.25; BhG VI.13; MṛgĀ yp 18b).

In Kāvya literature the use of the terms *rekhā, lekhā, lekha* or *lekhana* are found frequently. These terms are used to denote various meanings such as line, row, range, delineation, sketch, drawing or painting and engraving etc. Many compound words are formed by using *rekhā, lekhā,* such as *madarekhā, madalekhā, vidyullekhā, meghalekhā, anaṅgalekha* (Kuṁ I.7); *manmathalekha* (AbhŚāk III.24) etc. Often it is used to compare or describe the beauty of a lady. The beauty of Devī is described in the **Saundaryalaharī** in the following way:

गले रेखास्तिस्रो गतिगमकगीतैकनिपुणे
विवाहव्यानद्धत्रिगुणगुणसंख्याप्रतिभुवः ।
विराजन्ते नानाविधमधुररागाकरभुवां
त्रयाणां ग्रामाणां स्थितिनियमसीमान इव ते ॥

SLah 69 (cf. DPur III.2.26)

The three creases in your neck, O you who are skilled without compare in [the triple art of singing] theme, ornament, and song,

which correspond to the number of strands in the triple thread knotted [on your neck] at the time of marriage,

shine forth so that for those mines of manifold sweet musical modes,

the three kinds of basic scales, they seem to be lines for defining the [respective] limits. (Tr. W.N. Brown)

The description of Devī and Śiva, as they appear together in her mansion at the top of the cosmos, which is represented by the mystic diagram known as the *śrīcakra* is beautiful.

चतुर्भिः श्रीकण्ठैः शिवयुवतिभिः पञ्चभिरपि
प्रभिन्नाभिः शंभोर्नवभिरपि मूलप्रकृतिभिः ।
चतुश्चत्वारिंशद्वसुदलकलाश्रत्रिवलय-
त्रिरेखाभिः सार्धं तव शरणकोणाः परिणताः ॥

SLah 11

By reason of the four [triangles called] *śrīkaṇṭhas* and the five [triangles called] *śivayuvatis,*

which are pierced by the *bindu* and constitute the nine [basic triangles of the *śrīcakra* called] *mūlaprakṛtis,*

forty-four – along with the lotuses of eight and sixteen petals [outside the triangles] and the three circles [outside the lotuses]

and the three lines [outside the circles] – angles of your dwelling place are evolved. (Tr. W.N. Brown)

The famous poet Kālidāsa in his **Kumārasambhava** praises the beauty of Pārvatī whose eye-brows surpass the beautiful shape of the bow of the god of love.

तस्याः शलाकाञ्जननिर्मितेव कान्तिर्भ्रुवोरायतलेखयोर्या ।
तां वीक्ष्य लीलाचतुरामनङ्गः स्वचापसौन्दर्यमदं मुमोच ॥

Kum I.47

On seeing the beauty, charming in its sportiveness, of her long-arching brows, pencilled as it were with black paint, the bodiless God (Cupid) gave up all pride in the beauty of his own (curved) bow. (Tr. M.R. Kale)

Kālidāsa compares the beauty of Pārvatī with the increasing crescent of the moon (*lekhā*):

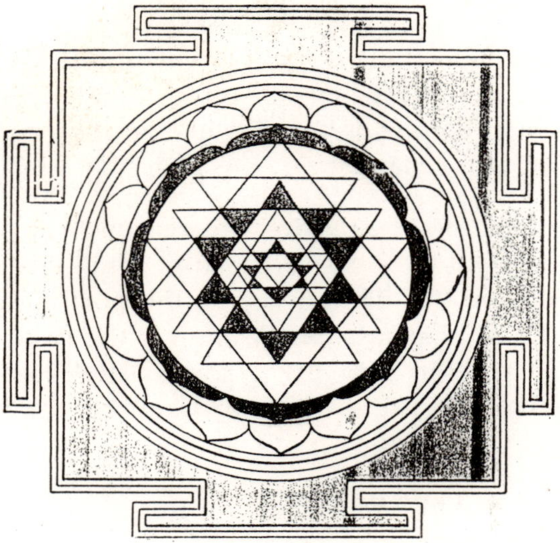

Figure 1: *Śrīcakra*

दिने दिने सा परिवर्धमाना लब्धोदया चान्द्रमसीव लेखा ।
पुपोष लावण्यमयान्विशेषाञ्ज्योत्स्नान्तराणीव कलान्तराणि ॥

Kum I.25

She, who had got her birth, growing day by day, developed extraordinary graces, as the newly-risen crescent of the moon, waxing day by day, (develops) other digits hidden in her lustre.
(Tr. M.R. Kale)

At another place *rekhā* has been used in the sense of measurement.

रेखामात्रमपि क्षुण्णादा मनोर्वर्त्मनः परम् ।
न व्यतीयुः प्रजास्तस्य नियन्तुर्नेमिवृत्तयः ॥

Ragh I.17

Acting like the rim of a wheel under a skilful driver, the subjects of him, their guide, swerved not even to the width of a line from the path that had been trodden from the days of Manu.
(Tr. M.R. Kale)

Sometimes another word *rāji, rājī* or *rājikā* is also used to denote a streak, line or row (cf. Ragh XIV.12 for *dhūmarāji*).

स न्यस्तचिह्नामपि राजलक्ष्मीं तेजोविशेषानुमितां दधानः ।
आसीदनाविष्कृतदानराजिरन्तर्मदावस्थ इव द्विपेन्द्रः ।

Ragh II.7

Possessing kingly fortune (or royalty) which, with its insignia cast aside, could be inferred from the super-eminence of majesty, he resembled a royal elephant, inwardly in condition of rut but without the lines of ichor manifested externally. (Tr. M.R. Kale)

Rekhā as the delineation of a portrait reveals as well as conceals the identity of the person represented. Sanskrit literature is full of examples where the hero or heroine falls in love by only seeing the portrait of the person. But king Duṣyanta in the **Abhijñānaśākuntala** notices the dissimilarity of the outlines of Śakuntalā's portrait with the original. After seeing the picture of Śakuntalā in the picture-board, brought by Caturikā, the king Duṣyanta says to Sānumatī:

यद्यत्साधु न चित्रे स्यात् क्रियते तत्तदन्यथा ।
तथापि तस्या लावण्यं रेखया किञ्चिदन्वितम् ॥

AbhŚāk VI.14

Whatever may not be right (is faulty) in (this) picture is corrected; yet her beauty is only partially represented by the delineation. (Tr. M.R. Kale)

The root *likh-* has been equally used by Kālidāsa in the sense of painting.

आलोके ते निपतति पुरा सा बलिव्याकुला वा
मत्सादृश्यं विरहतनु वा भावगम्यं लिखन्ती ।
पृच्छन्ती वा मधुरवचनां सारिकां पञ्जरस्थां
कच्चिद्भर्तुः स्मरसि रसिके त्वं हि तस्य प्रियेति ॥

Megh II.25

She will meet your sight (will be seen by you) either engaged in performing worship (for the propitiation of the deities) or painting the likeness of me emaciated by separation and perceivable (pictured) by imagination, or asking the sweet-voiced Sārikā, confined in the cage – O sweet-natured one, dost thou remember thy master? – for thou wast his favourite. (Tr. M.R. Kale)

Another example of the term *lekhā* used in the sense of painting is found in Bhavabhūti's **Mālatīmādhava** where Mādhava is trying to portray the picture of Mālatī by the advice of his friend Makaranda.

वारं वारं तिरयति दृशोरुद्गमं बाष्पपूर–

स्तत्संकल्पोपहितजडिम स्तम्भमभ्येति गात्रम् ।
सद्यः स्विद्यन्नयमविरतोत्कम्पलोलाङ्गुलीकः
पाणिर्लेखाविधिषु नितरां वर्तते किं करोमि ॥

MālMā I.35

The flood of tears again and again obstructs the function of my eyes; my body becomes paralysed owing to the dulness brought on by my picturing her in my mind; and when I proceed to paint her, this my hand, at once perspiring, has its fingers excessively shaking on account of incessant tremor. What can I do?
(Tr. M.R. Kale)

In one verse of the **Naiṣadhīyacarita** the word *lekhā* is used. In the description of five Nalas, where Indra and other gods have come to Damayantī by assuming the form of Nala to test her love, Damayantī addresses the gods:

ईशा ! दिशां नलभुवं प्रतिपद्य लेखा
वर्णश्रियं गुणवतामपि वः कथं वा ।
मूर्खान्धकूपपतनादिव पुस्तकाना-
मस्तङ्गतं बत परोपकृतिव्रतत्वम् ॥

NaiCa XIII.49

Ye gods, lords of the cardinal points, like as the beneficial mission of meritorious books, even after they have acquired a beauty of letters derived from reed pens, vanishes when the books fall into deep wells, to wit, into the possession of fools; so likewise, why hath your benevolent mission, virtuous as you are, disappeared, alas, even after you have assumed Nala's beautiful form.
(Tr. K.K. Handiqui)

Manifestation in the Arts

The most obvious use of lines is found in the visual arts where *rekhā* is a basic and indispensable element of form. In any art-form the line is not just a geometrical necessity, but is charged with symbolism and an inherent quality and power. Before coming to the individual manifestations in sculpture, painting, architecture and dance, it is therefore meaningful to treat the basic philosophy of the line in Indian art, as we find it most explicitly in the **Vāstusūtra Upaniṣad**, of Orissan origin. Other texts on Śilpa or Vāstu use various descriptions of lines, but do not give the reason of the line and its symbolism. Therefore this late Upaniṣad can throw light even on all the other art-forms.

Right at the beginning the text defines the artist or sculptor in this way:

वृत्तज्ञानं रेखाज्ञानं च यो जानाति स स्थापकः ॥

VSUp I.4

Who has the knowledge of circle and line is a *sthāpaka.*
(Tr. A. Boner and B. Bäumer, as also the following quotations)

Here it appears that *rekhā* denotes a straight line first and foremost, although a circle is also drawn by a line.

The text is mostly concerned with the composition of sacred images and image-panels, and it describes the compositional diagrams and their symbolism. This diagram is termed *pañjara, khilapañjara* or sometimes *rekhāvāsa,* 'an abode of lines'.

शैलं खिलपञ्जरं, कीलेन पञ्जराकृतिकोष्ठका रेखावासः तदा रूपाङ्गानि मर्माण्याश्रयन्ते तच्छैलभेदनम् ।

Comm. on VSUp I.8

(Six disciplines of Art are the following.) Knowledge of stones (*śailam*), compositional diagrams (*khilapañjara*) made with a peg, a net-work of lines for housing the image like a cage, in which the limbs of the image depend on the vital points (*marmāṇi*), the carving of stones (*śailabhedana*)...

Elsewhere the diagram is called *kīrtyāvāsa,* the term *kīrti* referring both to the temple and to the image, both being an abode of divine glory. The lines are first drawn on the dressed stone with powder, and slightly engraved (cf. VSUp II.4–5). Then the limbs of the images to be carved are placed in relation to these lines (*rekhānvaye sarvāṅgāni nyāsaya* – VSUp II.8). The drawing of the lines is called *bhedanakriyā,* dividing action (comm. on VSUp II.8), since the lines create divisions on the otherwise plain surface.

But the text goes further in the investigation of the meaning of form and line. Āṅgirasa said: I am asking the *brāhmaṇa* the venerable Pippalāda, two questions, whether he may tell me:

का रेखा, कस्तस्या भावः, कति भेदाः, ब्रूहि पिप्पलादेति ।
तान् ह स ऋषिरुवाच–आङ्गिरस, शिल्पकाश्यप शृणु रेखाव्याख्यानम् । तथा तासां भावञ्च । रेखा न्यासस्याधारः सा धारेव । सा कर्मप्रतीतेरधिभूतमधिदैवतञ्च ।
तेजांसि सरलरेखाः ॥
तद्रेखेण मण्डलं भिन्दन्ति, यथा कर्त्तारः कर्मणा विश्वं परिभिन्दन्ति .... ।

Comm. on VSUp II.8–9

What is the line? What is its character (*bhāva*)? How many varieties are there? Please tell, O Pippalāda.

To them the *ṛsi* said: O Āṅgirasa and Śilpakāśyapa, hear the explanation of the lines and their character (*bhāva*). The line is the support (determinant) of the composition, it is like a boundary (or like a stream, *dhārā*). It is that which corresponds to the fundamental elements (*adhibhūta*) and to the gods (*adhidaivata*) in the realisation of action.

Straight lines are as rays of light.

By the line they (the *sthāpakas*) divide the circle, as the creators by their action divide the world.

If the lines are identified with rays of light, *tejas*, this implies their straightness as well as their inherent energy. The drawing of the essential lines is thus as powerful as the creation, and hence the division of the field into four parts corresponds to the division of the world into four continents.

मण्डलमध्ये द्वे मध्यरेखे लिखन्ति मध्यरेखा मध्यप्रस्थरेखा भवति । सममानेन तत्रोपलभन्ते चतुष्खण्डक्षेत्राणि चतुर्द्वीपां पृथिवीमिव, एषा भूमिक्षेत्रस्य भावना ।

Comm. on VSUp II.13

They (*sthāpakas*) trace two centre-lines within the circle, they are the vertical middle line (*madhyarekhā*) and the horizontal middle line (*madhyaprastha rekhā*). There they obtain four parts of the same measure, like the four continents of the earth. This is the conception (*bhāvanā*) of the earth-field.

Just as the word is all-powerful for the poet, so is the line for the sculptor, painter and architect.

रेखाज्ञानं सर्वमिति ज्ञेयम् ॥

VSUp II.27

The knowledge of the line is to be known as all-comprehensive.

The most powerful line in any panel is the vertical middle line, called *brahmasūtra* or *brahmakīla*. The commentary gives a number of comparisons which are revealing:

ब्रह्मकीलमध्यगरेखया द्वैतांशे ब्रह्मकीलेन सह क्षेत्रं विभाजयन्ति । यथा धरायां मेरुकीलं, पशौ पृष्ठास्थि, वृक्षे सुषीरं, जीवे जीवात्मा, तथा रेखा हि सत्यम् । रेखा रूपस्य कारणम् । ततो रेखायां दशकोष्ठकान् विभाजयोत्तिष्ठक्रमेण, येन समोपक्षेत्राणि लभेरन् ।

Comm. on VSUp IV.26

They divide the field (panel) in two parts by the *brahmakīla* which is the vertical middle line, like the post of mount Meru (*merukīla*) on the earth, like the backbone in the animal, like the marrow of the tree, like the soul in the living being. Thus the line is verily a fundamental reality (*satyam*), it is the origin of form. Therefore, division in ten sections should be made by lines from below upwards, by which equal subdivisions may be obtained, thus some sections are divided.

It is due to the power of the compositional lines that images conforming to them become beautiful and harmonious (*surūpa* in II.20–21):

रेखासंयोगे तत्क्षेत्रेऽङ्गानि सौभगानि भवन्ति ॥

अग्निरेखायामुत्थिताङ्गानि । अप्पार्श्वगरेखायां स्थिराङ्गानि । मारुतरेखायां वेगप्रदर्शनाङ्गानि । एतन्निपातनेन रूपाणि मन आकर्षयन्ति ।

Comm. on VSUp IV.28

When the limbs in that panel adhere to the lines they become well-proportioned (harmonious).

On vertical lines erect limbs, on horizontal lines restful and quiet limbs, on diagonal lines limbs showing speed (movement). Setting them in this way the forms (images) attract the mind.

The verticals, horizontals and diagonals have each a different character and symbolism, which is compared to the nature of the primal elements:

रूपतत्त्वे विना रेखाकरणं रूपं हीनमिति ध्येयम् ।

उत्थितरेखा अग्निरूपा:, पार्श्वगा अब्रूपा:, तिर्यग्रेखा मरुद्रूपा इति ॥

रेखाप्रभेदे भावभेदा उपजायन्ते । रेखानुसृतं रूपं विभाति । रूपं सुरूपं भवतीति ।

Comm. on VSUp II.21–22

According to the principle of form it should be remembered that without tracing the lines (of the diagram) the form becomes deficient.

Vertical lines have the nature of fire, horizontal lines have the nature of water, diagonal lines have the nature of wind (*māruta*).

With the different lines the differences of characters (of images) arise. That form shines forth as determined by the lines and the form becomes perfect (*surūpa*).

This symbolism is then elaborated:

वज्रचूर्णेन लिखन्ति ।

तिस्रः रेखाः श्रेष्ठाः ॥

ऊर्ध्वरेखा अग्निरेखाः यथा शिखा उत्थिता प्रज्वलति । पार्श्वगा रेखा अप्छेदा यथा नदीनां प्रवाहः । कर्णक्षेत्रगा भेनकारेखा मारुतच्छेदा मारुतस्य तिर्यग्गतिरिव, उदाहृतरेखया शैलक्षेत्रे पञ्जराख्यं कोष्ठककर्माऽऽचरेत् । एष कोष्ठकः अग्न्यम्मारुतरेखासमष्ट्या संयोगेन सम्भवति ।

Comm. on VSUp VI.4–5

They (sculptors) trace them with white stone-powder.

Three (types of) lines are essential.

Vertical lines are fire-lines like a flame soaring upwards, horizontal lines are water-lines, like the flow of rivers, diagonal lines going to the corners are wind-lines, like the transversal motion of the wind. With the above-mentioned lines one should make a grid (*koṣṭhaka*) on the stone panel, which is called *pañjara*. This grid is the combination of the vertical, horizontal and oblique lines.

This exposition has shown not only the creative power of the lines of a diagram, but also the symbolism of the various types of lines, comparable only to a →*yantra*. The line itself is composed of chain of →*bindu*s although this formation often remains invisible. In the context of temple architecture the *yoginī-yantra* which is at the basis of a *śakti* temple, is described in the **Śilpa Prakāśa**, where the different lines are associated with the three *guṇa*s.

बिन्दुक्रान्ता तदा रेखा रजोरेखा हि कथ्यते ।
बाहुप्रान्तं समारभ्य योजयेत् तमसापि वा ॥
निम्ने तमोगुणा छेदा त्रिकोणविपरीतगा ।
ततः सत्त्वं मध्यभागे रेखाकरणमुत्तमम् ॥
तद्वत् तामसिके चैव निम्नरेखा च निम्नगा ।
योजयेत् त्रिभुजाकारे रजोबिन्दुं समाचरेत् ॥
ऊर्ध्वे निम्ने च पञ्चभ्यः त्रिकोणं यन्त्रमुत्तमम् ।
अन्ते पार्श्वद्वये तद्वत् त्रिकोणं रजसन्निभम् ॥
मध्ये योगिनीरेखा च सर्वयन्त्रसुभाविनी ।
सर्वत्रिकोणः बिन्दुश्च छेदिनी दण्डरूपिणी ॥

ŚiPrak I.93–97

The line passing through the *bindu*s is called *rajorekhā* (*rajas*-line). Beginning from the end of the line, the *tamas* (triangle) should be joined to it.

Below, the lines of this *tamoguṇa* form a triangle in opposite direction. Then it is best to draw a line across the middle of the *sattva guṇa*.

Similarly, in the *tamas trikoṇa* below turned downwards a line is going across. These (lines) are joined with the *rajobindu* (central point) forming triangles.

This best *yantra* is made of five triangles above and below. Finally, on both sides in the same way a triangle is joined to the *rajas* (*bindu*).

In the centre there is the Yoginī-line, giving the whole *yantra* a good aspect (*subhāva*). Like a rod it pierces all the points of the triangles. (Tr. A. Boner)

Here the lines of the *yantra* have a qualitative significance, being associated with the qualities of the three →*guṇa*s. These lines forming the *yantra*

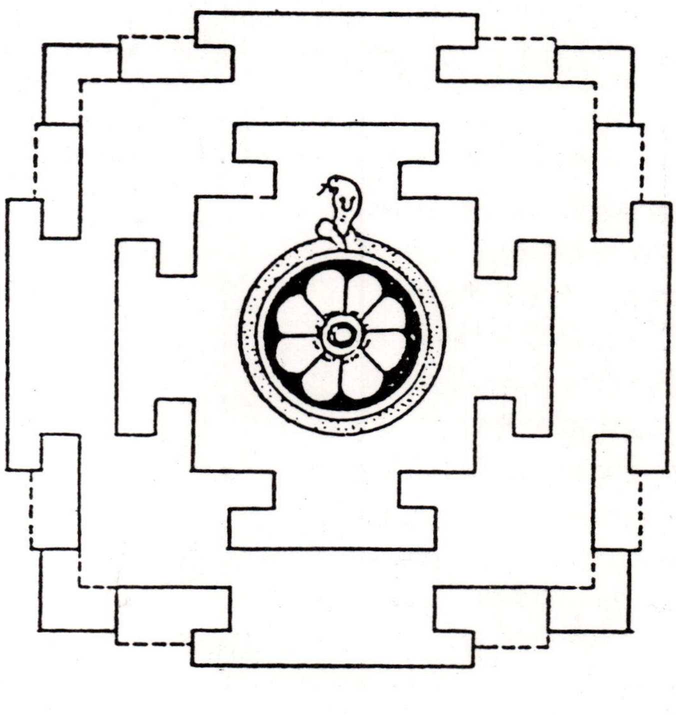

Figure 2: *Bhairavayantra*

become invisible when inserted in the foundation of a *śakti* temple. Similarly, the same text describes *yantras* underlying the composition of images, such as Bhairava (cf. ŚiPrak I.158–168; II.69–76). Line-incisions denoting bas-relief are an important decorative element of the temple.

> तदूर्ध्वे रेखकर्म च अपरवाडसन्निधौ ।
> छेदाकारे तदा रेखः चतुःपार्श्वे यथाक्रमे ॥
> शृणु गर्भ-रेख-कर्म प्रस्थाकारे विशेषतः ।
> द्विभागं वेदभागं वा भित्तिः किंवाकृतिर्बलिः ॥
>
> ŚiPrak II.48, 52
>
> Above that there is line-work along the breadth of the wall. That line-work is in form of incisions running around all four sides.
>
> Hear about the line-work on the *garbha* (running) mainly in the horizontal. This portion, divided into two or three parts (constitutes) the wall, in the form of mouldings (forming pillars) (in continuation of the five divisions of the lower wall).

In secular architecture *rekhā* is used for the lines of a ground-plan and of the *vāstupuruṣamaṇḍala* (cf. BṛSam LIII.42), and the outlines of the plan are drawn on the ground at the beginning of a construction (cf. BṛSam LIII.100). A similar process is followed in temple architecture and charged with symbolism. Thus the *garbhagṛha* is determined by the lines of the ground-plan:

> रोधयेत् रेखा पार्श्वेण अर्धभागे सुनिश्चिते ।
> आडरेखां समारभ्य गर्भरेखान्तचालनम् ॥
>
> ŚiPrak I.66
>
> These lines at the sides are arrested half-way. Starting from the *āḍa-rekhā*, going to the *garbha-rekhā*. (Tr. A. Boner)

The front-wall of the *mukhaśālā* of a temple is made with different designs where *rekhā* (line) plays a major role.

> शृणुष्व मुखशालासु सम्मुखा रेखाविधिं पुनः ।
> रेखाभेदस्तथा छेदः वसन्तफेणिकादयः ॥
>
> ŚiPrak I.203
>
> Hear about the method of designing the *mukhaśālā* front, the different lines (*rekhā*), divisions (*cheda*), creeper-bands (*vasanta*), cornices (*pheṇi*) and other things.
> (Tr. A. Boner)

The Kailāsa temple type is attractive with its various parts and divisions. Its walls are made with *jāṅghas* and *bandhanās*, where the *bandhanā* resembles lines.

> वर्धिता अर्धभागेन शिखरभूमिः जायते ।
> मध्यबन्धना संकीर्णे पञ्चरेखादिसन्निभम् ॥
>
> ŚiPrak II.32
>
> The base for the spire (*śikhara-bhūmi*) is projecting by half a part. The middle *bandhanā* is narrow, looking like five lines (with five parts conjoined). (Tr. A. Boner)

But apart from the ground-plan and decorative carvings, *rekha* (m.) assumes a technical meaning in the elevation of the temple *śikhara* of North Indian style. The reason for this terminology is that the vertical sections of the spire (it may be a *pañcaratha* or *saptaratha* temple) are rising upwards marking clear lines. The term *rekha* is masculine because it is related to →*prāsāda*, and a further reason is given in some Śilpa texts that the *śikhara* or *vimāna* represents the bridegroom, and the *śālā* the bride (cf.→*sandhi*).

> विश्वभागा कृता रेखा गर्भदेशे बलाकृतौ ।
> अपरभाग सम्पन्ने प्रस्तरस्य मुखे तथा ॥
>
> ŚiPrak I.504
>
> Inside the hall the entire part is in the shape of a rounded moulding. On the opposite side the stone remains complete (uncut, flat). (Tr. A. Boner)

> सर्वलक्षणसम्पन्नं विमानं पागधारिणी ।
> एवं कृत्वा तदा रेखकैलासं रथमन्दिरे ॥
>
> ŚiPrak II.133
>
> Endowed with all the features of the (big) *vimāna-pāga*, this (is made) according to the rules on the *rekha-kailāsa* and on the *ratha*-temple. (Tr. A. Boner)

> रेखनिर्देशरूपेणाचरेत् न मिश्रीकरणं कदा ।
> रेखः पुरुषाकारः मञ्जुश्री यन्त्रमन्दिरम् ॥
>
> ŚiRaKo 393
>
> (These *vimānikās* should follow) the *rekha* form. It (this type of temple) should never be mixed (with other forms). The *rekha*-temple has the form of *puruṣa*, whereas the Mañjuśrī is a *yantra*-temple.

In temple architecture the vertical and horizontal lines are in harmonious combination, and the basis is always the ground-plan or *yantra*.

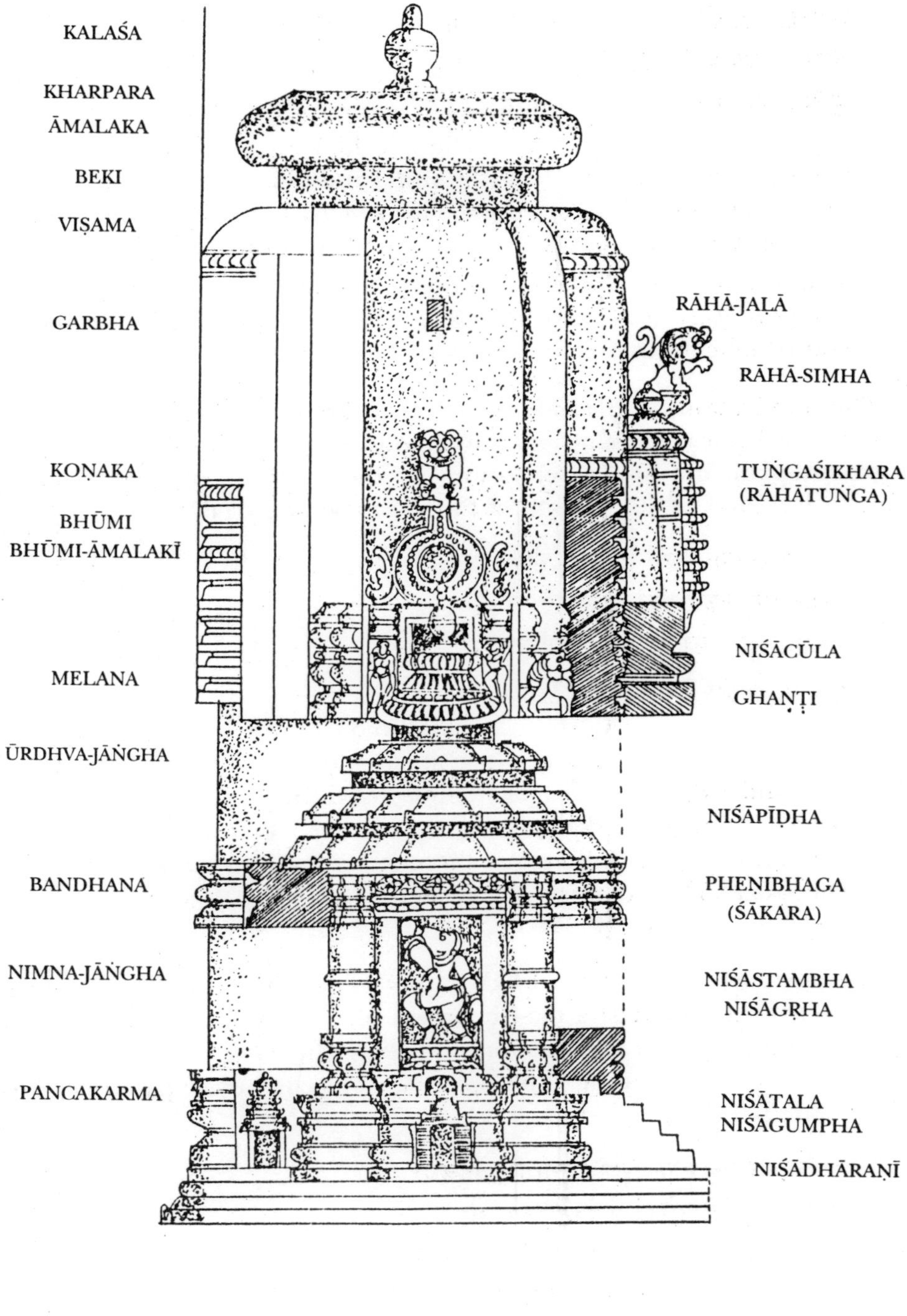

Figure 3: *Rekhā śikhara*

यन्त्रं रेखाकृतौ मुख्ये अलङ्कारेण मण्डयेत् ।
कोणकं पञ्चभागेन प्रतिभागं त्रिभागकम् ॥
छेदगुणान्वये भागः तद्भागः रेख उच्यते ।
मूलमारभ्य अन्ते च इषुसंख्यानुसारतः ॥

ŚiPrak II.84–85

Constructed on the lines of the *yantra* and decorated mainly with line-ornaments (flat carvings). The *koṇaka* is in five parts, and each of these parts has three (horizontal) sections (*bhūmis*).

The single parts linked together by line incisions (of small *vajramastakas*) are called *rekhā-bhāga.* From the base to the upper end (the neck) these are five in number. (Tr. A. Boner)

The implication of this statement is that the *rekha* temple has an emphasis on vertical lines, and the *yantra* temple is not only based on a →*yantra* in its ground-plan, but also in elevation. By the *yantra* form, called *meru*, the clear vertical lines of the sections of the *śikhara* get blurred.

प्रासादः रेखपीढाख्यः द्विविधः भास्करमते ।
विमानं पुरुषाकारं पीठात् ध्वजस्थलावधिः ॥
तामसराजस सत्त्वं गुणत्रयं क्रमोदितम् ।
भुवनभागसंयुक्तं रेखप्रासाद एव च ॥

ŚiRaKo 6–7

In the opinion of Bhāskara (architect) the temple is of two types: *rekha* and *pīḍha.* The *vimāna* (temple) is in the form of the Puruṣa (Man), from the *pīṭha* (plinth) up to the flag (on the top). In ascending order it follows the three *guṇas*: *tamas, rajas* and *sattva.* The *rekha* temple consists of fourteen parts.
(Tr. B. Bäumer & R.P. Das)

It is obviously in painting (*ālekhya, citrābhāsa*) where the line is an essential element. The **Abhilaṣitārtha-Cintāmaṇi** of Someśvara gives a very significant definition of *rekhā* as *ākārajanikā*, 'the mother of form', parallel to the definition of *lekhā* or drawing as *ākāramātṛkā*, in its chapter on painting (*ālekhya-karma*):

पश्चाच्चित्रं विचित्रं च तस्यां भित्तौ लिखेद्बुधः ।
नानाभावरसैर्युक्तं सुरेखं वर्णकोचितम् ॥
पूर्वं तिन्दुकलेख्यं स्याद् यद् वा वर्तिकया बुधैः ।
आकारमात्रिकां लेखां विना वर्णं लिखेत्पुनः ॥

आकारजनिकां रेखां तिन्दुवर्तिकनिर्मिताम् ।
लिखेत्तामेव लेखिन्या गैरिकोद्भूतवर्णतः ॥

Abhil I.3.150, 160–161

After this, the knowledgeable man should paint the picture (*citra*) and ornament (*vicitra*) on the wall, embodying diverse moods (*bhāva*) and passions (*rasa*), with clear outline (*surekhā*) and appropriate pigment (*varṇaka*).

By knowledgeable men, the drawing should first be made with the style (*tindukā*) or the crayon (*vartikā*), then again without colour line-in the draft (*lekhā*) which is the prototype of the representation (*ākāra-mātṛkā*).

But with the brush (*lekhanī*) and pigment prepared from ochre (*gairika*) line in that very outline (*rekhā*) which was done with the style or with the crayon, and is progenitive with respect to the representation (*ākāra-janikā*). (Tr. A.K. Coomaraswamy)

A similar definition is given in the **Śivatattva-Ratnākara** (v. 29) which speaks of *ākāra-nirmitāṃ rekhām* 'the outline defining the figure' (quoted in A.K. Coomaraswamy, "*The technique and theory of Indian Painting*", p. 13). Coomaraswamy adds a note to the above text: "... it is the model imitated in the first drawing to be put down on the wall, which drawing (*lekhā*) establishes the measure (*pramāṇa*) of and is progenitive-with-respect-to the finished-representation (*ākāra janikā*)" (*ibid.*, p. 15). The section starts with a definition of an expert painter:

प्रगल्भैर्भावुकैस्तज्ज्ञैः सूक्ष्मरेखाविशारदैः ।
विद्युन्निर्माणकुशलैः पत्रलेखनकोविदैः ॥
वर्णपूरणदक्षैश्च वीरणे च कृतश्रमैः ।
चित्रकैर्लेखयेच्चित्रं नानारससमुद्भवम् ॥

Abhil I.3.139–140

Artists who are proficient, endowed with feelings and knowing the subject, who are masters of the subtle line, who are capable of drawing a flash of lightning, who are experts in the art of calligraphy, who are skilful in filling in colour and who are hard-working should paint a picture which gives rise to various emotions (in the onlooker).

The line is not only important as outline or sketch, but also in painting details such as fine hair:

रोमराजिमितां कुर्यात् रेखां नानाविधामपि ।

वीरणैस्सूक्ष्मतुण्डाग्रैर्मृदुघर्षणयोगत: ॥

Abhil I.3.180

Make also the strokes (*rekhā*) that represent the growth of hair, in its various ways, working delicately with the tips of the fine points. (Tr. A.K. Coomaraswamy)

In fact, the line is important at two stages of drawing or painting: "First when the painter starts sketching and second, at the end, when he paints the final lines." In fact, the "line is a conceptual proposition in a work of art. It is elemental and abstract but has the potentiality of rendering shapes, forms and contents" (D. Pathy, *Essence of Orissan Paintings*, p. 43). There are certain art-forms which are entirely dependent on lines, such as palmleaf illustrations. There the lines are etched in with a stylus and cannot be erased or corrected. Other arts of the line are done with various media like rice-paste, either on the floor or on walls (*bhaumacitra*, etc.).

The **Viṣṇudharmottara Purāṇa** in its Citrasūtra contains an elaborate description of the process of painting. There are four ways of appreciation of a painting, of which the best is by the masters who know the line:

रेखा च वर्तना चैव भूषणं वर्णमेव च ।
विज्ञेया मनुजश्रेष्ठ चित्रकर्मसु भूषणम् ॥
रेखां प्रशंसन्त्याचार्या वर्तनां च विचक्षणा: ।
स्त्रियो भूषणमिच्छन्ति वर्णाढ्यमितरे जना: ॥
इति मत्वा तथा यत्न: कर्तव्यश्चित्रकर्मणि ।
सर्वस्य चित्तग्रहणं यथा स्यान्मनुजोत्तम ॥

VDhPur III.41.10–12

(Oh) best of men, in works of *citra*, delineation, shading, ornamentation and colouring should be known as decorative (i.e., as the elementation of visualisation).

The masters praise the *rekhās* (lines), the connoisseurs praise the display of light and shade, women like the display of ornaments, the rest of the public like richness of colours.

Considering this, great care should be taken in the work of *citra*, so that, (oh) best of men, it may be appreciated by every one. (Tr. S. Kramrisch)

Light and shade, or rather shading, is produced by three types of lines:

चित्रमिश्रं समाख्यातं समासान्मनुजोत्तम ।
तिस्रश्च वर्तना: प्रोक्ता: पत्राहैविकबिन्दुजा: ॥

पत्राकृतिभी रेखाभिः कथितात्र च वर्तना ।
अतीव कथिता सूक्ष्मा तथाहैरिकवर्तना ॥
तथा च स्तम्भनायुक्ता कथिता बिन्दुवर्तना ।
दौर्बल्यबिन्दुरेखत्वमविभक्तत्वमेव च ॥

VDhPur III.41.5–7

Methods of producing light and shade are said to be three:

(1) Crossing lines (lit. lines in the form of leaves, *patraja*), (2) by stumping (*airika*), and (3) by dots (*binduja*). The first method (of shading) is called (*patraja*) on account of lines in the shape of leaves. The *airika* method is called so because it is said to be very fine. The *binduja* method is called so from the restrained (i.e. not flowing) handling of the brush. (Tr. S. Kramrisch)

From the description of the defects (*doṣa*) in painting one can deduce the ideal of drawing or painting a line: feeble lines (*daurbalya*), broken lines (*bindurekhatva*), too thick lines (*sthūlarekhatva*) or crooked lines (*vakrarekhatva*) have to be avoided since they do not produce a good painting, and hence the opposite has to be the case. Lines have to be unbroken, equal, sure and yet fine, and even.

सुस्निग्धविस्पष्टसुवर्णरेखं विद्वान्यथादेशविशेषवेशम् ।
प्रमाणशोभाभिरहीयमानं कृतं भवेच्चित्रमतीव चित्रम् ॥

VDhPur III.41.15

A painting should be then very beautiful, when a learned (artist) paints it with golden colour, with articulate and yet very soft lines, with distinct and well arranged garments, and lastly not devoid of the beauty of (proportionate) measurement. (Tr. S. Kramrisch)

In the **Nārada Śilpa-Śāstra** (chapters on painting, edited by V. Raghavan), the importance of even lines is stressed:

तदिदं वै चित्रकाल्पनिकं त्रिधा विभक्तं – अथो भौमिकं, कुड्यकं, ऊर्ध्वकमित्याह भगवान् नारदः ।

तत्र वै नानाभेदकं ताक्षणिकात् (?) क्वचित्काल्पनिकात् (?) नानाद्रव्यकैः कृत्रिमाकृत्रिमरूपकैः, शाश्वतकं क्वचित् तात्कालिकमिति ह वै तत्र बहुधाकं चित्रं मानज्ञाः परिजकरेजककुम्भकभेदटंकवर्धनटंककैः (?) अभिवर्धयेयुः विविधेषु काल्पनिकेषु, यथामानं, अविषमरेखिकं, अविरुद्धसूत्रापातनिकमिति । .... सर्वत्र ह समरेखिकजुट्कं शान्तं नानालङ्कृत्युद्भासितं ।

NārŚiŚ pāṭha 71, p. 21

This painting is divided into three kinds, of the floor, of the wall and of the upper regions, says Nārada (1).

These various kinds of painting (2), sometimes on carvings (3), (with) various materials (4), (of) artificial designs and natural forms (5), permanent and temporary (6), those knowing measurements shall make in abundance (7), on various surfaces in accordance with general measurements, in even lines and in conformity to (the rules regarding) pose-lines (8). ...

In all places, (the *citra* shall be) in even lines, auspicious, shining with various ornaments and neither more nor less in respect of lines. (Tr. V. Raghavan)

Nārada mentions square shaped diagrams with lines, called *pañjara*, (*caturaśrāṃ madhyarekhikāṃ pañjarākṛtikam...* – NārŚiŚ pāṭha 71).

The evenness of the line is also enjoined in the **Devī Purāṇa** while drawing an image of the goddess:

समा रेखा तु कर्तव्याऽविच्छिन्ना पुञ्जवर्जिता ॥
अङ्गुष्ठपर्ववैपुल्या समा कार्या विजानता ।

DPur LXV.66cd–67ab

A line should be drawn uniformly without breaks and without any rewriting. Their breadth should not be greater than that of the thumb. (Tr. R.S. Bhattacharya)

In the making of a divine image the last act is the drawing of the eyes, corresponding to the 'opening of the eyes' (*netronmīlana*), accompanied by the *netramantra*:

हेमसूचीप्रहाराभ्यां पक्ष्मरेखां समालिखेत् ।
सितमण्डलमालिख्य दृष्टिमण्डलमालिखेत् ॥
ज्योतिर्मण्डलकं पश्चान्नेत्रमुच्चार्य लेखयेत् ।

RauUĀ Anubandha V.10–11ab

By the strikes of needle made of gold one should draw the eyelids. Then drawing the white eyeball one should draw the luminous dot of the eye sight. Then uttering *netra mantra* one should draw the circle of the halo. (Tr. H.N. Chakravarty)

रजतस्यैव सूच्या तु पक्ष्मरेखाश्च लेखयेत् ।
नेत्रमन्त्रं समुच्चार्य कृष्णमण्डलमालिखेत् ॥
ज्योतिर्मण्डलमालिख्य मध्वाज्यं च समर्पयेत् ।

RauUĀ XIII.5–6ab

But by the needle of silver one should draw lines of the hairs of the eye-lids and then uttering the *mantra* related to the eye he should draw the black eye-ball and then drawing the luminous disc (of it) he should offer honey and clarified butter.
(Tr. H.N. Chakravarty)

The golden needle used in this process is essential because of the sacredness of the divine eyes.

नेत्रमन्त्रमनुस्मरन्नजसूत्रं पार्श्वसूत्रं च ।
हाटकनिर्मितसूच्या आचार्यः संलिखेद् रेखाम् ॥

Mayam XXXIII.106

Bearing the Netra formula in mind, the Master roughs out the lines, the line of *aja* and the lateral ones, using a gold point to do so. (Tr. B. Dagens)

Rekhā in Music and Dance

In music, *rekhā* does not find a place because Indian thought has not emphasized the visual aspect of music in notation. In the Western tradition, music is 'seen' in notation and there naturally lines have an important place. The visual contemplation of *rāgas* and *rāgiṇīs* in Indian music pertains to the human or divine which belongs to the area of painting.

In dance, of course, *rekhā* is conceived as an important component of the dancer's regular practice. *Rekhā* has been defined as:

शिरोनेत्रकरादीनामङ्गानां मेलने सति ।
कायस्थितिर्मनोनेत्रहारी रेखा प्रकीर्तिता ॥

SR VII.1226 (cf. NN IV.2.343cd–344ab)

Rekhā is the posture of the body where limbs like the head, eyes, hands, etc. are 'unified' and which captures the heart and mind.
(Tr. P.L. Sharma)

The dancer is expected to practice *rekhā* among other things:

दण्डिकालम्बिनी कन्याभ्यस्येदङ्गविवर्तनम् ।
वलनं स्थापनं रेखां तालसाम्यं लयानपि ॥

SR VII.1232

The girl who hangs by the rod (that is fixed on two pillars) should practise the rotation of limbs, bending, steadiness, *rekhā*, unity with *tāla* and *laya* (control of speed). (Tr. **P.L. Sharma)**

Even today, the excellence of the gestures and postures of the dancers is described in terms of the clarity of 'lines', as in the following definitions of *rekhā* from the texts on dance:

> या शिरोङ्घ्रिकरनेत्रपङ्कजा-
> द्यङ्गमेलनविधौ सति स्फुटम् ।
> कें (? का) चिदत्र [च] दिश (? दृशा) मनोहरा
> सा स्थितिर्निगदितात्र रेखिका ॥
>
> NṛKo IV.4.11
>
> When the head, feet, hand, eyes are united to resemble a lotus and when the stance [produces] a beautiful sight [the effect] is known as *rekhikā.* (Tr. M. Bose)
>
> अङ्गप्रत्यङ्गकानां यः सन्निवेशो यथोचितः ।
> सैवोक्ता जनताचित्तनयनानन्ददायिनी ॥ इति रेखा ।
>
> SDar VII.106
>
> The arrangement of *aṅgas* and *pratyaṅgas* as they should be [and] pleasing to the soul and the eyes of people – such is *rekhā.* (Tr. M. Bose)

Process

The method of drawing lines depends on the medium and on the use. Lines drawn on the ground or on the surface of a stone are marked with coloured thread (→*sūtra*) – whether in the construction of Vedic altars, in marking the groundplan of a temple or in drawing *yantras* or *maṇḍalas,* as well as auspicious designs (in different Indian languages called variously *bhauma-citra, ālpanā, citā, koḷam,* etc.) in front of houses or shrines.

Lines on a permanent material such as stone or metal are engraved with a chisel or sharp instrument and thus remain permanently. Engraving is also the method used for inscriptions. Writing of manuscripts on a material such as palm-leaf is also done by engraving the lines with a stylus (*lekhanī*).

But drawing lines for a (*yantra* or *maṇḍala*) any sacred structure or diagram or sculpture is a ritual procedure which has to be prepared by the necessary purificatory rites and accompanied by the appropriate →*mantras.* The awareness that the drawing of a line is a participation in the creative and re-creative process of the universe is always present to a greater or lesser degree.

In painting, the drawing of the outlines precedes the application of colour – whether in a wall painting or in a painting on cloth or paper. Different instruments are used, and different methods, such as dotted lines, or fully drawn thin or thick lines. Thus drawing is the basis of painting.

Conclusion

In the visual and ritual arts, including architecture, the line (*rekhā*) is an essential structural and symbolical element. It delineates, separates and encloses, it creates structures and forms, and is therefore, an element of creation, of structuring the unstructured. Creating sacred space by the drawing of lines, whether in a two-dimensional →*maṇḍala* or in a three-dimensional temple, is a basic ritual and artistic action.

Bettina Bäumer

Select Bibliography

Boner, Alice: Principles of Composition in Hindu Sculpture, Delhi: IGNCA and MLBD, 2nd edn, 1990.

Coomaraswamy, A.K.: Abhilaṣitārthacintāmaṇi, The Technique & Theory of Indian Painting, in Journal of the U.P. Historical Society, Lucknow, Vol. XXIII, 1950.

Kramrisch, Stella: The Vishnudharmottara (part III), A Treatise on Indian Painting and Image-making, Calcutta: Calcutta University, 2nd edn, 1928.

Mishra, Haramohan: Dimensions of hṛllekhā, Abstracts of Xth World Sanskrit Conference, Bangalore, 1997.

Pathy, Dinanath: Essence of Orissan Paintings. Delhi: Harman Publishing House, 2001.

Raghavan, V.: Two chapters on Painting in the Nārada Śilpa Śāstra, in Journal of the Indian Society of Oriental Art, 3 (1), June 1935, pp. 15–32.

ĀKĀRA/ĀKṚTI

Overview

Ākāra (m.) and *ākṛti* (f.) generally stand for form and shape, *ākriyate anena iti ākāraḥ,* by which a form is shaped. Every thing in the world or universe must have some form. Most of the objects are recognised by their shape but there are a few things which although exist yet remain unnoticed. Even being invisible their presence is felt or experienced by external or internal faculties. The smell is felt but not seen, similarly air is felt but not seen. →*Ākāśa* (sky) is experienced but does not have visible shape.

There are some words which do convey the sense of *ākāra* or *ākṛti* but are written and pronounced differently, e.g. →*rūpa,* →*vigraha,* →*pratimā,* →*vastu,* etc. At the same time the terms *ākāra* and *ākṛti* have multiple meanings and explanations which depend on the situation and context. While in visual arts (art, architecture, iconography, sculpture, etc.) these are commonly accepted to express figure, form, shape, dimension and measurements, in the performing arts (music, dance and drama) *ākāra* and *ākṛti* denote gestures and expressions which are abstract.

At the philosophical plane the terms *sākāra* and *nirākāra* have altogether a different connotation as the manifest and unmanifest aspects of *brahman* are visualised. In the Sūtra literature and also at certain place in the **Mahābhārata** *ākṛti* stands for a person following the prescribed (good) code of conduct and *nirākṛti* suggest a person who transgressed the decent conventions.

The perusal of scriptures from the Vedic times to the modern period reveals that there are about sixty interpretations of these terms (*ākāra* and *ākṛti*) and their study becomes a very interesting subject.

Etymology and Related Words

Traditionally *ākāra* may be derived from the root *kṛ-* to manifest, preceded by the prefix *ā* and followed by the suffix *ghañ* in the instrumental voice. Thus *ākāra* as a compound denotes something by which a shape or form is manifested. Kṣīrasvāmin while commenting on the **Amara Kośa** (III.2.15, III.3.162) on *ākāra* agrees to this point, when he says *ākāra ākaraṇam,* i.e. *ākāra* means to give shape of something. As regards derivation of *ākṛti,* we find the same prefix and root; the only change is with the feminine suffix *ktin*; hence the word conveys the sense of shape or form itself.

However, scholars of modern age have tried to explain it in a different way. From Prabhupāda's observation in his translation on the **Bhāgavata Purāṇa** (III.4.28) we find a new approach on the etymological expression of the term – "*Ākṛti* means complete pastime; *ā* means complete and *kṛti* means transcendental pastime. *Ākṛti* also means signal."

Lexicographers have used *ākāra* and *ākṛti* almost synonymously to denote more or less same meaning, i.e. *iṅgita* (hint) and *ākṛti* (form).

आकाराविङ्गिताकृती ॥

AmKo III.3.162d (cf. VaiKo V.2.22; MedKo XXVII.115a)

Ākāra means hint and form. (Tr. R.S. Bhattacharya)

Kṣīrasvāmin has explained here *iṅgita* as expression or effort to suggest something (*bhāvasūcakaṃ ceṣṭitam*). Thus we find that they have explained *ākāra* and *ākṛti* from a common platform though some specific meanings are always there, e.g. physique, shape or structure, transformation, etc.

आकारस्त्वाकृतावात्मवैकृते ।

VaiKo VII.1.7ab

Ākāra denotes shape or formation (*ākṛti*) and transformation from original. (Tr. P. Ghosal)

आकारे देह आकृतिः ॥

VaiKo VII.2.2d

Ākṛti means physique or figure, i.e. body structure. (Tr. P. Ghosal)

आकृतिस्तु स्त्रियां रूपे सामान्यवपुषोरपि ।

MedKo XVI.95ab

Ākṛti in feminine gender means form, generality. (Tr. S. Das)

Layers of Meaning

The lexicons have unfolded several meanings of *ākāra* and *ākṛti* depending on the situation. Amarasiṃha prefers to accept the meaning as hint and form (AmKo III.3.162). The remark of Kṣīrasvāmin in this regard is noteworthy when he explains as under: 'hint (*iṅgita*) is the effort to suggest some purpose. Form (*ākṛti*) is colourlessness (or paleness) etc. and a collection.'

Sense of configuration is denoted when the **Nyāya-Sūtra** says:

आकृतिर्जातिलिङ्गाख्या ॥

NySū II.2.70

Configuration is that which indicates the generality and its characteristics. (Tr. G.N. Jha)

On the other hand we are informed by the **Viṣṇudharmottara Purāṇa** (III.3.7cd) that *ākṛti* is name of the metre having twenty two syllables. The **Artha-Śāstra** (I.15.7, 9) accepts word *ākṛti* for expression.

Ākṛti often stands for a person or personality and the citations from the **Mahābhārata** (I.8.17), **Raghuvaṃśa** (XV.28d), **Mālavikāgnimitra** (I, after verse 3) and **Abhijñānaśākuntala** (I, after verse 21) are interesting.

If the word is prefixed by *nir* it means Supreme Spirit (ViPur IV.11.4), and without form or formless according to the **Īśānaśivagurudeva Paddhati** (III.69)but as a vulgar fellow in the light of a verse in the **Mahābhārata** (I.122.34) and also a fool (XII.37.41).

We come across about sixty explanations of *ākāra* or *ākṛti* in the scriptures. These are appearance, arrangement, aspect, attributes, attribute-generic, beauty, body, class, concept or conceptual form, configuration, countenance, design, eternal, expression, fantasy, figure, form, frame, follower of discipline, fool, generality, genres, gesture, guide, hint, idea, identity, illusion, image, indication, like, locomotive, magnitude, maker, mansion, meaning, measurement, metre, mode, name, nature, object, perception, physique, planning, proto-type, representation, shape, sign, signal, similarity, size, species, structure, supreme spirit, synonymous, transcendent, vulgar, word, etc.

Development of the Concept

Ākāra or *ākṛti* is a term of great significance for more than one reasons. Firstly, whatever is visible in the universe it comes in the realm of *ākāra* or *ākṛti*. It may be larger than largest and smaller than the smallest. Even a point (→*bindu*) has a form which may be microscopic and not visible through eyes. Secondly, it has multiple meanings and their multiple explanations. There are instances where the word does not occur but its sense is there. When the measurements of a place, object, image or painting are given these result in making a form and *ākṛti* is conceived without being mentioned. Thus, like Brahman (Supreme Spirit) it is omnipresent and sometimes it is seen and sometimes it remains unseen.

Despite a number of connotations *ākāra* or *ākṛti* basically stands for form and shape and it is difficult to make any distinction between the two aspects.

A subtle difference may perhaps be visualised that the form '*ākāra*' is that stage when it has a finished exterior and the shape, *ākṛti* may be explained a stage of framing or shaping. This explanation finds support from the **Artha-Śāstra** (I.15.19). In both the cases a form is seen.

Ākṛti finds mention in the **Ṛgveda** and also in the **Atharvaveda** but with different sense like 'maker':

> यत् त्वा देव प्रपिबन्ति तत आ प्यायसे पुनः ।
> वायुः सोमस्य रक्षिता समानां मास आकृतिः ॥
>
> ṚV X.85.5
>
> O God (Soma), when they (the gods) drink thee, forth thenceforward thou thrivest again. Wind is the protector of Soma; the month is the maker of years. (Tr. L. Sarup)

The above hymn of the **Ṛgveda** is repeated in the **Atharvaveda** also (XIV.1.4) and has been translated as under:

> When they begin to drink thee, then, O God, thou Swellest out again.
>
> Vāyu is Soma's guardian God. The Moon is that which shapes the years. (Tr. R.T.H. Griffith)

With this translation of the same hymn *ākṛti* stands to mean as shape or form whether noun or verb.

The **Ṛgveda** records the word *ākṛta* which is to be explained as properly built or shaped house:

> यत् स्थो दीर्घप्रसद्मनि यद् वादो रोचने दिवः ।
> यद् वा समुद्रे अध्याकृते गृहेऽत आ यातमश्विना ॥
>
> ṚV VIII.10.1
>
> Whether ye travel far away or dwell in yonder light of heaven,
>
> Or in a mansion that is built above the sea, come thence, ye Aśvins hitherward. (Tr. R.T.H. Griffith)

The word *adhyākṛta* may also be interpreted as well proportioned or well placed or suitably set. The adjective *adhi* was probably found necessary as the house has been conceived in the sea and has to be well designed and properly shaped or finished to face the natural adversities of sea like storm, wild waves, winds, and even the aquatic creatures. If it were so, we may conjecture that the hymn suggests a ship. We are well aware of the fact that one stock of the Aryans was engaged in the navigational activities and for this purpose sturdy boats or ships looking like good houses *adhyākṛta gṛha* were built.

The purpose of *ākṛti* has been expressed by other terms or synonyms in the Vedic Saṃhitās, e.g. →*yoni* and →*rūpa* both occur in the following one *mantra*:

> विष्णुर्योनिं कल्पयतु त्वष्टा रूपाणि पिंशतु ।
>
> ṚV X.184.1ab
>
> May all pervading Viṣṇu fashion the womb and Tvaṣṭā render beauty in you. (Tr. H.N. Chakravarty)

In the later Vedic period *ākṛti* is used for nature and creation also.

> स वृक्षकालाकृतिभिः परोऽन्यो यस्मात् प्रपञ्चः परिवर्ततेऽयम् ।
> धर्मावहं पापनुदं भगेशं ज्ञात्वात्मस्थममृतं विश्वधाम ॥
>
> ŚvUp VI.6
>
> Higher and other than the world-tree, time, and forms.
>
> Is He from whom this expanse proceeds.
>
> The bringer of right (*dharma*), the remover of all evil (*pāpa*), the lord of prosperity –
>
> Know Him as in one's own self(*ātma-stha*), as the immortal abode of all. (Tr. R.E. Hume)

The gist is that the Creator of world is above His own creation in the same way as the magician remains free from the impact of his own magic or hypnotism. Here the trees etc. symbolise the nature, i.e. limbs or forms (*ākṛti*) of nature. At the same time, the term *prapañca* suggests different forms of *ākṛti*s, i.e. expansion of world. The Overlord of the universe has to be realised in the Cosmic Form (*viśvadhāma,* i.e. *viśvākṛti*).

The **Nirukta** uses the word *ākāra* in the sense of appearance of forms.

> अथाकारचिन्तनं देवतानाम् । पुरुषविधाः स्युरित्येकम् ।
>
> Nir VII.6
>
> Now (we shall discuss) the appearance of the gods. Some say that they are anthropomorphic ...

The **Kātyāyana Śrauta-Sūtra** discusses shapes in sizes of different ladles used for →*yajña*:

> बाहुमात्र्यः स्रुचः पाणिमात्रपुष्करास्त्वग्बिला हंसमुखप्रसेका मूलदण्डा भवन्ति ॥
> अरत्निमात्रः स्रुवोऽङ्गुष्ठ पर्ववृत्त पुष्करः ॥
> स्फ्योऽस्याकृतिरादर्शाकृतिः प्राशित्रहरणं चमसाकृति वा ॥
>
> KātŚrSū I.3.38–40

All the ladles are (made) one arm long, having a hand-size bowl with the cavity on the bark-side of the wood and having the discharging portion shaped like the beak of a swan. Its holding side should be located on the root side of the wood of which it is made. The *sruva* (dipping spoon) is made one cubit long (of the length of fore-arm) with a round bowl having a diameter equal to the size of one part of the thumb. (The wooden implement known as) '*sphya*' should be made of the shape of a sword and the '*prāśitraharaṇa*' (utensil used for taking the *brahmabhāga* of the *iḍā*) of the shape of a mirror or goblet (with four corners).
(Tr. H.G. Ranade)

The ladles have been differentiated as per their form, size, use and requirements. All these aspects ultimately result in a distinct shape (*ākṛti*). While one takes the shape of the beak of a swan, the other looks like a sword. Thus the hymn presents multiple facets of *ākṛti* through narrating the sacrificial instruments.

The **Āpastamba Śrauta-Sūtra** refers the term *ākṛti* to mean shape:

अतुङ्गमनपूपाकृतिं कूर्मस्येव प्रतिकृतिमश्वशफमात्रं करोति ॥

ĀpŚrSū I.25.4

(The Adhvaryu) prepares (the sacrificial cake which is) not too thick or raised, not like the shape of *apūpa* (cake) but (which looks like) the figure of tortoise and of the size of horse's hoofs.
(Tr. V.A. Kulkarny)

This preparation is for *darśapūrṇamāsa* sacrifice. It is noteworthy here that *ākṛti* stands for shape and →*pratikṛti* should be interpreted as copy or imitation. It means that exact and similar aspects are being dealt together in this *sūtra.*

The negative form of *ākṛti* has been suggested by the term *nirākṛti* in denouncing sense in the **Āpastamba Dharma-Sūtra**:

यश्च सर्वान् वर्जयते सर्वान्नी च श्रोत्रियो निराकृतिर्वृषलीपतिः ।

ĀpDhSū I.6.18.33

Likewise a learned *brāhmaṇa* who avoids everybody, or eats the food of anybody, or neglects the (daily) recitation of the Veda, (and) he whose (only living) wife is of the *śūdra* caste.
(Tr. G. Bühler)

The *sūtra* as cited above has used the word *nirākṛti* to convey the sense that a *brāhmaṇa* even well versed in scriptures, if does not follow the decent code of conduct he is to be treated as outcast or a person who has lost his identity (*nirākṛti*). This seems to be justified for the period when a person was to be recognised by following the *varṇadharma* (prescribed duties) and one who failed to do so, was derecognised (*nirākṛti*). In this context, the terms *ākṛti* and *nirākṛti* assume a special social significance. The commentary of the **Gautama Dharma-Sūtra** speaks almost the same language when it gives no place to a *nirākṛti*:

> निराकृतिः न क्वचिदाश्रमे व्यवस्थितः ।
>
> Maskarin's comm. on GauDhSū II.6.18
>
> A *nirākṛti* person (who has violated prescribed code of conduct) has no place to stay in any stage of life (*āśrama*). (Tr. P. Ghosal)

It is thus clear that in the philosophical context the code of conduct or discipline is responsible in true identification of a person and if one is devoid of such code he remains *nirākṛti* although his body (figure) exists.

In the context of *garbha-śuddhi* of a pregnant woman, the commentary on the **Logākṣi Gṛhya-Sūtra** with special reference to the **Ṛgveda** (X.184.1) further explains that Prajāpati in the form of sacrifice may fashion your womb in such a way that it may be able to bear the foetus. Tvaṣṭā, Āditya may render shape, form and beauty by means of powdering the elements of beauty and later adding them to you so that you may appear full of beauty. The term →*yoni* should better be explained a base or surface and should develop fertile for creation. On the other hand, →*rūpāṇi* are to be interpreted as forms or motifs, i.e. good *ākāra* or *ākṛti*.

The **Mahābhāṣya** of Patañjali unfolds various layers of *ākṛti* meaning form, changing form, genus, kind, species, name, indication, class, variety, etc.

> लोकेऽपि हि आकृतिमतो मांसपिण्डस्य देवदत्त इति संज्ञा क्रियते ।
>
> Mahābh I.1.1
>
> In worldly behaviour the name Davadatta is given to a lump of flesh having a form. (Tr. R.S. Bhattacharya)

Ākṛti has definitely been explained as form, shape or frame. We further understand that *ākṛti* is name and *anākṛti* is without form.

> अथवा अनाकृतिः संज्ञा । आकृतिमन्तः संज्ञिनः ।
>
> Mahābh I.1.1
>
> Or, things having names have forms, but the name has no form. (Tr. R.S. Bhattacharya)

This needs further elaboration, i.e. if there is no shape or form we call it *anākṛti* because those (things) which have form, this nomenclature persists.

Without name the form can not be grasped and without form no name can be given.

There is some deeper thought on the subject in the **Mahābhāṣya**:

आकृतावपि तत्वं न विहन्यते ।

Mahābh I.1.1

In the form also the essence is not destroyed. (Tr. K.C. Chatterjee)

This suggests that the basic element of form is not perishable.

In the **Mahābhāṣya** we find opinion of two groups of teachers: (i) those, who regard genus as the sense of word (*ākṛtipadārthavādin*-s), and (ii) those who regard individual as sense of word (*dravyapadārthavādin*-s). A thing to be noted here is that none of them nullify the other totally, as both have accepted the other to some extent, i.e. according to *dravyapadārthavādins,* individual is primary sense, genus comes there as secondary meaning and in view of *ākṛtipadārthavādin*-s genus comes as primary meaning, individual comes there as secondary one (Mahābh I.2.64). This shows the correlation of genus (*ākṛti*) with individual (→*dravya*).

But at some places *ākṛti* (genus) seems to be higher or of greater significance. Because genus is independent, it does not get destroyed even if the individual is destroyed (*ibid.,* I.2.64, p. 247). Hence genus is eternal, and the individual is transitory (*ibid.,* I.1.1, P. 7). The same tune is being echoed in the **Vākyapadīya** (III.2.4). In some other cases *dravya* gets upper hand, there *ākṛti* (form) becomes transitory (Mahābh I.1.1, p. 7). The confusion is due to the changing behaviour of *ākṛti* when it means genus, it is imperishable and it comes in prime order, but when it means form, it is perishable and gets secondary importance.

This is an important disposition for the fact that a subtle distinction between these two terms, i.e. *ākṛti* (genus) and *dravya* (individual) has been put forward. Generally, one thinks that both are interdependent as *ākṛti* should not be conceived without *dravya.* But in philosophic terminology genus (*ākṛti*) remains even if *dravya* perishes. The reason being that genus may be visualised at the mental or psychic plane even if the structure is gone (for further textual details, → *Dravya,* KTK Vol. IV, pp. 84–87).

The grammarians have considered the terms *ākāra* and *ākṛti* to denote different meanings, viz. form, shape, attributes, forms of time, figure, structure. The **Vākyapadīya** says:

घटादीनां न चाकारान् प्रत्याययति वाचकः ।
वस्तुमात्रनिवेशित्वात् तद्गतिर्नान्तरीयकी ॥

Vāk II.123

An expressive word (like *ghaṭa* = a jar) does not denote the shapes and forms of a jar as it rests only on the general idea (that is common to all the jars). One, however, inevitably understands them. (Tr. K.A.S. Iyer)

There are two distinct ways of understanding either *ākāra* or *ākṛti* (form). One is when the object is visual and the other is when we just feel its presence although it remains unseen. We see the jar or cloth but we do not see space, smell, wind, etc.

सुवर्णादि यथा भिन्नं स्वैराकारैरपायिभिः ।
रुचकाद्यभिधानानां शुद्धमेवैति वाच्यताम् ॥

Vāk III.2.4

(Or) it is like gold etc. which even though differentiated by different impermanent forms, remains in its pure form, the expressed meaning of words like *rucaka* and so on. (Tr. K.A.S. Iyer)

Stress has been laid on the significance of words which convey a larger sense and are not confined to the outer form only. When the word *rucaka* is used, it stands for the shape of the ornament as well as the basic element which in this case is gold. The form may be perishable or changeable but the element will remain intact whatever the shape is given. By using a form we restrict the expression of words (cf. Vāk III.2.5).

When we name an ornament like necklace, ring, torque or bangle we restrict ourselves to a particular fabrication although the basic material, i.e. gold or silver remains same and unchanged, even if it is not expressed through speech. The reason for this has been explained in the following verse where one can infer the distinction between form (*ākāra*) and the substance (*tattva*).

तेष्वाकारेषु यः शब्दस्तथाभूतेषु वर्तते ।
तत्वात्मकत्वात्तेनापि नित्यमेवाभिधीयते ॥

Vāk III.2.6

As for the word which conveys such (impermanent) forms, since these are essentially one with it (the substance), it also conveys the eternal. (Tr. K.A.S. Iyer)

The words convey the sense of a shape which may deteriorate or change but the element is understood to be of permanent nature. Besides, eleven forms of time have been indicated here, conditioned by action (cf. Vāk III.9.37). It is further interesting to note that *ākāra* or *ākṛti* to mean figure (Vāk III.1.19) and structure (Vāk III.4.316) also finds its place in the same text.

The term *ākāra* and *ākṛti* have been used variously in Āyurveda for studying the symptoms of diseases. Caraka has suggested different meanings by *ākṛti.*

> इह खलु वर्णश्च स्वरश्च गन्धश्च रसश्च स्पर्शश्च चक्षुश्च श्रोत्रं च घ्राणं च रसनं च स्पर्शनं च सत्त्वं च भक्तिश्च शौचं च शीलं चाचारश्च स्मृतिश्चाकृतिश्च ... परीक्ष्याणि प्रत्यक्षानुमानोपदेशैरायुषः प्रमाणावशेषं जिज्ञासमानेन भिषजा ।
>
> CarSam ISthā I.3
>
> The following entities should be examined by the physician desirous to know the remaining span of life with perception, inference and authoritative statements such as complexion, voice, smell, taste, touch, visual organ, auditory organ, olfactory organ, gustatory organ, tactile organ, psyche, inclination, cleanliness, conduct, behaviour, memory, facial expression .... (Tr. P.V. Sharma)

Ākṛti has been considered as synonym of *liṅga.*

> तत्र लिङ्गमाकृतिर्लक्षणं चिह्नं संस्थानं व्यञ्जनं रूपमित्यनर्थान्तरम् ॥
>
> CarSam NiSthā I.9
>
> *Ākṛti, lakṣaṇa, cihna, saṃsthāna, vyañjana* and *rūpa* these are synonyms of *liṅga.* (Tr. P.V. Sharma)

Ākṛti has been conceived as shape:

> संस्थानमाकृतिर्ज्ञेया सुषमा विषमा च सा ।
>
> CarSam ISthā VII.8ab
>
> *Saṃsthāna* means shape which may be symmetrical and asymmetrical. (Tr. P.V. Sharma)

At another place *ākṛti* has been explained as symptom.

> सर्वाणि रूपाणि तु वक्त्ररोगे भवन्ति यस्मिन् स तु सर्वजः स्यात् ।
> संस्थानदूष्याकृतिनामभेदाच्चैते चतुःषष्टिविधा भवन्ति ॥
>
> CarSam CiSthā XXVI.115
>
> These disorders of mouth according to location, pathogenic substratum, symptoms and name are of sixty four types.
> (Tr. P.V. Sharma)

Thus in Āyurveda *ākṛti* is used for examining the symptoms of ailments and signs of body.

The term *ākṛti* has been taken to mean feature in another famous treatise on Āyurveda, i.e. the **Suśruta Saṃhitā**.

अथातो नवग्रहाकृति विज्ञानीयमध्यायं व्याख्यास्यामः ।

SuSam Uttara Tantra XXVII.1

Now we shall discourse on the chapter which deals with the specific features (of the nine diseases of infant life, which are attributed to the influences) of the nine malignant *grahas* (*navagrahākṛti-vijñānam*). (Tr. K.L. Bhishagratna)

Ḍalhaṇa comments on the same:

आकृतिः आकारो लिङ्गं कार्यभूतं, न तु स्वभावाख्यम् ।

Connotation of *ākāra* or *ākṛti* is its distinctive property (*kāryabhūta liṅga*), not the inherent disposition. (Tr. P. Ghosal)

At another place *ākṛti* stands for shape or form:

शक्तिध्वजरथाः कुन्तवाजिवारणगोवृषाः ॥
येषु चाप्यवभासेरन् प्रासादाकृतयस्तथा ।

SuSam SūSthā XXVIII.18cd–19ab

An ulcer should be regarded as fatal, that is shaped like the bark of a spear, or a *kunta* (a kind of barked dart or spear), or like a banner, chariot, horse, or an elephant, or like a cow, an ox, a temple, or a palace. (Tr. K.L. Bhishagratna)

Ḍalhaṇa observes *akṛti* as vision:

आकृतिरत्र रूपमेव । रूपं च पञ्चेन्द्रियार्थमध्ये ।

Ākṛti stands only for vision (*rūpa*) which is, one of the five sensory faculties. (Tr. P. Ghosal)

When the **Aṣṭāṅga-Hṛdaya** suggests the measurements of twigs, an *ākṛti* is formed.

कनीन्यग्रसमस्थौल्यं प्रगुणं द्वादशाङ्गुलम् ।

AṣṭH SūSthā II.3ab

The twigs (for cleansing the teeth) should be of the size of the tip of the little finger in thickness and twelve *aṅgulas* in length. (Tr. H.N. Chakravarty)

The Astrological text **Sūrya-Siddhānta** mentions the term *ākṛti* and *ākāra* for form and shape of the cosmos:

ब्रह्माण्डमेतत् सुषिरं तत्रेदं भूर्भुवादिकम् ।
कटाहद्वितयस्येव सम्पुटं गोलकाकृति ॥

SūrSiddh XII.29

This Brahma-egg is hollow; within it is the universe, consisting of earth, sky, etc.; it has the form of sphere, like a receptacle made of a pair of cauldrons. (Tr. E. Burgess)

The universe has been compared with receptacle of two cauldrons, i.e. the world has been conceived to be round (*golākṛti*).

The same has been expressed in the following verse:

अल्पकायतया लोकाः स्वस्थानात् सर्वतो मुखम् ।
पश्यन्ति वृत्तामप्येतां चक्राकारां वसुन्धराम् ॥

SūrSiddh XII.54

Owing to the littleness of their own bodies, men, looking in every direction from the position they occupy, behold this earth, although it is globular, as having the form of a wheel. (Tr. E. Burgess)

The shape of earth is again described round resembling a wheel (*cakrākāra*).

The **Rāmāyaṇa** records the terms *ākāra* and *ākṛti* to mean form, shape, size, dimension, resemblance, etc.

अरत्निमात्राकृतयो भग्नगात्रा भयार्दिताः ।
ताः कन्या वायुना भग्ना विविशुर्नृपतेर्गृहम् ॥

Rām I.32.24

Their bodies being thus broken (and reduced to the size of thumb) by air, those damsels exceedingly agitated and overwhelmed with shame with tears in their eyes entered the residence of the king. (Tr. M.N. Dutt)

Besides this *ākṛti* stands for size (Rām IV.11.16) and →*rūpa* to denote form or figure (IV.11.25). Somewhere *ākāra* means resemblance whereas *ākṛti* indicates shape and better mood (V.1.49). Again, use of *ākāra* to mean resemblance or dimension has been traced in the same text (V.1.29). *Ākṛti* and *ākāra* have been expressed differently in the **Mahābhārata** like form, expression, person, design, appearance, etc.

सा दष्टा सहसा भूमौ पतिता गतचेतना ।
व्यसुरप्रेक्षणीयापि प्रेक्षणीयतमाकृतिः ॥

MBh I.8.17

Stung by that serpent, she instantly dropped senseless on the ground, her colour faded and all the graces of her person gone. And she who was agreeable to behold became on her death what was too painful to look at. (Tr. P.C. Roy)

Ākṛti mean here person or personality. Yet at another place the term means expression or countenance (I.150.2). Further, *ākṛti* is to be explained as forged appearance or guise (*vadhirākṛti*). Planning and design have also been suggested by *ākṛti* (MBh I.134.20). Likeness and resemblance also have often been conveyed by *ākāra* (MBh XII.47.71).

The chariots have been compared with towns or their shape was like towns. Actually, the front door of the large chariot looked like the city gate (*gopuram*) through which the cattle passed. The chariots with horses in front and the door of the carriage resembled the city gate.

The **Mahābhārata** refers to the words *nirākṛti* and *nirākāra* in the denouncing term as it has been discussed in the Sūtra literature:

> उपस्थितं तु द्रुपदः सखिवच्चाभिसंगतम् ।
> स मां निराकारमिव प्रहसन्निदमब्रवीत् ॥
>
> MBh I.122.34
>
> I (Droṇa) approached him confidently as a friend should. But Drupada laughing in derision cast me off as if I were a vulgar fellow. (Tr. P.C. Roy)

The term *nirākāra* has been used here as abuse and *nirākṛti* to mean an indisciplined person violating decent conventions (MBh XII.37.41).

The **Agni Purāṇa** refers to *ākṛti* and *ākāra* of different →*avatāras*:

> मत्स्याकारस्तु मत्स्यः स्यात् कूर्मः कूर्माकृतिर्भवेत् ॥
>
> AgPur XLIX.1cd
>
> The image of the Matsya and the Kūrma incarnations (of Viṣṇu) should be of the form of a fish and a tortoise respectively.
> (Tr. R.S. Bhattacharya)

At another place *ākāra* means figure:

> अलक्षणापि लक्षण्या यत्राकारस्ततो गुणाः ।
>
> AgPur CCXLIV.6ab
>
> A woman though bereft of auspicious signs if possesses a (good looking) figure, she is regarded as 'one possessing auspicious signs'. (Tr. H.N. Chakravarty)

The **Viṣṇu Purāṇa** conveys the similar sense when the earth is compared with lotus (*vasundharā padmākārā* – II.12.37).

The **Matsya Purāṇa** follows suit while dealing with the iconographic details of divinities (cf. CCLIX.1–2).

The **Viṣṇudharmottara Purāṇa** when describes the measurements of icons and their pedestals, actually gives their shape or forms.

चतुरस्त्रं भवेन्मूले ततो वृत्तं महाभुज ।
ततोऽल्पचतुरस्त्रं च चतुरस्त्रं ततो भवेत् ॥
ततोऽल्पचतुरस्त्रं च मेरु वत्संस्थितं ततः ।
भद्रपीठमिदं प्रोक्तं व्योमभागं तृतीयकम् ॥

VDhPur III.75.2–3

At the base it is square. Above it O big armed one, is round, still above it there is a square shorter than the former, then it is followed by another square, still followed by another shorter square and thus it is shaped like mount Meru rising vertically (describing a square). This is called *bhadrapīṭha* (auspicious seat base). (Tr. H.N. Chakravarty)

Ākṛti has also been suggested to be one of the *chandas* (metres).

द्वाविंशतिश्च कथितं तथैवाकृति संज्ञकम् ॥

VDhPur III.3.7cd

(A metre having) 22 syllables (per *pāda*) is called *ākṛti.*
(Tr. H.N. Chakravarty)

The **Bhāgavata Purāṇa** probably suggests different meanings of *ākṛti.*

निधनमुपगतेषु वृष्णिभोजेष्वधिरथयूथपयूथपेषु मुख्यः ।
स तु कथमवशिष्ट उद्धवो यद् हरिरपि तत्यज आकृतिं त्र्यधीशः ॥

BhāgPur III.4.28

The king inquired: At the end of the pastimes of the Lord of the three worlds, 'Śrīkṛṣṇa, and after the disappearance of the members of the Vṛṣṇi and Bhoja dynasties, who were the best of the great commanders, why did Uddhava alone remain? (Tr. Prabhupada)

Ākāra and *ākṛti* occur in the **Devī Bhāgavata Purāṇa** in varied ways.

तस्माच्छुकः समुद्भूतो व्यासाकृति मनोहरः ॥

DBhāgPur I.14.8cd

... when arose from that *araṇi* the wonderfully beautiful form of Śukadeva, looking like a second Vyāsa. (Tr. Vijnanananda)

At other place *ākṛti* means figure, body, shape or being (II.1.34b–35a), resemblance (IX.24.58) and likeness (IX.16.24, IX.19.29, XII.12.26). *Ākāra* is referred to for resemblance:

नवीननीरदाकारं लक्ष्मीनारायणाभिधम् ॥

DBhāgPur IX.24.58cd

The sacred stone (*śālagrāma*) which looks like fresh cloud is called Lakṣmīnārāyaṇa. (Tr. R.S. Bhattacharya)

Almost same meaning like or shape has been conveyed in a reference in the **Mārkaṇḍeya Purāṇa**:

इलावृतं तयोर्मध्ये चन्द्रार्धाकारवत् स्थितम् ।

MārkPur LIV.13

Ilāvṛta is situated between those halves, and is shaped like the half moon. (Tr. F.E. Pargiter)

Apart from *ākāra*, →*chāyā* (shadow) and →*rūpa* (form) also convey the same sense as these words indirectly bear the meaning of *ākṛti* or *ākāra*.

The **Artha-Śāstra** of Kauṭilya refers to the words *ākāra* and *ākṛti* for form and expression:

मन्त्रभेदो हि दूतामात्यस्वामिनामिङ्गिताकाराभ्याम् ।

ArthŚ I.15.7

Secret counsel is indeed betrayed by the gestures and the expressions of the envoy, the minister and monarch.

Again:

आकृतिग्रहणमाकारः .... ।

ArthŚ I.15.9

The putting on of an expression (of the face) is *ākāra*.
(Tr. R.P. Kangle)

Here a subtle distinction has been considered between *ākṛti* and *ākāra*. *Ākṛti* seems to be preparation of a particular form (guise) and *ākāra* an accomplished form.

The term *ākāra* has been accepted in the **Manu Smṛti** to convey the sense of aspects or gestures.

बाह्यैर्विभावयेल्लिङ्गैर्भावमन्तर्गतं नृणाम् ।
स्वरवर्णेङ्गिताकारैश्चक्षुषा चेष्टितेन च ॥
आकारैरिङ्गितैर्गत्या चेष्टया भाषितेन च ।
नेत्रवक्त्रविकारैश्च गृह्यतेऽन्तर्गतं मनः ॥

Manu VIII.25–26 (cf. Hit II.50)

By external signs let him discover the internal disposition of men, by their voice, their colour, their motions, their aspect, their eyes, and their gestures.

The internal (working of the) mind is perceived through the aspect, the motions, the gait, the gestures, the speech, and the changes in the eyes and of the face. (Tr. G. Bühler)

While the first verse through *ākāra* suggests the sense of aspect, the second verse conveys gestures. One can also recognise some difference between the *ākāra* and *vikāra*. *Ākāra* stands simply for formation and *vikāra* is used here to denote intentional movements of eyes.

The **Abhidharma Kośa Bhāṣya** includes *ākṛti* to convey form and conceptual form in womb.

अथ कां गतिं गमिष्यतः किमाकृतिरन्तराभवोऽभिनिवर्त्तते ।

एकाक्षेपादसावैष्यत्पूर्वकालभवाकृतिः ।

AbhidhKoBh III.13ab

What is the form of an intermediate being?

Being projected by the same action that projects the *pūrvakālabhava*, an intermediate being has the form of this being, that is, the being of the realm of rebirth to come after his conception. (Tr. L.M. Pruden)

The **Visuddhimagga** mentions *ākāra, ākṛti* and →*saṃsthāna* for appearance, form, shape and concept.

... तञ्च खो पन नेव वण्णवन्तं, न सण्ठानवन्तं । यदि हि तं ईदिसं भवेय्य, चक्खुविञ्ञेय्यं सिया ओळारिकं सम्मसनूपगं तिलक्खणब्भाहतं । न पनेतं तादिसं । केवलं हि समाधिलाभिनो उपट्ठानाकारमत्तं सञ्ञजमेतं ति । उप्पन्नकालतो च पनस्स पट्ठाय नीवरणानि विक्खम्भितानेव होन्ति, किलेसा सन्निसिन्ना व, उपचारसमाधिना चित्तं समाहितमेवा ति ॥

ViMag IV.31

But it has neither colour nor shape; for if it had, it would be cognizable by the eye, gross, susceptible of comprehension (by in sight ... see ch. XX, 2f.) and stamped with the three characteristics. But it is not like that. For it is born only of perception in one who has obtained concentration, being a mere mode of appearance. But as soon as it arises the hindrances are quite suppressed, the defilement subside, and the mind becomes concentrated in access concentration. (Tr. Bhikkhu Ñyāṇamoli)

At other place *ākāra* means aspects.

> कतमेहि चत्तारीसाय आकारेहि सम्मत्तनियामं ओक्कमती ... पञ्चक्खन्धे अनिच्चतो पस्सन्तो अनुलोमिकं खन्तिं पटिलभति ।
>
> ViMag XX.18
>
> By means of what forty aspects does he enter into the certainty of rightness? .... Seeing the five aggregates as impermanent he acquires liking that is in conformity. (Tr. Bhikkhu Ñyāṇamoli)

Here *ākāra* suggests aspects or steps for good conduct. The text also deals with nine aspects for purification (ViMag III, p. 250).

Another Buddhist text, the **Jātakamālā**, handles *ākṛti* to connote the sense of shape or species.

> सुखानुलोमे गुणबाधिनि क्रमे गुणानुकूले च सुखोपरोधिनि ।
> नरोऽपि तावद् गुणपक्षसंश्रयाद्विराजते किम्वथ तिर्यगाकृतिः ॥
>
> Jāmā VI.4
>
> If out of the two lines of conduct – that which complies with pleasures and checks virtue, and that which is in accordance with the virtue and obstructs pleasures ... a man applies himself to the virtuous side, he is already illustrious, how much more a being that has the shape of a beast. (Tr. J.S. Speyer)

The **Sarvārthasiddhi,** a Jaina text states that proper shape is *ākṛti.*

> संस्थानमाकृतिः-तद् द्विविधम् । इत्थं लक्षणमनित्थं लक्षणं चेति । वृत्तत्र्यस्र चतुरस्रायत परिमण्डलादीनामित्थं लक्षणम् । अतोऽन्यमेघादीनां संस्थानमनेकविधम् इत्थमिदमिति निरूपणाभावादनित्थं लक्षणम् ।
>
> SaSi on TaSū V.24
>
> Shape is of two kinds, that which can be defined and that which cannot be defined. The regular geometrical shapes such as the circle, the triangle, the rectangle, the square, the globe, etc. are instances of first variety. The clouds etc. may be of various irregular shapes, which cannot be exactly described. These are instances of the latter variety. (Tr. S.A. Jain)

Proper shape is figure and all the formations are the result of *ākṛti* which it is in shape of circle, triangle or rectangle.

At another place *ākṛti* appears in a new dimension when it stands for magnitude beside shape.

आकृतिः खलु परिमाणम्, इयत्ता ।

NySūBh III.1.60

Ākṛti, 'shape' stands for the exact limit of extent of magnitude. (Tr. G.N. Jha)

The **Nyāya-Sūtra Bhāṣya** under the topic *jātivāda* has defined *ākṛti* as generality and configuration.

यया जातिर्जातिलिङ्गानि च प्रख्यायन्ते तामाकृतिं विद्यात् ।

NySūBh II.2.70

That should be known as configuration which serves to indicate generality and the characteristic features of the generality. (Tr. G.N. Jha)

The **Yoga-Sūtra Bhāṣya** discusses how mind assumes different *ākāra*s according to the character of receivable support.

ग्राह्यालम्बनोपरक्तं चित्तं ग्राह्यसमापन्नं ग्राह्यस्वरूपाकारेण निर्भासते ।

YSūBh I.41

A mind set on subtle element and being engrossed in them is coloured by the nature of such subtle elements, while a mind absorbed in gross elements is coloured by their gross nature. (Tr. H. Aranya)

Ākāra means mutual characteristics in the **Yoga-Sūtra Bhāṣya**:

तत्र पार्थिवाद्याः शब्दादयो विशेषाः सहाकारादिभिर्धर्मैः स्थूल शब्देन परिभाषिताः ।

YSūBh III.44

In the [system] the [five elements] beginning with earth [which in essence are a generic form and a particular] have [as particulars] sounds and other perceptible things; [these] particulars, together with their properties (*dharma*), shape and the rest [which are to be described], are technically called 'coarse'. (Tr. J.H. Woods)

In the **Mīmāṃsā-Sūtra** and its commentary *ākṛti* is accepted as genus or similarity.

अथ गौरित्यस्य शब्दस्य कोऽर्थः । सास्नादिविशिष्टाकृतिरिति ब्रूमः ।

MīmSūBh I.1.5 (pp. 59–60)

What is the denotation of the word *gauḥ* (cow)? What we assert is that the class or (genus) characterised by the dewlap and other features is what is denoted by the word. (Tr. G. N. Jha)

The commentary hints that *ākṛti* is form or figure, for example, of the cow, but at the same time it does convey the idea of a person, animal or an object in the context, the term (*ākṛti*) is spoken.

Some scholars are inclined to take *ākṛti* as object smoke. But it is difficult to call smoke as object since it constantly changes and does not form a regular shape. At the most it (smoke) temporarily makes a frame and not a form. It may be called illusion or fantasy. Thus here *ākṛti* hints a stage when the form itself is in formation but not accomplished. Secondly, it may be just the conceptual form or illusion which may eventually lead to some form. For such conceptual ideas the analogy of *dhūma* seems to be befitting.

Beside *ākṛti*, the word *ākāra* appears in the same context but here the meaning is certainly form.

> स्यादेतदेवम् - यद्यर्थाकारा बुद्धिः स्यात् । निराकारा तु नो बुद्धिः । आकारवान् बाह्योऽर्थः ।
>
> MīmSūBh I.1.5 (p. 38)
>
> This would be so, if the cognition had the form of the object. As a matter of fact, however, our cognition is without form, it is the external object that has form. (Tr. G.N. Jha)

Ākāra in the present context should stand for form and *nirākāra* without form. This simple meaning is in contrast to the term *nirākāra* which conveyed the sense of indisciplined or outcaste as discussed above (cf. GauDhSū II.6.18, ĀpDhSū I.18.33). Here *ākṛti* has been conceived to express the class and individual.

> का पुनराकृतिः का व्यक्तिरिति द्रव्यगुणकर्मणां सामान्यमात्रमाकृतिः असाधारणविशेषा व्यक्तिः । ....
>
> MīmSūBh I.3.30 (pp. 235–237)
>
> What is class and what is individual? Among substances, qualities and actions – that factor which is common to several individuals is the class and that which possesses certain specific (uncommon) characteristics is the individual. (Tr. G.N. Jha)

Śabara in his commentary has tried to elucidate the subject as under:

> आकृतिः शब्दार्थः कुतः । क्रियार्थत्वात् श्येनचितं चिन्वीत इति वचनमाकृतौ सम्भवति, यद्याकृत्यर्थः श्येनशब्दः ... ।
>
> MīmSūBh I.3.33 (pp. 245–246)
>
> It is the class that is denoted by the word, why? For it is that which serves the purpose of actions. The injunction '*śyenacitam cinvīta*' one should erect the altar like *śyena* is possible only with refer-

> ence to the class (the communality), if the word *śyena* denotes the class. (Tr. G.N. Jha)

The **Prakaraṇa Pañcikā** of Śālikanātha Miśra has explained both *ākāra* and *ākṛti* from different angles, e.g. form (p. 77), bodily shape (p. 86), generic attitude (p. 96), etc. Here Śālikanātha has discussed on gross form of *saṃvid* (knowledge) which is last resort in ascertaining existence of objects (p. 77). He has shown the reason of explaining manifested form of knowledge, had it not been so, in that case it would be difficult to express that whose form is perceived in dream (p. 140). This *ākṛti*, when it means generic attitude, it is proved by perception (*pratyakṣapramāṇasiddhā*, p. 96).

Apart from this, the term *ākāra* is used to differentiate between various forms or aspects.

> एकाकारप्रतीतिरेव खल्वभेददर्शनम्, विलक्षणाकार प्रतीतिश्च भेददर्शनम् ।
>
> PraPañ p. 373
>
> Perception of non-difference consists in the apprehension of one single form or aspect and perception of difference consists in the apprehension of different forms or aspects. (Tr. R.S. Bhattacharya)

Actually, it is through *ākṛti* that the meaning of an object is grasped. Without frame of an item it cannot be understood. Even if something is not manifested or remains invisible, its shape is visualised by expression or words. At the emotional or devotional plane the *ākṛti* of a deity is conceived through meditation whether its figure is before us or not.

Besides *ākāra* and *ākṛti* formless mental modifications (*nirvikārā mānasikavṛtti*) also have been referred (cf. PraPañ p. 143).

The **Ślokavārttika** refers to *ākṛti* and *ākāra* to mean form, class and shape.

> आकारवत्त्वभेदो हि ज्ञात्वा शक्येत भाषितुम् ।
> प्राग्बुद्धिग्रहणादर्थे संवित्तिर्नेति साधितम् ॥
>
> ŚlVā (śūnyavāda) V.34
>
> Because, such an assertion could be made only after the difference between pure cognition and the cognition as endowed with a form has been only recognised. And prior to the comprehension of the cognition, there can be no comprehension of the object, as we have already proved. (Tr. G.N. Jha)

Accordingly, *ākāra* aims at differentiation of pure knowledge from ordinary knowledge and it seems to suggest somewhat secondary knowledge which depends on some form or shape. This has been suggested that it is not proper to explain *ākāra* as a property of contact of the cognition with the object. In that case there can be no such contact because of the difference of their position and because of the cognition being immaterial (and in corporeal) and the subject being material (and corporeal).

Form may not be just the outcome of contact which itself depends on several factors. The tussel between form and formless is noteworthy.

तेनाकारवतः क्लृप्ताद् ग्राह्यादाकार वर्जितम् ।
वस्त्वन्तरं प्रकल्प्यं स्याद् ग्राहकं निष्प्रमाणकम् ॥

ŚlVā (śūnyavāda) V.12

And in this, over and above the well-defined and ascertained cognisable object having a form, we would be postulating a groundless cogniser, which would be formless and something altogether foreign to the cognisable object. (Tr. G.N. Jha)

It is not proper to see a form everywhere and in all cases as the form may be the offshoot of formless. *Ākāra* has been accepted as shape at the philosophical plane (ŚlVā śūnyavāda, V.8–9). It has been suggested here that there is a close relation between the form and the object as no object can be seen or conceived without form.

Ākṛti has been explained as to mean only →*jāti* (class):

जातिमेवाकृतिं प्राहुर्व्यक्तिराक्रियते यया ।
सामान्यं तच्च पिण्डानामेकबुद्धिनिबन्धनम् ॥

ŚlVā (ākṛtivāda) V.3 (cf. ŚṛPrak VI, p. 205)

It is the class itself, that has been called '*ākṛti*', which signifies that by which the individual is specified (or characterized). It is that which is common to all the individual objects, and the means of a collective idea of all these (individuals) as forming one composite whole. (Tr. G.N. Jha)

The **Mānameyodaya** has discussed the forms of knowledge which are expressed in the external objects:

तस्माद् विज्ञानाकाराणाम् अनेकविधत्वदर्शनात् तत्तदाकारसमर्पणहेतुभूताः क्षणिकतरा बाह्यपदार्था अपि ज्ञानाकारविशेषदर्शनानुमेयाः ।

MāMey Prameya sec. on abhāva, after 50

Therefore since the forms of cognitions are seen to be various in nature, external objects, too, quite momentary, are to be inferred from the particularity seen in the forms of cognition, as forming the ground for conferring such and such forms.
(Tr. C.K. Raja and S.S.S. Sastri)

While the objects are perishable, these are to be recognised as basis of forms of knowledge and this aspect determines the significance of *ākāra.* This has further been reiterated as under:

> अस्तु ज्ञानं साकारम् । तथापि न बाह्यमर्थमपह्नोतुं शक्यम् ।
>
> MāMey Prameya sec. on abhāva, after 50
>
> Let it be that cognition has the form. Even then it is not possible to deny external reality. (Tr. C.K. Raja and S.S.S. Sastri)

Ākāra with cognition should mean perception. Here the metaphysical forms of things have been conceived:

> न चातीन्द्रियवस्तूनां प्राग्दृष्टाकारयोगिता ।
>
> MāMey Pramāṇa sec. on anumāna, 49ab
>
> And super-sensuous things are not associated with forms seen before. (Tr. C.K. Raja and S.S.S. Sastri)

Ākāra stands here for forms seen and super-sensuous things are *ākṛtis* which remain unseen by our eyes.

The Vedantins interpreted *ākṛti* as species. Śaṅkara while commenting on the **Brahma-Sūtra** states:

> आकृतिभिश्च शब्दानां सम्बन्धो न व्यक्तिभिः ।
>
> BrSūŚBh I.3.28
>
> It is with the species that the words are connected, not with the individuals. (Tr. G. Thibaut)

Now, let us see how the monistic philosopher handles *ākāra* (form) and *nirākāra* (formless).

> तस्मादेवं जातीयकेषु वाक्येषु यथाश्रुतं निराकारमेव ब्रह्म अवधारयितव्यम् । इतराणि तु आकारवद् ब्रह्म विषयाणि वाक्यानि न तत्प्रधानानि । उपासनाविधिप्रधानानि हि तानि .... ।
>
> BrSūŚBh III.2.14
>
> On the ground of such passages we therefore must definitely conclude that Brahman is devoid of form. Those other passages, on the other hand which refer to a Brahman qualified by form do not aim at setting forth the nature of Brahman, but rather at enjoining the worship of Brahman. (Tr G. Thibaut)

It is quite striking that *nirākāra* is not used here in abusive sense like indisciplined or wicked (which we find in Smṛti) but refers to the Supreme Spirit (Brahman) (BrSū II.2.1). The **Sarvadarśana-Saṅgraha** explains the term *ākāra* and *ākṛti* in various contexts like form, shape, mode, image, aspects, perception, etc.

तस्माद् बुद्धिरेव अनादिवासनावशाद् अनेकाकारावभासत इति सिद्धम् ।

SarDSaṅg (Bauddha) p. 33

Thus it has been evinced that intellect as affected by beginningless ideation, manifests itself under diverse forms. (Tr. A.E. Gough)

Here intellect (*buddhi*) has been conceived as root cause of *ākāra*. Another reference suggests *ākāra* as illusory form.

सत्यं वस्तु तदाकारैरसत्यैरवधार्यते ।

SarDSaṅg (Pāṇini) p. 306 (quoted from Vāk, Sambandhasamuddeśa)

The true Reality is ascertained by its illusory forms.
(Tr. E.B. Cowell)

Thus the illusory forms also sometimes lead to Reality. *Ākāra* occurs for aspect:

प्रकाश शब्देन तमोविरोध्याकारस्य विवक्षितत्वात् ।

SarDSaṅg (Śāṅkara) p. 457

Since the intended sense of the word *prakāśa* is the aspect (*ākāra*) opposite to darkness. (Tr. R.S. Bhattacharya)

Ākāra is explained as mode also (SarDSaṅg p. 32). It is interesting to note that *ākāra*, intellect and knowledge have great deal of affinity.

ज्ञानाकारेण ज्ञेयमनुमेयम् ।

SarDSaṅg (Bauddha) p. 36

... from the form of knowledge, a knowable may be inferred.
(Tr. A.E. Gough)

Here *ākāra* in case of knowledge may be accepted as discipline or branch because knowledge does not have a visible form.

For worshipping a deity or God an *ākāra* appears to be a must.

निराकारे ध्यानपूजाद्यसंभवेन भक्तानुग्रहकारणाय तत्तदाकारग्रहणाविरोधात् ।

SarDSaṅg (Śaiva) p. 179

... there is no contradiction in his assuming such forms to show his mercy to his devoted servants, since meditation, worship, etc. are impossible towards a being entirely destitute of form.
(Tr. E.B. Cowell)

It has thus been accepted that for the benefit of a devotee God assumes a form to accept his (devotee's) worship in order to please him. This is not possible through *nirākāra*, i.e. formless aspect of Brahman.

The **Tantrāloka** presents *ākāra* and *ākṛti* in different aspects like form, cosmic form, transformed stage, shape, etc.

> उक्तं च कामिके देवः सर्वाकृतिर्निराकृतिः ।
> जलदर्पणवत्तेन सर्वं व्याप्तं चराचरम् ॥
>
> TĀl I.66
>
> In the **Kāmikāgama**, it is stated that the Lord is immanent and yet transcendent. He pervades the mobile and immobile worlds like the water and the mirror. (Tr. H.N. Chakravarty)

Here all pervasive and inherent aspects of God have been conveyed by *sarvākṛti-nirākṛti* (TĀl IV.196).

The commentator Jayaratha explains that the Lord (*viśvākṛti*) does not have a specific form but can appear in any form male or female. In another place the text itself states that Supreme Spirit manifests (i.e. *viśvākṛti*) in any form male or female (TĀl IV.199). Here two types of aspirants have been described, one is desirous of world and its various enjoyments but the other who is intent on liberation, does not meditate only on deity with a particular form. The Lord in this immanent form is his object of meditation. Besides this, *ākāra* has been conceived as solid form of delight in the commentary on **Tantrāloka**:

> आश्यानं चिद् रसस्यौघः साकारत्वमुपागतम् ।
> जगद्रूपतया वन्दे प्रत्यक्षं भैरवं वपुः ॥
>
> Comm. on TĀl VIII.2
>
> The heap of the fluid or liquid of consciousness having dried up transformed itself into the universe, I pay obeisance to that perceptible form of Bhairava. (Tr. H.N. Chakravarty)

The **Yoginī-Hṛdaya** while furnishing the detailed account of *śrīcakra* uses the term *ākāra* to mean form.

> खेचर्यादि जयान्तार्णपरमार्थप्रथामयम् ।
> एवं शक्त्यनलाकारस्फुरद्रौद्रीप्रभामयम् ॥
>
> YoH I.18
>
> Thus the whole *cakra* with the form of both Śakti and Śiva (fire) (consisting of forty two triangles) is made of the rays Raudrī. (Tr. H.N. Chakravarty)

This point has been dealt with elaborately in the following verses:

दीपाकारो अर्धमात्रश्च ललाटे वृत्त इष्यते ॥
अर्धचन्द्रस्तथाकारः पादमात्रस्तदूर्ध्वके ।
ज्योत्स्नाकारा तदष्टांशा रोधिनी त्र्यस्रविग्रहा ॥

YoH I.28cd–29

Bindu is of the shape of the lighted lamp. It is located on the forehead and is circular. The subtle unit of time that is *ardhacandra* is also of the same shape (the shape of the lamp). The time unit is one fourth measure. It is located above it. *Rodhinī* is of luminous form of moonlight having the shape of a triangle and the time unit for its upgoing movement is one-eighth of a *mātrā*.
(Tr. H.N. Chakravarty)

It is a specific feature of Tantra school that different inner faculties and their symbols have been composed with some shape or the other. In order to discuss *ākāra* of Bāṇaliṅga the text states:

कादितान्ताक्षरोपेतं बाणलिङ्गं त्रिकोणकम् ।
कदम्बगोलकाकारं थादिसान्ताक्षरावृतम् ॥
सूक्ष्मरूपं समस्तार्णवृतं परमलिङ्गकम् ।
बिन्दुरूपं परानन्दकन्दं नित्यपदोदितम् ॥

YoH I.46–47

The Bāṇaliṅga is associated with the syllables beginning with '*k*' and ending with '*t*' (16 syllables). It is triangular in shape. The Itaraliṅga is round like the shape of *kadamba* flower and is associated with the syllables beginning with '*th*' and ending with '*s*' (16 syllables). The transcendent *liṅga* (*para*) is subtle and is associated with all the syllables. It is of the form of *bindu* and is the root of Supreme Bliss. It manifests itself as the first vibrative impulse (*prathama spanda*) to the view of yogin from the eternal sound.
(Tr. H.N. Chakravarty)

Apart from this *ākāra* occurs in the sense of shape when Śakti takes the form of hook in her latent form (YoH I.37).

Different shapes of holy pits have been described in the **Śāradā-Tilaka**:

चतुरस्रं योनिमर्द्धचन्द्रं त्र्यस्रं सुवर्त्तुलम् ।
षडस्रं पङ्कजाकारमष्टास्रं तानि नामतः ॥

ŚāTil III.49

(*Kuṇḍa*s) holy pits are of different shapes. They are known as square, the shape of the female organ, the shape of the half moon, triangular, fully round, hectagonal, lotus shaped and octagonal. (Tr. H.N. Chakravarty)

According to caste, the shape of →*kuṇḍas* has been described in a specific language.

विप्राणां चतुरस्रं स्याद्राज्ञां वर्त्तुलमिष्यते ॥
वैश्यानामर्द्धचन्द्राभं शूद्राणां त्र्यस्रमीरितम् ।
चतुरस्रं तु सर्वेषां केचिदिच्छन्ति तान्त्रिकाः .... ॥

ŚāTil III.87cd–88

The square shaped *kuṇḍa* is for *brāhmaṇa*s, for the king it is round, for the *vaiśyas* it is like the shape of the half moon and for the *śūdras* it is stated to be triangular. Some *tāntrika* thinkers prescribe the square shaped *kuṇḍa* for everybody. (Tr. H.N. Chakravarty)

The geometrical patterns of basic elements have been presented here.

वृत्तं दिवस्तत् षड्बिन्दु लाञ्छितं मातरिश्वनः ।
त्रिकोणं स्वस्तिकोपेतं वह्नेरर्धेन्दु संयुतम् ॥
अम्भोजमम्भसो भूमेश्चतुरस्रं सवज्रकम् ।

ŚāTil I.23–24ab

The void is circular in shape, the wind is also circular with six dots within, while the shape of fire is triangular (apex upward) lotus attached to the half moon (two lotuses are drawn at two ends of the moon). The earth is square with (*vajra*) crosses at each end of the lines. (Tr. H.N. Chakravarty)

Regarding this point the **Mṛgendra Āgama** (yp 37) opines almost similarly with a slight variation.

There are some references in which the term *ākāra* and *ākṛti* are not mentioned but the description leads to the form or shape, e.g. proper shape of sacrificial altar has been mentioned:

चतुरस्रां ततो वेदीं मण्डलाय प्रकल्पयेत् ॥

ŚāTil III.27cd

A square altar should be made for the purpose of drawing a *maṇḍala* there. (Tr. H.N. Chakravarty)

The same is inferred from the description of temple and its accessories:

मूलालयाग्रतो वैशे कल्पयेत्तरुणालयम् ।
त्रिचतुः पंचहस्तं वा तरुणालय विस्तृतम् ॥

RauĀ kp XXVII.5

In front of the main temple, in the north-east direction there should be a miniature temple, measuring three, four or five cubits in extension. (Tr. H.N. Chakravarty)

The description of a well in front of a temple suggests *ākāra* or *ākṛti* (RauĀ kp XX.13). In the **Āgama Rahasya**, the group of shapes has been accepted as important along with its base (knowledge).

आकार वर्ग उपरि प्रतिभासतेऽस्य
ज्ञानस्य साऽपि तव विश्वमयी विभूतिः ।
विश्वात्मकस्त्वमिति नागमसिद्धमेतत्
किन्तु स्वसंविदितरूपंतयापि सिद्धम् ॥

Āgama Rahasya 3

The best of shapes and forms which shine above this knowledge that also is your immanent glory. That you are immanent is not an established truth proved by the Āgamas, it is also proved even by one's own knowledge. (Tr. H.N. Chakravarty)

According to Śaiva Āgama shapes and forms shine above knowledge, like ice-berg floating on the surface of water. Here, water is knowledge and ice-berg is the shape. In the **Haṭhayoga Pradīpikā**, word *nirākāra* occurs in the context of God.

यस्तत्त्वान्तो निराकारः स एव परमेश्वरः ॥

HyPard IV.101cd

The Supreme Self is said to be *nirākāra* (formless).
(Tr. H.N. Chakravarty)

The **Īśānaśivagurudeva Paddhati** describes meditation on s*ākāra* and *nirākāra* both.

अथ ध्यानं द्विधा प्रोक्तं सकलं निष्कलं तथा ।
साकारं सकलं ध्यानं निराकारं तु निष्कलम् ॥

ĪśGP Uttarārdha yp III.69

Meditation is said to be of two types. It is either with parts and without parts. (Tr. H.N. Chakravarty)

The Agamic literature mentions the terms *ākṛti* and *ākāra* to mean form and shape (MṛĀ vp IX.20, XIII.43cd–44ab).

Although the words are not mentioned yet the following citation conveys the sense of *ākṛti* as the measurements make a shape.

जम्बूद्वीपं क्षितेर्नाभिस्तद्वृत्तं लक्षयोजनम् ॥

MṛĀ vp XIII.40cd

Jambūdvīpa is the navel of the earth. It is round and ten millions in extension. (Tr. H.N. Chakravarty)

Transparent form of Śīrṣa Īśāna has been recommended for meditation and liberation.

मुक्त्यर्थं स्फटिकाकारं प्रसन्नं चेतसा स्मरेत् ।

MṛĀ kp III.45cd

For the purpose of liberation the Lord Īśāna should be meditated upon as having crystal shape; that is, transparent and graceful. (Tr. H.N. Chakravarty)

The word →*rekhā* is used to make shape through powder of different colours the choice of which depends on the benefit accrued.

रेखा सच्छालिपिष्टेन सिता रक्ताद्रिधातुना ।
हरिद्रकादिना पीता कृष्णा दग्ध्यवादिना ॥
मुक्ताविद्रुमहेमाद्यैर्भूति सन्मङ्गलोदये ।
चिताभस्मेष्टकाङ्गारप्रमुखैश्चाभिचारके ॥

MṛĀ kp VIII.39–40

Those who are desirous of prosperity and attainment of auspiciousness should draw lines with the powder of pearl and coral but for the purpose of exorcising (*abhicāra*), the line should be drawn with ashes and bricks from the cremation ground. (Tr. H.N. Chakravarty)

All the five elements have some shape. The **Raurava Āgama** mentions *ākāra* or *ākṛti* to suggest form, shape and measurements.

वेदाश्रं योनिखण्डेन्दुत्रिकोणं वृत्तमेव च ॥
पंचाश्रं च षडश्रं च सप्ताश्रं चाष्टकोणकम् ।
पद्माकारं दशैतानि ... ॥

RauĀ kp XIV.1cd–2abc

The shapes of the *kuṇḍa* are of ten types – square, as that of the shape of the female organ (*yoni*), of the half-moon, triangular, round, five-cornered, six-cornered, seven-cornered, eight-cornered and of the form of the lotus. (Tr. H.N. Chakravarty)

Describing the erection of a *yajñamaṇḍapa* (pavilion of fire worship) the formation takes a good shape (RauĀ kp XXVIII.12cd–15ab).

Bhāsa in his **Pratimā Nāṭaka** used the word *ākṛti* to mean close resemblance.

... को नु खल्वयमासां प्रतिमानामल्पान्तराकृतिरिव प्रतिमागृहं प्रविष्टः ।

PraNāṭ III after 6

Who can, indeed, this be, possessing a form almost resembling (lit. differing very little from) the statues, that has entered the statue house. (Tr. M.R. Kale)

Personality of Bharata looked like the images or pictures of his ancestors displayed.

Aśvaghoṣa in the **Buddhacarita** has used *ākṛti* for appearance. Gautama's desire for renouncing this world was keenly excited by seeing an old man, overpowered with senility whose *ākṛti* was different from other men in the assembly.

दृष्ट्वा नरेभ्य:पृथगाकृतिं तम् ।

BudCa III.27b

Seeing him whose appearance was different from that of others. (Tr. S.S. Janaki)

Similarly, variance of appearance according to each season has been mentioned in the **Saundarananda** (X.19a). It is interesting to note that in the same text *ākāra* has appeared to mean facial expression: '*ākāreṇāvagacchāmi*' (Saun XI.23a).

Kālidāsa refers to the terms *ākāra* and *ākṛti* to mean differently. In the **Raghuvaṃśa** beautiful figure (*lobhanīyā ākṛti* – VI.58a) of Indumatī at the time of her *svayaṃvara* has been mentioned. Similarly sweet personality (*madhurākṛti* – Ragh XV.28c) of Śatrughna has been recorded. In the **Abhijñānaśākuntala,** Priyaṃvadā was impressed to see serene personality of King Duṣyanta and passed a remark "*ko nu khalveṣa caturagambhīrākṛtir madhuram*" (AbhŚāk I after 22). King's admiration of Śakuntalā's beauty even in forest wearing is also mentionworthy:

किमिव हि मधुराणां मण्डनं नाकृतीनाम् ॥

AbhŚāk I.18d

... to sweet forms ,what, indeed, is not an embellishment. (Tr. M.R. Kale)

Further, in the court scene King was attaracted to see Śakuntalā's charming beauty, whom he had forgotten already under the craze of Durvāsā's curse: *nanu darśanīyā punar asyākṛtir lakṣyate* (AbhŚāk V after 13). In the **Mālavikāgnimitra,** Mālavikā's attractive appearance draws attention of everybody (Māla I after 3). Here personality (*ākṛti* – Māla I after 5 & 11) does not simply mean physical appearance but it stands for status as well, earned through scholarship, virtues or rank in the society. In the **Mahāvīracarita** the form is concentrated upon for the purpose of identification:

> कोऽप्येष वीर शिशुकाकृतिः .... ॥
>
> MaCa II.39c
>
> Who is this strange person in the form of a brave child?
> (Tr. S.S. Janaki)

In the **Veṇī Saṃhāra**, Bhaṭṭanārāyaṇa has employed *ākāra* to mean sweet form of composition: *sālaṅkārārasa-prasannamadhurākārāḥ kavīnāṃ giraḥ* (VI.48c). Actually, the word *ākāra* has been used here in the invisible form at the abstract level.

In the **Kirātārjunīya**, *ākāra* conveys the sense of expression or appearance.

> आकारमाशंसितभूरिलाभं दधानमन्तःकरणानुरूपम् ।
> नियोजयिष्यन्विजयोदये तं तपः समाधौ मुनिरित्युवाच ॥
>
> Kir III.27
>
> The sage (Vyāsa), wishing to direct him (Arjuna) to the practice of penance for the attainment of success, thus addressed him whose bodily appearance foreshadowed the acquisition of great (or varied) success and which was in keeping with the high aspirations (enthusiasm) of his mind. (Tr. M.R. Kale)

Ākāra and *ākṛti* occur in the anonymous sayings (*subhāṣita*) also. Here *ākṛti* has been used for form and appearance.

> अस्या मनोहराकार कबरीभारवर्जिताः ।
> लज्जयेव वने वासं चक्रुश्चमरबर्हिणः ॥
>
> MSSaṅg 3993
>
> The chowrie-deer and the peacocks were ashamed of their tails on seeing the resplendent and charming tresses of this ladv and hence resolved to take their abode in woods.
> (Tr. A.A. Ramanathan)

Manifestation in the Arts

The works on performing and visual art, dramaturgy, Śilpa texts including art, aesthetics, sculpture, architecture, etc. have accepted the terms *ākṛti* and *ākāra* for form, shape, structure, genus, dimension, measurements, etc. The **Śṛṅgāra Prakāśa** being a text on Sāhitya-Śāstra (poetics) handles *ākṛti* in order to discuss the relation between word and meaning. Therefore Bhoja has meant *ākṛti* as shape or structure (*avayava-saṃsthāna*) of composition. According to him, replica of an individual is called *ākṛti*. It can be explained differently depending on the situation.

> व्यक्तेः प्रतिरूपमाकृतिः । सा त्रिधा, द्रव्याकृतिः, गुणाकृतिः, क्रियाकृतिश्च ।
>
> ŚṛPrak VI, p. 204
>
> The replica of an individual goes by the name *ākṛti*, the structure. That is threefold (on account of appearing in the form of) a thing (*dravya*), quality (*guṇa*) and action (*kriyā*). (Tr. P. Ghosal)

Bhoja in many places of his work has stated that Mīmāṃsā school designates genus (*jāti*) as *ākṛti* and explains it as *sāmānya* the generality, which makes us to find out commonness in the individuals belonging to same group (ŚlVā V.3; cf. ŚṛPrak VI, p. 205). The pseudo-followers of Vindhyavāsi school opine *ākṛti* (genus) is connotated by *pada* (ŚṛPrak p. 208). Bhoja has refuted this Mīmāṃsā theory and considered *ākṛti* as *saṃsthāna*.

> तत्राकृति पदेनेह संस्थानमभिधीयते ।
> लोके शास्त्रे च दृष्टत्वान्न जातिर्जैमिनीयवत् ॥
>
> ŚṛPrak VI, p. 208
>
> To this context, the term *ākṛti* refers to *saṃsthāna* the particular arrangement of components and not *jāti* 'the genus' as said by Jaimini. Because this is confirmed by the usage in practical life as well as in the scriptural texts. (Tr. P. Ghosal)

Here Bhoja has shown that in practical usage structure of thing is meant by *ākṛti* in which →*guṇa* resides almost compulsorily, while in scripture →*jāti* is connotated by *ākṛti*.

> लोके यथा – यत्राकृतिस्तत्र गुणा वसन्तीति । शास्त्रे यथा –
> आकृतिग्रहणा जातिः लिंगानाञ्च न सर्वभाक् ॥
>
> ŚṛPrak VI, p. 208
>
> So far as practical usage is concerned (it is seen) qualities always follow where there is any structure. The scripture shows, *jāti* is to be ascertained by *ākṛti* the structure; and that does not always affect genders. (Tr. P. Ghosal)

Thus, Bhoja has proved that in both the cases arrangement of component or structure of a thing (that may be a word also) is denoted by *ākṛti*. Hence, *ākṛti* should be declared as the meaning of word.

> उभयत्रापि चाकृति शब्देनावयवसन्निवेशविशेष उच्यते ।
> .... तस्मादाकृतिः पदार्थ इति ।
>
> ŚṛPrak VI, pp. 208–209
>
> In both the cases particular arrangement of components is referred to by the term *ākṛti* ... Therefore, *ākṛti* 'the structure' is to be meant by the word '*pada*'. (Tr. P. Ghosal)

Thus, we find that in other texts of Poetics, *ākṛti* is referred to in the context of discussing construction of literary composition. The **Kāvya Prakāśa** states that words make figures through particular arrangement of letters which make various *ākṛti*s (shapes) and create *citrabandha* (a specific type of literary composition).

> तच्चित्रं यत्र वर्णानां खड्गाद्याकृतिहेतुता ।
>
> KāPrak IX.85
>
> Where the letters assume the form of such objects as the sword and the like, it is the Figure Pictorial. (Tr. G.N. Jha)

The **Ujjvalanīlamaṇi** refers to the term *ākṛti* for image or figure.

> उपतरु ललितां तां प्रत्यभिज्ञाय सद्यः
> प्रकृतिमधुररूपां प्रेक्ष्य राधाकृतिं च ।
>
> UjNīl XIV.37ab
>
> Lord Kṛṣṇa tells his friend that he has recognised Lalitā hiding behind a tree and the image of Rādhā, who is beautiful by nature.

In the Śilpa text the terms *ākāra* and *ākṛti* have been used to connote different meanings like form, shape, measurements, representation, etc.

> व्यालेभसिंहभूतादिमण्डितं यत्तु मूलतः ।
> यथेष्टाकृतिसंयुक्तं तत्तन्नाम्ना समीरितम् ॥
>
> Mayam XV.20
>
> A pillar which, no matter what the form of its upper part, is decorated from the bottom up with *vyāla* or elephants, lions, dwarves, (etc.,) .... bears the name of its decoration. (Tr. B. Dagens)

Thus in decoration *ākṛti* plays a big role and the component of the building is called by the name of that figure. The **Śilpa Prakāśa** refers to *ākṛti* to suggest variety:

एकैके तु क्रमे यन्त्रं वक्ष्यामि पृथगाकृतिम् ।
कर्तव्यं तु तथा शिल्पी यन्त्रानुसारमाचरेत् ॥

ŚiPrak I.287

I am describing one by one the different *yantras*, according to which the Śilpin should make (the creeper or scroll ornaments).

Another verse suggests form:

अथवा तोरणं लक्ष्मीः शिल्पशास्त्रानुसारतः ।
कारयेत्तु तथा मूर्तिं भिन्नाकारे तथैव च ॥

ŚiPrak I.185

Or Toraṇa-Lakṣmī, can be made in different forms and other images as well as per canonical instruction where different forms of images of Lakṣmī on gate have been perceived.

The **Abhilaṣitārtha-Cintāmaṇi** accepts the word *ākāra* to mean formation or representation:

आकारजनिकां रेखां तिन्दुवर्तिकनिर्मिताम् ।
लिखेत्तामेव लेखिन्या गैरिकोद्भूतवर्णतः ॥

Abhil ālekhyakarma 161

But with the brush (*lekhanī*) and pigment prepared from ochre (*gairika*) like in that very outline (*rekhā*) which was done with the style or with the crayon, and is progenitive with respect to the representation (*ākāra-janikā*). (Tr. A.K. Coomaraswamy)

Expression *ākāra-janikā* is significant. It is line which is responsible to make a form. At another place *ākāra* denotes representation:

पूर्वं तिन्दुकलेख्यं स्याद् यद् वा वर्त्तिकया बुधैः ।
आकारमात्रिकां लेखं विना वर्णं लिखेत्पुनः ॥

Abhil ālekhyakarma 160

By knowledgable men, the drawing should first be made with the stylus (*tinduka*) or the crayon (*vartikā*), then again without colour line in the draft (*lekhā*) which is the prototype of the representation (*ākāra-mātrikā*). (Tr. A.K. Coomaraswamy)

The above text includes *ākāra* to denote representation (cf. Abhil ālekhyakarma 941).

Here *ākāra* should stand for primary lines which make a shape but it is not the end we have to go further or deeper to enjoy the real beauty of a picture.

Conclusion

The terms *ākāra* and *ākṛti* although convey the meaning of shape or form in general sense, yet the meaning is diversified as per their use in different contexts. We come across about sixty connotations of these words from the Vedic period to the late medieval period. These renderings enhance the significance of these terms considerably. What looks a solid form in architecture and sculpture becomes formless or abstract in philosophy and poetics. If used for gestures *ākāra* and *ākṛti* assumes a different dimension as hinted in the **Manu Smṛti** (VIII.25–26).

In the literary texts like Kāvya and Nāṭakas, the *ākṛti* generally stands for personality but the Sūtra literature offers a new explanation when *ākṛti* conveys the sense of good conduct and the person violating the prescribed norms is called *nirākṛti* and he has no place to stay in an *āśrama* (GauDhSū XV.17).

At the philosophical plane *ākṛti* is sometimes called eternal and sometimes non-eternal. Brahman has been conceived both as *sākāra* and *nirākāra* and as such the meaning of *nirākṛti* changes.

We may safely conclude that in case of these terms, *ākāra* and *ākṛti*, the situation of use results in changing their meaning and interpretations. We have to be careful in grasping the real sense of these words as there may be various layers which have to be unfolded before the hidden but real purport comes forth.

Ramesh Chandra Sharma

Select Bibliography

Jeschke, Erich: "Form and Meaning", in Concepts of Space-Ancient and Modern, Ed. Kapila Vatsyayan, New Delhi: IGNCA and Abhinav Publications, 1991, pp. 543–549.

Maxwell, T.S.: "Viśvarūpa: Time and Transformation", in Concepts of Time – Ancient and Modern, Ed. Kapila Vatsyayan, New Delhi: IGNCA and Sterling Publishers, 1996.

Umino, Takanori: "On the Concept of ākāra", in Journal of Indian and Buddhist Studies, Vol. XXXIII, Tokyo, 1968, pp. 434–439.

Vatsyayan, Kapila: "The Indian Arts – Their Ideational Background and Principles of Form", in Rūpa-Pratirūpa, Ed. Bettina Bäumer, Alice Boner Commemoration Volume, New Delhi: Biblia Impex, 1982.

RŪPA-PRATIRŪPA

Overview

In Indian tradition, both religious and secular, *rūpa* encapsulates a highly varied spectrum of meanings on the materialised, gross phenomena and has both aesthetic and philosophical import. Its connotations have a bewildering multiplicity, rich in content and magnitude, and it eminently meets the essential premise in regard to the constituted 'form' in Indian art, its aesthetics and philosophy specially, as it re-invents and transcribes experience into a visual structure or a representation. It interprets the categories of the gross (*sthūla*) in Indian philosophical systems, both *āstika* (theistic) and *nāstika* (atheistic). In Buddhism it is either the physical, corporeal category in the world of appearance or a psycho-physical factor which makes the gross phenomenon possible. In the *āstika* philosophies it is often the illusion that masks the reality gone into difference. In art, its major implication rests in the validity of 'form' through the argument of immanence in it of the essence that lies invariably behind it and of which it is the formal 'reflection'. It legitimates content in speech or in colour and is paired with *nāman* and *pratirūpa* as the principle of differentiation. *Rūpa* also defines the formal particularities in poetics, grammar, numismatics, visual and performing art, and in philosophy.

Etymology and Related Words

Rūpa, 'form', 'design', 'figure'; or, as explained by Monier-Williams, any outward appearance or phenomenon or colour, ... shape; Yāska (III.13) derives it from the root *ruc-*, 'to shine', but the derivation is uncertain. Quoting Pāṇini (PāDhā XXV.79), Monier-Williams regards *rūpa* as a nominative from *rūpa-* as in *rūpayati,* 'to form, figure, represent,.. exhibit by gesture, act, feign...'. Following perhaps Yāska (Nir III.13), he connects *rūpa* with the Vedic *varpa* or *varpas* which implies 'a pretended or assumed form, phantom' or 'any form or shape, figure, image, aspect...'. For instance, in the **Ṛgveda** (III.60.1) in connection with the Ṛbhus, the divine artificers, whose share in sacrifice was ensured, thank to their 'wondrous acts' which made meeting the needs possible - *yābhir māyābhiḥ pratijūti varpasaḥ*; or, in the **Ṛgveda** (I.117.9) where the Aśvins 'wearing many forms' bestowed bounties on their favourite: *purū varpāṃsyaśvinā dadhānā...*; or, in the **Ṛgveda** (VI.44.14) where Indra, the slayer of the demons is characterised as 'knowing' or 'skilled in many forms':

अस्य मदे पुरु वर्पांसि विद्वानिन्द्रो वृत्राण्यप्रती जघान ।

ṚV VI.44.14ab

In the wild joy of this hath Indra, knowing full many a form, struck down resistless Vṛtras... (Tr. R.T.H. Griffith)

The connotation of *varpas* as *rūpa*, 'form', is quite apparent in above citations, alongwith following *mantra* – *indro māyābhiḥ pururūpa īyate* (ṚV VI.47.18) – 'Indra moves multiform by his *māyā*'. The derivation of *rūpa* from *varpas* may thus be likely though not necessarily final for, other derivations and connections have also been indicated.

In the **Nighaṇṭu** (III.7), *varpaḥ, apsaḥ, psuḥ, apnaḥ, piṣṭam, peśaḥ, aruṣam, śilpam* are among the synonyms of *rūpa* under the sixteen terms for *śilpa.* Of these, the two terms *apnaḥ* and *śilpam* occur in the **Nighaṇṭu** (II.1) as synonyms of *karman.* This is significant in that the sense of artificing often lies inherent in such connections. Etymological and semasiological considerations relate the term *rūpa* to the root *rup-*, 'to pierce', a variant of the Indo-European *lup,* 'to break' (Pathak 1981). The latter, according to Carl D. Buck, is of a fairly wide occurrence in many Indo-European languages. Conceding the same continuity, Pathak holds that *rup-*, 'to pierce', as distinct from root *rup-*, 'to charm', "indicated breaking, piercing, and scratching" and thereby it implies 'an object imprinted with a design'. Craft and artificing and also the form so produced are thus latent in the root *lup-* and its variant *rup-* where the term *rūpa* may have derived. In that derivation it had a substantive Indo-European heritage as it came into the Vedic Sanskrit, as in the **Ṛgveda** (I.95.8) where, used in collocation with the root *mi-*, 'to kill' (e.g. *budhnaṃ pari marmṛjyate dhīḥ*) it implies devising 'a most noble form of splendour' (*tveṣaṃ rūpaṃ kṛṇuta...*), which is an act of Agni who himself is 'produced' by the ten daughters (i.e., ten fingers) of Tvaṣṭā(ṚV I.95.2). Similarly, in the **Ṛgveda** (V.42.13) Indra lays 'each varied form within his daughter's (i.e., Earth's) bosom'. The sense of 'breaking' in *rup-* is retained when it is explained as *rūpaṇāt rūpam iti* (AbhidhKoBh I.13), i.e., 'because of being broken, it is called *rūpa*' (tr. N.H. Samtani). The **Sphuṭārthā** commentary explains it as: *śalyaviddha iva asau rūpyate bādhyata ityarthaḥ-* 'As a person pierced with arrow is broken; "tormented" is the meaning' (tr. N.H. Samtani). The same implication of the term is found in Pali *ruppati,* 'to break', to destroy', as in *ruppanto rūpam* in the **Visuddhimagga** (588) or in the **Saṃyutta Nikāya** (III.86)- *ruppatī ti tasmā rūpan ti vuccati* (Pali English Dictionary, *s.v.*).

And yet *rūpa* also has another derivation, viz. from the root *rup-*, 'to charm' (Pathak 1981:2). In any case, the term has multiple meanings in different spheres. A wide range of connotation is attributed to it in the **Medinī Kośa** (XXI.9):

रूपं स्वभावे सौन्दर्ये नामगे पशुशब्दयोः ।
ग्रन्थावृत्तौ नाटकादावाकारश्लोकयोरपि ॥

MedKo XXI.9

The word *rūpa* means characteristic or manner, beauty, cattle, sound, acquiring familiarity with any book learning by heart, a drama etc., a form, and a poetic composition. (Tr. S. Das)

But in the early occurrences of the term its association with artificing is unmistakably apparent.

Layers of Meaning

In the Vedic texts, the term occurs often in conjunction with the roots or words denoting creative action which brings about different manifestations or supports and sustains them. Thus *rūpa* is sometimes the product of *māyā; māyā* being a 'marvellous act'; not guile or 'illusion', (as in DBhāgPur X.12.31 where the demon assumes various forms by his magic power) but an act of someone endowed with *prajñā*, as in the case of Indra in the **Ṛgveda** *ni māyino mamire rūpamasmin* (III.38.7b), where *māyinaḥ* is explained by Sāyaṇa as *prajñāvantaḥ*, i.e., 'endowed with intellect'. Those capable of producing 'varied forms' are also supposed to be *vidvān*, 'knowing', e.g., Tvaṣṭā, the Divine Artificer in the **Ṛgveda** who is 'knowing or skilled in many forms' – *tvaṣṭeva viśvā bhuvanāni vidvān*, (ṚV IV.42.3c) or Indra, who is in the 'habit of becoming form in every form' (Gonda 1959:1), for he is endowed with *māyā*:

रूपं रूपं मघवा बोभवीति मायाः कृण्वानस्तन्वं परि स्वाम् ।

ṚV III.53.8ab

Maghavan weareth every shape at pleasure, effecting magic changes in his body. (Tr. R.T.H. Griffith)

Here →*māyā* is a faculty that endows "a special ability to create form", an inexplicable power of a High Being to assume an outward appearance, "to appear in or as phenomenal world" (Gonda 1959:128). Neither illusion nor guile is intended here in the creative act of 'being the corresponding form in every form'.

In many other instances, similar ingenuous felicity of action signifying 'fashioning' with great creative elan is meant when *rūpa* occurs in conjunction with the root *piś*, 'to fashion', as in the **Ṛgveda**:

त्वष्टा रूपाणि पिंशतु ।

ṚV X.184.1b

May Tvaṣṭṛ duly shape the forms. (Tr. R.T.H. Griffith)

Or, the same ingenuity is conveyed when the term *rūpa* occurs in conjunction with *kṛ-*, or *vi+kṛ-*, 'to make', 'to modify', as in the **Taittirīya Saṃhitā:**

> यावच्छो वै रेतसः सिक्तस्य त्वष्टा रूपाणि वि करोति तावच्छो वै तत्प्रजायते ... ।
>
> TSam I.5.9.1-2
>
> ... as many modifications of seed when poured as Tvaṣṭṛ makes, in so many shapes does it become fruitful. (Tr. A.B. Keith)

Sometimes in such a creative act, mechanical device is also instrumentally involved. Thus in the **Atharvaveda** (XII.3.33) Tvaṣṭā creates form with a chisel (*svadhiti*) – *tvaṣṭeva rūpaṃ sukṛtaṃ svadhityainā.* Or, a 'wise one (*kaviḥ*) puts on all forms' (*viśvā rūpāṇi prati muñcate kaviḥ* – ṚV V.81.2). In the **Ṛgveda** a 'mould' is suggested where *rūpa* occurs in collocation with the root *han,* 'to mould'. Indra is here praised for 'laying' or 'moulding' form in the wombs (*vakṣaṇa*) of the daughters – *āhanā duhitur vakṣaṇāsu rūpā mināno* (ṚV V.42.13). That the act of creation not only involves begetting the mankind but also sustaining it, is clear from the **Ṛgveda** (III.55.19) where the divine Tvaṣṭā, the 'wearer of all forms' is supposed to do precisely that act – *devas tvaṣṭā savitā viśvarūpaḥ pupoṣa prajāḥ purudhā jajāna.* Or, in the **Ṛgveda** (I.188.9) he is the 'maker of all forms'– *tvaṣṭā rūpāṇi hi prabhuḥ.* The act of creating a 'noble form' involves not only the skill of hands but also *dhī,* 'wisdom', the mental capacity, as in the **Ṛgveda** (I.95.8) *tveṣaṃ rūpaṃ kṛṇuta ... kavirbudhnaṃ pari marmṛjyate dhīḥ,* which according to Pathak (1981:11) "refers to the shining form... of a big-bellied pot... where burnishing of the pot may be intended".

The association of *rūpa* with the roots and words denoting manual or mental action distinctly exemplifies the craft technology and the processes of artificing in which the contexts are mostly divine but implication often mundane in terms of the crafts. The Vedic *rūpa* as a creation of *māyā* indicates that creativity involved in corresponding forms was essentially the result of a 'marvellous' act, similar to that in the realm of →*śilpa,* e.g., *yadvai pratirūpaṃ tacchilpam* (ŚBr III.2.1.5). Artificing and skill is implicit in the instances above for, *rūpa* in those citations is coincident with the roots *piś,* 'to fashion', *han,* 'to mould', *kṛ-,* 'to make' *vi-kṛ-,* 'to modify', *rup-,* 'to break' etc., the processes which eventually 'produced' different forms. This reinforces the secular validity of the *rūpa-śilpa* interface in creativity and their reciprocity, inspite even of the instrumentality of the divine beings involved in such cases. No wonder, those with skilful hands have also the power and control over form, as was the case with Tvaṣṭā– 'deft-worker, skilful-handed, helpful, holy' (*sukṛt supāṇiḥ svavān ṛtāvā* – ṚV III.54.12).

In any case, the Vedic and subsequent usages of the term *rūpa* have a multiplicity in meanings:

रूपं द्विधा, वर्णः संस्थानं च ।

AbhidhKoBh I.10a

The visible matter (*rūpa*) is of two kinds – colour and shape. (Tr. N.H. Samtani)

And it is synonymous with many other terms like:

रूपं तत्त्वं सतत्त्वं च स्वरूपं च सलक्षणम् ।
सहजं निजमाजानं .... ॥

VaiKo V.2.1

Rūpa (formation), *tattva* (thatness or real truth), *satattva* (containing the real truth), *svarūpa* (actual feature), *salakṣaṇa* (having same feature), *sahaja* (innate), *nija* (original) and *ājāna* (cogenital), all are synonymous. (Tr. P. Ghosal)

Different usages of the term *rūpa* exemplify its varied connotations and implication depending on the contexts. *Rūpa* thus is relevant both in its manifested and latent, un-manifested variations. It may be manifested or materialised organically or mechanistically. Or it may be brought forth merely by a divine will so that it is there the moment it is so willed. Its manifestations implicate varied imageries and connotations– cosmogonic, verbal (as in a speech), symbolic, anthropomorphic and terrestrial including those faunal and even those relating to time and space. But it is fundamentally located in three major categories of embodied materiality, apart from its super-sensual, symbolic, notional character. These three categories about the embodied materiality of *rūpa* respectively refer to *rūpa* as:

1. colour signifying a varied symbology,
2. words or sounds as uttered in recited speech or verses that would constitute the contingent ritual,
3. creatures or things populating the universe and sensually perceived or experienced.

Of these, the first and third are relevant in arts and thought and the second is relevant to language, literature and all these are relevant to sacrificial rituals. In every case, the *rūpa-pratirūpa* continuity is invariably found interwoven together for, one is not possible without the other.

Rūpa as Colour and Speech

Rūpa as colour has Vedic antiquity. In the **Ṛgveda** (IX.71.8; IX.74.7), white or a 'radiant hue' are the *rūpas* which Soma is supposed to 'assume'.

Assuming the *rūpa* (colour) of a particular kind also means becoming endowed with the quality and function of the entity so represented. So, in the **Śatapatha Brāhmaṇa** (XII.1.4.1,3) Puruṣa as *samvatsara* (year) has the day and night latent in him as white and dark *rūpa.* Wearing those colours as a black garment with a black fringe (*kṛṣṇaṃ vāsaḥ kṛṣṇatūṣam* – TSam II.4.9.1), he represents Parjanya and causes clouds to rain. As colour, *rūpa* may symbolically identify all the three worlds (*lokas*) in a skin used in the *kṛṣṇa-ajina-dīkṣā* for, white and black there are supposed to be the images (*rūpa*) of sky as well as the earth while the brown in it symbolises the image of *antarikṣa* (ŚBr III.2.1.3; TSam II.4.9). Again, in the **Śatapatha Brāhmaṇa** (I.6.3.41), black and white are alternatively regarded as the *rūpa* of Agni and Soma and those colours embody their dry and moist quality which are respectively related to 'looking on' and 'being asleep'. A pairing (PraUp I.4) of *rūpa* in colours symbolises fecundity as in the case of the dark grey form of a bull on whose skin the dark grey and white hair occurring together are suggestive of coupling for procreation e.g., *dvandvaṃ vai mithunaṃ prajananam* (ŚBr V.2.5.8) 'two and two means a productive pair' (tr. J. Eggeling). In the **Chāndogya Upaniṣad** (VI.4.1-7), *rūpa* is interpreted primarily as colour and its multiplication implies a distinction between *rūpa* as the primary truth and its counterpart denoted by speech representing its designated (*nāmadheya*) modification. The same text (III.3.3; 8.3; 9.3; VI.2.3) conceives of different deities like Vāyu, Agni, Sūrya, Rudra, Āditya, Maruts and Soma in different *rūpa*s (forms, colours).

Words or speech (*vāk*), when articulated or verbalised, turns into *rūpa.* It is the uttered form of a word: *svaṃ rūpaṃ śabdasyāśabdasaṃjñā* (Pā I.1.68). And there is a dictum about it in the **Mahābhāṣya**:

> रूपनिर्ग्रहश्च शब्दस्य नान्तरेण लौकिकं प्रयोगम् ।
>
> Mahābh I.2.64
>
> The form of a word can be apprehended or received if it is not used in popular speech. (Tr. R.S. Bhattacharya)

Letters in the utterances have a differentiated form but sometimes accent is not so endowed: *na hi svaro rūpavān,* (Mahābh VII.1.6) 'Accent does not possess *rūpa*' (tr. R.S. Bhattacharya). In itself devoid of letters, accent is yet built into the former. Therefore *rūpa* in speech relates to sound and words and in that its primacy lies in the chant as recited in a sacrifice:

> आग्नावैष्णव्यौ रूपसमृद्धे एतद्वै यज्ञस्य समृद्धं यद्रूपसमृद्धं यत् कर्म क्रियमाणमृगभिवदति।
>
> AitBr I.4
>
> These two verses (addressed to Agni and Viṣṇu) are corresponding in their form. What is appropriate in its form is successful in

the sacrifice; that is to say when the verse which is recited refers to a ceremony which is being performed. (Tr. M. Haug)

Confirmity is essential to *rūpa* in sacrificial ritual as is indicated in the arrangement of bricks laid into an altar in imitations of the form of an animal (BŚulSū II.20); or when an effigy of man made of sticks is offered as part of expiatory rites (AitBr VII.2), or when the design of the sacrificial utensils has been knitted out in a garment (KātŚrSū XV.5.10), or when circular lines are drawn in the Pravargya ceremony on a mound of earth to represent Sun (ĀpŚrSū XV.14.9). A whole range of symbolic imagery and its signs are encapsulated in terms of *rūpa* as commoditised sacrificial objects in connection with the Sautrāmaṇi sacrifice in the **Yajurveda** (XIX.13–16). The correspondence of the words of →*mantra* in a sacrifice and the acts that go with it must necessarily match to qualify the 'form' of that particular sacrifice. This point is explicitly made in the commentary on the **Mīmāṃsā-Sūtra** (*rūpopadeśābhyām* – III.2.26):

रूपं चैषाम् तत्प्रकाशनसामर्थ्यम् ।

MīmSūBh III.2.26

(Here the term) *rūpa* denotes capacity of expressing (the sense of sentences). (Tr. P. Ghosal)

The word *rūpa* is used here as a technical word in the sense of power to express the sense (of words). But in essence, sacrifice must relate to a deity and the offerings made to that divinity.

यागस्य द्वे रूपे द्रव्यं देवता चेति ।

MīmNyPrak p. 57 (Edgerton edn)

A sacrifice has two aspects the material (which is offered) and the deity or divinity. (Tr. R.S. Bhattacharya)

Development of the Concept

The early Vedic *rūpa* is mostly expressed in terms of differentiation of identities whether in shape or colour, pliable in essence and generally controlled by the skill or power of divine personages, some of whom, e.g. Tvaṣṭā, Indra, Earth are adorned with it while others like Agni, Sūrya, besides Tvaṣṭā and Indra bring it forth or multiply it. But, for any form created there always has to be a creator. Once manifested *rūpa* turns into a phenomenal entity and in order to go back to the original manifestor the illusion of the manifested form has to be necessarily transcended. Embodied, structured construction is essential to form (*rūpa*) but as *tanu* 'body' the disembodied essence of divinities may rest pooled together in a depository in great multiplicity, yet remaining distinct even in such a combined togetherness (AitBr I.24). Form also has a validity in a ritual or sacrifice in that it must adhere to its sacrosanct verbal structure at the time of sacrifice and, when uttered, be faithful to its desired counterpart so addressed. In that situation its construction through speech (→*vāk*) is central to its efficacy and speech is clearly the mediator in making it, as for instance in the **Ṛgveda** (V.81.2) where Savitar 'arrays himself in every form when he hath looked on heaven's high vault after the outgoing dawn' (tr. R.T.H. Griffith). Perception in other contexts has to be visual. In that eventuality it is apparently supposed to rest in the eyes which make a vision of 'form' possible through *dṛṣṭi.* Such a perception regarding form rests fundamentally on its being the counterform or the reflection of the primal source from which it emanated and which it phenomenally signifies, provided the intervening illusion is crossed over. The esoterism of this formulation is particularly in evidence in the cosmogonic enunciations, specially in the Upanisadic discourse on →*sat* and the series of its multiple emanations through which the Universe came into being and was populated.

In the **Ṛgveda**, for any manifestation of form there is always a power or an instrument of action behind it. Still in some, the diverse forms are forever deposited. Among such repositories of *rūpa,* we have Earth in that it is perpetually endowed with all the forms:

पद्या वस्ते पुरुरूपा वपूंष्यूर्ध्वा तस्थौ .... ।

ṚV III.55.14ab

Earth weareth beauties manifold... (Tr. R.T.H. Griffith)

Seasons, guided by their divine lords modify (such) *rūpas* (*vikṛtāni rūpaśaḥ*):

तेषामिष्टानि विहितानि धामशः स्थात्रे रेजन्ते विकृतानि रूपशः ॥

ṚV I.164.15cd

Their good gifts sought of men are ranged in order due, and various in their form move for the lord who guides.
(Tr. R.T.H. Griffith)

The divine lords of the seasons themselves are not always visually perceived. Of the three such divinities, namely Agni, Sūrya, and Vāyu, the last one is ever illusive for his *rūpa* is unseen:

त्रयः केशिन ऋतुथा वि चक्षते संवत्सरे वपत एक एषाम् ।
विश्वमेको अभि चष्टे शचीभिर्ध्राजिरेकस्य ददृशे न रूपम् ॥

ṚV I.164.44

> Three with long tresses show in ordered season; one of them sheareth when the season is ended, One with his power the universe regardeth: of one the sweep is seen but not his figure.
> (Tr. R.T.H. Griffith)

Among the Vedic deities, Tvaṣṭā is intimately and profusely instrumental in multiplying *rūpa* in all its variety. He is *rūpa-vikartā* 'modifier of forms' (BṛDev III.25). His control over *rūpa* is legendary and this goes well with his reputation as the 'maker of fair things' and as one who 'expands' life (ṚV X.18.6) even as he rules the world with power (*gnābhiḥ*) (ṚV II.31.4). He is the first-born and the repository of whatever *rūpa* there might be and therefore himself the Viśvarūpa; he was in existence even before the *rūpa* differentiation came about:

> इह त्वष्टारमग्रियं विश्वरूपमुप ह्वये ।
>
> ṚV I.13.10ab
>
> Tvaṣṭar I call the earliest born, the wearer of all forms.
> (Tr. R.T.H. Griffith)

Possessed of all the *rūpa* and in that singularity, as the lord and the essence of all-*rūpa*, he merrily goes about adorning the heaven and earth with forms of all kind and thereby making 'the beauty perfect' (*deva tvaṣṭar yat ha cārutvamānaṭ* – ṚV X.70.9). Thus, he made the Heaven and Earth, the parents, creatures, the mankind and cattles in the field:

> य इमे द्यावापृथिवी जनित्री रूपैरपिंशद्भुवनानि विश्वा ।
> तमद्य होतरिषितो यजीयान्देवं त्वष्टारमिह यक्षि विद्वान् ॥
>
> ṚV X.110.9
>
> Hotar, more skilled in sacrifice, bring hither with speed today God Tvaṣṭar, thou who knowest.
>
> Even him who formed these two, the Earth and Heaven, the Parents, with their forms and every creature. (Tr. R.T.H. Griffith)

Deft of hand, holy and helpful, Tvaṣṭā (ṚV III.54.15) creates all forms:

> त्वष्टा रूपाणि हि प्रभुः पशून् विश्वान् त्समानजे । तेषां नः स्फातिमा यज ॥
>
> ṚV I.188.9
>
> Tvaṣṭar the lord hath made all forms and all the cattles of the field.
> Cause them multiply for us. (Tr. R.T.H. Griffith)

Vāyu, the formless and unseen (ṚV I.164.44), the one who is the lord of right, is his son-in-law (ṚV VIII. 26.21). Vāk cherishes and sustains him (ṚV X.125.2), and he the creator par excellence, begets mankind and sustains what he brings forth:

देवस्त्वष्टा सविता विश्वरूपः पुपोष प्रजाः पुरुधा जजान ।
इमा च विश्वा भुवनान्यस्य महद् देवानामसुरत्वमेकम् ॥

ṚV III.55.19

Tvaṣṭar, the God, the Omniform Creator, begets and feeds mankind in various manner,

His verily are all these living creatures, Great is God's Supreme and sole dimension. (Tr. R.T.H. Griffith)

He even engendered Agni in collaboration:

द्यावा यमग्निं पृथिवी जनिष्टामापस्त्वष्टा भृगवो यं सहोभिः ।

ṚV X.46.9ab

That Agni, him whom Heaven and Earth engendered, the Waters, Tvaṣṭar and with might the Bhrigus. (Tr. R.T.H. Griffith)

The **Śatapatha Brāhmaṇa** elaborates on the point in the context of the reestablishment of the sacred fire by Tvaṣṭā whereby Agni gave up to him both kinds of forms, domestic and wild: hence they call them Tvaṣṭā's forms, since it is *tasmādāhus tvāṣṭrāṇi vai rūpāṇīti, tvaṣṭurhyeva sarvaṃ rūpam* (ŚBr II.2.3.4) "from Tvaṣṭṛ that all forms proceed ....." (tr. J. Eggeling). In the Vedic texts, Tvaṣṭā's power over *rūpa* appears supreme for it encompasses the universe in its limitless dimensions and extends to heaven and earth and in such creativity he appears to be continually and immanently modified. Agni keeps a watch even as the shapes develop for, in the **Ṛgveda** (VIII.91.8), we have the wish expressed that Agni "may stand by us even as Tvaṣṭar comes unto the forms that must be shaped" (tr. R.T.H. Griffith).

As the fashioner of 'perfect beauty' (*tvaṣṭar yat ha cārutvamānat* ... – ṚV X.70.9) he adorns the universe with forms rendering them beautiful by his power and skill. He adorns the forms even in the womb in concert with other gods:

विष्णुर्योनिं कल्पयतु त्वष्टा रूपाणि पिंशतु ।
आ सिञ्चतु प्रजापतिर्धाता गर्भं दधातु ते ॥

ṚV X.184.1

May Viṣṇu form and mould your womb, may Tvaṣṭar duly shape the forms,

Prajāpati infuse the stream and Dhātar lay the germ for thee. (Tr. R.T.H. Griffith)

The implication of adornment is contextual for as explained by Yāska (Nir VIII.11), the word *peśas* implies 'beauty'; it being derived from the root *piś*, 'to adorn'.

In the later Vedic texts Tvaṣṭā's role as the one who modifies *rūpa* is upheld repeatedly. In the **Taittirīya Saṃhitā** (I.5.9.2) and in the **Taittirīya Brāhmaṇa** (I.8.1.2) we have Tvaṣṭā who modified the forms, *tvaṣṭā rūpāṇi vikaroti.* In the **Śatapatha Brāhmaṇa** (III.8.3.37; cf. TSam VI.3.11.2) he shapes the form (*rūpa*) endowing it with a uniformity of the signifier (*salakṣmā*): *salakṣmā yadviṣūrūpaṃ bhavātīti kṛtsnavṛtamevaitatkaroti.* As explained in the **Śatapatha Brāhmaṇa** (I.9.3.6; IV.4.3.14) such an act involves removing whatever is uneven, cut or defiled. He renders smooth what has been injured in our body and heals whatever is torn – *tanvo yad viliṣṭam iti yad vivṛḍhaṃ tat sandadhāti* (Chaturvedi 1993: 35). *Rūpa* is immanently located in him but he shapes out corporealities by his artificing skill and thereby adorns the Universe with multiple, pleasing forms (*rūpa*). Thus he is possessed of all the forms as the Viśvarūpa and he is also the creator of *rūpa*s in its multiple varieties. Yet he is not the sole creator of form nor the only one to have an exclusive control over it. Indra, Agni, Dyāvā-Pṛthivī, etc. have their share in this activity. So has the Sun. Even the day and night renovate themselves by transmutation while the Sun remains eternal:

> सनातनमेनमाहुरुताद्य स्यात् पुनर्णवः ।
> अहोरात्रे प्र जायेते अन्यो अन्यस्य रूपयोः ॥
>
> AV X.8.23
>
> Him (the Sun) too they call eternal: he may become new again today. Day and night reproduce themselves, each from the form the other wears. (Tr. R.T.H. Griffith)

In the later Vedic phase the pre-eminence of Tvaṣṭā as the fashioner of form (*rūpa*) or as its repository is taken over by other deities specially Brahman (ŚBr XI.2.3, 3 and 5), Prajāpati (TBr II.2.7.1), Puruṣa (MNUp 24, JaimUpBr I.27) the Great Soul (BṛUp I.4.6), and Sat (ChUp VI.2.1–4, VI.3.1–3). The contexts of *rūpa* and its differentiation are often cosmogonic. The Brahman descended into this universe by *nāma-rūpa* and thereby he 'extended' it:

> ... तत् द्राभ्यामेव प्रत्यवैत् । रूपेण चैव नाम्ना च । स यस्य कस्य च नामास्ति तन्नाम । यस्यो अपि नाम नास्ति । यद्वेद रूपेणेदं रूपमिति तत् रूपं । एतावद्वा इदं यावद्रूपं चैव नाम च।
>
> ŚBr XI.2.3.3
>
> It (the Brahman) then descended again by means of these two — Form and Name. Whatever has a name, that is name and that again which has no name, and which one knows by its form. 'This is (of a certain) form', that is form: as far as there are Form and Name so far, indeed, extends this (universe). (Tr. J. Eggeling)

And also:

ते हैते ब्रह्मणो महती यक्ष्ये । स यो हैते ब्रह्मणो महती यक्ष्ये वेद महद्धैव यक्ष्यं भवति । तयोरन्यतरत् ज्यायो रूपमेव । यद्यपि नाम रूपमेव तत् । स यो हैतयोर्ज्यायो वेद । ज्यायान् ह तस्मात् भवति । यस्मात् ज्यायान् बुभूषति ।

ŚBr XI.2.3.5

These indeed, are the two great manifestations of the Brahman and verily, he who knows these two great manifestations of the Brahman becomes himself a great manifestation. One of these two is the greater, namely, Form for whatever is Name, is indeed Form; and verily, he who knows the greater of the two, becomes greater than he whom he wishes to surpass in greatness. (Tr. J. Eggeling)

The cosmogonic discourse about extending the universe has a different shade of meaning in the **Taittirīya Brāhmaṇa** where the beings were indeterminate when created until Prajāpati himself entered into them, thus introducing identities, multiplicity and distinctions in the *rūpa*:

प्रजापतिः प्रजा असृजत । ताः सृष्टाः समश्लिष्यन् । ता रूपेणानु प्राविशत् । तस्मादाहुः । रूपं वै प्रजापतिरिति । ता नाम्नानुप्राविशत् । तस्मादाहुः । नाम वै प्रजापतिरिति ।

TBr II.2.7.1

Prajāpati created living beings. They, however, were in a shapeless state. He entered into them with form. Hence, men say 'Prajāpati is form'. He entered into them with name. Hence, men say: 'Prajāpati is name'. (Tr. J. Muir)

Yet another version of *nāma-rūpa* differentiation is attributed to Sat in the **Chāndogya Upaniṣad** (VI.2.1–4; VI.3.1–3). Sat is posited here as the Primal Being, 'one without a second', in its primary existence, i.e., before It wished (*aikṣat*) to multiply through *nāma-rūpa*. So, It created (*asṛjat*) the elements, namely fire (*tejas*) which by its will created water (*āpaḥ*) which, on its turn created food (*anna*). Evidently, these 'elements' came into existence, (in subtle form) merely by a wish about them to become. *Icchā* (desire) was the instrumental cause of these 'elements'. Then the Primordial Sat further 'modified' those elements into *nāma-rūpa* by 'entering' into them by means of 'living self' and with the pluck of a 'tripartite division'. In this division, the elements, viz. fire, water and earth were each the dividend factor while the *nāma-rūpa* pair was the divisor factor; hence the tripartite division. The coming of the populated universe with all the multiplicity of *nāma-rūpa* located in it was thus the result of a division of 'elements' with *nāma-rūpa* and it was brought into play at the will of the Primordial Sat:

सेयं देवतैक्षत - हन्ताहमिमास्तिस्रो देवता अनेन जीवेनात्मनानुप्रविश्य नामरूपे व्याकरवाणीति । तासां त्रिवृतं त्रिवृतमेकैकां करवाणीति । सेयं देवतेमास्तिस्रो देवता अनेनैव जीवेनात्मनानुप्रविश्य नामरूपे व्याकरोत् ।

ChUp VI.3.2–3

That Deity thought: "Let Me now enter into these three deities (Fire, Water and Earth) by means of this living self and let Me then develop name and form ".

That Deity having thought: "Let Me make each of these three tripartite, entered into these three deities by means of the living self and developed names and forms". (Tr. Nikhilananda)

It is later said in the **Chāndogya Upaniṣad** (VI.4.1–5) that the red, white and black *rūpa* in the recreated fire are the modifications of those elements in their original state and they become apparent temporally only in speech (*vāc-ārambhaṇaṃ vikāro nāmadheyam*). The knowledge of this truth, viz. 'the tripartite nature of things brought to experience by the device of *nāma-rūpa*', is the complete knowledge in itself:

यदु रोहितामिवाभूदिति तेजसस्तद्रूपमिति तद्विदाञ्चक्रुः । यदु शुक्लमिवाभूदित्यपां रूपमिति तद्विदाञ्चक्रुः । यदु कृष्णमिवाभूदित्यन्नस्य रूपमिति तद्विदाञ्चक्रुः ॥ यद्वविज्ञातमिवाभूदित्येतासामेव देवतानां समास इति तद्विदाञ्चक्रुः ।

ChUp VI.4.6–7

Whatever appeared red they knew to be the colour of fire; whatever appeared white they knew to be the colour of water; whatever appeared black they knew to be the colour of earth.

Whatever appeared to be unknown they knew to be the combination of these three deities (i.e. colours). (Tr. Nikhilananda)

It is thus argued that all the truth about the universe is realised by means of *rūpa* (or by *nāma-rūpa*) in their elemental or differentiated state which are but the modifications of the Primordial Sat. Thereby Sat is known through the instrumentality of *nāma-rūpa* in which *nāma* is only a manner of speech that formalises the truth. *Rūpa* here, as in many other instances in the Upaniṣads is apparently the specific form or nature of the thing; and *nāma* is the sign signifying the particularity of each form. The *nāma-rūpa* compound therefore interprets the particularity of a thing and also its 'determinate character'.

Rūpa is compounded with *nāma* in the **Atharvaveda Pariśiṣṭa** (I.16.1) where it is one of the twelve entities, viz. *prāṇa, apāna, vyāna, samāna, udāna, cakṣus, śrotra, vāk, manas,* etc. But it is every where in the universe, and even in the remnant:

उच्छिष्टे नाम रूपं चोच्छिष्टे लोक आहितः ।

AV XI.7.1ab

In the remnant (are set) name and form, in the remnant (is) set the world. (Tr. W.D. Whitney)

The *nāma-rūpa* duo is supposed to be the basis of all empirical knowledge for, *indriyas*, 'sense organs' as well as the →*manas* have to function within the realm of *nāma-rūpa.* A cognition of *rūpa* is considered possible only when it is brought into the range of the visual; till then an experience is bound to remain latent in the *manas* (mental state). Hence the dictum:

प्रिया च मानसी । प्रतिरूपा च चाक्षुषी ।

KauṣUp I.3

... the beloved *mānasī* (mental) and her counterpart *cākṣuṣī* (visual). (Tr. R.E. Hume)

Within such a structure of material particularities, the Upaniṣads offer a highly complex ideology of the One differentiated into many, the many being the transient materiality of the original repository of *rūpa.* Forms thus descend from that intransient, subtle Creator who divides itself and yet remains complete. This Creator is subtle and unseen. It is more than the aggregate of its parts and the parts are always transient, unreal and mutable, only ethereal constructions even though they signify the One from whom they derive or eventually pass into and merge. This convergence and differentiation motif is written large in the entire Upanisadic idealism:

न संदृशे तिष्ठति रूपमस्य न चक्षुषा पश्यति कश्चनैनम् ।
हृदा मनीषा मनसाऽभिक्लृप्तो य एतद्विदुरमृतास्ते भवन्ति ॥

KaṭhUp VI.9

His form (*rūpa*) is not to be beheld.
No one soever sees Him with the eye.
He is framed by the heart, by the thought, by the mind.
They who know that become immortal. (Tr. R.E. Hume)

Yet the store house of all forms, Puruṣa in this instance is the Ultimate Refuge where identities are lost and a total merger is achieved:

यथा नद्यः स्यन्दमानाः समुद्रेऽस्तं गच्छन्ति नामरूपे विहाय ।
तथा विद्वान्नामरूपाद्विमुक्तः परात्परं पुरुषमुपैति दिव्यम् ॥

MuṇḍUp III.2.8

As the flowing rivers in the ocean,
Disappear quitting name and form,

So the knower, being liberated from name and form,
Goes into the heavenly person, higher than the high.
(Tr. R.E. Hume)

This Puruṣa, the Ultimate Refuge has a plurality in that He is differently conceived, in an ascending order, as →*puruṣa, atipuruṣa,* and *paramapuruṣa,* intimately related to *anurūpa, pratirūpa* and *sarvarūpa* respectively:

स हैषोऽमृतेन परिवृढो मृत्युमध्यास्तेऽन्नं कृत्वा । अथैष एव पुरुषो योऽयं चक्षुषि । य आदित्ये सोऽतिपुरुषः । यो विद्युति स परमपुरुषः । एते ह वाव त्रयः पुरुषाः । आ हाऽस्यैते जायन्ते । स योऽयं चक्षुष्येषोऽनुरूपो नाम, अन्वङ् ह्येष सर्वाणि रूपाणि, तमनुरूप इत्युपासीत । अन्वञ्चि हैनं सर्वाणि रूपाणि भवन्ति । य आदित्ये स प्रतिरूपः प्रत्यङ् ह्येष सर्वाणि रूपाणि, तं प्रतिरूप इत्युपासीत । प्रत्यञ्चि ह्यैनं सर्वाणि रूपाणि भवन्ति । यो विद्युति स सर्वरूपः । सर्वाणि ह्येतस्मिन् रूपाणि। तं सर्वरूप इत्युपासीत । सर्वाणि हास्मिन् रूपाणि भवन्ति । एते ह वाव त्रयः पुरुषाः । आ हाऽस्यैते जायन्ते य एतदेवं वेदाथो यस्यैवं विद्वानुद्गायति ॥

JaimUpBr I.27.1–7

Having been strengthened by *amṛta* (the nectar) and (having) consumed the *mṛtyu* (the death) He stays. Now, who is in eyes, He is *puruṣa* (the Man). He, who is in the Sun, is *atipuruṣa* (the Superman). He, who is in the lightning is *parama puruṣa,* (the Supreme Person). These three are the forms of *puruṣa.* All the beings spring forth unto Him.

He, who is in the eyes is called by the name *anurūpa* (the Conform One). All the forms are corresponding to This One. He should be meditated as *anurūpa* (the Conform One). Having followed Him all *rūpas* (forms) take place. He, who is in the Sun, is *pratirūpa* (the Reflection). All the forms are equal to This (One). He, should be meditated on as *pratirūpa* (reflection). Having been occidental to This, all the forms take place. He, who is in the lightning, is *sarva-rūpa* (the Universal Form). All the forms manifest in This One. He should be meditated as *sarva-rūpa* (the source of all the forms). All the forms are merged in This One. These are the three forms of *puruṣa.* He, who knows this One (as source of all forms) as such and he, who having known This One as such sings on – finds everything in Himself. (Tr. P. Ghosal)

Brahman is the producer of *nāma, rūpa* and *anna* (MuṇḍUp I.1.8) and meditation leads an aspirant to him through a congery of superfluous experiences:

नीहारधूमार्कानलानिलानां, खद्योतविद्युत् स्फटिकशशीनाम् ।
एतानि रूपाणि पुरःसराणि ब्रह्मण्यभिव्यक्तिकराणि योगे ॥

ŚvUp II.11

When *yoga* is practised, the forms which appear first and which gradually manifest *brahman* are those of snow flakes, smoke, sun, fire, wind, fire-flies, lightning, crystal and the moon.
(Tr. Nikhilananda)

Yet the Brahman's form is beyond comprehension:

बृहच्च तद् दिव्यमचिन्त्यरूपं सूक्ष्माच्च तत्सूक्ष्मतरं विभाति ।
दूरात्सुदूरे तदिहान्तिके च पश्यत्स्विहैव निहितं गुहायाम् ॥

MuṇḍUp III.1.7

That *brahman* shines forth vast, self-luminous, inconceivable, subtler than subtle. He is far beyond what is far, and yet here very near at hand. Verily, he is seen here, dwelling in the cave of the heart of the conscious beings. (Tr. Nikhilananda)

Subtler than subtle is →*ākāśa* which unfolds forms in the **Chāndogya Upaniṣad**:

आकाशो वै नामरूपयोर्निर्वहिता । ते यदन्तरा तद् ब्रह्म, तदमृतं स आत्मा ।

ChUp VIII.14.1

That which is called the *ākāśa* is the revealer of names and forms. That within which these names and forms exist is, verily, *brahman*. That is the Immortal; that is the self. (Tr. Nikhilananda)

And the knowledge of →*brahman* liberates: it accords to such a knower the propensity to assume the desired form, in other words, the propensity to transcend form: *imāṃllokān kāmānnī kāmarūpyanusañcaran* (TUp III.10.5; cf. also ĪśUp 16), leading one on to realisation of vision of the most beautiful form (*kalyāṇatamaṃ rūpam*) of *puruṣa*.

The Upaniṣads also bring out the *ātman*'s interface with *rūpa* in many ways. *Ātman* thus creates *nāma-rūpa* (*tannāmarūpābhyāmeva vyākriyat asau nāmā'yamidaṃrūpa iti* – BṛUp I.4.7). In its embodied existence, it is shrouded in multiple corporealities of this universe constituted of *nāma*, *rūpa* and *karma* (*ibid.*, I.6.1). The →*ātman* is soundless, intangible, formless, undecaying, tasteless, eternal and odourless, without a beginning and unchanging (KaṭhUp III.15). But It tends to come into its own form in certain eventuality:

> ... in the common conscious existence of man, the *ātman* can not be realised because he is not-total (*asarva*), reality being differentiated... through name-and-form (BṛUp I.4.7). But in a peculiar condition of 'knowledge', in the ecstatic unification of man's

being in which the *prāṇas* are immobilised, ... the re-constituted *ātman* having left bodily differentiated existence and reached supernal Light, comes forth in his own Form (*svena rūpeṇābhiniṣpadyate*), that is, in one-and-total *rūpa* of the universal, Supreme Puruṣa (ChUp VII.12.3) (Maryla Falk 1943: 15–16).

Ātman is also the entity which makes the sense-experience possible; these 'senses' are mentioned in the **Kaṭha Upaniṣad** (IV.3) as consisting of *rūpa* besides taste, smell, sound, touch and carnal pleasures. These are supposed to be experienced through the instrumentality of the *ātman*. It being the Pure Consciousness even as the senses being the inert matter-devoid of consciousness – are capable of perceiving the externality. The non-duality of the *ātman*, whatever be its manifestation, is interpreted further with the instances of Agni, Vāyu and Sūrya whose forms (*rūpa*) go into divergence in the world of experience. →*Ātman* remains un-divided despite the diversification that may flow from It, and significantly It stays outside such divisions in Its Supreme Oneness. It is thus sited both in the manifestation of experience and outside of it; both in and out; many in its multiplicity and yet Single in its ultimate state of Oneness:

एकस्तथा सर्वभूतान्तरात्मा रूपं रूपं प्रतिरूपो बहिश्च ॥

KaṭhUp V.9cd

Ātman, dwelling in all beings, becomes different according to whatever It enters. And It exists also without. (Tr. Nikhilananda)

And it is explicitly stated in the same Upaniṣad:

एको वशी सर्वभूतान्तरात्मा एकं रूपं बहुधा यः करोति ।

KaṭhUp V.12ab

There is One Supreme Ruler, the inmost Self of all beings, who makes His one form manifold. (Tr. Nikhilananda)

The Upaniṣads conceive this universe as constituted of *nāma, rūpa* and *karma* (BṛUp I.6), a universe in which *rūpa* and other senses of perception derive from and are experienced through the instrumentality of the *ātman* (KaṭhUp IV.3), Sun makes the perception of *rūpa* possible. The running continuity of individual *rūpa* with its counterpart resting in the Sun is exemplified in the **Chāndogya Upaniṣad** where the individual self and the Supreme Self are the same in their names – *yannāma tannāma*:

तस्यैतस्य तदेव रूपं यदमुष्य रूपम् ।

ChUp I.7.5

The form of this person (in the eye) is the form of that Person (in the Sun). (Tr. Nikhilananda)

This is so because the essence (*rasa*, ChUp III.1.3) is said to have turned tangible in the Sun (*ibid.*, III.1.4). The idea is quite in conformity with the **Ṛgveda** where forms are rendered perceivable only in the light of the sun; where *kavi* (sapient one) is supposed to make all eternal objects visible at sunrise, and he does it thanks to Savitar: *viśvā rūpāṇi pratimuñcate kaviḥ* (ṚV V.81.2; AV XIII.1.11). Vaiśvānara-Sūrya is *viśvarūpa*:

> स एष वैश्वानरो विश्वरूपः प्राणोऽग्निरुदयते ... ॥
>
> PraUp I.7
>
> The Sun, which is the soul of all creatures, the soul of all forms, which is life and fire. (Tr. Nikhilananda)

> विश्वरूपं हरिणं जातवेदसं परायणं ज्योतिरेकं तपन्तम् ।
> सहस्ररश्मिः शतधा वर्तमानः प्राणः प्रजानामुदयत्येष सूर्यः ॥
>
> PraUp I.8
>
> (The wise know him who) is in all forms, full of rays, all knowing, non-dual, the support of all life, the eye of all beings, the giver of heat, the thousand-rayed, existing in a hundred form, the life of all creatures. (Tr. Nikhilananda)

Sun here is indeed life (→*prāṇa*), the creation of Prajāpati who desired progeny, performed penance and produced a pair consisting of the moon and the sun, and bade them to produce the creatures for him (PraUp I.4). This pair signifies both the active element (i.e. sun as *prāṇa*) and the stuff (i.e. moon as food) on which creation depends and is sustained. Prajāpati is the cosmic principle who pairs energy and matter in which sun, representing energy is *viśvarūpa* – the soul of all forms and the soul of all creatures.

The foregoing underscores *rūpa* in terms of empirical entities populating the universe and wrought by divinities like Indra, Tvaṣṭā, Prajāpati with whom it identifies severally. Or else it is lodged in particular deities like Earth or is unseen, as in Vāyu. Indra, Tvaṣṭā, Prajāpati, and Sat differentiate it by their power, will or skill. But the Vedic argument about the omniscience as well as an engineered multiplicity of the primal form or stuff, e.g., Indra (of the Vedas), is more formally hypothesised in the Upanisadic discourse on the Primordial Principle and its secondary manifestations. These are comprehended respectively at suprasensual and sensual level in which each passes into the other and the latter constitutes the transitory world of experience as extended in the universe that is brought into being. The Primordial Principle is thus valid in its immanence even as it has its suprasensual entity beyond the experiential reality. The realisation of the Supreme Principle is thus posited on the grounds of its immanence in 'form' through the suggestion of *nāma-rūpa* . This concept of *rūpa* permeates through the entire discourse in that it posits a primal creator beyond and above, who brings about the *tattvas,* e.g., water, fire, air, etc., some of which are subtle and some subtler than subtle. To be received, they are phenomenally sited in their material counterparts which make the world of experience possible. In time, the notion of *vidyā-avidyā, nitya-anitya, vyakta-avyakta, saśarīram-aśarīram* came to be applied to the entire discourse in the dualist or non-dualist philosophies down to the Vedānta.

In such Vedic, specially the Upanisadic concept of *rūpa,* sun is the prime agent of perception of form (PraUp I.5–8). *Cakṣu* (eyes, symbolising sun) and *rūpa* are reciprocally implicated in the Upaniṣads. Heart is the locus of *rūpa* but eyes manifest it (*rūpāṇāṃ cakṣurekāyanam* – BṛUp II.4.11). *Vāk* (BṛUp I.6.1), in particular, brings them forth and extends them:

> कस्मिन्नु चक्षुः प्रतिष्ठितमिति ? रूपेष्विति, चक्षुषा हि रूपाणि पश्यति । कस्मिन्नु रूपाणि प्रतिष्ठितानीति ? हृदय इति होवाच, हृदयेन हि रूपाणि जानाति । हृदये ह्येव रूपाणि प्रतिष्ठितानि भवन्तीति ।
>
> BṛUp III.9.20
>
> 'And on what is the eye based?'
> 'On appearance, for with the eye one sees appearances.'
> 'And on what are appearances based?'
> 'On the heart,' he said, 'for with the heart one knows appearances, for on the heart alone appearances are based.' (Tr. R.E. Hume)
>
> चक्षुर्वै ग्रहः स रूपेणातिग्राहेण गृहीतश्चक्षुषा हि रूपाणि पश्यति ।
>
> BṛUp III.2.5
>
> The eye, verily, is an apprehender. It is seized by appearance as an over-apprehender, for by the eye one sees. (Tr. R.E. Hume)

Or,

> अथ रूपाणां चक्षुरित्येतदेषामुक्थम् । अतो हि सर्वाणि रूपाण्युत्तिष्ठन्ति । एतदेषां सामैतद्धि सर्वैः रूपैः समम् । एतदेषां ब्रह्मैतद्धि सर्वाणि रूपाणि बिभर्ति ।
>
> BṛUp I.6.2
>
> Now of forms. – That which is called the Eye is their hymn of praise (*uktha*), for from it arise (*ut-thā*) all forms. It is their Sāman (chant), for it is the same (*sama*) as all forms. It is their prayer (*brahman*), for it supports (*bhar-*) all forms. (Tr. R.E. Hume)

Rūpa is variously interpreted in Indian philosophical systems, both orthodox and heterodox, *āstika* and *nāstika.*

In Buddhist philosophy, *rūpa* together with *nāma* signifies 'changing entity known as self' and refers to 'aggregate of perception and experience' with *nāma* implying psychical factors and *rūpa,* the physical body, put together in a particular way. Eyes perceive it eminently-*cakṣurindriya gocaro'rthaḥ* (Abhidh Samu 3). But *rūpa,* like anything else in Buddhism, is constantly changing and continually decaying (*pratighātorūpeṇetyapare* – AbhidhKoBh I.13). Alone, it signifies 'matter' or 'corporeality'.

> रुप्पन लक्खणं वा रूपं ।
>
> Aṭṭh II.42
>
> States (or bodies) which possess property of matter in an inseparable state are termed 'Material'. (Tr. Pe Maung Tin)

Or,

> रूपनट्ठेन रूपं ।
>
> Aṭṭh II.55
>
> Matter is that which changes its state or condition.
> (Tr. Pe Maung Tin)

Rūpa is one of the five aggregates:

> ... खन्धा ति पञ्च खन्धा - रूपक्खन्धो वेदनाक्खंधो सञ्ञाक्खंधो, सङ्खारक्खंधो, विञ्ञाणक्खंधो ति ।
>
> ViMag XIV.33
>
> ... the aggregates here are the five aggregates, that is to say, the materiality aggregate, the feeling aggregate, the perception aggregate, the formation aggregate and the consciousness aggregate.
> (Tr. Bhikkhu Ñyāṇamoli)

All the five *skandhas,* 'aggregates' are 'transitory', 'unsubstantial' 'unindividual' and 'injurious' - *capalānasārān anātmakāṃścaiva badhātmakāṃśca* (Johnston, Saun XVIII.15a). In its wider relations, *rūpa* is not merely a →*skandha* but it also includes 'ten elements of matter' (*daśarūpa dhātu*), the 'ten spheres of matter' (*daśarūpa āyatana*)' and 'matter' in the sphere of *dharmadhātu* (mental objects) (AbhidhSamu 16). It derives from the four elements - *pathavī* (earth), *āpo* (water), *tejo* (fire) and *vāyu* (air):

> तत्थ कतमं सब्बं रूपं ? चत्तारो च महाभूता, चतुन्नं च
> महाभूतानं उपादाय रूपं, इदं वुच्चति सब्बं रूपं ।
>
> DhSaṅ (Rūpakaṇḍa) p. 584

What is form ?
The four great phenomena and the form which is derived from them. (Tr. Rhys Davids)

Citta which is formless, is the locus of *rūpa* for its consciousness is aroused there:

नारूप्ये रूपसद्भावः रूपोत्पत्तिस्तु चित्ततः ॥

रूपस्य चित्तादेवोत्पत्तिस्तद्विपाकहेतुपरिभाविताल्लब्धवृत्तितः । कथमनाश्रित्य रूपं चित्तं वर्तते? कस्मान्न वर्तितव्यम् ? इहैवमदर्शनात् । कवडीकारान्तरेणापि विना रूपधातौ न वर्तितव्यम् । किं कारणम् ? इहैवमदर्शनात् । उक्तं यथा वर्तते ।

AbhidhKoBh VIII.3cd

There is no *rūpa* in the *arūpyas.* Physical matter arises from the mind (*citta*).

A cause was formerly produced – a certain action, etc., which should ripen in physical matter; a trace (*vāsanā*) of this cause remains in the mind; its efficacy now matures; the physical matter that now arises from the mind. But how can a mind in *arūpyadhātu* exist without being supported by physical matter, *rūpa*? Because it never happens here below that a mind exists without a body.But by virtue of this same reasoning, you should deny that beings in *rūpadhātu* live on material food. Moreover, we have already explained how a mind in the *arūpadhātu* has *nikāya* (genre) and *jīvita* (Life) as its support. (Tr. L. Pruden)

Rūpa is closely connected with *āsrava,* a principle (→*tattva*) in Jainism. In its philosophical discourse, →*indriyas* (senses), and also the karmic actions produced from them, are supposed to bind the soul and, the state of →*karma* coming over to soul is called *āsrava* which is one of the seven *tattvas,* 'principles', in Jain thought. *Rūpa* figures as the component of *āsrava,* thus in Jain thought:

इन्द्रियद्वारा हि पौरुषं ज्योतिर्विषयान् स्पृशद् रूपादि ज्ञानरूपेण परिणमते ।

SarDSaṅg (Jaina) p. 74

... the light of the soul, coming in contact with external objects by means of the senses, becomes developed as knowledge of form etc. (Tr. E.B. Cowell)

Form is cognised by the sense of vision, in the same system:

... अपगततिमिरादि प्रतिबन्धं लोचनविज्ञानं रूपसाक्षात्कारि ।

SarDSaṅg (Jaina) p. 57

... the sense of vision cognises form directly, the hindrances of darkness, etc., are removed. (Tr. E.B. Cowell)

In attempting to explain the Universe, including its framework, property and relation, the Nyāya-Vaiśeṣika systems deal with *dravyas* and *padārthas* in which *rūpa* is regarded as the attribute of *guṇa*:

रूपरसगंधस्पर्शाः ... गुणाः ॥

VaiśSū I.1.6

Colour, taste, smell, touch ... are attributes. (Tr. R.S. Bhattacharya)

Colour (*rūpa*) is said to exist in earth, water and fire only (VaiśSū II.1.1-3). It is supposed to have a genus as well as a differentia and is identified by its particular mark:

चक्षुर्मात्रग्राह्यो गुणो रूपम् । तच्च शुक्लनीलपीतरक्तहरितकपिशचित्रभेदात् सप्तविधं पृथिवीजलतेजोवृत्ति । तत्र पृथिव्यां सप्तविधम् । अभास्वरं शुक्लं जले । भास्वरं शुक्लं तेजसि ।

TarkSaṅg 19

Rūpa (colour) is the (special) quality which is cognised by eye alone. It (colour) is of seven kinds in accordance to its distinctiveness as white, blue, yellow, red, green, brown and variegated and resides in earth, water and light. All the seven are found in earth, pale in water, and brilliant white in light. (Tr. M.R. Bodas)

Or,

रूपत्वं नाम नीलसमवेतगुणत्वापरजातिः ।

SarDSaṅg (Vaiśeṣika) p. 220

The class or genus of colour (*rūpa*) is that which is subordinate to quality and exists with intimate relation in blue. (Tr. E. B. Cowell)

It is essentially *anitya*, 'non-eternal' (VaiśSū VII.1.2) though it is a fundamental component of universe and its perception depends on a medium without which a form may remain illusive:

प्रदीपस्याभावाद्रूपस्यादर्शनमिति ।

NySūBh IV.2.33

There is non-perception of colour when the lamp is absent. (Tr. G.N. Jha)

It changes under different impacts and yet it remains existent in *dravya*:

नात्यन्तं रूपोपरमो द्रव्यस्य, श्यामरूपे निवृत्ते पाकजं गुणान्तरं रक्तं रूपमुत्पद्यते ।

NySūBh III.2.48

In the case of the object cited (i.e. the jar), there is not a total disappearance of all colour; all that happens is that the dark colour having disappeared, another colour red, is produced by baking. (Tr. G.N. Jha)

The **Vaiśeṣika-Sūtra** (I.1.28) explains *rūpa* essentially as the joint effect or product of many colours (*rūpāṇāṃ rūpam*). The interpretation invokes the rule that many attributes produce but one attribute even as different *dravya*s are made of different *rūpa*s (VaiśSūBh p. 65, 88). Eyes however are central to perceiving *rūpa* and quite a lot is included among the things that eyes perceive:

संख्याः परिमाणानि पृथक्त्वं संयोगविभागौ परत्वापरत्वे कर्म च रूपिद्रव्यसमवायात् चाक्षुषाणि ॥

VaiśSū IV.1.11

Number, magnitude, separateness, etc. are said to be objects of visual perception since they are inherently connected with things possessing colour. (Tr. R.S. Bhattacharya)

Yet, *rūpa* is perceived only when it is there, not otherwise:

अरूपिष्वचाक्षुषाणि ॥

VaiśSū IV.1.12

Number, magnitude, etc. (stated in IV.1.11) are not the objects of visual perception if they do not possess colour.

In the Nyāya-Vaiśeṣika atomic theory *rūpa* is supposed to originate in the coming together of two atoms which thus form a 'binary compound' for it must be produced because in the first place, it is already there in the causal substance:

... आरब्धे द्व्यणुके कारणगुणादिभ्यः कार्यगुणादीनां रूपादीनामुत्पत्तिरिति यथाक्रमं नव क्षणाः ।

SarDSaṅg (Vaiśeṣika) p. 225

... from the qualities etc., of the cause (i.e., the, atoms) are produced colour etc., the qualities of the effect (i.e., the *dvyaṇuka*). Such is the order of the series of nine moments. (Tr. E.B. Cowell)

Rūpa is perceived even beyond the 'binary compound' (*dvyaṇuka*) in a triad (*tryaṇuka*) when it develops to the degrees of appreciability (*udbhūtatva*) and unobscured (*anabhibhūta*) state:

अनेकद्रव्यसमवायाद् रूपविशेषाच्च रूपोपलब्धिः ।

VaiśSū IV.1.8

Colour is perceived, provided it becomes associated with more than one substance [i.e., with *tryaṇuka* molecule] and it contains some peculiarity [i.e., *udbhūtatva* and *anabhibhūta*].
(Tr. R.S. Bhattacharya)

Visual perception is not unlimited and it is possible only within certain range of dimensionality:

महत्यनेक द्रव्यवत्त्वाद् रूपाच्चोपलब्धिः ॥

VaiśSū IV.1.6

Visual perception takes place provided the thing has a medium dimension, is composed of many parts, and has (manifested) colour. (Since in an atom, *paramāṇu,* all these three conditions are absent, it is incapable of being perceived).
(Tr. R.S. Bhattacharya)

In the Sāṃkhya-Yoga systems *rūpa* qualifies all that is 'manifested' in the cycle of evolution of the universe when →*prakṛti* is transformed from its state of equilibrium to the state of dissolution and thereby starts a chain of manifestations from *mahat* principle down to *ahaṃkāra* and then on to the group of sixteen *tattvas* (principles), e.g., the five *tanmātras* and eleven *indriyas* including *manas.* Then the five →*mahābhūtas* are produced out of five →*tanmātras* (SāṃKā 22). And that completes the cycle of the manifestation of the universe:

तत्र रूपप्रवृत्तिफललक्षणं व्यक्तम् । रूपं पुनः महानहंकारः पञ्च तन्मात्राणि एकादशेन्द्रियाणि पञ्चमहाभूतानि ।

YuDīp on SāṃKā 2

The manifest is characterised by form or aspect (*rūpa*), activity (*pravṛtti*) and result (*phala*). The aspects are (the principles namely) *mahat, ahaṃkāra,* the five *tanmātras,* eleven *indriyas* and the five *mahābhūtas.* (Tr. R.S. Bhattacharya)

A cognition of *rūpa* is rendered possible through the sense organs:

रूपादिषु पञ्चानामालोचनमात्रमिष्यते वृत्तिः ।

SāṃKā 28ab

Mere awareness (sensation) concerning colour etc. is regarded as the function of five sense organs. (Tr. R.S. Bhattacharya)

This is so because of the Sāṃkhya dictum:

शक्यमिदमस्य शक्तश्चायम् अस्येत्ययं नियमः सतां दृष्टः । तद् यथा चक्षुषो रूपस्य ।

YuDīp on SāṃKā 9

In the sphere of existent things a law is observed as: 'an adequate thing can be effected by a potent cause and a potent cause can effect only that of which it is capable'. As for example, the eye is the potent cause and colour is the adequate effect (i.e., to be perceived by the eye). (Tr. R.S. Bhattacharya)

The perception of *rūpa* may however, be subdued by exercising restraint (*saṃyama*):

कायस्यरूपे संयमाद् रूपस्य या ग्राह्या शक्तिस्तां प्रतिष्टभ्नाति ।

YSūBh III.21

When *saṃyama* is practised on the (visible) appearance of the body, the property of perceptibility possessed by it becomes ineffective (i.e., the *yogin* can remain unseen by others on account of this *saṃyama*. This shows that *rūpa* is seen in a particular state only which is capable of being subdued). (Tr. R.S. Bhattacharya)

In the Yoga system, *rūpa* also signifies a *bindu*, 'point' located on the forehead where alone the experience is supposedly arrested. It is from that spot on the forehead that the final experience of the aspirant about form and colour begins even as such an experience tends to end there. The location of →*bindu* is named *rūpa* and among others, it needs being transcended in order to achieve meditation:

पिण्डरूप पदग्रन्थि भेदनाद् विघ्नभेदकम् ।

YoH III.94ab

One is able to get rid of obstacles by penetrating *piṇḍa*, location of *kuṇḍalinī*. That is *rūpātīta*, beyond all forms.
(Tr. H.N. Chakravarty)

However, in the Mīmāṃsā system, the cognition of *rūpa* is dependent on *sannikarṣa*, for:

सन्निकर्षस्येव रूपादिज्ञाने ।

MīmNyPrak p. 6

As the operative relation (*sannikarṣa*) (of sense organs) is (the producer) of the cognition of colour (*rūpa*) and the like.
(Tr. R.S. Bhattacharya)

This is specially so because apprehension is totally dependent on eyes and it is the outcome of vision; it cannot happen in any other way:

... यथा चक्षुषा रूपमुपलभ्यते इति दर्शनादेवावगतम् ।

MīmSū Bh I.1.2

... just as the fact that colour (*rūpa*) is apprehended by the eye is deduced only from the fact that the man sees it. (Tr. G.N. Jha)

न चार्थव्यपदेशमन्तरेण बुद्धेः रूपोपलम्भनम् ।

MīmSūBh I.1.5

Further, the form of the cognition is never apprehended except in terms of the objects (which could not be the case if both cognition and objects were cognised by sense perception). (Tr. G.N. Jha)

... एतद् वै देवानां रूपं यदुदगयनं, पूर्वपक्षोऽहरिति । न च वयं देवादीनां रूपं विद्मः । अथ त्वेषु कालेषु दैवानि क्रियन्ते, तत एतेन संबन्धेन रूपवचनमवकल्पते ।

MīmSūBh VI.8.23

.... (the *daiva* acts are to be done at these stated times) the Northern Solstice and the days of the earlier fortnight constitute the very form of divine beings. As a matter of fact, we do not know the form of divine being but the fact that '*daiva* acts' are done at the stated times indicated this relationship of forms of those beings. (Tr. G.N. Jha)

Other philosophical systems also contain significant postulates about *rūpa.* For instance, *rūpa* signifies a 'distinction' (*rūpabheda*) and in that sense it also implies distinction in action (BrSūŚBh III.3.1). Śaṅkara accepts the possibility of assuming another form without leaving one's 'own form'. This he terms as *vivarta* (SarDSaṅg p. 420). Rāmānuja (SarDSaṅg p.109) speaks of dissolution of *nāma-rūpa* in a state when body returns to its state of *prakṛti* — a state of imperceptibility, when it is the 'absolute spirit' and the 'emanative cause'. According to the **Pauṣkarāgama**, (quoted in the SarDSaṅg p. 179), Śiva's form is invoked for the express purpose of preservation of the devotees. In any case, the concept of *rūpa* as found in the different philosophical systems affords sufficient content to underscore its multiple interpretations. In essence, it occurs both as the 'manifested phenomenon' open to cognition through the senses of experience and as the 'manifested phenomenon' again which masks the reality. The reality in its absoluteness is its cause and thereby *rūpa* is only a part of that Absolute Entity.

These different concept and connotation of *rūpa* do not entirely exhaust the multiplicity of its varying usages. There is more to it as regards defining particular phenomena in the spheres of poetics, drama, arts and in the fields of medicine, coinage and currency. As in the **Aṣṭādhyāyī**, so also in the **Artha-Śāstra**, it is commoditised even as it specifically implies a coin. In the **Aṣṭādhyāyī** (*rūpādāhatapra-śaṃśayoryap* – Pā V.2.120) it means both form and figure. The example is *rūpyaḥ gauḥ* (a bull of praiseworthy form); the example of the latter is *rūpyaṃ kārṣāpaṇam*; the ancient coin *kārṣāpaṇa* bore a figure (symbol) which was struck with a punch (*nighātikā-tāḍanādinā*, hence *rūpyaṃ kārṣāpaṇam* – Kāśikā). *Rūpa* implies a coin in the **Artha-Śāstra**:

> एकरूपं चात्र हिरण्यं पूर्वनिखातम् ।
>
> ArthŚ V.2.61
>
> And from a place where money consisting of a single coin is buried before hand ... (Tr. R.P. Kangle)

Or, it interestingly, implies a stolen article found on or with a person (ArthŚ IV.6.3). Or, it qualifies an impost or surcharge in the context of a penalty:

> दण्डकर्मसु सर्वेषु रूपमष्टपणं शतम् ।
> शतावरेषु व्याजीं च विद्यात् पञ्चपणं शतम् ॥
>
> ArthŚ III.17.15
>
> In all cases of fine one should know that there is an impost of eight *paṇas* per hundred but in those above one hundred, a surcharge in addition of five *paṇas* per hundred. (Tr. R.P. Kangle)

Rūpa also signifies an animal branded with a mark, as in:

> परपशूनां राजाङ्केन परिवर्तयिता रूपस्य पूर्वं साहसदण्डं दद्यात् ।
>
> ArthŚ II.29.17
>
> He who changes the cattle of another with the royal mark shall pay the lowest fine. (Tr. R.P. Kangle)

'*Rūpasya*' here means 'for each animal'. These passages qualify *rūpa* as money, property, or revenue, essentially a quantity of value sometimes fit for a monetary transaction.

In ancient Indian works on medicine, *rūpa* stands for the symptoms of a disease and is supposed to assist in the prognosis of particular afflictions:

> यत् पित्तमूष्मा च यो या च भाः शरीरे तत् सर्वमाग्नेयं रूपं दर्शनं च ।
>
> CarSam ŚāSthā VII.16
>
> *Pitta*, heat, lustre along with vision and visual sense are *āgneya* (predominant in agni *mahābhūta*). (Tr. P.V. Sharma)

प्रादुर्भूतलक्षणं पुनर्लिङ्गम् । तत्र लिङ्गमाकृतिर्लक्षणं चिह्नं संस्थानं व्यञ्जनं रूपमित्यनर्थान्तरम् ।

CarSam NiSthā I.9

Liṅga consists of the manifested signs and symptoms of the disease. *Ākṛti, lakṣaṇa, cihna, saṃsthāna, vyañjana* and *rūpa* – these are synonyms of *liṅga.* (Tr. P.V. Sharma)

In Indian Poetics, *rūpa* is sometimes an indicator of embellishment, e.g.:

अङ्गान्यभूषितान्येव केनचिद्भूषणादिना ।
येन भूषितवद्भाति तद्रूपमिति कथ्यते ॥

UjNīl XI.23

Through which the unadorned organs look like ornamented is *rūpa.* (Tr. S. Punjani)

But according to the **Kāvya-Mīmāṃsā** (quoting the Jain ācārya Pālyakīrti), the relish, taste (or appreciation) is obtained not by a form or a shape (*rūpa*) but by the manner of its construction by a poet or an orator. Thus in the dialectics of literary criticism in terms of relish or taste, *rūpa* is a pliable quantity relished or run down depending on the nature of its narrative woven by poet.

यथा तथा वास्तु वस्तुनो रूपम् । वक्तृप्रकृति विशेषायत्ता तु रसवत्ता । तथा च यमर्थं रक्तः स्तौति तं विरक्तो विनिन्दति ... । .... विदग्ध भणिति भङ्गिनिवेद्यं वस्तुनो रूपं, नियतस्वभावम्, इति अवन्तिसुन्दरी ..... ।

KāMīm IX, pp. 115–116

It implies that 'whatever be the form of a thing its relish depends on how charmingly it is stated: the stated form may alternatively be admired or run down respectively by those with empathy or indifference. So, Avantisundarī says that the shape of an object has no fixed nature. It would appear in the manner it is stated by a great poet or orator. (Tr. H.N. Chakravarty)

As in philosophy, so in poetics, epistemological stand is necessary for a perception of form:

अर्थादेवेति रूपादेस्तत एवेति न्यायतः ।
अन्यथा घटविज्ञानमन्येन व्यपदिश्यते ॥

Kāvyāl V.10

By the principle that conceptions (for example, conceptions of attributes etc.) spring from what is the objective *arthādeva*, it fol-

> lows that *rūpa* can be produced only from object (of cognition). Otherwise the idea of a pot may be supplanted with the attributes of something else. (Tr. P.V. Naganatha Sastry)

Inference of identity in transmutation of *rūpa* may still be possible:

> अतद् रूपस्यान्यथाध्यवसानमतिशयार्थमुत्प्रेक्षा ॥
>
> KāvyālSū IV.3.9
>
> The poetic imagination (*utprekṣā*) is one in which the poet ascertains the existence of the one in a place which is different from it for the purpose of adding excellence to it. (Tr. H.N. Chakravarty)

From *rūpa* we have *rūpaka* and *daśarūpaka* (KāvyālSū I.3.30), the particular types of poetic compositions. *Rūpaka* is defined in the **Vakroktijīvita** as:

> उपचारैकसर्वस्वं (यत्र तत्) साम्यमुद्वहन् ।
> यदर्पयति रूपं स्वं वस्तु तद्रूपकं विदुः ॥
>
> VaJī II.21
>
> That content which conveys a similarity implicitly by virtue of an essentially metaphorical usage of words, is termed 'metaphor' (*rūpaka*) since it involves surrender of its own form in favour of another. (Tr. K. Krishnamoorthy)

Yet, sometimes the similarities in form (*rūpa*) have to be viewed with caution, warns the **Mahābhāṣya**:

> अन्यस्मिंश्चान्यस्मिंश्च रूपसामान्यात् तदेवेदम् इति भवति ।
>
> Mahābh I.19, āh2
>
> On account of similarity in form the notion of identity arises in things that are different. (Tr. R.S. Bhattacharya)

In the Puranic discourse, *rūpa* is reckoned in many ways, either in its significant togetherness with →*liṅga, guṇa, nāma-rūpa, māyā, sūkṣma* or *sthūla* phenomenon or it is considered as a secondary manifestation open to cognition through the senses, including *manas, buddhi,* or *cakṣus.* In these conjunctions, it is also supposed to be the subtle element (*tanmātra*) derived from →*tejas* or *vāyu,* the →*mahābhūta*s 'cosmic elements' which on their turn originate from a subtler than subtle agency, or sometimes through the mysterious power – *māyā.* The latter as the faculty of the Supreme Power fabricates the forms in the world of experience. These ideas fundamentally reflect the Upanisadic sensibilities or even those of the Sāṃkhya, Nyāya, Vaiśeṣika or Mīmāṃsā philosophies about the manifestation of the diverse phenomena in the Universe and their perception even as they are essentially the reflection of a supreme entity which is beyond and above the notion of form. *Rūpa* is thus regarded as a notional or material manifestation of a divine personage, e.g., Devī, Brahmā, Viṣṇu (Hari, Vāsudeva, Puruṣottama included), Śiva, Sūrya, etc. who are primarily, on different occasions, its cause or repositories in that they may have a subtle or subtler than subtle or even a macrocosmic (*virāṭ*) form, to be so perceived, meditated upon or worshipped. →*Bhakti*, 'devotion', characterized by a total surrender to the God and desiring his grace by invoking the Godhead with prayers, repeatedly occurs in relation to *rūpa*, specially that of a divinity. These observations are exemplified below, starting with the togetherness of *rūpa* with *guṇa* and *māyā* etc. The need to discern *rūpa* in its essence arises from the need to dispel ignorance:

> न चास्य कश्चिन्निपुणेन धातुरवैति जन्तुःकुमनीष ऊतीः ।
> नामानि रूपाणि मनोवचोभिः सन्तन्वतो नटचर्यामिवाज्ञः ॥
>
> BhāgPur I.3.37
>
> Just as an ignorant spectator is not able to recognize the actor behind his make up so also no one having a limited and perverted intelligence depending on his skill in logic can understand the mystery of the Creator manifested into countless names and form. (Tr. Tapasyananda)

The **Devī Bhāgavata** (V.8.58-59) reiterates this observation. Ignorance apart, form, along with *guṇa, nāma, māyā,* etc., are regarded essentially as creations of a Supreme Being:

> येन स्वधाम्न्यमी भावा रजःसत्वतमोमयाः ।
> गुणनामक्रियारूपैर्विभाव्यन्ते यथातथम् ॥
>
> BhāgPur VI.1.41
>
> Nārāyaṇa is He who creates in Himself creatures out of qualities of *sattva, rajas* and *tamas,* characterized by distinctions of forms, names and actions. (Tr. Tapasyananda)

Rūpa is co-existent with *liṅga* and *nāma* also:

> स एव देवतालिङ्गैर्नामरूप विकल्पितैः ।
> इज्यते भगवान् पुम्भिः .... ॥
>
> BhāgPur VI.18.34
>
> It is Him ... that men worship in image under different forms and names... (Tr. Tapasyananda)

Māyā is the mysterious power that brings form before eyes:

एतद्रूपं भगवतो ह्यरूपस्य चिदात्मनः ।
मायागुणैर्विरचितं महदादिभिरात्मनि ॥

BhāgPur I.3.30

In the Supreme Being, who is the pure and formless Spirit, His own power *māyā* fabricates all forms with her evolutes like *mahattattva* and other categories. (Tr. Tapasyananda)

Yet, having been created by →*māyā,* such substances are impermanent and illusive; only God is adorable whose form is indescribable:

यद्रूपमेतन्निजमाययार्पितमर्थस्वरूपं बहुरूप रूपितम् ।
संख्या न यस्यास्त्ययथोपलम्भनात्तस्मै नमस्तेऽव्यपदेशरूपिणे ॥

BhāgPur V.18.31

This world of multiplicity projected by Thy *māyā* as a factually perceived universe is verily Thy form. It is seen as a countless multiplicity because it is viewed apart from Thee. Salutations to Thy indescribable form. (Tr. Tapasyananda)

A more philosophical attitude is in evidence in the Purāṇas about *rūpa* as the *tanmātra* (subtle aspect) which is consorted with the elements like *vāyu* (cf. ŚBr XI.8.3.8) and *tejas* (or Agni):

वायोश्चस्पर्शतन्मात्राद्रूपं दैवेरितादभूत् ।
समुत्थितं ततस्तेजश्चक्षू रूपोपलम्भनम् ॥

BhāgPur III.26.38

Through the functioning of the providence the element air which in its subtle *tanmātra* condition is identical with touch, produces the *tanmātra* of *rūpa* (form or perception), out of which is born the element *tejas* (brilliance, fire). The eyes perceive form and colour which are variations of *tejas.* (Tr. Tapasyananda)

Rūpa in concert with *tejas* is the subject of discourse many a times in the **Bhāgavata Purāṇa** (III.5.27-29; III.26.41) and it is argued that *tejas* is perceived by eyes in the manner of Agni which is like eyes of the world (BhāgPur III.5.33). *Dhī,* 'intellect' too discerns *rūpa,* whatever be its nature:

श्रुत्वा स्थूलं तथा सूक्ष्मं रूपं भगवतो यतिः ।
स्थूले निर्जितमात्मानं शनैः सूक्ष्मं धिया नयेदिति ॥

BhāgPur V.26.53

The rule is that the aspirant should hear about the gross and subtle forms of the Lord. Then after attaining concentration on the gross form, he should gradually draw his mind towards the subtle form. (Tr. Tapasyananda)

Besides intellect, *cakṣus*, 'eyes' and *manas*, 'mind', also render the discernment of *rūpa* possible:

यत् किञ्चिन्मनसा ग्राह्यं यद् ग्राह्यं चक्षुरादिभिः ।
बुद्ध्या च यत् परिच्छेद्यं तद्रूपमखिलं तव ॥

ViPur I.4.19

Whatever may be apprehended by the mind, whatever may be perceived by the senses, whatever may be discerned by the intellect, all is but a form of Thee. (Tr. H.H. Wilson)

The **Bhāgavata Purāṇa** reiterates the point about the capacity of eyes to perceive form, when it says that *cakṣuṣāṃśena rūpāṇāṃ pratipattiryato bhavet* (III.6.15cd) – "with the eyes forms are perceived". Cognition apart, the forms in all their multiplicity are but the varied distinctions of the Supreme Deity manifested in a series of categories from subtle onwards:

रूपं महत्ते स्थितमत्र विश्वं ततश्च सूक्ष्मं जगदेतदीश ।
रूपाणि सर्वाणि च भूतभेदास्तेष्वन्तरात्माख्यमतीव सूक्ष्मम् ॥
तस्माच्च सूक्ष्मादि विशेषणानाम् अगोचरे यत् परमात्मरूपम् ।
किमप्यचिन्त्यं तव रूपमस्ति तस्मै नमस्ते पुरुषोत्तमाय ॥

ViPur I.19.74-75

The universe is Thy intellectual form, whence proceeded by subtile form, this world: thence art Thou all subtile elements and elementary beings, and the subtile principle that is called soul, within them. Hence, the supreme soul of all objects, distinguished as subtle or gross, which is imperceptible, and which cannot be conceived, is even a form of Thee. Glory be to Thee, Puruṣottama. (Tr. H.H. Wilson)

A hierarchical distinction in the particular, mundane forms and their distinctions (*rūpabheda*) is postulated in the **Bhāgavata Purāṇa** (III.30.30) in case of the footed creatures. As for the divinities, they are supposed to be 'eternally, formless though continually manifested and open to all kinds of divisions and distinctions which may be non-eternal:

आद्यन्तं यत् परं सूक्ष्ममरूपं परमं स्थितम् ।
ओमित्युक्तं मया विप्र तत्परं ब्रह्म तद्वपुः ॥

MārkPur XCVIII.27

The word '*om*' which I have uttered O *Brahman*, which has a beginning and an end, which is sublime, subtle, formless, most sublime, permanent – this is the Supreme Spirit, yea his body. (Tr. F.E. Pargiter)

Such attributes in their wide multiplicity figure out many a divinities and even the amorphous Reality. The instances follow, starting with *brahman*:

द्वे रूपे ब्रह्मणस्तस्य मूर्तं चामूर्तमेव च ।
क्षराक्षरस्वरूपे ते सर्वभूतेष्ववस्थिते ॥

ViPur I.22.55

There are two states of this *Brahman*, one with and one without shape, one perishable and one imperishable; which are inherent in all beings. (Tr. H.H. Wilson)

Such attributes qualify Devī in the **Devī Bhāgavata**:

सा नित्या सर्वदैवास्ते देवकार्यार्थसिद्धये ।
नानारूपा त्वेकरूपा जायते कार्यगौरवात् ॥

DBhāg V.8.57

She (Devī) is constant, She is always existent, though She is the one yet She assumes different forms for fulfilment of the Devas' ends, whenever their position becomes serious. (Tr. Vijnanananda)

There is supposed to be an intrinsic quintessentiality about the being of the subtle form which is understood mainly in terms of *tattvas* howsoever they may be sensed or described:

एतद्धि यन्मया प्रोक्तं मम रूपमलौकिकम् ।
अव्याकृतं तदव्यक्तं मायाशबलमित्यपि ॥

DBhāg VII.32.24

The *tattva* (reality) that I have spoken to you is most excellent and it is my extra-ordinary Form merely. In the Vedas it is known as *avyākṛta* (unmodified), *avyakta* (unmanifested) *māyā śabala* (divided into various parts) and so forth. (Tr. Vijnanananda)

Such attributes qualify other deities also, like Mahādeva:

अमूर्तं चैव मूर्तं त ज्योतीरूपं हि तत् स्मृतम् ।
तस्योपलब्धिमन्विच्छन् यत्नः कार्यो विजानता ॥
गुणैर्वियुक्तो भूतात्मा एवं वक्तुं न शक्यते ।
शक्यते यदि वक्तुं वै दिव्यैर्वर्षशतैर्नवा ॥

MatPur CLXXXIII.58–59

The true nature of mine is really formless. But that which is manifested as my form is merely consisting of light to realise which a learned man ought to make great efforts. The Lord of the universe in his formless condition cannot be described, it can be described, if at all, by the persistent efforts of hundreds of years. (Tr. H.H. Wilson)

Or, Viṣṇu:

तच्च विष्णोः परं रूपमरूपाख्यमनुत्तमम् ।
विश्वस्वरूपवैरूप्य लक्षणं परमात्मनः ॥

ViPur VI.7.54

That is supreme, imperishable form of Viṣṇu, who is without (sensible) form, and is characterised as a condition of the supreme soul, which is variously modified from the condition of universal form. (Tr. H.H. Wilson)

Or, even other divinities like Sūrya, Vāsudeva, Hari, etc. However, the forms that a divinity may assume are often intended to gratify the devotees, which underscore the conjunction of *bhakti* with philosophical ruminations in regard to the 'formless', Supreme Deity differentiated into multiplicity of form. This is largely true whether in the case of Mahāviṣṇu or others:

रूपं भगवता त्वेतदशेषक्लेशसंक्षयम् ।
आविष्कृतं नः क्लिष्टानां किमन्यदनुकम्पितम् ॥

BhāgPur IV.30.27

To us who are subject to threefold misery of life, what also can be a greater mercy and blessing than this-that. Thou has graciously revealed this divine form of Thine which dispels all the woes of life. (Tr. Tapasyananda)

The same is true of the Devī also Who assumes forms to gratify Her devotees:

सेयं शक्तिर्महामाया सच्चिदानन्दरूपिणी ।
रूपं बिभर्त्यरूपा च भक्तानुग्रहहेतवे ॥

DBhāgPur IX.38.29

She is the Mahāmāyā, of the nature of everlasting existence, intellect and bliss. Though formless, She assumes forms for the gratification of the desires of Her *bhaktas*.
(Tr. Vijnanananda)

The form is thus an aid to the devotee in order to be invoked for his gratification or even for assisting him in concentrating upon the deity. The idea is succinctly stated in the **Pauṣkara Āgama** as cited in the commentary of Nīlakaṇṭha on the **Mṛgendra Āgama**:

> साधकस्य तु लक्ष्यार्थं तस्य रूपमिदं स्मृतम् ।
>
> MṛgĀ vp III under 9
>
> For concentration of the aspirant this form of Lord Śiva (*pañcamantratanu*) is known. (Tr. H.N. Chakravarty)

Rūpa also implies beauty – beauty of well endowed physical attributes specially in human beings. As such, the delicate charm and resplendance of *rūpa* is sensually received and may be a cause of much sensual delight: its attraction lying in its visual appeal. In such contexts, *rūpa* is understood in terms of →*saundarya* or *lāvaṇya*. *Rūpa* as beauty and charm however, is extolled or reviled depending upon who, with what pursuits, is exposed to it. Occurrence of the term *rūpa* as beauty is common to varied types of texts, including even those on Yoga and Medicine. For instance, Ḍalhaṇa, in his commentary on the **Suśruta Saṃhitā**, interprets *rūpa* as *saundarya* (beauty).

> रूपमिह लावण्यं विवक्षितं, यत्पर्यायः सौन्दर्यम् ।
>
> Ḍalhaṇa comm. on SuSamSūSthā V.27
>
> Hence, by the term *rūpa*, *lāvaṇya* (glamour or beauty) is meant; *saundarya* (beauty) is synonymous to it. (Tr. P. Ghosal)

In the original passage of the text, a wish is expressed that both *rūpa* and its shadow may be preserved by the stars and night respectively: *nakṣatrāṇi sadā rūpaṃ chāyāṃ pāntu niśāstava* (SuSamSūSthā V.27cd). The idea seems to be in conformity with the belief (BṛSam XV.26) that Aśvinī, a stellar deity, rules over handsome persons. There is a complete chapter in it (chapter CV: *Rūpasatra*) devoted to the methods of worship to get a good physical feature:

> नक्षत्रपुरुषकोऽयं कर्त्तव्यो रूपमिच्छद्भिः ॥
>
> BṛSam CV.5cd
>
> In this manner, the form of the Stellar Deity has to be constituted by those who wish for good physical features. (Tr. M.R. Bhat)

As in the text on medicine, quoted above, so in the **Haṭhayoga Pradīpikā**, *rūpa*, 'beauty', is consorted with *lāvaṇya* in reference to women: '*rūpalāvaṇyasampannā .... strī*' (III.25) – 'a woman possessing beauty and charming complexion' (tr. R.S. Bhattacharya).

According to the commentary however, *rūpa* is *saundarya* (beauty), and *lāvaṇya* is a quality that attracts the eye (*cakṣuḥ-priyo guṇaḥ*). Visual perception as the cause of delight is stressed elsewhere also, in a Tantric work:

> नयनयोरपि हि रूपं तद्वीर्यक्षोभात्मकमहाविसर्गविश्लेषणयुक्त्या एव सुखदायि भवति .... ।
>
> PTrīVi p. 16
>
> Even a (beautiful) figure brought into prominence by the meeting of two eyes affords delight only by the device of its union with the mighty seminal energy which stirs up the energy of the eyes. (Tr. J. Singh)

But *rūpa* undeniably is 'beauty' or a 'natural beautiful shapeliness', as in the **Bhāva Prakāśana**:

> आवेध्यारोप्यनिक्षेप्यबन्धनीयैरभूषितम् ।
> यद्भूषितमिवाभाति तद्रूपमिति कथ्यते ॥
>
> BhPrak III.94
>
> [When the person] inspite of not being adorned with ornaments like *āvedhya* (a special type of ear ornament), *āropya* (necklace etc.), *nikṣepya* (wristlet or anklet) and *bandhanīya* (*śroṇī sūtra, aṅgada,* etc. to be worn round the loins or upper arm) appears to be adorned should go by the name *rūpa* 'the beauty'. (Tr. P. Ghosal)

Beauty however evokes different responses:

> दृष्ट्वैकं रूपमन्यो हि रज्यतेऽन्यः प्रदुष्यति ।
> कश्चिद् भवति मध्यस्थस्तत्रैवान्यो घृणायते ॥
>
> Saun XIII.52
>
> On seeing a certain form one man is attracted, another dislikes it and a third is indifferent, while yet another feels compassionate disgust for the same object. (Tr. E.H. Johnston)

Beauty may even be impermanent like other short-lived personal possessions and proficiencies:

> बलं च रूपं च नवं च यौवनं तथावगच्छामि यथावगच्छसि ।
> अहं त्विदं ते त्रयमव्यवस्थितं यथावबुद्धे न तथावबुध्यसे ॥
>
> Saun IX.5
>
> I am aware, as you are aware, of your strength, beauty and young manhood but you do not understand as I understand, these three to be transitory. (Tr. E.H. Johnston)

And moral indictments have been inflicted on beauty time and again due to the ascetic values which advocate freedom and emancipation from sensual delights. In many such postures, beauty of form is denounced unequivocally:

अभिध्या प्रियरूपेण हन्ति कामात्मकं जगत् ।
अरिर्मित्रमुखेनेव प्रियवाक्कलुषाशयः ॥

Saun XIII.46

The desire of possession destroys the passion-filled world by means of attractive forms, like an enemy with friendly face, having pleasant words on his lips and evil in his heart. (Tr. E.H. Johnston)

But it is in the Kāvya literature that the delicate charm of *rūpa* 'beauty' is most illuminatingly articulated. Kālidāsa's narratives are typical in this regard. He aggregates different kinds of *rūpa* in terms of beauty in his inimitable poetic imageries. He professes, as it were, a hierarchy in *rūpa* describing with an ecstatic flourish, the delectable charm of divine, semi-divine and human *rūpa* (beauty) and finally making a categorical statement. That, 'beauty of form does not lead to sin' – *na rūpaṃ pāpavṛttaye.* Pārvatī, Urvaśī, Yakṣī, Mālavikā and Śakuntalā are the archetypal models of beauty in Kālidāsa, each with their respective unmatched attraction and charm. Urvaśī of lovely form (*manoharamidaṃrūpam*) born of 'that aged anchorite' (the sage Nārāyaṇa) who has grown dull through the study of the Vedas... (tr. C.R. Devadhar), was an Apsaras who surpassed even Śrī in beauty *pratyādeśo rūpagarvitāyāḥ śriyāḥ* (Vik I, prose under 3). In contrast, the *rūpa* of the other Apsaras Menakā is mentioned in terms of its "intoxicating charm" (*unmādayitṛ rūpa* – AbhŚāk under verse 22). Śakuntalā, her daughter, on the other hand, had, as it were, an unearthly form:

मानुषीषु कथं वा स्यादस्य रूपस्य संभवः ।
न प्रभातरलं ज्योतिरुदेति वसुधातलात् ॥

AbhŚāk I.23

How could any woman give birth to such a lovely form? The light that sparkles with tremulous beams does not rise from the surface of the earth. (Tr. C.R. Devadhar)

Mālavikā's 'flawless form' (*rūpa*) was delectably suitable for dance:

दीर्घाक्षं शरदिन्दुकान्तिवदनं बाहू नतावंसयोः
संक्षिप्तं निबिडोन्नतस्तनमुरः पार्श्वे प्रमृष्टे इव ।
मध्यः पाणिमितो नितम्बि जघनं पादावरालाङ्गुली
छन्दो नर्तयितुर्यथैव मनसः श्लिष्टं तथास्याःवपुः ॥

Māla II.3

Her long eyes; her face lovely like the moon of the autumn; the arms sloping at the shoulders; her compact bosom with plump and swelling breasts; her sides as if polished; her waist measurable by the palm of hand; her hips expansive; her feet with their curved toes; her whole body thus seems formed to suit the fancy of her teacher of dancing. (Tr. C.R. Devadhar)

The Yakṣiṇī of the **Meghadūta** is similarly described:

तन्वी श्यामा शिखरिदशना पक्वबिम्बाधरोष्ठी
मध्ये क्षामा चकितहरिणीप्रेक्षणा निम्ननाभिः ।
श्रोणीभारादलसगमना स्तोकनम्रा स्तनाभ्यां
या तत्र स्याद्युवतिविषये सृष्टिराद्येव धातुः ॥

Megh II.22

The Creator's prototype of a luscious women, slender, youthful, with (proper line of) teeth, and lips red like a *bimba* fruit, a thin waist and a glance like that of a startled deer; she has a deep navel, with measured gait owing to the weight of the hips, and she is slightly stooping from the weight of her bosom. (Tr. C.R. Devadhar)

Pārvatī's divine beauty, however, surpassed them all. Tempered with the discipline of *tapas* (austerities), it was, in every way, the essence of purity:

यदुच्यते पार्वति पापवृत्तये न रूपमित्यव्यभिचारि तद्वचः ।
तथा हि ते शीलमुदारदर्शने तपस्विनामप्युपदेशतां गतम् ॥

Kum V.36

What they say that beauty of form does not lead to sin is infallibly true; for thy character, O lady, large eyed, is an examplar even to the sages. (Tr. C.R. Devadhar)

The construction of the dictum that 'beauty of form does not lead to sin' is apparently based on the premise that beauty (*rūpa*) is something ideal and sin arises from confusing it with the body. In substance beauty is here regarded as an accidental property — a *daihika upādhi*— accidently superimposed on a person, and sin arises from confusing beauty with body. In the **Kumārasambhava** (V.1), Pārvatī herself deprecates that kind of *rūpa* which rests in its beauty alone for it is ephemeral and destructible, as was the case with the mind-born →*kāma* whose fate lay in his immolation. She blamed in her heart her beauty and, to her, that alone was beauty which would "win the heart of the husband": *nininda rūpaṃ hṛdayena pārvatī priyeṣu saubhāgyaphalā* *hi cārutā* (Kum V.1). Hence it was, that Pārvatī decided to invest her beauty with the discipline of penance: *iyeṣa sā kartumavandhya rūpatāṃ samādhimāsthāya tapobhirātmanaḥ* (Kum V.2).

Pārvatī and her consort Śiva were doubtlessly the ultimate models of 'form' but for whose manifestation the Creator's endeavour to create beauty would have utterly failed:

> परस्परेण स्पृहणीयशोभं न चेदिदं द्वन्द्वमयोजयिष्यत् ।
> अस्मिन् द्वये रूपविधानयत्नः पत्युः प्रजानां विफलोऽभविष्यत् ॥
>
> Kum VII.66
>
> If the Creator had not designed this couple for each other whose beauty was to be aspired by all, the Creator's endeavours to endow the two with beauty would have been in vain.
> (Tr. C.R. Devadhar)

As for Pārvatī, she was the epitome of beauty:

> सर्वोपमाद्रव्यसमुच्चयेन यथाप्रदेशं विनिवेशितेन ।
> सा निर्मिता विश्वसृजा प्रयत्नादेकस्थसौन्दर्यदिदृक्षयेव ॥
>
> Kum I.49
>
> She was created by the Creator, with great effort, from all materials of comparison moulding each limb as if the world's Creator would behold all beauty centred in a single mould.
> (Tr. C.R. Devadhar)

Rūpa as beauty in such contexts refers often to ideal physical attributes. Among other illustrative examples, besides those mentioned above, reference may be made to Rāma and to his consort Sītā, as in the **Rāmāyaṇa**. Rāma is described as equal to Kandarpa in beauty (*rūpavān subhagaḥ śrīmān kandarpa iva mūrtimān* – Rām V.34.30ab; cf. VI.95.6), as he was possessed of ideal physical attributes (→*lakṣaṇas*, Rām I.1.9-11), which are graphically described (Rām V.35.15-20). Sītā was similarly endowed (*rūpam aṅgapratyaṅga sauṣṭhavam* – Rām V.15.51b), as the details reveal in glowing terms(Rām III.46.14-24).

Yet, it must be cautioned that *rūpa* does not always signify 'beauty' for, *rūpa* may vary in many ways and may stand for even an ugly, unattractive, 'modified' (*vikṛta*) or 'horrid' (*ghora*) form (Rām I.1.55) and thus be *virūpa*, the opposite of 'beautiful' (Rām III.17.28; III.18.20, 23, 25). In general, it is supposed to be an appearance specific to its abode; an external physical construct, a kind of covering. It may even be assumed by guile as in the case of Indra in the **Rāmāyaṇa** (I.48.28) who assumed the *rūpa* of Gautama to entice Ahalyā (*mamarūpa samāsthāya* ..).

Nāma-rūpa

As noticed above, *rūpa* is often paired very significantly with *nāma*. Apart from what has been adduced above on *nāma-rūpa*, some more passages may be quoted here to explain their complementarity. The duo occurs together in its almost Vedantic connotation in the **Atharvaveda**:

को अस्मिन् रूपमदधात् को मह्यानं च नाम च ।
गातुं को अस्मिन् कः केतुं कश्चरित्राणि पूरुषे ॥

AV X.2.12

Who set form in him? Who both bulk (*mahmānam*) and name? Who (set) in him progress (*gātu*)? Who display (*ketu*)? Who (set) behavior (*caritra*) in man? (Tr. J. Muir)

This creator is identified in the **Taittirīya Brāhmaṇa** (II.2.7.1) with Prajāpati who produced 'shapeless things' and then entered into them by name and form. The transient, mutable nature of the duo is apparent time and again:

निस्तत्त्वे नामरूपे द्वे जन्मनाशयुते च ते ।
बुद्ध्या ब्रह्मणि वीक्षस्व समुद्रे बुद्बुदादिवत् ॥

Pañcad XIII.79

Both name and form are without any real existence, because they are subject to creation and destruction. So know them as superimposed by the intellect on *brahman*, just as waves and foam on the ocean. (Tr. Swahananda)

Temporally, name and form are basic to every manifest phenomenon and are significant in their manifested corporeality as well as in regard to the entity from which they are derived. In the latter aspect *nāma* and *rūpa* go into a series of differentiation where each of such manifestation may be a continuum from subtle to the gross. In such a continuum every subsequent emanation implies in it the inherent plausibility of the Being so diversified or represented. In arts, this continuity re-states the correspondence of formal and representational elements by a rhetoric of the implied suggestion:

ब्रह्मण्येते नामरूपे पटे चित्रमिव स्थिते ।
उपेक्ष्य नामरूपे द्वे सच्चिदानन्दधीर्भवेत् ॥

Pañcad XIII.93

Just as many objects are seen in a picture, so the various names and forms exist in the *brahman*. By negating both names and forms one can understand that what remains in existence, consciousness and bliss. (Tr. Swahananda)

Nāma-rūpa thus turn out to be both subtle in derivation and gross in materiality; functioning merely as limiting adjuncts:

चेतनाचेतनेष्वेषु सच्चिदानन्दलक्षणम् ।
समानं ब्रह्म भिद्येते नामरूपे पृथक् पृथक् ॥

Pañcad XIII.92

Brahman, characterised as existence, consciousness and bliss is the common basis of both the animate and inanimate objects; they differ only in their names and forms. (Tr. Swahananda)

Or, as implicit in reference to their originator and explicit in their revelation:

विचित्य सर्वरूपाणि कृत्वा नामानि तिष्ठति ।
अहं व्याकरवाणीमे नामरूपे इति श्रुतेः ॥

Pañcad XIII.64

After creating names and forms *brahman* remains established in His nature, i.e. remains as immutable as ever, says, the Śruti, while another Śruti says that *brahman,* as the Self reveals names and forms. (Tr. Swahananda)

Or, they extend the world:

जगदव्याकृतं पूर्वमासीद्व्याक्रियताधुना ।
दृश्याभ्यां नामरूपाभ्यां विराडादिषु ते स्फुटे ॥

Pañcad IV.8

It is also said that before its manifestation the whole world existed in *brahman* in a potential form; then assuming name and form it came into being as *virāṭ.* (Tr. Swahananda)

Or, even get reduced and dissipated:

नामरूपान्यथात्वेऽपि कूटस्थं ब्रह्म नान्यथा ॥

Pañcad XIII.100cd

... while names and forms constantly change, the unchanging *brahman* does not become otherwise. (Tr. Swahananda)

The *nāma-rūpa* categories in tandem are valid only in the empirical world for, *nāma* identifies any or all distinctions that *rūpa* may potentially assume. The Kṣīrasvāmin's commentary on the **Amara Kośa** (I.6.3) explains *nāma* as one through which something is called: *namatyanena nāma.*

Nāma was there at the very beginning before the creation because it identifies a-sexual Primordiality:

संज्ञाया आदित्वात् ॥

VaiśSū IV.2.9

(The existence of a-sexual bodies is proved) from the primitiveness of the name. (Tr. N.L. Sinha)

Elsewhere, a different view is expressed in that it is said that names surfaced after the Primordial Being:

इदं सर्वं पुरा सृष्टेरेकमेवाद्वितीयकम् ।
सदेवासीन्नामरूपे नास्तामित्यारुणेर्वचः ॥

Pañcad II.19

Before all this was created there was Being alone, one only without a second, there was neither name nor form, so said Āruṇi. (Tr. Swahananda)

In essence, names are taken to originate in many ways, one of them being their adherence to forms which makes their own differentiation multiply. The **Bṛhaddevatā** (I.25–26) explains such origins and other connections of 'name' and its multiplicity.

In the Upaniṣads name and form are clearly the "negative, mortal, differentiated conditions of one *nāma*, all-conscious, co-substantial with one *rūpa*, the Universe as the latter's 'own form'. While *nāma* is the inner power of individual being or thing, the *rūpa* is its sensuous appearance. *Rūpa* is realised by perception (*dṛṣṭi*) or imagination (*saṃkalpa*)... and *nāma* by audition (→*śruti*) or thought (*dhī*)" (Maryla Falk 1943: 19–20). The belief in *nāma-rūpa* being the categories of identity of things is continued all through the tradition, and this is stressed even in the later works, as in the Purāṇas:

नामरूपं च भूतानां कृत्यानां च प्रपञ्चनम् ।
वेदशब्देभ्य एवादौ देवादीनां चकार सः ॥

MarkPur XLV.42

And he (the Lord, Creator) assigned the names and shapes of created things, and propounded the duties of the gods and other beings even by words of the Veda at the beginning. (Tr. F.E. Pargiter)

Nāma-rūpa distinguishes the existential nature of things that inhabit the world of experience:

नामरूपव्याकृतं हि वस्तु सच्छब्दार्हं लोके प्रसिद्धम् ।

BrSūŚBh II.1.17

Those things which are distinguished by name and form are in ordinary language called 'existent'. (Tr. G. Thibaut)

Yet, this *loka-prasiddhi*, 'common knowledge', does not guarantee that such things would constitute the essence of the un-differentiated Entity:

> न नामरूपं वस्तूनां विकल्पा वाचकाश्च यत् ।
> विश्वकल्पाः प्रवर्तन्ते यथाभ्यासमभेदिनि ॥
>
> TaSaṅg I.31
>
> The name of things is not their 'Essence' (nature, form) because all kinds of 'conceptions' and 'verbal expressions' proceed through habit with reference to the undifferentiated (Immaculate Entity). (Tr. G.N. Jha)

Rūpa-pratirūpa

Rūpa is also posited as the essence resting in the transcendental or notional, un-verbalised, un-manifested primary cause which goes into difference in all imaginable variety. And in that sense, it invokes the primary source from which it derives and thus serves as the mediating factor, linking the source with its materialised manifestation. Thus Indra, the 'wearer of every shape at pleasure' (ṚV III.53.8) is one in many:

> रूपं रूपं प्रतिरूपो बभूव तदस्य रूपं प्रतिचक्षणाय ।
> इन्द्रो मायाभिः पुरुरूप ईयते .... ॥
>
> ṚV VI.47.18
>
> In every figure he hath been the model: this is his only form for us to look on.
> Indra moves every form by his illusion.... (Tr. R.T.H. Griffith)

The phenomenon of form-counterform is categorically an act of great skill (*yadvai pratirūpaṃ tat śilpam* – ŚBr III.2.1.5). It is central to the vision of the archetypal model even as that model may tend to divide and diversify itself in the act of creation. In every subsequent materialisation of itself the archetypal model is also supposed to be inherently and transiently arrested; and such secondary forms serve as symbolic devices to comprehend the latent force behind it. The reconstituted, material phenomenon thus brought about may be epistemologically perceived or understood as the reflection of the unmanifested in its multiplicity. Essentially *rūpa* is of two kinds:

> द्वे वाव ब्रह्मणो रूपे । मूर्तं चैवामूर्तञ्च । मर्त्यं चामृतं च ।
> स्थितञ्च यच्च । सच्च त्यं च ॥
>
> BṛUp II.3.1
>
> There are, assuredly, two forms of *brahman*: the formed (*mūrta*) and

the formless, the mortal and the immortal, the stationary and the moving, the actual (*sat*) and the yon (*tya*). (Tr. R.E. Hume)

Rūpa in a *pratirūpa* is premised, whether stated or not so stated as the potential factor in the manner of →*śabda,* sound (as heard in the *dundubhi,* →*śaṅkha* or *vīṇā* – BṛUp II.4.7-9) which accords efficacy to the verses (AitBr I.21). Here the verses (or the uttered words in those verses) recited by priest 'extends' and 'far extends' Bṛhaspati and makes him "possessed of body and form" – *satanumevainaṃ tatsvarūpaṃ karoti.* Similarly, in the **Aitareya Brāhmaṇa** (I.6) Virāja is a meter (*chandas*) of strength for, as the immanent principle in its *padas,* it accumulates in itself the unity (*sāyujyam*) and identity of form (with) the World (*sarūpatāṃ salokatām aśnute*); and then, a mere utterance of the *mantra* – *preddho agna imo agna iti* 'Kindled O Agni' and 'These O Agni' is enough to invoke and materialise that strength. This utterance and *rūpa* combination is essentially a *rūpa-pratirūpa* continuity un-stated in that catch-phrase yet involving the unity of the vocalised words with their contingent form. Later, in the philosophies in Mīmāṃsā for instance, and in Kāvya, *śabda* has the authority of being a →*pramāṇa,* 'proof' of knowledge which makes perception possible. In its transcendental character the divinity however is without a form (*rūpādi rahita*) according to the Jaiminīya philosophy (SarDSaṅg p.125).

The **Kaṭha Upaniṣad** (II.2.9–10) speaks of Agni and Vāyu multiplying by assuming the form of the things in which they find an abode, but unlike them, the *ātman,* even while inhabiting all beings and thereby going into differentiations, manages yet to exist 'without'.

The formal entity of the Supreme self is conceived in terms of Its Singleness (*ekarūpa* which It multiplies – *ekaṃrūpaṃ bahudhā yaḥ karoti* (KaṭhUp V.12). But the Brahman, beyond the counterform, may be comprehended in a subtle way, e.g. as seeing oneself in a mirror (thereby seeing the self) (KaṭhUp VI.5). Deduction by the process of intellection is supposed to lead to the perception of the Sole Reality here. In these details, a mirror figures along with the likes of it such as dream, water, light and shade which are all among the transient categories; and all these are hierarchically contrasted with Self, the *pitṛloka, gandharvaloka* and *brahmaloka* which make the higher world where a vision of the Reality may be possible.

The imagery of 'reflection in mirror' or in water is fairly pervasive right from the Vedic times (Misra 1980: 179f.). In the **Chāndogya Upaniṣad** (VIII.8.1), we have Prajāpati directing the representatives of the gods and demons to look at their shadow in water in order to make them able to realize the →*ātman.* All of them were, in that manner, immediately though erroneously satisfied, for:

तौ होचतु: – सर्वमेवेदमावां भगव आत्मानं पश्याव
आ लोमभ्य आ नखेभ्य: प्रतिरूपमिति ॥

ChUp VIII.8.1

Then the two said: we see everything here, sir, a self corresponding exactly, even to the hair and finger-nails. (Tr. R.E. Hume)

The Person whose reflection in water (*ya evāmyamādarśe puruṣaḥ sa eṣaḥ*) identifies him, is supposed to rest in *rūpa* (*rūpāṇyeva yasyāyatanam*), which is his abode, and the *rūpa-pratirūpa* combination is evident here too. The combination is explicit in describing Indra's multiplicity (BṛUp II.5.19).

An organic unity is essential in the *rūpa-pratirūpa* continuity for, a son is ideally a *pratirūpa*:

मनसा वै सम्राट् स्त्रियमभि हर्यति तस्यां प्रतिरूप: पुत्रो जायते स आनन्द: ।

BṛUp IV.1.6

Verily, your Majesty, by the mind one betakes himself to a woman. A son like himself is born of her. He is bliss. (Tr. R.E. Hume)

प्रतिरूप इति वा अहमेतमुपास इति । स य एतमेवमुपास्ते प्रतिरूपं
हैवैनमुपगच्छति, नाप्रतिरूपम् । अथो प्रतिरूपोऽस्माज्जायते ॥

BṛUp II.1.8

I worship him verily as the counterpart (of the phenomenal objects). His counterpart comes to him (in his children), not that which is not his counterpart. His counterpart is born from him. (Tr. R.E. Hume)

Disparate forms are also made to correspond:

दिवं गच्छ सुव:पत रूपेण वा रूपमभ्यैमि वयसा वय: ।

TSam I.4.43.1–2

Go to the sky, fly to heaven, with my form I approach your form; with my age your age. (Tr. A.B. Keith)

A spatial dimension in relativity is accorded to *rūpa-pratirūpa* symbolism in connection with sacrifice and its follow up:

य आदित्ये स प्रतिरूप: । प्रत्यङ्ङ्ह्येष सर्वाणि रूपाणि ।
तं प्रतिरूप इत्युपासीत । प्रत्यञ्चि हैनं सर्वाणि रूपाणि भवन्ति ॥

JaimUp I.27.5

He, who is in the region of Sun, is the counterpart.
He is in occidental direction to all the formations.
He should be worshipped as the counterpart. (And now)
all the formations become occidental to him. (Tr. P. Ghosal)

The *rūpa-pratirūpa* correspondence is also expressed in terms of *pratibimba, anurūpa, tulyarūpa* and →*sādṛśya* which are all different from *tathārūpa* (Rām IV.6.2), i.e., the form specific to its particular category. Thus the well endowed (*rūpa-sampanna*) Lava and Kuśa were possessed of the form and marks in the mirror-image of Rāma – *bimbādi ādhṛtaṃ bimbau rāmadehāttathāparam* (Rām I.4.11) or, *ubhau rāmasya sadṛśau bimbād bimbamivotthitau* (Rām VII.94.14). Similarly, the likeness of Śacī is mentioned in the **Rāmāyaṇa** (III.48.24b): *śacīṃ pradhṛṣyā pratirūpa rūpām.* Or, it is said that Indrajit was in the likeness of Rāvaṇa in austerities and strength (Rām V.48.6). Or, identical forms of Bālī and Sugrīva in ornaments, dress, measure and movement (*alaṃkāreṇa veṣeṇa pramāṇena gatena ca*) are mentioned in the **Rāmāyaṇa** (IV.12.30ab). Sometimes not only the beings but even things are similarly described, e.g., **Rāmāyaṇa** (V.7.7d) – *gṛhottamaṃ hyapratirūpa rūpam.* Or, sky and sea look alike (*tulyarūpa* or *tadrūpa*) where they join the horizon (Rām VI.4.21). This similarity could even be created by guile as in the case of Rāma's figure made by Vidyujjihva which looked alike in face, eyes, and complexion (Rām VI.31.8; VI.32.2) so much so that Sītā, in desperation, made a request to pair her with Rāma in the later's measure: *śirasā me śiraścāsya kāyaṃ kāyena yojaya* (Rām VI.32.32ab).

Manifestation in the Arts

Rūpa, whether conceptual or representational (→*avyakta* or *vyakta,* ŚiRaKo p. 174) figures centrally in arts (*rūpavidyā,* comm. on VSUp) and connotes an 'image' or 'sculpture' (VSUp I.2, III.7; Mayam XV.28, etc.) as well as its characteristic. The explicit compositional structure and the →*bhāva* ('mood', 'implication', 'nature') in a form together constitute *rūpavidyā* which interprets both the concept and principles of composition. In that sense, whatever is crafted morphologically is also validated aesthetically, in concurrence. The re-constitution of *rūpa* in an image is canonically described as *rūpa-nirmāṇa* for instance in the **Viṣṇudharmottara Purāṇa** in which compositional features have to be 'purposive' (*sahetuka,* VDhPur p. 41) in import. While a divine entity in a state of its consciousness may bring about the forms merely by its will (*icchā,* VDhPur p. 16), an artist renders the experience of his creative consciousness into a representational reality in conformity with the principles of composition. Identities are thereby inferred in plastic art with the help of *lakṣaṇa* and *pramāṇa* (Misra 1994: 105-106). In any case, *rūpa* in arts is often supposed to arise from the 'formless', so a *rūpa-pratirūpa* continuum is implicit in →*śilpa.* Equally implicit in it is *bhāvarūpa* for, whatever is created in arts, has to be the counterpart of the archetypal form, rediscovered or reincarnated, as it were, in its formal (*nāma-rūpa*) materiality. These ideas occur repeatedly in the texts.

Rūpa implies both the material form and its property:

सदैकरूपरूपाय विष्णवे सर्वजिष्णवे ॥

ViPur I.2.1cd

We pay obeisance to the Being. It is the only characteristic of the One Who has that form. (Tr. H.N. Chakravarty)

The verse is addressed to Viṣṇu, the 'victorious of all' and here 'the first *rūpa* means the characteristic and the second means body (*vigraha*)', according to the commentary. Even the 'formless', if it comes into the ambit of *nāma-rūpa* (form), is realised in arts, regardless of its being invisible:

अप्रत्यक्षेऽपि एवं नामरूपं लिख्यते ।

Nāgā p.58

Though invisible her form is (nicely) painted. (Tr. N.C. Panda)

Or, as in the **Viṣṇudharmottara Purāṇa** the form of even the 'incomprehensible' is suggestively rendered tangible.

एतद्धि तस्याप्रतिमस्य रूपं तवेरितं सर्वजगन्मयस्य ।

VDhPur III.48.20ab

Thus has been stated to you the form of the incomprehensible One Who pervades the world. (Tr. D.C. Bhattacharya)

This is so much in conformity with the temporal immanence of divine entity whose manifestation, beautiful and effulgent, like a painting, are simply willed and so they are there:

स्वेच्छा विश्वमयोल्लेख खचितं विश्वरूपकम् ।
चैतन्यमात्मनो रूपं निसर्गानन्द सुन्दरम् ॥

YoH I.50

The Supreme Consciousness in its immanence is adorned with the painting of the Universe born of its will. The very nature of the self as light is its self-reflection (*cidvimarśa*). It is beautiful by virtue of its innate blissful nature. (Tr. H.N. Chakravarty)

Similarly, in the Pāśupata philosophy (Sharma, SarDSaṅg p. 263) art, as dependent on the Īśvara, is split into *kāryākhyā* and *kāraṇākhyā* categories or, in other words into the *indriyarūpā kalā* (art of the sensual perception) and *viṣayarūpā kalā* (art of the consciousness). On the other hand, the plastic art is given to creating identities of form by manual skill. So, we have in the **Viṣṇudharmottara Purāṇa**:

देवतारूपनिर्माणं कथयस्व ममानघ ।
यस्मात् सन्निहिता नित्यं शास्त्रवत्साकृतिर्भवेत् ॥

VDhPur III.2.1

O sinless one, how should I then question as to how should one make the form of gods so that the image made according to rules may always manifest (the deity)? (Tr. P. Shah)

In a similar fashion, the **Vāstusūtra Upaniṣad** goes into conceptual as well as compositional details of reconstitution of diverse forms, even as it lays stress on conformity of a composed image with its archetypal model. It visualises both the primary and secondary form:

अरूपाद्रूपं .... ॥

VSUp V.21

From the formless arises form. (Tr. A. Boner)

The commentary explains that "...due to diversity of conceptions arises the form of the divinity, and through the form arises diversity. That becomes the images (*pratirūpa*, or secondary form)" (tr. A. Boner). Reconstitution of *rūpa* therefore has to be understood as *bhāvarūpa* only:

तद् भावाद्रूपं रूपं प्रतिरूपं जायते ... ।

Comm. on VSUp IV.2

The image corresponding to every (original) form arises on the basis of that nature (*bhāva*). (Tr. A. Boner)

This commentary on the **Vāstusūtra Upaniṣad** (*rūpādaṅgāni sañ-jāyante* – IV.2) offers a different interpretation of *bhāvarūpa* in arts than that in philosophy. The Advaita philosophy interprets *bhāvarūpa* as the resultant of *avidyā* (nescience), leading up to misapprehension (Hiriyanna 1964: 354). In arts it seems to signify the latent in the manifested form which makes a comprehension possible by suggestion, much in the manner of 'moon reflected in water' (Misra 1989: 179). Therefore, the dictum – *rūpasya bhāvo mukhyaḥ* – (VSUp III.1) 'the character of the form is essential', in the act of carving.

A re-constitution of form in arts is appropriately dependent on *śilpa*:

षट् शिल्पाङ्गप्रयोगेण प्रजनयन्ति रूपाणि ॥

VSUp I.2

Art forms are produced by means of six disciplines. (Tr. A. Boner)

Or,

शिल्पात् प्रतिमा जायन्ते ॥

VSUp I.5

By *śilpa* images are produced. (Tr. A. Boner)

This 'production' requires the 'knowledge of stones' (*śailam*), 'compositional diagrams' (*khilapañjara*), 'carving of stones' (*śailabhedana*), 'arrangement of limbs or parts' (*aṅgaprayoga*), 'the emotional disposition, evoked by the composition' (*nyāsabhāvanā*), and 'the understanding of the integration of the composition' (*sambandhaprabodha*) (comm. on VSUp I.8; tr. A. Boner).

In the discourse, form is essentially archetypal in character and instrumental in making the implicit principle comprehensible. The non-visual modes like recitation of songs and myths are supposed to mediate in making the comprehension possible. But in any case, the conceptual *rūpa* is the primal source of the end-product in the entire compositional programme in art:

> रूपात् क्रमेण प्रतिमायास्तत्त्वबोधो जायते । तत्त्वबोधाद् धारणेति । धारणाया गाथा, कथा प्रसरति लोके गाथाया रूपाण्युत्पादयन्ति स्थापकाः ..... ।
>
> Comm. on VSUp I.7
>
> From the archetype gradually arises the knowledge of principle of images, from the knowledge of principle comes clear conception, from clear conception sacred songs and myths arise among people. From sacred song (*gāthā*) the *sthāpakas* derive images. (Tr. A. Boner)

This experiential series is designated in the text as *rūpavāstu ṣaḍaṅgaṃ śilpam,* (comm. on VSUp I.8) 'six branches of the art of image making'. *Rūpa* thus has an absolute primacy in sculpture or in visual arts. Its reconstitution by a *sthāpaka* is possible when its →*tattvas* (principles), *dhāraṇā* (conception) and *gāthā* (mythical content) have been reappropriated in an image. Reconstituting *rūpa,* in the situation, requires translating one mode into another whereby the concepts and principles turn into myths which then help in composing the image (*rūpa*). The images have to necessarily conform to their conceptual content:

> यथा प्रकृतिस्तथा रूपलक्षणम् ।
>
> VSUp III.15
>
> The features of image are conform to nature. (Tr. A. Boner)

The commentary on the *sūtra* (III.15) explains the point further by introducing →*hṛdaya* as the element of action in comprehending the *rūpa*:

> रूपस्य स्वभावानुक्रमेण रूपाणि भवन्ति । तेषां तत्तद् गुणाः प्रभवन्ति कामचारिणां हृदये इति ।
>
> Comm. on VSUp III.15

The forms of images are according to their own nature. They manifest their qualities corresponding to each form as they arise in the heart of those who are moved by creative impulse (*kāmacārin*). (Tr. A. Boner)

Artisanal modes are prescribed in the canon of art to materialise a *rūpa*, 'image' or 'sculpture', with the aid of practical artificing devices. In such application, *rūpa* (image) conforms to its conceptual and material format:

यन्त्रानुसारि यद्रूपं ध्यानानुसारितं तथा ।

ŚiPra II.192ab

His (Nāṭambara's) form should be in accordance with the *yantra* and with the *dhyāna.* (Tr. A. Boner)

Artist is required to make a linear grid (on a stone, comm. on VSUp VI.4) for making an image (VSUp IV.6), as in:

तत्त्वज्ञानेन रूपार्थं कोष्ठका मुख्याः ॥

VSUp IV.4

According to the knowledge of the principles for making images, a grid is most important. (Tr. A. Boner)

A grid of sixteen compartments is supposed to be ideal for image-making:

षोडशकोष्ठकमध्ये रूपाणि प्रभवन्ति तद्रूपार्थं श्रेष्ठम् ॥

VSUp VI.7

The forms appear within the grid of sixteen compartments, this is best for making images. (Tr. A. Boner)

The second chapter of the **Vāstusūtra Upaniṣad** on Khilapañjara-jñānam prescribes the use of compositional diagrams for image making. It recommends drawing circles and lines on a stone piece and suggests that once a diagrammatic format has been systematically laid out, the *rūpakarma,* 'image-making', should proceed from the centre:

नाभौ रूपकर्म प्रारभ्यते ॥

VSUp II.10

The creation of the image starts from the navel. (Tr. A. Boner)

"Infusion of feelings" (→*bhāva*) is specially enjoined in the *rūpakarma* (VSUp V.1) and *rūpa* in an image may vary depending upon the *rasas* to which it may relate (VSUp V.3).

In all these details, *rūpa* in arts, specially in sculpture, seems to encompass the creative process which brings out the conceptual into the range of sensual perception and aesthetic appreciation. Despite the fact that *rūpa* in spiritual domain is considered as *anitya*, 'transient' or 'impermanent', its significance in arts and aesthetics is appropriately established as something pleasing to senses and valid both in secular and religious domain (Misra: 1994).

Conclusion

Rūpa in ancient Indian tradition, represents a major concept with a great multiplicity in its connotations. Yet, phenomenally, even in its remarkable diversity, it is a specific category which maintains its diversity and ensures specific identities. *Rūpa* is supposed to be there noumenally also as the causative property of its repository which is capable of endless differentiations which on their turn constitute the empirical world. *Rūpa* also defines specific categories in Indian philosophical systems. In literature and arts it qualifies beauty, taste and relish which invoke delight. In plastic art it is reconstituted by translating the conceptual into representational, and manual skill plays a significant part in the process. *Rūpa* qualifies beauty in its resplendent, delectable physical charms as also in its enchanting, ensnaring propensities. Essentially, a transient, impermanent, phenomenal stuff or quality signifying matter as well as its properties and characteristics, *rūpa* pervades the world of experience for, but for its being there, the phenomenal world in all its diversity would not be explained, in tradition.

Rama Nath Misra

Select Bibliography

Bäumer, Bettina: "Puruṣa and The Origin of Form", in Rūpa Pratirūpa, Alice Boner Commemoration Volume, Ed. Bettina Bäumer, New Delhi: Biblia Impex Ltd., 1982, pp.27–31.

Chaturvedi, Prem Sagar: The Technology in Vedic Literature, Delhi: Books and Books, 1993.

Devadhar, C.R. (Ed. & Tr.): Works of Kalidasa, Vols 1–2, Delhi: Motilal Banarsidass, 1984–1991 (Rpt.).

Falk, Maryla: Nāma-rūpa and Dharmarūpa, Calcutta: University of Calcutta, 1943.

Gonda, J.: Four Studies in the language of the Veda, Gravenhage: Mouton & Co., 1959.

Hiriyanna, M.: Outlines of Indian Philosophy, London: George Allan and Unwin, (Rpt.), 1964.

Misra, R.N.: "Śilpa" in Kalātattvakośa,Vol. I. Gen. Ed. Kapila Vatsyayan, Delhi: IGNCA and Motilal Banarsidass, 1988.

— "Indian Śilpa Tradition, Śilpī and Aesthetics" in Śāstric Tradition in Indian Arts, Ed. A.L. Dallapiecola, Stuttgart: Steiner Verlag, 1989.

— "Perceptions of India's Past: Tradition and Artist" in Perception of South Asia's Visual Past, Eds. Catherine B. Asher and Thomas R. Metcalf, New Delhi : Oxford and I.B.H., 1994.

— "Art and Religion: A Study of Relations in Early India", a Paper presented in the Seminar on Indian Art: Forms, Concerns and Development, New Delhi : I.C.P.R. 1994.

Pathak, V.S.: Presidential Address (to the 68th Annual Conference of the Numismatic Society of India) Pune, 1981.

Pathak, V.S. and Misra, R.N.: "Words and Image in Reference to Technique in Indian Art" in Journal of Asiatic Society, Vol. 56–59, 1981–84, Bombay: Asiatic Society, 1986.

SAKALA-NIṢKALA

Overview

The two characteristics of the individual and whole are analogous to aspects of shapeless and shaping. Parts are subsumed in the whole so that we may visualize the wholeness of something we do not take into account in its parts. But on the other hand, when we visualize the whole blossoming out into different parts, we see the whole in every part. *Sakala* having parts and *niṣkala* having no parts are two aspects of its reality at every level. To have a full understanding of the two terms, the different usages of its components, *kalā* is very relevant. These usages present a clear idea of what *sakala* is and what the transcendental *niṣkala* is. These usages will bear out the basic Indian view of creativity that the whole has to realise its wholeness through its manifestation in parts and this urge itself is the root of every act of creation, be it the original event of Cosmic Creation or the happening in the presence of some created arts.

Etymology and Related Words

The term *sakala* derived from the root *kal-*, 'to enumerate', 'to count', bears the etymological sense of possessing all its component parts (*kalayā saha vartamānam*), i.e. *sa* (an indeclinable, used in the sense of 'having') + *kalā* (portion of a whole) the term *niṣkala* is also derived from the same root, *kal-* and is used to denote 'without parts'.

The word *sakala* is recorded in the **Amara Kośa** in the list of words, conveying the sense of entirety or all:

...... अथ समं सर्वम् ॥
विश्वमशेषं कृत्स्नं समस्तनिखिलाखिलानि निःशेषम् ।
समग्रं सकलं पूर्णमखण्डं स्यादनूनके ॥

AmKo III.1.64d–65

The following terms are synonymous as denoting plenty, not deficient (*anūna*), viz. *sama* (together), *sarva* (entire), *viśva* (all), *aśesa* (whole), *kṛtsna* (complete), *samasta* (complete), *nikhila* (completed), *akhila* (combined), *niḥśeṣa* (without remainder), *samagra* (put together), *sakala* (having parts), *pūrṇa* (full) and *akhaṇḍa* (without fragments). (Tr. P.K. Agrawala)

The **Vaijayantī Kośa** records the use of the word *sakala* also in the sense of totality and entirety:

> समग्रं सकलं सर्वं समस्तं निखिलाखिले ।
>
> VaiKo V.4.85cd
>
> *Samagra, sakala, sarva, samasta* (all these are used to cover the sense of) totality (*nikhila*) and entirety (*akhila*). (Tr. P. Ghosal)

The related term *niṣkala* is recorded in the **Nānārtha Mañjarī** as follows:

> निष्कला विगतार्तवा ।
> कलाहीने ... ।
>
> NāMa 1700–1701
>
> The term *niṣkala* means a woman of post menstruation while used in feminine gender but it denotes artless (while used in all the three genders). (Tr. S. Chattopadhyay)

The **Medinī Kośa** reflects almost the same concept:

> निष्कलस्तु कलाशून्ये नष्टवीर्ये च वाच्यवत् ॥
>
> MedKo XXVIII.103cd
>
> The term *niṣkala* means devoid of any part or division and impotent as well; it occurs according to the substantive. (Tr. P. Ghosal)

The **Vaijayantī Kośa** records the term *niṣkalā* to denote a menopaused woman:

> ... अनृतुर्वधूः निष्कला ... ॥
>
> VaiKo IV.4.16
>
> The menopaused woman should be called by the name *niṣkalā*. (Tr. P. Ghosal)

Layers of Meaning

The juxtaposition of *sakala* and *niṣkala* can be best understood through the second segment of these two words which has five demonstrations: two primary and three secondary. The primary meanings are division of time and the secondary meanings are gradual increase in the size of the moon and each phase of increase is known as *kalā* (digit). So *kalā* is spatio-temporal measure. It is analogous to →*māyā* which is also basically a measurer or a mapping out, then unfolding process, subsequently a matrix of all creation. *Kalā* also, though seems only divisive in meaning, in essence, is a creative process. The fourth meaning of →*kalā* is by extension 'arts', as gathered from the famous verse about Śiva:

निरुपादान सम्भारमभित्तावेव तन्वते ।
जगच्चित्रं नमस्तस्मै कलाश्लाघ्याय शूलिने ॥

Stavacintāmaṇi 9

My obeisance to the trident bearer Śiva who is admired for His art and also for the moon digit on His forehead, who draws a great painting of the Universe with no canvas, with no brush, with no colour box and such a wonderful work.

Other secondary meaning of *kalā* is one of the five sheaths (*kañcuka*) of Śiva. It is a limitation of making *niyati, kāla, kalā, vidyā,* and *māyā.* The last meaning of *kalā* is artfulness – artfulness in every field. Even stealing could be developed into such subtle devices that these could be called art. Some 64 such *kalā*s have been identified in the **Kāma-Sūtra** (I.3.14–15).

The concept of *sakala* consequently subsumes the above meanings of *kalā* and the term conveys much more. While *sakala* means all the parts *vikala* means having some parts removed or missing. The concept of *sakala* is further elaboration of the concept of *sarva,* 'all'. We have a dictum in the Upaniṣad: *sarvaṃ hi paśyan paśyati* (MaitUp VII.11). He who sees all is in reality seeing from which it follows that if you do not see all in one particular thing, you miss a great deal about it. This all is undivided.

Development of the Concept

Sakala is a whole but a whole with all its parts remains distinct and bound together. The following passages in the Vedic literature bear out this meaning of *sakala*:

असूतिका रामायण्यपचित् प्र पतिष्यति ।
ग्लौरितः प्र पतिष्यति सकलं तेन शुध्यति ॥

AV (p) I.21.4

Barren shall the *apacit,* daughter of the black one, fly forth; the boil (*glau*) shall fly forth from here; thereby it dries wholly up.
(Tr. W.D. Whitney)

चतुष्पात् सकलो यज्ञश्चातुर्हौत्रविनिर्मितः ।
चतुर्विधै स्थितो मन्त्रैर्ऋत्विग्भिर्वेदपारगैः ॥
प्रायश्चित्तैरनुध्यानैरनुज्ञानानुमन्त्रणैः ।
होमैश्च यज्ञविभ्रंशं सर्वं ब्रह्मा प्रपूरयेत् ॥

GoBr II.2.5

The whole sacrifice having four parts is attended by the function of four chief priests (*cāturhautra vinirmitaḥ*) and is established in four types of *mantras* cited by priests well versed in Vedas. All the shortcomings of sacrifice should be complemented by Brahmā priest with the aid of expiation, meditation, assention, invocation and performance of *homa*s. (Tr. P. Ghosal)

उद्यन्तमस्तंयन्तमादित्यमभिध्यायन्कुर्वन्ब्राह्मणो विद्वान्थ्सकलं भद्रमश्नुतेऽसावादित्यो ब्रह्मेति ब्रह्मैव सन् ब्रह्माप्येति य एवं वेद ॥

TĀr II.2

Meditating upon the rising and setting sun and knowing the yonder sun as the Supreme Brahman, being identical with Brahman one attains Brahman, the *brāhmaṇa* obtains all good fortune. (Tr. S. Chattopadhyay)

Kalā as explained above is one of the sixteen phases of the moon – fifteen visible and sixteenth invisible:

षोडशकलः सोम्य पुरुषः । पञ्चदशाहानि माऽऽशीः । काममपः पिब । आपोमयः प्राणो न पिबतो विच्छेत्स्यत इति ॥

ChUp VI.7.1

O good looking one, a person has sixteen parts. Do not eat for fifteen days. Drink water as much as you like. The vital force is made up of water. It will depart if you do not drink.
(Tr. Gambhirananda)

तं होवाच – यथा सोम्य महतोऽभ्याहितस्यैकोऽङ्गारः खद्योतमात्रः परिशिष्टः स्यात् । तेन ततोऽपि न बहु दहेत् । एवं सोम्य ते षोडशानां कलानामेका कलाऽतिशिष्टा स्यात् । तयैतर्हि वेदान्नानुभवासि । अशान । अथ मे विज्ञास्यसीति ॥

ChUp VI.7.3

To him he said, 'O good-looking one, as a single ember of the size of a fire-fly remains as a residue of a big fire, and by that nothing bigger than that is burnt – in this way, O good looking one, one of your sixteen parts remains as a residue. With that you do not remember the Vedas at this time. Eat and then you will understand me'. (Tr. Gambhirananda)

एवं सोम्य ते षोडशानां कलानामेका कलाऽतिशिष्टाऽभूत् । साऽन्नेनोपसमाहिता प्राज्वाली । तयैतर्हि वेदाननुभवसि ।

ChUp VI.7.6

[To him he said] ....

Similarly, O good looking one, a single one of your sixteen parts had continued as a remnant. It has blazed up by being nourished with food. With that you can now understand the Vedas. (Tr. Gambhirananda)

This is further coroborated by another observation in the **Bṛhadāraṇyaka Upaniṣad**:

स एष संवत्सरः प्रजापतिः षोडशकलः, तस्य रात्रय एव पञ्चदश कलाः, ध्रुवैवास्य षोडशीकला । स रात्रिभिरेवा च पूर्यतेऽप च क्षीयते, सोऽमावास्यां रात्रिमेतया षोडश्या कलया सर्वमिदं प्राणभृदनुप्रविश्य ततः प्रातर्जायते ।

BṛUp I.5.14

This Prajāpati (Hiraṇyagarbha) has sixteen digits and is represented by the year. The nights (and days) are his fifteen digits, and the constant one is his sixteenth digit. He (as the moon) is filled as well as wasted by the nights (and days). Through this sixteenth digit, he permeates all these living beings on the new moon night and rises the next morning. (Tr. Gambhirananda)

यो वै स संवत्सरः प्रजापतिः षोडशकलः । अयमेव स योऽयमेवंवित् पुरुषः । तस्य वित्तमेव पञ्चदशकलाः । आत्मैवास्य षोडशी कला । स वित्तेनैवा च पूर्यतेऽप च क्षीयते, तदेतन्नभ्यं यदयमात्मा, प्रधिर्वित्तम् ।

BṛUp I.5.15

That Prajāpati, who has sixteen digits and is represented by the year, is indeed this man who knows as above. Wealth constitutes his fifteen digits and the body his sixteenth digit. He is filled as well as wasted by wealth. This body stands for a nave and the wealth is the felloe. (Tr. Madhavananda)

The sixteenth is the digit of the *amāvāsyā* night and is called →*amṛta*, the one which refuses to die. The fifteenth night of the dark half of the month, analogous to this is the anatomical division of the Cosmic Person, →Puruṣa, five senses, five organs of action, five elements and the invisible mind. So *sakala* means imbued with all the parts and so fold. It is borne out by these references:

भगवन् हिरण्यनाभः कौसल्यो राजपुत्रो मामुपेत्यैतं प्रश्नमपृच्छत । षोडशकल भारद्वाज पुरुषं वेत्थ । ... तं त्वा पृच्छामि कासौ पुरुष इति ।

PraUp VI.1

Venerable Sir! Hiraṇyanābha, a prince of Kosala approached me and put this question, "Bhāradvāja, do you know the Puruṣa, possessed of sixteen parts" ... Of that Puruṣa, I ask you, O Sir! Where does He exist? (Based on the tr. by Gambhirananda)

तस्मै स होवाच । इहैवान्तः शरीरे सोम्य स पुरुषो यस्मिन्नेताः षोडश कलाः प्रभवन्तीति ।

PraUp VI.2

To him, he (Pippalāda) said: O amiable one, here itself inside the body is that Puruṣa in whom originate these sixteen digits. (Tr. Gambhirananda)

स यथेमाः नद्यः स्यन्दमानाः समुद्रायणाः समुद्रं प्राप्यास्तं गच्छन्ति, भिद्येते तासां नामरूपे । समुद्र इत्येवं प्रोच्यते । एवमेवास्य परिद्रष्टुरिमाः षोडश कलाः पुरुषायणाः पुरुषं प्राप्यास्तं गच्छन्ति, भिद्येते चासां नामरूपे, पुरुष इत्येवं प्रोच्यते । स एषोऽकलोऽमृतो भवति ।

PraUp VI.5

Just as these flowing rivers that have the sea as their goal, get absorbed after reaching the sea, and their names and forms are destroyed, and they are called merely the sea, so also these sixteen parts of the all – seeing Puruṣa, that have the Puruṣa as their goal, disappear on reaching the Puruṣa, when their names and forms are destroyed and they are simply called as Puruṣa. Such a man of realization becomes free from the parts and is immortal. (Tr. Gambhirananda)

अरा इव रथनाभौ कला यस्मिन् प्रतिष्ठिताः ।
तं वेद्यं पुरुषं वेद यथा मा वो मृत्युः परिव्यथा इति ॥

PraUp VI.6

You should know that Puruṣa who is worthy to be known and in whom are transfixed the parts like spokes in the nave of a chariot wheel, so that death may not afflict you anywhere.
(Tr. Gambhirananda)

Coming to *niṣkala,* it is not something opposite to *sakala.* It is only an aspect of the same Supreme Reality which when so wills is endowed with parts, otherwise is by nature undivided whole. Therefore, it follows from this that *niṣkala* does not mean bereft of *kalā.* It only means a reality yet to unfold, or the primordial state of Supreme Reality. In the post-Vedic literature, we find these two qualifiers of Ultimate Reality as *saguṇa* and *nirguṇa* with slight shift in the meaning. This shift is from subtle to gross. The word *kalā* is more abstract and conceptual than the word →*guṇa* (property). But even *saguṇa* and *nirguṇa* are in juxtaposition and not in opposition. The following Vedic passages bring out the meaning of *niṣkala*:

हिरण्मये परे कोशे विरजं ब्रह्म निष्कलम् ।
तच्छुभ्रं ज्योतिषां ज्योतिस्तद्यदात्मविदो विदुः ॥

MuṇḍUP II.2.10

In the highest golden sheath
Is Brahma, without stain, without parts.
Brilliant is It, the light of lights –
That which knowers of the Soul (*ātman*) do know! (Tr. R.E. Hume)

न चक्षुषा गृह्यते नापि वाचा नान्यैर्देवैस्तपसा कर्मणा वा ।
ज्ञानप्रसादेन विशुद्धसत्त्वस्ततस्तु तं पश्यते निष्कलं ध्यायमानः ॥

MuṇḍUp III.1.8

Not by sight is It grasped, not even by speech,
Not by any other sense-organs (*deva*) 'austerity' or work.
By the grace of knowledge (*jñāna-prasāda*), one's nature purified –
In that way, however, by meditating, one does behold Him, who is without parts. (Tr. R.E. Hume)

In support of what has been said about *kalā*, a few quotations from the **Chāndogya Upaniṣad** would be quite apt:

ब्रह्मणश्च ते पादं ब्रवाणीति । ब्रवीतु मे भगवानिति । तस्मै होवाच । प्राची दिक्कला, प्रतीची दिक्कला । दक्षिणा दिक्कला । उदीची दिक्कला । एष वै सोम्य चतुष्कलः पादो ब्रह्मणः प्रकाशवान्नाम ॥

ChUp IV.5.2

(The bull said) 'I wish to tell you of one foot of Brahman.' (Satyakāma said) 'Please tell me, revered sir'. To him he said: 'The eastern side is one part, the western side is one part, the southern side is one part, the northern side is one part. 'O good looking one surely this is one foot of Brahman consisting of four parts and called the Manifested (Prakāśavān)'. (Tr. Gambhirananda)

पृथिवी कला । अन्तरिक्षं कला । द्यौः कला । समुद्रः कला । एष वै सोम्य चतुष्कलः पादो ब्रह्मणोऽनन्तवान्नाम ॥

ChUp IV.6.3

Earth is one part, inter-mediate – space is one part, heaven is one part, ocean is one part, O good looking one, of Brahman, this is surely one foot called Limitless, having four parts.
(Tr. Gambhirananda)

अग्निः कला । सूर्यः कला । चन्द्रः कला । विद्युत् कला । एष वै सोम्य चतुष्कलः पादो ब्रह्मणो ज्योतिष्मान्नाम ॥

ChUp IV.7.3

Fire is one part, the sun is one part, the moon is one part, lightning is one part. O good looking one, of Brahman this is surely one foot called the Effulgent, having four parts. (Tr. Gambhirananda)

प्राणः कला । चक्षुः कला । श्रोत्रं कला । मनः कला । एष वै सोम्य चतुष्कलः पादो ब्रह्मण आयतनवान्नाम ॥

ChUp IV.8.3

The vital force is one part, the eye is one part, the ear is one part, the mind is one part. O good looking one, of Brahman this is surely one foot named Āyatanavān (possessed of an Abode) having four parts. (Tr. Gambhirananda)

In these passages, spatial division is *kalā*. But these divisions are not metaphysical rather physical. These passages clearly explain as to how the Universal Person (Puruṣa) is conceived of sixteen phases and without the 16th phase, the Person is not complete.

In the light of what has been said above, the realisation of the Ultimate Reality requires complete withdrawal from all kind of pluralities and activity:

निष्कलं निष्क्रियं शान्तं निरवद्यं निरञ्जनम् ।
अमृतस्य परं सेतुं दग्धेन्धनमिवानलम् ॥

ŚvUp VI.19

To Him, who is without parts, without activity, tranquil (*śānta*),
Irreproachable, spotless,
The highest bridge of immortality,
Like a fire with fuel burned. (Tr. R.E. Hume)

Niṣkala could also be called *akala* and the juxtaposition of *sakala* and *niṣkala* could be as that of finite versus infinite as in this passage:

अथ य प्रागादित्यात् सोऽकालोऽकलः । अथ य आदित्याद्यः स काल सकलः । सकलस्य वा एतद्रूपं यत् संवत्सरः ।

MaitUp VI.15

That which is prior to the sun is the Timeless (*a-kāla*), without parts (*a-kala*). But that which begins with the sun is Time, which has parts. Verily, the form of that which has parts, is the year. (Tr. R.E. Hume)

The visualization of finite time can be experienced at the spiritual level any time, even during the dream state. This is well explained in the following passage:

स्वप्ने स जीवः सुखदुःखभोक्ता स्वमायया कल्पितजीवलोके ।
सुषुप्तिकाले सकले विलीने तमोऽभिभूतः सुखरूपमेति ॥
पुनश्च जन्मान्तरकर्मयोगात् स-एव जीवः स्वपिति प्रबुद्धः ।
पुरत्रये क्रीडति यश्च जीवस्ततस्तु जातं सकलं विचित्रम् ।
आधारमानन्दमखण्डबोधं यस्मिँल्लयं याति पुरत्रयं च ॥

KaivalyaUp 13–14

On the dream state the *jīva* feels pleasure and pain in a sphere of existence created by his own *māyā* or ignorance. During the state of profound sleep when everything is dissolved (into their causal state), he is overpowered by *tamas* or non-manifestation and comes to exist in his form of Bliss. Again, through his connection with deeds done in previous births, that very *jīva* returns to the dream state or the waking state. The being who sports in the three cities (viz. the states of wakefulness, dream and profound sleep) – from Him has sprung up all diversity. He is the substratum, the bliss, the indivisible consciousness in whom the three cities dissolve themselves. (Tr. Madhavananda)

In the later Upaniṣads, the juxtaposition of the differentiated versus the undifferentiated aspect of the Supreme Reality has been described not as a juxtaposition of opposites but of complementary aspect of the same. The text bear out the unity of the Supreme Reality. The seemingly decotomous these two aspects are creational necessities. Manifestation involves differentiation and understanding of unmanifest necessitates an understanding of the manifest. To be manifested is to bloom out as a full limbed body. At the same time, the manifestation process itself needs a substratum and a whole which is not in entirety manifested, as indicated in the Puruṣa Sūkta. One part loomed out as the manifest universe while three parts which are imperishable, immutable and immortal, are there in the World of Light.

पादोऽस्य विश्वा भूतानि त्रिपादस्यामृतं दिवि ॥
त्रिपादूर्ध्व उदैत् पुरुषः पादोऽस्येहाभवत् पुनः ।

ṚV X.90.3cd–4ab

So mighty is his greatness; yea, greater than this is Puruṣa. All creatures are one-fourth of him, three-fourths eternal life in heaven. With three-fourths Puruṣa went up one-fourth of him again was here. (Tr. R.T.H. Griffith)

The illustrations which follow from the later Upaniṣads all indicate this identity of the two aspects and the necessity of visualizing the one beyond immobilization or predication or even intellection through the manifested – formed and uttered aspect.

मय्येव सकलं जातं मयि सर्वं प्रतिष्ठितम् ।
मयि सर्वं लयं याति तद्ब्रह्माद्वयमस्म्यहम् ॥

KaivalyaUp 19

All the beings have been originated in me, established in me and all these are re-absorbed in me, I am That Brahman, the Secondless. (Tr. P. Ghosal)

In some passages the indifferentiated aspect of the Supreme Reality is described as negation as that in manifest, as in the following verse. But this negation is only an assertion of transcendence and not an indication of rejection of the differentiated.

न भूमिरापो न च वह्निरस्ति न चानिलो मेऽस्ति न चाम्बरं च ।
एवं विदित्वा परमात्मरूपं गुहाशयं निष्कलमद्वितीयम् ॥
समस्तसाक्षिं सदसद्विहीनं प्रयाति शुद्धं परमात्मरूपम् ।

KaivalyaUp 23–24ab

For me there is neither earth, nor water, nor fire, nor air, nor ether. Thus realising the Paramātman who lies in the cavity of heart, who is without parts, without a second, the witness of all, beyond both existence and non-existence – one attains the pure Paramātman Itself. (Tr. Madhavananda)

प्राणो ह्येष आत्मा । आत्मनो महिमा बभूव देवानामायुः, स देवानां निधनमनिधनं दिव्यब्रह्मपुरे विरजं निष्कलं शुभ्रमक्षरं यद्ब्रह्म विभाति स नियच्छति, मधुकर राजानं माक्षिकवत् ।

BrahmaUp 1

That is *prāṇa,* the *ātman.* He constitutes the glory of the *ātman,* the life of the *devas.* He represents both the life and death of the *devas.* That Brahman who shines within the divine *brahmapura* (or body) as the faultless one, devoid of manifested effects, self-effulgent, all-pervading, He (it is who) controls (the *jīva*), like a spider controlling the king of bees. (Tr. Madhavananda)

This point will be borne out by the passages of the **Dhyānabindu Upaniṣad** where the *sakala* aspect, the differentiated aspect is also visualized as an abstraction of the concrete and therefore described by way of a concrete metaphor:

वृक्षं तु विद्याच्छाया सकलं तस्यैव निष्कला ।
सकले निष्कले भावे सर्वत्रात्मा व्यवस्थितः ॥

DhyānabinduUp 8

Know the tree to be possessed of parts (*sakala*) while its shadow is (*niṣkala*) partless. In (both the stages) possessed of parts and partless – the Self pervades everywhere. (Tr. P. Ghosal)

शिखा ज्ञानमयी यस्य उपवीतं च तन्मयम् ।
ब्राह्मण्यं सकलं तस्य इति ब्रह्मविदो विदुः ॥

BrahmaUp 3

The person whose *śikhā* (plume or top-knot) indicates wisdom and *upavīta* (sacrificial thread) is absorbed in that – thereby brahminhood becomes complete – so says the *brahmavid* (the wise). (Tr. P. Ghosal)

The point of 'Puruṣa', the Universal Person, having sixteen *kalā*-s or digits is further supported by these passages in the **Nṛsiṁhapūrvatāpanīyopaniṣad**:

अथ षोडशारं षोडशपत्रं चक्रं भवति, षोडशकलो वै पुरुषः ... ।

NṛpūUp V.1

Further, the *cakra* (wheel) should have sixteen spokes and sixteen petals, because the Puruṣa possesses sixteen parts or limbs. (Tr. P. Ghosal)

षोडशसु पत्रेषु मातृकाद्याः सबिन्दुकाः षोडश कला भवन्ति ।

NṛpūUp V.2

In sixteen petals (of a lotus) all the syllables or *mātṛkās* with a dot on each (sixteen vowels from *a* to *ah* should be written on each with a dot). They represent sixteen parts (of Puruṣa).
(Tr. H.N. Chakravarty)

By way of digression, a brief discussion on the semantic aspect of the word *niṣkala* would be relevant. The term in the **Vaijayantī Kośa** is compared to 'yet to menstruate'. This is an apt simile for the unmanifest with a prospect of flowering out. The description in the **Brahmabindu Upaniṣad** of this word is through giving two adjuncts to it: unstained and quietened (*nirmala, śānta* and untransformable). This also suggests that there is a possibility of other aspects – stained and interconnection:

तदेव निष्कलं ब्रह्म निर्विकल्पं निरञ्जनम् ।
तद्ब्रह्माहमिति ज्ञात्वा ब्रह्म संपद्यते ध्रुवम् ॥

BrahmabinduUp 8

That Brahman is devoid of any parts (*niṣkala*) free from any differentiation (*nirvikalpa*) and pure (*nirañjana*). I am That Brahman – having realised this Truth, Eternal Brahman can be attained. (Tr. P. Ghosal)

निष्कलं निर्मलं शान्तं तद्ब्रह्माहमिति स्मृतम् ॥

BrahmabinduUp 21cd

I am considered [to be] That Brahman (which is) devoid of any parts, unstained and calm. (Tr. P. Ghosal)

रेचकेन तु विद्यात्मा ललाटस्थं त्रिलोचनम् ।
शुद्धस्फटिकसंकाशं निष्कलं पापनाशनम् ॥

DhyānabinduUp 32

With the aid of *recaka* (the exhalation – one of the three *prāṇāyāmas*) one should meditate on the Self-identical with the *vidyā* (the concerned *mantra*) who is in the third eye, seated on the forehead who is pure and as transparent as crystal, devoid of any parts and who destroys the evils. (Tr. P. Ghosal)

Furthermore, the word *sakala* has its purposiveness as borne out by the passage in the **Nirukta** where *sakala* is used as adjective for 'all'.

स्थाणुरयं भारहारः किलाभूदधीत्य वेदं न विजानाति योऽर्थम् ।
योऽर्थज्ञ इत्सकलं भद्रमश्नुते नाकमेति ज्ञानविधूतपाप्मा ॥

Nir I.18

He is the bearer of a burden only – the blockhead who having studied, does not understand the meaning of the Veda. But he who knows the meaning obtains all good fortune and, with his sins purged off by knowledge, attains heaven. (Tr. L. Sarup)

To sum up the discussion related to passages in the Vedic literature and its ancillaries, we may say that the process of creation is a journey from the unmanifest to manifest, from abstract to concrete and from undifferentiated to differentiated. But the approach towards the manifest, the concrete and the differentiated is a holistic one because all these aspects are viewed as components of one whole and the vision of allness is never lost sight of. This is reflected in the meaning of the word *sakala* as 'all', total, all the parts linked together. This agrees with the meaning of the word *sākalya* as allness. This term is used for all the various components of an offering ('*tila*' black sesame, clarified butter, barley, rice, yellow sandalwood and other fragrance materials) and this putting together all the different kinds of offerings towards the final offering is a symbolic act of offering all and all linked together to the all in One, Universal Person on behalf of all.

A second point has also emerged from the discussion, viz. the undifferentiated or the unsplit does not stand in opposition to the differentiated. The differentiated through its all-pervasiveness leads to the goal, all in one which ultimately is undifferentiated. Vice-versa, the undifferentiated splits itself into parts so that it is understood bit by bit and this understanding leads to its power to expand into immeasurable ways. Such a two-way understanding of the unity of things and all beings is essential.

Now we shall take up very briefly the treatment of these two mutually related concepts in the Agamic literature which has a striking similarity. One could easily conclude that the Agamic view of reality is derived from the Vedic world-view. The main text which has been considered as basis, is the **Tantrāloka**.

The Epic and Purāṇas are in a way bridge between the Vedic and the Agamic literature because they give a clear indication of comprehending and elaborating Vedic ideas and also of absorbing Agamic perceptions, that hold striking similarity with the Vedic perceptions. The **Agni Purāṇa** speaks of five-fold aspect of *sakala* comprising respectively of heart, throat, palate, forehead and →*prāṇa*, visualized as the five gods namely Brahmā, Viṣṇu, Rudra, Maheśvara and Śiva:

पञ्चधा सकलः प्रोक्तो विपरीतस्तु निष्कलः ॥

AgPur CCXIV.32cd

The *sakala* form of the divine deity has five varieties; the opposite form is known to be *niṣkala* (*sakala* = with *kalās*, parts).
(Tr. R.S. Bhattacharya)

The same Purāṇa speaks of *sakala-niṣkala* juxtaposition in terms of being embodied or disembodied.

देहस्थः सकलो ज्ञेयो निष्कलो देहवर्जितः ।

AgPur CCXIV.29ab

The divine is known to be *sakala* (with parts) when residing in the body; it is known to be *niṣkala* (without parts) when it is not associated with the body.

Both the aspects are one is indicated by another passage where Viṣṇu has been termed as both *sakala* and *niṣkala.*

सकलो निष्कलो ज्ञेयः सर्वज्ञः परमो हरिः ।

AgPur CCCLXXIV.10ab

The omniscient Supreme Hari (Viṣṇu) is to be known as possessing parts or characteristics and also as bereft of parts or characteristics.

A similar unity of the two aspects has been indicated in the **Mārkaṇḍeya Purāṇa** where the Supreme Deity is described both as *sakala* and *niṣkala*:

एवं देवि त्वया व्याप्तं सकलं निष्कलं जगत् ॥

MārkPur XXIII.46cd

Thus O goddess, that which has parts is pervaded by thee, and so also that which has no parts. (Tr. F.E. Pargiter)

Sakala has been used in the **Mahābhārata** to mean sum total:

चतुष्पादं दशविधं धनुर्वेदमरिन्दमः ।
अर्जुनाद्वेद वेदज्ञात्सकलं दिव्यमानुषम् ॥

MBh I.213.65

(That) victorious (lad) learnt ten branches of archery having four (sub) - sections from Arjuna and from the scholars well versed in Vedas (learnt) all the human and divine (sciences). (Tr. P. Ghosal)

But at the same time the **Mahābhārata** also uses *sakala-niṣkala* concept as differentiated and non-differentiated.

आत्मदेहे मयासृष्टा प्रकृतिः क्षेत्रमेव च ।
सकलं तु भवेत् क्षेत्रं निष्कलं परमं पदम् ॥

MBh VI, app. 3.6

The innate nature (*prakṛti*) and (its) sphere of action (*kṣetra*) have been created by me in my own body. The *kṣetra* is *sakala* (constituting of parts) while the Supreme One is *niṣkala* (without any parts). (Tr. P. Ghosal)

The **Mahābhārata** has referred to a *ṣoḍaśīkalā*, sixteenth digit by which everything is merged into. So in a way this is analogous to the moon's unseen digit on the fifteenth day of dark fortnight (MBh VI, app. 3.29–30).

Corresponding to the sixteen digits of the moon, there are sixteen digits of Soma as enumerated in the following verse:

पूषा यशा, सुमनसा रतिः प्राप्तिस्तथा धृतिः ।
ऋद्धिः सौम्या मरीचिश्च तथा चैवांशुमालिनी ॥
अङ्गिरा शशिनी चेति छाया सम्पूर्णमण्डला ।
तुष्टिश्चैवामृता चेतिं कलाः सोमस्य षोडश ॥

KāmSū cited in ŚaKal II, p. 428

The digits of Soma (moon) are sixteen in number, viz. *pūsā, yaśā, sumanasā, rati, prāpti, dhṛti, ṛddhi, saumyā, marīci, amśumālinī, angirā, śaśinī, chāyā, sampūrṇa-maṇḍalā, tuṣṭi* and *amṛtā*. (Tr. P. Ghosal)

The Agamic tradition has often been misunderstood in some of the grammars and Upaniṣads. The text concerned here may belong to a later date but the Agamic tradition was co-existent with the Vedic one and through interaction with one tradition which leads a life-force today in which they are merged. The **Rudra Yāmala** gives a list of sixteen digits of the moon and also refers to a *kalāvatī dīkṣā.* It is an initiation into a mystic and into an Agamic practice.

तन्त्रोक्ताः षोडशकलाः –
अमृता मानदा पूषा पुष्टिस्तुष्टी रतिर्धृतिः ।
शशिनी चन्द्रिका कान्तिर्ज्योत्स्ना श्रीः प्रीतिरङ्गदा ॥
पूर्णापूर्णामृताकामदायिन्यः शशिनः कलाः ।
आसां प्रयोजनं कलावतीदीक्षादौ पूजनम् ।

Rudra Yāmala cited in ŚaKal II, p. 428

Amṛtā, mānadā, pūṣā, puṣṭi, tuṣṭi, rati, dhṛti, śaśinī, candrikā, kānti, jyotsnā, śrī, prīti, aṅgadā, pūrṇā and *pūrṇāmṛtā* – these (sixteen) are digits of moon, granting desires (of the aspirant). The purpose of it is to worship in the *kalāvatī-dīkṣā.* (Tr. P. Ghosal)

The **Tantrāloka** brings out more elaborately a definitive aspect of *kalā*:

कलाव्याप्त्यन्तचर्चने, इति – अमाख्यकलास्वरूपस्फारसिद्धान्त विचारावसरे इत्यर्थः ।

Viveka on TĀl III.140

Kalāvyāptyanta carcane – while discussing the limit of the pervasiveness of *kalā,* here *kalā* means the *kalā* known as *amākalā.* The commentator explains the phrase thus: the final opinion regarding the expansion of the real nature of *kalā* named *amā* – this is the meaning. (Tr. H.N. Chakravarty)

The **Viveka** commentary on the same refers to *kalā* analogous to the moon. Person also comprises sixteen parts.

पुरुषे षोडशकले तामाहुरमृतां कलाम् । इत्याद्युक्त्या अन्तःकरणप्रभृतीनां षोडशानामपि कलानामाप्यायकारित्वात् नित्योदितत्वेन च अनस्तमितरूपत्वात् अमृताकाररूपिणी येयं चिन्मात्रस्वभावा कौलिकीति, परेति एवमादिशब्दव्यपदेश्या हकारार्धार्धरूपिणी अमाख्या सप्तदशीकला ।

Viveka on TĀl III.140

Person composed of sixteen portions – that one is called *amṛtākalā* – the deathless portion as it replenishes all the sixteen inner organs and others representing sixteen *kalās* and as it remains ever arise it does not have any setting – it is of the nature of nectar. It is of the nature of consciousness alone. It is also designated by the name *kaulikī* or *parā*. It is the half of *ha* sound designated as *amā*, the seventeenth portion. (Tr. H.N. Chakravarty)

ज्ञानाकलस्य मानं तु गलद्विद्या कलावृति ।
अशुद्धविद्याकलनाध्वंस संस्कारसंगता ॥

TĀl X.14

The soul known as *vijñānākala* having its instruments *vidyā* and *kalā* are going to dissolve. Its contact with impure *vidyā* in the form of the residue (*saṃskāra*) of the destruction of the activating force of *kalā* is absent therein. (Tr. H.N. Chakravarty)

The sixteenth *kalā* is a merger of other *kalā*s which are differentiated parts. It is through this *kalā* that things emanate from.

आ शिवात् सकलान्तं ये मातरः सप्त ते द्विधा ।
न्यग् भूतोद्रिक्तशक्तित्वात् तद्भेदो वेद्यभेदकः ॥

TĀl X.18

Beginning from Śiva and ending in *sakala*, these knowing agents are seven and are classified under two groups. The power of some are relegated to subordination while others are possessed of powers remain active. (Tr. H.N. Chakravarty)

The sixteenth *kalā* is half of the sound *visarga* and is in fact the activity at the pure consciousness. The same text in another reference explains a note fairly where *kalā* implies the rising of the six-fold sheaths, the unfolded portions starting from the *aśuddhavidyā*, impure consciousness and coming up to the earth element.

यत्तूच्यते कलाद्येन धरान्तेन समन्विताः ॥
सकला इति तत्कोश षट्कोद्रेकोपलक्षणम् ।
उद्भूताशुद्धचिद्राग कलादिरसकञ्चुकाः ॥

TĀl X.98cd–99

What has been stated (in the Mālinīvijaya Tantra) that the souls who are associated with *kalā* first and later all the evolutes ending in the earth make it *sakala*, but *kalā* implies the rising of the sixfold sheathes. The impure consciousness (*aśuddha vidyā*), attachment, *kalā* and thus the sixfold sheathes make them *sakala*. (Tr. H.N. Chakravarty)

Kalā as one of the five sheaths is a limitation of activities and regency. This meaning of *kalā* is very significant because it suggests that a creative activity emanates from something of the nature of the undifferentiated stage of being. This is identified by the undifferentiated stage, *niṣkala*:

न कलापिण्डसंबद्धः संबद्धोऽसौ यथा पशुः ॥
कदाचिदेव देवेशस्तस्माद् गीतस्तु निष्कलः ।

MKā 38cd–39ab

The Lord is never associated with *kalā* (the limited form of activity) and a body like a bonded being. On account of this He is called *niṣkala*, free from *kalā*s. (Tr. H.N. Chakravarty)

The **Sārdhatriśatikālottara Tantra** defines *kalā* as manifested in the entire body and so this body is called *sakala* (with all the differentiations well articulated). The transcendent is *niṣkala*:

देहस्थः सकलो ज्ञेयो निष्कलो देहवर्जितः ।

SākāT XXIII.2ab

(The spiritual teacher when abides in the body) is known to be *sakala* having all the qualities of a *paśu* unliberated Soul but he is known as *niṣkala* when he becomes identified with Śiva (*śivasamānadharmā*). (Tr. H.N. Chakravarty)

The **Svacchanda Tantra** explains *niṣkala* as the undifferentiated that means something which has no roots, no beginning, no peak. It is all the way something which makes all things transformed remaining itself unfound:

यस्य नाग्रं च मूलं च न दिशो विदिशस्तथा ॥
न शब्दो नापि चाकाशम् .... ।

SvT III.29cd–30a

It (*niṣkala*) does not have any top, nor root, neither does it have directions, it is not sound, nor is it the void. (Tr. H.N. Chakravarty)

This text also explains *sakala* as *saguṇa* where all the attributes are well manifest but devoid of all these is *niṣkala* and is further concretised by Śiva.

सगुणः सकलो ज्ञेयो निर्गुणो निष्कलः शिवः ॥
सकलो ग्रहसंयुक्तो निष्कलो भावमाश्रितः ।

SvT VI.17cd–18ab

Śiva is known to be (*sakala*) with *kalā* because of its association with attributes (*guṇa*), but Śiva is (*nirguṇa*) without any attribute, therefore He is known as *niṣkala*. *Sakala* is associated with *graha* (=*uccāra*), but *niṣkala* is characterised by *bhāva* (=*sphurattā* = self-reflective light). (Tr. H.N. Chakravarty)

तदूर्ध्वे सकलं देवं स्वच्छन्दं परिकल्पयेत् ॥

SvT I.40cd

Above it (*cinmūrti,* form of consciousness) one should conceive Lord Svacchanda as of *sakala* form. (Tr. H.N. Chakravarty)

The external worship is always directed towards the manifest and undifferentiated, the primordial being while the worship of *niṣkala* is purely an activity of the soul.

कर्मकाले तु सकलाञ्छिरः पाण्यादिभिर्युतान् ।
जपेत्तु सकलान्देवि निष्कलेन समन्वितान् ॥

SvT VI.46

While performing rituals of the *sakala* divinities, they should be meditated upon as having heads and arms and so on but he should repeat the *mantra* of the *sakala* deities, O goddess, as rested in *niṣkala* aspect, that is the one who is partless. (Tr. H.N. Chakravarty)

यावदुच्चार्यते वाचा यावल्लेख्येऽपि तिष्ठति ॥
तावत् स सकलो ज्ञेयः .... ।

SvT VII.238cd–239a

The one which is pronounced by speech and abides in the form of written scripts, is known to be *sakala,* the one with parts. (Tr. H.N. Chakravarty)

The **Svacchanda Tantra** also explains *niṣkala* as indivisible:

निष्कलो भेदवर्जितः ।

SvT VII.239b

The partless one is without any division. (Tr. H.N. Chakravarty)

A transcendence of the sixteen digits is the seventeenth one which according to commentary on the **Tantrāloka** is nectar.

कला सप्तदशी यासावमृताकाररूपिणी ।

Viveka on TĀl I.1

The portion known as the seventeenth is of the nature of nectar (implying immortality). (Tr. H.N. Chakravarty)

It is further elaborated in the **Tantrāloka** that the creation emanates from the seventeenth part (or rather partless part) and is the starting point of pulsation (*spandana*):

उक्तं च त्रिशिर:शास्त्रे कला व्यास्यन्तचर्चने ॥
कला सप्तदशी तस्मादमृताकार रूपिणी ।
परापरस्वस्वरूप बिन्दुगत्या विसर्पिता ॥

TĀl III.137cd–138

The text called Triśirabhairava while discussing the scope of *kalāvyāpti,* that is how far does the *kalā* reach, speaks of the seventeenth *kalā* with the nature of immortality. Its expansion occurs in two ways, *parāpara* the beyond-non-beyond and *aparā,* the non-bey-ond by means of the pulsative flow of *bindu.*
(Tr. H.N. Chakravarty)

The **Sūrya-Siddhānta** has defined *kalā* as division of time and *vikala* is a further division of the unit *kalā.*

विकलानां कला षष्ट्या तत्षष्ट्या भाग उच्यते ।
तत् त्रिंशता भवेद्राशिर्भगणो द्वादशैव ते ॥

SūrSiddh I.28

Sixty seconds (*vikala*) made a minute (*kalā*); sixty of these, a degree (*bhāga*); of thirty of the latter is composed of a sign (*rāśi*); twelve of these are as evolution (*bhagaṇa*). (Tr. E. Burgess)

Kalā as a referent of time presents a view of time which has two aspects – finite and infinite. The finite aspect is visualized as a part of the process of manifestation (SūrSiddh IV.11).

Manifestation in the Arts

Finally, →*kalā* would be in fuller meaningfulness in the text on art and architecture. The **Śiva Saṃhitā** gives a description of the process of creation wherein the sun is the nucleus of twelve digits, *kalā*:

मेरुमूले स्थितः सूर्यः कलाद्वादश संयुतः ।
दक्षिणे पथि रश्मिभिर्वहत्यूर्ध्वं प्रजापतिः ॥

ŚSam II.10

At the bottom of the Meru there is the sun having twelve *kalā*s. In the right side path (*piṅgalā*) the lord of creatures carries (the fluid) through its rays upwards. (Tr. S.C. Vasu)

Another important reference to this is the body (*piṇḍa*) itself a microcosmos and having its manifestation into eight *kalā*-s:

ब्रह्माण्ड संज्ञके देहे यथादेशं व्यवस्थित: ।
मेरुशृंगे सुधारश्मिर्बहिरष्टकलायुत: ॥

ŚSam II.6

In this body, which is called *brahmāṇḍa* (microcosm, literally the mundane egg), there is the nectar-rayed moon, in its proper place, on the top of the spinal cord, with eight *kalā*s (in the shape of a semi-circle). (Tr. S.C. Vasu)

The **Mayamata** is an important text of art and architecture which refers to *kalā* as clearer bearing on the meaning of *kalā* as used today in reference to arts. Some relevant passages may be quoted from the **Mayamata** in which *sakala* and *niṣkala* both are represented in a *vāstu* (in a layout of a house).

सकलं निष्कलं मिश्रं कुर्यात् पुंशिलया सुधी: ।

Mayam XXXIII.10ab

The sage makes an iconic, symbolic or mixed representation with a 'male' stone. (Tr. B. Dagens)

The house is a representation of the Cosmos (unmanifest and manifest) and the intervening half-manifest and half-unmanifest form (Mayam XXXIV.72).

Sakala in another passage is referred to of a icon (a symbol of the Divine unmanifest):

मुनिकराग्रजमादितयोदयं नयनमात्रविवर्धनया ततम् ।
नवविधं तरुणप्रतिमोदयं सकलकेऽसकलं च यथा कुरु ॥

Mayam XXXV.54

There are (potentially) nine heights for a provisional image, starting with seven digits and adding two each time. The procedure for a manifest representation is as for an unmanifest one. (Tr. B. Dagens)

Representation can be visualized as under:

निष्कलं सकलं मिश्रं लिङ्गं चेति त्रिधा मतम् ।
निष्कलं लिङ्गमित्युक्तं सकलं बेरमुच्यते ॥
मुखलिङ्गं तयोर्मिश्रं लिङ्गोच्चाकृतिसन्निभम् ।

Mayam XXXIII.1–2ab

It is said that there are three sorts of representation of the god, symbolic, iconic and mixed. Those which are symbolic (*niṣkala*) are called Liṅga, the iconic (*sakala*) are called image, the Mukhaliṅga is a combination of these two and is similar to the Liṅga as to shape and height. (Tr. B. Dagens)

Conclusion

To sum up, the different treatments of the concept of *sakala* and *niṣkala* (differentiated and undifferentiated) all together bring out a holistic view of manifestation as compulsion both at the levels of micro-cosmos and macro-cosmos. It also brings out the principle of continuous interaction between the two aspects so that neither the undifferentiated slips out of mind nor the differentiated. Analogous to this position is the gradual concretisation of the highest view *parā śakti* into *paśyantī* (unmanifest state), go into the stage of manifest-unmanifest (*madhyamā*) reaching or opening out at *vaikharī* (the articulate speech). In a way externalisation of the original pulsation perceived by the ear is half *ha* sound (*visarga*). It also brings out a close affinity between the activity of the speech and all other activities. The entire tradition is marked by a process of continuous interaction and also unfolding and folding the mysteries of life and its activity.

Vidya Nivas Misra

Select Bibliography

Kaviraj, Gopinath: "Nāda, bindu and kalā", in Journal of the Ganganath Jha Research Institute, Vol. 3, Allahabad. 1945–46, pp. 47–62.

Sastri, P.S.: "Nature of the integral whole", in Prabuddha Bharata, Vol. 74, Calcutta, 1969, pp. 465–474.

ARCĀ

Overview

Arcā (f.) is a widely known term for denoting worship, veneration or adoration; *arcanā* (f.) is an allied abstract noun derived from the same root *arc-*, 'to worship'. *Arcā* came to acquire also the sense of an object or form that is worshipped, such as an image, or venerable object. Already in Vedic thought, the concept of *arcā* finds frequent occurrence for praying, praising, or even venerating. The grammarian Patañjali also gives *arcā* in its definitive sense of an icon or a fashioned deity-image. In the Great Epics as well as the Purāṇas both the connotations of *arcā* are found, besides *arcanam, arcanā* and the verb forms of *arcā.* The Purāṇas have given details of various iconographic and iconoplastic conventions about deity-images (*arcā*), essential for offering worship (*arcanā*) to the gods. The Mahāyāna Buddhist texts enumerate aspects of cult rituals pertaining to the worship of the Buddha, the Bodhisattvas and allied Tantric practices. The Jaina canonical literature has also laid emphasis on the *arcanā* of images.

Arcā and *arcanā* have been explained in Vedantic thought as indicating the mental, the vocal and the physical aspects of worshipping a god, an external means needed essentially for common worldly folk.

Arcā worship has been treated at great length by several sectarian schools of Brahmanical fold; particularly, the Vaikhānasa and Pāñcarātra Saṃhitās, Śaiva Āgamas and Tantra works afford valuable presentation of the relevant traditions.

Etymology and Related Words

From etymological viewpoint, the term *arcā* (f.) is derived from the root *arc-*, 'to worship' (*arc pūjāyām*) added with suffix *a* (as per rule *guruśca halaḥ* – Pā III.3.103).

According to the **Amara Kośa**, *arcā* meaning 'worshipful image', is synonymous with such other words:

प्रतिमानं प्रतिबिम्बं प्रतिमा प्रतियातना प्रतिच्छाया ॥
प्रतिकृतिरर्चा पुंसि प्रतिनिधिः ...... ।

AmKo II.10.35cd–36a

The terms (of similar meaning) are *pratimāna* (counterpart), *pratibimba* (counter-reflection), (*pratimā*) (image), *pratiyātanā* (statue), *praticchāyā*, (counter-shadow), *pratikṛti* (counter figure, image), *arcā* (idol), *pratinidhi* (representation; in masculine gender).

As Kṣīrasvāmin has explained the term *arcā* here: *arcyate arcā*, 'that which is worshipped is called *arcā*.' Elsewhere, the same lexicon gives this word in the sense of 'worship', 'veneration', being an abstract noun also:

पूजा नमस्याऽपचितिः सपर्याचार्हणाः समाः ॥
वरिवस्या तु शुश्रूषा परिचर्याप्युपासना ।

AmKo II.7.34cd–35ab

The terms synonymous are *pūjā* (veneration), *namasyā* (bowing down), *apaciti* (reverence), *saparyā* (service), *arcā* (worship), *arhaṇā* (honouring), *varivasyā* (adoration), *śuśrūṣā* (attendance), *paricaryā* (waiting upon) and *upāsanā* (homage).

The **Vaijayantī Kośa** says:

पूजाऽर्चना नमस्याऽर्चा सपर्येज्याऽर्हणाऽञ्चनम् ।

VaiKo III.6.39ab

The terms synonymous with *arcā* (worship) include *pūjā* (veneration), *arcanā* (adoration), *namasyā* (bowing down), *saparyā* (service), *ijyā* (sacrifice), *arhaṇā* (honouring), and *añcanā* (paying of homage).

Elsewhere, the same lexicon states summarily:

अर्चा पूजाप्रतिमयोः ।

VaiKo VI.2.1

The term *arcā* is used to denote 'worship' and an image (that is worshipped).

Both the above senses of the term are indicated by other medieval lexicons using almost similar expressions (cf. MedKo IV.1; Ane Saṅg II.54, the gloss thereof has explained, *arcanam arcyate'sau iti vā arcā*, 'the act of worship or the object that is worshipped, is meant by *arcā*').

Layers of Meaning

As early as the **Ṛgveda**, the root *arc-* occurs frequently in the sense of doing 'praise' or veneration through prayers and sacrificial rites:

अर्चन्तस्त्वा हवामहेऽर्चन्तः समिधीमहि ।
अग्ने अर्चन्त ऊतये ॥

ṚV V.13.1

With songs of praise we call on thee, we kindle thee with songs of praise,

Agni, with songs of praise, for help. (Tr. R.T.H. Griffith)

गायन्ति त्वा गायत्रिणोऽर्चन्त्यर्कमर्किणः ।
ब्रह्माणस्त्वा शतक्रत उद्वंशमिव येमिरे ॥

ṚV I.10.1

The chanters hymn thee, they who say the word of praise magnify thee.

The priests have raised thee up on high, O Śatakratu, like a pole. (Tr. R.T.H. Griffith)

It is significant to notice that the word *arka,* 'the worshipful one', used in collocation of the verb *arcā* here comes from the same stem. In the opinion of Yāska:

अर्को देवो भवति । यदेनमर्चन्ति । अर्को मन्त्रो भवति । यदनेनार्चन्ति । अर्कमन्नं भवति । अर्चति भूतानि । अर्को वृक्षो भवति । संवृत्तः कटुकिम्ना ।

Nir V.4

Arkaḥ means a god, (so called) because they worship him. *Arkaḥ* means a stanza (so called) because it is by means of a stanza that they worship (gods). *Arkam* means food: it causes created beings to shine. *Arkaḥ* means a tree (*Calotropis gigantea*): it is compressed with bitterness. (Tr. L. Sarup)

Another word of cognate derivation is *arcis,* meaning 'a spark of fire', 'a flame', besides having the implication of an offering in fire-sacrifice, or of a lighted lamp to the deity (so worshipped in the later form of *pūjā*; cf. *arcibhir arcitam* (BhāgPur IV.21.2), 'worshipped with lamps').

The meaning of *arcā* as worship may have been initially connected with the concept of fire-offering, as is seemingly implied by the term *arcis* too. The same Vedic rite of making an oblation into a fire-flame can be said to have been subsequently reduced to or symbolised as an offering of a lamp or lamps lit in honour of the deity.

From the frequent use of the verb *arcā,* there evolved quite logically such phrases as *arcā, arcanā, abhyarcanā, arcanam,* and so on, all implying worship, the act of veneration or honouring. One of the significant terms as found in later Vedic texts is *arcā,* denoting 'a prayer', or invocation addressed to the deity, thereby introducing a meaning of the term also for a hymn or a stanza used for a deity's worship.

Patañjali records the word in its definitive sense of an icon or a fashioned out deity-image as follows:

> मौर्यैर्हिरण्यार्थिभिरर्चाः प्रकल्पिताः ।
>
> Mahābh V.3.99
>
> Being greedy of gold the Mauryan rulers caused images of deities to be made.

Development of the Concept

In several Vedic passages the divine worship is expressly enjoined:

> प्र वः पान्तमन्धसो धियायते महे शूराय विष्णवे चार्चत ।
>
> ṚV I.155.1ab
>
> To the great Hero, him who sets his mind thereon, and Viṣṇu, praise aloud in song your draught of juice. (Tr. R.T. H. Griffith)

Likewise, we find in the **Sāmaveda**:

> अर्चत प्रार्चता नरः प्रियमेधासो अर्चत ।
> अर्चन्तु पुत्रका उत पुरमिद् धृष्ण्वर्चत ॥
>
> SV I.4.2.3
>
> Sing, sing ye forth your songs of praise, men, Priyamedhas, sing your songs:
>
> yea, let young children sing their lauds: yea, glorify our firm stronghold. (Tr. R.T. H. Griffith)

In the Brāhmaṇa texts it is significant to find the word *arcā* as already evolved to convey the concept of worship, ritual performance or devotion offered to a deity. As it occurs in the **Śatapatha Brāhmaṇa**:

> यज्ञो हि विष्णुस्तस्माद् वैष्णव्यर्चा जुहोति ।
>
> ŚBr III.6.3.16
>
> For Viṣṇu is the sacrifice: therefore he offers with a verse addressed to Viṣṇu. (Tr. J. Eggeling)
>
> यूपं व्रक्ष्यन् वैष्णव्यर्चा जुहोति । वैष्णवो हि यूपस्तस्माद् वैष्णव्यर्चा जुहोति ।
>
> ŚBr III.6.4.1

Being about to cut the sacrificial stake, he offers with a verse addressed to Viṣṇu. For the stake belongs to Viṣṇu, therefore he offers with a verse addressed to Viṣṇu. (Tr. J. Eggeling)

वारुणो वै पाशो वरुणपाशादेव तत्प्रमुच्यते वारुण्यर्चा
स्वेनैव तदात्मना स्वया देवतया वरुणपाशात्प्रमुच्यते ।

ŚBr VI.7.3.8

The noose belongs to Varuṇa, thus he frees himself from Varuṇa's noose. He does so with a verse to Varuṇa (*vāruṇī, arcā*): he thus frees himself from Varuṇa's noose by its own self, by its own deity. (Based on the tr. by J. Eggeling)

Such a verse is already under reference and specified by the ritual tradition, as in the last case it is **Yajurveda** (YV XII.12 =ṚV I.24.15). As it is ordained in the following rule of Paninian grammar:

साधुनिपुणाभ्यामर्चायां सप्तम्यप्रतेः ।

Pā II.3.43

In the event of expressions indicating respectfulness or devotion (*arcāyām*), the seventh case-ending is used with the words *sādhu* and *nipuṇa* apart from the cases in which *prati* is used with accusative.

In the usages, there evolved a word *ārca*, denoting a person with *arcā*:

प्रज्ञाश्रद्धार्चावृत्तिभ्यो णः ।

Pā V.2.101

From the terms *prajñā, śraddhā, arcā* and *vṛtti* are formed, by adding *taddhita* affix *ṇa*, the phrases *prājña* (having *prajñā*), *śrāddha* (having or belonging to *śraddhā*), *ārca* (having *arcā* or possessing an object of worship), *vārtta* (having *vṛtti*), respectively.

Here, it is remarkable that the Paninian rule also covers, besides a worshipful person, the concept of one who has an object or symbol of worship in possession.

It is apparent from the **Bṛhaddevatā** that the verb *arcā* came to indicate the proper act of worshipping an object or entity, embodied or incarnate:

तत्रार्बुदस्तु ग्रावाणं मूर्तिमन्तमिवार्चति ॥

BṛDev VII.146cd

In that hymn [*tatra* referring to ṚV X.94], *Arbuda* adores the pressing-stone as if incarnate. (Based on the tr. by A.A. Macdonell)

As we see in an apocryphal section of the **Mānava Śrauta-Sūtra**:

सुगुप्तदेशे गोचर्ममात्रेऽस्थन्स्वनुलिप्ते वा लिङ्गपद्माकृतिं प्रकल्प्य प्रोक्ष्य "मा नो महान्तमिति" स्थापयेत्, "नमः शम्भवे" चेत्यर्चयेत् ।

MānŚrSū XI. 7.1.13

In a fully secluded place, sitting on a spot covered by a cow-hide, or a site well-besmeared by cow-dung paste, having made a symbolical shape of the lotus diagram, sprinkling it and setting it up, with the verse '*mā no mahāntam*', should worship the same with the formula '*namaḥ śambhave*'.

Recording an illustration to the rule referred above (Pā V.3.99), the word *arcā* has been specifically shown to denote a symbol or image of divinities. Likewise, Patañjali also preserves the following examples current in the language as specifying divine idols with their peculiarity in representational details:

दीर्घनासिकी अर्चा, तुंगनासिकी अर्चेति ।

Mahābh IV.1.54

An image with long nose; an image with high nose-ridge.

For a person worthy of respect as well as for devotion to the deities, the expressions derived from the verb *arcā* are quite common in both the Epics. For example:

अथो पुनरिदं वाक्यं प्राजापत्यो नरोऽब्रवीत् ।
राजन्नर्चयता देवानद्य प्राप्तमिदं त्वया ॥

Rām I.16.18

Now again the divine person presiding over generation spoke these words: 'By worshipping the gods, O king, you have gained today this' [reward of a milky food from the gods].

देवागाराणि शून्यानि न भान्तीह यथा पुरा ।
देवतार्चाः प्रविद्धाश्च यज्ञगोष्ठास्तथैव च ॥

Rām II.71.40

The shrines here being dissolute now do not look charming as (they were) before, and also are likewise the deity images as well as the sacrificial sheds deserted.

तस्मिन्नध्यासति गुरावासनं परमार्चितम् ।
ततो वक्ष्यसि यत्त्वां स प्रक्ष्यति द्विजसत्तमः ॥

MBh I.4.7

When he is seated on his highly respected seat, you will answer what that best of *dvijas* shall ask of you. (Tr. P.C. Roy)

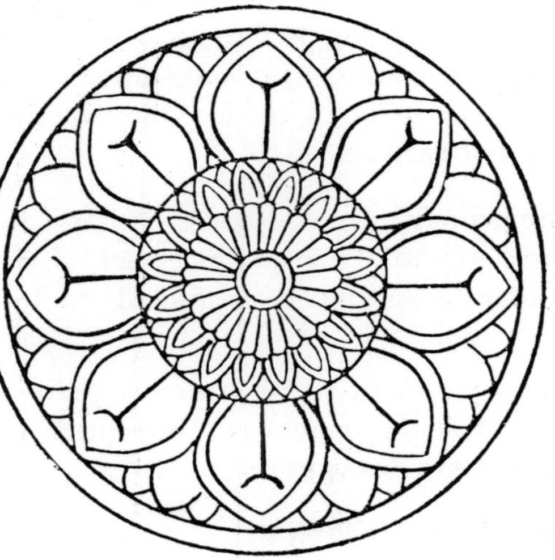

Figure 4: Lotus shaped symbol of divine worship

Side by side the sense of 'adoration' the word had well acquired currency for a divine statue or worshipful symbol; this fact is thus apparent from the **Mahābhārata** (VII.172.86cd–87).

According to a view as given in the **Harivaṃśa Purāṇa**, the gods came to be paid worship from a specific time in hoary antiquity:

देवताऽर्च्याश्च पूज्यन्ते तदाप्रभृति भारत ।
तेषां ब्रह्मविदां राजन् पृथिव्यां ब्रह्मवादिभिः ॥

HarPur III.24.2

O King, the gods worthy of homage (*arcya*) came to be worshipped from then onwards on the earth by the Brahman-preachers amongst those who knew (the real essence of) Brahman-doctrine.

A figure or diagram of the lotus-shaped symbol (→*padma, padma-maṇḍala*) has been described so frequently to form the centre or means of divine worship (*arcanā*) and meditation:

पद्मस्वरूपं तव वच्मि राजन् यत्रार्चनं कार्यमथेश्वराणाम् ॥
सौवर्णं राजतं ताम्रमारकूटमयं तथा ।
द्विहस्तमात्रं कर्तव्यं कमलं चारुकेसरम् ॥
तस्याष्टभागाः कर्तव्याः कर्णिका नृप वर्तुला ।

VDhPur III.44.21cd, 45.1–2ab

O king, I shall tell you of the form of lotus symbol, wherein the worship of gods is performed. The lotus symbol can be made of gold, silver, copper or brass, two *hasta*-units in size, consisting of charming filaments; its eight sections are divided, (the first being) the round pericarp.

According to the principles of widespread Smārta and Āgama-Tantra worship, such a →*padma* was to serve not as common symbol but as the very 'body' or 'image' of one specific deity for whom that was dedicated (cf. VDhPur III.45.5–9).

Under the general theme of ritual practices (*kriyā-yoga*), an enumeration of the main features of divine images is found incorporated in some of the Puranic texts. As the **Matsya Purāṇa** says:

क्रियायोगं प्रवक्ष्यामि देवतार्चानुकीर्तनम् ।
भुक्तिमुक्तिप्रदं यस्मान्नान्यत् लोकेषु विद्यते ॥
प्रतिष्ठायां सुराणां तु देवतार्चानुकीर्तनम् ।
देवयज्ञोत्सवं चापि बन्धनाद् येन मुच्यते ॥

MatPur CCLVIII.2–3

I would tell the ritual system and an enumeration of the deity images (as well as worship). In the worlds, there exists nothing else which can bestow both joys and redemption (simultaneously). In the installation ceremonies of the gods, there take place a glorification of the divine images and also sacrificial festivities dedicated to the gods, through which men gain release from (mundane) bondages.

'Worship' is said to have a wider perspective:

अर्चायामेव हरये पूजां यः श्रद्धयेहते ।
न तद्भक्तेषु चान्येषु स भक्तः प्राकृतः स्मृतः ॥

BhāgPur XI.2.47 (also cf. III.29.22,24)

One who wishes to do worship of Viṣṇu in the image (alone) and does not show reverence to his devotees and others, is known to be a votary of the *prākṛta* type (i.e. a commoner, a novice).

On the ritual level, the *arcā* has been categorically analysed to be of two types:

वैदिक्यर्चापि द्विविधा मूर्तिभेदेन भूधर ।
वैदिकी वैदिकैः कार्या वेददीक्षासमन्वितैः ।

DBhāgPur VII.39.4

It is of two kinds: one is the Vedic worship and the other, O King, is differentiated as of image-worship. The Vedic type is performed by those who are initiated in that following.

The occasional disturbances when remarked in the divine images are stated to portend ill effects. Such of unnatural activities are enlisted to occur in this context:

देवतार्चाः प्रनृत्यन्ति वेपन्ते प्रज्वलन्ति च ।
वमन्त्यग्निं तथा धूमं स्नेहं रक्तं तथा वसाम् ॥
आरटन्ति रुदन्त्येताः प्रस्विद्यन्ति हसन्ति च ।
उत्तिष्ठन्ति निषीदन्ति प्रधावन्ति धमन्ति च ॥
भुञ्जते विक्षिपन्ते वा कोशप्रहरणध्वजान् ।
अवाङ्मुखा वै भवन्ति स्थानात् स्थानं भ्रमन्ति च ॥
एवमाद्या हि दृश्यन्ते विकाराः सहसोत्थिताः ।

MatPur CCXXX.1–4ab

The deity images appear as dancing, as shaking, as catching fire, as exuding fire-flames, or smoke, oily substance, blood or fat. They (sometimes) cry, weep, sweat and laugh, or stand up, or get seated, and also appear running or melting. Or they appear as swallowing or throwing wealth, weapons or banners. They get upturned with face downwards or appear as moving from one place to another. May be these and other kinds of abnormalities are seen occurring all of a sudden (i.e. without no obvious explanation).

In such cases detailed pacificatory rituals are prescribed in the text.

A great emphasis has been laid on the proper preparation of a deity-image, well complete in its iconographic details and features:

प्रासादकरणं पुण्यं देवार्चाकरणं तथा ।
सुरार्चापूजनं पुण्यं तत्र पुण्या नमस्क्रिया ॥
तस्मात् सर्वप्रयत्नेन सुरार्चां लक्षणान्विताम् ।
कारयेत्पूजयेद् विद्वान् न त्वलक्षणसंयुताम् ॥

VDhPur III.1.11–12

The making of a temple is meritorious, the making of deity images is likewise (auspicious). Then, the worship of deity images is auspicious, and there the act of bowing down (to a deity) is auspicious. Therefore, the learned should get the deity image, carefully made, as endowed with characteristic marks, and worship it; but not an image that is deficient of such features (should be worshipped).

As it has been observed in a general way:

अर्चायां कारयेद् देवं चित्रे वा पुस्तकर्मणि ।

VDhPur III.44.9ab

The god should be represented in the image form, in a painting, or in stucco-work.

The worship of the invisible *pitṛs* is thus indicated:

अर्चितानाममूर्तानां पितृणां दीप्ततेजसाम् ।
नमस्यामि सदा तेषां ध्यानिनां दिव्यचक्षुषाम् ॥

MārkPur XCVII.3

I bow down to those manes, who are worshipped, have no bodily form (but only) luminous splendour, and are rapt in meditation, having divine insight.

The merit of Śiva's five-syllabled →*mantra* and its devout muttering has been given as follows:

भक्त्या पंचाक्षरेणैव यो हि मां सकृदर्चयेत् ।
सोऽपि गच्छेन्मम स्थानं मंत्रस्यास्यैव गौरवात् ॥
तस्मात्तपांसि यज्ञाश्च व्रतानि नियमास्तथा ।
पंचाक्षरार्चनस्यैते कोट्यंशेनापि नो समाः ॥

ŚPur VII.2.13.12–13

[Śiva says to the goddess:] Whosoever even once worships me with devotion alone by the formula consisting of five syllables, he also goes to my abode through the high merit of this *mantra* (namely, '*namaḥ śivāya*'). For all sorts of penances, sacrifices, vows and moral observances are not at par even with one billionth part of the merit accruing from the veneration (done of me) with the five-syllabled *mantra.*

With respect to the need as well as the mode of image worship the sage Mārkaṇḍeya has thus remarked in the following Puranic passage:

कृतत्रेताद्वापरेषु नराः पश्यन्ति देवताम् ।
तिष्यं प्राप्य न पश्यन्ति पूजास्त्वर्चागता यतः ॥
कृतादिष्वपि दृष्ट्वा च देवान्मनुजसत्तम ।

अर्चागतविशेषेण पूजयन्ति विधानतः ॥
चित्रसूत्रविधानेन देवतार्चां विनिर्मिताम् ।
सुरूपां पूजयेद् विद्वांस्तत्र सन्निहिता भवेत् ॥

VDhPur III.1.5–7

During the Kṛta, Tretā and Dvāpara ages men could see the gods. However, having reached the stage of Kali age, they do not see them, hence they (the gods) are (seen as) staying in the images. O best of men, even in the Kṛta and other (two succeeding) ages, side by side seeing the gods, men (did) worship them, with proper rituals, as staying specifically in the images. Thus, the learned should worship the divine image, well-shaped and made in accordance of the Citrasūtra manual, so that the deity assumes the identity with it.

Manu has laid down certain daily duties to be diligently performed by a householder:

नित्यं स्नात्वा शुचिः कुर्याद् देवर्षिपितृतर्पणम् ।
देवताभ्यर्चनं चैव समिदाधानमेव च ॥

Manu II.176

Every day, having bathed, and being purified, he must offer libations of water to the gods, sages and manes, worship (the images of) the gods, and place fuel on (the sacred fire). (Tr. G. Bühler)

According to Yājñavalkya a person may normally take gifts for such pious intentions:

देवातिथ्यर्चनकृते गुरुभृत्यार्थमेव वा ।
सर्वतः प्रतिगृह्णीयादात्मवृत्त्यर्थमेव च ॥

YājSm I.9.216

For the sake of divinities, guest and worship as well as for (supporting the elders (or teachers) and the servants, one may accept the charities and also for one's own living.

The trial named as *Kośapāna* is enjoined by the law as follows:

देवानुग्रान्समभ्यर्च्य तत्स्नानोदकमाहरेत्।
संस्राव्य पाययेत्तस्माज्जलं तु प्रसृतित्रयम् ॥

YājSm II.7.112

Having worshipped the violent divinities (such as Durgā, Sūrya, etc.) the water of their (ritual) bathing should be taken and filtered; then the suspect under trial should be asked to drink three handfuls of that water.

As enumerated in the **Divyāvadāna**, the holy places connected with the Buddha's life were visited by the Maurya emperor Aśoka with monk Upagupta who thus explained their significance one after the other:

इदं महाराज शाक्यवर्धं नाम देवकुलम् । तत्र बोधिसत्त्वो जातमात्र उपनीतो देवमर्चयिष्यतीति ।

Divyāv p. 249

This is, O monarch, the holystead Śākyavardha by name. Here the Bodhisattva when taken after his birth would offer his worship to the god.

In the **Kuṇālāvadāna**, it is mentioned that for perpetuating the worship of the Buddha, Aśoka ordered monumental symbols to be installed at the main sites related with the Lord (Divyāv p. 248). The same text further records a semi-historical legend about contemporary attempts of making a cloth-painting directly from life by drawing the likeness or →*pratimā* of the Buddha (cf. Divyāv p. 466).

The concept of the Buddha image and its worship has been thus given in the **Divyāvadāna** (XXVI.48).

The Gilgit manuscripts prescribe the worship of holy spots as under:

शुचौ प्रदेशे बुद्धाधिष्ठिते गन्धपुष्पैर्ध्वजपताकैः पूर्णकुम्भैरभ्यर्च्य स पृथिवीप्रदेशः स च धर्मभाणकः शुचिः सुस्नातगात्रः श्वेतवस्त्रप्रावृतो नानापुष्पमाल्यगन्धैरभ्यर्च्य लिखापयितव्यः सर्वसत्त्वासाधारणानि कुशलमूलानि कृत्वा सर्वसत्त्वमैत्रचित्तेन दयाचित्तेन करुणाचित्तेन तथागतगुरुगौरवं चित्तमुपस्थाप्य तेन दिने दिने लिखता ताव लिखे यावदर्धदिवसम् ।

Gilgit Ms., Vol. I, p. 68

Meditating on such a pious spot, consecrated by the Buddha, worshipping that (earthly spot) with perfumes, flowers, banners, buntings, and full vases, the same earthly site and the preacher of religion, who is pious, has his body bathed properly, is clad in white garments, is to be drawn with due service performed with various flowers, wreaths, and perfumes, having done welfare rites for all sentient beings, with mind intent upon the good-will for all sentient being, with mind full of compassion, with mind full of piety, having settled the mind on the glory of the arch-teacher Tathāgata, – with this procedure, day by day he should describe that drawing till the midday.

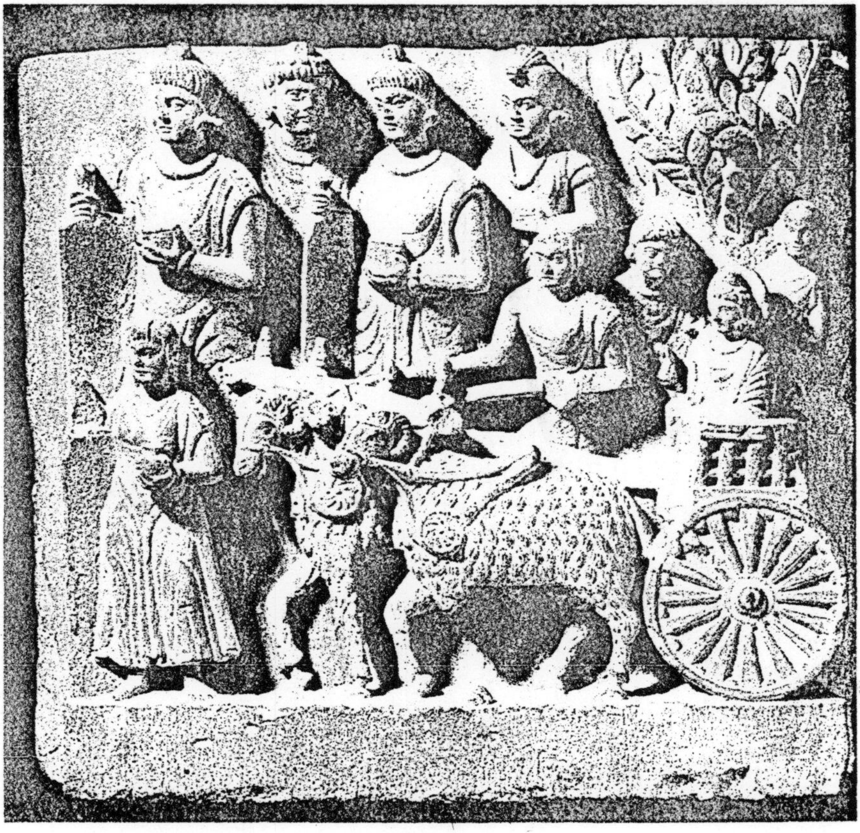

Figure 5: Life events of Buddha

For honouring of a respected guest the expression *arcana* occurs quite frequently. For example:

> अथ स राजा शुद्धोदनोऽसितस्य महर्षेरर्घपाद्यमर्चनं च कृत्वा साधु सुष्ठु च परिगृह्य आसनेनोपनिमन्त्रयते स्म ।
>
> LVi VII, p. 73
>
> Now, the king Śuddhodana, having made the due offering of water for washing his feet and also having done his veneration (*arcana*), together with a seat invited the great sage Asita with the words, 'O worthy, welcome, take (the seat)'.

In several of the Sanskrit Buddhist scriptures, the Lord Buddha is given the following description:

देवनागयक्षासुरगरुडकिन्नरमहोरगाभ्यर्चितो बुद्धो भगवान् ।

AvaŚa I.4

The worshipful Lord Buddha, who is worshipped by (all) the gods, serpents, Yakṣas, demons, Kinnaras and great dragons.

The *mantra* of Kārttikeya as an attendant or aspect of Mañjuśrī runs as follows:

ॐ। कुमार महाकुमार क्रीड क्रीड षण्मुख बोधिसत्वानुज्ञात मयूरासनसद्योद्यतपाणि रक्ताङ्ग रक्तगन्धानुलेपनप्रिय ख ख खाहि खाहि खाहि । हुं नृत्य नृत्य रक्तपुष्पार्चितमूर्ति समयमनुस्मर । भ्रम भ्रम भ्रामय भ्रामय भ्रामय । लहु लहु मा विलम्ब । सर्वकार्याणि मे कुरु कुरु चित्ररूपधारिणे । तिष्ठ तिष्ठ हुं हुं सर्वबुद्धानुज्ञात स्वाहा ।

MMK II.17 (prose after verse 17)

Om. Kumāra, Great Kumāra, disport disport, O you six-faced One, who is known to be endowed with the Bodhi-essence, has the seat of a peacock, has the (right) hand raised forthwith (i.e. in pose of amnesty), red-limbed, whom red perfumes and unguents are dear, *kha, kha,* consume, consume, consume! *Hum,* dance, dance! O you, having the person worshipped with red flowers, remember the vow. move around, move around, make others bewildered (*bhrāmaya*), *bhrāmaya, bhrāmaya.* Quick, quick, do not be late. O, you, who has variegated form, accomplish, accomplish all my deeds. Stay, stay, *hum, hum.* Known to (or knowing) all the Buddha. I offer oblation (*svāhā*).

Likewise, a sacred Sūtra or text is claimed to have divine efficacy:

देवगण अर्चितोऽयं देवेन्द्रनमस्कृतश्च सूत्रेन्द्रः ।
आरक्षितश्चतुर्भिर्महर्द्धिकैर्लोकपालैश्च ॥

SuSū VII.15

This best of scriptures is venerated by the host of gods, and is honoured by the god Indra, and is well-protected by the greatly prosperous lords of the world (Lokapālas, i.e., the four Great Regents of Quarters).

As the expression occurs in a Jaina canon, *accana* (=*arcana,* meaning adoration, prayer, worship) was connected with images also:

जिणपडिमाणं अच्चणं करेइ ।

Ṇāyādhammakahāo XVI

She performs the worship of the Tīrthaṅkara icons.

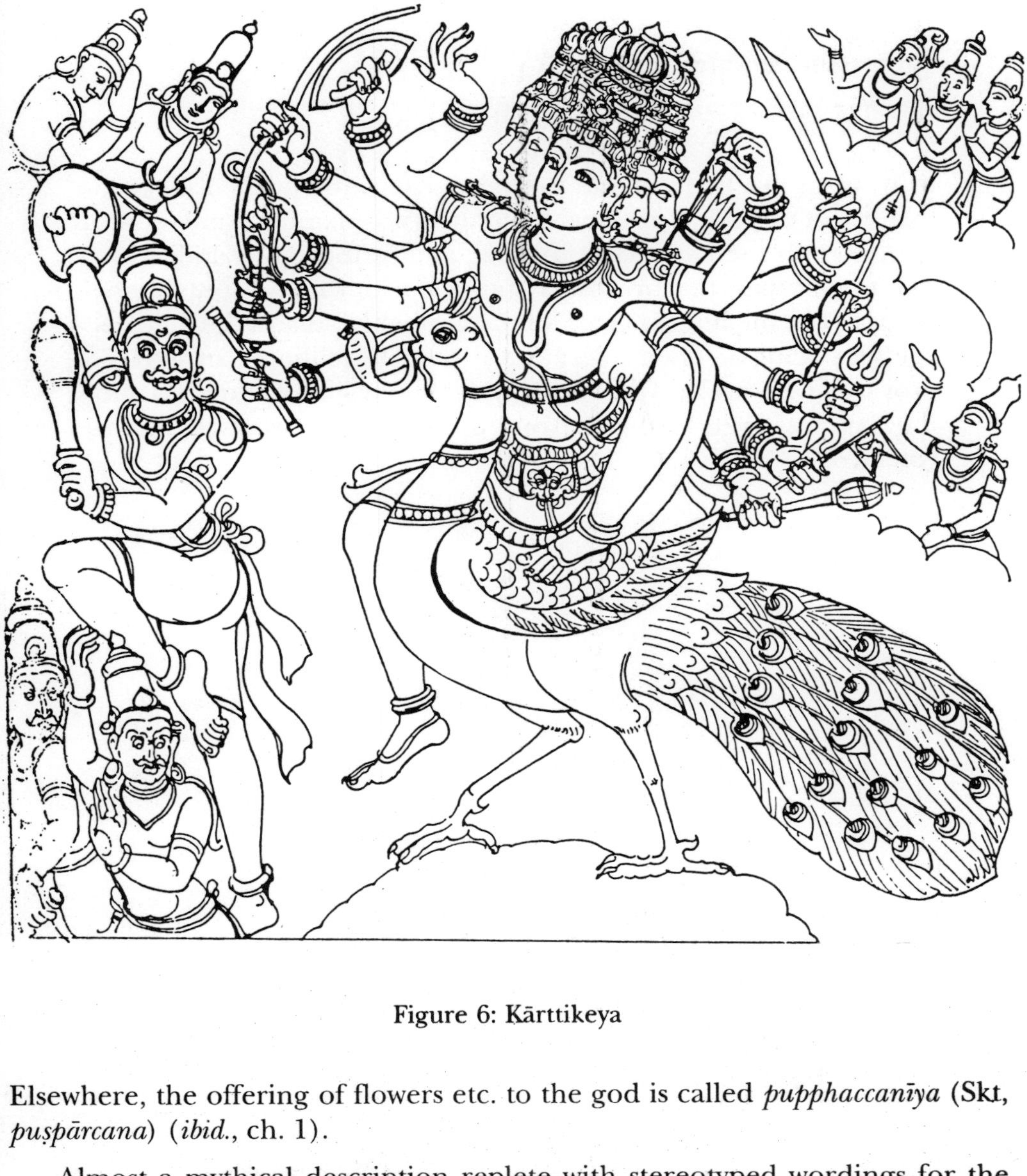

Figure 6: Kārttikeya

Elsewhere, the offering of flowers etc. to the god is called *pupphaccanīya* (Skt, *puṣpārcana*) (*ibid.*, ch. 1).

Almost a mythical description replete with stereotyped wordings for the grandiose complex of a Jaina edifice runs in its relevant part as in the **Lokavibhāga** of Siṃhasūri:

अस्त्यग्रे जिनवासस्य मञ्जुलो मुखमण्डपः ।
ध्वजादिभिश्च संयुक्तस्तस्मात्प्रेक्षणमण्डपः ॥

आस्थानमण्डपस्तस्मात् स्तूपा नव पुरः पुरः ।
द्वादशाम्बुजवेदीभिर्जिनसिद्धार्चाभिरन्विताः ॥
ततो द्वादशवेदीभिर्जिनसिद्धार्चाभिरन्वितौ ।
चैत्यसिद्धार्थवृक्षौ स्तस्ततोऽपि च महाध्वजाः ॥

Lok I.309–311

In front of the Jina's abode there is a charming portico; next to that is the theatrical pavilion, decorated with banners and so on; then there is the pavilion for resting, and further preceding it are the nine Stūpas, that are (next) provided with twelve lotus-altars, occupied by the images (*arcā*) of the Tīrthaṅkaras and the Siddhas (perfect beings). Then, there are two Wishfulfilling Caitya-trees, provided with twelve altars beset with the images of the Jinas and the Siddhas. Even further beyond there are the Great Standards (erected).

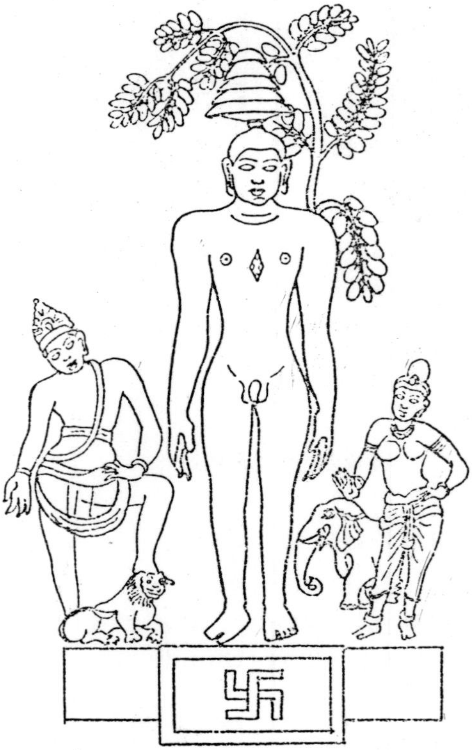

Figure 7: Supārśvanātha

The term *abhyarcana* is also used in the same or similar connotation:

क्षेत्रपालस्य तैलाभिषेकाभ्यर्चनविधिं विधाय .... ।

Prati II, p. 114

Having arranged the mode of worship with the oil-anointing of the Kṣetrapāla image.

In view of the evolved notions of *arcana*, the great teacher Śaṅkara has so aptly observed in his gloss of the **Viṣṇu-Sahasranāma**:

अर्चयन्नित्यनेनोभयविधमर्चनमुच्यते । ध्यायंस्तुवन्नमस्यंश्चेत्यनेन मानसं वाचिकं कायिकं चोच्यते ।

ViSahasrBh I.5

By the expression 'worshipping' (*arcayan*) both kinds of procedural worship (*arcana*) is indicated. By 'meditating', 'praying' and 'paying homage' are indicated, respectively, the mental, the vocal and the physical modes of worship.

In a fine passage of the **Yoga-Vāsiṣṭha** the worldly need of external means of worship is thus indicated.

प्रबुद्धस्त्वं मुनिश्रेष्ठ तेनेदं तव कथ्यते ।
नातिदेवार्चने योग्यः पुष्पधूपचयो महान् ॥
अव्युत्पन्नधियो ये हि बालपेलवचेतसः ।
कृत्रिमार्चामयं तेषां देवार्चनमुदाहृतम् ॥

YVās VI.1.30.4–5

O best of sages, you are well awakened so it is being told to you. Huge collection of flowers and incenses is not needed at all for worshipping the excellent god. However, for those who are not of enlightened mind and have just child-like tender understanding the god's worship consisting in artificial means of worshipful images is recommended.

The same work maintains from a Vedantic standpoint as follows:

शमबोधादिभिः पुष्पैर्देव आत्मा यदर्च्यते ।
तत्तु देवार्चनं विद्धि नाकारार्चनमर्चनम् ॥
आत्मसंवित्तिरूपं तु त्यक्त्वा देवार्चनं जनाः ।
कृत्रिमार्चासु ये सक्ताश्चिरं क्लेशं भजन्ति ते ॥

YVās VI.I.29.128–129

That worship, which the soul offers to the god with the flowers of self-control, awakening, etc. should be known as the (real) divine worship, and not the service done to the shaped form as (real) worship. Those folk who are devoted to artificial images (*arcā*) as relinquishing the worship of the divinity in shape being the self-sentiency (or knowledge of inner spirit), are likely to soon land in trouble (of delusion).

Referring to the Vaishnavite doctrine of Rāmānuja *arcā* is thus indicated:

तत्रार्चा नाम प्रतिमादयः ।

SarDSaṅg (Rāmānuja) p. 115

In the (present) context *arcā* indicates 'images', etc.

तदर्चाविभवव्यूहसूक्ष्मान्तर्यामिसंज्ञकम् ।

SarDSaṅg (Rāmānuja) p. 120

They (i.e. the emanations of the Lord) are by designation *arcā* (image-form), *vibhava* (emanation), *vyūha* (manifold epiphanies), *sūkṣma* (subtle) and *antaryāmin* (all-pervasive Soul).

Showing the difference between →*dhyāna* and *arcanā*, Abhinavagupta has thus remarked:

तत्रार्पणं हि वस्तूनामभेदेनार्चनं मतम् ।
तथा सम्पूर्णरूपत्वानुसंधिर्ध्यानमुच्यते ॥

TĀl XII.9

Offering of articles to the divinity entertaining no difference (*abhedena*) of them (from the deity) is called worship (*arcana*). Likewise, the unified experience of all forms (of expressing homage by external and internal means) as one complete identity is called meditation (*dhyāna*).

Summarising the tenets of Bhagavatism (=Vaishnavism), Parāśara-bhaṭṭa has made the following observation referring to the *vibhava*- emanations of the Lord.

In view of the material means and items of offering, the *arcana* is stated to be of two kinds in certain ritual texts:

अनिर्माल्यं सनिर्माल्यमर्चनं द्विविधं स्मृतम् ।
दिव्यं मनोभवैर्द्रव्यैर्गन्धपुष्पैः स्रगादिभिः ॥
यदर्चनमनिर्माल्यं दिव्यभोगापवर्गदम् ।
ग्रामारण्यादिसम्भूतैर्यागद्रव्यैर्मनोहरैः ।

भक्तैर्यत् क्रियते सम्यक् सनिर्माल्यं तदर्चनम् ॥

Tattvasāgara Sam as quoted in Tārābhaktisudhārṇava, V, sec. on tarpaṇa

The worship (*arcanā*) is known as of two kinds: without *nirmālya* and with *nirmālya.* [*Nirmālya* denotes the remainder of objects in service of a deity, such as that are personally acceptable to the ritualist and some of them can also be distributed to votaries as *prasādam.*]

The first one is the worship which is carried out without using any (actual) objects but all such items of offering being conceived on a celestial level only through mental imagination as the incenses, flowers, garlands, etc. This *a-nirmālya* worship bestows divine enjoyments and final release.

We are told by the famous master Vedānta-deśika (1260–1370A.D.) in his **Pañcarātrarakṣā** (p. 66, 2nd ch., Adyar Library edn, 1942) about the harms of not worshipping the image of Keśava.

In a Vaikhānasa Āgama text, *arcā* or *arcanā* has been expressly mentioned as a form of the Lord's assumed presence to be conceived of under two main heads:

अमूर्तेति समूर्तेति द्विविधा साऽर्चना मता ॥
अमूर्ताऽग्न्याहुतिः प्रोक्ता समूर्ता प्रतिमार्चना ।

Samū I.28cd–29ab

The worship is considered to be of two kinds, namely, one related to the formless and the other, belonging to the imaged deity. The formless kind is said to be done with fire-oblations, and the *samūrta* worship is the adoration made to the image.

Regarding *arcā* worship in the Vaikhānasa shrines, M.R. Kavi has so aptly observed, "Besides *dhruva* image, *kautuka* idol is essential in every shrine. *Kautuka* or *arcāmūrti* is used for all *arcanās* (worship), *snapana* for baths, and *utsava* for taking out in processions." The same author makes it further clear that 'There is another *mūrti* (image) called *bali* made of a metal (one of the selected five metals) of a slightly larger size than that of *kautuka.* This is taken out every day round the central *ālaya* (shrine) at the time of offering the *bali* to *lokapālas* and *dvārapālas*" (Samū Introduction, p. xii).

About the daily service in the Vaiṣṇava shrines, it is observed:

नित्यार्चनमविच्छिन्नं कारयेत् तु विधानतः ।
नित्यार्चने तु विच्छिन्ने यजमानो विनश्यति ॥

आचार्यस्थापकादीनामर्चाहीने महद्भयम् ।
आद्योऽर्चकोऽथ पुत्रादिस्तन्नियुक्तोऽथवार्चयेत् ॥

Samū IV.40–41

There should be an arrangement made for the daily worship (of the god in the temple). For in the event of the daily worship being interrupted the patron perishes. If there were no (daily) worship for the preceptor, the consecrator (or builder) and the like would have fear. Thus, the worship must be done either by the primary priest or even by his son deputed for the purpose (in case of any urgency).

However, the **Lakṣmī Tantra**, a text of the Pāñcarātra Vaiṣṇava fold, comments thus:

अनिरुद्धस्य विस्तारो दर्शितस्तस्य सात्वते ।
अर्चापि लौकिकी या सा भगवद्भावितात्मनाम् ॥

LT II.59

In the Sātvata tradition (or text), an unfoldment of Aniruddha's forms is shown; the *arcā* is the worldly aspect (i.e. image-incarnation) which is enjoined for those whose self (soul, being) is inspired with the notion of the Lord.

As the same Tantric text observes further:

देवर्षिपितृसिद्धाद्यैः स्वयं वा जगतां हिते ।
निर्मितं भगवद्रूपमर्चा सा शुद्धचिन्मयी ॥

LT IV.31

God's image conceived by Himself or by various deities, sages, manes, or demigods for favouring the worlds are His forms consisting of pure knowledge. (Tr. Sanjukta Gupta)

Elsewhere (NārSam XIII.3–4), the *arcā* is taken to be of five kinds, viz. *śilāmayī*, of stone, *lohamayī*, of metal, *maṇimayī*, of gems, *kāṣṭhajā*, of wood, and *mṛṇmayā*, of clay.

Referring to the temple cult, the **Sātvata Saṃhitā** furnishes a detailed explanation (XXV.308–315).

F. Otto Schrader has observed, "Even among inanimate objects an image of Kṛṣṇa, the Man-lion, Garuḍa, etc. becomes an *avatāra* of Viṣṇu (endowed with a certain miraculous power felt by the worshipper) as soon as it is duly consecrated according to the Pāñcarātra rites, it being supposed that Viṣṇu, owing to His omnipotence, is capable of 'descending' into such images with a portion of His *śakti*, that is, with a subtle ('divine', 'non-natural') body. This is the *arcā avatāra* or incarnation for the purpose of ordinary worship. It is exhaustively treated in the **Viṣvaksena Saṃhitā**" (*Introduction to the Pāñcarātra and the Ahirbudhnya Saṃhitā*, pp. 48–49, Madras, 1916, pp. 48–49).

As regards the position of 'ritual substitutes' representing the main deity (*dhruva, mahābera*), the **Viṣvaksena Saṃhitā** ordains:

मत्स्यादिदशमूर्तीनां पूजाबिम्बं चतुर्भुजम् ।
मूलबेरे तु यत्प्रोक्तं तथैव मुनिसत्तम ॥
अवतारेऽथवा कुर्याद् अर्चनाबेरमत्र वै ।

VSam XI.311–12

The icon of worship should be made four-armed in case of the ten forms, the fish, etc. Or, what rules have been laid down (earlier) for the main idol, the same O best of sages, are applicable here for making an image-of-worship (*arcanā-bera*).

In such contexts the terms *pūjā-bimba, arcanā-bera, arcā-vigraha, arcā-mūrti* and the like as formed in the so pregnant Sanskrit vocabulary appear as synonymous.

The commentator Alaśiṅga Bhaṭṭa on the **Sātvata Saṃhitā** has, however, made the following observation on the concept of *arcāvatāra*(*arcā* + *avatāra*, i.e. the Lord's epiphany as *arcā* in certain worthies or in cult-icons):

नन्वर्चावतारस्यापि प्रादुर्भावेष्वन्तर्भावो वक्तव्यः ।

Comm. on SātSam I.27

Well, it may be said that *arcāvatara* is included within (the category of) *prādurbhāvas*, 'incarnations'.

He further cites the authority of the **Lakṣmī Tantra** (II.58cd–61) supporting the opinion, to which there is no technical objection to be maintained, that the *arcāvatāra* should be indicated first in the list.

Different types of ancillary images have been enumerated in the **Pādma Saṃhitā** (XIX.1–3).

The purpose of representing several *arcā* images in a Vaiṣṇava temple is thus enumerated in the Pāñcarātra works:

कर्मार्चादिविशेषाणां संज्ञाभेदं च लक्षणम् ।
उपयोगस्तथैतेषां कथ्यते कमलेक्षणे ॥
कर्मार्चा चोत्सवार्चा च बल्यर्चा च तथापरे ।
तीर्थस्नानोभये स्यातामपरा शयनार्थिका ॥

ŚrīSam XIV.1–2

O lotus-eyed, now is expounded here the defining distinctions and features as well as their use of images of ritual purpose specified for the ritual and other activities. They are *karmārcā, utsavārcā, balyarcā, tīrthārca, snāna-arcā,* and *śayana-arcā,* etc.

In case of the human image of Vāsudeva in the sanctum, the **Pādma Saṃhitā** enumerates his ancillary divinities as represented around him with specific features. They are enjoined to be shown in standing postures:

स्थानके स्थानकाः प्रोक्ता आसीनेऽपि तथा भवेत् ॥
चतुर्भुजा तु कर्मार्चा द्विभुजा वापि सा भवेत् ।
उत्सवार्चाप्रतिकृतिः सर्वा चैव चतुर्भुजा ॥
मानुष्यं वासुदेवस्य प्रोक्तं संक्षेपतो विधिः ।

PSam kp XVI.65cd–67ab

For the standing idol, the ancillary icons are the standing ones; for the seated also they are likewise. The ritual image is four-armed, or can also be two-armed. However, all the festive images are to be four-armed. This procedural system is briefly stated in case of the human Vāsudeva.

A ritual identity of the deity's →*mantra* having essentially a 'body' of six parts is stated to be brought about with the concrete frame of the image:

अर्चायां देहविन्यासं मन्त्रस्य विदधीत च ।

ViśSam X.107

One should make an implacement of the (six fold) body of the *mantra* into the limbs of the image.

For having the deity-concept of the Lord to descend and take its stay in the image-body a detailed procedure of sanctificatory rites and transforming preliminaries was undertaken. To have a glimpse of such details, we may cite here the following:

अर्चागतस्यापि विभोरेकसंधानकारणात् ।
घृतेन दध्ना पयसा मधुना च क्रमाद् द्विज ॥
अङ्घ्रिनाभीश्च हृदयं स्पृष्ट्वा मूर्धानमेव च ।
अनिरुद्धादिभिर्मन्त्रैर्हुत्वान्ते प्रोक्षयेत् क्रमात् ॥

ViśSam XIV.126–127

Owing to the condition that the Lord's identity gets merged with the material image as one, O wise, the same should be anointed, after due worship of the fire-oblations with the *mantras* of

'Aniruddha' and so on, having touched in sequence the feet, the navel, the heart and the head, by ghee, yogurt, milk and honey, respectively.

The Pāñcarātra devotees are strictly prohibited to keep away from such places and peoples who have no set-up of Vaiṣṇava service:

विष्ण्वर्चारहिते ग्रामे विष्ण्वर्चारहिते गृहे ।
न कुर्यादन्नपानादि न तत्र दिवसं वसेत् ॥

BhārSam IV.28

One should not accept food, drink, etc. in a village devoid of the images of Viṣṇu, neither even in a house having no Vaiṣṇava images, nor he should stay there even for a day.

However, it is advised that one should not take image-worship as one's profession:

न च मन्त्रोपजीवी स्यान्न चाप्यर्चोपजीविकः ।

BhārSam IV.29

A (Pāñcaratra) follower should not earn his livelihood from *mantra* practices nor should he take to image-worship as his profession.

In the Kāvya literature, the concept of *arcanā* and the image worship would be found to have numerous occurrences. We may give here only a few instances.

Worship of deities without Vedic →*mantras* is thus mentioned:

कामं दैवतमित्येव युक्तं नमयितुं शिरः ।
वार्षलस्तु प्रणामः स्याद् अमन्त्रार्चितदैवतः ॥

PraNāṭ III.6

I allow that it is proper to bend the head just thinking these to be (the statues of) deities; but my salutation will be in the manner of a Vṛṣala (*śūdra*) wherein a deity is worshipped without (the accompaniment of) *mantras*. (Tr. M.R. Kale)

Kālidāsa uses several expressions for the worshipful activities:

अनर्घ्यमर्घ्येण तमद्रिनाथः स्वर्गौकसामर्चितमर्चयित्वा ।
आराधनायास्य सखीसमेतां समादिदेश प्रयतां तनूजाम् ॥

Kum I.58

The mountain-lord, having worshipped, with the customary offerings, him who was of inestimable worth and was adored by the gods (lit., denizens of heaven), directed his daughter of restrained soul, together with her two female friends to wait upon (or to propitiate) him. (Tr. M.R. Kale)

यथाविधिहुताग्नीनां यथाकामार्चितार्थिनाम् ।

Ragh I.6ab

Who offered oblations in the sacrificial fire according to the rules ordaining them, who honoured those desiring any thing from them by granting all that they desired. (Tr. C. Sivaramamurti)

The worship of god Cupid with flowers is indicated elsewhere:

मधुकरिका – सहि । अवलम्ब मं जाव अग्गपादट्ठिआ भविअ चूदकलिअं गेण्हिअ कामदेवाच्चणं करेमि ।

[सखि । अवलम्बस्व मां यावदग्रपादस्थिता भूत्वा चूतकलिकां गृहीत्वा कामदेवार्चनं करोमि ।]

परभृतिका – जइ मम वि क्खु अद्धं अच्चणफलस्स ।

[यदि ममापि खलु अर्द्धमर्चनफलस्य ।]

AbhŚāk VI.2 (prose)

Madhu. – Friend, support me, while, standing on tip-toe I pluck a mango blossom and worship the God of Love.

Para. – (I will), if half the merit of the worship be mine. (Tr. M.R. Kale)

Even in the animal stories of the **Pañcatantra** we hear of divine worship:

यावदहं नदीं गत्वा स्नानं देवार्चनाविधिं कृत्वा गच्छामि, तावत्त्वयात्राप्रमत्तेन भाव्यम् ।

Pañc I, Kathā 16 (p. 77)

[The lion said,] "Till I go to the river, take a bath and return back after doing rites of worship to the god, you should without being negligent remain here".

The worship of Jina images by pious devotees has been described by poet Jaṭānandī at several occasions:

नन्दीश्वरेऽर्हत्प्रतिमार्चनाय समुद्यमन्ते प्रतिवर्षमिन्द्राः ।
कथं न कुर्याम वयं जिनार्चां संसारपाशच्छिदुरप्रभावाम् ॥

VaCa XXII.37

Every year in the Nandīśvara Dvīpa, the Indras arrange with great eclat for the worship of the Jina's image. Why should not we, therefore, perform the worship of Jina here, which has the effect of destroying worldly bondage.

General worship of gods is thus indicated in Bāṇa's **Harṣacarita**:

विश्रान्ता च नातिचिराद् उत्थाय सावित्र्या सार्धमुच्चितार्चनकुसुमा सस्नौ ।

Haca I, p. 8

Then after resting she soon arose, and having with Sāvitrī gathered flowers for worship, bathed. (Tr. E.B. Cowell and F.W. Thomas)

The poet Daṇḍin has included in his prose-romance **Avantīsundarī Kathā** an instance of a master-sculptor who had renovated one of the hands of a Śeṣaśāyī image built in a stone temple on the sea-shore of Mahāmallapuram:

पारावारशीकरसलिलबिन्दुभिरवहितेन चक्षुषान्ततस्तदर्चाशरीरमभिनिरूप्य क्वचिदप्यनधिगतघटनाप्रस्थानभेदस्तमेव स्थपतिमालोक्य 'अपचयितस्य पुस्तकर्मणः काष्ठेयम्, अत्र तु कस्त्वया प्रतिसंहितकर' इत्यभाषत ।

AvK p. 15

Having inspected the body of the image quite closely with his eyes, made intensely attentive by the drops of water coming from the sea sprays, and finding nowhere any secret departure in the execution of the image, he looked at the sculptor-architect (*sthapati*) and thus said, 'This is the acme of a coraplast's work of repairing a deficiency (in sculpture). Which one of the hands have you repaired here (i.e. in this image)?'

Likewise, Bhavabhūti's lines may be quoted here as follows:

अपि प्रभोर्वः कुशलं तस्य यस्यार्चत्यसौ शासनम् ।
मूर्ध्ना स्खलत्किरीटेन शासनं पाकशासनः ॥

MaCa I.29

Does your lord do well whose orders are obeyed by Indra with his crown slipping from his bowed head?

कण्डूलद्विपगण्डपिण्डकषणोत्कम्पेन संपातिभि-
र्धर्मस्रंसितबन्धनैः स्वकुसुमैरर्चन्ति गोदावरीम् ।

UttCa II.9ab

[The trees on the banks having nests of birds on them are] honouring the Godāvarī with their flowers having their stems loosened by the heat and dropping down on account of the violent shaking caused by the elephants rubbing their itching temples against them. (Tr. M.R. Kale)

A charming analogy has been thus drawn by royal poet Bhoja:

जग्राह जनकात्सीतां तातादेशेन राघवः ।
आम्नायशासनेनार्चां यजमानादिवानलः ॥

CaRām I.108

From her father Janaka, the Raghu-scion Rāma took away Sītā (in marriage) just as the fire accepts worship (*arcā*) offered by a sacrificer with due traditional rites.

There are many a beautiful poetic description of divine worship occurring in the **Naiṣadhīyacarita** of Śrīharṣa:

अर्चयन्हरकरं स्मितभाजा नागकेसरतरोः प्रसवेन ।
सोऽयमापयदतिर्यगवाग्दिक्पालपाण्डुरकपाल विभूषाम् ॥

NaiCa XXI.35 (also cf. XI.4, XIII.48, XVI.29, XVIII.86)

Worshipping Śiva's hand with a smiling Nāgakesara flower, he seemed to decorate it with the white skull of Brahmā, the ruler of the region which exists neither sideways nor below (i.e. the upper regions). (Tr. K.K. Handiqui)

In early epigraphs, the word *arcā* is of rare occurrence (the terms *pratimā* and *mūrti* being popular). The Mora (Mathura) stone-inscription of the time of Śaka ruler Śodāsa (early 1st cent. A.D.) thus records the dedication of the stone-images:

भगवतां वृष्णीणां पंचवीराणां प्रतिमाः शैलदेवगृहे .... । (line - 2)
अर्चादिशां शैलां [read: अर्चास्तेषां शैलाः] पंच ज्वलत इव परम-वपुषा । (line - 5)

In the lithic temple, (five) images of the five worshipful heroes of the Vṛṣṇis [the clan-name of Kṛṣṇa's families] .....

Their stone images (representing them) like the five flaming ones with superb bodily form .... (?)

Manifestation in the Arts

Varāha mihira is one of the earliest writers summarising the iconographic and ritual rules on the making and installation of deity-images. He has devoted several chapters of his **Bṛhat Saṃhitā** to these topics coming under the purview of ancient Indian astronomical tradition. The terms →*pratimā*, →*mūrti*, *arcā*, etc. are used by him as popular synonyms. However, *arcā* denoting a deity's image occurs in such of the following passages:

अनिमित्तभङ्गचलनस्वेदाश्रुनिपातजल्पनाद्यानि ।
लिङ्गार्चायतनानां नाशाय नरेशदेशानाम् ॥

BṛSam XLVI.8

If there occur without reasons any cracks, displacement, sweating, weeping, talking, etc. in the divine symbols (*liṅga*), images (*arcā*) or shrines, such (happenings) are the cause of destruction of rulers and people.

अर्चार्थममुकस्य त्वं देवस्य परिकल्पितः ।
नमस्ते वृक्ष पूजेयं विधिवत् सम्प्रगृह्यताम् ॥

BṛSam LIX.10

O tree! You have been selected (by us for providing the wood) for the image of that certain deity. Please accept this worship offered (by us) to you with due procedures.

The above formula forms part of the ritual of selecting and felling a tree in the forest for the purpose of obtaining wood for an image. Likewise, a detailed procedure is given of sacred ceremonies undertaken while installing the image in a shrine and properly invoking the specific deity as to come to stay into that image as its permanent spirit within direct reach of common devotees (cf. ch. LIX).

In the opinion of an old authority, viz. sage Kāśyapa, we are told that different mediums of art manufacture employed in making deity-figures were believed to give distinct religious fulfilment:

यार्चा मृद्दारुसम्भूता सायुःश्रीबलदा मता ।
सौवर्णी पुष्टिदा ज्ञेया रत्नजा हितकारिणी ॥
राजती कीर्तिदा ज्ञेया ताम्रजा जनवर्धनी ।
महत् करोति भूलाभं यार्चा पाषाणनिर्मिता ॥

(Cited by commentator Utpala on
BṛSam LIX.4–5)

The image which is made of clay or wood is enjoined to bestow life, dignity and power. The golden one is known to give nourishment; the jewel-made icon causes welfare. The silver one is known to give fame; the copper icon is for the increase of people. The image that is made of stone induces great acquisition of lands.

However, the **Matsya Purāṇa** gives a general list of the following kinds of images fit for worship:

सौवर्णी राजती वापि ताम्री रत्नमयी तथा ।
शैली दारुमयी चापि लोहसंघमयी तथा ॥
रीतिकाधातुयुक्ता वा ताम्रकांस्यमयी तथा ।
शुभदारुमयी वापि देवतार्चा प्रशस्यते ॥

MatPur CCLVIII.20–21

The image of a deity is laudable as made (of different substances recommended), viz. the one in gold, or silver, or in copper, or in jewel, in stone, wood or in an alloy of several metals, such as the brass, or the bronze or also of an auspicious kind of wood.

According to the **Pratiṣṭhālakṣaṇa-sāra-samuccaya** of Vairocana, a medieval compendium on the features of Saivite consecration the *arcā* (images) are classified into seven general categories with respect to their iconographic specification and the iconometric representation:

सालंकारास्त्रिधा भूता वेताला: स्थूलवामना: ।
पंगुरूपाश्च कूष्माण्डा: सप्तधार्चाश्च वर्तयेत् ॥

PLSSamu V.10

The *arcā*s of sevenfold division are to be made, namely [1–3] three types of standard vogue having ornaments [this refers to the *aṣṭatāla, navatāla* and *daśatāla* types, as indicated further in the text and described with minute details]; [4] Bhūtas and Vetālas; [5] Sthūlas, huge-size attendants, and Vāmanas, dwarfs; [6] squat-footed shapes; and [7] the Kūṣmāṇḍas (i.e. Kumbhāṇḍās), ithyphallic gnomes.

These types of figures are thus explained later:

तालैकादशभिर्कुयात् भूतवेतालरक्षसाम् ।
द्वे द्वे चैवांगुले देये वक्त्रादिषु यथाक्रमम् ॥
किंकरा: स्थूलरूपाश्च सप्ततालोच्छ्रया मता: ।
वामन: पञ्चतालश्च भूतांशै: पङ्गुकुब्जकौ ॥
कूष्माण्डकश्चतुस्तालैरुन्मानेन प्रकल्पयेत् ।
बुद्ध्वा बुद्ध्वा तु यत्नेन सूक्ष्मदृष्ट्या विचक्षण: ॥
पोषणं हरणं कुर्यात्सर्वस्मिन्नेव रूपके ।
अथैतन्मानत: कार्या: सर्वावयवभूषिता: ॥

PLSSamu V.66–69

Figures of Bhūtas, Vetālas and Rakṣases should be made with the measure of eleven *tāla*s, in their face and other limbs two *aṅgula*s each are to be increased (over the proportions enjoined in case of the *daśatāla* division). Kiṅkaras (attendants) of the voluminous bodily form are known to be seven *tāla*s in height. Vāmana is a form of five *tāla*s; both squat-footed and dwarf figures are made by five *tāla*s. The Kūṣmāṇḍa gnomes are carved in their height with the standard of four *tāla*s. The expert artisan should induce an increase or a decrease in proportions of measurement with regard to such of these model forms having thought of them in fine perspective again and again with proper care. Thus, they are to be made in this (proportionate) measurement as ornamented with all the limbs.

An image is termed as *vyaktārcā*, fully 'manifested image', as compared to the symbol representations which show fully aniconic type or with partial figure of deity on it (e.g. *mukha-liṅgas*). The complex iconometric procedure normally followed in making divine statues has been so aptly summarised by Vairocana in his excellent treatise on Śaivite images (cf. PLSSamu V.11–17).

For a household shrine the image height is prescribed not to exceed the proportionate limit of one hand-unit when this latter is said to be technically consisting of twentyfour-*mātrā*-digits, i.e. arrived at from the breadth of patron's middle finger-joint:

मात्राङ्गुलिवशेनैव गृहार्चामानकल्पनम् ।
नाधिकं हस्तमानाच्च न न्यूनं द्वादशाङ्गुलात् ॥

PSam XXXII.28

The dimension (i.e. height) for an image to be worshipped in the house (*gṛha-arcā*) should be devised as per the *mātrā-aṅgula* measure. It is not to be more than one *hasta* (i.e. 24 *aṅgulas*) and also not less than twelve *aṅgulas.*

The **Aparājita Pṛcchā** of Bhuvanadeva, an outstanding treatise of Indian Śilpaśāstra, extant in more or less its fuller form, has to comprehensively observe on the subject of relative size of a cult-image (*arcā*) with reference to the dimensions of its temple:

प्रासादमानोद्भवार्चा प्रमाणैस्त्रिविधोदिता ।
सीमा-गर्भ-द्वारमानं तुर्यो हस्ताङ्गुलैर्विधिः ॥
आदौ सीमा पुनर्गर्भं द्वारमानं तृतीयकम् ।
हस्ताङ्गुलक्रमोक्तं च आर्चामानं चतुर्थकम् ॥

AparPṛ CCIX.1–2

The image originating from the dimensions of the temple is stated to be of three kinds with respect to its sizes. The technical procedure (involves) either the measure of its *sīmā* [i.e. boundary], or its *garbha* or its doorway; the fourth one is with respect to the hand and *aṅgula* units. First consideration is in relation to the 'boundary measure' of the temple; next is with regard to the sanctum sanctorum (*garbhgṛha*); the third is in relation to the doorway height (*dvāra-māna*); and the fourth is said to be in consideration with the height of the temple, i.e. (the choice for the image height being) as many *aṅgula*-digits as is the (temple height measured in) *hasta*-units.

The fuller system for arriving at these four alternatives of the image-height is given further in the same text (cf. verses 3–20).

The convention of installing an extra large image under open sky is hinted at as follows:

दशहस्तादितो याऽर्चा प्रासादेन विनाऽर्चयेत् ॥

Rūp I.8cd

The image which is (in height) beyond the ten *hasta* units should be worshipped without installing it in a temple.

Certain restrictions regarding worship of deities in one's household set-up are thus summarised by Maṇḍana:

गृहे लिङ्गद्वयं नार्च्यं गणेशत्रयमेव च ।
शक्तित्रयं तथा शङ्खं मत्स्यादिदशकाङ्कितम् ॥
द्वे चक्रे द्वारिकायास्तु शालिग्रामद्वयं तथा ।
द्वौ शङ्खौ नार्चयेत् तद्वत्सूर्ययुग्मं तथैव च ॥
तेषां तु पूजनान्नूनमुद्वेगं प्राप्नुयाद् गृही ।
तुलस्या नार्चयेच्चण्डीं दीपं सूर्यं गणेश्वरम् ॥

Rūp II.2–4

In the house, two Śiva-liṅgas are not be worshipped; and likewise, three images of lord Gaṇeśa, nor three Śakti representations; neither a conch-shell incised with the Fish and other ten incarnations of Viṣṇu; nor two *cakra*-stones of Dvārikā; neither a pair of Śālagrāma stones; nor two conch-shells are to be worshipped, neither, likewise a pair of two Sūryas. By their (simultaneous) worship the householder gets disturbance. One should not worship the goddess Caṇḍī, with basil leaves and also not the Sun-god and Gaṇeśa (be worshipped) with lamps.

As regards the proportionate measurements fixed by the architectural tradition as per the ratio of dimensions between that of the image and its shrine, the Śilpaśāstra tradition has thus observed:

> अर्चालिङ्गोद्भवं मानं वेश्मांशे त्वपराजित ।
> न्यूनाधिको न कर्तव्यः प्रासादः सूत्रतः क्रमात् ॥
> वेश्म न्यूनाधिकं शस्तं स्वभुबाणे च रत्नजे ।
> घटितेषु विधिः ख्यातो ह्यर्चालिङ्गेषु तत्वतः ॥
>
> ApaṛPr CCII.15–16
>
> O Aparājita, the measurement is to be arrived at with reference to the image or *liṅga* in case of its shrine (to be set up). The shrine should not be made more or less with reference to that sequence of dimensions (arrived at) in accordance of the measuring rules (*sūtrataḥ*). The shrine dimensions even less or more are laudable in case of a *liṅga*, of the Svabhu or Bāṇa type, and also of a jewel one. However, the procedural rules are described (to be followed) as per its true principle (*tattvataḥ*).

The Śilpa treatises also give the rules of orientation for the image in the shrine (cf. AparPṛ CVIII.4, 25).

Referring to the images set up for household worship (*gṛha-arcā*) in a personal shrine of the devotee the **Bhārgava Tantra** has thus enjoined:

> गृहार्चा-स्थापने सर्वं प्रतिष्ठाकर्म पूर्ववत् ।
> गृहवंशर्द्धिकृद्देवः सदनस्थापितो हरिः ॥
> मंदिरे स्थापितो देवः पालयेद्भुवनत्रयम् ।
>
> BhāT XV.41
>
> With respect to the consecration of an *arcā* in one's house, all ritual performances as described earlier (in the case of a temple) are prescribed. The Lord Hari as installed in one's residence bestows prosperity on the house and family. However, the god set up in a temple protects the three worlds.

In Vāstu treatises the ritual installation for an image has been also specified as follows:

> रत्नन्यासं ततः कुर्याल्लिङ्गार्चायां विचक्षणः ।
> धात्वौषधीश्च रत्नानि धान्यान्यष्ट तथैव च ॥
>
> AparPṛ CXLVIII.28
>
> Next, the expert should make the deposit of jewels (*ratna-nyāsa*) in (case of the installation of) a *liṅga* or an image (*arcā*). And also

are (deposited thus) the eight *dhātus* (minerals or metals), herbs, jewels and grains.

For the temple cult, as evolved in the Vaiṣṇava tradition, there are found several ancillary *arcā*-images prescribed for various ritualistic occasions and performances. Thus we have it ordained from the viewpoint of image-making in a Pāñcarātra Saṃhitā (cf. VisSam XXII.36–39, 41–45).

The ritual treatises have generally used the terms *arcā, bimba, mūrti, bera, vigraha,* etc. as synonyms (VisSam XXII.36–39, 41–45). Likewise, another Pāñcarātra Saṃhitā observes:

नवतालप्रमाणेन देवीकर्मार्चनादिकम् ।
षट्कौतुकसमोपेतं बहुबेरमुदाहृतम् ॥
एकबेरं तथा प्रोक्तं शिलार्चेति द्वयं विना ।
कर्मार्चा स्नपनं चैव स्थापने कर्मकौतुकम् ॥
आत्मार्थं च परार्थं च द्विविधं स्थापनं भवेत् ।
गृहेषु स्थापितं पूर्वमालये चापरं भवेत् ॥
आत्मार्थं गृहरक्षा स्यादालयं ग्रामरक्षकम् ।
मुख्यस्थाने स्थितो देवो राजराष्ट्रस्य रक्षकः ॥
अन्योन्यसङ्गतौ स्यात् तु राष्ट्रक्षोभो यथारुचि ।
कर्मार्चा चोत्सवार्चा च बल्यर्चा च तथैव च ॥
स्नानतीर्थोभयार्चा च स्वापोत्थानार्चया सह ।
प्रतिमा षड्विधा प्रोक्ता उत्तमा समुदाहृता ॥

AniSam XII.14–19

That is called the *bahubera* ('having many idols') set-up which has the images (*arcanā*) of the goddess and (of the god meant) for ritual usage, made in the nine *tāla* measurement of height, thus (the set of images) consisting of six ceremonial images (*kautuka*). That mode is called of the *ekabera* ('one image') kind which has a single image, made in stone, but without the two (above-mentioned) image types.

And in the installation service, bathing and other ceremonial rites are done on the 'ritual image' (*karma+arcā*).

There can be two installation modes, one for the self and the other, on behalf of others. The former is meant for household images and the latter for temple images. The one for the self saves the household, while the other for the temple protects (whole community in) the village. The god installed at a principal centre is in fact the saviour of kingdom and people.

If both the procedural conventions are arbitrarily mixed up, there would be turmoil in the state.

The set of six images is mentioned and praised to be the best, comprising *karma-arcā* (ritual image), *utsava-* (festivity-image), and likewise *bali-* (offering image), *snāna-* (bathing-image), *tīrtha-* (procession-image), along with *svāpa-* (sleeping image), and *utthāna-* (rising images).

About the relative measurement of a →*pīṭha*, dais or pedestal into which the deity image is affixed, the general rule prescribed in another Pāñcarātra text reads as follows:

अर्चायामं त्रिधा कृत्वा पीठमेकेन कल्पयेत् ॥
उपानहादिपञ्चांगयुक्तं वृत्तं सुखावहम् ।
अथवा चतुरस्रं वा विस्तारतुलितायति ॥

BhāT IV.111–112

Having divided the height of the image into three parts, the pedestal should be made of one part, in shape being round and pleasant as decorated with five mouldings, namely *upāna*, regulating course, etc. (other four beings *jagatī*, plinth moulding; *kumuda*, lotus; *kampa*, fillet; and *vājana*, string-course moulding).

Or, it can be oblong (*caturasra*, lit., four-cornered), or of square shape having the width as equal to its length.

Summarising the iconographic injunctions as regards the decorative elements to be carved in the background frame (*arcā-parikara*) of the seated or standing images, i.e. the minor details of carving in the setting of the deity-figure against its image-slab representation in high relief, the **Aparājita Pṛcchā** has emphasised the following points:

आसनस्था तथैवार्चा शयनस्था विशेषतः ।
तासामनुक्रमं युक्तिं वक्ष्ये परिकरादिकम् ॥
पूर्वमानान्विताः कुर्यादर्चा वै सर्वशोभनाः ।

AparPṛ CCXVI.1–2ab

The image is either (shown as) seated, and likewise in lying posture specifically, (as well as in standing attitude). I shall speak about the combination of their framing, etc. (to be made) in proper arrangement. The images should be made as having standard proportions of measurement (*māna*), detailed earlier, so that they are truly attractive in all manners.

For a *mukhaliṅga* the same text uses quite significantly the word '*liṅga-arcā*', i.e. phallic symbol with partial manifestation. As it enjoins:

लिङ्गार्चा पृथुमानं तद्विभक्तं द्वादशाङ्गुलम् ।
चतुर्विंशतिकोच्छ्राये वक्त्रं वै द्वादशाङ्गुलम् ॥
ललाटं द्व्यङ्गुलं प्रोक्तं भ्रूनेत्रं द्व्यङ्गुलं तथा ।
नासिका द्व्यङ्गुला प्रोक्ताऽधरौ चैककाङ्गुलौ ॥
शङ्खाकृतिः कण्ठरेखा हनुकाद्व्यङ्गुलायता ।
वेदाङ्गुलं पृथुवक्रं द्व्यङ्गुला नासिकापुटिः ॥
द्व्यङ्गुलायतकं नेत्रं तन्मानं नेत्रकान्तरम् ।
चापाकारा च दृष्टिः स्यात् भ्रूलता चाङ्गुलायता ॥
द्वादशाङ्गुलविस्तारे कर्णाविकैककाङ्गुलौ ।
भ्रूसमोत्सेधकौ चैव उभौ कर्णौ समानतः ॥
जटामुकुटसंयुक्तं शशाङ्ककृतशेखरम् ।
शिवाननं कुण्डलादि-दिव्याभरणभूषितम् ॥

Apar Pṛ CCIV.9–14

The width-measure of a Liṅgārcā [i.e, *liṅga* with partial *arcā* emanation on it, one-faced Śivaliṅga] is divided into (its own) twelve digits. When the height (of this portion, which is 1/3 of the total *liṅga* height) is of twentyfour relative digits, the face is twelve digits. Thus there should be as stated, the forehead two digits, the (height of) eye-brows two digits and the nose two digits; one digit each are the two lips. The shape of the temporal bone, the throat line, and the chin are each two digits in height. The mouth is four digits wide and the nostrils two digits. The eyes are in extent two digits and the same is the interval between the two eyes. The gaze is of bow-shape, while the extent of the eye-brows one digit. In case of the total width being twelve digits two ears are one digit each, while they are equal in height with that of the eye-brows. The Śiva's face is marked by a crown of matted locks, has the digit of moon on it and decked with celestial ornaments such as the ear-rings, etc.

According to the conventions of Śilpa, there is further a kind of twofold classification of the cult-images:

मूर्तयः द्विविधा ज्ञेया अर्चा मण्डना एव च ।
अर्चा पूजनकर्मार्थं मण्डना पार्श्वदेवता ॥

ŚiRaKo 451

Images are known to be of two kinds, viz. (1) *arcā* and (2) *maṇḍanā*. The *arcā* image is for cult purposes while the *maṇḍanā* implies figures of attendant divinities (being simply decorative elements).

Conclusion

Arcā and *arcanā*, two allied terms derived from root *arc-* as conveying the idea of 'worship', 'honour', or respect, are well explained from their frequent usages in the Vedic, Epic and Puranic texts. Successively, the term *arcā* came also to denote an object of worship, an image, signifying in itself the very notion of worshipfulness as well as the divine aspect paid devotional service. As regards the *arcā* doctrine, says the **Viṣṇudharmottara Purāṇa**:

अर्चागतविशेषेण पूजयन्ति विधानतः ।
चित्रसूत्रविधानेन देवतार्चां विनिर्मिताम् ॥
सुरूपां पूजयेद् विद्वांस्तत्र सन्निहिता भवेत् ।

VDhPur III.1.7

With proper rituals men worship (the gods) as staying specifically in the images (*arcāgata*). Thus, the learned should worship the divine image, well-shaped and made in accordance with the Citrasūtra manual, so that the deity assumes the identity with it.

From the common Buddhist standpoint, the **Divyāvadāna** states that the likeness of the gods are worshipped as the gods designate. In view of the evolved notion of *arcanā*, Śaṅkarācārya has aptly observed, "By the expression 'worshipping' both kinds of procedural worship is indicated. By 'meditating', 'praying', and 'paying homage' are indicated, respectively the mental, the vocal and the physical modes of worship."

Even *arcā* is seen by a Vaikhānasa text as a form of the Lord's assumed presence at two levels of the votaries experience: *amūrta* and *samūrta*. Elaborate rituals and systematised practices came to evolve around image-worship in the sectarian treatises. Likewise, a specialised branch of Śilpa knowledge, found incorporated in the Purāṇas, Śilpa-Śāstra manuals, Pratiṣṭhā ('installation') treatises as well as Tantra-Āgama works, appertains to certain iconoplastic and iconometric aspects, ritual and cultic specifications for the deity images and their worship.

Prithvi Kumar Agrawala

Select Bibliography

Agrawala, V.S.: Studies in Indian Art, Varanasi: Vishwavidyalaya Prakashan, 1987.

Alper, Harvey P.: Understanding Mantras, Delhi: Motilal Banarsidass, 1991.

Banerjea, J.N.: Development of Hindu Iconography, Calcutta: University of Calcutta, 1956.

Kane, P.V.: History of Dharmaśāstra Vol. – III, Poona: Bhandarkar Oriental Research Institute, 1946.

Schrader, F. Otto: Introduction to the Pāñcarātra and the Ahirbudhnya Saṃhitā, Madras, 1916.

MŪRTI

Overview

The term *mūrti* (f.), denoting formal aspect of a concept, or a formed entity, image, icon, is one of the most significant ideas of Indian philosophy, cultural thought and Sastric symbology, art and architecture. Basically it implies the sense of stupefying or congealing, and later on the concept of solidifying as an embodiment or imaged representation.

In the Vedas, *mūrti* symbolised earthly or formed aspect as opposed to the formless (*amūrta*) or abstract vision. According to the Vedic exegesis, the form or *mūrti* is said to typify the principle of individuation. In ancient astronomy, thus time is of two kinds: *mūrta,* tangible and *amūrta,* intangible. In view of Sāṃkhya, an effect is defined as the assuming of a gross limited form by the subtle. The Nyāya thought employs the concept of *mūrti* to explain the successive evolution of distinctive qualities in a body. In the Jaina doctrine, →*jīva* is said to be on the empirical level to assume form through karmic bondage. By the phrase *mūrtimat,* the *pudgala* aspect of matter is implied while the rest is known as *amūrta.*

On the concrete level of art creations and worship, *mūrti* is a formed portrayal of the deity, its image or the very body wherein the abstract divinity assumes its identity, representation or temporal stay. In fact, this practical aspect of *mūrti* forms the central theme of the Epics, Dharmaśāstras, Purāṇas, Tantras, Āgamas, Kāvyas as well as the Śilpa-Śāstras.

In the Purāṇas, the Supreme Divine Entity is said to manifest as well as permeate the Universe. The formless lord is visualised for the devout into multiple aspects of *mūrtis*. A detailed list of *mūrtis*, their symbolical and iconographic definitions, mantric forms, creeds and rituals of worship, etc. occur in the Tantra-Āgama literature that is also found treated in the Purāṇas from an eclectic standpoint. In the Śilpa Śāstras and Vāstu-Śāstras as well as in the numberless variety of divine portrayals, *mūrti* is handled in specific details, laying emphasis on their iconological and iconographic, iconometric and technical contents, classification and specification.

Etymology and Related Words

The term *mūrti* derived from the root *mūrcch-*, imbibes the basic idea of "congealed", "solidified", "embodied", "shaped" 'image', also its concretised representation as an icon or symbol, specifically of a divinity. It is one of the oldest terms occurring for denoting form, image, and allied notions; *mūrta-* of connected etymology, also conveys the identical or similar notions and is, however, an adjectival phrase which changes according to the qualified principle.

According to the **Amara Kośa** the term *mūrti* is used to denote hardness and a body (or embodiment): *mūrtiḥ kāṭhinyakāyayoḥ* (AmKo III.3.66cd).

As Kṣīrasvāmin's gloss explains, it is derived from the root *murch-*, *mūrcchanaṃ mūrcchati ca mūrtiḥ*, i.e. the act of becoming dumb, and the one coagulated. According to Pāṇini, *mūrchā mohasamucchrāyayoḥ* (PāDhā, *bhvādi* 212), "the root *mūrchā* is meant in case of delusion and elevation"; the first meaning referring to the concept of stupefying, congealing, becoming dumb or shaped. When "in case of feminine the suffix *kti* is added" (Pā III.3.94) to this root, the word *mūrti* is derived (as per rule *rāllopaḥ*, Pā VI.4.21, *ca* is dropped). Elsewhere Pāṇini himself has used the word in the sense of 'solidifying' *mūrtau ghanaḥ* (Pā III.3.77).

The same is reflected in:

द्रवमूर्तिस्पर्शयोः श्यः ॥

Pā VI.1.24

Samprasāraṇa (vocalization) of the semi-vowel of the verbal stem *śyai-* (= *śyā*) 'to go' takes place to denote coagulation (*drava-mūrti*) or touch (*sparśayoḥ*). (Based on the tr. by S.M. Katre)

The **Amara Kośa** reads:

मूर्च्छाले मूर्तमूर्च्छितौ ॥

AmKo II.6.61d

In the sense of 'fainted' occur 'insensible' and 'stupefied'.

Elsewhere, the same lexicon gives twelve words for a body and a bodily limb, including the term *mūrti*, with such others as: *kāya, deha, tanu, gātra, vapu, saṃhanana, śarīra, varṣman, vigraha, aṅga, pratīka, avayava, apaghana* and *kalevara*. Or in the sense of 'hardened', 'aged', 'stiff' or 'stern' are given *mūrta* 'embodied' as well as *mūrtimat*, 'having a body or shape' (AmKo III.1.76).

The **Vaijayantī Kośa** explains the term in two senses of body (physical form) and image (imaged figure): *mūrtirdeha pratimayoḥ* (VaiKo VI.2.28cd).

Likewise, the great polymath Hemacandra opines:

मूर्तिः पुनः प्रतिमायां कायकाठिन्ययोरपि ।

AneSaṅg II.191

'*Mūrti* is again used in denotation of image, as well as body and hardness.'

In view of Jaina terminology, Dhanañjaya observes:

मूर्तिमत्सु पदार्थेषु संसारिण्यापि पुद्गलः ।

Anekārthanāmamālā 42

In case of embodied objects or substances as well as living beings the word *pudgala* 'matter' is used.

Layers of Meaning

The word *mūrti*, or *mūrta*, or its connected derivatives, do not occur in the **Ṛgveda**. However, it begins to occur with the other Saṃhitās and later Vedic texts quite frequently in diverse contexts of evolved ideas and connotations. The Paippalāda recension of the **Atharvaveda** (besides *mūrchām* in III.40.2) uses *mūrtam* as follows:

हृदयं परि वर्जयाक्ष्यौ कामेन शोचया ।
मूर्तं माम् अपश्यत वयम् (?) इत् त्वामग्निर् आ नयत् ॥

Av(p) XX.60.8

Burn the heart with passion having agitated the limbs. You have seen me as "stupefied" or "shaped" ... (?) ....

The root *mūrcha-* occurs in the **Maitrāyaṇī Saṃhitā** in the express sense of coagulating:

अथ श्वेताँ श्वेतवत्सां दुहन्ति, तत् स्वयं मूर्छति, स्वयं मथ्यते, स्वयं विलीनमाज्यं भवति ।

MaitSam II.6.6

They milch the white cow, who bears a white calf; that (milk) gets by itself coagulated; that (coagulated) gets churned by itself, and there appears by itself the butter saturated within.

स ईक्षत – इमे नु लोकाः । लोकपालान्नु सृजा इति । सोऽद्भ्य एव पुरुषं समुद्धृत्यामूर्च्छयत् ॥

AitUp I.1.3

He bethought himself: 'Here now are worlds. Let me now create world-guardians.' Right (*eva*) from the waters he drew forth and shaped (*mūrch*) a person. (Tr. R.E. Hume)

As noted by Yāska, the form symbolised an earthly aspect:

पृथिव्या मूर्तिः ।

Nir XIV.5

From the Earth is derived the (material, physical) form.

And a figure of human or animal entity is symbolically recognised from its head:

मूर्धा मूर्तमस्मिन्धीयते ।

Nir VII.27

The head is (so-called because) the body depends on it.
(Tr. L. Sarup)

Mūrti denoting image belongs to the second stage of Vedic ideologies on worship, offered to divinities, firstly conceived in the abstract medium of poetic words and visions, but now also on the concrete level of art creations showing an aniconic or figural representation, namely a formed portrayal of the deity, as a shape, an image, sketched on the earth, a hide or a cloth; or modelled in clay, paste or such other materials; or incised on a piece of brick, stone or sheet of metal; or carved in stone, cast in metal and so on. Hence, the word came to imply the 'congealed' or 'concretised' aspect of a thing, as a 'physical shape' and a shaped image.

Śaṅkarācārya has thus summarised the allied ideas conveyed by *mūrti*:

देहसंस्थानलक्षणा मूर्च्छिताङ्गावयवा मूर्तयः ....

BhGŚBh XIV.4

Mūrtis are those which are featured by a body and a designed frame, or own integrated concrete parts and limbs......

Mūrta and also phrase *mūrti-mat*, 'having a figure', 'incarnate', 'personified', evolved to convey the idea of an abstract symbol brought to the level of physical entity; it sometimes expressly denoted 'he' or 'she' of an animate or an inanimate object, or even a quality or a concept. It is this aspect of 'personalisation' which is clearly exposed by Śaunaka in his **Bṛhaddevatā**:

यज्ञस्य वो वैश्वदेवे प्रैत इत्युत्तरं तु यत् ।
तत्रार्बुदस्तु ग्रावाणं मूर्तिमन्तमिवार्चति ॥

BṛDev VII.146

'Of your sacrifice' (*yajñasya vaḥ-*, ṚV X.92.1a) are two addressed to the All-gods (92, 93): but in that which comes next, 'Forth these' (*praite-* X.94.1a), Arbuda adores the pressing-stone as if incarnate. (Tr. A.A. Macdonell)

As it occurs in the **Rāmāyaṇa**:

कन्दर्पो मूर्तिमानासीत् काम इत्युच्यते बुधैः ।

Rām I.23.10

There was Kandarpa himself (*mūrtimān,* incarnate), whom the learned call Kāma (Passion) by name.

Conveying this popular denotation, many allied compounds can be noticed; e.g. *mūrti-saṃsthita* in the great Epic:

चोदयामास वज्रं स दिव्यास्त्रं मूर्तिसंस्थितम् ।

MBh XII.31.27

Indra commanded his celestial weapon thunder, standing before him in embodied shape, ... (Tr. P.C. Roy)

Some significant layers of meaning that evolved around the *mūrti* are as follows:

(i) descending to the level of hardened shape,

(ii) manifestation as a form,

(iii) incarnation or personalisation,

(iv) image or icon fashioned in a material medium , and

(v) the concept of a deity and the deity-image.

Development of the Concept

In early Vedic Saṃhitās the word *mūrti* as well as the concept allied with it may not be clearly traced, but in later Vedic texts the term occurs in its definitive connotation of an object or even an abstract notion, viewed as a formed entity or shape. For example, the following Brāhmaṇa passage goes to define *mūrti* as the principle of individuation evolved from *ṛk* or *mantra* revelation:

ऋग्भ्यो जातां सर्वशो मूर्तिमाहुः ।
सर्वा गतिर्याजुषी हैव शश्वत् ॥
सर्वं तेजः सामरूप्यं ह शश्वत् ।
सर्वं हेदं ब्रह्मणा हैव सृष्टम् ॥

TBr III.12.9.1–2

That which is born wholly from the *ṛk* is called *mūrti* (form). All motion is truly ever derived from the *yajus.* All that is glory (*tejas*) is ever of the form of *sāman*. The entire Veda (knowledge) is verily created by Brahman.

As one of the leading authorities on Vedic exegesis has explained, "The form is spoken of in the Brāhmaṇas as *mūrti*. Thus we get two principles, viz. the power or motion in the centre typified as *yajus* and its becoming manifest as diametre, i.e. *ṛk*. *Yajus* is *gati* and *ṛk* is *mūrti* .... As soon as *ṛk* or form is created, the circumscribing principle of limitations is at once implied. This principle of circumscribing is the *maṇḍala* symbolised as *sāman*" (V.S. Agrawala, *Vedic Lectures*, 2nd edn, 1981, p. 20). The same idea is summarily repeated elsewhere:

ऋचा मूर्तिर्याजुषी गतिः साममयन्तेजः ।

GoBr I.2.9

Ṛcā is *mūrti*; that which is derived from the *yajus* is motion, and glory consists of *sāman*.

At the earliest, the arch-theory of twofold Brahman, Ultimate Reality, occurs in the **Bṛhadāraṇyaka Upaniṣad** which evinces a definite growth of metaphysical layers of meaning woven around the words *mūrta* and its abstract counterpart *amūrta*:

द्वे वाव ब्रह्मणो रूपे । मूर्तं चैवामूर्तं च । मर्त्यं चामृतं च । स्थितं च यच्च सच्च त्यं च ॥

BṛUp II.3.1

There are, assuredly, two forms of Brahman: the formed (*mūrta*) and the formless, the mortal and the immortal, the stationary and the moving, the actual (*sat*) and the yon (*tya*).
(Tr. R.E. Hume)

The formation of *mūrti*, a shaped form, got further related to the process of heating of the primordial waters (liquid substance) to shape 'it' into a defined figure as it were by a creator. However, the **Śatapatha Brāhmaṇa** makes significant use of the word *mūrta* together with its semantically associated root *pramūrccha*, i.e. *mūrccha-* with prefix *pra*, for conveying the notion of becoming grossly consistent, to gain shape with reference to a Vedic theory of cosmogony preaching the successive evolution of material forms from the abstract concept of mind:

नेव वा इदमग्रेऽसदासीत्, नेव सदासीत् । आसीदिव वा इदमग्रे नेवासीत् । तद्ध तन्मन एवास ॥ तदिदं मनः सृष्टमाविरबुभूषत् । निरुक्ततरं मूर्ततरं तदात्मानमन्वैच्छत् । तत्तपोऽतप्यत । तत्प्रामूर्च्छत् ।

ŚBr X.5.3.1,3

> Verily, in the beginning this (universe) was, as it were, neither non-existent nor existent; in the beginning this (universe), indeed, as it were, existed and did not exist: there was then only that Mind. This Mind, when created, wished to become manifest -- more defined, more substantial: it sought after a self (body). It practised austerity: it acquired consistency.

About the origin of 'form' from the heating principle operative upon the primeval waters, we have the following statement:

> सोऽपोऽभ्यतपत्ताभ्योऽभितप्ताभ्यो मूर्तिरजायत । या वै सा मूर्तिरजायतान्नं वै तत् ।
>
> AitĀr II.4.3
>
> He brooded over the water. From the waters brooded over form was born. The form that was born was indeed food.
> (Tr. A.B. Keith)

A creative process is said to have started from the dual principle of a male and a female uniting to produce a shape:

> स मिथुनमुत्पादयते रयिं च प्राणं चेति । ... आदित्यो ह वै प्राणो रयिरेव चन्द्रमाः ।
> रयिर्वा एतत्सर्वं यन्मूर्तं चामूर्तं च । तस्मान्मूर्तिरेव रयिः ॥
>
> PraUp I.4–5
>
> He produces a pair, matter (*rayi*, f.) and life (*prāṇa*, m.) .... The sun, verily, is life; matter, indeed, is the moon. Matter, verily, is everything here, both what is formed and what is formless. Therefore material form (*mūrti*) indeed is matter. (Tr. R.E. Hume)

Elsewhere, the word *mūrti* presents a notion of formal identity:

> वह्नेर्यथा योनिगतस्य मूर्तिर्न दृश्यते नैव च लिङ्गनाशः ।
> स भूय एवेन्धनयोनिगृह्यस्तद्वोभयं वै प्रणवेन देहे ॥
>
> ŚvUp I.13
>
> As the material form (*mūrti*) of fire when latent in its source (i.e. the fire-wood)
>
> Is not perceived – and yet there is no evanishment of its subtile form (*liṅga*) –
>
> But may be caught again by means of the drill in its source,
>
> So, verily, both (the universal and the individual Brahma) are (to be found) in the body by the use of *om*. (Tr. R.E. Hume)

As given in the following observation made on the Yoga concept of a meditative symbol:

तत्तारकं द्विविधं, मूर्तितारकम् अमूर्तितारकं चेति । यत् इन्द्रियान्तं तत् मूर्तिमत् । यत् भ्रूयुगातीतं तत् अमूर्तिमत् । सर्वत्र अन्तःपदार्थविवेचने मनोयुक्ताभ्यास इष्यते ... ।

AdvayatārakaUp I

That Tāraka (the Liberating principle conceived as a stellar spot between the eye-brows, a symbol for *oṃkāra* in Yoga practices) is of two kinds, viz. formed Tāraka and formless Tāraka. The formed one is that which is realised externally by sense-organs, as existing between the pair of eye-brows. The other one is the formless which is beyond the pair of eye-brows. However, in all such cases of deliberations aimed at internal objectives, a recourse to mind-harnessing practices is essentially intended.

According to the **Sūrya-Siddhānta** definition, the hymns, songs and liturgy are the three bodies of scripture known as the **Ṛgveda, Sāmaveda** and **Yajurveda**. The **Ṛgveda** is conceived of as the peripheral aspect of the solar disk while the **Yajurveda** represents this form itself:

प्रकाशात्मा तमोहन्ता महानित्येष विश्रुतः ।
ऋचोऽस्य मण्डलं सामान्युस्रामूर्त्तिर्यजूंषि च ॥

SūrSiddh XII.17

He (the sun) is extolled as natural illuminator, destroyer of darkness, great. The hymns (*ṛcas*) are his disk, the songs (*sāmāni*) his beams, the liturgy (*yajūṃṣi*) his form. (Tr. E. Burgess)

Relative time is said to be of two kinds: *mūrta*, tangible and *amūrta* intangible. According to the **Sūrya-Siddhānta** man's normal vital-breath (inspiration and expiration) duration is the unit of tangible time (SūrSiddh I.10–11ab).

In the different philosophical schools the term *mūrti* conveys various ideas. As has been the primary sense of the term *mūrti* commented upon by Śabara in the tradition of Vedic epistemology:

सांनाय्यविकारोऽपि दध्नो विकारः स्यात् पशुः, न पयसः । कुतः । मूर्तिसामान्यात् । घनत्वं मूर्तिः ।

MīmSūBh VIII.2.15

Even though the 'animal-offering' is a modified form of the curd-butter-offering, yet it should be treated as a modified form of the curds, not of the milk – why so? – because the shape is similar to it, the shape meant here, is solidity. (Tr. G.N. Jha)

In the Vedānta concepts, along with 'form' there is essentially a defining 'name':

संज्ञामूर्तिक्लृप्तिस्तु त्रिवृत्कुर्वत उपदेशात् ॥

BrSū II.4.20

But the fashioning of names and forms belongs to him who renders tripartite, on account of the teaching (of scripture).
(Tr. G. Thibaut)

On the evolution of diverse forms Śaṅkara makes the following comment:

कल्प्यमाने तावदुपचितापचितगुणत्व उपचितगुणानां मूर्त्युपचयादपरमाणुत्वप्रसंगः ।

BrSūŚBh II.2.16

For if we assume that some kinds of atoms have more numerous qualities, it follows that their solid size (*mūrti*) will be increased thereby, and that implies their being atoms no longer.
(Tr. G. Thibaut)

In Vedantic point of view, we find the great teacher Śaṅkara as explaining the two juxtaposed concepts of *mūrti* and *amūrti* in the following manner as taking a clue from the Vedic sources on one hand and seeing the same as being evolved, on the other, to the threshold of monistic dualism:

मूर्तिः घनरूपं धारणसमर्थं चराचरलक्षणम्, 'ताभ्योऽभितप्ताभ्यो मूर्तिरजायत' (ऐ. उ. IV.3) इति श्रुतेः। तद्रहित इति अमूर्तिः । अथवा देहसंस्थानलक्षणा मूर्च्छिताङ्गावयवा मूर्तिः; तद्रहित इति अमूर्तिः ॥

ViSahasrBh 102

Mūrti is the solidified or coagulated form which has the capacity of bearing (*dhāraṇa-samartham*), (and is thus) a characteristic trait of the mobile and the immobile. This is a citation from the *śruti* [AitUp IV.3.7]: 'From those (female principles, i.e. *āpaḥ*, waters) when agitated (or lit. heated), there ensued the Formed One (*mūrti*).' (Therefore) the principle devoid of that (formed one) is the formless (*a-mūrti*). Or the formed (*mūrti*) is (to be explained) as having limbs and minor limbs that are solidified, being characterised in the framework of a body (*deha-saṃsthāna*).

The initial meaning of 'hardness' as implied in the term *mūrti* is connected in the Yoga philosophy with the earthly body or material bindings:

मूर्तिर्भूमिः .... ।
पृथिवी मूर्त्या न निरुणद्धि योगिनः शरीरादिक्रियाम् .... ।

YSūBh III.44–45

For example the feature of earth is its natural hardness.

The inability of the earth, through its hardness, to arrest the functioning of the organs of the Yogin's body. (Tr. H. Aranya)

As the same is explained further:

मूर्तिः सांसिद्धिकं काठिन्यम् .... ।

TaVai on YSūBh III.44

The concept *mūrti* represents elemental hardness.

As contrasted to the material form, it is said:

तया अमूर्तस्यानावरणदर्शनाद् विभुत्वमपि प्रख्यातमाकाशस्य ।

YSūBh III.41

By that (observation), owing to the non-appearance of any delimiting principle (*āvaraṇa*, covering) — the all-pervasiveness of (formless) *ākāśa* (space) is well explained.

Thus, it is observed that the primal cause is above such defining principles.

मूर्तिव्यवधिजातिभेदाभावान् नास्ति मूलपृथक्त्वम् ।

Quoted in YSūBh III.53

Since there is no diversity in characteristics, shape and species in the primal cause, there is no distinction or perceptible heterogeneity therein. (Tr. H. Aranya)

Mūrti has been thus defined in the Sāṃkhya deliberations:

सूक्ष्माणां मूर्तिलाभः कार्यम् ।

YuDīp on SāṃKā 3

An effect (*kārya*) is nothing but the assuming of a *mūrti* (gross limited form) by the subtle entities (which are its causes).
(Tr. R.S. Bhattacharya)

मूर्तिमता अवयवेन (अवयवी) समानदेशः स्यात् ।

YuDīp on SāṃKā 9

Owing to its being as framed into limbs, he, the limbed one (*avayavin*) would exist here or there occupying the same space as occupied by the limbs.

The individual ego assumes smaller or bigger body :

स (अहंकारः) च मूर्तिप्रत्ययाभ्यां महतः स्थूलतरः ।

YuDīp on SāṃKā 24

It (i.e. the dynamic ego, *ahaṃkāra*)is more gross than the *mahat* (*buddhi*-principle, I-sense) on account of its delimiting formal attributes (*mūrti*) and awareness (*pratyaya*). (Tr. R.S. Bhattacharya)

It is amusing to find that the principle of *mūrti* has been thus substantiated from the Vedic myths :

श्रुतिरपि चास्य मूर्तिमाचष्टे कृत्तिवासाः ... ।

YuDīp on SāṃKā 15

The Vedas also speak of Its (God's) form or figure by using such words as 'one having skin garment' the hide of an animal as the cloth' (*kṛttivāsas*).

In the Nyāya philosophy, the term *mūrti* is significantly used to define the process of evolution:

यो गुणविशेषाणां स्पर्शान्तानां गुरूत्वघनत्वसंस्काराणामव्यापिनः परिमाणस्याश्रयो यथासम्भवं तद् द्रव्यं मूर्तिः, मूर्च्छितावयवत्वादिति ।

NySūBh II.2.69

A material body is called a '*mūrti*' because it is composed of parts and which according to circumstances, is the receptacle of the distinctive qualities of (odour, taste, colour), touch, gravity, solidity, fluidity and faculty and of the non-pervasive dimension. (Tr. G.N. Jha)

This is explained from the observation that owing to its possession of the attributes of activity, the mind has its physical stay (*mūrtatvam*):

क्रियावत्त्वान्मूर्तत्वम् ।

VaiśSūBh sec. on dravya (p. 225)

Having action, it (*manas*) must be corporeal or material. (Tr. G.N. Jha)

The principle of '*mūrti*', i.e. congealing into a body or physical form, has been thus defined in the **Vaiśeṣika-Sūtra Bhāṣya**:

मूर्तिरसर्वगतद्रव्यपरिमाणं तदनुविधायिनी च क्रिया ।

VaiśSūBh sec. on karma (p. 734)

'Corporeality' implies a non-pervading (limited) dimension; and action is concomitant with corporeality. (Tr. G.N. Jha)

According to the Nakulīśa-Pāśupata system, there are five principles leading to initiation (*dīkṣā*) in the Pāśupata fold:

दीक्षाकारिपञ्चकं चोक्तम् – "द्रव्यं कालः क्रिया मूर्तिर्गुरुश्चैव हि पञ्चमः" इति ।

SarDSaṅg (Nakulīśa Pāśupata) p. 164

There are five aspects stated to be operative as the causes of initiation, viz. the material, the proper time, the rite, the image and the spiritual guide as the fifth.
(Based on the tr. by E.B. Cowell & Gough)

As regards the Śaivite thought, it has been thus further observed on the compulsory guidance to be essentially given by the preceptor to spiritually awaken his disciple:

तत्परिपाकाधिक्यानुरोधेन शक्त्युपसंहारेण दीक्षाकरणेन मोक्षप्रदो भवति आचार्य-मूर्तिमास्थाय परमेश्वरः ।

SarDSaṅg (Śaiva) p. 186

... the Supreme, having assumed the form of a teacher, stops the continued accession of maturity and contracts his manifested power, and ultimately grants to them liberation by the process of initiation. (Tr. E.B. Cowell & Gough)

With respect to the formless and the formed aspects seen in the world, the Jaina thinkers raise an objection worded as follows:

अमूर्तस्याकाशस्य मूर्त्तस्य पृथिव्यादेश्चैककारणकत्वायोगात् ।

Prameyaratnamālā (p. 153)

It is not justified to say that Brahma is the sole cause simultaneously of both the formless sky and of the earth etc. having form.

According to the Jaina belief, a combination of the invisible →*jīva* (life-principle) with the visible material aspect should be thus analysed:

वण्ण रस पंच गंधा दा फासा अट्ठ णिच्चया जीवे ।
णो संति अमुत्ति तदो ववहारा मुत्ति बंधादो ॥
वर्णाः रसाः पञ्च गन्धौ द्वौ स्पर्शाः अष्टौ निश्चयात् जीवे ।
नो सन्ति अमूर्त्तिः ततः व्यवहारात् मूर्त्ति बन्धतः ॥

DSaṅg 7

In view of the (true) logic of the Doctrine, i.e. absolute viewpoint, *jīva* is without form, because of five kinds of colour and taste, two kinds of smell, and eight kinds of touch are not present in it. On the contrary, it is only for the practical purposes (i.e. from the empirical viewpoint) that *jīva* is said to have form through the bondage (of *karma*). (Based on the tr. by S.C. Ghoshal)

As it is described by poet Jaṭānandī in his **Varāṅgacarita**:

परिणामाज्जीवभावान्नित्यात्कारणादपि ।
कर्तृत्वात्सत्क्रियत्वाच्च मूर्तिमत्त्वाद्विभुत्वतः ॥
एकक्षेत्रात्तथैकत्वात् सप्रदेशाद्यथाक्रमम् ।
सर्वं तद् विविधं (द्विविधं) द्रव्यं विज्ञातव्यं विचक्षणैः ॥
जीवाश्च पुद्गलाश्चैव परिणामगुणान्विताः ।
परिणामं न गच्छन्ति शेषाणीति विदुर्बुधाः ॥
जीवद्रव्यं हि जीवः स्याच्छेषं निर्जीव उच्यते ।
मूर्तिमत्पुद्गलद्रव्यममूर्तं शेषमिष्यते ॥

VaCa XXVI.33–36

Owing to the nature of growth or evolution (*pariṇāma*), the state or mode of sentiency (*jīvabhāva*), the perpetuality (or indestructibility, *nityatva*), and also the causation (*kāraṇa*), the assumption of being a doer (*kartṛtva*), the assumption of activity, the state of assuming a body (*mūrtimat-tva*), the assumption of ownership or possession (*vibhūtva*), the state of occupying a place (*ekakṣetra*), the being as a unit and the identity with that place, *dravya* (the substance) is in sequence (of the above considerations) knowable to be of diverse kind by the learned.

The *jīvas* (living beings) as well as the *pudgalas* (material bodies) are endowed with the quality of developing (*pariṇāma*). All other principles do not undergo any development. Thus it is known to the learned.

The substance endowed with the life-principle (*jīva-dravya*) is (known as) the very sentient being (*jīva*); the rest is called *nirjīva* (without life). Likewise, by the term *mūrti-mat* 'having a body, form or frame', the *pudgala* 'the matter' aspect of substance is intended; the rest is conveyed by the expression *a-mūrta* (formless).

According to the non-dual philosophy as enumerated in the **Laghu Yoga-Vāsiṣṭha**, the formed bodies are not real in themselves but mere appearances:

जगन्तीमान्यमूर्तानि मूर्तिमन्ति मुधाग्रहात् ।

LYVās III.2.99ab

On account of vain affection toward the world, all objects appear to possess a particular form, though they really do not have any form. (Tr. H.N. Chakravarty)

In the Rāmānuja system of Vaiṣṇava thought, the Supreme Lord is believed to assume five secondary emanations:

तदर्थं लीलया स्वीयाः पञ्च मूर्त्तिः करोति वै ।

SarDSaṅg (Rāmānuja) p. 116

For that aim, He has verily transformed Himself into His own Five Embodiments just by way of recreation.

स एव करुणासिन्धुर्भगवान् भक्तवत्सलः ।
उपासकानुरोधेन भजते मूर्तिपञ्चकम् ॥

SarDSaṅg (Rāmānuja) p. 119

The Lord Himself, being an ocean of compassion and kind to His worshippers, assumes in fact, a set of His five forms for the cause of His votaries.

With respect to the worship of them, it is further observed:

तत्र पूर्वपूर्वमूर्त्युपासनया पुरुषार्थपरिपन्थिदुरितनिचयक्षये सत्युत्तरोत्तरमूर्त्युपास्त्यधिकारः ।

SarDSaṅg (Rāmānuja) p. 116

By the worship of these divine emanations, one by one, as mentioned in the order, a quantity of sins hindering his path in reaching the (final) human goal (*mokṣa,* deliverance) is destroyed and the devotee gets entitled of changing over to the worship of each next of the emanations in sequence (up to the foremost).

According to the philosophy of Sanskrit Grammar, *mūrti* or formed aspects have for their base a proportionate share of elements.

सर्वाश्च पुनर्मूर्तय एवमात्मिकाः संस्त्यानप्रसवगुणाः, शब्दस्पर्शरूपरसगन्धवत्यः ।
यत्राल्पीयांसो गुणास्तत्रावरतस्त्रयः शब्दः स्पर्शो रूपमिति । रसगन्धौ न सर्वत्र ।

Mahābh on Pā I.2.64

Likewise natured all objects with forms, have natural aspects of decrease and increase; they have the features of sound, touch, colour, taste and smell. The material objects that contain fewer attributes, must contain at least three, namely sound, touch and colour. Taste and smell do not reside in all objects having forms. (Based on the tr. by R.S. Bhattacharya)

येन मूर्तीनामुपचयाश्चापचयाश्च लक्ष्यन्ते तं कालमित्याहुः ।

Mahābh on Pā II.2.5

That is called time through which the growth and decay of material things (or things having limited dimension) are duly observed. (Tr. R.S. Bhattacharya)

Bhartṛhari takes light as the primary cause illuminating manifestation:

वैकृतं समतिक्रान्ता मूर्तिव्यापारदर्शनम् ।
व्यतीत्यालोकतमसी प्रकाशं यमुपासते ॥

Vāk I.19

The light which those worship who have passed beyond the manifested state consisting of the cognition of things and actions and beyond light and darkness. (Tr. K.A.S. Iyer)

According to the Ayurvedic viewpoint it is observed by Caraka:

तस्य पुरुषस्य पृथिवी मूर्तिः ।

CarSam ŚāSthā V.5

Of the man the congealed form is (due to) the Earth.

सौम्याः खल्वापोऽन्तरिक्षप्रभवाः प्रकृतिशीता लघ्व्यश्चाव्यक्तरसाश्च, तास्त्वन्तरिक्षाद्भ्रश्यमाना भ्रष्टाश्च पञ्चमहाभूतगुणसमन्विता जङ्गमस्थावराणां भूतानां मूर्तीरभिप्रीणयन्ति, तासु मूर्तिषु षडभिमूर्च्छन्ति रसाः ।

CarSam SūSthā XXVI.39

The waters are innately composed of Soma, generated in atmosphere, and by nature they are cold, light and contain *rasa* yet not manifest. They, while falling from the atmosphere, get endowed with the properties of five primary elements (*mahābhūtas*) and thus dropped (on the ground) nourish the physical forms of moving as well as fixed beings; in those physical forms the six *rasas* are congealed (respectively, of the property of Soma, Earth, Fire, Waters, Air and Sky in their combined evolution in them with more or less quantity).

As stated in the **Gītā**, the worldly forms are created by the formless lord:

मया ततमिदं सर्वं जगदव्यक्तमूर्तिना ।
मत्स्थानि सर्वभूतानि न चाहं तेष्ववस्थितः ॥

BhG IX.4

As the formless (creator) I have unfolded this entire world by Me. All elements (*bhūtas*, i.e. beings, expressed entities) exist or depend on Me, and I am not dependent on them.

A spiritual embodiment or subtle image is called *yoga-mūrti* in the great epic:

संगम्य सा तु धर्मेण योगमूर्तिधरेण वै ।
लेभे पुत्रं वरारोहा सर्वप्राणभृतां वरम् ॥

MBh I.114.3

Having united with the god Dharma, who had verily descended by assuming a yogic body, the excellent lady Kuntī obtained a son, who was best among all human beings.

The multiple aspects of one single god-head are explained as evolved through the Yogic power:

योगेन बहुधात्मानं कृत्वा तिष्ठामि मूर्तिषु ।
अग्निहोत्रेषु सत्रेषु क्रियास्वथ मखेषु च ॥

MBh I.7.6

By ascetic power, having multiplied myself, I am present in various forms, in places of the daily *havana*, at a sacrifice extending for years, in places where holy rites are performed (such as marriage, etc.) and at other sacrifices. (Tr. P.C. Roy)

In the **Manu Smṛti** the body (*śarīra*) is defined as formed of six constituents:

यन्मूर्त्यवयवाः सूक्ष्मास्तस्येमान्याश्रयन्ति षट् ।
तस्माच्छरीरमित्याहुस्तस्य मूर्तिं मनीषिणः ॥

Manu I.17

Because his (i.e. creator's) six kinds of minute bodily constituents (*mūrtyavayavāḥ*) enter these creatures, so by the wise His (creator's) *mūrti* (=corporeal body) is called bodily frame (*śarīra*).

It further observes:

यदाणुमात्रिको भूत्वा बीजं स्थास्नु चरिष्णु च ।
समाविशति संसृष्टस्तदा मूर्तिं विमुञ्चति ॥

Manu I.56

When, being clothed with minute particles (only), it enters into vegetable or animal seed, it then assumes, united (with the fine body), a (new) corporeal frame. (Tr. G. Bühler)

आचार्यो ब्रह्मणो मूर्तिः पिता मूर्तिः प्रजापतेः ।
माता पृथिव्या मूर्तिस्तु भ्राता स्वो मूर्तिरात्मनः ॥

Manu II.226

The teacher is the image of Brahman, the father the image of Prajāpati (the lord of created beings), the mother the image of the earth, and an (elder) full brother the image of oneself. (Tr. G. Bühler)

To explain the interconnection of formless and formed entities both are thus significantly compared with the vowel and consonant sounds, respectively:

> यच्चामूर्तं यच्च मूर्तं समस्तं ... ।
> .... त्वत्संबद्धं त्वत्स्वरैर्व्यञ्जनैश्च ॥
>
> MārkPur XXIII.47
>
> Everything – both that which is destitute of visible shape, and that which has visible shape ... is connected with thee by thy vowels and by thy consonants. (Tr. F.E. Pargiter)

The Great Goddess is eulogised to permeate as well as manifest the universe:

> नित्यैव सा जगन्मूर्तिस्तया सर्वमिदं ततम् ।
>
> MārkPur LXXXI.47ab
>
> She exists eternally, embodied as the world. By her this universe was stretched forth. (Tr. F.E. Pargiter)
>
> देव्या यया ततमिदं जगदात्मशक्त्या निःशेषदेवगणशक्तिसमूहमूर्त्या ।
>
> MārkPur LXXXIV.2ab
>
> The goddess, who stretched out this world by her power,
>
> Whose body comprises the entire powers of all the hosts of gods. (Tr. F.E. Pargiter)

The Supreme Lord Viṣṇu or Nārāyaṇa is stated to have his single *mūrti* transformed into four aspects:

> एका मूर्तिरनिर्देश्या शुक्लां पश्यन्ति तां बुधाः ।
> ज्वालामालोपरुद्धांङ्गी निष्ठा सा योगिनां परा ॥
> द्वितीया पृथिवी मूर्ध्ना शेषाख्या धारयत्यधः ।
> तामसी सा समाख्याता तिर्यक्त्वं समुपासिता ॥
> तृतीया कर्म कुरुते प्रजापालनतत्परा ।
> सत्वोद्रिक्ता तु सा ज्ञेया धर्मसंस्थानकारिणी ॥
> चतुर्थी जलमध्यस्था शेते पन्नगतल्पगा ।
> रजस्तस्या गुणः सर्गं सा करोति सदैव हि ॥
>
> MārkPur IV.45, 48–50
>
> His first form is inscrutable; the wise behold it bright; it is covered with garlands of flame; it is the acme of perfection to devotees; ... His second form, called Śeṣa, supports the earth below with its head; it is described as being characterized by the quality of darkness; it belongs to the brute creation. His third form is active, and devoted to the preservation of creatures; it is to be

considered as consisting chiefly of the quality of goodness; it is the fashioner of virtue. His fourth form abides in water; it lies on a serpent as its bed; its attribute is passion; and it is always indeed active. (Tr. F.E. Pargiter)

The *mūrta* and *amūrta* aspects are explained as belonging to the Lord:

मूर्तामूर्तमदृश्यं च दृश्यं च पुरुषोत्तम । .... तत् सर्वं त्वम् ..... ॥

ViPur I.4.24

... all that is formless, or that has form, all that is visible, or invisible; that all is you, o Puruṣottama. (Based on the tr. by H.H. Wilson)

As it is put elsewhere in a similar strain of metaphysical realisations:

द्वे रूपे ब्रह्मणस्तस्य मूर्तं चामूर्तमेव च ।
क्षराक्षरस्वरूपे ते सर्वभूतेष्ववस्थिते ॥

ViPur I.22.55

There are two states of this Brahma: one with, an one without shape; one perishable, and one imperishable; which are inherent in all beings. (Tr. H.H. Wilson)

While speaking of the two kinds of knowledge about mysteries of the Great Lord, the same Purāṇa thus further alludes to the truth of all devotional enquiries:

द्वे विद्ये त्वमनाम्नाय परा चैवापरा तथा ।
त एव भवतो रूपे मूर्तामूर्तात्मिके प्रभो ॥

ViPur V.1.35

O Lord, there are two gnostic approaches, one is superior while the other is even beyond that. Both of them are to refer to your two aspects, the former is an imaged form while the latter has a formless nature.

Even for the yogic practitioners, the initial stage of their endeavour is stated to be inspired by the formed glorification of the deity.

सर्वशक्तिमयो विष्णुः स्वरूपं ब्रह्मणः परम् ।
मूर्तं यद् योगिभिः पूर्वं योगारम्भेषु चिन्त्यते ॥

ViPur I.22.61

The supreme condition of Brahman, which is meditated by the yogis in the commencement of their abstraction, as invested with form, is Viṣṇu composed of all the divine energies.
(Tr. H.H. Wilson)

Without any perceptible base, no mental apprehension (of Viṣṇu's form) can be realised (by common folks).

यच्च मूर्तं हरे रूपं यादृक् चिन्त्यं नराधिप ।
तच्छ्रूयतामनाधारा धारणा नोपपद्यते ॥

ViPur VI.7.79

The retention or apprehension by the mind of that visible form of Viṣṇu, without regard to subsidiary forms, is thence called Dhāraṇā, and I will describe to you the perceptible form of Hari, which no mental retention will manifest. (Tr. H.H. Wilson)

Answering to the question as to why an image is essential for the worship of a deity, the **Agni Purāṇa** has thus observed:

तच्च विष्णोः परं रूपमरूपस्याजमक्षरम् ।
अशक्यं प्रथमं ध्यातुमतो मूर्त्यादि चिन्तयेत् ॥

AgPur CCCLXXIX.35

That supreme form of the formless Viṣṇu is beginningless and imperishable; it is impossible to meditate on it at first. Therefore, one should meditate on the *mūrtis* (idols or images) and the like. (Tr. R.S. Bhattacharya)

The four aspects of Viṣṇu, the supreme godhead, as one composite form are thus given in the **Bhāgavata Purāṇa**:

नमो भगवते तुभ्यं वासुदेवाय धीमहि ।
प्रद्युम्नायानिरुद्धाय नमस्सङ्कर्षणाय च ॥
इति मूर्त्यभिधानेन मन्त्रमूर्त्तिममूर्त्तिकम् ।
यजते यज्ञपुरुषं स सम्यग्दर्शनः पुमान् ॥

BhāgPur I.5.37–38

We all meditate upon (your glory) and pay homage to you, O Lord; (it is you who) assumes the (fourfold) forms by the designations of Vāsudeva, Pradyumna, Aniruddha and Saṅkarṣaṇa: to them (all), we pay homage. A person with real vision worships you, the same He-of-the Sacrifice, who is though formless, yet transforms (his self) in four *mantra*-images.

An image from Mathura represents this aspect when Vāsudeva Kṛṣṇa is the central figure and from whose shoulders emerge other family members. Saṅkarṣaṇa with cap and snake canopy is clear and the other figures are gone. The sculpture is recovered from the Mathura Museum compound well belongs to the Kushana period (1st – 2nd cent. A.D.).

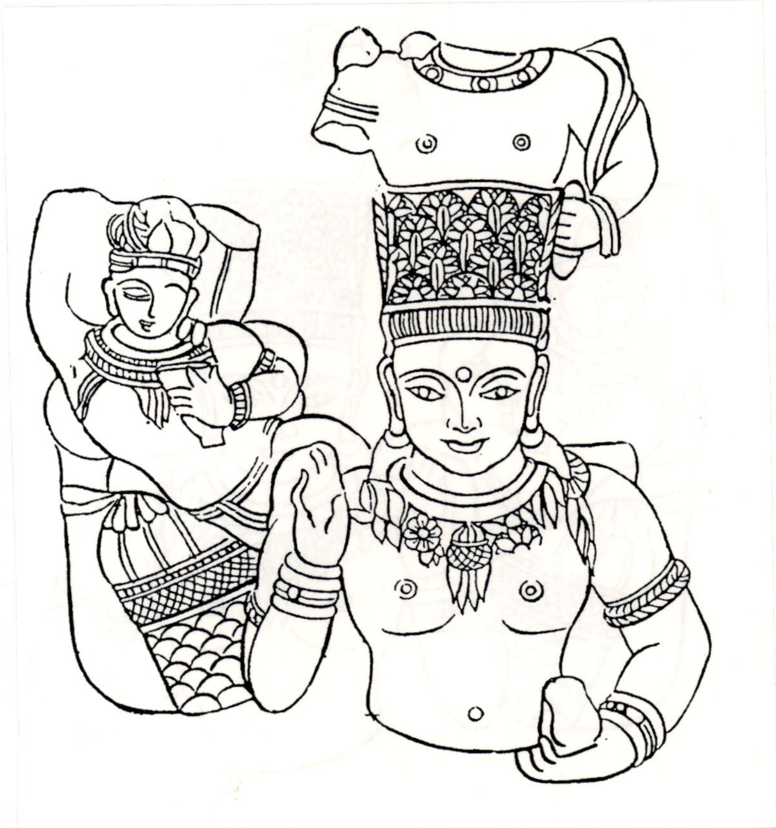

Figure 8: Composite form of Vāsudeva Viṣṇu (Kushana period, Mathura Museum)

The Lord is stated to meditate on his own fourth aspect:

.... सर्वभूतहितेच्छया ।
तां तामसीं तुरीयां च मूर्तिं प्रकृतिमात्मनः ॥
उपधावते चैकाग्रमनसा भगवानजः ।

DBhāgPur VIII.8.11b–12ab

For the well-being of all creatures the Unborn Lord (Brahmā) adores with intent mind his own fourth form, that is of the nature of *tamas.*

An aspect of the Goddess is named Trimūrti:

त्रिमूर्तिश्च त्रिवर्षा च ..... ॥

DBhāgPur III.26.41c

Trimūrti is the name (of the virgin Goddess), represented by a girl of three years.

The personified Vedas and other scriptures are mentioned as follows:

वेदाः सर्वे मूर्तिमन्तः शास्त्राणि विविधानि च ॥
स्मृतयश्च पुराणानि मूर्तिमन्ति वसन्ति हि ।

DBhāgPur XII.11.86cd–87ab

Verily there stay all the Vedas in embodied form, various Śāstras (scriptures of traditional treatises), the Smṛtis (law books) as well as the Purāṇas (works of ancient lores) as it were in their incarnate presence.

सततं मूर्तिमन्तश्च वेदाश्चत्वार एव च ।
सन्ति यस्याश्च जिह्वाग्रे सा च वेदवती श्रुता ॥

DBhāgPur IX.16.63

She was known as Vedavatī, 'possessing Vedas', for the four Vedas as if incarnate in form were ever present on the tip of her tongue.

Observing on the supreme aspect of the Lord Śiva and his manifestations for creative unfoldment, the Purāṇa writers have expressed their analysis as follows:

मूर्तात्मा सकलः कश्चित्स चान्यो निष्कलः शिवः ।
शिवेनाधिष्ठितश्चेति सर्वत्र लघु कथ्यते ॥
मूर्त्यात्मैव तदा मूर्तिः शिवस्यास्य भवेदिति ।
तस्यां मूर्तौ मूर्तिमतोः पारतन्त्र्यं हि निश्चितम् ॥
अन्यथा निरपेक्षेण मूर्तिः स्वीक्रियते कथम् ।
मूर्तिस्वीकरणं तस्मान्मूर्तौ साध्यफलेप्सया ॥
न हि स्वेच्छाशरीरत्वं स्वातंत्र्यायोपपद्यते ।
स्वेच्छैव तादृशी पुंसां यस्मात्कर्मानुसारिणी ॥

ŚPur VII.30.10–13

The wise have said that the embodied *ātman* is *sakala*; the unembodied Śiva is *niṣkala*. The embodied *ātman* is presided over by Śiva.

If it is contended that the embodied *ātman* is the form of Śiva, the dependence of the embodied on the form becomes certain. How can we explain that?

Otherwise how is the form adopted by the non-dependent? The adoption of form is with a purpose to get the fruit of his desire.

The assuming of physical bodies out of wish is not consistent with freedom. Such a wish too follows the activities of men.
(Tr. Board of Scholars)

आत्मोपमोल्बणं साक्षान्मूर्तिरेव हि काचन ।
शिवस्य मूर्तिर्मूर्त्यात्मा परस्तस्योपलक्षणम् ॥
यथा काष्ठेष्वनारूढो न वह्निरूपलभ्यते ।
एवं शिवोऽपि मूर्त्यात्मन्यनारूढ इति स्थितिः ॥

ŚPur VII.31.13–14

Some form, intense with the similarity of *ātman*, is Śiva's idol. The other, the great one, the *ātman* of the *mūrti* is its implication.

Just as fire cannot be obtained without its being mounted in the twigs so also Śiva is not known or understood without its being superimposed in the idol. (Tr. Board of Scholars)

The Purāṇas mention Mūrti as the personal name of Dharma's wife. She was one of the thirteen daughters of Arch-creator Dakṣa whom he married to Dharma:

मूर्तिः सर्वगुणोत्पत्तिर्नरनारायणावृषी ॥

BhāgPur IV.1.52

Mūrti being an origin-ground of all high merits, gave birth to the sages Nara and Nārāyaṇa.

मूर्त्तिश्च धर्मपत्नी सा कान्तिरूपा मनोहरा ॥

DBhāgPur IX.1.115cd

Mūrti was the wife of god Dharma. She was of shining form and fascinating.

The *caturviṃśati mūrtis* (twentyfour image-types) of Viṣṇu are enumerated in brief by the author of the **Garuḍa Purāṇa** (XLV.2–13) may be tabulated as follows:

Deities	**Attributes**			
Keśava	Conch	Wheel	Mace	Lotus
Nārāyaṇa	Lotus	Mace	Wheel	Conch
Mādhava	Wheel	Conch	Lotus	Mace
Govinda	Mace	Lotus	Conch	Wheel
Viṣṇu	Lotus	Conch	Wheel	Mace
Madhusūdana	Conch	Lotus	Mace	Wheel
Trivikrama	Mace	Wheel	Conch	Lotus
Vāmana	Wheel	Mace	Lotus	Conch

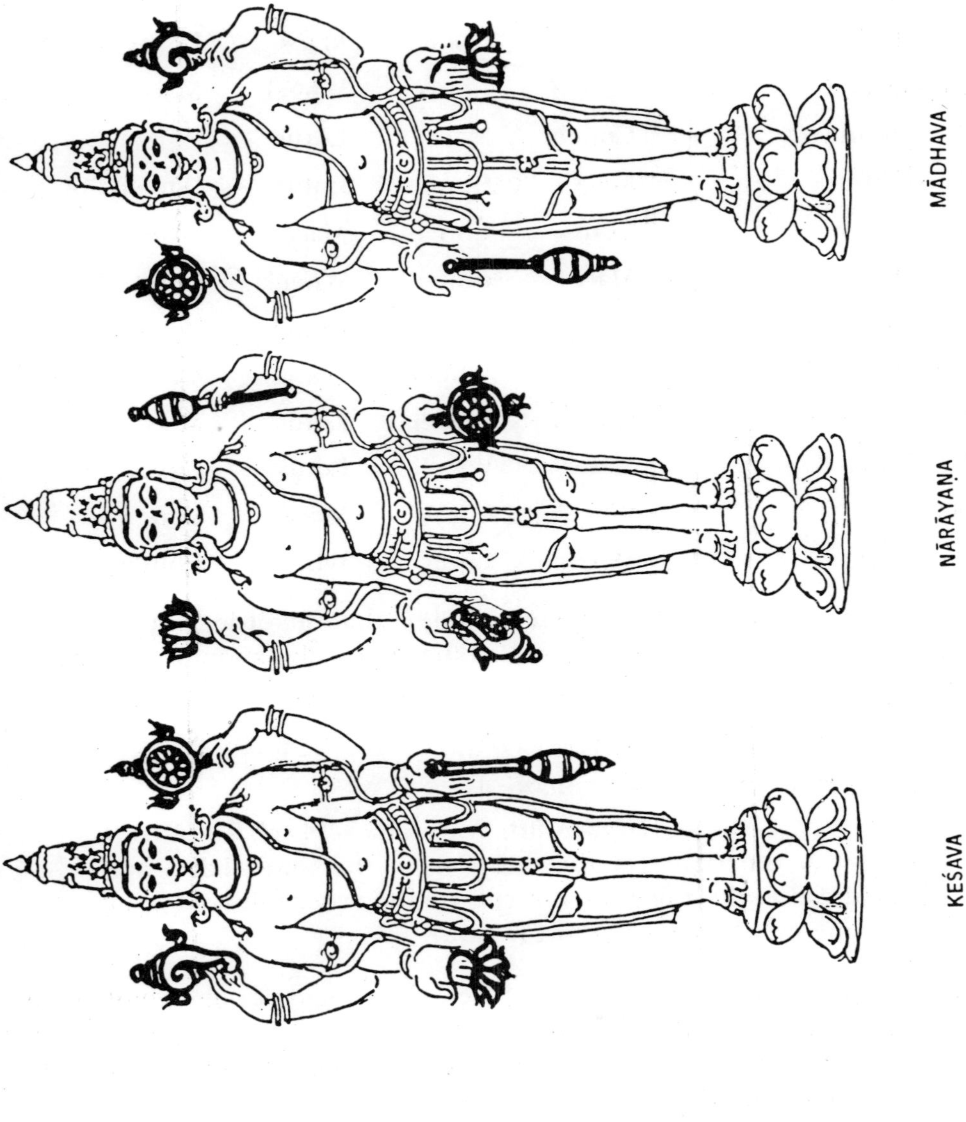

Figure 9: Keśava, Nārāyaṇa and Mādhava with *āyudhas*

Śrīdhara	Wheel	Lotus	Conch	Mace
Hṛṣīkeśa	Lotus	Mace	Conch	Wheel
Padmanābha	Lotus	Wheel	Mace	Conch
Dāmodara	Conch	Wheel	Mace	Lotus
Vāsudeva	Wheel	Conch	Mace	Lotus
Saṅkarṣaṇa	Conch	Lotus	Wheel	Mace
Pradyumna	Conch	Mace	Lotus	Wheel
Aniruddha	Mace	Conch	Lotus	Wheel
Puruṣottama	Lotus	Conch	Mace	Wheel
Adhokṣaja	Mace	Conch	Wheel	Lotus
Nṛsiṃha	Lotus	Mace	Conch	Wheel
Acyuta	Lotus	Wheel	Conch	Mace
Janārdana	Conch	Wheel	Lotus	Mace
Upendra	Mace	Wheel	Lotus	Conch
Hari	Wheel	Lotus	Mace	Conch
Śrī Kṛṣṇa	Mace	Lotus	Wheel	Conch

It should be remarked in the present context that the order of placement followed for the four *āyudhas* (attributes) in the above tabulation of twentyfour *mūrtis* was presumably the one that is given by the master-artist Maṇḍana:

अधरं दक्षिणे हस्तमारभ्य सृष्टि [माग्रत:] मार्गत: ।
चतुर्विंशतिमूर्त्तीनां सर्वत्रेना [त्रैवा] युधक्रम: ॥

Devtā Mūrti Prakaraṇa V.14 (cf. Rūp III.19)

Starting on the right (of the deity) from the lower hand and going ahead in the clockwise direction is the order followed in all case of the twentyfour *mūrtis* (of Keśava).

For the installation ceremony, there were appointed certain numbers of persons, called *mūrtipas*, who officiated as "protectors of the image" or bearers of the image before the same was brought by them under strict care to the place of consecration:

अत: परं प्रवक्ष्यामि मूर्तिपानां तु लक्षणम् ।
मूर्तिपास्तु द्विजाश्चैव कुलीना ऋजवस्तथा ॥
द्वात्रिंशत् षोडशाथापि अष्टौ वा श्रुतिपारगा: ।

ज्येष्ठमध्यकनिष्ठेषु मूर्तिपा वा प्रकीर्तिताः ॥

MatPur CCLXV.1ab, 5cd–6

Now further on I would expound upon the characteristics of the *mūrtipas,* 'bearers of the image', they are twice-born, of noble birth and upright in character. They are known to be thirtytwo, or sixteen or even eight such persons, well-versed in the Vedic tradition, (and appointed) for the respective cases of the superior, the middling and the inferior types of images.

The four sons of Daśaratha are described as the four incarnations of the Supreme Spirit:

तस्योदये चतुर्मूर्तेः पौलस्त्यचकितेश्वराः ।
विरजस्कैर्नभस्वद्भिर्दिश उच्छ्वसिता इव ॥

Ragh X.73

At the advent of that four-fold incarnation (of him in the four forms) the (four) quarters whose tutelary deities were made to tremble by Paulastya, breathed a breath of relief as it were by means of the breezes which were free from dust.
(Tr. G.R. Nandargikar)

Śakuntalā has been beautifully mentioned as the pious virtue incarnate of the holy sages:

त्वमर्हतां प्राग्रसरः स्मृतोऽसि नः शकुन्तला मूर्तिमती च सत्क्रिया ।
समानयंस्तुल्यगुणं वधूवरं चिरस्य वाच्यं न गतः प्रजापतिः ॥

AbhŚāk V.15

You are known to us as the foremost of the worthy, and Śakuntalā is virtue incarnate. It is after a long time that the Creator, (thus) bringing together a bride and a bridegroom of equal merit, has not incurred censure. (Tr. M.R. Kale)

An elephant is likened to the obstacle personified, for the presiding deity of obstacles is well-known in Indian myths as the elephant-faced god Gaṇeśa:

मूर्तो विघ्नस्तपस इव नो भिन्नसारङ्गयूथो
धर्मारण्यं विरुजति गजः स्यन्दनालोकभीतः ॥

AbhŚāk I.30cd

Scared by the royal chariot in its course with headlong haste an elephant invades the hallowed precincts of our sacred grove; Himself the terror of the startled deer, an embodied hindrance to our rites. (Tr. M. Monier-Williams)

The river Chambal is poetically seen by Kālidāsa as a stream descended on the earth as incarnating the glory of a past king's sacrificial undertakings:

व्यालम्बेथाः सुरभितनयालम्भजां मानयिष्य-
न्स्रोतोमूर्त्या भुवि परिणतां रन्तिदेवस्य कीर्तिम् ॥

Megh I.48cd

You should descend to pay respect to the glory of Rantideva who offered thousands of cows in *yajña* on the bank of river whose water also looked reddish (as was also the colour of cows).
(Tr. R.C. Sharma)

The three supreme gods are described as aspects of the one great principle:

एकैव मूर्तिर्बिभिदे त्रिधा सा सामान्यमेषां प्रथमावरत्वम् ।
विष्णोर्हरस्तस्य हरिः कदाचिद्वेधास्तयोस्तावपि धातुराद्यौ ॥

Kum VII.44

The one only form was divided three-fold. Sometimes Hara or Śiva was senior to Viṣṇu or Hari or Viṣṇu to him and Brahmā to both; and they too Viṣṇu and Śiva were sometimes prior to Brahmā.
(Tr. H.H. Wilson)

The ascetic practices of the lord Śiva are so beautifully described as follows:

तत्राग्निमाधाय समित्समिद्धं स्वमेव मूर्त्यन्तरमष्टमूर्तिः ।
स्वयं विधाता तपसः फलानां केनापि कामेन तपश्चचार ॥

Kum I.57

The eight-formed Śiva, having there set up a fire lighted by sacrificial wood, another of his own forms, himself the dispenser of the fruits of asceticism, practised asceticism actuated by some desire which none could guess. (Tr. H.H. Wilson)

The primal division into Female and Male of the divine entity is thus hinted at by Kālidāsa:

स्त्रीपुंसावात्मभागौ ते भिन्नमूर्तेः सिसृक्षया ।
प्रसूतिभाजः सर्गस्य तावेव पितरौ स्मृतौ ॥

Kum II.7

Male and female are but parts of thy body who wert divided into two forms by desire of creation. They themselves are held as parents of creation. (Tr. H.H. Wilson)

The procreative mystery as evolved from the Supreme Self is thus indicated by Bhāravi:

अविग्रहस्याप्यतुलने हेतुना समेतभिन्नद्वयमूर्ति तिष्ठतः ।
तवैव नान्यस्य जगत्सु दृश्यते विरुद्धवेषाभरणस्य कान्तता ॥

Kir XVIII.33

Even though having no body of any comparison, owing to certain unknown reason, you stay as a unison appearing as consisting of two distinct bodies (of male and female), – it is only yours and of none else that the beauties appear there in the worlds as clad in opposite dresses and ornamental attributes.

The worship of Śiva's eight forms with due rituals is thus described by Bāṇabhaṭṭa:

पुलिनपृष्ठप्रतिष्ठितसैकतशिवलिङ्गा च भक्त्या परमया पञ्चब्रह्मपुरःसरां सम्यङ् मुद्राबन्धविहितपरिकरां ध्रुवागीतिगर्भामवनिपवनवनगगनदहनतपनतुहिनकिरण यजमानमयीर्मूर्तीरष्टावपि ध्यायन्ती सुचिरमष्टपुष्पिकामदात् ।

HaCa I, p. 30

Next, having in Śiva's honour erected sand *liṅgas* on the sand-isles, she with deep devotion performed in full the ritual of clasping of fingers together with the Dhruvā hymn and preceded by the Pañcabrahma prayer; lastly after long meditation on the eight incarnate forms, earth, wind, water, sky, fire, sun, moon, sacrificer, she presented the eightfold offering of flowers.
(Tr. E.B. Cowell and F.W. Thomas)

The king Harṣa evokes a charming analogy for the full moon risen in sky:

दृष्ट्वा बिम्बं हिमांशोर्भयकृतवलयां संस्मरन् शेषमूर्तिम् ।

Nāgā IV.25ab

By looking at the disc of the moon (and thus) recounting of the body as it were of the serpent king Śeṣa, coiled up in fear.

An outstanding piece of poetic fancy comes from the classic epic of Jaṭānandin conceiving the newly-wed royal couple as reflecting the righteous acts embodied of the whole capital:

एवं तयोस्तु प्रथितोरुकीर्त्योः परस्परोद्वर्तितभोगरत्योः ।
विश्रम्भभावानुगतप्रणीत्योः कालो व्यतीतः पुरपुण्यमूर्त्योः ॥

VaCa XIX.38

Thus, the time passed of that couple, who had their fame far extended, had mutually acted in enjoyment of marital pleasures and amours, had acquired the policy of surrender (to each other) in intense faith, and had, as it were, incarnated as the (pair of) merits of the city.

While describing the sage Nārada, a beautiful poetic imagery has been thus evoked by Māgha:

रथाङ्गपाणेः पटलेन रोचिषामृषित्विषः संवलिता विरेजिरे ।
चलत्पलाशान्तरगोचरास्तरोस्तुषारमूर्तेरिव नक्तमंशवः ॥

Śiśu I.21

The (white) bodily glimpses of the sage (Nārada) shone as mixed up with the mass of shining glitters of Kṛṣṇa's (complexion), just like the rays of the snow-bodied (moon) that shine during the night being filtered through the moving leaves of a tree.

The arch-deity of creation is lauded by the same poet:

अनन्यगुर्वास्तव केन केवलः पुराणमूर्तेर्महिमावगम्यते ।
मनुष्यजन्मापि सुरासुरान्गुणैर्भवान्भवच्छेदकरैः करोत्यधः ॥

Śiśu I.35

Even though you have taken a human birth, you put down all the gods as well as the demons by your attributes capable of cutting worldly bondages. Who can know the sole glory of your primordial and the highest Man-image?

The poet Bhavabhūti has brought in his unique way several imageries underlining embodiments of emotions:

परिपाण्डुदुर्बलकपोलसुन्दरं दधती विलोलकबरीकमाननम् ।
करुणस्य मूर्तिरथ वा शरीरिणी विरहव्यथेव वनमेति जानकी ॥

UttCa III.4 (also cf. IV.7; VI.10)

The daughter of Janaka, her countenance charming owing to its pallid and emaciated cheeks and her loosened braids waving about, coming to the wood like the very image of pity, or rather like the pain of separation incarnate.

Another excellent imagery is found couched in select phraseology of the poet Murāri:

एताभिस्तव कौतुकोक्तिभिरपि त्रैविद्यमूर्त्तैरिव
त्वष्टस्यामरशिल्पिना दिनकृतोऽच्छेदवेदाक्षरैः ।

Anargharāghava I.34

[King Daśaratha's answer to Viśvāmitra]

By your such amusing words, which are derived from specifically analysed Vedic syllables by you, who is himself the triple Veda incarnate, are like the (bodily) particles of the Sun-god, turned on a lathe by the divine craftsman (Viśvakarmā).

The following vignettes of beautiful analogies as evoked by king Bhoja in his prose-romance here and there are quite remarkable:

वामनमूर्तिरिव निजविक्रमाक्रान्तत्रिभुवना ।

Śṛṅgāramañjarīkathā, p. 15

(The bawd), though dwarfish in stature, was like the (Trivikrama incarnation of Viṣṇu) traversing the three world by her own (cunning) means.

लोहाकारभस्त्रेवाध्मातमूर्तिः ।

Śṛṅgāramañjarīkathā, p. 17

(The bawd) was plump in her form like, as it were, the bellows of an iron-smith.

पारदमूर्तिरिव सुवर्णमादाय पाण्डूकरोति ।

Śṛṅgāramañjarīkathā, p. 17

(The bawd) makes the customers pale by snatching away their gold, as is the (metal) image, besmeared with mercury, rendered golden (by heating).

The poet Soḍḍhala employs the term *mūrti* as denoting a pictorial portrait:

चित्रकरेण शिल्पकलाकौशलमात्मनो दर्शयता रतिरूपस्पर्धया यत्र त्वदीया मूर्तिरालिखिता तं पटम् ।

Udayasundarīkathā, p. 103

The same cloth-picture, in which the painter, by showing his own expertise of craftsmanship, has drawn your portrait that vies with the beauty of goddess Rati.

The great poet Śrīharṣa has drawn some excelling imageries dwelling upon the term *mūrti*, signifying both 'body' and 'image' as well as embodiment:

तमेव लब्ध्वावसरं ततः स्मरः शरीरशोभाजयजातमत्सरः ।
अमोघशक्त्या निजयेव मूर्तया तया विनिर्जेतुमियेष नैषधम् ॥

NaiCa I.43 (also cf. I.124; III.57, 102; VI.8; XXI.41)

So getting an opportunity, Cupid, who was jealous, because he was surpassed by Nala in beauty, wished to conquer him by means of Damayantī, the embodiment of Cupid's own unfailing strength. (Tr. K.K. Handiqui)

Describing a Jina temple the poet Jaṭānandin has thus drawn a charming imagery:

अन्तर्बहिश्चापि समाप्तकर्मा प्रमाणसंवर्धितदिव्यमूर्तिः ।
जिनेन्द्रगेहो रमणीयरूपः पुरस्य भूतांगणितां जगाम ॥

VaCa XXII.73

Featured with beautiful forms, that temple of Lord Jina – being completed in its construction work, both inside and outside, and thus assuming well-developed form in its divine nature in accordance with the proper measurements, had (as if it were) attained the position of the central court of the city.

The Jaina poet Amaracandra Sūri has devised the following imagery in a unique manner:

तत्खड्गयोः प्रभुर्धाराचतुष्के प्रतिबिम्बितः ।
पञ्चमूर्तिरभूत् पञ्चेन्द्रियारिविजयोद्यतः ॥

PadMa XIII.67

In the four sides of their two swords there reflected four images [of the Jina], and thus [the Lord] appeared to be of five forms, risen, as it were, to conquer the five enemies of (the form of) five sense-organs.

The horse as one of the seven jewels of a sovereign monarch is thus conceived by the same poet:

मूर्तिमन्तमिवोत्साहं देहस्थमिव साहसम् ।
पिण्डीभूतमिवागण्यं पुण्यं भरतचक्रिणः ॥

PadMa XV.243

[The horse jewel] was like the embodied fortitude, or as it were, like the valour personified, or as the immense merit of Bharata, the sovran, shaped into a solid body.

Some of the charming literary pieces to be found in the classical epigraphs may be cited further:

खिन्नस्येव विसृज्य गां नरपतेर्ग्गामाश्रितस्येतरां
मूर्त्या कर्म्म-जितावनिं गतवतः कीर्त्या स्थितस्य क्षितौ ।
शान्तस्येव महावने हुतभुजो यस्य प्रतापो महा-
न्नाद्याप्युत्सृजति प्रणाशितरिपोर्यत्नस्य शेषः क्षितिम् ॥

Mehrauli Iron-pillar Ins, verse 2

He, the remnant of the great zeal of whose energy, which utterly destroyed (his) enemies, like (the remnant of the great glowing heat) of a burned-out fire in a great forest, even now leaves not the earth; though he, the king, as if wearied, has quitted this earth, and has gone to the other world, moving in (bodily) form to the land (of paradise) won by (the merit of his) actions, (but) remaining on (this) earth by (the memory of his) fame.
(Tr. J.F. Fleet)

जयति धरण्युद्धरणे घन-घोणाघात-घूर्ण्णित-महीद्ध्रः ।
देवो वराहमूर्त्तिस्त्रैलोक्य-महागृह-स्तम्भः ॥

Eraṇ Stone Boar Ins of Toramāṇa, verse 1

Victorious is the God (Viṣṇu), who has the form of a Boar, who, in the act of lifting up the earth (out of the waters), caused the mountains to tremble with the blows of (his) hard snout; (and) who is the pillar (for the support) of the great house which is the three worlds. (Tr. J.F. Fleet)

यस्याष्टमूर्तिरभवत्स्वयमर्ध मूर्तियन्नाभिपङ्कजभुवो जगतां प्रसूतिः ।
यस्यानिशं प्रथमवाग्विवृणोति सत्त्वं स श्रीधरो दिशतु विश्वपतिः श्रियं वः ॥

Udayendiram Copperplates of Hastimalla,
South Ind. Ins II (p. 382)

May that Śrīdhara, the Lord of the universe, half of whose body was taken up by the eight-bodied Śiva, the one born of whose navel-lotus is the cause of the worlds, and whose glory is explained by the first utterances of Brahma (Veda).
(Tr. C. Sivaramamurti)

तस्य पुत्रो महातेजाः कन्दर्प इव मूर्तिमान् ।
धर्मज्ञश्च कृतज्ञश्च पार्थतुल्यपराक्रमः ॥

Satara Copperplate of Eastern Chālukya king
Viṣṇuvardhana, Indian Antiquary, XIX (p. 309)

His son is of great prowess, like Cupid as if in person (*mūrtimān*), righteous, grateful and equal to Arjuna in gallantry.

Specific definitions comprising more than one aspect of Mūrti

There are some popular definitions, occurring frequently in the Purāṇa, Tantra, Āgama and allied literature, which denote certain groups of more than one aspect or form of a deity or several divinities such as Trimūrti, Pañcamūrti, Aṣṭamūrti, and so on:

एका मूर्तिस्त्रयो देवा ब्रह्मविष्णुमहेश्वराः ।
रजःसत्त्वतमोभिश्च संयुताः कार्यकारकाः ॥

DBhāgPur I.8.4

The Trinity Brahmā, Viṣṇu and Maheśa are really one form, indeed, Trinity in Unity and Unity in Trinity. Being endowed respectively with *sattva, rajas,* and *tamas guṇa*s they do their respective works. (Tr. Vijnanananda)

The concept of Hindu Trinity, comprising of Brahmā, Viṣṇu and Śiva is thus explained by classical poet Kālidāsa:

नमस्त्रिमूर्तये तुभ्यं प्राक्सृष्टेः केवलात्मने ।
गुणत्रयविभागाय पश्चाद्भेदमुपेयुषे ॥

Kum II.4

Salutation to thee, three-formed, existing as one spirit before creation but afterwards betaking to distinctive forms for the separation of three qualities *sattva, rajas* and *tamas.* (Tr. H.H. Wilson)

चतुर्मूर्तिः ... ।

चतस्रो मूर्तयो विराट्सूत्राव्याकृततुरीयात्मानोऽस्येति चतुर्मूर्तिः । सिता रक्ता पीता कृष्णा चेति चतस्रो मूर्तयोऽस्येति वा ।

ViSahasrBh 95a

Of four forms.

The four forms are (Virāj, Sūtrātman, Avyākṛta and Turīya; or He who has white, red, yellow and dark-blue bodies. (Tr. R.A. Sastry)

At times the Caturvyūha is also explained as a fourfold representation of *mūrtis*:

मथुरायां महाभागे साक्षाद्देवो हरिः स्थितः ।
चतुर्व्यूहस्वरूपेण माथुराणां विमुक्तिदः ॥
एका वाराहमूर्तिश्च परा नारायणाह्वया ।
वामनाख्या तृतीया च चतुर्थी हलधारिणी ॥

NārPur II.79.48–49

O blessed lady, in the city of Mathura the Lord Hari Himself is stationed in His fourfold *vyūha* form as granting redemption to the citizens of Mathura. One of them is Varāha *mūrti,* the other is Nārāyaṇa designate, the third is Vāmana by name and the fourth is that of the plough-bearer (Balarāma).

The fourfold *mūrti* or aspects of yet another god are thus enumerated in the Puranic lore:

चतुर्मूर्तेः कुमारस्य रूपं ते वच्मि यादव ।
कुमारश्च तथा स्कन्दो विशाखश्च गुहस्तथा ॥

VDhPur III.71.3

O Yādava, I would now tell you the form of Kumāra (Skanda-Kārttikeya), who has four aspects, viz. Kumāra, Skanda, Viśākha and Guha.

As says the **Agni Purāṇa**:

ब्रह्मा विष्णुस्तथा रुद्र ईश्वरश्च सदाशिवः ।
एते च पञ्चमूर्त्तीशा .... ॥

AgPur XCII.50

There are five deities called *mūrttīśas* (lords of images), namely Brahmā, Viṣṇu, Rudra, Īśvara and Sadāśiva. (Tr. R.S. Bhattacharya)

क्षमाग्नियजमानार्क जलवातेन्दुखानि च ।
प्रतितत्त्वं न्यसेदष्टौमूर्तीः .... ॥

AgPur XLVIII.47

Eight *mūrti*s (of Śiva) are to be assigned to the following eight *tattvas*, namely earth, fire, sacrificer (i.e. the self), sun, water, air, moon, and sky. (Tr. R.S. Bhattacharya)

Elsewhere, the same idea has been so poetically stated in the **Śivamahimna-stotra** (26) and **Abhijñānaśākuntala** (I.1).

As pointed out by V.S. Agrawala, "Under Aṣṭamūrti the **Śabdakalpadruma** makes a significant statement on the authority of the **Kālikā Purāṇa** that the eight forms of Śiva are the eight feet of his Śarabha incarnation (*etāḥ śarabha-rūpi-śivasyaṣṭapādāḥ iti kālikāpurāṇam*)" [*Sparks from the Vedic Fire*, p. 121].

This has further been explained by V.S. Agrawala (*op. cit.*, p. 119). The Purāṇas designate the *yajamāna* as *dīkṣita brāhmaṇa*:

आत्मा तस्याष्टमी मूर्तिर्यजमानाह्वया परा ॥ ....
दीक्षितं ब्राह्मणं प्राहुरात्मानं च मुनीश्वराः ॥

LPur II.12.43cd, 44cd

The *ātman* is his (Śiva's) eighth image, being the supreme one designated as *yajamāna*; the chief sages have styled the same *ātman* also by the term *dīkṣita brāhmaṇa*.

From the viewpoint of his images couched in different aspects the god Śiva is thus invoked in a verse by Kṣemarāja:

अष्टमूर्ति विश्वमूर्ति यदमूर्ति प्रगीयते ।
मंत्रमूर्ति नुमो नेत्रं तच्चिन्मूर्ति महेशितुः ॥

Comm. on NT II.1

We pay homage to the Eye of Lord Maheśa, that is of His form as Sentiency, His *mantra* aspect, is also the same that lauded as the *mantra*-image, is of his eight-forms, comprises of all forms, and yet is formless (*amūrti*).

A group of twelve forms (*dvādaśa-mūrti*) or aspects of Gaurī images are found detailed in the medieval iconographic works:

उमा च पार्वती गौरी ललिता च श्रियोत्तमा ।
कृष्णा हेमवती रम्भा सावित्री च तथैव च ॥
त्रिषंडा तोतला चैव त्रिपुरा द्वादशी मता ।
एवं द्वादशमूर्तिश्च [र्तीश्च] कुर्याद्वै शिवशासनीः ॥
अक्षसूत्रं चाम्बुजं च दर्पणश्च कमण्डलुः ।
एवं भवेद् उमामूर्तिः पूजिता त्रिदशैरपि ॥

AparPṛ CCXXII.6–8 (also cf. 9–19)

One should make the twelve *mūrtis* (of the goddess Gaurī), as belonging to the Śaivite lore, namely Umā, Pārvatī, Gaurī, excellent Śriyā (= Śrī), Kṛṣṇā, Hemavatī, Rambhā, Sāvitrī, and likewise Triṣaṇḍā, Totalā, and Tripurā the twelfth. (With the attributes in her four hands, viz.) of *akṣa*-rosary, lotus, mirror and water-pot, would be the form of Umā, venerated even by the gods.

The **Jayākhya Saṃhitā** mentions the meditational procedure of visualizing the deity-figure in one's heart for concentrating on Him with due invocations:

ध्यानोक्तां कल्पयेन्मूर्त्तिं तस्य हृत्पद्ममध्यगाम् ।

JaySam XII.53ab

One should imagine the image of the god, as given in his *dhyāna*, in the centre of the lotus heart.

The mantric image of the god Viṣṇu is thus described in the **Lakṣmī Tantra**:

सर्वलक्षणसम्पन्ना सर्वाधारमयी परा ।

नित्या सम्पूर्णषाड्गुण्या या विष्णोर्मूर्तिरुज्ज्वला ॥
सैवेयं कथ्यते मूर्त्तिर्मान्त्री मन्त्रैश्चिदात्मकैः ।

LT XXXVI.80–81ab

The bright form of Viṣṇu, which is full of all (lucky) signs and consists of the substratum of all, which is supreme and eternal and possesses all the six (divine) attributes in their totality, is said to be the *mantra*-embodiment. (Tr. Sanjukta Gupta Gombrich)

The fourfold transformation of the goddess Śrī is thus explained in the same Pāñcarātra treatise:

विभजामि स्वया शक्त्या चतुर्धात्मानमात्मना ।
लक्ष्मीः कीर्त्तिर्जया माया चतस्रो मूर्त्तयश्च ताः ॥

LT XLV.2

As operating with my divine power I divide on my own part my own innate nature into fourfold self – they are Lakṣmī, Kīrti, Jayā and Māyā, my four *mūrti*s (manifestations or aspects).

The features of four attending goddesses are given in the **Lakṣmī Tantra** (XLVII.4cd–5ab).

The four types of temples are prescribed for enshrining four images of different gods, set up at the four corners of the main temple:

अतः परं प्रवक्ष्यामि चतुर्मूर्तिप्रभेदकम् ।
नागरं द्राविडं चैव वेसरं मिश्रकं तथा ॥
चतुरश्रं चतुर्वृत्तं त्वष्टाश्रं चैव वर्तुलम् ।
कल्पयेत्तु चतुर्मूर्ति प्रासादं कृतवास्तुभिः ॥

RauUtĀ II.1–2

Now I shall tell four distinctive features of *prāsāda* for four types of images. They are *nāgara, drāviḍa, vesara* and the mixed type. They are square, apsidal, octagonal and round. One should design four temples suitable for four forms of images.
(Based on the tr. by H.N. Chakravarty)

पूर्वे च दक्षिणे चैव पश्चिमे चोत्तरेऽपि च ।
इन्द्रमूर्तिस्तु पूर्वे स्याद्दक्षिणामूर्तिर्दक्षिणे ॥
पश्चिमे विष्णुमूर्तिश्च ब्रह्ममूर्तिस्तथोत्तरे ।

RauUtĀ II.3–4ab

In case the subsidiary shrines are to be in the east, the south, the west and also in the north, (the temple) for the image of Indra should be in the east, Dakṣiṇāmūrti in the south, the image of

Viṣṇu should be installed in the west, while the image of Brahmā is to be placed in the north. (Based on the tr. by H.N. Chakravarty)

Śiva is enumerated to transform himself into five aspects that appear in his five-faced image as assuming five heads:

तद्वपुः पञ्चभिर्मन्त्रैः पञ्चकृत्योपयोगिभिः ॥
ईशतत्पुरुषाघोरवामाजैर्मस्तकादिकम् ।
ईष्टे येन जगत्सर्वं गुणेनोपरिवर्तिना ॥
स मूर्धसमदेशत्वान्मूर्धा नावयवस्तनोः ।

MṛgĀ vp III.8cd–10ab

That body of the Lord is endowed with five *mantras* for functional operating of the five forms of activities, which are represented in the form of Īśāna, Tatpuruṣa, Aghora, Vāmadeva and Sadyojāta, having separate heads and other (bodily attributes). Being equivalent of the supreme position *śīrṣasthānīya* it is called 'head' though it can not be really referred to as a (common place) limb of the body.

The expression *mūrti* employed in case of a God has been explained further in the **Mṛgendra Āgama**:

न जातु देवतामूर्तिरस्मदादिशरीरवत् ।
विशिष्टैश्वर्यसंपन्ना सातो नैतन्निदर्शनम् ॥

MṛgĀ vp I.11

The form (image) of the divinity is not at all like the body of beings such as us (men). It is endowed with a specific supernatural power. Therefore your (i.e. Indra's) comparison is not valid. (Tr. H.N. Chakravarty)

Thus we find one of the forms explained in the **Mataṅgapārameśvara Āgama**:

मूर्त्तिः शरीरं यत्तस्य स्ववीर्यविभवात्मकम् ॥
सद्योजातं पराद्भावात्सुव्यक्तं क्रीडनाय तत् ।
स्वभावस्यापरो भावः सा क्रीडेत्युपचर्यते ॥
सद्यो मूर्तित्वमापन्नं सद्यो मूर्तिस्ततः स्मृतः ।

MPĀ vp IV.28cd–30ab

That form or body of his, which comprises the Lord's own virile power and magnanimity is Sadyojāta. This form (Sadyojāta) has emerged distinct from the transcendent state just for the play (of creation). That play is another (secondary) expression of (primordial) nature and thus entertained (adored) as such. As that state of being (*bhāva*) assumed immediate emanation so it is known as the Sadyojāta *mūrti.*

The primal form of the God is conceived to evolve in the following process:

शक्तेर्नादोऽभवद्बिन्दुरक्षरं मातृका ततः ।
मूर्तिराद्या महेशस्य सर्ववाच्यानुयायिनी ॥

MṛgĀ kp I.2

From *śakti* (*kuṇḍalinī śakti*) *nāda,* the unstruck sound (*anāhata*) evolved. When this sound solidifies itself it appeared as a mass of *bindu,* otherwise known as a drop from which *akṣara* known as immutable *oṃkāra* emerges. It is the first form of Lord Maheśa. It permeates all signified objects. (Tr. H.N. Chakravarty)

The *mantra* form of the deity is thus given:

मूर्तिं हंसाक्षरेणैव बिन्दुभिन्नेन कल्पयेत् ॥

SvT I.39cd

One should conceive the form of the deity (here Svacchanda Bhairava) by means of the syllables *haṃsaḥ* which are penetrated by the *bindu.* (Tr. H.N. Chakravarty)

The concept of *mūrti* as referring to physical substances or material varieties is explained by Abhinavagupta as follows:

पदार्थस्य स्वं रूपं मूर्तिः, तस्या यत् वैचित्र्यं विभेदः, तद् यथा गृहमिति अन्यत् स्वरूपं, प्राङ्गणमिति अन्यत्, विपणिरिति अन्यत् । देवकुलमिति अपरम्, उद्यानमिति अन्यत्, अरण्यमिति तदन्यतरत् ।

ĪPraVim II.1.5

Mūrti means the body of the object and *vaicitrya* means variety of it (*mūrti*). The variety of external bodies such as the house is different from the other, the courtyard is also each different, the market; the temple, the garden or the forest is different from the rest. (Tr. H.N. Chakravarty)

तस्यां दिवि सुदीप्तात्मा निष्कम्पोऽचलमूर्तिमान् ।
काष्ठा सैव परा सूक्ष्मा सर्वदिक्कामृतात्मिका ॥
प्रध्वस्तावरणा शान्ता वस्तुमात्रातिलालसा ।
आद्यन्तोपरता साध्वी मूर्तित्वेनोपचर्यते ।

TĀl I.203–204

In that brilliance (*śakti*) stays as the resplendent, flickerless light who has his own changeless form (*mūrti*). That very *śakti* is His excellence. She is transcendent and subtle and encompasses all the directions. She is of the characteristic of immortality. She has torn asunder all limitations, being of the nature of pure consciousness; becomes exceedingly desirous, her being the aggregate of all objects. She has neither beginning nor the end and is ever faithful (to the Lord). Thus, she is entertained as the form (*mūrti*) of the Lord in the secondary sense. (Based on the tr. by H.N. Chakravarty)

The primary creative impulse is thus explained:

निस्तरङ्गध्रुवधामरूढस्य दृष्टिस्वाभाव्यात् या किल आद्या स्पन्दकला सैव मूर्तिः .... ।

TSā XIII

Of the One, – who is though ultimately congealed as the static light-principle while in the waveless unchangeable state, and is however, by nature ever intent on beholding (worldly manifestation), – the first or primary aspect (*kalā*, attribute) is the vibration (*spanda*). This very same aspect is (called) *mūrti*.

In astrology the term *mūrti* is also employed in the technical sense of the first →*bhāva* (place, state) of *lagna* (or *janma-lagna* = birth sign as one of the twelve zodiacal figures):

मूर्त्तौ करोति दिनकृद् विधवां कुजश्च ... ।

BṛSam CIII.1a

If the Sun or Mars occupy the ascendant at a marriage, the girl would become a widow. (Tr. M.R. Bhat)

As it is elsewhere explained with reference to its results:

मूर्तिमायुश्च कीर्त्तिश्च साङ्गोपाङ्गं निरूपयेत् ।
स्थितिं स्वरूपं सम्पत्तिं जन्मलग्राद् विचिन्तयेत् ॥

Madhya Pārāśarī IX (Bhāvavicārādhyāya).1

There should be indicated in every detail the form, living and fame; (thus) on the basis of the birth-sign (*janma-lagna*) of a person his status, personal aspect, property should be considered.

यदि मूर्त्तो भविचारी शिरोऽथवा भवति मण्डली राहुः ।

BṛSam V.4ab

In case Rāhu has a body, moves in the zodiac, possesses only the head and a circular shape.... (Tr. M.R. Bhat)

Manifestation in the Arts

As the worship of images gained wide popularity by the 3rd-2nd cent. B.C. there came to evolve successively a tradition of art manufacture related to the religious needs of various sects and creeds and their iconic conventions specifying features and attributes of diverse images. Thus, we see a significant branch of knowledge taking definite shape during the Kushana and Gupta periods (i.e. from 1st cent. to 6th cent. A.D.), that fully established itself far and wide and developed through the corridors of time further into distinctive themes of iconography, discussed and treated in great details by the followers of diverse faiths for their own usages and practices, and also for instructing the *śilpin* (both artisans and architects), required to accomplish the work assigned to them by the priestly community. A rich corpus of →*vāstu* and →*śilpa* manuals is found, quite befittingly to have developed and put to writing in various regions and art traditions of which only a few are now fully or partially extant. However, there is also vast amount of useful material incorporated in the religious texts dealing with cult worship, rituals and sacred consecration (*mūrti-pratiṣṭhā*) of images such as the Tantras, Āgamas, Purāṇas, encyclopaedic digests (*nibandhas*), as well as the Jaina and Buddhist works of allied nature.

The common synonyms used in the texts for an image of deity are given as follows:

बिम्बमूर्ति शरीराभा विश्वमूर्तिस्वरूपकैः ॥
चिह्नदेह प्रतिच्छन्दप्रतिमाङ्कैस्तु नामभिः ।
दृश्यदेवः समाख्यातो .... ॥

Mayam XXXIII.2cd–3abc

The manifestation in the form of an image is analogous to a body and is provided with one of the specific aspects of the universal form of the god. Images incorporate the characteristic signs (of each of the forms of god) and the god is designated by the names which correspond to these images. (Tr. B. Dagens)

The **Devī Purāṇa** describes a number of substances in which the images of the goddess are supposed to have been worshipped by various deities for gaining Her specific favour (ch.XXX). Such mediums enlisted there range from a mental image to icons fashioned out in metals or jewels, viz. *mantraśaktimayī*, i.e. one of an abstract forms meditated upon with a rosary representing the Alphabet-as-Goddess (*mantra-mātṛkā*); those made of stone, blue sapphire, gold, silver (*raupya*), brass, bell-metal, clay (→*pṛthivī*), crystal, jewel (*ratna*), copper, pearl, coral, *rīti* (a kind of bronze), tin and lead (*trapu-*

sīsa), alloy of three metals (*triloha*, often explained as consisting of gold, silver and copper), steel (*vajraloha*) and gem (*maṇi*).

It may be further remarked that several works on Pratiṣṭhā and a few extant treatises on medieval iconography mention various mediums, recommended or otherwise, for fashioning a symbol of worship such as an image or a →*liṅga*. For example, the **Śilparatna Kośa** (uttara I.38–41) mentions gold, silver, copper, tin, bronze, brass, octoalloy, *triloha*, diamond, pearl, topaz, cat's eye (*vaidūrya*), ruby, blue sapphire, etc. *Aṣṭaloha* or octo-alloy is specially recommended for making religious implements and images. According to the tradition recorded elsewhere:

हैमं रौप्यं तथा ताम्रं कांस्यं च पित्तलं तथा ।
त्रपु नागः सप्तमः स्यात्कृष्णलोहं तथाऽष्टमम् ॥
इति चाष्टौ लोहकाद्या धातवः परिकीर्तिताः ।
कामदानि च कार्याणि अष्टलोहमयानि च ॥

ApaрPṛ CXCIX.13–14

Gold, silver, copper, bronze and brass, tin, lead as the seventh and the eighth being black iron – these are the eight metals known as the *loha* and others. The *liṅgas* made of an alloy of these eight metals should be made for fulfilling one's desires.

Bhartṛhari has drawn an analogy from the process of painting to explain the 'images' formed in understanding of →*śabda*:

यथैकबुद्धिविषया मूर्त्तिराक्रियते पटे ।
मूर्त्यन्तरस्य त्रितयमेवं शब्देऽपि दृश्यते ॥

Vāk I.52

Just as the unified image of an original figure is drawn on cloth (in three stages), so does one see the three stages in the case of the word also. (Tr. K.A.S. Iyer)

We can analyse the above observations, in the context of painting which may be equally applicable also to the process of image-making:

1. the first image is the one which the painter (or a sculptor) knows properly in his mind through the knowledge of the figure complete in all its parts;

2. the second is that which he invokes in his mind for painting (or carving) as taking its different parts and shapes one by one;

3. the third image is that which is given its complete (composite) shape and finished by him on the canvas (*paṭe*) (or fashioned out in stone or other medium) (P.K. Agrawala, *On the Ṣaḍaṅga Canons of Painting*, pp. 33–34).

How certain iconographic traits finding occasional mention in contemporary literature can be usefully analysed against their chronological setting may be demonstrated here by the following pieces of evidence:

मूर्ते च गङ्गायमुने तदानीं सचामरे देवमसेविषाताम् ।
समुद्रगारूपविपर्ययेऽपि सहंसपाते इव लक्ष्यमाणे ॥

Kum VII.42

Though in form different from rivers yet recognised, as it were, by being accompanied by flights of swans, Gaṅgā and Yamunā too, in embodied forms, served the god with chowries. (Tr. H.H. Wilson)

This reference to two river-goddesses appearing in human form as attending upon the god with fly-whisks in their hand must be viewed against its proper setting of art history (Kalātattvakośa Vol. III, fig. 37). As identified by Prof. V.S. Agrawala, "This was the most typical decoration on the door-jambs of the Gupta temple. No specimen of early or late Kushana art has so far been found portraying this feature. Indeed, with the emergence of the flat-roofed small shrines in the early Gupta period (4th century A.D.), the framework of the entrance to the temple received special attention and various elements of decoration were introduced to impart beauty, grace and life to the architectural portion leading to the place of the deity in the shrine" (*Studies in Indian Art*, p. 211). Thus, we see the two goddesses shown in person as riding on their respective vehicles, *makara* (alligator) and *kūrma* (tortoise), and holding a *ghaṭa* in the hand, e.g. at Deogarh temple.

Kālidāsa has further alluded also to the human images of Viṣṇu's weapons, characterised by their specific cognisances, presumably on the head.

गुप्तं ददृशुरात्मानं सर्वाः स्वप्नेषु वामनैः ।
जलजासिगदाशार्ङ्गचक्रलाञ्छितमूर्तिभिः ॥

Ragh X.60

The queens saw in their dreams that they (on account of the presence of the Vaishnava *teja* within their wombs) were guarded by dwarfish beings bearing the symbols of conch, sword, mace, bow and disc. (Tr. V.S. Agrawala)

It is remarkable here that this iconographic convention of showing the personified weapons of Viṣṇu appears to have evolved for the first time in the Gupta period sculpture, to which date the great poet Kālidāsa has been referred to by modern historians.

As a preamble to the detailed enumeration of Brahmanical iconography the Puranic doctrine on basic unity of three principal gods, viz. Brahmā,

Viṣṇu and Śiva, is analysed with reference to their personal aspects which largely explain their features:

आदावेव प्रवक्ष्यामि त्रिमूर्तेस्तव पार्थिव ॥
विष्णोरमितवीर्यस्य प्रतिमालक्षणं शुभम् ।
ब्राह्मी तु राजसी मूर्तिस्तस्य सर्वप्रवर्तिनी ॥
सात्त्विकी वैष्णवी ज्ञेया संसारपरिपालिनी ।
तामसी च तथा रौद्री ज्ञेया संहारकारिणी ॥

VDhPur III.44.2cd–4

O King, I shall tell you in the beginning about iconographic features of the god Viṣṇu, who is of boundless virility and triple-imaged (*tri-mūrti*, or transforms himself in three divine images): the image that is (known as) his *rājasa* aspect is Brahmā, unfolding the entire creation; the one known to be his *sāttvika* image is Viṣṇu, who supports these worlds; and the one known as his *tāmasa* form is Rudra, bringing about contraction (or destruction of universe).

The arch-artificer god Viśvakarmā is described in his imaged form as follows:

विश्वकर्मा तु कर्तव्यः सूर्यरूपधरः प्रभुः ।
सन्दंशपाणिर्द्विभुजस्तेजोमूर्तिधरो भवेत् ॥
विश्वं करोति वै यस्माद्विश्वकर्मा ततः स्मृतः ।
विश्वकृद्भगवान् विष्णुर्विश्वकर्मा स उच्यते ॥

VDhPur III.71.17–18

Viśvakarmā should be made as having a physical appearance (generally) akin to the Sun god (i.e. wearing northerner's dress, etc.). He should be resplendent in form, two-armed as bearing a pair of princers (or the hand-pose called *sandaṃśa*). Indeed, he creates the world, so he is known by the name Viśvakarmā. It is the world-creator aspect of the lord Viṣṇu himself, that is styled as Viśvakarmā.

The image of Narasiṃha incarnation is stated to be a form of the Saṅkarṣaṇa aspect of Viṣṇu (VDhPur III.78.7–10).

Likewise, on the symbolical significance of the image of the Varāha incarnation, the same Purāṇa observes:

मूर्तिमन्तमनैश्वर्यं हिरण्याक्षं विदुर्बुधाः ।
ऐश्वर्येण वराहेण स निरस्तोऽरिमर्दनः ॥

VDhPur III.79.8

The knowledgeable sages know Hiraṇyākṣa to be the personified non-*aiśvarya*; by the divine faculty of Supremacy (*aiśvarya*) personified in Varāha, the same demon, vanquisher of (other) enemies was destroyed.

About the placement of *āyudhas* in the hands of Vaiṣṇava forms, the **Matsya Purāṇa** indicates thus:

चतुर्भुजस्य वक्ष्यामि यथैवायुधसंस्थितिः ॥
दक्षिणेन गदापद्मं वासुदेवस्य कारयेत्।
वामतः शङ्खचक्रे च कर्तव्ये भूतिमिच्छता ॥
कृष्णावतारे तु गदा वामहस्ते प्रशस्यते ।
यथेच्छया शंङ्खचक्रे चोपरिष्टात्प्रकल्पयेत् ॥

MatPur CCLVIII.8cd–10

Of the four-armed Lord (Viṣṇu) I expound the manner regarding the position of his weapons. Of Vāsudeva one should make a club and a lotus on the right and a conch and a discus on the left. In the image representing the Kṛṣṇa incarnation, the club is preferably made in the left hand and the conch and the discuss may be shown over and above as per one's desire.

The five *mūrti*s of Śiva are specified as follows:

स्फटिकाभं चतुर्बाहुं फलशूलधरं शिवम् ॥
साभयं वरदं पञ्चवदनं च त्रिलोचनम् ।
पत्रेषु मूर्त्तयः पञ्च स्थाप्यास्तत्पुरुषादयः ॥
पूर्वे तत्पुरुषः श्वेतो अघोरोऽष्टभुजोऽसितः ।
चतुर्बाहुमुखः पीतः सद्योजातश्च पश्चिमे ॥
वामदेवः स्त्रीविलासी चतुर्वक्त्रभुजोऽरुणः ।
सौम्ये पञ्चास्य ईशाने ईशानः सर्वदः सितः ॥

AgPur CCCIV.23cd–26

Śiva has crystal-like white complexion, five-faced, three-eyed (in each of his face), four armed as holding a fruit, a lance and showing the *abhaya* and *varada* poses. On the (five peripheral) petals, his five aspects, viz. Tatpuruṣa and others, are to be assigned. In the east is Tatpuruṣa, who is white; (in the south) is eight-armed Aghora, who is black in colour; in the west is Sadyojāta, having four arms and four faces, (yellow in colour). Vāmadeva is in the north, being four-faced and four-armed, red in colour, and having the graceful bearing like a female; in the north-eastern point is the five-faced Īśāna, white in colour and all-bestowing.

There is a list of sixteen images of Śiva that are commonly named and described with respect to their mythical legends and forms, iconometric and iconographic specifications as well as installation rites in the sections, that treat such subjects in the Śaiva Āgamas and also in allied Śilpa works, such as the **Kāśyapa Śilpa, Sakalādhikāra, Mānasara, Mayamata, Īśānaśivagurudeva Paddhati, Śilparatna Kośa,** etc. As it is given in the **Sakalādhikāra**, ascribed to Agastya:

सोमास्कन्देश्वरं सेन्दुशेखरं वृषवाहनम् ।
नटेश्वरं तथा गङ्गाधरं च त्रिपुरान्तकम् ॥
कल्याणसुन्दरं चार्धनारिं पाशुपतं तथा ।
कङ्कालं केशवार्धं च भिक्षाटनमतः परम् ॥
चण्डेशानुग्रहं दक्षिणेशं कालविनाशनम् ।
लिङ्गोद्भवं च मूर्तीनां भेदः षोडशधा भवेत् ॥

Sakala I.6–8

The division of Śiva's images is of sixteenfold, including (the forms known as) Somāskanda-mūrti, Candraśekhara, Vṛṣavāhana, Naṭarāja, Gaṅgādhara, Tripurāntaka, Kalyāṇasundara, Ardhanārī, Pāśupata, Kaṅkāla, Keśavārdha, Bhikṣāṭana, Caṇḍeśānugraha, Dakṣiṇāmūrti, Kālāntaka, and Liṅgodbhava-mūrti.

Of them, the image of Dakṣiṇāmūrti is thus described elsewhere in its iconographic details:

त्र्यक्षं चतुर्भुजं शान्तमार्जवमार्द्रवान्वितम् ॥
अन्योन्याङ्घ्रितलौ द्वौ च स्फिक्पिण्डाधः प्रकल्पयेत् ।
हृदये ज्ञानमुद्रा तु ह्यभ्यन्तरमुखं करम् ॥
वरदं वामहस्तं तु कटिसूत्रोपरि न्यसेत् ।
दक्षिणे परहस्तेऽक्षमालाधृग्वामसूचिका ॥
नासाग्रं तु समीक्ष्याक्षि स्वल्पासितप्रकाशकम् ।
अपरे पार्श्वयोश्चैव जटाधाराः प्रलम्बयेत् ॥
ऋषयः पार्श्वयोश्चैव नीत्या तृप्तिं प्रकल्पिताः ।
बाह्वोश्चैव जटाभारे व्याला यानसमन्विताः ॥
मृगपक्ष्यादयश्चैव योगाभ्यासं प्रचारिताः ।
दक्षिणामूर्तिराख्याता .... ॥

RauĀ kp XXXV 287cd-292abc

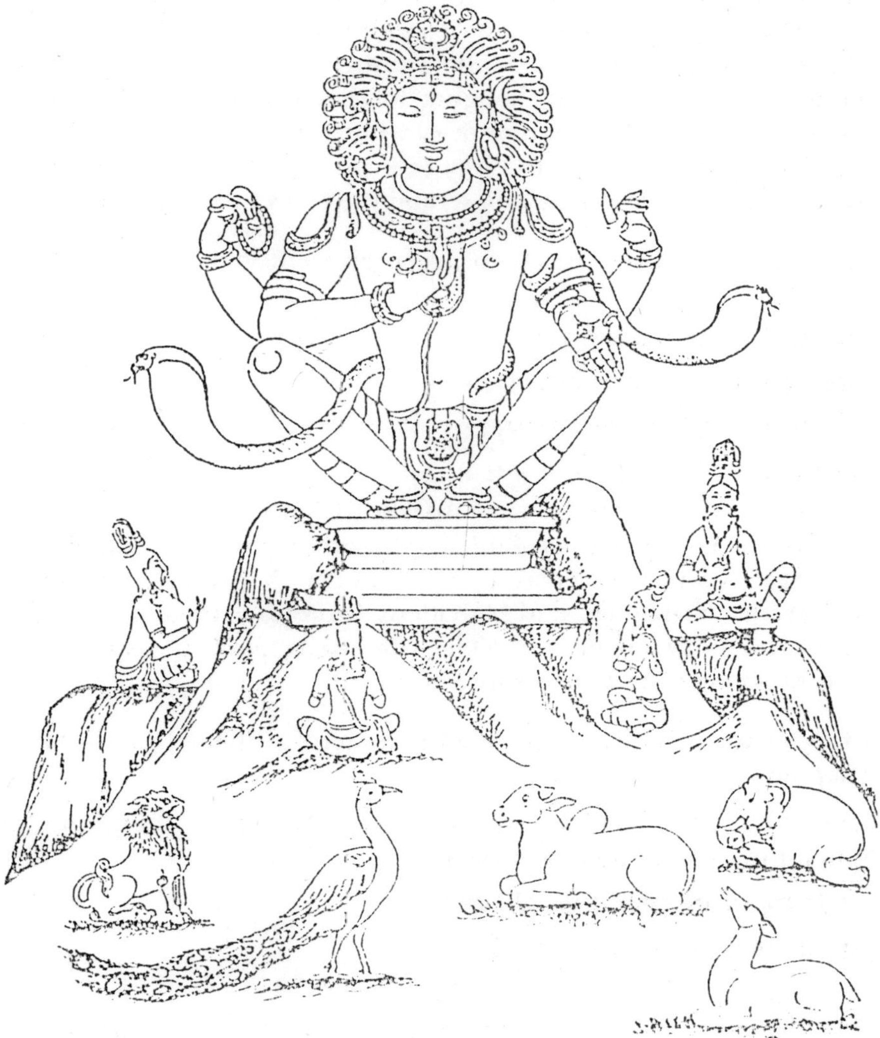

Figure 10: Dakṣiṇāmūrti

He is three-eyed, four-armed and graceful, straitforward, and soft-hearted. His two feet are to be placed under the mass of hips. Before the heart the *jñānamudrā* (i.e. the fingers and palm of the hand raised up as turned towards the chest) while the left hand should be in the *varada* pose (i.e. boon-granting) as placed over the waistband, the lower right hand bears the rosary and the left one is held as showing the *sūcikā* pose (i.e. the tips of fingers as raised up with the index-finger slightly bent like a needle). His eyes gazing at the tip of the nose are open just as much as only a slight glimpse of the dark eye-ball is visible. His matted hair should be shown flowing as dangling on both the sides and back. Seers on both of his sides are to be shown seated in ever satisfied mood. On his arms and hanging locks are serpents with open fangs. Deer, other animals and wild birds are to be shown there as gathered about and engaged in yoga practices. Thus Dakṣiṇāmūrti is described. (Based on the tr. by H.N. Chakravarty)

However, there are twelve image-forms of Śiva enlisted and described elsewhere:

सद्यो वामोऽघोरतत्पुरुषावीशान एव च ।
मृत्युंजयश्च विजयः किरणाक्षोऽघोरास्त्रकः ॥
श्रीकण्ठश्च महादेवो रुद्राश्चैकादश स्मृताः ।
द्वादशकलासम्पूर्ण-मूर्तिश्चैवं सदाशिवः ॥

AparPṛ CCXII.1–2

There are known eleven Rudras, namely, Sadyojāta, Vāmadeva, Aghora, Tatpuruṣa, Īśāna, Mṛtyuñjaya, Vijaya, Kiraṇākṣa, Aghorāstra, Śrīkaṇṭha, and Mahādeva. Sadāśiva is thus the twelfth one, who is an image complete with twelve *kalās* (= aspects or constituents of the Lord's supreme form).

Each of these icons is given a detailed treatment in the verses (8–34) of the same chapter.

An image of the Great Goddess, made in clay, is especially mentioned in the Devī Māhātmya of **Mārkaṇḍeya Purāṇa**:

तौ तस्मिन् पुलिने देव्याः कृत्वा मूर्तिं महीमयीम् ।
अर्हणां चक्रतुस्तस्याः पुष्पधूपाग्नितर्पणैः ॥

MārkPur XC.7

Having made an earthen image of the goddess on that sand-bank, they both paid worship to her with the offering of flowers, incense, fire-sacrifice and water-libations.

The best of the Northern temples described in Vāstu treatises of medieval period is styled as the *meru* or *mahāmeru prāsāda* fit only for the trinity of leading Hindu gods:

कर्णे श्रृङ्गत्रयं चैव एकोत्तरशताण्डकः ।
मेरुश्चापि समाख्यातः कर्तव्यश्च त्रिमूर्तिके ॥

AparPṛ CLIX.65

[By adding further] three more spires on the corners thus is (made) the temple having a hundred *aṇḍakas* (i.e. superstructure-units, *śikharas*), known as the *meru*, to be made (only) in case of Brahmanical Trinity.

The choice of gods in such a triple group is restricted only to the following:

हरो हिरण्यगर्भश्च हरिर्दिनकरस्तथा ।
एते देवा: स्थिता मेरौ नान्येषां स कदाचन ॥

AparPṛ CLIX.67 (also cf. CLXXXIII.12)

In a *meru* are stationed only these gods: Śiva, Brahmā and Hari or the Sun. The *meru* must never be made for any other deities.

The **Aparājita Pṛcchā** mentions a rare group of four types of Brahmā's icons:

ब्रह्मा पितामहश्चैव विरञ्चि: कमलासन: ।
एकैकस्य यथा प्रोक्ता मूर्ति: स्यात्परमेष्ठिन: ॥

AparPṛ CCXIV.2

(There are) Brahmā, Pitāmaha, Virañci and Kamalāsana. Of them, each (specific) image of Parameṣṭhin (Brahmā) should be as it is described.

Their iconographic characteristics are distinctly treated in the text. Accordingly, Kamalāsana has four hands carrying a rosary and a ladle (*sruk*) in the right ones and a book and a water pot in the left. Virañci has the rosary and book in his right hands while the left ones hold a ladle and a waterpot. Likewise, Pitāmaha is specified by his attributes of a waterpot and a rosary in the right hands and a ladle (*sruva*) and a book in the left ones. Brahmā's form is defined by a book and a rosary in his right hands and a *sruva* and a waterpot in the left hands (cf. verses 3–9; also reproduced in Rūpamaṇḍana).

The fourfold *vyūha* images of Viṣṇu are seen as related to the pattern of quadruple symbology:

अथात: संप्रवक्ष्यामि विष्णुमूर्तेश्च लक्षणम् ।
मूर्तयो वासुदेवाद्या युगादिवर्णभेदत: ॥
कृते युगे वासुदेवस्त्रेतायां कृष्ण एव च ।
प्रद्युम्नो द्वापरे चैवानिरुद्धश्च कलौ युगे ॥
वासुदेवो भवेद्विप्रे क्षत्रे संकर्षण: शुभ: ।
प्रद्युम्नश्च तथा वैश्ये शूद्रे चैवानिरुद्धक: ॥

AparPṛ CCXVII.1–3

Now I shall tell the features of Viṣṇu's image. The (four) images of Vāsudeva and others are taken as represented in accordance with the (four) ages (*yugas*) and the (four) *varṇas*; for Kṛta is

Vāsudeva, Tretā is Kṛṣṇa, Dvāpara is Pradyumna and Kali is Aniruddha. In case of the four *varṇas*, there are the gods Vāsudeva, Saṅkarṣaṇa, Pradyumna and Aniruddha respectively.

The text goes on as describing their iconographic forms in great details and has treated further the sequence of *āyudhas* (weapons, attributes) to be shown in the two sets of their twelve and twenty-four emanations (*dvādaśa-mūrtayaḥ* and *caturviṃśati-mūrtayaḥ*) with respect to the four hands of each of such forms, known by a specific name as popular in the orthodox Pāñcarātra tradition of Medieval Iconology (cf. AparPṛ CCXVII.4–33).

On the worship of nine planets or *navagraha* representations, the **Yājñavalkya Smṛti** prescribes their manufacturing medium differently:

सूर्यः सोमो महीपुत्रः सोमपुत्रो बृहस्पतिः ।
शुक्रः शनैश्चरो राहुः केतुश्चेति ग्रहाः स्मृताः ॥
ताम्रकात्स्फटिकाद्रक्तचन्दनात्स्वर्णकादुभौ ।
राजतादयसः सीसात्कांस्यात्कार्या ग्रहाः क्रमात् ॥
स्ववर्णैर्वा पटे लेख्या गन्धैर्मण्डलकेषु वा ।

YājSm I.296–298ab

There are known the Sun-god with the planets, viz. the Moon, Mars, Mercury, Jupiter, Venus, Saturn, Rāhu and Ketu. Their representations are to be made respectively in copper, crystal, red-sandal wood, the next two being of gold, in silver, iron, lead and bronze in the order (of their mention). Or, these may be drawn on a cloth in their specific colours, or they be just represented on the diagrammatic circles, done in (coloured) fragrant substances [as the commentary adds, *yathāvarṇam*, i.e. as per their respective colours].

According to the commentary of Vijñāneśvara, they are to be shown in the *graha-pūjā*, planet worship, as two-armed deity-figures, in accordance with the iconographic details, laid down in the **Matsya Purāṇa** (XCIII.1–8).

In the chapter on iconographic features of deity images, Varāhamihira has thus described the forms of the Buddha and the Jaina Tīrthaṅkara:

पद्माङ्कितकरचरणः प्रसन्नमूर्तिः सुनीचकेशश्च ।
पद्मासनोपविष्टः पितेव जगतो भवति बुद्धः ॥
आजानुलम्बबाहुः श्रीवत्साङ्कः प्रशान्तमूर्तिश्च ।
दिग्वासास्तरुणो रूपवांश्च कार्योऽर्हतां देवः ॥

BṛSam LVIII.44–45

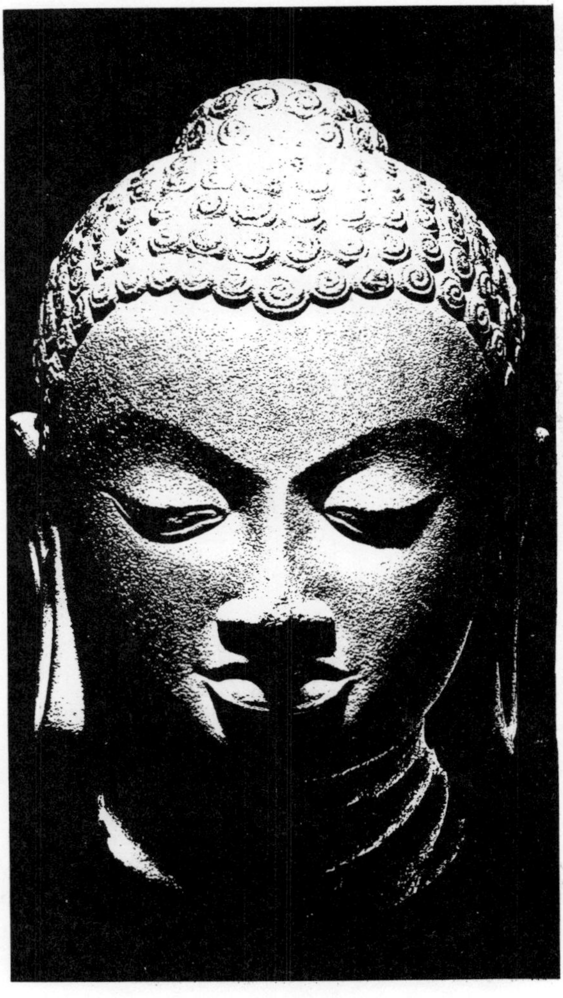

Figure 11: Buddha as *dakṣiṇāvartamūrdhā*

Buddha, as if he were the father of mankind, should be represented with a placid countenance, seated on a lotus seat, with the palms and soles bearing lotus marks and very short hair (*sunīcakeśaḥ*) (a variant reading is *sunītakeśaḥ* which would mean 'well-arranged' – perhaps referring to the 'short curls on the Buddha-head turning from left to right, *dakṣiṇāvartamūrdhaja*, a characteristic sign of Buddha). The god of the Arhats (the Jainas, i.e. any of the 24 Tīrthaṅkaras) should be shown nude young and beautiful in appearance with a tranquil expression and arms reaching down to the knees; his breast should have the (auspicious) *śrīvatsa* mark. (Tr. J.N. Banerjea)

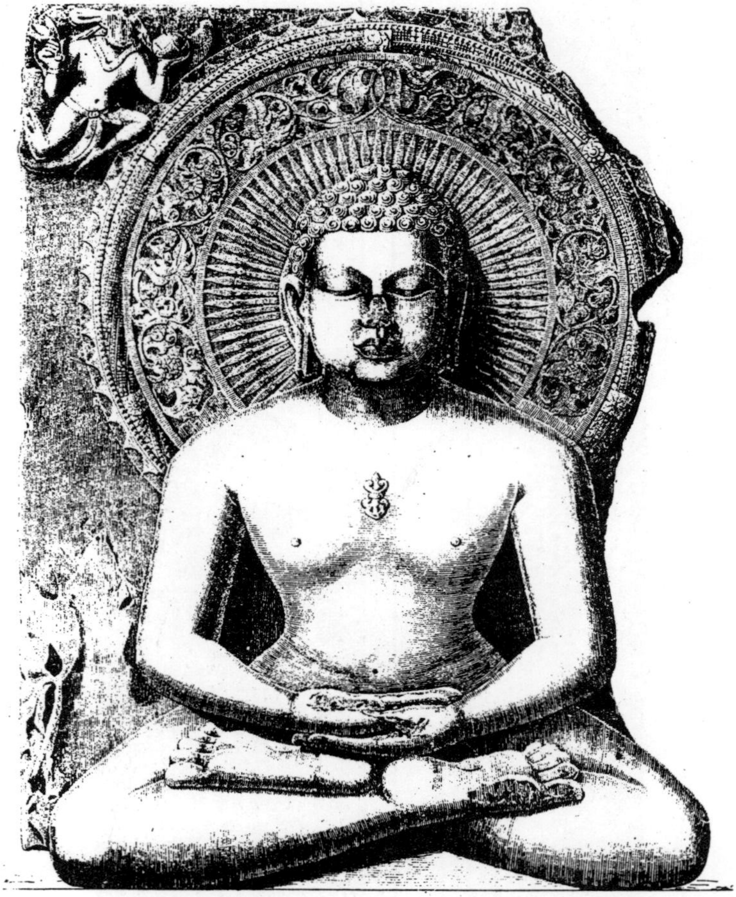

Figure 12: Jaina Tīrthaṅkara with *śrīvatsa* mark

जिनस्य मूर्तयोऽनन्ताः पूजिताः सर्वसौख्यदाः ।
चतस्रोऽतिशयैर्युक्तास्तासां पूज्या विशेषतः ॥
श्री आदिनाथो नेमिश्च पार्श्वो वीरश्चतुर्थकः ।
चक्रेश्वर्यम्बिका पद्मावती सिद्धायकेति च ॥

Rūp VI.25–26

There are numerous images of the Jina that being worshipped bestow happiness. Particularly four of the Tīrthaṅkaras are worshipped owing to their miraculous powers, viz. Ādinātha (Ṛṣabha), Neminātha, Pārśvanātha and Mahāvīra as the fourth. (Their attendant Yakṣīs or Śāsanadevīs) are Cakreśvarī, Ambikā, Padmāvatī, and Siddhāyakā.

By meditating upon the deity, a votary visualises Him as assuming a specific image before his mind's eye:

संहरंश्चाचिन्त्यमूर्त्तिरुदेति ।

Niṣpannayogāvalī, p. 1

And comprehending thus, the one (i.e., Vajrasattva) with unimaginable form (*mūrti* or image) rises up.

Having described the formation of certain →*maṇḍalas* or deity-circles, as visualised in the Vajrayāna liturgy, the author Abhayākaragupta has thus stated in the concluding lines of the work:

कथ्यमानाऽपि तथा अमेया मूर्त्तिसम्पदः ।
अम्भोभृदुद्वहत्यम्बुवारिधेरक्षयं पयः ॥
श्रीवज्रभृन्मूर्त्यामृतप्रवाहादुदञ्चदुच्चैः सुकृतामृतौघैः ।
निःसीममूर्त्येव परस्पराभिः परार्थकृत् स्यादभयः कृतीशः ॥

Niṣpannayogāvalī, p. 93

Due to his immortalising mass of meritorious deeds, the writer Abhaya may achieve the supreme goal by the grace of the mutually allied ones, – who, by enumerating the unfathomable wealth of such image-forms, has just acted highly like a cloud lifting up inexhaustible water from the ocean, owing to the nectar-flow of innumerable image-forms of the illustrious lord Vajradhara (bearer of the thunderbolt), possessing the boundless image-unity.

Comments of the **Śukranītisāra** on the features of cult images and *liṅgas* are also pertinent:

यथोपाधिप्रभेदेन ससंयोगविभागतः ।
समस्तव्यस्तवर्णादिभेदज्ञानं प्रजायते ॥
लेख्या लेप्या सैकती च मृन्मयी पैष्टिकी तथा ।
एतासां लक्षणाभावे न कश्चिद्दोष ईरितः ॥
बाणलिङ्गे स्वयंभूते चंद्रकान्त समुद्भवे ।
रत्नजे गंडकोद्भूते मानदोषो न सर्वथा ॥

ŚNSā IV.4.151–153

In accordance with difference of attributes and specification of groupings there arises the knowledge of distinctive colours etc. and of single or collective arrangement. Any lack of features is not considered a demerit in case of a painted, plastered, sand-made, clay-made or dough-made image. (Likewise) any deficiency in *māna* (= standard measure) does not altogether hold good, in case of the Bāṇa, or Svayambhū liṅga, neither in case of a *liṅga* made of moon-stone or of jewel, nor in case of a pebble-symbol originating from the Gaṇḍakī river.

Process

As regards procedural details of technique, employed in the manufacture of a clay or stucco image for setting up in the sanctum of a shrine, the description in the **Śrīpraśna Saṃhitā** (XIII.2–8) is note worthy.

The mode of working out the plastering of images, to be done in sequence, stage by stage, in case the principle image is desired to be made in clay – (i) wooden armature; (ii) binding of cords; (iii) plastering with clay; (iv) fixing of tubes or channels; (v) binding with cocoanut coir; (vi) plastering with mixed clay; (vii) another binding of (finer) cords; (viii) plastering of gritty material; (ix) setting of cloth-pieces; (x) application of decoration; (xi) imparting white base; and finally (xii) application of various colours according to the choice of specific images. However, the application of colours is enjoined for the figures other than the principal image. The main image is besmeared only by sandal paste, agallochum paste, and oil etc.

With reference to the renovation procedure enjoined for an idol, the Pāñcarātra authority's declaration is as under:

या मूर्तिर्येन तन्त्रेण यादृशेनाधिकारिणा ।
प्रथमे कल्पने सैव द्वितीये कल्पने भवेत् ॥
मूर्तिस्तदेव तन्त्रं च स एव स्थापकः पुनः ।
तन्त्राधिकारिमूर्तीनां व्यत्यये कल्पिते सति ।
नृणां नरपतेश्चापि राष्ट्रस्य च भवेत् क्षयः ॥

PSam cp XVII.29–30

Which kind of image has been formerly (originally) set up, under which creed, and by which sort of officiating teacher the same kind (of every order) should be maintained in the subsequently done renovation; there has to be again the image of the same kind, the same tradition of creed, and the same sort of officiating preceptor. If there takes place any inversion of order, that would cause destruction of the people, the king as well as the kingdom.

About renovation of an old image the prescription given in the **Agni Purāṇa** is worth noticing:

जीर्णोद्धारविधिं वक्ष्येऽभूषितां स्नपयेद् गुरुः ।
अचलां विन्यसेद् गेहे अतिजीर्णां परित्यजेत् ॥
व्यङ्गां भग्नां च शैलाढ्यां न्यसेदन्यां च पूर्ववत् ।
संहारविधिना तत्र तत्त्वान् संहृत्य देशिकः ॥
सहस्रं नारसिंहेन हुत्वा तामुद्धरेद् गुरुः ।
दारवीं दाहयेद् वह्नौ शैलजां प्रक्षिपेज्जले ॥
धातुजां रत्नजां वापि अगाधे वा जलेऽम्बुधौ ।
यानमारोप्य जीर्णाङ्गं छाद्य वस्त्रादिना नयेत् ॥
वादित्रैः प्रक्षिपेत्तोये गुरवे दक्षिणां ददेत् ।
यत्प्रमाणा च यद्द्रव्या तन्मानां स्थापयेद्दिने ॥

AgPur LXVII.1–5

I would tell now the procedure for renovating an old image. The teacher should anoint (and decorate afresh) the one without ornaments and consecrate it in the shrine if it is of the immovable type. In case it is greatly damaged it should be discarded. (In place of) the stone image broken in its major limbs, a new one should be consecrated (with due rituals) as laid down before. By collecting back the elements in a counter-clockwise manner, the ritualist should withdraw that (broken one) while performing a thousand oblations with the Nārasiṃha *mantra* and should destroy it in fire if the image is of wood; in case it is the stone one it should be thrown into water. Also the metallic or the jewel one should (be immersed) in some fathomless water-reservoir. The image broken in its limbs should be taken away as covered with a cloth on a vehicle, in accompaniment of instruments sounded and thrown into water. The teacher (priest) should then be given gifts. (The new image) to be consecrated on an auspicious day should be of the same size and of the same material (as was the former one).

The Śilpa text **Rūpamaṇḍana** comments on the worthiness of generally recommended images and also on the rule for repairs in case of damaged ones:

अष्टलोहमयी मूर्तिः शैलरत्नमयी शुभा ।
श्रेष्ठवृक्षमयी वापि प्रवालादिमयी शुभा ॥
अतीताब्दशता मूर्तिः पूज्या स्यान्महत्तमैः ।
खण्डिता स्फुटिताऽप्यर्च्या अन्यथा दुःखदायका ॥
धातुरत्नविलेपोत्था व्यङ्गा संस्कारयोग्यका ।
काष्ठपाषाणजा भग्ना संस्कारार्हा न देवता ॥

Rūp I.10–12

> The image made in an alloy of eight metals [or in eight different metals], and the images carved in stone or jewels are of auspicious nature. Or, also that which is carved in the wood from the best of trees and also the one made in (gems like) coral and others. An image older by a hundred years is worthy being worshipped by eminent persons; on the contrary, an image if broken or fragmentary causes trouble. However, the image made in metal, or jewel or in paste-substance is worthy of proper repairs even in case of deficiency of limbs. A broken deity-image if made of wood or stone is not worthy of repairs.

For a resume of the processes operative in the field of age-old Mūrti-Śāstra we may review here the contents of a canonical work compiled at the fully evolved stage of the subject – by a great practical master of his times (15th cent. A.D.).

The title Devatāmūrtiprakaraṇa of **Sūtradhāra Maṇḍana** is indeed a handy treatise of medieval Indian Iconography and Iconometry. Divided into well-defined eight chapters (*adhyāyas*) on the subject of deity images (*devatā-mūrtis*), it deals with the following topics:

i) The examination and selection of stone, wood, etc.; the dimension of image types; merits and demerits thereof; and portents and omens.

ii) The units for measurements and *tālamāna* (iconometry).

iii) Position and facing of cult images in temple plan.

iv) Various images – Brahmā, Sūrya, nine Planets, and ten Dikpālas.

v) Vaiṣṇava images.

vi) Images of Rudra and Liṅgas.

vii) Twentyfour Tīrthaṅkara images, their attendant Yakṣas and Yakṣīs (*śāsanadevatās*).

viii) Images of various goddesses.

Conclusion

The concept *mūrti* evolved along the root-meaning of *mūrch-*, to congeal, to assume shape as a body or formed image. Thus, it served as a handy term to underline the notion of an abstract entity as *amūrta, amūrti*; when conceived on a material or concrete level the form or a concept thereof is given a tangible identity or definition as *mūrta* or *mūrti*. The formless or abstract principle is the subtle source of ideas, attributes, qualities or aspects. however, the *mūrti* is a form which imbibes and sets forth on those aspects, ideas or attributes on a definitive visualisation. Thus, in all major traditions of Indian thought, the god-head is described to assume *mūrta* or formed aspect. He or She is conceived as transforming Himself or Herself into various images, incarnations, emanations or personalised divine entities. As it is aptly put by Gauḍapāda:

> मूर्त इति मूर्तविदोऽमूर्त इति च तद्विदः ॥
>
> MāṇḍKā II.23cd
>
> It is the *mūrta* for those who know the formed aspect and for those who know that as noumenon it is formless one.

There evolved successively the worship of divine images or *mūrtis* with various religious creeds and sects that gave birth to a rich tradition of image making and iconography. Thus, a remarkable material of actual art specimens as well as a large number of literary texts are to present various aspects of this development through the ages. Many Śilpa treatises, either independent or as incorporated in their summary form in the religious works such as the Purāṇas, Tantras, Āgamas, ritual digests, etc., are of immense help for understanding the nature and growth of Indian images, their ritual background, manufacture and techniques, iconometry and iconological principles.

Prithvi Kumar Agrawala

Select Bibliography

Agrawala, P.K.: On the Ṣaḍaṅga Canons of Painting, Varanasi: Prithivi Prakashan, 1981.

Agrawala, V.S.: Spark from Vedic Fire, Varanasi: Prithivi Prakashan, 1961.

— Studies in Indian Art, Varanasi: Vishwavidyalaya Prakashan, 1965.

— Vedic Lectures, Varanasi: Prithivi Prakashan, 2nd edn, 1981.

Banerjea, J.N.: Development of Hindu Iconography, Calcutta: University of Calcutta, 2nd edn, 1956.

PRATIMĀ-PRATIKṚTI

Overview

Pratimā, an image, icon, figure, likeness, similitude, reflection; model, model-type, representative; counterpart, copy, duplicate, an adversary; etc. derived from the root *mā-*, to measure, with prefix *prati*, towards, in accordance, or comparison with, or in opposition to, the word generally refers to images of deities, figures and representations of ideas in a concrete form or imagination. Almost similar in connotation is the word *pratikṛti*, although less frequent in usage it specifically denotes an image, a portrait, a counterpart; it usually has the sense of opposition, retaliation; an adversary, etc.; derived from the root *kṛ-*, to do with prefix *prati*.

The word *pratimā* has been used in several Vedic contexts to denote a measured representative, the representation or symbol of something. It implies, at times, a counterpart or model, while elsewhere, a surrogate. Being evolved on the basic concept of likeness, affinity or comparison, the term *pratimā* came to convey the idea of an image, symbolic figure, even divine image. As early as the formation of the later Vedic texts and Epics, this meaning is well evidenced for *pratimā* while the cognate *pratikṛti* also implies an effigy or likeness of person. Pāṇini gives a rule regarding words denoting *pratikṛti* as figures in the likeness of an original subject.

The Purāṇas devote detailed discussion on the divine images, their installation ritual, manufacture, iconography, aesthetic and devotional aspects, etc. The texts on the Dharmaśāstra and Arthaśāstra also treat images against their various settings. In the Buddhistic tradition, once the Buddha image was introduced during the first-second cent. A.D., there evolved a widespread following of image-worship in an ever-developing pantheon. Besides the Jina images and cults of various divinities, the Jaina ethics uses the word *pratimā* in an exclusive sense of rules or standards of conduct.

In Vedānta, *pratimā* denotes a measured aspect, also an image of a deity. Image-worship forms the core of Vaiṣṇava and Śaiva philosophies while the Tantras and Āgamas define the divine symbols on several levels of visualisation, as image, symbolic shapes, diagrams, mental notions, etc.

In the art conventions and iconography there developed an enormous body of shastric injunctions treating *pratimākaraṇa* (image-making) and →*tālamāna* (iconometry), aesthetic and dedicatory ideals, etc.

Etymology and Related Words

By way of etymology the term *pratimā* is derived from the root *mā-*, 'to measure' and 'to sound' (*māṅ māne śabde ca* – PāDhā XXV.6), being prefixed with *prati* and added by the verbal suffix *aṅ* (Pā III.3.106).

Pratikṛti is a feminine noun derived from the root *kṛ-* 'to do', being prefixed with *prati* and followed by the suffix *ktin* (Pā III.3.93).

According to the **Amara Kośa**, *pratimā* and *pratikṛti* have the following common synonyms:

> प्रतिमानं प्रतिबिम्बं प्रतिमा प्रतियातना प्रतिच्छाया ॥
> प्रतिकृतिरर्चा पुंसि प्रतिनिधिरुपमोपमानं स्यात् ।
>
> AmKo II.10.35cd–36ab
>
> The terms (of similar meaning) are *pratimāna* (counterpart), *pratibimba* (counter-reflection), *pratimā* (image), *pratiyātanā* (statue), *praticchāyā* (counter-shadow), *pratikṛti* (counter-figure, image), *arcā* (idol), *pratinidhi* (representation; in masculine gender), *upamā* (simile) and *upamāna* (analogy).

As Kṣīrasvāmin remarks *pratimīyate'neneti pratimānaṃ pratimā ca* – (AmKo II.10.36), 'that by which something is known as comparison is *pratimāna* also *pratimā*.'

As **Medinī Kośa** (XVI.212cd) puts it, *pratikṛtirathārcāyāṃ pratinidhi-pratīkārayośca strī,* 'the word *pratikṛti,* feminine in gender, denotes an *arcā* (image, effigy), a *pratinidhi* (representative) and *pratīkāra* (revenge).'

The **Vaijayantī Kośa** (III.9.20cd) has stated: *praticchāyā pratikṛtiḥ pratimā pratiyātanā* – *praticchāyā* (reflection), *pratikṛti* (counterpart), *pratimā* (image) and *pratiyātanā* (figure) – all are synonymous.

The **Anekārtha Saṅgraha** of Hemacandra states:

> प्रतिमा प्रतिरूपके, गजस्य दन्तबन्धे च ।
>
> AneSaṅg III.1069–70
>
> The word *pratimā* is used for 'image' and also for 'the part of an elephant's head between the tusks'.

The **Śabdaratnāvalī** of Mathureśa explains:

> प्रतिमानुकृतौ कुम्भिदन्तबन्धेऽपि च स्त्रियाम् ।
>
> ŚaRa p. 255 (cal. edn, 1970)
>
> The term *pratimā* denotes a 'resemblance' and also 'the ornament decorating the middle part of an elephant's tusks.

Layers of Meaning

The word *pratimā* occurs as early as the **Ṛgveda** in the sense of 'model', 'measure' or a 'representative'; as we find it used in the **Atharvaveda**:

अपां यो अग्रे प्रतिमा बभूव .... ।

AV IX.4.2a

In principio, who became or existed as the representative [or in the 'likeness'] of the waters.

Here the second layer of meaning evolving towards the denotation of 'likeness' and even 'image', can be well noticed. However, there are many later Vedic passages which still used the word in the sense of a representative, or rather 'symbol' standing for an idea, form or concrete object. For example:

संवत्सरस्य प्रतिमा वै द्वादश रात्रयः ।

TBr I.1.9.10

Verily the twelve nights are the 'representative' of year.

पुरुषो वै सहस्रस्य प्रतिमा ।

ŚBr VII.5.2.17

Verily, man is the 'symbol' of a thousand.

असौ वै लोकः प्रतिमैष ह्यन्तरिक्षलोके .... ।

ŚBr VIII.3.3.5

Yonder world is the model (*pratimā*); this (i.e. terrestrial world) is, as it were, countermeasured in the atmospheric world.

पशोर्वै प्रतिमा पुरोडाशः ।

TBr III.2.8.8

Puroḍāśa (offering) is a representative (i.e. surrogate) for the animal (offering).

Another meaning evolved around the term indicating an image, an icon or statue, or deity, besides a likeness made after an object or a person or creature.

मूषानिषिक्तद्रुत-ताम्रादि-प्रतिमावत् ।

BrSūŚBh I.1.12

... just as the statue possesses the form of the mould into which the molten brass has been poured. (Tr. G. Thibaut)

One of the meanings that came to be associated with *pratimā* is coequal with 'reflection' 'a reflected figure or image'.

This last connotation even leads us to yet another implication arrived at in the classical language, namely a 'comparison', 'analogue' or analogy:

अप्पटिमो बुद्धो ति ।

MilPañ 239

The Lord Buddha is without comparison.

Another special sense of the term *pratimā* (also *pratimāna*) is often found, recorded by the medieval lexicons (MedKo XXV.48cd).

Pratikṛti in the sense of representation, representative symbol is of quite rare occurrence; it denotes a symbol or form employed as a proxy in certain rituals or sacraments for the one lost or destroyed; for example, in case of one's loss in a distant land the funeral rites by the relatives were performed over a 'representation' or *pratikṛti* made of cane, etc. Likewise, for gaining religious merit on another's behalf his supposed *pratikṛti*, nicknamed as *darbha-baṭu*, i.e. manikin made in *kuśa* grass, is enjoined to be immersed in the holy waters of a →*tīrtha* (cf. Smṛtitattva of Raghunandana, Vol. I, p. 492). In case of *abhicāra* or incantational practices intended to kill or harm a rival; or for subjugating the heart of others, or to bring somebody under one's control, his/her *pratikṛti* is said to be used in different rituals. As we find in the **Tantrasāra Saṅgraha** of Nārāyaṇa:

प्रज्वाल्याग्निमपामार्गैरेवं वश्यो भवेद् द्विजः ।
दीप्ते वह्नौ चिताकाष्ठैः प्रतिकृत्या तथा हुनेत् ॥
राजा वशीभवेदेवं वश्यं स्याद्वैश्यशूद्रयोः ।

TSāSaṅg XXIV.28–29ab

(By incantational rites done) in the fire lighted from (the faggots of) *apāmārga* (achyranthus aspera) plant the twice-born is put under (one's) control. In the fire lighted from the wood of funeral pyre, one should sacrifice the likeness (of that person) into it. Thus a person of the *kṣatriya* caste comes under one's control; (this is also the practice) for subduing a *vaiśya* or *śūdra.*

Thus, a specialised connotation of the word appears later to have evolved for the 'portrait' or picture of a person.

In a charming stanza found in the Junagarh rock-inscription of emperor Skandagupta, *pratikṛti* seems to denote both the above meanings:

नरपतिभुजगानां मानदर्पोत्फणानां प्रतिकृति-गरुडाज्ञां निर्विषीं चावकर्ता ।

– Select Inscription, D.C. Sirkar, Vol. I, p. 308

(And the king) has made the antidote in the form of the Garuḍacommands which are remedy against the serpent-like princes raising their hands in pride and arrogance.

Pratikṛti for figure is suitable as the Gupta Imperial seal and ensign bore the representation of Garuḍa, and the sense of *pratikāra* is also poetically evoked as the specific action was a retaliatory or punitive measure against enemies.

Development of the Concept

In a famous stanza of the **Ṛgveda** the word *pratimā* appears to have been used as signifying 'image' or 'model':

कासीत् प्रमा प्रतिमा किं निदानमाज्यं किमासीत् परिधिः क आसीत् ।

ṚV X.130.3ab

What was the fore-measure, what the image, and what the symbol (primordial cause) was? What was the molten butter (offering), what the wooden fenders were?

Elsewhere, we find the phrase used in a general sense of denoting the concept of affinity or comparison:

न वः प्रतिमै सुकृतानि .... ।

ṚV III.60.4c

Your well-created products are not for comparison.

In a similar strain the term *pratimāna* presumably refers to the concept of a 'representative', 'counterpart' or 'countermeasure':

त्वं भुवः प्रतिमानं पृथिव्या ऋष्ववीरस्य बृहतः पतिर्भूः ।

ṚV I.52.13ab

Thou art the counterpart of earth, the Master of lofty heaven with all its mighty heroes. (Tr. R.T.H. Griffith)

In the **Yajurveda** we find the concept of a measured layout or design of a sacrificial altar being implied by the term *pratimā* as follows:

मा छन्दः प्रमा छन्दः प्रतिमा छन्दो अस्रीवयश्छन्दः .... ॥

YV XIV.18

Mā metre. Pramā metre. Pratimā metre. Asrīvayas metre. (Tr. R.T.H. Griffith)

It may however, be remarked that the term →*chandas* or metre appears to have been used in its specific context of →*vāstu* definition meaning plan, ground-plan or layout under which the *pratimā*, 'counter-measure', was a name for the type of altar layout of bricks meant to represent symbolically the mid-air region. [For the later, usage of the word *chandas,* see *adhaḥchanda, tālachanda, ūrdhvachanda,* etc. in SamSūt and other architectural treatises.]

Elsewhere, the term seems to evolve beyond its rudimentary denotations and has its significant implication of an image or counter-image more or less specified in the following passage:

> न तस्य प्रतिमा अस्ति यस्य नाम महद्यशः ।
> हिरण्यगर्भ इत्येष मा मा हिंसीदित्येषा यस्मान्न जात इत्येषः ॥
>
> YV XXXII.3
>
> There is no *pratimā* (perhaps, image, formal representation) of Him whose glory is verily great, – (the same which is sung) in the passages, viz. *hiraṇyagarbha* .... etc.

However, the term *pratimāna* retains well the concept of counter-measure or retaliation in certain contexts:

> नार्वागिन्द्रं प्रतिमानानि दभ्नुवन्ति । यैरेनं प्रतिमिमते नैनं तानि दभ्नुवन्ति । अर्वागेवैनमप्राप्य विनश्यन्तीति ।
>
> Nir V.12
>
> All the counter-measures do not deceive Indra, i.e. the counter-measures which they adopt against him are of no avail before Indra: they perish before they reach him, i.e. without reaching him at all. (Tr. L. Sarup)

As noted earlier, the concept of a 'representative' or symbolic model appears well implied in the **Atharvaveda**. Likewise, we find the same concept conveyed through the word in numerous Vedic passages. For example:

> संवत्सरस्य या पत्नी सा नो अस्तु सुमङ्गली ॥
> संवत्सरस्य प्रतिमां यां त्वा रात्र्युपास्महे ।
>
> AV III.10.2cd–3ab
>
> The night who is the consort of the year may be auspicious for us. O night, you are whom we revere as a representative symbol of the year.
>
> वैश्वानरस्य प्रतिमोपरि द्यौः .... ।
>
> AV VIII.9.6a
>
> The Dyaus above is the *pratimā* (representative symbol or image) of Vaiśvānara or universal man.

Perhaps, the passage indicates that as the fire is in earthly reference so is the Dyaus for higher regions.

संवत्सरस्य प्रतिमां यां त्वा रात्र्युपासते । प्रजां सुवीरां कृत्वा विश्वमायुर्व्यश्नवत् ॥

TSam V.7.2.1

O night, you are whom men revere as a representative symbol of the year. May he enjoy all life by making his progeny rich in hero-sons.

यावानेष संवत्सरस्तावन्तस्संवत्सरस्य प्रतिमाः ।

JaimBr III.361

As is the extent of the year so is the extent of the symbol-images of the year.

नवाहो वै संवत्सरस्य प्रतिमा ।

ṢaḍBr IV.6.4

The nine-day rite is verily a model or symbol of the year.

Commentators like Sāyaṇa often render the word *pratimā* by *sadṛśa*, meaning similar, similarity or likeness.

भागसंधान्तयज्ञैः प्रतिमा नरचतुर्थे ।

MānŚrSū X.3.5.1

The given division of the layout, being in size a one-fourth of the man's measure are for offerings of the junctions of parts.

As showing the concept of an image or figure the term finds occurrence in several later Vedic texts:

चित्रं देवानाम् इत्यर्धर्चाभ्यामक्षिछिद्रयोर्हुत्वा पश्चात् पुरुषशिरसः पुरुषचितिमुपदधाति पुरुषस्य प्रतिमाम् ।

VŚrSū II.1.7.7

Having offered the oblations in the two holes reciting the half *ṛc, citraṃ devānām* and after muttering the *puruṣa-śiras mantra,* (the Adhvaryu) places an idol of a person on the *puruṣa* bricks.
(Tr. V.A. Kulkarny)

There are rites given to eradicate evil effects of such abnormalities that are seen miraculously to occur in divine images:

देवतायतनानि कम्पन्ते, दैवतप्रतिमा हसन्ति, रुदन्ति, गायन्ति, नृत्यन्ति, स्फुटन्ति, स्विद्यन्ति, उन्मीलन्ति, निमीलन्ति ।

ṢaḍBr VI.10.2

(When) the abodes of deities tremble, the images of the gods appear laughing, weeping, singing, dancing, breaking into pieces, perspiring, opening and closing the eyes.

भूमिकम्पो भवेद् यत्र देवता प्रतिमा हसेत् ॥
देवता भ्रमते यत्र मृत्युस्तत्र विनिर्दिशेत् ।

AVPari LXX.23.1cd-2ab

Where the image of deity laughs, there happens earthquake; similarly where the (idol of a) deity roams, there will be death. (Tr. R.S. Bhattacharya)

According to the **Anukramaṇī** of Śaunaka even the inanimate objects employed in the service of divinities or holy rituals being taken as items or symbols of worship came to be known as images (*pratimā*), thought to be presided over by a 'he' or 'she' of that object:

अनः शाखोखाशम्योपवेषकपालेध्मोलूखलादयश्च प्रतिमाभूताः ।

Anukramaṇī I.1

They are (taken to be the) 'iconic beings', images, such as the cart, branch of a tree, cooking pot, wooden wedge, stick, bowl or sherd, fuel, mortar, and others.

Likewise, *pratikṛti* also occurs as denoting the concept of a symbolic representation or image in the later Vedic passages:

अथ सुवर्णमयीं भूमिं भूमेः प्रतिकृतिं गोचर्ममात्रां कृत्वा ... ।

AVPari X.1.8

Now, (while gifting a piece of land) a golden image of the earth-goddess be made as representative of a *go-carma* – measure of the land.

The concept of *pratikṛti* as representing a human being in his or her figural form came to be quite popular in the *abhicāra* or incantational rites. Such practices were meant either to kill or harm a rival, or to win over the heart of a beloved. It can be well traced back as early as the **Kauśika-Sūtra** of the **Atharvaveda**:

प्रतिकृतिमवलेखनीं दार्म्यूषेण भाङ्गज्येन कण्टकशल्ययोलूकपत्रयासितालकाण्डया हृदये विध्यति ॥

KauśSū XXXV.28

By means of a bow, which is made of the *kuśa*-root and has a bow-string of hemp, with an arrow whose barb is of a splinter, of a porcupine, whose plumage is of an owl's feather, whose shaft is made of black *āla* wood, he pierces in the heart of a painted effigy (of the woman he wishes to control).

Likewise, we read in the **Sāmavidhāna Brāhmaṇa**:

पांसुभिः प्रतिकृतिं कृत्वा प्राक्शिरसं पूर्वाह्ने दक्षिणशिरसं मध्याह्ने प्रत्यक्शिरसमपराह्णेऽर्द्धरात्र उदक्शिरसं तस्या हृदयदेशमधिष्ठाय ... वा सर्वेषां सौवर्णीं प्रतिकृतिं कुर्याद् ब्राह्मणस्य राजतीं क्षत्रियस्यौदुम्बरीं वैश्यस्यायसीं शूद्रस्यौदुम्बरीं वा सर्वेषां ... ।

SViBr II.5.4

Having made with mud a likeness or effigy of the person (a woman or a man whom he wishes to inflict), and putting the same as east-facing in the morning, or south-facing during the noon, or west-facing during afternoon, or north-facing during the night time, he being seated on it.... (recite respective formulae, or the stanza) ... in case of all. Or, he should make a golden effigy in case of the Brāhmaṇa caste, a silver one in case of the *kṣatriya*, a copper one of the *vaiśya*, an iron one (*āyasī*) of the *śūdra*, or the copper image in all such cases, ...

For destroying the enemy army, the same Brāhmaṇa gives the following rite:

हस्त्यश्वरथपदातीनां पिष्टमयीः प्रतिकृतीः कृत्वा पिष्टस्वेदं स्वेदयित्वा सर्षपतैलेनाभ्यज्य तासां क्षुरेणाङ्गान्यवदायाग्नौ जुहुयादभि त्वा शूर नोनुम इति रहस्येन .... ।

SViBr III.6.11

Having the effigies (or likeness, i.e. figurines) of elephants, horses and footmen made of paste, and later drying out the moister of that paste medium, as besmearing them with the mustard oil, he should sacrifice them into fire by cutting their limbs with a knife..., reciting the efficacious charm '*abhi tvā śūra nonuma*' etc. [Sāma Āraṇya Gāna V.5.129.1].

The relative merit of *pratimā* or icon, useful essentially for devotional concentration by the common folk, is explicitly stated in the **Jābāladarśanopaniṣad**:

शिवमात्मनि पश्यन्ति प्रतिमासु न योगिनः ।
अज्ञानां भावनार्थाय प्रतिमाः प्रतिकल्पिताः ॥

JāDarUp IV.59

The yogis see Śiva not in the icons but in their own self. The icons are fashioned for the purpose of effecting meditation of the ignorant.

अविमुक्ते तव क्षेत्रे सर्वेषां मुक्तिसिद्धये ।
अहं संनिहितस्तत्र पाषाणप्रतिमादिषु ॥

RāmUttUp 5

[Says Rāma to Śiva] In your abode called Avimukta, meant for the attainment of redemption of all people, I myself stay there as merged into the images of stone etc.

Pratikṛti as denoting the shape or likeness occurs in the **Āpastamba Śrauta-Sūtra**:

अतुङ्गमनपूपाकृतिं कूर्मस्येव प्रतिकृतिमश्वशफमात्रं करोति ॥

ĀpŚrSū I.25.4

It (the sacrificial cake) he prepares in the shape of a tortoise (as appearing) similar to a horse's hoof neither too high nor (too low) like a sweet-bread.

The concept of a deity image or icon is also implied by this word occurring in the Pariśiṣṭas of the Gṛhyasūtras:

अथ प्रतिमाद्रव्याणि मुक्ताफलशिलादारुहेमताम्ररजतकांस्यमृत्तिकादीनि ।

ĀśvaGṛhSūPari IV.3

Now the materials for (preparing) images, viz. pearl, stone, wood, gold, copper, silver, bronze, clay, etc.

देवस्य प्रतिकृतिं कृत्वाऽक्षतपुष्पैर्यथालाभमर्चयित्वा ... ।

BGṛhSūPari II.14.2

Having prepared the image of the god and worshipping it with unbroken rice and flowers as available....

ईशानस्य प्रतिकृतिं कृत्वा तस्य दक्षिणप्रत्यग्देशे तन्मुख स्थित्वा आत्मनि देवताः स्थापयेत् ।

BGṛhSūPari II.18.1

Having made an image of the god Īśāna (Śiva), and being seated on its south-west side as facing it, he should implace the divinities on various limbs of his self (or body).

With regard to the question of anthropomorphic character and natural rudiment inhering the forms of gods as evolved in the imagination of Vedic seers, some observations made by Yāska reflect significant views prevailing in his time:

अथाकारचिन्तनं देवतानाम् । पुरुषविधाः स्युरित्येकम् । ... अपुरुषविधाः स्युरित्यपरम् ।

... अपि वोभयविधाः स्युः। अपि वा पुरुषविधानामेव सतां कर्मात्मान एते स्युः। यथा यज्ञो यजमानस्य। एष चाख्यानसमयः ॥

Nir VII.6–7

Now follows discussion of the form of the gods. Some say, they resemble human beings in form (*puruṣavidhāḥ*); ... Others say, the gods do not resemble human beings in form (*apuruṣavidhāḥ*); ... Or the gods may both resemble human beings in form as well as may not resemble human beings in form. Or the gods who do not resemble human beings in form exist in the form of *karman* (sacrifice); as for instance, the sacrifice performed by the *yajamāna* (sacrificer). This is the opinion of those who know the legends.

Pāṇini in his **Aṣṭādhyāyī** (V.3.96) uses the word *pratikṛti* for a likeness, a figure showing a likeness, an image. As the **Kāśikā** explains: *pratikṛtiḥ pratirūpakaṃ praticchandakam/aśva ivāyam aśvapratikṛtiḥ aśvakaḥ.* The grammatical tradition implies that a likeness or figure of a horse made in a medium such as grass, hide or wood is called *aśvaka*, i.e. its *pratikṛti.* Likewise, the images of Śiva, Skanda, Viśākha were known by Śivaka, Skandaka and Viśākhaka, respectively.

The term *pratikṛti* denoted the concept of alikeness or portrait also as it is hinted at by Patañjali as follows:

ननु चोक्तं नैवं शक्यमिह हि दोषः स्यात् काश्यपप्रतिकृतयः काश्यपा इति।

Mahābh IV.1.89

Indeed, it is stated (in this context) that this (i.e. *añ* suffix) is not applicable here since there would be a defective expression in saying that 'the Kāśyapas' is indicative of the images of the (several) persons of the Kāśyapa lineage.

It has been further commented upon thus by Bhartṛhari:

उपमानस्य भेदाच्च बहुषु स्यादञो विधिः।
काश्यपा इति लोपः स्यात् तथा प्रतिकृतिष्वपि ॥
एकस्यापि प्रतीयेत भिन्ना प्रतिकृतिः सह।
काश्यपस्येति तेनायं प्रत्येकमवतिष्ठते ॥

Vāk III.14.592, 604

If the standard of comparison becomes many, then the suffix *añ* would be expressive of the plural and then, even in the sense of images, there would be elision of the suffix *añ* in *kāśyapa* (resulting in the form *kāśyapāḥ*).

The different images might be understood as similar to one Kāśyapa. Therefore, it (the standard of comparison) is connected with each object of comparison. (Tr. K.A.S. Iyer)

The concept of *pratimā* as denoting image or likeness would be found well implied by several passages of the great epics. For example:

काञ्चनप्रतिमैकाग्रं मणिविद्रुमतोरणम् ।

Rām II.15.32ab

[The palace of Rāma] was embellished with a gateway made of gems and corals, as having golden images adorning its facade.

आदर्शतलसंकाशा ततो वै पृथिवी मया ।
अलातचक्रप्रतिमा दृष्टा गोष्पदवत्कृता ॥

Rām IV.46.13

[Says Sugrīva to Rāma] at that moment when I was running around being pursued by Bālī), I saw, indeed, the earth like the (dazzling) surface of a mirror, or like a whirling wheel of the fire-brand, or made as it were (a small place of shelter) or the size of a hoof-mark.

Describing Rāvaṇa, the king of ogres, the poet Vālmīki has drawn series of similes hinting at his opposing features:

स कल्पवृक्षप्रतिमो वसन्त इव मूर्तिमान् ।
श्मशानचैत्यप्रतिमो भूषितोऽपि भयंकरः ॥

Rām V.22.29

He was (shining with ornaments) like a wishfulfilling tree, or appeared, like the spring season incarnate, yet looked dreadful as a *caitya* (tree or building) of the sepulchral ground even being well-decorated.

The **Mahābhārata** also employs the term *pratikṛti* for conveying the concept of one's figure or portrait:

भीमसेनानुरोधाय हनूमान्मारुतात्मजः ।
आत्मप्रतिकृतिं तस्मिन्ध्वज आरोपयिष्यति ॥

MBh V.57.8 (cf. BORI edn, Vol. VI, p. 266)

From the request of Bhīmasena, there on that flag (of Arjuna), Hanūmān, son of the god Wind, would put his own likeness or figural form.

In several such passages the term *pratimā* denotes the concept of a figure in art representations:

तां सुमध्यां पृथुश्रोणीं प्रतिमां काञ्चनीमिव ।
प्राप्तेयं देवकन्येति दृष्ट्वा संमेनिरे जनाः ॥

MBh III.277.26

Seeing her the people came to think that she was a divine damsel come there as endowed with a fine waist, broad hips and beauty like a golden image.

As Rāma said to the sages as inviting their opinion about his wish to perform an Aśvamedha sacrifice even in absence of his spouse in person:

सौवर्णी प्रतिमाकार्या जानकी सदृशी प्रभो ।
तादृश्या सीतया सार्धं करिष्ये व्रतमुत्तमम् ॥

MBh Jaiminīyāśvamedha XXIX.48

O lord, an image of gold in the likeness of (my wife) Jānakī may be made, and thus together with such of Sītā's likeness, I would undertake the excellent vow (namely *asipatra-vrata*, essential for the purpose).

From the theoretical point of view the most important aspect of *pratimā* in the temple cult is its installation (*pratiṣṭhā*) inducing the spirit (→*prāṇa*) of the deity to get merged into it for ever, while in the household images or similar images employed for temporary ritual *āvāhana* and *visarjana* of the deity for that image is required to be made daily or whenever worshipped. Thus, the essential placement-and-merger of the deity spirit in the image is indicated by the doctrine of *sannihita* or *sannidhi, sānnidhya*, for attaining the aim of which there evolved a complex canon of rites on image consecration, merits of the priests, patrons, devotees, site, material, auspicious moment or occasion, iconography, aesthetic norms, etc. For example, the injunctions on avoiding certain defects or demerits in an image from the ideal of natural and pleasing form are mentioned to be aimed for the same purpose (cf. VDhPur III.38.13–23).

We are expressly reminded by the Puranic writer of the truth that the →'*rūpa*' (form) described as such refers to the divinity, who is without image in the ultimate reference (*apratima, aprameya*). Of that Supreme Spirit there are two forms: *prakṛti* and *vikṛti*; his invisible form is known as →*prakṛti* and his derivative forms or *vikṛti* are the shaped ones described as the whole world. Thus the worship, meditation, etc. are possible in case of the shaped only:

प्रकृतिर्विकृतिस्तस्य रूपेण परमात्मनः ।
अलक्ष्यं तस्य तद्रूपं प्रकृतिस्सा प्रकीर्तिता ॥

साकारा विकृतिर्ज्ञेया तस्य सर्वं जगत्स्मृतम् ।
पूजाध्यानादिकं कर्तुं साकारस्यैव शक्यते ॥

VDhPur III.46.2–3

Of that Supreme Lord three are two formal aspects, viz. *prakṛti* (basic nature) and *vikṛti* (creation or modality). That which is His invisible form is known as *prakṛti*. The formed aspect of His is knowable as *vikṛti* or creation, which is thought of the world. One is capable of doing worship and meditation etc. only of the formed aspect.

The basic idea of knowing the differentiated icons of deities as derivatives, reflections or representatives of the Ultimate Reality or the undifferentiated One is well understood and remarked in so many ways in the texts. As noted by Prof. V.S. Agrawala:

"That which is *parama rūpa* is *arūpa*; the Highest Form is identical with the Formless, so says the **Viṣṇu Purāṇa** – *tacca viṣṇoḥ paramarūpam arūpākhyamanuttamam, viśva-svarūpa-vairūpya-lakṣaṇaṃ paramātmanaḥ* (ViPur VI.7.54). The cosmic forms constitute the *vairūpya*, the manifold appearances of the deity. Each of them in its strict definition is an apparition, a *yakṣa*, merely name and form without real substance. The yogin alone can comprehend the higher form (*pararūpa*); others can think only of the material forms of images. Meditation of images is essential, the normal way for the functioning of the mind" (*Studies in Indian Art*, p. 23).

As says the **Śiva Purāṇa**:

हृदि संसारिणः साक्षात्सकलः परमेश्वरः ।
इति विज्ञानयुक्तस्य किं तस्य प्रतिमादिभिः ॥
इति विज्ञानहीनस्य प्रतिमाकल्पना शुभा ।
पदमुच्चैः समारोढुं पुंसो ह्यालम्बनं स्मृतम् ॥
आलम्बनं विना तस्य पदमुच्चैः सुदुष्करम् ।
निर्गुणप्राप्तये नृणां प्रतिमालम्बनं स्मृतम् ॥

ŚPur II.1.12.62–64

Lord Śiva is within the heart of beings in this world. Of what avail are the idols to those who have this real knowledge?

Having an idol is very auspicious for a person who has no such knowledge. It is a ladder that enables him to climb to a higher position.

It is very difficult to climb to a position without a support. The idol is only a means to achieve the *nirguṇa* Śiva. (Tr. J.L. Shastri)

About the image worship of the Great Goddess, we have the following statements made in the **Devī Bhāgavata Purāṇa**:

प्रतिमां कारयित्वाऽथ मुहूर्तेऽथ शुभे दिने ।
द्विजानाहूय वेदज्ञान् स्थापयामास भूपतिः ॥

DBhāgPur III.25.32

Then the king Sudarśana had an image of the Devī nicely built and got that installed with the help of the Pandits, versed in the Vedas, on an auspicious day and at an auspicious moment. (Tr. Vijnanananda)

सुबाहुरपि काश्यां तु दुर्गायाः प्रतिमां शुभाम् ।
कारयित्वा च प्रासादं स्थापयामास भक्तितः ॥

DBhāgPur III.25.41

On the other hand, the king Subāhu established the image in Benares, had temples built and worshipped there the Devī. (Tr. Vijnanananda)

As says the **Śiva Purāṇa**:

संशोध्य गन्धचूर्णेन पेषयित्वा सुमण्डपे ।
हस्तेन प्रतिमां कुर्यात् क्षीरेण च सुसंस्कृताम् ॥
अङ्गप्रत्यङ्गकोपेतामायुधैश्च समन्विताम् ।
पद्मासनस्थितां कृत्वा पूजयेदादरेण हि ॥

ŚPur I.1.16.6–7

It (clay) should be washed well and pasted with scented powder and milk. The idol should be made with the hands on a raised platform.

All the limbs, joints, etc. should be perfectly shaped with the respective weapons of the deity concerned. It should be seated on *padmāsana* (the lotus pose) and worshipped respectfully. (Tr. J.L. Shastri)

The deities are to be installed as facing the town and not as facing the opposite direction:

नगराभिमुखाः स्थाप्या देवा न च पराङ्मुखाः ॥

AgPur XXXIX.9cd

The images of deities are to be installed facing the town and not otherwise.

According to the **Devī Purāṇa**:

प्रतिमा पूजिता स्वप्ने क्षिप्रं सिद्धिफलप्रदा ।

DPur XII.16

An idol (of a deity) worshipped in dreams affords success immediately. (Tr. R.S. Bhattacharya)

प्रतिमां शोभनां वत्स महासुरक्षयङ्करीम् ॥
पूजयेद् रथविन्यस्तां सर्वमङ्गलमङ्गलाम् ।

DPur XXX.6cd–7ab

O my child, one should worship the beautiful and universally auspicious idol (of Devī) which is the destroyer of great demons placing it on a car (chariot). (Tr. R.S. Bhattacharya)

The making of image in a material medium is thus alluded to elsewhere:

मद्रूपां प्रतिमां कृत्वा नगर्यन्ते तथैव च ।
ततः स्वप्ने यथोद्दिष्टं सर्वं कारितवान्नृप ॥

HarPur I.29.48

Having set up likewise an image of my form in the outskirts of the city, the king then performed all those rituals as were ordained in the dream.

त्वत्तोऽश्मभिश्च प्रतिमां कारयित्वा हि भक्तितः ।
शुश्रूषयन्ति ये नित्यं मम यास्यन्ति ते गतिम् ॥

HarPur II.74.52

Those who having made the image from your stones with due veneration offer worship to it daily, would go to my station.

Likewise (NārPur I.114.34cd–48) in the procedural details of the worship of seven sages their images in gold are enumerated to be consecrated and gifted away to seven Vedic *brāhmaṇas* with due rites:

कश्यपोऽत्रिर्भरद्वाजो विश्वामित्रोऽथ गौतमः ॥
जमदग्निर्वसिष्ठश्च सप्तैते ऋषयः स्मृताः ।
प्रतिमाः सप्त कुर्वीत सुवर्णेन स्वशक्तितः ।
जटिलाः साक्षसूत्राश्च कमण्डलुसमन्विताः ॥

NārPur I.114.37cd–38ab, 41

The seven sages are known as Kaśyapa, Atri, Bharadvāja, Viśvāmitra, Gautama, Jamadagni and Vasiṣṭha. The images of these seven should be made in gold as per one's resources. They are (to be shown as) having matted locks, carrying a rosary and a water-pot.

Classification

Classification of images is noticed mainly in the puranic texts. The **Bhāgavata Purāṇa** classifies it under two main types:

चलाचलेति द्विविधा प्रतिष्ठा जीवमन्दिरम् ।
उद्वासावाहने न स्तः स्थिरायामुद्धवार्चने ॥

BhāgPur XI.27.13

(Kṛṣṇa said to Uddhava) An image, which is a temple of the Lord is (again) of two varieties, movable and immovable. (The ceremonies of) invoking the presence of or bidding farewell to a deity are not necessary in worship done through the medium of an immovable one. (Tr. C.L. Goswami)

However, on the basis of their material medium the images are further classified under several types:

शैली दारुमयी लौही लेप्या लेख्या च सैकती ।
मनोमयी मणिमयी प्रतिमाष्टविधा स्मृता ॥

BhāgPur XI.27.12

An image has been declared to be of eight kinds according as it is carved out of (a block of) stone or wood, made of (molten) metal (such as brass or bronze), clay or sandal-paste etc., painted (on a wall etc.) made of sand or carved out of a precious stone or conceived by the mind.

Seven kinds of images are mentioned by the **Agni Purāṇa** (XLIII.9cd–10ab); made of clay (*mṛnmayī*), wood (*dārughaṭitā*), metal (*lohajā*), jewel (*ratnajā*), stone (*śailajā*), fragrant substance (*gandhajā*), and flower (*kausumī*):

मृन्मयी दारुघटिता लोहजा रत्नजा तथा ॥
शैलजा गन्धजा चैव कौसुमी सप्तधा स्मृता ।

AgPur XLIII.9cd–10ab

Images are of seven kinds which are being made of clay, wood, metal, gem, stone, fragrant substance and flower.

Likewise, the **Matsya Purāṇa** enumerates:

सौवर्णीराजतीवापि ताम्रीरत्नमयी तथा ।
शैलीदारुमयीचापि लोहसंघामयी तथा ॥
रीतिकाधातुयुक्तावा ताम्रकांस्यमयी तथा ।

शुभदारुमयीवापि देवतार्चा प्रशस्यते ॥

MatPur CCLVIII.20–21

An image may be made of gold, silver, copper, gems, precious stones, stone, wood, iron brass, compound of copper and bell-metal, sandal-wood or other beautiful wood.

As it has been so aptly observed by J.N. Banerjea, "Very great importance is assigned to the images of the gods in the **Manu Smṛti** and there are various passages in the work which lay down that *daivatam* (images of gods) are to be circumambulated (IV.39), that one should not voluntarily step over the shadow of the gods (IV.130), that at the *parvans* one should go to the images for protection (IV.153), and that he who destroys a bridge, the flag of a temple (really the votive column in front of it), a pole (really a pillar) or images (*saṃkramadhvaja-yaṣṭīnāṃ pratimānāṃ ca bhedakaḥ*) shall repair the whole (damages) and pay 500 (*paṇas*) as fine (IX.285)" (*Development of Hindu Iconography*, p. 87).

Medhātithi gives one specific line of argument as maintained by certain 'traditionalists' and thinkers on the worship of deities as follows:

अत्र केचिच्चिरन्तना विचारयांचक्रुः – का एता देवता नाम यासामिदमभ्यर्चनमुच्यते ? यदि तावच्चित्र पुस्तकन्यस्तः चतुर्भुजो वज्रहस्त इत्यादयः, 'प्रतिकृतय' इति लौकिका व्यवहरन्ति, अतो गौणस्तत्र देवताव्यवहारः । ... अतः प्रतिमानामेवैतत्पूजाविधानम् ।

Medhātithi on Manu II.176

In this context some traditionalists have thus pondered upon: "What are these *devatā* (deities) by name? If the folk call them in normal usage as 'representatives' 'images' (*pratikṛti*) that are placed in a painted book showing them as 'four-armed' 'holding a *vajra*' etc., the implication of the deity-concept is then only secondary ... " Therefore, this injunction for worship is laid down just for the images of deities.

Kauṭilya has also referred to deity images in several such contexts:

चैत्यदैवतप्रतिमां वा तेजनतैलेनाभ्रपटलच्छन्नेनाग्निना वा रात्रौ प्रज्वाल्य तथैव ब्रूयुः । तदन्ये ख्यापयेयुः । दैवतप्रतिमानामभ्यर्हितानां वा शोणितेन प्रस्रावमतिमात्रं कुर्युः ।

ArthŚ XIII.2

... or spies may set fire to an altar or an image of a god covered with a layer of mica besmeared with burning oil at night, and shout aloud as before. Others may spread this news abroad; or they may cause (by some contrivance or other) blood to flow out in floods from revered images of gods. (Tr. R. Shamasastry)

मैथुने द्वादशपणः तिर्यग्योनिष्वनात्मनः।
दैवतप्रतिमानां च गमने द्विगुणस्मृतः॥

ArthŚ IV.13

When a senseless man has sexual intercourse with beasts, he shall be fined 12 *paṇas*; when he commits the same act with idols (representatives) of goddesses (*daivata-pratimā*), he shall be fined twice as much. (Tr. R. Shamasastry)

...... नागप्रतिमायामन्तश्छिद्रायां चैत्यच्छिद्रे वल्मीकच्छिद्रे वा सर्पदर्शनमाहारेण प्रतिबद्धसंज्ञं कृत्वा श्रद्धानानादर्शयेत्।

ArthŚ V.2

Or they may place in a bore-hole made in the body of an image of a serpent, or in a hole in the corner of a temple, or in the hollow of an ant-hill, a cobra, which is, by diet, rendered unconscious, and call upon credulous spectators to it (on payment of a certain amount of fee). (Tr. R. Shamasastry)

In Buddhism the symbols preceded the icons and this stage continued for some time due to canonical interdiction as followed in the pre-Christian centuries. At the initiative of Mahāsāṅghika or Mahayanists the anthropomorphic representation of the Buddha was introduced. Earlier either symbols or Jātaka narrations conveyed the presence of the Buddha.

The images of Indra are mentioned as installed in the heavenly abode of the Cāturmahārājika gods:

एवं अस्स चातुम्महाराजिकदेवलोकं दस्सेत्वा पुरतो रथं पेसेत्वा तावतिंसभवनस्स चित्तकूटद्वारकोट्ठकं परिवारेत्वा ठिता इन्दपटिमा दस्ससे, तं दिस्वा राजा पुच्छि,
इतरो पि 'स्स आचिक्खि: अनेकरूपं रुचिरं नानाचित्रं पकासति
आकिण्णं इन्दसदिसेहि व्यग्धेहे' व सुरक्खितं।

Jā VI.125

Thus he showed the heaven of the four great kings, and drove on until he could show the statues (*pratimā*) of Indra which stood around the great Cittakūṭa gateway of the heaven of the thirty-three. At this sight the king asked, and the other answered.

"This place so fine, elaborate, adorned,
Set round with Indra's statues, (*sadṛśa*), as it were
By tigers guarded ...." (Tr. E.B. Cowell and H.T. Francis)

In Buddhist monastic set-up also there came to develop a devotion to the image worship:

विहारपूजादीसु हि 'तानि चेतियानि चेव पटिमायो च वन्दिस्सामि, पोत्थकम्म-
चित्तकम्मानि च ओलोकस्सामी' ति ।

Aṭṭh IV.98 (rūpakaṇḍa, p. 458)

In case of the worship in Vihāras (it occurs to him) that, 'I would thus pay homage to those holysteads as well as to the images (*pratimā*), and I would see the work of plastering as well as of painting.'

A life-size image is styled as the *kāyapramāṇikā pratimā*:

ततस्तेन च तत्र क्रकुच्छन्दस्य सम्यक्संबुद्धस्य कायप्रमाणिका प्रतिमा, बभूव विशीर्णा,
सा अभिसंस्कृता ... ।

Divyāv XXXVII.160 (prose)

Then, by him a life-size statue of the enlightened lord Krakucchanda, that had disintegrated, was got properly renovated there.

Seeing the personal elegance and divine charm of prince Siddhārtha the sages proclaimed in wonder:

रूपं वैश्रवणातिरेकवपुषं व्यक्तं कुबेरो ह्ययं
आहो वज्रधरस्य चैव प्रतिमा चन्द्रोऽथ सूर्यो ह्ययम् ।
कामाग्राधिपतिश्च वा प्रतिकृती रुद्रस्य कृष्णस्य वा
श्रीमान् लक्षणचित्रिताङ्गमनघो बुद्धोऽथ वा स्यादयम् ॥

LVi XI.3

Oh, the beauty, appearing as the unique body excelling Vaiśravaṇa, may be he is Kubera himself; or is that an image or likeness (*pratimā*) of Vajradhara; or he is the moon, or the sun. He is perhaps the presiding lord of passions, or a counter-image or model of Rudra or of Kṛṣṇa. Or, he being endowed in the body with the characteristic marks (of a superman), illustrious, free from sins, may be the enlightened one himself.

According to the **Divyāvadāna**, it is the popular faith of a divinity that inspires people to pay homage to an image though its substance may appear a dead material only:

मृण्मयेषु प्रतिकृतिष्वमराणां यथा जनः ।
मृतसंज्ञामनाहत्य नमत्यमरसंज्ञया ॥

Divyāv XXVI.49

As it is in case of the clay figures (of the gods), that the folk discarding their inanimate identity, bow down as taking them to be divinities incarnate.

Certain abnormal activities appearing in the divine statues portend evil events:

प्रतिमाः परिवर्तन्ते धूमायन्ते रुदन्ति च ।
प्रस्विद्येयुः प्रधावेयुरन्यो राजा भविष्यति ॥

Divyāv XXXIII.504

When the images turn about, exude smoke or weep, perspire or run about, someone else would become the king.

The *pratikṛti* or likeness of a person has been prescribed to be used in incantational rites effecting harm or control over the subject:

रेखां ददाति ध्यात्वा तु मन्त्रज्ञो यस्य कस्यचित् ।
शत्रोः प्रतिकृतिं कृत्वा म्रियते नात्र संशयः ॥

GuhyaT XV.24

There is no doubt that the enemy dies when the expert knowing *mantra* draws a line while meditating and making likeness of that enemy.

शत्रोः प्रतिकृतिं कृत्वा चिताङ्गारतुषादिभिः ।
नग्नो मुक्तशिखो भूत्वा त्रैलोक्यमपि नाशयेत् ॥
शत्रोः प्रतिकृतिं कृत्वा श्मशानचितिभस्मना ।
सहस्राष्टशतेनापि म्रियते नात्र संशयः ॥

GuhyaT XV.74–75

The practitioner would destroy even the three worlds when he as having made a likeness or figure of the enemy with the straw, and charcoal, etc. from a pyre, and untying his knot [stalks] naked.

There is no doubt that the enemy dies when the expert has made the likeness of that enemy with the ashes from a pyre of the funeral yard and [performs the rite] a thousand and eight hundred times.

In the Mahāyāna as well as the Buddhist Tantric tradition the images of a huge pantheon came to be developed:

ततो मण्डलाचार्येण भगवतः शाक्यमुनेः प्रतिमाया दक्षिणे पार्श्वे द्वौ प्रत्येकबुद्धौ पद्मासनोपविष्टौ पर्यङ्केनोपविष्टौ कार्यौ । तयोरधस्ताद् द्वौ महाश्रावकौ धर्मं शृण्वन्तः कार्यौ ।

MMK II.52, p. 40

Then, by the preceptor performing the circle-rite, there on the right side of the image of the worshipful lord Śākyamuni should be made two Pratyeka-buddhas, seated on a lotus-seat and posed in the *paryaṅka* (cross-legged) attitude. Below them there should be made two great disciples listening to the religious preaching.

दन्तमयीं प्रतिमां कृत्वा देवीनां कन्यसाङ्गुलिप्रमाणामतिगुप्ते प्रदेशे आहूय मूलमन्त्रैः वामहस्तेन धूपं दत्वा जयाया मूलमन्त्रं जपेत् । ...
जया स्वकल्पं भाषते । मरकतेन्द्रनीलपद्मरागस्फटिकादिभिः प्रवालाङ्कुराश्मवैदूर्य-रत्नविशेषैः सुवर्णरूप्यमयैर्वा प्रतिमां कृत्वा ... ।

MMK XLVIII.104, pp. 538–539

Having made the ivory images of the goddesses, of the size of the little-finger, and invoking them in a highly secret place with the root-*mantras* and having offered the incense with his left hand he should recite the root-*mantra* of goddess Jayā....

The goddess Jayā relates her own ritual. Having made the image in certain jewels, viz. emerald, blue sapphire, ruby, crystal, etc., in the stone of coral shoot and cat's eye, or made of gold or silver.

Besides images, the replicas prepared through lost wax process (*madhūcchiṣṭam*) have also been referred to in this text.

राजानं राजमात्रं वा वशीकर्तुकामः तस्य मधूच्छिष्टकेन प्रतिकृतिं कृत्वा निर्धूमाङ्गारेषु क्षिपेत् सप्तरात्रम् । स वशो भवति ।

MMK LV, p. 670

One who wishes to gain control over a king or a king's minister, as having made his likeness in wax, should throw (the same) into smokeless fire-coals for seven nights. That (person) comes under control.

One of the inauspicious or unworthy happenings is given as follows:

स्तूपानां प्रतिमानां च दीपव्युच्छेदः ।

Mahākarmavibhaṅga after 9 (prose)

Discontinuity or violation of lamps (is) for *stūpas* and images.

मांसरुधिरभक्षान् यक्षराक्षसान् पूजयन्ति । तस्य शत्रोर्नाम वा शरीरप्रतिमं वा कृत्वा तत्र घोरविद्यां साधयन्ति ... ।

Bhaiṣajyaguruvaidūryaprabharāja-Sūtra (Gilgit Mss, Vol. I, p. 13)

(There are people) who worship those Yakṣas and Rakṣasas who eat flesh and blood. Having executed the name or a bodily likeness of (this or) that enemy accomplish the practices of hideous lore.

कारेथ बुद्धप्रतिमां रुचिरां रत्नामयीं सुपरिकर्मकृताम् ।
प्रासादिकां परमसुदर्शनीयां नाचिरेण लप्स्यथ समाधिवरम् ॥

SamāRājSū XXIX.52

You should make an image of the Buddha, charming, jewel-made (or consisting of jewels), fashioned in fine artistic work, pleasing and highly worth-seeing. You would gain before long the excellent (state of) meditation.

तस्मिन्महाशालवृक्षः । तत्रैकेन भगवतः प्रतिमा कारिता । द्वितीयेन विहारः प्रतिष्ठापितः ... ।

Cīvaravastu (Gilgit Mss, Vol. III, part 2, p. 9)

In the city (of Vaiśālī) there is a huge *śāla* tree. A person got an image of the Lord made there. Another got a monastery erected.....

The worship of images has been mentioned with respect to ritual offerings and other procedural details in the **Bodhicaryāvatāra** of Śāntideva:

सर्वसद्धर्मरत्नेषु चैत्येषु प्रतिमासु च ।
पुष्परत्नादिवर्षाश्च प्रवर्तन्तां निरन्तरम् ॥

BoCar II.21

May an incessant rain of flowers and gems shower on all the *caityas* and images of all the jewels of noble *dharma.* (Tr. P.N. Sharma)

A technical process of gilding the metal images has been thus alluded to:

अशुचिप्रतिमामिमां गृहीत्वा जिनरत्नप्रतिमां करोत्यनर्घाम् ।
रसजातमतीव वेधनीयं सुदृढं गृह्णत बोधिचित्तसंज्ञम् ॥

BoCar I.10

It (i.e. *bodhicitta*) takes this unclean form (i.e. body) and transforms it into the pure and priceless form of a *jina* or conqueror. It is like the priceless gold-making elixir and has the quality of transforming everything. So, hold on fast to *bodhicitta.*

In Jainism the image worship found favour from early period. Of course it was preceded by the large number of symbols on the *āyāgapaṭṭas* (stone tablets for worship). There was no objection to icon worship in this faith hence it gained momentum.

The Jaina ethical discipline employs the term *pratimā* (*paḍimā*) yet in another specific context of the ascetic codes of conduct both for the laity and the mendicant recluse, which in the former case are counted as eleven in number while in the latter they make a list of twelve *pratimā*s (cf. Daśāśrutaskandha, daśā 6; Vyavahārasūtra, uddeśa 5; Samavāyāṅga, samavāya 11 and 12; Niśīthacūrṇi, uddeśa 5; etc.). A similar tradition prevails both in the Śvetāmbara and the Digambara folds although some difference of nomenclature can be found to occur in their respective listing that may be, however, reconciled to a great extent on critical scrutiny. In fact, the *pratimā*s form progressive stages of ethical resolution in the path of spiritual attainment recommended for an *upāsaka* or a *bhikṣu*.

According to the **Samavāyāṅga**, the eleven (kinds of) *paḍimā*s essential for a laity are as follows:

> एक्कारस उवासगपडिमाओ पण्णत्ता तंजहादंसणसावए, कयव्वयकम्मे, सामाइअकडे, पोसहोववासनिरए, दिया बंभयारी, रत्ति परिमाणकडे, दिआ वि राओ वि बंभयारी, असिणाई विअडभोई मोलिकडे, सचित्तपरिण्णाए, आरंभपरिण्णाए, पेसपरिण्णाए, उद्दिट्ठभत्तपरिण्णाए, समणभूए, आदि भवई समणाउसो ।
>
> Samavāyāṅga XI.1

There are the eleven *paḍimās* prescribed for a lay devotee, viz.: (defining the stages when he has)

1. Heard the knowledge,
2. observed the vows,
3. observed the *sāmayikas,* i.e. resolutions,
4. devoted to *poṣadhopavāsa,* i.e. the fasting on holy days,
5. kept continence by day and restricted himself in copulating (with wife) by night,
6. kept continence both by day and night, avoiding daily bath, left meals after evening, stopped wearing a crown, etc.,
7. renounced the use of articles having life,
8. renounced attending to business duties,
9. renounced advising other family members,
10. renounced the world (for forest-dwelling) and accepted forest-dwelling , and
11. almost become a monk, or has reached on the verge of monkship.

The group of *pratimā*, 'ideals', denoting eleven steps of the ladder in

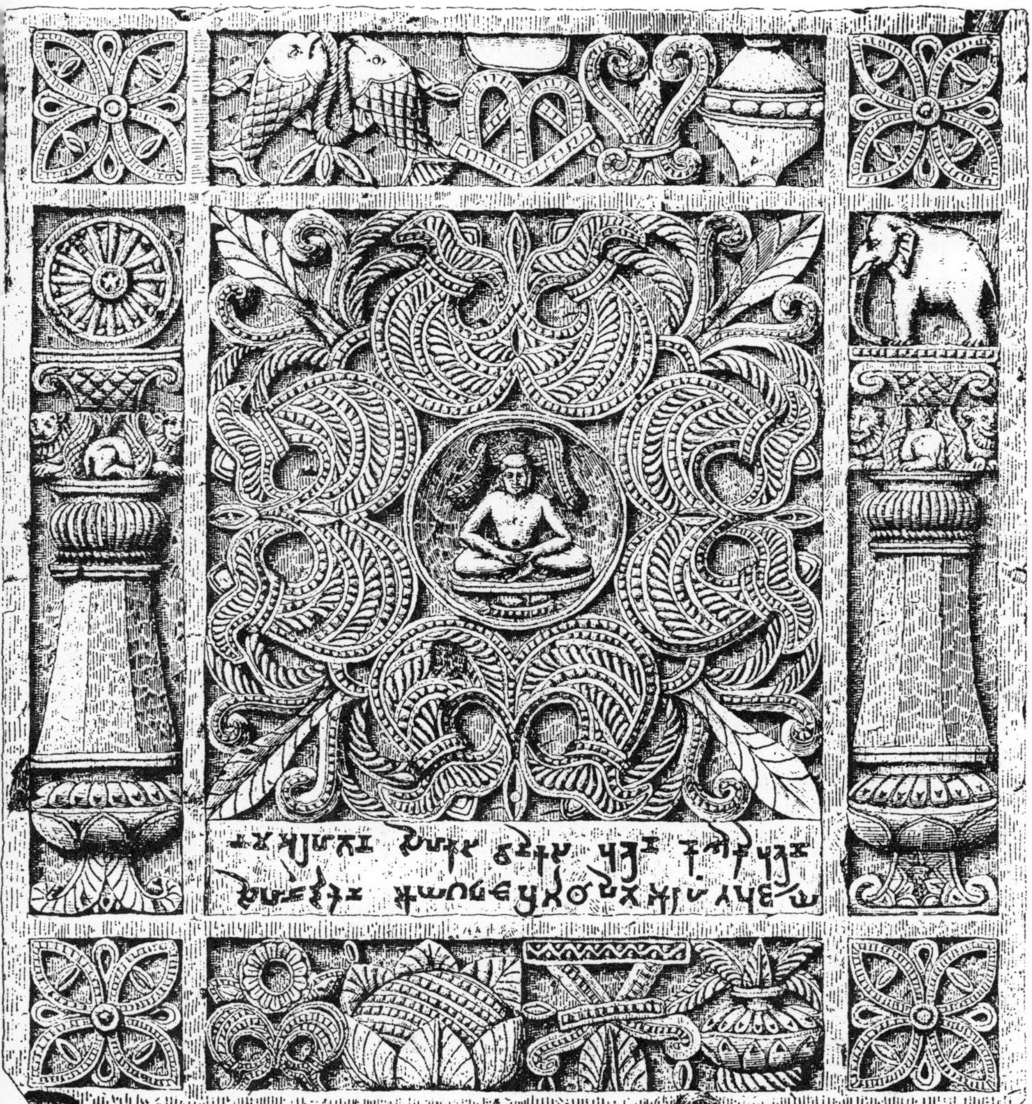

Figures 13: Symbols on the *āyāgapaṭṭa*

spiritual progress for the aspirant. In brief, the following chart of the *pratimā* advancements can be thus given here:

1. *darśana pratimā* : the first stage, of holding right views and connected observances; it comprehends almost all aspects of Jainistic religio-ethics,
2. *vrata pratimā* : the second stage, of holding scrupulous observances referring to the *aṇuvratas, guṇavratas*, etc.,
3. *sāmayika pratimā* : the third stage, of holding the practice of *sāmayika*, i.e. resoluteness of mind, body and speech, and certain daily observances,
4. *posadha pratimā* : the fourth stage, of holding fasts on certain prescribed norms and occasions,
5. *sacittatyāga pratimā* : the fifth stage, of renouncing impure articles of nourishment,
6. *rātribhukti (-tyāga) pratimā* : the sixth stage, of holding abstinence from sexual intercourse (by day) or and of not eating food at night,
7. *brahmacarya pratimā* : the seventh stage, of keeping absolute continence,
8. *ārambha-tyāga pratimā* : the eighth stage, of abandoning all vocational endeavours,
9. *parigrahaṇatyāga pratimā* : the ninth stage, leading to the abandonment of all kinds of acquisitions (excepting clothes and food),
10. *anumati-tyāga pratimā* : the tenth stage, of relinquishing all interest in household matters, and
11. *uddiṣṭa-tyāga pratimā* : the eleventh stage, of renouncing home and specially prepared food. [Or, in the Śvetāmbara explanation, the stage of renouncing the world to become a forest-dweller as initiated mendicant.]

The twelve *bhikṣupratimās* or standards of austere practices for the monk are given as follows:

बारस भिक्खुपडिमाओ पण्णत्ताओ, तंजहा – मासिआ भिक्खुपडिमा, दोमासिआ भिक्खुपडिमा, तिमासिआ भिक्खुपडिमा, चउमासिआ भिक्खुपडिमा, पंचमासिआ भिक्खुपडिमा, छमासिआ भिक्खुपडिमा, सत्तमासिआ भिक्खुपडिमा, पढमा सत्तराइंदिआ भिक्खुपडिमा, दोच्चा सत्तराइंदिआ भिक्खुपडिमा, तच्चा सत्तराइंदिआ भिक्खुपडिमा, अहोराइआ भिक्खुपडिमा, रग्गराइया भिक्खुपडिमा ।

Samavāyāṅga XII.1

There are the twelve standard observances prescribed for a monk, viz. the first lasting one month, the second lasting two months, the third lasting three months, the fourth lasting four months, the fifth lasting five months, the sixth lasting six months, the seventh lasting seven months, the eight as the first one lasting seven days and nights, the ninth as the second one lasting seven days and nights, the tenth as the third one lasting seven days and nights, the eleventh lasting one day and night, and the twelfth lasting one night only.

The list of twelve *paḍimā* (*pratimā*) ideals for a monk or recluse (*bhikkhu, śramaṇa*) is altogether different and solely refers to the monk's austere life of wandering (*vihāra*) in utter isolation of worldly associations as practising long-term observances of bodily mortification based mainly on fasting, meditation and peculiar bodily postures. The first seven *paḍimās* are in sequence of one month each leading to a complete duration of seven months although they are termed as *eka-māsikī, dvi-māsikī,* etc. due to the fact of successive increase in the dole of food and water received by the monk from alms-begging.

In the first *pratimā* stage, the monk attempts at forgetting all bodily emotions and attachments, pains and afflictions, etc. He is advised not to stay at one place for more than a night or two and to keep restricted attention to his food and physical emotions. And while his time in prayers and meditations, this mode of austere conduct is continued in its order up to the seventh *pratimā* with the identical rules and restrictions except for the increase in acceptance of food and water from two, three, four, five, six and seven *dattis* from alms-begging (a *datti* indicates one-time gift of cooked food or water poured without break by the giver into the monk's bowl).

The eighth *pratimā* lasts for seven days and nights when the monk remains sitting or lying in meditation and keeps fast without water. The ninth *pratimā* is called the second *saptarātridivasa pratimā.* The tenth is similarly styled as the third *saptarātridivasa pratimā.* From the eighth to the tenth, the three *pratimās* last together for a duration of twenty-one days in all. The eleventh *pratimā* is of a day-and-night duration. The monk stays in the *kāyotsarga* pose.

The twelfth *pratimā* lasts only for a night's duration while the monk remains standing in the strict *kāyotsarga* pose as meditating with the gaze fixed on a spot. This prolonged course of *pratimā* austerities is advised to be undertaken by the monk in view of his wishes and spiritual requirements according to the prescribed religious dictates and rules with all the purity of conduct and thought as having the mind engrossed in the ideals of the tīrthaṅkara.

In the story of a householder named Ānanda we find it described as follows:

> तए णं से आणंदे समणोवासए उवासग-पडिमाओ उवसंपज्जित्ताणं विहरइ । पढमं उवासग-पडिमं अहा-सुत्तं अहा-कप्पं अहा-मग्गं अहा-तच्चं सम्मं काएणं फासेइ, पालेइ, सोहेइ, तीरेइ, कित्तेइ, अराहेइ ॥
>
> तए णं से आणंदे समणोवासए दोच्चं उवासग-पडिमं, एवं तच्चं, चउत्थं, पंचमं, छट्ठं, सत्तमं, अट्ठमं, नवमं, दसमं, एक्कारसमं, ... जाव ... आराहेइ ॥
>
> तए णं से आणंदे समणोवासए इमेणं एयारूवेणं उरालेणं विउलेणं पयत्तेणं पग्गहिएणं तवो-कम्मेणं सुक्के ... जाव ... किसे धमाणिसंतए जाए ॥
>
> Uvāsagadasāo I.70–72
>
> Then that Ānanda, the disciple of the monk, engaged in conforming himself to the standards of an *uvāsaga*. Perfectly in his (thought, word, and) deed, he practised, maintained, satisfied, accomplished, proclaimed and completed the observance of the first standard of an *uvāsaga*, according to the sacred writing, according to rules (prescribed in them), according to the right way, (and) according to the truth.
>
> Then, indeed, that Ānanda the disciple of the monk, completed the observance of the second standard of an *uvāsaga* and in the same way, of the third, fourth, fifth, sixth, seventh, eighth, ninth, tenth and eleventh standards.
>
> Then, indeed, that Ānanda the disciple of the monk, through these lofty, abundant, persevering and intense practices, became withered, emaciated and reduced to a skeleton. (Tr. N.A. Gore)

As it is observed by N.A. Gore on this passage:

An *upāsaka* who is desirous of reaching higher stage in the upward path than that attained by keeping the twelve vows is asked to observe the eleven *pratimās*, which lead him gently towards the point where he will be able to adopt the five great vows (*pañca mahāvratāni*) of the ascetic. Each *pratimā* is to be observed for the same number of months as the number it occupies in the list, i.e. the first *pratimā* is to be observed for the same number of months as the number it occupies in the list, i.e. the first *pratimā* is to be observed for one month, the second for two months and so on. The total period for eleven *pratimās* thus comes to five years and six months. The *upāsaka* who is observing these *pratimās* sits in a meditative posture during the period prescribed, thinking of the particular vow in question (*Uvāsagadasāo*, tr. by N.A. Gore, Poona, 1953, p. 159).

Describing the severe penances of tīrthaṅkara Mahāvīra, the **Āvaśyaka-Niryukti** refers to the *paḍimā* austerities:

भद्दं च महाभद्दं पडिमं तत्तो अ सव्वओ भद्दं ।
दो चत्तारि दसेव य दिवसे ठासी यमणुबद्धं ॥

ĀNi (Bhāvanagar edn) p. 100

For the durations of two, four and ten days respectively, he stood as performing the strict vows of *paḍimā*, called *bhadda, mahābhadda* and then *sarvao-bhadda* by name.

In the sense of rules or standards prescribed for ascetic conduct, the **Uttarādhyayana-Sūtra** also refers to the *pratimā*:

पिण्डोग्गह-पडिमासु, भयट्ठाणेसु सत्तसु ।
जो भिक्खू जयई णिच्चं, से ण अच्छइ मण्डले ॥
मयेसु बम्भगुत्तीसु, भिक्खूधम्मम्मि दसविहे ।
जे भिक्खू जयई णिच्चं, से ण अच्छइ मण्डले ॥
उवासगाणं पडिमासु, भिक्खूणं पडिमासु य ।
जे भिक्खू जयई णिच्चं, से ण अच्छइ मण्डले ॥
पिण्डावग्रहप्रतिमासु, भयस्थानेषु सप्तसु ।
यो भिक्षुर्यतते नित्यं, स न तिष्ठति मण्डले ॥
मदेषु ब्रह्मगुप्तिषु, भिक्षुधर्मे दशविधे ।
यो भिक्षुर्यतते नित्यं, स न तिष्ठति मण्डले ॥
उपासकानां प्रतिमासु, भिक्षूणां प्रतिमासु च ।
यो भिक्षुर्यतते नित्यं, स न तिष्ठति मण्डले ॥

USū XXXI.9–11

A monk who always exerts himself with regard to the (seven) rules of accepting alms, and the seven causes of danger (to other men) will not stand in the circle (of transmigration).

A monk who always exerts himself with regard to the (eight) objects of pride, to that which protects his chastity, and to that tenfold law of the monks.

A monk who always exerts himself with regard to the (eleven) duties of the *upāsakas,* and the (twelve) duties of the *bhikṣus,* will not stand, etc. (Tr. H. Jacobi)

The ideal of *pratimā* practices is thus given elsewhere:

पडिमं पडिवज्जिआ मसाणे, नो भीयए भयभेरवाइं दिस्स ।

विविहगुणतवोरए अ निच्चं, न सरीरं चाभिकंखए जे स भिक्खू ॥
प्रतिमां प्रतिपद्य श्मशाने, नो बिभेति भयभैरवाणि दृष्ट्वा ।
विविधगुणतपोरतश्च नित्यं, न शरीरं चाभिकांक्षेत यः स भिक्षुः ॥

DaSū X.12

He is a true monk (*bhikṣu*) who, having assumed a vow of austerity (*pratimā*) in the funeral ground, is not afraid from seeing any fearful and dreadful things, and being ever engaged in various multiplicities of austere practices never wishes for the bodily existence.

नासाग्रन्यस्तनयनः प्रलम्बितभुजद्वयः ।
प्रभुः प्रतिमया तत्र तस्थौ स्थाणुरिव स्थिरः ॥

Triṣaṣṭiśalākāpuruṣacarita X.3.16

Like a fixed log or pillar (*sthāṇu*) the Lord stood there motionless by assuming the image-like standard stance (*pratimā*), with his both hands suspended below and having his gaze fixed at the tip of the nose.

The designation *pratimā* or image has been thus explained in a specific context of the Jaina tradition:

विहरदि जाव जिणिंदो सहसट्ठसुलक्खणेहिं संजुत्तो ।
चउतीस अइसयजुदो सा पडिमा थावरा भणिया ॥

DaPā XXXV.27.11

Onwards the moment of gaining enlightenment the Jina's body, endowed with 1008 kinds of excellent signs and with 34 kinds of spiritual glories is called his *sthāvara-pratimā*, 'staying image', uptill his wandering presence in the world.

According to the commentary thereof:

सा प्रतिमा प्रतियातना प्रतिबिम्बं प्रतिकृतिः स्थावरा भणिता इह मध्यलोके स्थितत्वात् स्थावर प्रतिमेत्युच्यते । मोक्षगमनकाले एकस्मिन्समये जिनप्रतिमा जंगमा कथ्यते ।

That is called by the expression of the stationary image with terms such as *pratimā, pratiyātanā, pratibimba, pratikṛti.* From the fact of his staying (or living) in this middle world (in his bodily form) the same is called the stationary image. However, at the time of his entering into final release is for an occasion that the Jina's same bodily image is styled as migrating (*jaṅgamā*) image.

Elsewhere the person of a Jaina monk is styled to be a *pratimā* or *jaṅgamā pratimā* designate:

चेइय बंधं मोक्खं दुक्खं सुक्खं च अप्पयं तस्स ॥
सपरा जंगमदेहा दंसणणाणेण सुद्धचरणाणं ।
णिग्गंथवीयराया जिणमग्गे एरिसा पडिमा ॥

BoPā 9cd–10

The 'self' undergoing bondage, liberation, sorrow and joy is worshipful. The other (material aspect) is the moving body, of the persons (i.e. of Jaina monks or pontiffs), who have, with the proper viewpoint and knowledge, achieved pure conduct, and have in the path of the Jina freed themselves from all the bonds and passions. Such (person) is indicated by the term (*jaṅgama* = moving) *pratimā* or image.

The mention of a gold-made *paḍimā* in one's own likeness is significant and indicates the use of the word in the sense of *pratikṛti*, portrait (cf. Nāyādhammakahāo, ch. VIII).

A large metal image (*paḍimā*) of the →Yakṣa Moggarapāṇi as installed and worshipped in his shrine is mentioned to bear a huge iron club of a thousand *pala*-weights:

मोग्गरपाणिस्स जक्खस्स जक्खाययणे होत्था पोराणे दिव्वे सच्चे जहा पुण्णभद्दे । तत्थ णं मोग्गरपाणिस्स पडिमा एगं महं पलसहस्सणिप्फण्णं अयोमयं मोग्गरं गहाय तिट्ठति ।

Antagaḍadasāo VI.13

(There was) a Yakṣa shrine sacred to the Yakṣa Moggarapāṇi, ... ancient, divine, truth-telling, and so forth, like Puṇṇabhadda's. In it there stood a figure of the Yakṣa Moggarapāṇi holding a great iron mace a thousand *palas* in weight. (Based on the tr. by L.D. Barnett)

Elsewhere, the same Jaina canon describes the worship of an image of the god Hariṇegamesi:

तए णं सा सुलसा बालप्पभिइं चेव हरिणेगमेसीभत्तया यावि होत्था । हरिणेगमेसिस्स पडिमं करेइ, कल्लाकल्लिं ण्हाया जाव पायच्छित्ता उल्लपडसाडया महरिहं पुप्फच्चणं करेइ ।

Antagaḍadasāo III.38

Now Sulasā was from childhood a worshipper of the god Hariṇegamesi. She caused to be made an image of Hariṇegamesi, and every morning she bathed... performed the lustratory rites, and with a moist robe made flower-offerings of great worth....
(Tr. L.D. Barnett)

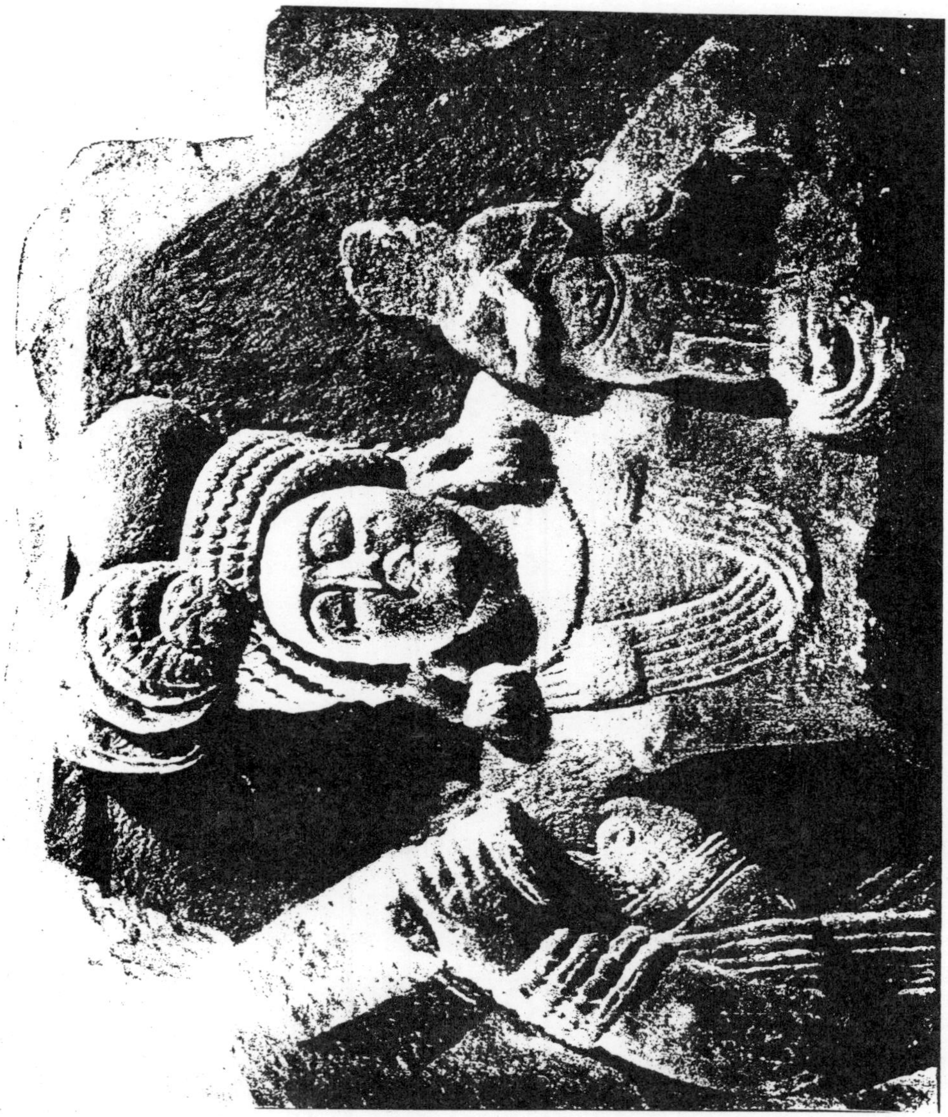

Figure 14: Yakṣa Moggarapāṇi

The process of carving out an image or figure in a log of wood is alluded to in the following observation by a Jaina teacher on the subject of liberation:

अव्वुच्छेओ भव्वाण अणंतभावेण । एअमणंताणं तयं समया इत्थ नायं । भव्वत्तं जोग्गयामेत्तमेव केसिंचि पडिमाजोग्गदारुनिदंसणेण । ववहारभयमेअं ।

Pañcasutta V.6

The number of liberable souls can never be exhausted because it is infinite; that number is infinite by infinite as understood from the scriptures. Liberality is merely the fitness on the analogy of the wood fit for cutting out an image. The statement that a liberable soul attains liberation is true from the practical standpoint of view. (Tr. A.N. Upadhye)

Commenting on the divine images the gloss on the **Darśana Pāhuḍa** has thus observed:

व्यवहारेण तु चन्दनकनकमहामणिस्फटिकादिघटिता प्रतिमा स्थावरा । समवशरण-मण्डिता जंगमा जिनप्रतिमा प्रतिपाद्यते ।

Comm. on DaPā XXXV.27.13

In practical reference, the image carved in sandal-wood, or gold, precious jewels, crystal, etc. is the *sthāvara* (=stationary) icon. However, the *jaṅgama* (=moving) Jina image is prescribed to have a set-up in the *samavaśaraṇa*, or preaching procession [=model or tableau for congregational display of Jina's preaching-session on the earth or elsewhere].

Reference may be made to certain mythical insets of tīrthaṅkara images found in a Digambara text:

वरचामरभामंडलठत्ततयकुसुमवरिसपहुदीहिं ।
संजुत्ताओ तेसु जिणवरपडिमाओ राजंति ॥

Tipa IV.1694

In them there shine the images of the foremost tīrthaṅkaras as endowed with best of flywisks, halo, triple parasol, rain of flowers, etc. (features).

सिंहासणादिसहिदा चामरकर-णाग-जक्खमिहुण-जुदा ।
णाणाविह-रयणमया जिणपडिमा तेसु भवणेसुं ॥

TiPa III.52

In those mansions are the tīrthaṅkara images, made of various kinds of jewels, and provided with the lion-throne etc., and the pairs of Nāgas and Yakṣas holding flywisks in hand.

जाव सहसा दिट्ठा तेलोक्क-बंधुणो भगवओ अरहओ मउडम्मि पडिमा मुत्तासेल-विणिम्मिआ ।

यावत् सहसा दृष्टा त्रैलोक्यबन्धोः भगवतः अर्हतः मुकुटे प्रतिमा मुक्ताशिला-विनिर्मिता ।

महतीं दिव्य-यक्ष-प्रतिमाम् ।

Kuvalayamālā, sec. CXCIX, pp. 115, 119

The great divine image of Yakṣa all of a sudden was seen in the crown (of his image) a (miniature) icon made in marble of the worshipful lord Arhat, who is the shelter for the three worlds.

The defect in an image causes harms of different types as referred to in the **Pratiṣṭhāpāṭha** of Vasunandī (IV.75.80).

The image of tīrthaṅkara in his pre-enlightenment existence was technically called Jīvanta-svāmī *pratimā*:

पूर्वं भरतो राजा श्रीमालपुरे श्रीशत्रुञ्जये सोपारकेऽष्टापदे च जीवितस्वामिप्रतिमाश्चकार ।

Purātanaprabandha-Saṅgraha XLII.31–32

Formerly, the king Bharata got the 'life-time statues of the Lord' (*svāmī* = tīrthaṅkara) set up at Śrīmālapura, Śrī-Śatruñjaya, Sopara and the Aṣṭāpada hill.

जीवन्तस्वामी-श्रीऋषभप्रतिमा-वन्दनार्थम् ।

PrabandhaKośa of Rājaśekhara XLVIII.21

For paying homage to the 'life-time' statue of the lord Ṛṣabha.

Such of the Jaina images have been discovered and identified by U.P. Shah and the origin of these images goes back to the 5–6th cent. A.D. (cf. *Jaina-Rūpa-Maṇḍana*, New Delhi, 1987, pp. 33–40). This image type was presumably akin and most probably inspired by the iconographic conversion of a Bodhisattva, evidenced earlier in Buddhist art and rendered by the Jaina communities in their own way.

The practice of inlaying deity images with a golden forehead-mark formed part of one's votive offering:

उवरिनिवेसियमाणिक्कमणहरे कणगनिम्मिए तिलए ।
चउवीसं जिणपडिमाओ जुग्गे कारवइ वीरमई ॥
अन्नदिणे अट्ठावयगिरिम्मि गंतुं इमा सपरिवारा ।
पूजं कुणइ जिणाणं ण्हवणविलेपणबलिप्पमुहं ॥
जिणपडिमाण निलाडेसु ताइं तिलयाइं ठवइ भत्तीए ।
तप्पुण्णपायवस्स व जाइं विरायंति कुसुमाइं ॥

Nalacarita (of Somaprabha) V.101–103

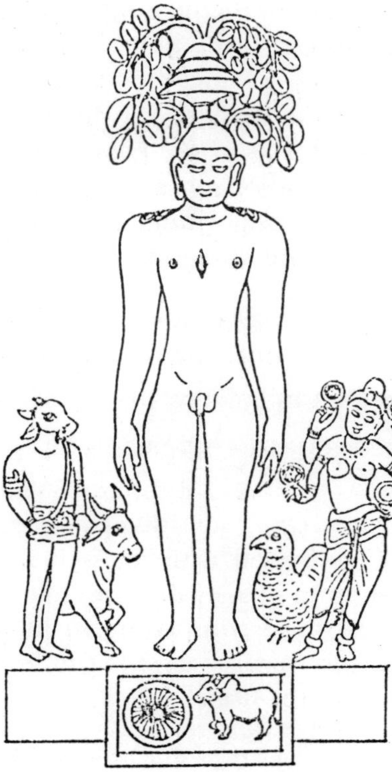

Figure 15: Statue of Ṛṣabhanātha

Vīramati got the idols of the twenty four Jinas made in pairs and also golden *tilaka*s studded with beautiful jewels, fixed above.

Then she went with her attendants to the mount Aṣṭapāda and worshipped the Jina idols, bathing them (with proper rites), preceded by anointing and offerings.

With deep devotion, she fixed those *tilakas* on the foreheads of the Jina-idols, that shone as if they were the flowers of the tree of her merit. (Tr. N.V. Vaidya)

Referring to many an Upanisadic statement supposed to identify Brahman or sole divine entity with the individual self, Śaṅkarācārya has thus explained the Vedānta viewpoint:

यदुक्तं प्रतीकदर्शनमिदं विष्णुप्रतिमान्यायेन भविष्यतीति तदयुक्तं गौणत्वप्रसङ्गात् । वाक्यवैरूप्याच्च । यत्र हि प्रतीकदृष्टिरभिप्रेयते सकृदेव तत्र वचनं भवति । यथा – 'मनो ब्रह्म' (छां॰ उप॰ III.18.1), 'आदित्यो ब्रह्म' (छां॰ उप॰ III.19.1) ।

BrSūŚBh IV.1.3

As for the argument that on the analogy of an image being Viṣṇu, this is only a meditation with the help of an image (which in this case is "I"), that is improper, since that would amount to a figurative interpretation (of the texts about unity). It is also improper because the syntactical forms of the passages are different. Where the intention is that a symbol should have an idea superimposed on it, a sentence occurs only unilaterally, as for instance, 'The mind is Brahman', 'The Sun is Brahman'. (Tr. Gambhirananda)

Explaining the Vedantic analogy alluded to in the **Yoga-Vāsiṣṭha** (IV.44.25), the commentator Ānandabodhendra Sarasvatī observes:

मूषा प्रतिमाकारनभोगर्भमृत्पिण्डस्तदन्तर्निषिक्तद्रुतहेमाभं बहिःस्थूलभास्वरमन्तःसूक्ष्म-भास्वरं स्थूलदेहसंवलितं वक्ष्यमाणसंनिवेशमुपादत्ते तत्तेजः ।

Comm. on YVās IV.44.25

That luminous essence (*tejas*, i.e. life-principle) acquires the spoken residing place, endowed with gross material body, shining subtle inside and shining grossly outside, like the poured-in molten gold into the clay-mass comprising in its interior a space of the shape of an image, that represents the hollow mould (*mūṣā*, lit. crucible-shaped mould) itself.

Investigating the question whether worldly attachments of a being stay in the sentiency or in the corporality the **Yoga Vāsiṣṭha** makes the following observation:

चिच्चमत्कारमात्रं स्वं स्वात्माङ्गं दृश्यमद्वयम् ।
सरूपमेव नीरूपं सकारणमकारणम् ॥
दधत्याश्चित्स्वभावायाः संस्काराद्यभिधाः कृताः ।
प्रतिमायाः प्रभाविन्या न संस्कारादयः पृथक् ॥

YVās VI.2.144.10-11

Of a distinguished imaged entity (*pratimā*), sentient by its innate nature, there are no experiences different from it, but they are known as such by the name of its experiences for the same (imaged one) carries them (as its traits) being just an entity of wonderful sentiency, embodied in a body but appearing as non-dual, formed as well as formless, with a cause or without a cause.

The term *pratimā* as implying the concept of 'reflection' occurs in the following splendid passage of the **Yoga Vāsiṣṭha**:

स्वारोपशान्त्या स्वादर्शो यथैति प्रतिमा-स्थितिम् ।

YVās VI.1.31.25

As a good mirror being cleansed of its incrustations attains the state of reflecting.

The **Pañcadaśī** argues, the presence of a divinity is commonly acceptable in the image for practical purposes of devotion:

अपरोक्षशिलाबुद्धिर्न परोक्षेशतां नुदेत् ।
प्रतिमादिषु विष्णुत्वे को वा विप्रतिपद्यते ॥

Pañcad IX.23

The perception of stone image is not opposed to an indirect knowledge of the deity whom the image represents. Which devotee contradicts the idea of Viṣṇu in the image?
(Tr. Swahananda)

From the standpoint of Nyāya philosophy, it is observed:

किं बहुना, यं कारवोऽपि विश्वकर्मेत्युपासते, तस्मिन्नेवं जातिगोत्रप्रवरचरण-कुलधर्मादिवदासंसारं सुप्रसिद्धानुभावे भगवति भवे तत्त्वसन्देह एव कुतः । किं निरूपणीयम् ।

NyKu I.3.(1) prose

Why farther detail? Whom even the artisans themselves worship as the great artisan, Viśvakarman – although, I say, with regard to that Being, the adorable Śiva, whom all recognize throughout the world as universally acknowledged like castes, families, family invocations of Agni, schools, social customs, etc., how can there arise any doubt? And what then is there to be ascertained?
(Tr. E.B. Cowell)

As the commentary of Rāmabhadra Sārvabhauma explains the above context:

लोकव्यवहारसिद्धः प्रतिमाद्याकारः ।

Comm. on NyKu I.3

The (divine) form as image etc. is obtained as regards the worldly tradition (though they are not in ultimate sense visible).

Referring to the efficacy of ritually evoking the divinity in an image, the same commentator observes:

एवं प्रतिष्ठादिना प्रतिमादौ शक्तिविशेषो जन्यते ।

Comm. on NyKu I.11

Thus, in the deity-images a specific 'power' (*śakti*, divine essence) is produced through the rituals of consecration, etc.

In view of the Vaiṣṇava philosophy of Rāmānuja the images worshipped in the temple etc. are the *arcā* or *pratimā* aspects of the Lord:

प्रतिमादिकमर्चा स्यादवतारास्तु वैभवाः ।

SarDSaṅg (Rāmānuja) p. 116

The *pratimā* (images) etc., are the *arcās* or worshipful symbols (of the Lord). The incarnations are (His) emanations (*vaibhava*).

Yāmunācārya has specifically observed about the Bhāgavata beliefs regarding the merit of one's attending upon the images and their worship. As he cites in support:

सात्वतानां च देवायतनशोधनं, नैवेद्यभोजनं, प्रतिमासंरक्षणम् इति ।

Āgama Prāmāṇya, p. 150

The duties of the Sāttvata followers include the act of cleansing the divine abode, of eating the *naivedya* (i.e. offerings made to the deity) and of keeping guard of the image.

According to the **Kulārṇava Tantra**, the symbols of the divine may differ in view of several levels of visualisation:

अग्नौ तिष्ठति विप्राणां हृदि देवो मनीषिणाम् ।
प्रतिमास्वल्पबुद्धीनां सर्वत्र विदितात्मनाम् ॥

KulT IX.44

The *brāhmaṇas* find their deity as abiding in the (sacred) fire, the wise in their heart and those who are not enlightened, find it in the image but those who have realized their self find god everywhere. (Tr. H.N. Chakravarty)

The image in view of iconological features (*pratimālakṣaṇa*) is specified to be of three kinds as follows: 1. fully manifest image form, →*vyakta*, 2. unmanifest image-form as symbol, *avyakta*, and 3. *vyaktāvyakta*, image-form combined with symbol. The type *vyakta* is also called →*sakala*, 'complete' or without fragments, full in its shape. For the *vyaktāvyakta* type an example is the *mukhaliṅga*, Śaivite symbol with a face shown on it:

अतः परं प्रवक्ष्यामि प्रतिमालक्षणं श्रृणु ।
त्रिविधं व्यक्तमव्यक्तं व्यक्ताव्यक्तं तथैव च ॥
व्यक्तं तु सकलाकारमव्यक्तं लिङ्गमुच्यते ।
मुखलिङ्गमिति प्रोक्तं व्यक्ताव्यक्तं प्रजायते ॥
अधुना प्रोच्यते सर्वं सकलानां तु लक्षणम् ।

चलं चलाचलं चैव अचलं च त्रिधा भवेत् ॥
चलं धातुमयं ज्ञेयं शैलं चलाचलं स्मृतम् ।
अचलं मृण्मयं ज्ञेयं भित्तिचित्रपटं तथा ॥
चित्रहीनं चलं शैलमचलं चित्रयुक्सदा ।

Kāraṇāgama I.11.1–5ab

Now, it is proposed to tell the features of images that you listen. There are kinds of images, namely manifest (*vyakta*), unmanifest (*avyakta*), and likewise unmanifest with manifest features (*vyaktāvyakta*). That is manifest which is full in the round; the unmanifest is a symbol (such as a) phallic emblem. However, it is said that the *vyaktāvyakta* type is produced when a *liṅga* has a face carved on it.

Here is now being told all about the features of *sakala*, complete form, which is of three types, viz. the movable (*cala*), the movable as well as stationary (*calācala*) and the stable image (*acala*). A metallic image is known as the movable, a stone image is regarded as the *calācala* while a clay-image is known to be an *acala* one as are those painted on a wall or a pictorial plane (*citrapaṭa*). A stone image without painting may be (sometime taken as) a movable one (*cala*).

The **Suprabheda Āgama**, another Agamic text, divides the →*sakala* variety of images as under:

एतानि सकलादीनि त्रिविधानि मयोच्यते ।
चित्रं चित्रार्धमेवं तु चित्राभासं तथैव च ।
सर्वावयवसम्पूर्णं दृश्यं तच्चित्रमुच्यते ।
अर्धावयवसंदृश्यमर्धचित्रं तथैव च ।
पटे भित्तौ च यो लिख्यं चित्राभासमिहोच्यते ।

SupĀ I.34.1–3

These *sakala*, etc. are described by me to be of three kinds, viz. *citra, citrārdha* and likewise *citrābhāsa.* In which all the limbs are fully seen is called the *citra*; likewise where only half portions of the bodily details are seen is called *ardhacitra.* In this context that is called *citrābhāsa* which is painted on a cloth or a wall-surface.

Almost same concept has been explained in the **Sanatkumāra Saṃhitā** (Brahmarātra VII.36cd–41ab). We find the canonical principles of Iconometry or →*tālamāna* briefly indicated in the **Dīptāgama** as follows:

प्रतिमायाममानं तु तालगण्येन भाजितम् ।
लब्धोत्सेधस्य मानं तु चतुर्विंशच्छतं कुरु ॥
तद्वद् भागैकमानं यत्तदङ्गुलमिति स्मृतम् ।

DīĀ XVI.34–35

The length, i.e. the height of the (proposed) image is to be divided by the count of the *tāla.* (In case it is *uttama daśatāla*) make the measure of the obtained height a one-hundred-and-twenty-fourth part. The same in this case is taken to be the measure of one *aṅgula*-unit.

As the great preceptor Īśāna-śiva has made it expressly clear:

प्रतिमाकरणं तत्तद् देहलब्धाङ्गुलेन तु ॥

ĪśGP kp XLI.47cd

The making of image in this case or that case is in accordance with the *dehalabdhāṅgula,* i.e. the relative digit obtained from the (available or accepted) body-measure (of the specific image).

Other relative measurements enjoined for the image size are given in the Tantric tradition (RauĀ kp XXXVII.8cd–11ab).

The procedure of making unbaked and baked clay figurines and their use are specified in the commentary of **Tantrasamuccaya** (XI under verse 112).

Elsewhere, in a Śaivite manual on Pratiṣṭhā, the images are said to be of five types with respect to their posture: (1) standing (*ūrdhva*); (2) seated (*āsīna*); (3) riding a vehicle (*yānastha*); (4) lying or sleeping (*supta*); and (5) flying in the air (*antarikṣaga*) (PLSSamu VI.40).

The same concept prevails in the Pāñcarātra and Vaikhānasa Saṃhitās as well as in the Puranic literature and later Pratiṣṭhā texts belonging to various creeds and schools.

In the religious vogue of common people the image or formal representation of the divinity is proclaimed essential. As stated by the **Viṣṇu Saṃhitā**:

न च रूपं विना देवो ध्यातुं केनापि शक्यते ॥
सर्वरूपनिवृत्ता हि बुद्धिः कुत्रास्य तिष्ठति ।

ViSam XXIX 55cd–56ab

Without a form the god cannot be meditated upon by any one. Where would the intellect stay if taken away from all the formal features?

संकल्प्य प्रतिमामेकां शिलायां वृक्ष एव वा ।

नान्यां तु प्रतिमां कुर्यात् कृता भवति निष्फला ॥

ViSam XIV.45

Initially having conceived one image-form in a piece of stone or wood another must not be carved out of the same piece; if carved that bears no fruit.

Image-making has been thus classified in the Tantra-Āgama literature:

त्रिविधं प्रतिमाकर्म शास्त्रज्ञाः संप्रचक्षते ॥
चित्रं चाप्यर्धचित्रं च चित्राभासं तथैव च ।
दृश्यन्तेऽवयवा यस्याः प्रतिमायाः समन्ततः ॥
मानोन्मानप्रमाणा हि सा चित्रमिति कीर्तिता ।
शिलागताया यस्यास्तु पृष्ठभागो न दृश्यते ॥
मानप्रमाणसंयुक्ता सार्धचित्रमिति स्मृता ।
या स्थितालेख्यरूपेण लिखिता वापि शिल्पिभिः ॥
मानप्रमाणसंयुक्ता सा चित्राभासमुच्यते ।
उत्तमं तु फलं चित्रे मध्यमं चार्धचित्रके ॥
आलेख्ये त्वधमं प्रोक्तं प्रतिमाकर्मणि क्रमात् ।

SanSam Brahma VII.36cd–41ab

Those who are experts of the *śāstra* proclaim the work of image as comprising of three kinds, viz. *citra, ardhacitra* and likewise *citrābhāsa.* That image is called of the *citra* kind of which the bodily details are seen on all its sides as (fashioned out) in true proportions of its measurements and height. That is known as *ardhacitra,* though made in true proportions of its measurements and height is not seen in its back portion which is merged in the stone-slab. The one which exists in the form of a pictorial representation, or is just engraved by the sculptors is called the *citrābhāsa* type being endowed in true proportions of its measurement and height. The merit accruing from the work of image-making is said to be the best in case of a *citra* (sculpture in the round), the middling in case of an *ardhacitra* (bas-relief), and the inferior in case of an *ālekhya* (picture).

The stones are described to be of three kinds to be employed for different parts of an image:

या पुलिङ्गशिला प्रोक्ता तया तु प्रतिमा भवेत् ।
अतो नपुंसकाख्यां च रत्नन्यासाय कल्पयेत् ॥

स्त्रीलिङ्गेति च या प्रोक्ता सा भवेत् पादपीठिका ।
शिलायाश्च शिरो ज्ञात्वा कारयेत् प्रतिमां ततः ॥
कांस्यघण्टाध्वनिर्यत्र तच्छिलायाः शिरो भवेत् ।

SanSam Brahma VII.26–28ab

The image is (made) of that stone which is said to be of the male variety. The neuter variety of stone should thus be employed for the rite of implacing the jewels. The stone variety which is said to be of female gender is meant for the pedestal. One should make the image after ascertaining the head of the stone; there the head of the stone is the portion where a sound like that of a bronze bell (is produced).

The images are further classified under two heads viz. *saumya* (placid) and *āgneyī* (fiery) as per their nature (cf. SanSam Brahma VII.59cd–63ab).

The relative dimensions of a doorway (Kalātattvakośa Vol. III, fig. 4) to the shrine are thus specified:

गर्भपादेन विस्तीर्णं द्वारं द्विगुणमुच्छ्रितम् ॥
उच्छ्रायात्पादविस्तीर्णा शाखा तद्वदुदुम्बरः ।
विस्तारपादप्रतिमं बाहुल्यं शाखयोः स्मृतम् ॥
त्रिपञ्चसप्तनवभिः शाखाभिस्तत्प्रशस्यते ।
अधश्शाखाचतुर्भागे प्रतिहारौ निवेशयेत् ॥
शेषं मङ्गल्यविहगैः श्रीवृक्षस्वस्तिकैर्घटैः ।
मिथुनैः पत्रवल्लीभिः प्रतिमाभिश्च शोभयेत् ॥
द्वारमानाष्टभागोना प्रतिमा स्यात् सपिण्डिका ।
द्वौभागौ प्रतिमा तत्र तृतीयांशश्च पिण्डिका ।

BhāT III.14cd–18

In width the (temple) doorway is one-fourth of the sanctum sanctorum and in height twice (its own width). A one-fourth of its height gives the width of its side-jamb; so is the lintel (in width). The depth of two door-jambs is equal to a one-fourth of this width. (The doorframe) is commendable to have three, five, seven or nine jambs. In the one-fourth lower portion of the door-jambs should be placed the two door-keeper figures. The rest of (its height) should be embellished with the figures of auspicious birds, *śrīvṛkṣa* (wood-apple fruit or foliage design), *svastika,* full vases, amorous couples, scrolls and images. The image together with its pedestal is a one-eighth part less than the doorway height. (Out of it) two one-third parts make (the height of) the image and a one-third the pedestal.

The procedure of image-making is stated to be governed by the following iconometric proportions:

ऋज्वीमेकां पुरा भूमौ मूर्तिं शिल्पी विलेखयेत् ।
तत्र मानादिकं सर्वमादाय तदनन्तरम् ॥

ŚrīSam XIII.9

Firstly, on the ground the sculptor should draw an image straight in its stance. As taking thereon all the (standard units of) dimension he may next (start on the actual image).

प्रतिमायास्तथायामो विभज्य दशभागकैः ॥
भागस्य द्वादशांशस्तु निर्दिष्टं स्वकमङ्गुलम् ।
तेनैवाङ्गुलमानेन तालं वै द्वादशाङ्गुलम् ॥

NārSam XIII.126cd–127

And having divided the height of the image into ten (equal) parts, a one-twelfth of that one unit is indicated as (forming) one own *aṅgula*-unit (of the image). With the same measurement of an *aṅgula*, a *tāla* comes to comprise twelve of them.

The preliminaries to the consecration of an image included a ritual of its purification by immersing it under water with due ceremonies (cf. BhāT VII.25cd–27). For the *kautuka* images, ancillary to the main idol, the Vaikhānasa scripture has discussed in details (cf. Atriprokta-Samūrtārcanādhikaraṇa XXV.21–27).

For proper orientation of the enshrined image with respect to the facade of the temple, the norms are laid down in the **Sanatkumāra Saṃhitā** (Brahma VII.28cd–32ab).

The renovation of an old shrine or an image is prescribed as under:

लुप्ते पुरातने धाम्नि प्रतिमा वा पुरातनी ।
न ज्ञायते चाधिकारी पुनः सृष्टिर्यथेच्छया ॥

BhāT XXII.100

When the older shrine has been effaced or the ancient image has been lost and when the official creed is even not known, there may take place fresh construction as per one's own desire.

The word *pratikṛti* is found normally preferred for an effigy made of an individual in Tantric or *abhicāra* practices to harm the subject or gain over control; however, terms like *mūrti*, *pratimā*, *puttalī* (doll), are also found in such contexts:

कृकलासवसासाध्यपादपांसुः कुलालमृत् ॥
तैः कृतां प्रतिमां मूत्रस्थाने खन्याद्वशीक्रिया ।

TSāSaṅg XVII.13cd–14ab

The rite of gaining control (over someone) includes the practice of making an image of that person with the fat of a chameleon, the dust of that person's feet and the potter's clay and depositing the same in (his or her) urinating ground.

Bhāsa uses the motif of a shrine containing statues of departed kings in his **Pratimā Nāṭaka** based on the **Rāmāyaṇa** story:

अहो क्रियामाधुर्यं पाषाणानाम् । अहो भावगतिराकृतीनाम् । दैवतोद्दिष्टानामपि मानुषविश्वासताऽऽसां प्रतिमानाम् ।

PraNāṭ III.5

Oh, the attractiveness of the workmanship of (exhibited on) the stones. How wonderful the life-lineness (lit., the expression of inward feelings on the faces) of the images. These statues, though meant to be of deities, convey the conviction that they are human. (Tr. M.R. Kale)

Likewise, the poet Bhāsa is the earliest author using the term *pratikṛti* for denoting a painted portrait:

अथ चावाभ्यां तव च वासवदत्तायाश्च प्रतिकृतिं चित्रफलकायामालिख्य विवाहो निर्वृत्तः । एषा चित्रफलका तव सकाशं प्रेषिता । एतां दृष्ट्वा निर्वृतो भव ।

Svap VI.11 (prose)

Thereafter we had the portrait of you and of Vāsavadattā painted on a picture-board and celebrated the wedding. Here is the picture-board sent to you. Be looking at it and comfort yourself. (Tr. M.R. Kale)

Kālidāsa has drawn a number of charming pictures using the concept of *pratimā* as image or likeness (cf. Ragh XVII.36). For convening the specific concept of a person's portrait or likeness, the great classical poet uses the term *pratikṛti*:

सीतां हित्वा दशमुखरिपुर्नोपयेमे यदन्यां तस्या एव प्रतिकृतिसखो यत् क्रतूनाजहार ।

Ragh XIV.87ab

That the enemy of the ten-headed demon did not marry a second wife after he had abandoned Sītā, and that he performed sacrifices being accompanied by the image of herself. (Tr. G.R. Nandargikar)

Pratikṛti as denoting the concept of a man's representative in his son is thus brought out by Śūdraka:

नृणां लोकान्तरस्थानां देहप्रतिकृतिः सुतः ।
मयि यो वै तव स्नेहो रोहसेने स युज्यताम् ॥

Mṛcch IX.42

The son is the embodied image of men staying in the other world (that is, dead). Whatever affection indeed you felt towards me, that (same) should be bestowed on Rohasena.
(Tr. R.D. Karmarkar)

For conveying the idea of counter-action or retaliatory measure, the same term has been used in a proverbial statement of the **Pañcatantra**:

कृते प्रतिकृतिं कुर्याद्धिंसिते प्रतिहिंसितम् ।
न तत्र दोषं पश्यामि दुष्टे दुष्टं समाचरेत् ॥

Pañc V.80

In case of an action done, one should make a counter-action; when one is attacked he should counter-attack in return. I do not see any fault in such cases, for a wicked should be meted out with the same coin.

A charming analogy based on *pratimā* as denoting reflection of form occurs as follows:

श्रिया हसद्भिः कमलानि सस्मितैरलंकृताम्बुः प्रतिमागतैर्मुखैः ।
कृतानुकूल्या सुरराजयोषितां प्रसादसाफल्यमवाप जाह्नवी ॥

Kir VIII.44

The river Gaṅgā gained true significance of the clarity (of her waters) being favoured by the celestial women who adorned those waters by their smiling faces, appearing like the blossoming lotuses, being reflected therein.

Elsewhere, the *pratikṛti* or 'likeness' of a Yakṣī and its pictorial merits as a portraiture are mentioned using choice phraseology of classical art-aesthetics:

तत्र तत्र ततस्तेन पश्यता तत्तदद्भुतम् ।
यक्षी-प्रतिकृतिर्दृष्टा विन्यस्ता चित्रकर्मणि ॥
निर्जीवापि स्फुरन्तीव मूकापि मृदुवागिव ।
चित्रे न्यस्तापि सा तेन चित्ते न्यस्तातिरागिणा ॥

BṛSaṅg XIX.76–77

While going around those wonder-evoking scenes (in his visit to a *Yakṣa* festival), *pratikṛti* executed in painted work. That was though lifeless appeared pulsating with life, though dumb yet speaking as it were in a soft voice. She was depicted only in a painted surface but got expressly incised in his heart being overpowered with intense passion.

The Jaina poet Jaṭānandī has several beautiful stanzas using the term *pratimā* for divine images as well as the concept of similitude:

प्रतिमाः स्थापितास्तत्र नानारत्नविनिर्मिताः ।
भृंगारादर्श शंखादिपरिवारोपशोभिताः ॥

VaCa XV.139

There were set up the (tīrthaṅkara) images, made of various jewels and embellished with the (symbols of) spouted jars, mirrors, conch-shells, etc. and the encircling retinue (of attendant divinities).

The *pratimā* is employed quite ingeniously by the poet Bāṇa as conveying, through *double entendre,* two meanings, one as 'likeness' and the other indicating, the space between the tusks in an elephant's mouth or the ornament embellishing that portion of the elephantine god, who has but one tusk:

सकलमहीभृत्कम्पकृदुत्पद्यत एक एव नृपवंशे ।
विपुलेऽपि पृथुप्रतिमो दन्त इव गणाधिपस्य मुखे ॥

HaCa IV.2

Like the tusk set at a wide interval in the capricious mouth of the elephant-headed god, so in a royal house though populous, there arises but one like to Pṛthu, causing all monarchs to shake.
(Tr. E.B. Cowell and F.W. Thomas)

The gloss of Śaṅkara explains the term here as *pratimā sādṛśyaṃ dantakośaśca,* '*pratimā* denotes likeness as well the tusk-cover.'

In the description of king Harṣa's elephant the poet Bāṇa seems to imply in his phrase *sa-kāñcana-pratimām,* as also indicated by the commentator – two different meanings of the word, namely an ornate covering for the tusk of an elephant; and a figure of divinity (*pratimā dantakośaḥ; devatākṛtiśca*) (Nirnaya Sagar edn, p. 68).

To convey the concept of reflected images, the poet Māgha has likewise employed the term in the following stanzas:

रत्नस्तम्भेषु संक्रान्तप्रतिमास्ते चकाशिरे ।
एकाकिनोऽपि परितः पौरुषेयवृता इव ॥

Śiśu II.4

Although present all alone, they (viz. Kṛṣṇa, Balarāma and Uddhava) appeared, as it were, accompanied around by a host of men for they (themselves) shone as so many reflected images on the jewel-made columns.

Bhavabhūti refers to a golden likeness of Sītā by the term *pratikṛti*:

अरुन्धती – जगत्पते रामचन्द्र ।
नियोजय यथाधर्मं प्रियां त्वं धर्मचारिणीम् ।
हिरण्मय्याः प्रतिकृतेः पुण्यां प्रकृतिमध्वरे ॥

UttCa VII.19

Arundhatī – O Lord of the world, pious Rāma. As per the holy injunctions, you should associate in the sacrifice, your beloved and virtuous wife in the auspicious form (or nature, *prakṛti*) of her likeness (*pratikṛti*) made of gold.

In several passages of his excellent prose-romance, Dhanapāla has described divine images in beautiful phraseology:

परिपूर्णसर्वावयवां सर्वप्रतिमालक्षणोपेतां सर्वालंकारभूषितवपुर्लतां सर्वलोक-लोचनानन्दजननीं सर्वदोषनिर्मुक्तामत्युदारमुक्ताशैलदारुसंभवां भगवत्याः श्रियः प्रतिकृतिं यथाविधि प्रतिष्ठाप्य ..... ।

Til p. 34

Having consecrated with due rituals the icon (*pratikṛti*) of the Goddess Śrī, that was complete in all her limbs, as endowed with all the iconographic features, having the bodily frame as adorned with all the ornaments, evoking a pleasing sight to the eyes of all the world, being fully devoid of any (carving) defects, and produced in the wood coming from the high pearl-mountain, ...

Referring to a pictorial portrait or *pratikṛti* of a princess the poet paints a pen-picture (Til, Nirnaya Sagar edn, pp. 174–175).

Pratimā as denoting both the concepts of similitude and images occur in several select stanzas of the **Naiṣadhīyacarita** (I.23, VI.39, XII.I.42, XV.24).

पश्याः पुरन्ध्रीः प्रति सान्द्रचन्द्ररजःकृतक्रीडकुमारचक्रे ।
चित्राणि चक्रेऽध्वनि चक्रवर्तिचिह्नं तदङ्घ्रिप्रतिमासु चक्रम् ॥

NaiCa VI.39

The circle in his footprints, a mark of emperors, which was visible on the way where a crowd of young princes was playing with a thick mass of camphor powder, caused amazement to the elderly ladies who were looking at it. (Tr. K.K. Handiqui)

The specific Jaina concept of *pratimā* as ascetic ideal is thus conveyed by the poet Amaracandra Sūri:

स्थितः प्रतिमया मौनी, निर्ममो निष्परिग्रहः ।
ताभ्यामित्यर्थितो नाथः, क्व विवेकोऽथवार्थिनि ? ॥

PadMa XIII.56

The lord, who was poised silent in observance of the ascetic standard (*pratimā*), was indifferent, and had no possessions, was thus requested by them. In case of a petitioner where lies any discrimination?

Both the Buddhist and the Jaina donors who caused images of the respective pontiffs of their faith during the Kuṣāṇa and later periods are found to refer such statues in their dedicatory records by the word *pratimā* – quite commonly preferred. For example, a headless Buddha image in stone (Mathura Museum, No. 1557) dated in the year 22, is styled in its pedestal description as follows:

ओं सिद्धं (सं) २०+२ गृ २ दि ३० अस्यां पूर्व्वायां
प्रावारिक – विहारे बुद्ध-प्रतिमा प्रति(ष्ठा) पिता ।

Mathura Museum, No. 1557

Om Success! on the 30th day of the 2nd (month) of summer, in the year 22 on this occasion as specified, (this) image of Buddha was installed in the Prāvārika-vihāra .... (Tr. V.S. Agrawala)

A Kuṣāṇa stone Buddha (Mathura Museum, No. 270), standing on a lotus, and attended by two or more associated figures, bears an inscription on its rim, which reads:

भगवतो शाक्यमुनिस्य प्रतिमा प्रतिष्ठापिता भिक्षु ... ।

An image of Bhagavān Śākyamuni is set up by the monk ....

As pointed out by Prof. V.S. Agrawala, "It is remarkable that the standing image is definitely identified with Śākya Muni, which was the title of Gautama Buddha usually referring to him in his stage of Bodhisattvahood" (*Mathura Museum Catalogue,* Vol. I, Lucknow, 1948). An inscription carved on the pedestal of a Kuṣāṇa image, dated in the year 84 of the time of emperor Vāsudeva mentions the image as *pratimā* of Ṛṣabhanātha the first Jaina pontiff:

भगवतो अर्हतो ऋषभस्य प्रतिमा प्रतिष्ठापिता धरसहस्य कुटुम्बुनि ... गुत्त-कुमारदत्तस्य निर्वर्त्तन ।

Mathura Museum, No. B.4

.... has erected an image of the Lord, the Arhat Ṛṣabha at the request of Kumāradatta ... (Tr. V.S. Agrawala)

Another donative record in Prakrit of the same Kuṣāṇa year, calls the statue installed as that of Tīrthaṅkara Vardhamāna:

कुटुबीणिये दताये दानं वर्धमान-प्रतिमा प्रतिथापिता ।

... (this) image of Vardhamāna, a gift of Okhārikā the daughter of Damitra, and Datā (Sanskrit Dattā), the wife of a householder, was set up. .... (Tr. V.S. Agrawala)

A peculiar type of collective representation of the four Tīrthaṅkaras is already popular in the Jaina images of the first-second century A.D. showing one image on each face or side of a square stele or pillar. It was so aptly called by the term *pratimā sarvatobhadrikā,* the Prakrit form of which occurs as early as a donor's record dated A.D. 93 (Lucknow Museum, No. J.230; also cf. No. J. 235). According to V.A. Smith, "The expression *pratimā sabbato bhadrikā,* 'beautiful on all sides' is a technical term for quadruple image" (*The Jaina Stūpa,* p. 46). Later it came to be also styled as the *catuṣki* (*kā*), *caumukhī, catuṣtīrthī,* or *caturbimba* (cf. a Mathura quadruple image-inscription of A.D. 1023). There developed also other collective-image types in the Jaina worship and art, namely *dvitīrthī, pratimā, pañcatīrthī* (also, *pañcaparameṣṭhī; pañcendra,* cf. Gupta pillar and its inscription at Kahaum); *caubīsī* or *caturviṃśatikā;* etc.

भगवतोऽर्हतः चन्द्रप्रभस्य प्रतिमेयं कारिता ... ।
भगवतोऽर्हतः पुष्पदन्तस्य प्रतिमेयं कारिता ... ।
भगवतोऽर्हतः पद्मप्रभस्य प्रतिमेयं कारिता ... ।

Vidisa Jina-image Ins of Ramagupta's time (ca 365-367 A.D.)

One of the primary meanings of the word *pratimā* seems to be 'comparison' as the expression *a-pratima* commonly denotes, 'without comparison', 'with no counterpart', 'matchless'. The idea of a well-known **Yajurveda** stanza had been so beautifully handled in a Gupta pillar-inscription from Bhitari:

[न यस्य] प्रतिमा काचित्प्रतिमां तस्य शार्ङ्गिणः ।

The image of God Viṣṇu who has (in truth) no formal model or figure.

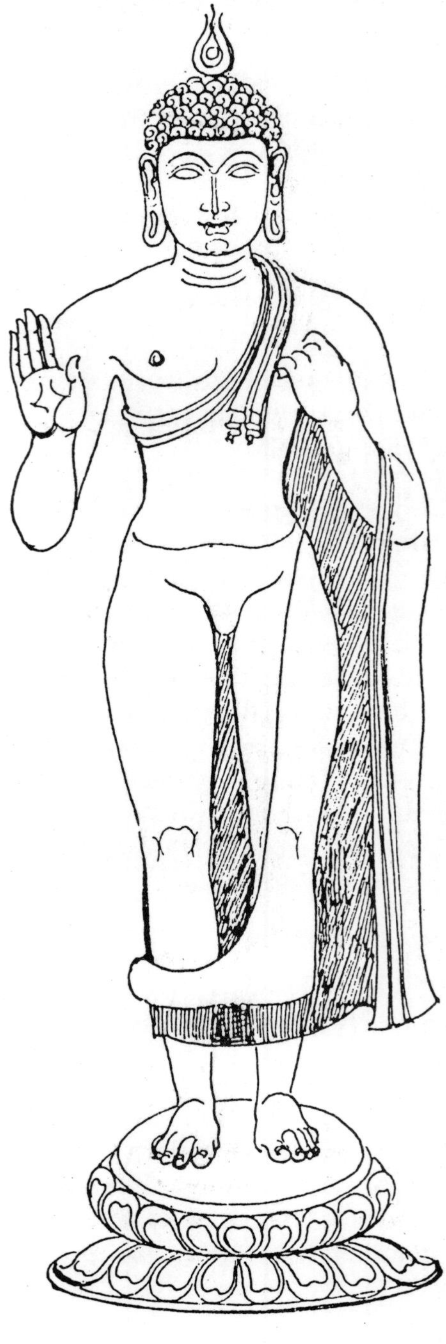

Figure 16: Buddha standing on a lotus

It compares well with the statement found in a Sarnath Buddhist record of the Gupta period:

भक्त्यावर्जित-मनसा पतिना पूजार्थमभयमित्रेण ।
प्रतिमाऽप्रतिमस्य गुणैरपरेऽयं कारिता शास्तुः ॥

The dying Buddha or *parinirvāṇa* image at Kasia (Kusinagar) bears the name of its sculptor who executed this Gupta period sculpture of enormous size:

प्रतिमा चेयं घटिता दिन्नेन माथुरेण ।

Archaeological Survey of India Report, 1906–7, pp. 45–50

This image has been carved by the artist Dinna of the Mathura atelier.

There are quite a few masterpieces of the same great artist now known from their contemporary donative records (cf. P.K. Agrawala, *Gupta-kālīna kalā evam vāstu*, Varanasi, 1994, pp. 26–27).

A beautiful picture of the wife's jealousy against her co-wife getting favour from the husband occurs in the following benedictory stanza of a Pallava inscription:

स्वस्ति श्रीकण्ठकण्ठाभरणभुजगराण्मूर्ध्नि माणिक्यमध्ये
दृष्ट्वात्मीयां सलज्जा प्रतिकृतिमपरामङ्गनां शङ्कमाना ।
आश्लेषालोलचित्तं कृतचरणनतिप्रार्थनं वो भवानी
दिश्यात्पश्यन्त्यधीरं निजपतिमनिशं सेर्ष्यमर्धेक्षणेन ॥

Thiruvalangadu Copper-plates
(South Indian Ins, Vol. III, p. 383)

Hail! May Bhavānī (Pārvatī) grant you prosperity who, seeing a reflection of herself in the gem on the head of the lord of serpents (serving as) neck-jewel of Śrīkaṇṭha (Śiva), and suspecting that to be another woman, and (consequently) bashful and jealous tremulously looks askance all the time at her husband praying prostrate at her feet with his heart yearning to embrace her. (Tr. C. Sivaramamurti)

In an 11th–12th cent. A.D. inscription, originally fixed in the Ananta-Vāsudeva temple at Bhubaneswar, the term *pratikṛti* occurs in the sense of a reflected image or shadow cast on the surface of water:

प्रासादाग्रे स खलु जगतः पुण्य-पण्यैव
चक्रे वापीं मरकत-मणि-स्वच्छ-सुच्छाय-तोयां (म्) ।

मध्ये वारि प्रतिकृतिमिषाद्दर्शयन्तीव तादृग्
विष्णोर्द्धामाद्भुतमहिकुलस्याधिकं या चकास्ति ॥

(Bhavadeva's Bhubaneswar Stone Ins, V.31 E.I., VI, pp. 203f.)

In front of the temple, he got a water-reservoir (*vāpī*, or step-well) made, which was as it were like a sole causeway for the world to the market of righteous deeds, which was full of clean and lustrous water resembling the sheen of emeralds. By way of showing as if a reflection of the image (of the god) from the abode of Viṣṇu of the kind (as described earlier in preceding verses), that (*vāpī*), in the middle of its water, shone as being miraculous even more than that (mythical abode of the lord's) serpent seat.

Manifestation in the Arts

One of the primary texts on art conventions as contained in the **Viṣṇudharmottara Purāṇa** includes a section (consisting chs. 44–85) which is appropriately named as the '*pratimā-lakṣaṇa*' (III.86.1: 44.3; also colophon to ch. 38); this seems to be the name for the subject which dealt with the common features of the image and included also certain comments and injunctions on Iconometry. The rules of its general norms are states to be closely allied to those of painting:

चित्रसूत्रं न जानाति यस्तु सम्यङ् नराधिप ।
प्रतिमालक्षणं वेत्तुं न शक्यं तेन कर्हिचित् ॥

VDhPur III.2.2

He who has not properly known the rules of painting cannot be able to ever know the rules of image-making.

However, the phrase *rūpa-nirmāṇa* denoting image making, finds specific favour from this author.

According to Varāhamihira, the images of various materials bestow merits of specific kinds:

आयुःश्रीबलजयदा दारुमयी मृण्मयी तथा प्रतिमा ।
लोकहिताय मणिमयी सौवर्णी पुष्टिदा भवति ॥
रजतमयी कीर्तिकरी प्रजाविवृद्धिं करोति ताम्रमयी ।
भूलाभं तु महान्तं शैली प्रतिमाथवा लिङ्गम् ॥

BṛSam LX.4–5

A wood-carved image is the giver of life, dignity, strength and victory; similar is the merit gained of a clay figure. The jewel-made one is for acquiring welfare of the world; the golden image is the bestower of nourishment. The silver-cast one gives fame; the copper image is for the increase in progeny. An image or a *liṅga* made of stone bestows great acquisition of lands.

Varāhamihira has summarily discussed the regional conventions and features to be followed in image-making as follows:

देशानुरूपभूषणवेषालंकारमूर्त्तिभिः कार्या ।
प्रतिमा लक्षणयुक्ता सन्निहिता वृद्धिदा भवति ॥

BṛSam LVIII.29

An image is to be made by representing in its form the characteristics, dress and ornaments in agreement of the region: an image made as per the iconographic rules and properly consecrated with the divine-spirit bestows growth.

As a rule the image or symbol in wood was to be made as per the nature of the tree, i.e. upper and lower parts of the wood were to be likewise maintained in the carved image. Thus while obtaining a tree its top and bottom as well as different sides (front, right, left, back) (*yathādiśam*) were to be carefully marked:

लिङ्गं वा प्रतिमा वा द्रुमवत् स्थाप्या यथादिशं यस्मात् ।
तस्माच्चिह्नयितव्या दिशो द्रुमस्योर्ध्वमथवाधः ॥

BṛSam LIX.7

Since an Emblem of Śiva or any image should be installed according to the directions of the tree, the different directions as well as the upper and lower parts should be marked on the tree.
(Tr. M.R. Bhat)

As explained by M.R. Bhat, "the different directions and tip and bottom of the tree should be marked, so that the idol may have the eastern part for its face, the western one for its back, the lower part for its feet and upper one for its head. If the image is made contrary to the directions of the tree, it will prove harmful to the maker as well as to the worshipper." The same principle had been thus stated by sage Kāśyapa, an authority earlier to Varāhamihira:

वृक्षवत्प्रतिमा कार्या प्राग्भागाद्युपलक्षिता ।
पादाः पादेषु कर्तव्याः शीर्षमूर्ध्वे तु कारयेत् ॥

Quoted in BṛSam LIX after 7

Similar injunctions on the iconoplastic concepts, ritual consecration and worship are also found treated by Vardhamāna Sūri in his **Ācāra Dinakara**, a Śvetāmbara Jaina text of great authority. As the author observes:

अग्नौ देवोऽस्ति विप्राणां हृदि देवोऽस्ति योगिनाम् ।
प्रतिमा स्वल्पबुद्धीनां सर्वत्र विदितात्मनाम् ॥

ĀcD I.12

In the fire is the god-head of the Brāhmaṇas; in the heart is the god-head of the Yogins; in the images (*pratimā*) is the god-head of those who are of lowly intelligence; and, everywhere is the god-head of those who have realised the soul.

Certain rules of image-making and the defective features to be avoided in iconic representation of deities are further enumerated (ĀcD II.33.13–20). With regard to the size and art medium the position has further been explained (ĀcD II.33.21–25).

Sometimes, the image of deity or pontiff is referred to in the dedicatory inscription engraved on its pedestal. This has been quite an ancient practice well traceable back to the beginning of the Christian era. For example, Vardhamānapratimā (Lucknow Museum, No. 490); *bhagavato arhato ṛṣabhasya pratimā* (Lucknow Museum, No. B.4). But the deity-image is mostly mentioned in such donative records simply by the name of that deity without using the word *pratimā* or *arcā*; or by addressing directly the divinity with a wish. In some rare occurrences the images are indicated by the imprint of the name of its donor; *jinadāsīya pratimā* (Lucknow Museum, No. B.2); *dattasāgarasya pratimā* (Mathura Museum, No. 268, which is first mentioned in line 1 of the record as *ṛṣabhasya pratimā*). This last convention is significantly referred to be Vardhamāna Sūri:

चैत्ये गृहे नवं बिम्बं कारयन्स्नातकः कृती ।
सप्तधा निजनामार्हं जैनबिम्बं विधापयेत् ॥

ĀcD II.33

Having got a new image made the pious and initiated householder should consecrate in a *caitya* or house the image of the Jina, bearing his own name, in accordance with the seven kinds of purifications.

The Mathura Lakulīśa pillar-inscription of A.D. 360 refers presumably to two Śiva-*liṅgas*, Upamiteśvara and Kapileśvara marked in the name of two teachers Upamita and Kapila. Besides naming the deity-image and thus its shrine after one's own name, of this practice there are numerous instances found in medieval epigraphs and the Puranic Māhātmyas, sometimes the image was dedicated as bearing the name of one's parent, teacher or friend, or even of a distant relative of the patron. The **Viṣṇudharmottara Purāṇa** (III.96.132–134ab) gives the general rule on the naming of the images,e.g. Viṣṇu, Brahmā, Śiva, etc. The well-defined code for this convention is briefly but very clearly indicated by the Śaiva author Vairocana in his **Pratiṣṭhālakṣaṇa-sāra-samuccaya**:

> प्राक्कर्तारख्येश्वरान्तं च लिङ्गं तत्प्रतिमापि वा ।
> दुर्गायामीश्वरी भानावादित्यो माधवो हरौ ॥
>
> PLSSamu XVI.127
>
> In case of both the *liṅga* or the image of Śiva the first element of its name is after the name of the maker (i.e. the patron, *yajamāna*) and the second part or ending is marked as *īśvara.* In case of Goddess Durgā it is (to end in) *īśvarī*; in case of Sun, Āditya; and in case of Viṣṇu, Mādhava.

As a major rule, the **Matsya Purāṇa** (CCLVIII.22–23) prescribes that in the household worship, a *pratimā* beginning with the size of one's own thumb-joint to a *vitasti* (12 *aṅgulas*) measure should be made. By the wise a bigger one is not commended. For installation in a temple the image can be up to the measure of 16 (*vitastis* or *talas*; equal to 8 *hasta*s or hands) but not beyond that.

The same text mentions as *svakīyāṅgulamāna* the relative unit of proportionate division of an image arrived at from its own accepted dimension and thus states briefly the convention:

> स्वकीयांगुलमानेन मुखं स्याद्द्वादशांगुलम् ।
> मुख्यमानेन कर्तव्या सर्वावयव-कल्पना ॥
>
> MatPur CCLVIII.19
>
> By taking the *mukha* [face, according to the general canon its height being 12 *aṅgulas* of the whole as per the ratio of image type in *tālamāna*] as the first basic unit all other limbs of the body be designed.

This *ūrdhvamāna* of the *navatāla* proportion may be tabulated on the basis of **Matsya Purāṇa** (CCLVIII.26–30a) as under:

1.	Face	one unit of *tāla*
1a.	*grīvā*	four *aṅgulas*
2.	*grīvā* to *hṛdaya*	one unit of *tāla*
3.	*hṛdaya* to *nābhi*	one unit of *tāla*

[3a.	*nābhi*	one *aṅgula*]
4.	*nābhi* to *meḍhra*	one unit of *tāla*
5.	*ūru* (thigh)	two units or two *tālas*
5a.	*jānu* (knee-joint)	four *aṅgulas*
6.	*jaṅghā*	two units or two *tālas*
6a.	*pāda* (foot)	four *aṅgulas*

One *tāla* (12 *aṅgulas*) + 8 units of *tālas* = nine →*tālas* or 108 *aṅgulas* or digits of an image's selfsame proportion. However, the image measured in its face or head portion two *aṅgulas* more when it wore a crown, i.e. fourteen digits in place of twelve.

One of the earliest extant treatises on the subject of *pratimā-lakṣaṇa* would be found as incorporated in the **Bṛhat Saṃhitā** of Varāhamihira of which several of the following chapters directly reproduce in nut-shell the main canons and principles regarding the deity images and their features as prevailing during the time.

On the priestly canons of *pratiṣṭhā* or ritual installation of images, we have an enormous body of literature included in proper contexts of the Puranic rites, both Śaivite and Vaiṣṇava Āgamas and Saṃhitās, Tantras and also encyclopaedic digests besides independent works or manuals directly devoted to the subject.

Conclusion

The term *pratimā* indicating such notions as counter-measure, likeness or image evolved quite early in the Vedic language. In many a passages it implies the sense of a representative or even symbol. For a similar concept the cognate term of *pratikṛti* also occurs from the later Vedic texts onwards.

For *pratimā* the sense of deity-image came to be well defined in the epics, Purāṇas and other literary traditions. The Purāṇa and Āgama-Tantra works describe various forms of divine images, their worship procedures and rituals, aesthetic merits, iconological and iconographic details, etc. *Pratimā* is explained as the concrete representative of the Ultimate Reality. In place of doctrine of an abstract God, the cult of *pratimā* signified divine being with a personality or formed entity to be worshipped with devotion and love and not only through *tapas* and *yoga* austerities. This aspect of image-worship became a common legacy of all Indian sects and beliefs.

The Jainas define an ideal of ethical codes and vows under the head of *pratimā*, both for a common devotee as well as monk.

In temple cult, the image or *pratimā* formed its nucleus and in Vāstu and Śilpa tradition many conventions and rules were evolved and prescribed with respect to image making as iconoplastic concepts, ritual consecration and installation, varieties of images, naming of an image, ancillary and surrounding (*āvaraṇa*) deities, demigods, etc.

Prithvi Kumar Agrawala

Select Bibliography

Agrawala, P.K.: Guptakālīna kalā evam Vāstu, Varanasi: Books Asia, 1994.

Agrawala, V.S.: Studies in Indian Art, Varanasi: Vishwavidyalaya Prakashan, 1981.

Banerjea, J.N.: Development of Hindu Iconography, Calcutta: University of Calcutta, 1956.

Kane, P.V.: History of Dharmaśāstra, Vol. II, Poona: BORI, 1946.

Sircar, D.C.: Select Inscriptions, Vol. I, Motilal Banarsidass: New Delhi, 1991.

VIGRAHA

Overview

Vigraha (m.) (derived from the root *graha-*, with the prefix *vi*) denotes in diverse contexts the meanings such as 'spreading', 'taking up', 'assuming' as well as 'a physical form', 'body' or 'image'. From a different viewpoint it signifies dissension, struggle or war. In grammar, it means separation of words, resolution of a compound or a sentence into its constituent parts. As part of Vedic worship, the term sometimes stands for a special *graha*, i.e. a ritual item or a verse used in offering of oblations. In the Epics, the word suggests an embodiment or incarnate entity by such phrases as *vigrahavat, vigraha-rūpin*, besides being employed to convey the concept of war. In the Purāṇas, all these meanings of the word are implied of various levels of expression, the most significant one being the sense of a body or form, both visible and invisible. In Āyurveda, it signifies an embodied existence or physical being.

The Buddhist and Jaina literatures use the word for an image or figure besides the meaning of fight or dissension implied in different contexts. In the Jaina philosophy, *vigraha-gati* refers to a specific type of transmigratory motion of mundane soul. In the Vedānta philosophy, *vigraha-vattva* or corporeality of the Ultimate Reality is a moot point of discussion. Likewise, the Āgama-Tantras raise the question of whether the gods possess a body or have no physical form. In the Vaiṣṇava Saṃhitās, *vigraha* occurs in the special sense of *upacāra*, i.e. items of divine service, or ritual means of offering. In the **Artha-Śāstra** or Indian Polity, *vigraha* evolves as one of the six codes of diplomatic relationship (*ṣāḍguṇya*); *vigraha* relates to the policies of war, which covered diverse situations and recourses of diplomatic struggles and expeditions both offensive as well as defensive.

In the manifestation of arts, *vigraha* successively evolves to denote the symbolic or iconic "body" or figure of a deity. In art-technical contexts, *vigraha* or image of the god is seen to pass through three stages of sculptor's work, viz. selecting a piece of stone, fashioning the figure and finally finishing it. Several early texts describing metal-casting procedure refer to the figural form by the phrase *vigraha* both for its mould-state as well as the case specimen.

Etymology and Related Words

According to the **Amara Kośa**, the term *vigraha* is one of the twelve synonyms denoting 'physical body':

अङ्गं प्रतीकोऽवयवोऽपघनोऽथ कलेवरम् ।
गात्रं वपुः संहननं शरीरं वर्ष्म विग्रहः ॥
कायो देहः क्लीबपुंसोः स्त्रियां मूर्तिस्तनुस्तनूः ।

AmKo II.6.70–71ab

As Kṣīrasvāmin has commented:

विगृह्यते विग्रहः, "ग्रहवृदृ-" (Pā III.3.58) इति अप् ।

Kṣ on AmKo II.6.70–71ab

That which is grasped is called *vigrahaḥ* (masculine in gender); it is derived from the root *graha-* with the suffix *ap* added to it (and prefix *vi* meaning diverse, specific).

Or, as the gloss Rāmāśramī notes:

विविधं सुखादि गृह्णाति । अच् (Pā III.1.134) । विविधैर्व्याधिभिर्गृह्यते वा ॥

Rāmāśramī on AmKo II.6.70–71ab

As it takes (experience of) various (denoted by prefix *vi*) pleasures, etc. it is *vigraha*; (from the root *graha-*) being added by suffix *ac*. Or, it is (explained) to be afflicted by various ailments.

The term also occurs in several other senses, such as:

विस्तारो विग्रहो व्यासः स च शब्दस्य विस्तरः ।

AmKo III.2.22ab

Vigraha means spreading out, width and the analysis of word.

अस्त्रियां समरानीकरणाः कलहविग्रहौ ॥

AmKo II.8.104cd

Samara (battle), *anīka* (army), *raṇa* (war), *kalaha* (quarrel) and *vigraha* (struggle, opposition) are (synonyms) used in masculine and neuter genders.

Layers of Meaning

All such meanings of the term are summarised together by the **Medinī Kośa**:

विग्रहः कायविस्तारविभागे ना रणेऽस्त्रियाम् ।

MedKo XXXIII.23cd

The term *vigraha*, masculine in gender, is used in the sense of body, breadth or extension and division (i.e. resolution by analysis of parts of a word or a sentence); and also as both masculine and neuter, in the sense of fight or war.

For the last mentioned meaning the **Agni Purāṇa** says: *apakārastu vigrahaḥ* (CCXXXIV.18), 'doing harm' is meant by *vigraha.*

The meaning 'division' is explained by the phrase *padavigraha = padavicchedaḥ*, i.e. separation of words, resolution of a sentence into its constituent parts (V.S. Apte, *Sanskrit-English Dictionary*). The same usage is explained by Yāska and Śaunaka as follows:

अथ यस्यागमाद् अर्थपृथक्त्वमह विज्ञायते न त्वौद्देशिकमिव विग्रहेण पृथक्त्वात् स कर्मोपसंग्रहः ।

Nir I.4

Now a conjunctive particle is that by whose addition separateness of notions is indeed recognised, but not like an enumerative one, i.e. because of a separation by isolation. (Tr. L. Sarup)

विग्रहान्निर्वचः कार्यं समासेष्वपि तद्धिते ।
प्रविभज्यैव निर्ब्रूयाद् दण्डार्हो दण्ड्य इत्यपि ॥
अनेकं सत्तथा चान्यद् एकमेव निरुक्तवान् ।
अरुणो मा सकृन्मन्त्रे मासकृद्विग्रहेण तु ॥

BṛDev II.106, 112

In compounds, as well as in a secondary derivative, explanation (*nirvacas*) should proceed from analysis: one should explain after separating (the parts); thus 'punishable' (*daṇḍya*) as 'deserving punishment' (*daṇḍārha*).

Similarly, another (expression) which is not one (word), he has explained as one only by (his) analysis as 'month-maker' (*māsakṛt*) in the formula, 'the ruddy one me once' (*aruṇo mā sakṛt* – ṚV I.195.18). (Tr. A.A. Macdonell)

Through specific usages in the language (*vi* + *gṛha* = to seize, to grab) another layer of meaning that evolved around the term is dissension, opposition, war:

गजपादयुक्तमिव बलवद्विग्रहः ।

Cāṇakya-Nītisūtra 57

The dissension or quarrel with a stronger enemy is just likened to the fight of a foot-soldier with an elephant.

As we find the same idea expressed in a general context of the following proverbial advice:

शत्रौ मित्रे पुत्रे बन्धौ मा कुरु यत्नं विग्रहसन्धौ ।

Dvādaśapañjarikā Stotra 7ab

You should not ever make an attempt of entering into dissension or alliance with a (natural) enemy, a friend, a son or a relative.

However, the word *vigraha* was given preference over its other synonyms (used for this specific implication) in the works of ancient Indian Polity which use it as a technical designation for denoting diplomacy of war as part of the sixfold state policy:

संधिर्ना विग्रहो यानमासनं द्वैधमाश्रयः ॥

षड्गुणाः .... ।

AmKo II.8.18cd–19a

The six state policies are concerning (1) *sandhi* (peace), (2) *vigraha* (war), (3) *yāna* (marching), (4) *āsana* (quite post), (5) *dvaidha* (double-dealing), and (6) *āśraya* (friendship).

Development of the Concept

The word *vigraha* as such is not found in any of the early Vedic Saṃhitās and Brāhmaṇas, though the root *graha* appears frequently used in its primary sense of 'taking', 'holding', 'assuming'. However, it begins to occur only from the later group of Upanisadic texts.

Besides extensive use of the root *graha* for its common denotation to take, to accept, to seize, the term *graha* is met as a popular Vedic name for ritual items such as a vessel, ladle, or any container of offering. Thus, *vigrahaṇa* (*vi-grahaṇa*) in the **Taittirīya Saṃhitā** is taken to imply "a verse supporting to offer oblations to various deities" [Suryakanta, *A Practical Vedic Dictionary*]. The term *vigraha* first occurs in a similar context of ritual vocabulary, preferring to indicate *vigraha* as a partial *graha* ("vessel"), a specific *graha* or offering divided in several portions for specific intention:

यस्य विग्रहस्तस्य प्रथमं चमसमुन्नयति ।

KātŚrSū IX.14.14

The Unnetṛ fills the goblet of the priest first with whom is connected the Ukthya-*vigraha* (i.e. one-third portion, namely, the Prastotṛ, Brāhmaṇācchaṃsin and Acchāvāka respectively).

However, an evolution in the meaning and concept of this word for a deity's form, body or image is well evidenced in the following Upanisadic passage:

खल्वात्मनोऽत्मा नेताऽमृताख्यश्चेता मन्ता गन्तोत्सृष्टानन्दयिता कर्ता वक्ता रसयिता घ्राता द्रष्टा श्रोता स्पृशति च विभुर्विग्रहे सन्निविष्ट इत्येवं ह्याह ।

MaitUp VI.7

For, thus, it has been said, 'assuredly the Soul (*Ātman*) of one's soul is called the Immortal Leader. As perceiver, thinker, goer, evacuator, begetter, doer, speaker, taster, smeller, seer, hearer– and he touches–the All-Pervader (i.e. the Soul, the *Ātman*) has entered the body (*vigraha*). (Tr. R.E. Hume)

Most probably from its (of such a vessel, offering-container) being a means in the act of homage offered to a deity, the same implication of the word *vigraha* reappeared as denoting an item of service or attendance to the deity (the other more popular term being *upacāra*). There came to be evolved several sets of such *vigrahas* (or *upacāras*), mentioned in the texts for general vogue of worship followed in accordance to one's means or the ritual occasion enjoined by the tradition.

Vigraha-vān for an embodied entity or personification occurs in the following imagery of the **Maitrī Upaniṣad**:

विग्रहवान् एष कालः सिन्धुराजः प्रजानाम् । एष तत्स्थः सविताख्यः ।

MaitUp VI.16

The Time is this embodied Horse of the Sind breed. Of the generations, this rider on it is the Savitā by name.

Vigraha as conveying the sense of 'bodily remains', or skeletal bones appears in the **Rāmapūrvottaratāpanī Upaniṣad:**

स तु रामे शङ्कितः सन्प्रत्ययार्थं च दुन्दुभेः ।
विग्रहं दर्शयामास यो रामस्तमचिक्षिपत् ॥

RāmPUp IV.21

He (the monkey-chief Sugrīva), being doubtful as to the prowess of Rāma, showed him to ascertain truth (the heap of) bodily relics (*vigraha*) of *Dundubhi*, which the celebrated Rāma kicked away (easily).

The same Upaniṣad preaches the worship of a →*yantra* as the very 'body' or representation of its presiding god:

सोऽभयस्यास्य देवस्य विग्रहो यन्त्रकल्पना ।
विना यन्त्रेण चेत्पूजा देवता न प्रसीदति ॥

RāmPUp I.13

Of this protection-granting Lord the *yantra* (= sacred diagram) design is His real form (*vigraha,* 'body', nature, representation). In case the worship is offered without *yantra* the divinity is not pleased.

Some of the earliest usages of the word as denoting body or form occur in **Vālmīki's Rāmāyaṇa**:

रामो विग्रहवान् धर्मः साधुः सत्यपराक्रमः ।
राजा सर्वस्य लोकस्य देवानामिव वासवः ॥

Rām III.37.13

Rāma is as it were the embodied righteousness or law (*dharma*) itself; being pious and having truthful valour he ruled over the world like Indra amongst the gods.

तदलं कालपाशेन सीताविग्रहरूपिणा ।
स्वयं स्कन्धावसक्तेन क्षेममात्मनि चिन्त्यताम् ॥

Rām V.51.35

Away with that noose of Death which in shape is the form of Sītā you got yourself affixed to your shoulder. (Therefore) you worry about your welfare.

Referring to the other significant concept of war or opposition we find the following instance:

संधिविग्रहतत्त्वज्ञाः प्रकृत्या सम्पदान्विताः ।

Rām I.7.18

(Those ministers) who are experts in the knowledge of war and peace naturally endow the state with prosperity.

तस्य ते विग्रहे ताभ्यां युगग्रहणमस्थिरम् ।
वृत्रस्येवेन्द्रबाहुभ्यां बाहोरेकस्य विग्रहे ॥

Rām V.21.32

[Sītā warns Rāvaṇa] In your encounter with both of them (i.e. Rāma and Lakṣmaṇa) your bearing the yoke (of battle) is uncertain as it was for the demon Vṛtra's one arm to meet both the arms of Indra in that war (of yore).

In the great epic **Mahābhārata,** also *vigraha* occurs frequently as denoting the concept of form, body or embodiment:

दिव्यरूपा हि सा देवी गङ्गा त्रिपथगा नदी ।
मानुषं विग्रहं श्रीमत्कृत्वा सा वरवर्णिनी ॥

MBh I.92.39

That celestial lady, Gaṅgā of the three courses, assuming a human form of exceeding beauty and excellent feature. (Tr. M.N. Dutt)

शुभमौर्वं नवं कृत्वा महापुरुषविग्रहम् ।
ईजिवांस्त्वं जपैर्होमैरुपहारैश्च मानद ॥

MBh VII.172.84

Creating [afresh] a white image of that foremost of male beings, O Bestower of honour, you adored him with homage, offerings and reiterating prayers. (Tr. M.N. Dutt)

सोऽभिगम्य महात्मानं विष्णुं पुरुषविग्रहम् ।
उवाच मधुराभाषः स्मितपूर्वमिदं तदा ॥

MBh XII.45.16

Approaching the high-souled one who was Viṣṇu himself in incarnate form, king Yudhiṣṭhira addressed him sweetly and smilingly. (Tr. P.C. Roy)

न वर्तयन्त्याहुतिभिस्ते नाप्यमृतभोजनाः ।
तथा दिव्यशरीरास्ते न च विग्रहमूर्तयः ॥

MBh III.247.21

They do not live on oblations or on ambrosia. They possess such celestial forms that they cannot be perceived by the senses.

The other context of war is implied in the typical usage *sāndhivigrahika* (MBh XII.86.29), besides many a passage using the word for diverse situations of enmity.

As the concept of an embodied form the term *vigraha* occurs quite frequently in the Purāṇas:

स्थूलं शब्दमयं रूपं विग्रहं बाह्यमिष्यते ॥

AgPur XXX.25cd

The *mantra* aspect (of a deity) consisting in mere words is laid down as its external gross form or image.

The *vigraha* of a deity has been conceived on several levels of religious symbolism as conforming to multiple experiences arrived at in the ritual practices:

ध्यायेत्खं तस्य मूर्तिं तु पृथिवी तस्य पीठिका ॥
कल्पयेद् विग्रहं तस्य तैजसैः परमाणुभिः ।
जीवमावाहयिष्यामि पञ्चविंशतितत्त्वगम् ॥
चैतन्यं परमानन्दं जाग्रत्स्वप्नविवर्जितम् ।
देहेन्द्रियमनोबुद्धि-प्राणाहङ्कार-वर्जितम् ॥

ब्रह्मादिस्तम्बपर्यन्तं हृदयेषु व्यवस्थितम् ।
हृदयात् प्रतिमाबिम्बे स्थिरो भव परमेश्वर: ॥
सजीवं कुरु बिम्बं त्वं सबाह्याभ्यन्तरस्थित: ।

AgPur LX.18cd–22ab

His *mūrti* should be meditated as being the sky (or space) of which the socle is the earth itself. His bodily form should be imagined as consisting of (subtle) energy particles. I would invoke therein the life-principle inherent in the twenty-five elements, that sentiency is the supreme beatitude, devoid of any awakened or inert (lit., sleeping) state, that which stays in the heart (or centre) of creatures beginning from Brahmā up to a blade of grass; O Ultimate Lord, from that heart you (descend to and) be stationed in the icon-image (*pratimā-bimba*). Ever staying within and without, you please make the (present) image endowed with that life-principle.

The five-faced lord Sadāśiva is conceived of thus in His all-transcending aspect:

तस्य देवाधिदेवस्य मूर्ति: साक्षात्सदाशिव: ।
पञ्चमन्त्रतनुर्देव: कलापञ्चकविग्रह: ॥

ŚPur VI.12.15

The image of the Lord of gods is Sadāśiva himself, the Lord with five *mantras* for his body and the five digits for his physical form. (Tr. Board of translators)

The river-goddess Gaṅgā is stated to have emanated from the limb of god Viṣṇu:

विष्णुविग्रहसंभूता द्रवरूपा सनातनी ।

DBhāg IX.1.60

She has sprung from the bodily part (i.e. the feet) of Viṣṇu and has the eternally present form of a flood.

There are numerous such expressions occurring in the Puranic literature as may be found useful for underlining different shades of concepts that evolved, through many enlightened usages of the poet-philosophers, around the very same notion of *vigraha*, denoting body or form, both visible and invisible, on various levels of efficacious understanding. Some of the choice instances indicating various connotations of the term are given here as follows: *saccidānandavigraha* (DBhāg VII.32.25; comprising the form of truth, sentiency and bliss); *jñānavigraha* (BhāgPur X.40.6; comprising the form of knowledge); *kāraṇa-vigraha* (BhāgPur V.12.1; DBhāg IX.1.50, being the cause incarnate); *śrīyukta-vigraha* (DBhāg IX.4.46, being the embodied lustre); *śānta-vigraha* (DBhāg IX.13.101, the peace incarnate); *bhaktānugraha-vigraha* (DBhāg IX.15.36, being the embodied compassion to the devotees); *śuddha-vigraha* (LPur I.98.51, being of the pure form; the embodied purity); *vigraho vigrahārhāṇām* (VāPur II.35.43; BraPur LXX.47; HarPur I.40.47, etc; 'who is the ultimate form of all those who deserve embodiment'); *varāha-vigraha* (LPur I.96.48, the Boar-incarnation).

> ये ब्रह्मविग्रहाः सन्ति गायत्री-विग्रहाश्च ये ॥
> व्याहृतीनां विग्रहाश्च ते नित्यं तत्र सन्ति हि ।
>
> DBhāg XII.11.87cd–88ab
>
> All the *avatāras* of Brahmā, Gāyatrī and Vyāhṛtis that exist in this Brahmāṇḍa, all live here. (Tr. Vijnanananda)

From the Ayurvedic point of view, the life's descent into an embodied existence has been explained by Caraka in the following way:

> स सर्वगुणवान् गर्भत्वमापन्नः प्रथमे मासि संमूर्च्छितः सर्वधातुकलुषीकृतः खेटभूतो भवत्यव्यक्तविग्रहः सदसद्भूताङ्गावयवः ॥
>
> CarSam ŚāSthā IV.9
>
> Featured with all the qualities the being (in seed form) thus finding the embryo state is congealed in the first month, turbid with all the constituent vital secretions becomes of phlegm shape, without being yet expressed in physical features is a composite of existent as well as non-existent bodily limbs.

It is interesting to note that the mythical origin of fever is thus conceived of in the medicinal tradition:

> तस्य क्रुद्धस्य वै वक्त्राद्ब्रह्मणस्तेजसो निधेः ।
> क्रोधो विग्रहवान् भूत्वा निपपातातिदारुणः ॥
>
> SuSam KaSthā III.19
>
> At this the omnipotent god Brahmā, verily grew extremely wrathful and this highly vehement wrath then emanated from his mouth as becoming an embodied entity.

In the astronomical tradition, the term *vigraha* indicates a kind of state observed with respect to unfavourable stellar conjunction or position of more than one constellation:

आसन्नावप्युभौ दीप्तौ भवतश्चेत् समागमः ।
स्वल्पौ द्वावपि विध्वस्तौ भवेतां कूटविग्रहौ ॥

SūrSiddh VII.22

Even when closely approached, if both are brilliant, it is 'conjunction' (*samāgama*): if the two are very small, and struck down, it is 'front' (*kūṭa*) and 'conflict' (*vigraha*), respectively. (Tr. E. Burgess)

An analogy of a golden figure with human person has been thus induced in the Pali canon:

सेय्यथापि, भन्ते, सोवण्णो विग्गहो मानुसं विग्गहं अतिरोचति; एवमेव खो, भन्ते, यदा ब्रह्मा सनङ्कुमारो देवानं तावतिंसानं पातुभवति, सो अञ्ञे देवे अतिरोचति वण्णेन चेव यससा च ।

DīghNik II.210 (II.226)

Just, lord, as a figure made of gold outshines the human frame, so, when Brahmā Sanaṅkumāra appears before the thirty-three gods, does he outshine the other gods in colour and in glory. (Tr. T.W. Rhys Davids and C.A.F. Rhys Davids)

Likewise, to refer a human body the term *vigraha* has been used:

यो भिक्खु मनुस्सविग्गहं जीविता वोरोपेति, अन्तमसो गब्भपातनं उपादाय, अस्समणो होति असक्यपुत्तियो ।

VinPiṭ I.97

A Bhikkhu who intentionally kills a human being, down to procuring abortion, is no Samana and follower of the Sakyaputta. (Tr. T. W. Rhys Davids and H. Oldenberg)

One proverbial statement occuring in the **Jātaka** text says:

ञातकानं अञ्ञमञ्ञं विग्गहो नाम न युत्तो ।

Jā I.208

Within the community of relations it is not befitting to have dispute with one another.

For dispute or controversy the same term has been thus employed:

ते समत्थं अविञ्ञाय, मेण्ढके जिनभासिते ।
अनागतम्हि अद्धाने विग्गहो तत्थ हेस्सति ॥

MilPañ IV.90

Not knowing the real meaning of the statements made by the Jina in the Meṇḍaka section, there in future times will be people having dispute (*vigraha*) over them.

An interesting term occurring in the Sanskrit Buddhist text is *dhātu-vigraha* (cf. Kalātattvakośa, Vol. IV, p. 128, fig. 3), for the "relic-body" of the Buddha (e.g. SaddhPuSū CCCCXXX.6).

The represented figures and shapes are, likewise, indicated by the term:

अपि च लङ्काधिपते भित्तिखचितविग्रहसमः सत्त्वप्रचारः । विश्लेष्टो लङ्काधिपते लोक-संनिवेशः कर्मक्रियारहितोऽसत्त्वात्सर्वधर्माणाम् । न चात्र कश्चिच्छृणोति श्रूयते वा । निर्मितप्रतिमो हि लङ्काधिपते लोकसंनिवेशः ।

LaSū I.43

Lord of Laṅkā, beings are appearances, they are like figures painted on the wall, they have no sensibility [or consciousness]. Lord of Laṅkā, all that is in the world is devoid of work and action because all things have no reality, and there is nothing heard, nothing hearing. Lord of Laṅkā, all that is in the world is like an image magically transformed. (Tr. D.T. Suzuki)

The images or depicted pictures of deities are also designated as *vigraha*:

तेषु च पद्मेषु निषण्णानि अष्टौ महाबोधिसत्त्वविग्रहानभिलेख्याः ।

MMK IV, p. 62

On those lotuses, there should be drawn eight images of the great Bodhisattvas.

सर्व एव कनकवर्णाः तथागतविग्रहाः कार्याः अभयप्रदानकराः ।

MMK IV, p. 64

All the images of the Tathāgatas should be made of golden complexion, and with their hand (held) in *abhaya* attitude.

वैडूर्यमयमनेकदिव्यरत्नप्रत्युप्तं तथागतविग्रहं दिव्यातिक्रान्तेन गन्धेन स्फुटम् । ... तेषु पर्यङ्केषु दिव्यान्यनेकरत्नप्रत्युप्तानि तथागतविग्रहाणि पद्मानि प्रादुर्भूतानि ।

SuSū II, p. 4

The Tathāgata (Buddha) image, made of cat's eye, and studded with many celestial jewels, diffusing excellent divine fragrance ... On those seats (or couches) there manifested the lotuses with images of the Tathāgatas, inlaid with many divine jewels.

A Jaina monk is advised to keep himself away from fight, or from making professies regarding outcome of a fight or struggle between two parts:

देवाणं मणुआणं च तिरिआणं च वुग्गहे ।
अमुगाणं जओ होउ, मा वा होउ त्ति नो वए ॥

देवानां मनुजानां च तिरश्चां च विग्रहे ।
अमुकानां जयो भवतु, मा वा भवत्विति नो वदेत् ॥

DaSū VII.50

In case of a fight of the gods (i.e. divine elements or forces), men or birds a monk must not forecast that this or that party will win or would not win.

Yet at another place danger of association has been explained:

जहा कुक्कुडपोअस्स, निच्चं कुललओ भयम् ।
एवं खु बंभयारिस्स, इत्थीविग्गहओ भयं ॥

यथा कुक्कुटपोतस्य नित्यं कुललतो भयम् ।
एवं खलु ब्रह्मचारिणः स्त्रीविग्रहतो भयम् ॥

DaSū VIII.53

As an infant of cock is ever in danger from a cat, so is there *brahmacārī* (i.e. a monk keeping the vow of celibacy) ever in danger from a female person (whether living or a representation).

In the Jaina philosophical deliberations, *vigraha-gati* has been thus specified with respect to transmigratory souls:

विग्रहगतौ कर्मयोगः ॥ अनुश्रेणि गतिः ॥ अविग्रहा जीवस्य ॥ विग्रहवती च संसारिणः प्राक्चतुर्भ्यः ॥ एकसमयाऽविग्रहा ॥

TaSū II.25–29

In the transmigratory motion of the *vigraha* kind, only *karmic* body activity takes place. The other kind of motion is in straight line. This (latter) motion, which is *avigraha* (i.e. having no turn and being not for a mundane soul) belongs to the liberated soul.

The *vigrahavatī* (i.e. the transmigration of *karmic* body) motion of a worldly soul takes place before four *samayās* at the most. (The soul takes one *samayā* in going in one direction. Each turning means one *samayā*.) Where the passage is straight and there is no turning, it takes only one *samayā*. (Based on the tr. by J.L. Jaini)

In view of the Vaiśeṣika tradition an intelligent *ātman* can be well guessed to govern the body (*vigraha*) as its controller:

रथकर्मणा सारथिवत् प्रयत्नवान् विग्रहस्याधिष्ठातानुमीयते .... ।

VaiśSūBh p. 199

As from the motion of the chariot we infer the existence of an intelligent guiding agent in the shape of the charioteer, so also we infer an intelligent guiding agent for the body. (Tr. G.N. Jha)

The **Sarvadarśana-Saṅgraha** epitomises the doctrine of Jaimini's Mīmāṃsā philosophy:

स्वभावतोऽशरीरस्यापि तस्य भक्तानुग्रहार्थं लीलाविग्रहग्रहणसंभवात् ।

SarDSaṅg (Mīmāṃsā) p. 273

Though the Lord is by his own nature without any body (or corporeality), still for the sake of his showing kindness to the votaries it is possible [to mention] that he assumes a body (*vigraha*) himself through *līlā* (sport, or divine prank).

In his **Bhāṣya** on the **Brahma-Sūtras**, Śaṅkarācārya poses the following question about the nature of Ultimate Reality:

कथं पुनरदृश्यत्वादिगुणकस्य भूतयोनेर्विग्रहवद् रूपं संभवति ।

BrSūŚBh I.2.23

But how can a bodily form be ascribed to the source of all beings which is characterized by invisibility and similar attributes? (Tr. G. Thibaut).

A probable answer to the above question is possible to be offered and defended to an extent only as follows:

विग्रहवत्त्वादृत्विगादिवदिन्द्रादीनामपि स्वरूपसंनिधानेन कर्माङ्गभावोऽभ्युपगम्यते ।

BrSūŚBh I.3.27

We shall have to admit, in consequence of that corporeality (*vigraha-tva*) that Indra and the other gods stand in the relation of subordinate members (*aṅga*) to sacrificial acts by means of their being present in person just as the priests are. (Tr. G. Thibaut)

The Vedantic viewpoint on this matter is further elaborated elsewhere:

तेन विग्रहादिमदधिष्ठानयोग्यमेवचेतनं चेतनाधिष्ठितमिति व्याप्तिराश्रयणीया ।

PraPañ p. 308

Accordingly, that invariable concomitance is to be accepted which shows that the non-intelligent *adhiṣṭhāna* (seat) possessing a body and the like (*vigraha-ādi*) is presided over by an intelligent entity. (Tr. R.S. Bhattacharya)

अपि च व्याप्तिग्रहणपूर्वकमनुमानम्, अन्वयव्यतिरेकाभ्यां च व्याप्तिरवगम्यते । यथा च चैतनोऽधिष्ठातेति प्रतीयते, तथा विग्रहादिमानपि ।

PraPañ p. 308

Moreover, inference is based on the knowledge of invariable concomitance; this concomitance in turn is known through the methods of agreement and difference. That process of inference through which (the existence of) an intelligent superintendent (of the world) is known, his possessing a body and the like is also known. (Tr. R.S. Bhattacharya)

However, the Raseśvara philosophy preaches, like many other Brahmanical creeds, the notion of an incarnation or *saguṇa* god representing the Ultimate →Brahman:

सच्चिन्नित्यनिजाचिन्त्यपूर्णानन्दैकविग्रहम् ।
नृपञ्चास्यमहं वन्दे श्रीविष्णुस्वामिसंमतम् ॥

SarDSaṅg (Raseśvara) p. 207

I glorify the man-lion set forth by Viṣṇu-svāmin, whose only body is existence, intelligence, and eternal and inconceivably perfect beatitude. (Tr. E.B. Cowell & A.E. Gough)

On the mysterious nature of a divine entity the **Netra Tantra** aptly raises the following question:

अमूर्तत्वात् कथं तेषां कर्तृत्वं चोपपद्यते ।
विग्रहेण विना कार्यं कः करोति वद प्रभो ॥

NT XXI.3

From the condition (or nature) of their formlessness how are they (=the divinities) capable of performing any deed? Tell us, O Lord, who can without having a body (or material form) perform any act?

A lengthy discussion on the question of whether the gods possess a body has been thus initiated by the commentator in his gloss on a similar passage of the **Mṛgendra Āgama**:

शब्दव्यतिरिक्ता हि यदि देवता विद्यते, किं विग्रहवती अविग्रहा उभयरूपानुभयरूपा वा ।

Comm. on MṛgĀ vp I.8

If the divinity is different from the word (i.e. name) (there arises a set of queries) whether it possesses a body or not or is of both the natures.

An old verse current in the doctrine (*siddhānta-vacana*) explains:

विग्रहो विग्रही चैव सर्वविग्रहविग्रही ।

Comm. on PrH IV

One body and embodied really include all the bodies and embodied. (Tr. J. Singh)

In the metaphysical parlance, unknown or undefinable noumenon is indicated by such expressions as *a-vigraha, saccidānanda-vigraha, amūrtavigraha, adṛṣṭavigraha,* and the like:

अदृष्टविग्रहायातं शिवात्परमकारणात् ॥
ध्वनिरूपं सुसूक्ष्मं तु सुशुद्धं सुप्रभान्वितम् ।
तदेवापररूपेण शिवेन परमात्मना ॥
मन्त्रसिंहासनस्थेन पञ्चमन्त्रमहात्मना ।
पुरुषार्थं विचार्याशु साधनानि पृथक् पृथक् ॥

SvT VIII.27–29

From Śiva, who is of imperceptible form, the supreme cause (of all emanations), has come the primordial sound, that is very subtle, quite pure, and highly glorious. By that yonder formed Śiva, the transcendent spirit, who is poised upon the lion-seat of *mantras,* and has the great soul consisting of five-*mantra* aspect, having expressly thought of the human goal the expedient agents are (produced) one distinct from another.

In the list of 193 *pāśas* or bonds, as enumerated in the Śaiva Tantras, one group of eight elements coming next to the eightfold host of *nāḍi-vidyās,* is styled as *vigrahāṣṭaka*:

अथोपरिष्टाद् देवेशि विग्रहाष्टकमुच्यते ॥
कार्यं च करणं चैव सुखदुःखकरं तथा ।
ज्ञानं साध्यं च विख्यातं साधनं कारणं तथा ॥

SvT X.1088cd–1089

Now, O Goddess, next in the order is called *vigraha-aṣṭaka,* group of eight (male) entities, namely, (1) the cause (*kārya*), (2) the means (*karaṇa*), (3) the effecting joy and pain (*sukhaduḥkhakara*), (4) the knowledge (*jñāna*), (5) the goal (*sādhya*), (6) the apparent (*vikhyāta*), (7) the inner spirit (*sādhana*), and (8) the primary cause (*kāraṇa*).

The Agamic ritual of *sakalīkṛta-vigraha* is defined as follows:

प्रलम्ब्य विग्रहे पाशसूत्रकं मस्तकादधः ।
पश्येत्तद्गतमध्वानं शिष्यदेहे स्वविग्रहे ॥

MṛĀ kp VIII.70

The teacher should hang the (plumb-line) chord representing

the bond from the head of the disciple downward and should view all the paths (of bondage) abiding therein, i.e. the body of the disciple and in (homology of) his own (transformed) body. (Based on the tr. by H.N. Chakravarty)

A hell called *jatupaṅka* is mentioned in the Tantric literature as:

जतु पङ्को ज्वलल्लाक्षाप्रलेप-प्लुष्ट-विग्रहः ।

Parākhya Saṃhitā (quoted in Luptāgama Saṃgraha, Vol. II, p. 110)

[It is so named as] there are 'figures' (*vigraha*) ever on fire from their coatings of inflamable lac.

In certain Pāñcarātra works, *e-kāra* is mystically stated to be denoted by the term *vigraha* or *avigraha*:

त्र्यस्त्र एकार-संज्ञस्तु जगद्योनिरविग्रहः ।

JaySam VI.37

The triangle is expressed by the designation of *ekāra*, the source of the creation, and also known as *avigraha.* (without form or body).

However, the following statement occurring in the **Ahirbudhnya Saṃhitā,** uses the word *vigraha* in similar context:

एकारस्तु जगद्योनिस्त्र्यश्रो विग्रह एव च ।

AhSam XVII.9

E-kāra is the source of the creation, it is (symbolised as) the triangle, known as *vigraha.*

In view of the elaborate of Tantric and Agamic worship, *vigraha* also denotes or refers to the specific rite of *sakalīkaraṇa* making one's body endowed with divine elements, 'transforming the human body in the elevated identity with the deity'; the same is also termed by such other expressions as *sakalīkṛta-vigraha, deha-nyāsa, vigraha-nyāsa* (cf. JaySam XI.21–23; 37–40).

The word *vigraha* is often preferred to other allied phrases (such as →*mūrti*) in case a personification of some charm (→*mantra*) or object, or an abstract concept is implied (cf. JaySam XIII.129; 138).

The *mantra-vigraha*, or the deity's body as conceived in and as his specific sacred prayer – which is indeed the receptacle (→*pada*) of all such *mantras* – is stated to be a thought on material level on which is ritually made to emerge the supreme concept of Him (→*para*). Likewise, that *para* which is beyond any receptacle as yet is invoked now to have entered the lotus-of-the heart, which is the means of soliciting sanctification of the devotee.

With the aid of sacred prayers, ritual gestures and the *pūraka* ('inhaling of breath'), one should experience the body as pervaded, from one's feet to head, by the Supreme Self. In case the body of the disciple shakes, due to the sacred prayer (→*mantra*) thus entered into it, the specific *mantra* is taken to find fulfilment with him without any further effort on his part (JaySam XV.235–239).

The letters of the alphabet (*mātṛkā*) are enumerated to emanate as parts (*aṃśas*) of the Lord and are, thus, of shining body or form (*bhāsvara-vigraha*, JaySam VI.59). The procedure of implacing the signs or characters of the alphabet on one's own body (*svavigraha*, JaySam VI.24) is an essential part of the ritual connected with various types of worship, accomplishing control over a *mantra*, etc. Its 'elevation' or 'lifting up' (*uddhāra*), worship and complete proficiency are further directed to be done on an eight-spoked *cakra* (circle-diagram), drawn for the purpose as containing the letters of the alphabet as divided into eight groups, each group being written on one spoke with the →*praṇava* (*oṃkāra*) in the centre.

The word is found used in a special context of denoting diverse items of deity's service as described in certain Vaiṣṇava treatises on the ritual procedure belonging to the Vaikhānasa school (cf. *arcanopacāra vidhi* – Samū ch. XLIII). It is more or less a synonym for *upacāra*, 'the means of doing worship', attendance or service to a deity. As it is explained in the **Samūrtārcanādhikaraṇa** of Atri, an article for expressing homage to the imagined or imaged divinity (*samūrta-arcana*) is called '*vigraha*' as it is taken up or held (*grahaṇa, graha*) particularly for the purpose.

अर्चनार्थं विशेषेण ग्रहणाद् विग्रहः स्मृतः ।
देवोपचारहेतुत्वाद् उपचारः प्रकीर्तितः ॥

Samū XLIII.2

As it (i.e. an item of homage or reverence) is specifically 'taken up' for the purpose of worship so it is called a *vigraha*. The same is well-known by the term *upacāra* as for the reason of its rendering worship to the god.

अथातो विग्रहाः । पूजाङ्गोपचारा विग्रहा इत्युच्यन्ते । द्वात्रिंशन्नवविंशति सप्तविंशतिस्त्रयोदशाष्टौ षड् विग्रहा इति समूर्तार्चनस्योपचाराः षड्विधा भवन्ति ।

Kāśyapa Jñānakāṇḍa LXXIII

Now the *vigrahas* (are treated). Various parts of worship which are attendance of service to a deity (*upacāras*) are also called *vigrahas*. There are six sets of *upacāras* current for the worship of an imaged deity, viz. comprising thirty-two, twenty-nine, twenty-seven, thirteen, eight and six *vigrahas* respectively.

The text even mentions elsewhere a set of twenty-five items (ch. LXXI). Thus, there were several sets of *vigrahas* or *upacāras* popular in general practice and followed in accordance to one's means, or the ritual occasion or exigencies enjoined by the tradition. According to the **Samūrtārcanādhikaraṇa** also:

एकविग्रहमाद्यं तु द्वितीयं स्याद्द्विविग्रहम् ।
षड्विग्रहं तृतीयं स्याच्चतुर्थं चाष्टविग्रहम् ॥
एकादशोपचारं च सप्तविंशति विग्रहम् ।
नवविंशतिकं चैव द्वात्रिंशद्विग्रहं तथा ॥

Samū LXIII.3–4

The set of one *vigraha* is the first; the second should be that consisting of two *vigrahas*; the third kind is that with six *vigrahas*; the fourth set consists of eight *vigrahas*; (next is the) set of eleven items of service (*upacāras*), and (then is) the set of twenty seven *vigrahas*; (then are) the set of twenty nine and that of thirty-two *vigrahas*.

The word *vigraha* as conveying the concept of an embodiment, figure or image with varying shades of poetic charm, is found frequently occurred in the Kāvya literature:

वनिताविग्रहो युद्धे महासुरभयंकरः ।
प्रयाति गगने शीघ्रं महोल्केव विभात्ययम् ॥

Dūt I.50

(Engaged) in war a fierce demon of the form of a female moves swiftly through the sky and it blazes like a meteor (or fire-brand).

वज्रपातोऽचलेन्द्राणां श्येनः सर्वपतत्त्रिणाम् ।
मृगेन्द्रो मृगसंघानां मृत्युः पुरुषविग्रहः ॥

MVy I.7

He is the Death (personified) in human form as if the thunder bolt for high mountains, an eagle for all birds and a lion for the herd of deer.

अत्र रामश्च सीता च लक्ष्मणश्च महायशाः ।
सत्यं शीलं च भक्तिश्च येषु विग्रहवत् स्थिताः ॥

PraNāṭ IV.4

Here (live) Rāma, Sītā and Lakṣmaṇa, of great fame, in whom dwell in a bodily form truthfulness, conduct and devotion (respectively). (Tr. M.R. Kale)

Another concept implied by the word is that of war, struggle, of opposition or hostility:

मम दारापहारेण स्वयंग्राहितविग्रहः ।
आगतोऽहं न पश्यामि द्रष्टुकामो रणातिथिः ॥

AbhNāṭ IV.22

From the event of my wife's abduction I have come (here) being desirous of meeting as a guest in the battlefield (the enemy whom) yet I do not see.

त्वत्पादयोर्निपतितं पतितस्य भूमा वेतच्छिरः प्रथममद्य विमुञ्च रोषम् ।
जीवन्तु ते कुरुकुलस्य निवापमेघा वैरं च विग्रहकथाश्च वयं च नष्टाः ॥

Urbh I.31 (also cf. Ragh XIX.38)

[Duryodhana with broken thighs addresses Baladeva] Of the person now fallen on the ground, this head has been bowed down earlier at your feet, so (I request) you may please give up this anger. Let the clouds opportuning the seeds (of your favour) towards the Kuru race live long: as the enemity, this narrative of war as well as we are (now all) destroyed.

Likewise, we have the term denoting the concept of body or figure in several such passages of poetic excellence:

ततः परं तेन मखाय यज्वना तुरंगमुत्सृष्टमनर्गलं पुनः ।
धनुर्भृतामग्रत एव रक्षिणां जहार शक्रः किल गूढविग्रहः ॥

Ragh III.39

After this, it is said that Śakra, with his person invisible, carried away even in the presence of the archers, his guards, the sacred steed which was let loose unrestrained again by him the sacrificer with a view to perform the last sacrifice. (Tr. G.R. Nandargikar)

Kālidāsa has drawn a beautiful imagery of the god Viṣṇu's form in a posture of sitting on the coiled body of the primordial serpent Ananta-śeṣa:

भोगिभोगासनासीनं ददृशुस्तं दिवौकसः ।
तत्फणामण्डलोदर्चिर्मणिद्योतितविग्रहम् ॥

Ragh X.7

The denizens of heaven saw him poised on a seat (or throne) made up of the body of the serpent (Śeṣa). His (the Lord's) body (*vigraha*) was illuminated by the luminous gems on (the serpent's) expansive hoods. (Based on the tr. by G.R. Nandargikar)

This image form appears for the first time in Gupta iconography as we find it shown in the central inset of Devagarh temple doorway-lintel. The **Viṣṇudharmottara Purāṇa** also refers to the same type of iconic representation as *bhogibhogāsanāsīnaṃ sthānakāmastu pūjayet* (VDhPur III.118.6).

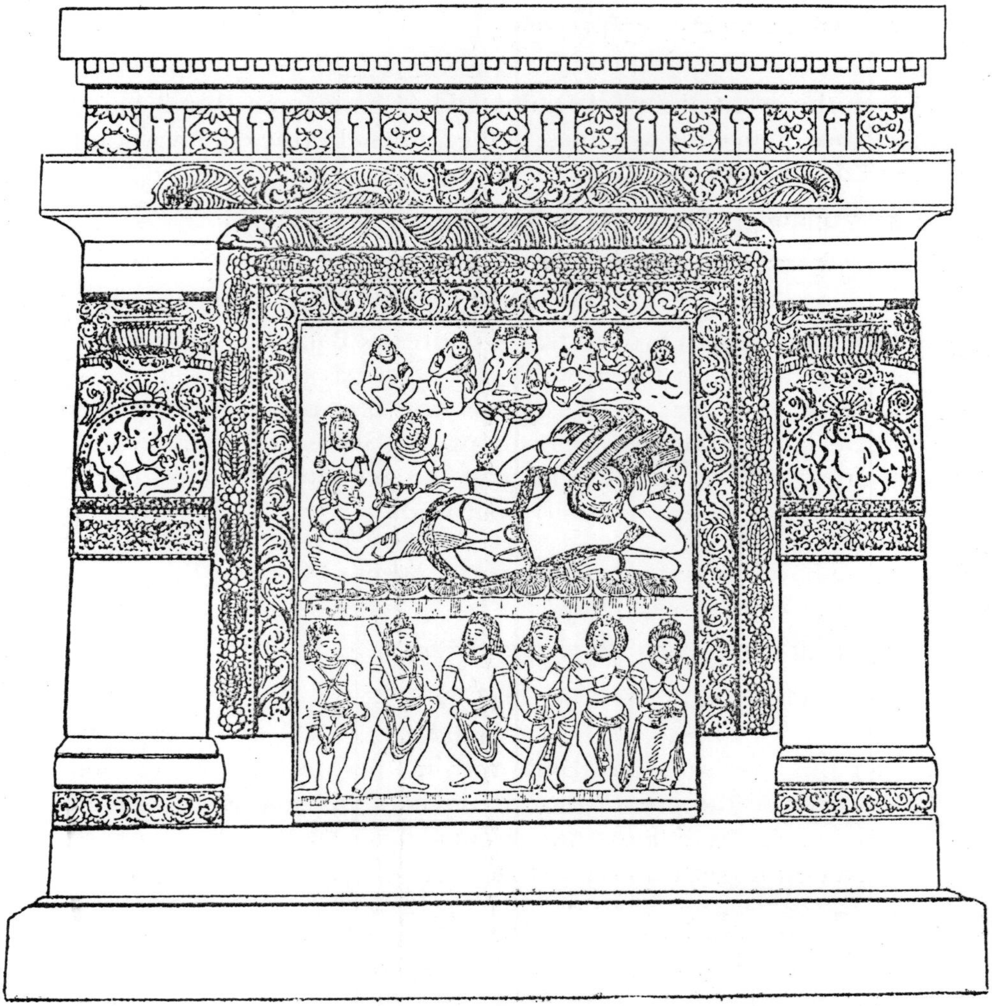

Figure 17: *Śeṣaśāyī* Viṣṇu, Devagarh temple doorway-lintel

रङ्गभङ्गच्युतं रेतस्तदामोघं सुदुर्वहम् ।
त्रिजगद्दाहकं सद्यो मद्विग्रहमधि न्यधात् ॥

Kum X.12

Being impeded in the enjoyment of sexual intercourse the infallible and unbearable semen of the lord penetrated into the body of the Fire-god. (Tr. H.H. Wilson)

मङ्गलालंकृता भाति कौशिक्या यतिवेषया ।

त्रयी विग्रहवत्येव सममध्यात्मविद्यया ॥

Māla I.14

[I see her, who indeed], decked with the auspicious ornaments, accompanied by Kausiki in the dress of an ascetic, shines like the three Vedas incarnate accompanied by the knowledge of the Supreme Soul. (Tr. C.H. Tawney)

सरसि नलिनीपत्रेणापि त्वमावृतविग्रहां ननु सहचरीं दूरे मत्वा विरौषि समुत्सुकः ।

Vik IV.20ab

When the person of your mate is concealed (from your sight) even by a lotus-leaf in the lake, you consider her to be at a great distance from you, and wail anxiously..... (Tr. M.R. Kale)

द्विरदेन्द्रगतिश्चकोरनेत्रः परिपूर्णेन्दुमुखः सुविग्रहश्च ।
द्विजमुख्यतमः कविर्बभूव प्रथितः शूद्रक इत्यगाधसत्त्वः ॥

Mṛcch II.3

With gait like that of the Lord of elephants, with eyes like those of the cakora (bird), with a face like the full moon (complete with all digits), and possessed of a handsome body, was a well-known poet by name Śūdraka, the most eminent of the twice-born (and) possessed of unbounded (lit. unfathomable) energy (or courage). (Tr. R.D. Karmarkar)

Some charming insets of poetic excellence are likewise remarkable in other Kāvyas:

अणुरप्युपहन्ति विग्रहः प्रभुमन्तःप्रकृतिकोपजः ।
अखिलं हि हिनस्ति भूधरं तरुशाखान्तनिघर्षजोऽनलः ॥

Kir II.51

Even a very small disturbance (revolt) caused by the disaffection of the internal constituents of a kingdom kills a king. The fire produced by the friction of the points of the branches of a tree burns the whole mountain. (Tr. M.R. Kale)

Vigraha denoting quarrel occurs in this piquant stanza of **Amaruśataka:**

कोपो यत्र भृकुटिरचना विग्रहो यत्र मौनं
यत्रान्योन्यस्मितमनुनयो दृष्टिपातः प्रसादः ।
तस्य प्रेम्णस्तदिदमधुना वैशसं पश्य जातं
त्वं पादान्ते लुठसि न च मे मन्युमोक्षः खलायाः ॥

Amaruśataka 33

O, behold, what a disaster has befallen that (former) love of ours; when a wrinkling of the brow was anger, when silence was strife, when a mutual smile was reconciliation and a glance a favour! Today, on the other hand, you wallow at my feet, and yet my wicked self cannot get rid of anger. (Tr. C.R. Devadhar)

As we have the term referring to an embodied form or entity:

अविग्रहस्याप्यतुलेन हेतुना समेतभिन्नद्वयमूर्ति तिष्ठतः ।
तवैव नान्यस्य जगत्सु दृश्यते विरुद्धवेषाभरणस्य कान्तता ॥

Kir XVIII.33

Even though having no body of any comparison, owing to certain unknown reason, you stay as a unison appearing as consisting of two distinct bodies (of male and female), – it is only yours and of none else that the beauties appear there in the worlds as clad in opposite dresses and ornamental attributes.

परीतमुक्षावजये जयश्रिया नदन्तमुच्चैः क्षतसिन्धुरोधसम् ।
ददर्श पुष्टिं दधतं स शारदीं सविग्रहं दर्पमिवाधिपं गवाम् ॥

Kir IV.11

After the bull had fallen, he (i.e. Arjuna) saw that loudly bellowing bull, chief of cattle, appearing like the damaged river-bank, endowed with glory of victory, and having the growth of an autumnal cloud overhanging it and as it were the haughtiness incarnate (*darpam iva savigraha*).

Describing the Mandākinī river, the poet Bāṇa has thus observed in his unrivalled style:

अनेकनाकनायकनिकायकामिनीकुचकलशविलुलितविग्रहाम् ।

HaCa I, p. 8

Rippled was its surface with the cup-like bosoms of unnumbered beauties of Indra's court. (Tr. E.B. Cowell and F.W. Thomas)

Elsewhere, he uses the word in a most befitting context:

विग्रहव्याप्तदिङ्मुखा गिरय इव भूभृत्प्रवरात् ।

HaCa IV, p. 196

[From the king Puṣpabhūti], the best of rulers, there (issued a line of kings) that had extended (their sway) in all the directions just as are the hill-ranges covering the direction-fronts issued out from the chief mountain.

Here, the word can also convey the concept of victorious 'war' implied, by way of the *double entendre,* in case of the king.

Likewise, the poet Māgha employs the term in both of its denotations:

> करुणमपि समर्थं मानिनां मानभेदे
> रुदितमुदितमस्त्रं योषितां विग्रहेषु ॥
>
> Śiśu XI.35cd
>
> In the event of dissension with haughty lovers even the sentiment of pity is powerful for it is said that 'crying' is a weapon of women in love-quarrels.

Bhavabhūti uses the term in the sense of hostility:

> दत्तेन्द्राभयदक्षिणैर्भगवतो वैवस्वतादा मनो-
> दृप्तानां दहनाय दीपितनिजक्षत्रप्रतापाग्निभिः ।
> आदित्यैर्यदि विग्रहो नृपतिभिर्धन्यं ममैतत्ततो
> दीप्तास्त्रस्फुरदुग्रदीधितिशिखानीराजितज्यं धनुः ॥
>
> UttCa VI.18
>
> If there would be a fight with the kings of the solar race, who from the time of the revered Manu, the son of Vivasvat, have granted protection from danger to Indra and who have kept the fire of their natural martial vigour ever blazing for the destruction of the haughty, then blessed will be this bow of mine, with its string lighted up with the flames of the fierce rays shooting forth from the blazing missiles. (Tr. M.R. Kale)

Both the concepts of 'body' and 'war' have been brought out so aptly by Bhoja in the following:

> तत्काले लङ्काधिदेवतात्मना सह विग्रहं विधातुं गृहीतयुवतिविग्रहां मार्गप्रसारस्यार्गलीभूय भूयसा तर्जयन्तीं निर्जित्य ..... ।
>
> CaRām V.21
>
> At that moment, (Hanumān) having conquered the presiding city-goddess of Lanka, who had assumed a young woman's form for waging a battle against him and was much threatening him as it were like an obstruction in the wide stretched road, ...

Śrīharṣa also comes out with several charming descriptions by using the term in its various implications:

प्रकाममादित्यमवाप्य कण्टकैः करम्बितामोदभरं विवृण्वती ।
धृतस्फुटश्रीगृहविग्रहा दिवा सरोजिनी यत्प्रभवाप्सरायिता ॥

NaiCa I.115

A lily growing on the pool was intensely thrilled in contact with the sun, and emitted an exuberance of fragrance. With lotus blooms for its body, it looked like a nymph during the day. (Tr. K.K. Handiqui)

As we have a Jaina poet writing in a didactic tone:

तद्-धुनी-वन-बिलागसागरै, रुद्धमस्ति न कियद् धरातलम् ।
भूलवोऽयमपि तद्वदुच्यतां, मुच्यतां सह कुलेन विग्रहः ॥
विग्रहः सह कुलेन नौचितीं, यात्यरातिकुलकल्पपादपः ।
प्रीतिमेति न वने वनचरः, कश्चिरं रणभरेण सिंहयोः॥

PadMa XVII.235–236

How much surface of the earth is not covered by the rivers, forests, hollows, mountains and oceans? Tell, then, how much is the small area of land (your own)? (Thus,) you should leave the enimity against (your) family members. The inimical relationship with one's own family members does not reach any justified end. One who takes the enemies as (his) wishfulfilling tree does not find friendship any where. For, who as a forest-dweller can, in the forest, last long while taking the burden of strife with two lions (at a time).

A charming stanza occurring in the Prakrit Anthology compiled by Jayavallabha (between the 8th and 12th cent. A.D.) is further remarkable:

गुरुविरहसंधिविग्गहणिम्मवणो अत्थि को वि जइ मन्तो ।
पढमिक्कमजरिं अंगुलिं व उब्भेइ सहयरो ॥

गुरुविरहसंधिविग्रहनिर्माता अस्ति कोऽपि यदि मत्तः ।
प्रथमैकमंजरीमङ्गुलिमिव ऊर्ध्वयति सहकारः ॥

Vajjālaggam Stotra DCXLI.1

The mango tree puts forth its first, unique spray of blossom, as if it were a finger lifted up to proclaim: "Is there any one other than I who is able to create peace (accord) and quarrel among lovers plunged in long separation?" (Tr. M.V. Patwardhan)

Eulogising the Kadamba ruler Kākutsthavarman, the poet Kubja records thus in the Talaguṇḍa pillar-inscription:

ज्यायोभिस्सह विग्रहोऽर्थिषु दया सम्यक्प्रजापालनं ।
दीनाभ्युद्धरणं प्रधान-वसुभिर्मुख्यद्विजाभ्यर्हणम् ॥

Talagunda Ins of Kadamba ruler Śāntivarman's time (ca 455–70 A.D), verse 28ab, (cf. Ep Ind, Vol. VIII, No. 5, p. 478)

Him, to whom war with the stronger, compassion for the needy, proper protection of the people, relief of the distressed, honour paid to the chief twice-born by (the bestowal of) pre-eminent wealth. (Tr. F. Kielhorn)

As we find another charming imagery in a medieval inscription:

कलियुगपराक्रमकलितविग्रहस्य समुच्छ्वास इव भगवतो धर्मस्य ।

Nidhanapur plates of Bhāskaravarman (Ep Ind XI, p. 118)

Like the revived breath of the Lord of Righteousness whose body was overcome by the power of the Kali age. (Tr. C. Sivaramamurti)

The Rāṣṭrakūṭa emperor Jagattuṅga alias Govinda III has been eulogised in a copper-plate inscription (Śaka 836 = 915 A.D.) from Vajirkheda as follows:

यस्याद्यापि प्रचण्डासिपातविश्लिष्टविग्रहाः ।
हतशेषा विमुंचन्ति गूर्जरा न भयज्वरम् ॥

Jaina Śilālekha Saṅgraha, Vol. VI

The fever of whose fear cannot be abandoned even today by those Gurjaras, who survived slaying (at his hands) in the battle-field where the bodies (of their soldiers) got severed by the impetuous fall of his sword.

In an inscription of the time of the Gahaḍavāla ruler Jayacandra, dated 1204 A.D., a medieval poet has a pair of stanzas playing upon the word *vigraha* in such an interesting fashion:

बुद्धो विशुद्धबुद्धिस्तस्य सुतोऽजनयदुद्धुरं जन्यम् ।
विग्रह इति कृतविरहश्शत्रुवधूनां ततो जज्ञे ॥
विग्रह-विग्रह-जातो ब्रह्मेति बभूव भूवधुदयितः ।
विग्रह-निग्रह-करणे शक्तिर्यस्याभवद् रिपुषु ॥

Ep Ind I, pp. 112 ff.; II, pp. 482 ff.

His son Buddha, a man of pure intellect, begot an excellent son, Vigraha by name, who caused the wives of his enemies suffer separation (from their husbands). From him was born Brahmā who emanated as the very *vigraha* or body of (his father) *vigraha* and became the lord of the lady earth. It was he who possessed the power of punishing (*vigraha*) and subjugating (*nigraha*) his enemies.

Under a different context of numismatical conventions, the word *vigraha* came to denote a coinage issued by a King named Vigrahapāla. However, this development refers itself to the significant expressiveness of Indian vocables, Sanskrit as well as Prakrit, that facilitated by usage certain new concepts to gain currency around a word, mostly through abbreviation. Thus, we find the following coin names connected with this term *vigraha*:

Vigrahapāla-dramma, a coin minted by a King Vigrahapāla = *vigraha-dramma* or *vigraha-pālīya-dramma* =(simply) *vigraha*.

Vigrahatuṅgīya-dramma = a coin named after a king Vigrahatuṅga (cf. D.C. Sircar, *Indian Epigraphical Glossary*).

From the above coin named there came to derive yet another concept of a land measure, called *bighā, bīghā* (*vigraha*) for which the agricultural revenue, as per the land mensuration fixed during late medieval times, amounted to be equal to one *dramma* of Vigrahapāla denomination (cf. Sircar, *op. cit.*, pp. 59–60).

Vigraha in the Political Theories

Under the comprehensive code of *ṣāḍguṇya*, the ancient Indian theorists analysed a standard policy of diplomatic relations as worthy of king or state with respect to the activities of the other diplomats and rulers, namely, →*sandhi* or peace, *vigraha* or the state of war or hostility, →*āsana* or remaining indifferent as maintaining a quiet stand against an enemy, *yāna* or preparedness for attack, *saṃśraya* or friendship, and *dvaidhībhāva* or double-dealing or duplicity. There, in the Śāntiparva (MBh XII.69.65–66), are treated some general principles of state policies regarding *ṣāḍguṇya*. The king is advised to acquire conquest without battles and detest war as far as possible to manage the course of activities through other means of diplomacy. A victory gained through battles is of the worst type from its being obviously a cause of much losses to men and property.

Elsewhere, the Epic uses the term in a general way:

यदि न स्युर्मनुष्येषु क्षमिणः पृथिवीसमाः ।
न स्यात्संधिर्मनुष्याणां क्रोधमूलो हि विग्रहः ॥
MBh III.30.25

If there were not persons amongst mankind equal to the earth in forgiveness there would be no peace amongst them but perpetual dissensions engendered by anger. (Tr. M.N. Dutt)

As a policy of war the term finds its place in the following passages:

न तु तस्मिन्प्रदेयं स्यात्तथा कार्यगतिः प्रभो ।
विग्रहः समुपारब्धो न हि शाम्यत्यविग्रहात् ॥

MBh V.86.6

But circumstances are such, my lord, that nothing should be given to him (Kṛṣṇa). War having been decided and will not turn into peace by delaying the former or giving presentations.
(Tr. M.N. Dutt)

एतत्सुबहुवृत्तान्तं पञ्चमं पर्व भारते ।
उद्योगपर्व निर्दिष्टं संधिविग्रहसंश्रितम् ॥

MBh I.2.151

These all have been described in the fifth parvan called Udyoga of the Bhārata, abounding with incidents appertaining to war and peace. (Tr. P.C. Roy)

In the Smṛti and Nīti literature also the concept is well indicated by this term:

स्वयंकृतश्च कार्यार्थमकाले काल एव वा ।
मित्रस्य चैवापकृते द्विविधो विग्रहः स्मृतः ॥

Manu VII.164

War is declared to be of two kinds, (viz.) that which is undertaken in season or out of season, by oneself and for one's own purposes, and (that waged to avenge) an injury done to a friend.
(Tr. G. Bühler)

सन्धिं च विग्रहं यानमासनं संश्रयं तथा ।
द्वैधीभावं गुणानेतान् यथावत् परिकल्पयेत् ॥

YājSm I.13.347

Let him employ as the occasion may require these (following) measures: alliance, war, marching, sitting, seeking, protection and distribution. (Tr. S.C. Vidyaranya)

तदेनं गत्वा भयकारणं विज्ञाय संधि-विग्रह-यान-आसन-संश्रय-द्वैधीभावानामेकतमेन संविधास्ये ।

Pañc I, p. 10

> Having gone there and knowing the cause of fear I shall win over him by one of the proper recourses undertaken as per the state policies of peace, war (*vigraha*), marching, sitting quiet, resorting to a safe place, and duplicity.

The above aspects of the 'sixfold diplomacy' are found already well treated in the **Artha-Śāstra** of Kauṭilya, who devotes pointed attention to the subject as an outstanding measure for maintaining well-balanced foreign relations by a conqueror (*vijigīṣu*). Besides, including armed contests (called *sāṃgrāmika* in ArthŚ X.1), the concept of *vigraha* must be said to have covered diverse situations and resources of diplomatic struggles and expedients – either offensive or defensive – with respect to both rival and friendly, neutral and ambitious rulers in view of one's own defences and external affairs (ArthŚ VII.1–11). Assuming a specific situation in one's diplomatic struggle, the great teacher has, for example, summed up the measures one may decide upon from diverse reasoning as follows:

> यदि वा पश्येत् – "आयुधीयप्रायश्श्रेणीप्रायो वा मे जनपदश्शैलवननदीदुर्गैकद्वाराररक्षो वा शक्ष्यति पराभियोगं प्रतिहन्तुमिति, विषयान्ते दुर्गमविषह्यमपाश्रितो वा शक्ष्यामि परकर्माण्युपहन्तुमिति, व्यसनपीडोपहतोत्साहो वा परस्संप्राप्तकर्मोपघातकाले इति, विगृहीतस्यान्यतो वा शक्ष्यामि जानपदमपवाहयितुम्" इति विग्रहे स्थितो वृद्धिमातिष्ठेत् ॥ यदि वा मन्येत् ... ॥
>
> ArthŚ VII.1.33
>
> Or if a king thinks, "That as my country is full of born soldiers or of corporations of fighting men, and as it possesses such natural defensive position as mountains, forests, rivers, and forts with only one entrance, it can easily repel the attack of my enemy; or having taken my stand in my impregnable fortress at the border of my country, I can harass the works of my enemy; or owing to internal troubles and loss of energy, my enemy will early suffer from the destruction of his works; or when my enemy is attacked by another king, I can induce his subjects to immigrate into my country", then he may augment his own resources by keeping open hostility with such an enemy. Or if a king thinks, ... (Tr. R. Shamasastri)

Some ancient theorists believed that the set of *ṣāḍguṇya* really represents variant aspects of the two basic measures of peace and war (*sandhi* and *vigraha*). But according to Kauṭilya and his followers a sixfold division is essentially called for due to common policies conditioned by differing situations. However, these six policies were further classified in view of the normally adopted course or courses of activities by a ruler from different involvements. In the fifteenth section, called *vigraha-vikalpa-prakaraṇa,* of the **Kāmandakīya Nīti Sāra** (a versified treatise of the 4th–5th cent. A.D. belonging to the Kautiliyan School), we find some such of the aspects of the *vigraha* expedient treated in brief, which may be outlined here as follows:

1) Causes of *vigraha.*

2) Conciliatory measures to pacify such a cause and remedy the situation.

3) Avoidance of different types of war-situations through withdrawal from the contest, forbearance, indifference, respect, restitution of favour.

4) Five types of hostilities: (a) *sāpatnya,* i.e. which exists among foes; (b) *vāstuja,* related to land and properties; (c) *strīja,* related to women; (d) *vāṅjāta,* related to insult or misunderstanding due to words; (e) *aparādhaja,* arising from guilt or transgression.

5) According to Bahudantīputra, hostility is of four types: (a) caused by the invasion of one's territory; (b) caused by damages to the regal powers (*śakti-vighātajam*); (c) disputes over the boundaries; and (d) due to disturbance relating to the balance of power in the →*maṇḍala* ('circle of a king's near and distant neighbours').

6) The followers of Manu recognise simply two kinds of hostilities: (a) *kulaja,* i.e. inherited; and (b) *aparādhaja,* caused by wrongs and transgressions.

7) Sixteen kinds of hostilities or hostile situations that must be avoided by a prudent ruler are enumerated.

8) Types of situations in which war be sought as a preferable measure, etc.

However, the **Agni Purāṇa** (CCXL.15–24) has also described diverse causes leading to warfare and its sixteen situations with reference to resultant outcome.

Vigraha as a 'policy-of-war' further finds varied mention in discussions given by ancient authors on many a kind of combined or conditional situations arising in practice from the other affiliated polices of *ṣāḍguṇya.* We may refer to the subject of *vigraha* as found noticed in brief or at times treated in considerable details in several traditional texts on Hindu Polity (cf. P.V. Kane, *History of Dharmaśāstra,* Vol. III, pp. 223–224).

We may refer here, for example, to one aspect as given by king Bāsava in his **Śivatattvaratnākara**, reproducing faithfully a handy gist of the traditional Hindu knowledge on the subject as successively evolved and studied. It gives an interesting list (apparently after Abhil II.12; Baroda edn, Vol. I, pp. 95–96) of the eight causes or types of hostilities arising from →*kāma* (love or sex), *lobha* (greed), *bhū* (territory), →*māna* (wounded pride), *abhaya* (assurance or promise for security), *icchā* (ambition), *mada* (haughtiness), and *ekadravyābhilāṣa* (wish for gaining a particular object):

> शूरत्वेन सहायेन सामर्थ्येन बलेन च ॥
> मन्त्रहीनेन भूपालः सार्धं कुर्वीत विग्रहम् ।
> कामजो लोभजश्चैव भूभवो मानसंभवः ॥
> अभयाख्यः समाख्यात इच्छाजोऽथ मदोत्थितः ।
> अर्थशास्त्रे परिख्यात एकद्रव्याभिलाषकः ॥
> इत्यष्टौ विग्रहाः प्रोक्ताः नवमो नोपलभ्यते ।
>
> Śivatattvaratnākara (of Bāsavarāja of Keladi) V.11.34cd–37ab
>
> A king should enter into war with an enemy who is destitute of proper counsel. However, he should himself be aided by heroism, friends or associates, prowess and army. There are eight kinds of hostility (*vigraha*) described (as per an involved situation in each of them) in the science of Polity, namely (1) born of desire or love (2) caprice (3) land (4) pride (5) promise of security to some one (6) ambition (7) haughtiness, and (8) the wish to gain a specific object. There is no other type that may be listed as the ninth.

By the same text each one of the above causes of hostility is further explained and commented upon in detail (Śivatattvaratnākara, verses 37–43).

A state minister or military secretary dealing in matters of war and peace appears to have been an important member in the council of ministers. Although early texts, including Kauṭilya, do not use any regular designation for him but from the 3rd–4th cent. A.D. the same appears frequently mentioned both in inscriptions and literature as *sāndhivigrahika,* even sometimes *mahāsāndhivigrahika,* who was evidently an expert in diplomacy being entrusted the charge of ministerial portfolio in state's dealings with her allies and foes.

A minister was normally required to be a person conversant with diverse situations pertaining or leading to dissension (*vigraha*). However, as for the qualifications of a *sāndhivigrahika,* the medieval digest **Vīramitrodaya** has reproduced the following verse from the **Viṣṇudharmottara Purāṇa** (cf. I.14.6):

> षाड्गुण्यविधितत्त्वज्ञो देशभाषाविशारदः ।
> सांधिविग्रहिकः कार्यो राज्ञा नयविशारदः ॥
>
> Vīrmi V, p. 231

A *sāndhivigrahika* to be appointed by the king should be an expert in the essence of six state policies and law; should have the expert knowledge of local dialects; and also an expert of Polity (*naya-nīti*).

As part of essential duty of this portfolio was also the burden of preparing and issuing of *rāja-śāsana*, i.e. royal edicts, charters, treaties, other proclamations such as land-grants, etc. Not only the texts but numerous epigraphical records also provide evidence for it. The **Vīramitrodaya** states in this regard:

संधिविग्रहकारी तु भवेत्तस्य लेखकः ।
स्वयं राज्ञा समादिष्टः स लिखेद् राजशासनम् ॥

Vīrmi VI, p. 130

The officer in-charge of executing (edicts of) *sandhi* and *vigraha* should be himself its writer. He must write the royal edict as per the dictates of the king personally.

Manifestation in the Arts

From very early times there have been discussions on the nature and antiquity of images in the Vedic rituals and pantheon. The orthodox opinion has often rejected the viewpoint of tracing back the concept of concrete images to the ancientmost hymnal anthologies of Vedic tradition, which generally continued to maintain its independent character through the ages.

स्मृतिश्च नः प्रमाणम् । तथा विग्रहवतीं देवतामुपचरन्ति । यमं दण्डहस्तमालिखन्ति, कथयन्ति च ।

MīmSūBh IX.1.6

Our authority (next to the Vedas) is the tradition (or scriptures imbibing its Smṛti). In this way, there are people who treat (or entertain) the deity as having a bodily form (*vigraha*); for instance, they make a drawing of Yama as carrying a staff in his hand and also describe him as such.

A similar observation has been made by Vairocana in his ritual text evolving within the Śaiva-Āgama fold:

न विग्रहात्मका देवा वेदेषु स्तुतिपूर्वकाः ।
सिद्धिमुक्ती विना सर्वे शब्दमात्रपरा मताः ॥

PLSSamu II.216

> The gods are not known as figures (or images) represented in the Vedas, they are (only) accompanied with hymns: they all are though to be mere verbal symbols without granting the gain of any accomplishment or liberation.

It may be noted that most of the modern authorities on Hindu iconography also hold a similar opinion. For instance, Prof. J.N. Banerjea arrived, after critically examining all the data available for early Vedic times at the conclusion as follows: "... it can be confidently observed that, even when some references to symbols or sensible representations are found in the Vedic and Brahmanic texts, this does not necessarily mean that they were the images proper of the respective deities" (J.N. Banerjea, *Development of Hindu Iconography*, p. 61).

Both the meanings of the word *vigraha* as by and struggle or dissension have enabled several classical poets to draw beautiful descriptions based on double entendre. Perhaps the most attractive of them is by Subandhu in his **Vāsavadattā** (p. 147, line 30) while describing a king: *jarāsandha iva ghaṭita-sandhivigrahaḥ.*

In case of the Magadhan king Jarāsandha of the **Mahābhārata** legend it implies so well that the two-halves of Jarāsandha's body (born of two mothers) were known to have been welded or joined into one unit (by a demoness called Jarā). (But in a general manner the expression indicates that) the king had acquired proper relations in war-and-peace (*sandhi* and *vigraha*) with his neighbours. However, a third meaning of this simple passage refers to the great poet's observation about an artist's workmanship: as the image (*vigraha*) which developes holes or fissures (*sandhi*) due to old age (*jarā*) or antiquity is repaired in such of its chasms or broken portions.

The compound *ghaṭita-sandhi-vigraha* expressly suggests the work of image repairs, for *sandhi-vigraha* first implies the concept of *sandhita-vigraha,* i.e. of which *vigraha* = a break or damage, 'cleavage' has been repaired; →*sandhi* = a 'joiner', 'joint' or joining. But by the *double entendre, vigraha* still means a statue or image, of which the *sandhi,* now giving the sense of 'breakage' has been made up; *ghaṭita,* 'repaired'. The work of image repairs, besides other normal cases, was sometimes done being permitted for those cult images that were considered prestigeous or worthy of worship even after sustaining minor injuries.

A beautiful description of the work of image repairs occurs in the introductory part of Daṇḍin's prose-romance called **Avantisundarī Kathā** now extant only in a fragmentary state (cf. AvK pp. 13–15, ed. by S.K. Pillai).

Another literary piece of excelling beauty may be cited here from Bāṇa's **Harṣacarita** (78): *pustakarmaṇā pārthivavigrahaḥ.*

The first implication is referring to the achievements of king Harṣa, while by *double entendre,* it suggests, on the other hand, the figurines of clay done in the medium of coroplasts, as it is shown by V.S. Agrawala (*Deeds of Harsha,* p. 67). Thus, the passage may be rendered in the following way: "By issuing written edicts (*pusta-karman*) the king achieved dissension (*vigraha*) amongst the rulers themselves. Or, the clay-figurines (*pārthiva-vigraha*) were made by the art of *pusta*-working (*pusta-karman*)".

Making a reference to art manufacture techniques, the poet Daṇḍin has also devised a charming imagery:

पीडनोच्छेदनकर्शनैस्त्रिभिर्दीप्तरूपश्चक्षुभिरिवैति शोभामीश्वरस्य विग्रहः ।

AvK p. 209

The image (*vigraha*) of the god obtains beauty worthy for the eyes by three operations (done to it by the sculptor), viz. the breaking (figuratively, cutting to size), the carving and the rendering it lean (i.e. finishing it by smoothening the sculpted surface).

One of the earliest usages of this word in art-technical context seems to occur in the **Mahābhārata** as follows:

यथा हि लोहनिष्यन्दो निषिक्तो बिम्बविग्रहम् ।
उपैति तद्वज्जानीहि गर्भे जीवप्रवेशनम् ॥

MBh XIV.18.8

As liquid iron being poured out assumes the form of the image (in the mould of which it is poured), such you must know is the entrance of the soul into the foetus.

Here the formation of an embryo in the womb is likened with the process of casting a metal image in the mould by pouring liquid metal into it. The compound phrase *bimba-vigraha* is significant and appears to imply two stages in the casting of a metal image, namely *bimba,* the original model, and *bimba-vigraha,* the moulded form or cast image (i.e. *vigraha* from the z̲*bimba*); while the intervening stage of the wax-mould may be well guessed from the word *garbha* occurring in the human analogy (cf. the phrase *bimba-garbha* for the mould in the text on lost-wax process, in the VaiĀ p. 79).

A similar art imagery recurs in the section on embryology in the **Caraka Saṃhitā**:

तत्र जरायुजानामण्डजानां च प्राणिनामेते गर्भकरा भावा यां यां योनिमापद्यन्ते, तस्यां तस्यां योनौ तथातथारूपा भवन्ति, तद् यथा – कनकरजतताम्रत्रपुसीसकान्यासिच्यमानानि

तेषु तेषु मधूच्छिष्टबिम्बेषु, तानि यदा मनुष्यबिम्बमापद्यन्ते, तदा मनुष्यविग्रहेण जायन्ते, तस्मात् समुदायप्रभवः सन् गर्भो मनुष्यविग्रहेण जायते, मनुष्यश्च मनुष्यप्रभव उच्यते, तद् योनित्वात् ॥

CarSam ŚāSthā III.16

Therefore of the *jarāyuja* (viviparous) and the *aṇḍaja* (egg-born) species of the creatures, the impregnating conditions when brought about in the particular kind of the womb, assumes the particular form in that womb according to its (own) kind, – as the (molten) gold, silver, copper, tin and lead when poured into the particular kinds of wax-moulds (assume that particular form in the mould). As they (the metals) get the mould of human figure, they are produced in the form of human image; likewise, the foetus, becoming......

Here the wax-mould is apparently indicated by *madhūcchiṣṭavigraha,* which signifies the form or shape in wax as well as the mould created after the wax is melted out; from it the *manuṣya-bimba* (=human image, cast by the metal poured into that mould) is turned out as are the *manuṣya-vigraha* (=human bodies) created in the mother's womb. It is remarkable that some later texts dealing with the *cere perdue* casting likewise use the word →*arcā* or →*bimba* for the wax-image and also for its hollow mould stage (temporarily existing there on a core and within an outer clay cover after the wax is drained out) ready to receive the molten metal for final casting (cf. Abhil I.87, 91, 94; Samū XXV.7, 11–12; MāSā LXVIII.13; ViSam XIV.65; etc.).

The **Śilpa Prakāśa** indicates that the images were believed to conform to the symbolic pattern of Tantric →*yantras,* or mysterious diagrams:

अत्र मुख्यं प्रवक्ष्यामि शक्तिगृहार्थमुत्तमम् ।
महाविद्यादियन्त्राणि यदनुसारविग्रहः ॥

ŚiPrak I.258

Now I speak in particular on the characteristics of the Śakti-temple. The images are made in accordance with the *yantra*s of the Mahāvidyās. (Tr. Alice Boner)

It is observed thus as regards the main image for which the whole paraphernalia of a temple set-up arose:

वक्ष्यामि शिष्यसुधीवृन्द विबोधनार्थं श्रीविग्रहावसतिश्रेष्ठविमानभागम् ॥

ŚiPrak II.1cd

For the sake of enlightening all groups of disciples and the learned I shall speak of the illustrious deity-image (*śrī-vigraha*) which is installed in the sanctum sanctorum marked by the best of parts that is the *vimāna* (= the spire on the *garbhagṛha*).

Elsewhere, the images are classified into three major categories after their physiognomical traits:

विग्रहस्त्रिविधः श्रेष्ठः लास्य उग्रो भयंकरः ॥
गुणत्रयविधानेन सत्त्वरजस्तमः क्रमात् ।
सौम्याननकराणि च मांसपेशीविवर्जितः ॥
सदायौवनसम्पन्नो लास्यविग्रहलक्षणम् ।
अंगानि सौम्यरूपेण मुखोग्रमुग्रलक्षणम् ॥
देह विक्षिप्तमास्यं यत् विकटं तत् भयंकरम् ।
रुच्यनुसारतः कर्माङ्गं मण्डयेत् रूपमण्डने ॥

ŚiRaKo Pratimālakṣaṇa 18cd–21

Three types of images are best: *lāsya, ugra,* and *bhayaṅkara* (gentle, powerful, terrifying), corresponding to the three *guṇas: sattva, rajas* and *tamas* respectively. Peaceful face, gentle hands, absence of muscles, always endowed with youthfulness, these are the features of the gentle image (*lāsya-vigraha*). The characteristics of a powerful image (*ugra*) are beautiful limbs and a fierce face. A terrifying (*bhayaṅkara*) image has scattered limbs and a dreadful face. The sculpting of the decoration of the parts of the body (of the image) can be done according to one's taste. (Tr. B. Bäumer)

On the question of replacing an old image by a newly made one, the Śilpa tradition has to observe as follows:

जीर्णदेहे तदा कुर्यात् भावानुसारविग्रहम् ।

ŚiRaKo Pratimālakṣaṇa 27ab

A damaged idol should be then replaced by a (fresh) image following strictly the mode of being (*bhāva*) of the former.

A rare description of the Haṃsa incarnation of Viṣṇu occurs in the **Īśvara Saṃhitā** as follows:

हंसमूर्त्तिमथात्मानं ज्ञानयज्ञभुजं स्मरेत् ।
कुन्देन्दु-स्निग्धकान्तिं च हेमतुण्डं महातनुम् ॥
रजस्तमोङ्घ्रि सत्सत्त्वविग्रहं परमेश्वरम् ।
धर्माधर्मेक्षणे ध्यायेदग्नीषोमात्मकेन तु ॥
दक्षिणोत्तरसंस्थेन पक्षयुग्मेन राजितम् ।

बहिस्तमेवोदकस्थं तुहिनाचलसन्निभम् ॥
ध्यात्वाऽर्चयेत्तु विधिवत् हंसविग्रहमच्युतम् ।

ĪśSam XXIV.232–235ab

One shall think of the Supreme Self of the form of *haṃsa* who partakes of the sacrifice of knowledge. He is of a splendour, tender like the Kunda flower and moon, having a golden beak, huge body, the Supreme Lord, having *rajas* and *tamas* as feet, *sattva* quality for his body and *dharma* and *adharma* as eyes. He shall be meditated upon as shining with a pair of wings, situated in the right and left portions, of the nature of Agni and Soma, who stays in water which is external *tamas* and who is like the hill of snow. After meditation, Acyuta, who has the body of swan shall be duly worshipped. (Tr. L.N. Thathacharya)

The **Raurava Āgama** although indicates fourteen image aspects of Śiva but furnishes the list of eight only:

द्विसप्त विग्रहे भेदाः स्यात्तदादौ सुखासनः ॥
सोमेश्वरो द्वितीयः स्यात्सोमास्कन्देश्वरस्ततः ।
उक्षारूढश्चतुर्थश्च पञ्चमः स्यात्पुरारिकः ॥
चन्द्रशेखरमूर्त्तिस्तु षष्ठस्तु परिकीर्तितः ।
सप्तमः कालहारी स्यात्कल्याणश्चाष्टमो भवेत् ॥

RauĀ kp XXXV.1cd-3

Among the fourteen kinds of images the first is Sukhāsana, the second is Someśvara, then comes Umāskandeśvara, the fourth is the Ukṣārūḍha (bull-seated one), the fifth is the Tripurāri, the sixth is known as Candraśekhara, the seventh is Kālahārī, and the eighth is Kalyāṇa. (Tr. H.N. Chakravarty)

Recording the technique of applying a shining lustre of golden hue to the painted surface, the following statement is interesting:

वाराहदंष्ट्रया तत्तु घट्टयेत्कनकं शनैः ।
यावत्कान्तिं समायाति विद्युच्चकित-विग्रहम् ॥

Abhil Ālekhyakarma 186

Slowly burnish the gold with a boar's tooth until it attains a "glimpse" (form, *vigraha*) seen in the lightning flash.
(Based on the tr. by A.K. Coomaraswamy)

Conclusion

One aspect of etymological connotations related to *vigraha* with the concept of assuming a dimension (breadth), which evolved, in later Vedic period as to denote a physical embodiment or formed shape, a body or imaged figure. Another aspect concerns with its meaning of dissension, hostility or war. Yet a third dimension of meaning attached to this term the notion of division or analysis of words in a compound or in a sentence.

In Vedic ritualism, *vigraha* sometimes occurs as denoting a specific *graha,* the latter being a popular name for ritual items, implements of sacrifice or offering as well as the supporting verse or group of verses used in making offerings to deities. This age-old meaning of *vigraha* presumably reappears in a slightly changed ritual context of Pāñcarātra and Vaikhānasa worship signifying an *upacāra,* i.e. item or constituent of attendance or service to a deity.

Ancient political theorists propounded a doctrine of sixfold diplomacy, including the topic related to various aspects and measures of state policy, named *vigraha,* regarding warfare and hostile relations with enemies. Already in Kauṭilya, this theme is found as given a fuller treatment discussing earlier opinions and a detailed analysis, diplomatic struggles and armed contests. *Vigraha* as a "policy-of-war" finds varied treatment in later works of Hindu Polity, sometimes in brief or in greater details by some such authorities as the **Agni Purāṇa, Viṣṇudharmottara Purāṇa**, Somadeva Suri's **Nītivākyāmṛta**, Someśvara's **Mānasollāsa,** etc.

Vigraha as the term for a deity's figure, form or image presumably evolved only in the post-Vedic tradition, represented by the Vedāṅgas, Epics, Pali canon, Jaina Aṅgas and the Purāṇas. In several ancient texts describing the procedure of 'lost wax' technique of casting metal images, the word *vigraha* together with *bimba* appears to have a specific Śilpa-Śāstra connotation, implying a 'figural form' in its several specific stages of production.

Prithvi Kumar Agrawala

Select Bibliography

Agrawala, V.S.: Deeds of Harsha, Varanasi: Prithivi Prakashan, 1981.

Banerjea, J.N.: Development of Hindu Iconography, Calcutta: University of Calcutta, 2nd edn, 1956.

Kane, P.V.: History of Dharmashastra, Vol III, Poona: Bhandarkar Oriental Research Institute, 1946.

Sircar, D.C.: Indian Epigraphical Glossary, Delhi: Motilal Banarsidass, 1966.

BANDHA-PRABANDHA

Overview

Bandha (m.) (lit. bondage or binding) stands for metrical or compositional forms in literature, specific posture of the body in Haṭhayoga and acrobatic postures in dance. Thus, it is definitely associated with form. There is no form without the act of 'binding' or tying of the components relevant to the context in order to keep them together. The act of limiting or binding is essential. *Pra-bandha* (m.) has special significance in music and literature for a definite musical and poetic form. In philosophy, *bandha* as bondage has a negative connotation but there also it endows the →*jīva* the functions of being the doer (*kartā*) and enjoyer (*bhoktā*). Hence, it can be said that form is the underlying idea in *bandha* and *prabandha*. Without limitation of space and time, form does not come into being and without form nothing becomes functional. In this way, *bandha* or binding is the basis of form and form is that which bestows specificity and the capacity to function, which in turn reveals the essence.

Etymology and Related Words

The word '*bandha*' is derived from the root *bandh-* to which the suffix '*ghañ*' is added. In '*prabandha*', the prefix '*pra*' is also added. The literal meaning of *bandha* is the act of binding, limiting, bondage, tie. The prefix '*pra*' adds the meaning of excellence to the above meanings. Tying together different components or elements and constructing a specific form is *bandha* in the arts. In ordinary usage, it is the putting together or tying together things like pieces of wood or books or clothes etc. Since a person whose liberty is taken away is also tied up in a sense, the act of arresting or putting in prison is also known as *bandha*. In philosophy, *bandha* stands for bondage of the individuated soul (*jīva*) which is the opposite of →*mokṣa* or liberation.

'*Prabandha*' stands for specific forms in music and literature. '*Nibandha*' and '*anibandha*' are derivatives of the root *bandh-* and have different layers of meaning in Saṅgīta-Śāstra.

The following compounds of *bandha* and *prabandha* are well-known in literature, music and dance: (i) *citra-bandha* in *kāvya*, (ii) *piṇḍī-bandha* in dance, (iii) *vādya-prabandha* in music, (iv) *prabandha-gāna* in music, (v) *sarga-bandha, gadya-bandha, padya-bandha, rasa-bandha, chandobandha*, etc. in literature.

In Haṭhayoga, *bandha* stands for specific formations of the limbs in different *āsanas*, e.g. *uḍḍīyāna-bandha, mūla-bandha, jālandhara-bandha*, etc.

In Odissi dance, some acrobatic formations are known as *bandhas*, e.g. *gaṅgāvataraṇa-bandha.*

In Śilpa-Śāstra, including architecture and sculpture, *bandhas* are described as a frieze or row of figures.

Layers of Meaning

In all the positive meanings of *bandha*, the idea of tying together different components in order to give a specific form is there in one way or the other. In the negative meaning of the loss of liberty in the physical, psychological or spiritual sense, also, the meaning of limiting is there. Form cannot be constructed without limiting space or time. The primordial process of creation is also one of limiting or contracting alongwith the act of expanding. Hence, there is an underlying unity in all levels of *bandha* through the act of limiting or curtailing. Architecture, sculpture, painting create limitations or enclosures of space. Music does so in the dimension of time; dance and drama deal with both space and time. Literature, basically, deals with time but with the introduction of printing, the dimension of space has also come to be associated with it, since the length of a literary composition is perceived through the space it occupies in print.

In the meaning of the loss of liberty, only the sense of curtailing or limiting operates and the sense of putting together or tying together different components is not there.

Development of the Concept

The term '*bandha*' is used in the sense of stalk or stem, a connecting part of plant with fruit or flower indicating the idea of bondage or binding in the Saṃhitās.

> त्र्यम्बकं यजामहे सुगन्धिं पुष्टिवर्धनम् ।
> उर्वारुकमिव बन्धनान्मृत्योर्मुक्षीय मामृतात् ॥
>
> ṚV VII.59.12 (cf. YV III.60)
>
> Tryambaka we worship, sweet augmenter of prosperity. As from its stem the cucumber, so may I be released from death, not reft of immortality. (Tr. R.T.H. Griffith)

In the Upaniṣads, the mind has been said to be 'bound' with *prāṇa*:

स यथा शकुनिः सूत्रेण प्रबद्धो दिशं दिशं पतित्वाऽन्यत्रायतनमलब्ध्वा बन्धनमेवोपश्रयते ।
एवमेव खलु सोम्य तन्मनो दिशं दिशं पतित्वाऽन्यत्रायतनमलब्ध्वा प्राणमेवोपश्रयते ॥

ChUp VI.8.2

Just as the bird, that is tied with a thread, after flying in various directions, not finding a resting place anywhere else, takes refuge in the state of tying itself, similarly O blessed one! the mind, after flying in various directions, not finding a resting place anywhere else, takes refuge in *prāṇa* itself.

Bondage is described in relation to the Ātman that is *anīśa,* not its own master:

अनीशश्चात्मा बध्यते भोक्तृभावाज्ज्ञात्वा देवं मुच्यते सर्वपाशैः ॥

ŚvUp I.8cd

The *anīśa* Ātman gets bound because of becoming the enjoyer. He gets liberated of all bonds when he comes to know 'Deva' (self-luminous Reality).

The mind is said to be the cause of bondage and liberation:

मन एव मनुष्याणां कारणं बन्धमोक्षयोः ।
बन्धाय विषयासङ्गि मोक्षे निर्विषयं स्मृतम् ॥

MaitUp VI.34

Mind alone is the cause of bondage and liberation of human beings. When it is attached to the object of enjoyment it brings about bondage and when it is not attached to any object, it brings about liberation.

→*Kāma* or desire gives rise to *adhyavasāya* (apprehension, the function of *buddhi*), *saṅkalpa* (volition, the function of *manas*), *abhimāna* (self-conception, the function of *ahaṅkāra*):

स हि सर्वकाममयः पुरुषोऽध्यवसायसङ्कल्पाभिमानलिङ्गो बद्धः । अतस्तद्विपरीतो मुक्तः ।

MaitUp VI.30

The *puruṣa* full of *kāma* or desire is bound having *adhyavasāya, saṅkalpa* and *abhimāna* as his *liṅga*s (characteristics). He who is the opposite of this is liberated.

The bondage of *saṃsāra* (this world) gets strengthened in the mind that is engrossed in the act of *manana* (thinking).

मननोत्थे मनस्येष बन्धः सांसारिको दृढः ॥

AnnaUp II.24cd

This bondage of *saṃsāra* (the world) is strong in the mind in which *manana* (thinking) takes place.

The purport is that when the act of *manana* is eradicated, then there is no question of bondage or liberation:

को बन्धः कश्च वा मोक्षो निर्मूलं मननं कुरु ॥

AnnaUp II.25cd

What is bondage and what is liberation? Just uproot *manana*.

Duality pervades all bondages. The **Bhagavad-Gītā** says that one who has transcended duality gets liberated:

निर्द्वन्द्वो हि महाबाहो सुखं बन्धात् प्रमुच्यते ॥

BhG V.3cd

O Arjuna! one who has become devoid of duality gets easily liberated.

In the **Brahma-Sūtra,** *saṅkalpasṛṣṭi,* i.e. creation out of the mind has been said to be the progenitor of bondage and contemplation of *paramātman* or Supreme Soul is the bestower of liberation:

पराभिध्यानात् तु तिरोहितं ततो ह्यस्य बन्धविपर्ययौ ॥

BrSū III.2.5

(The identical nature of *jīva* with *paramātman*) is concealed; with the contemplation of the Supreme it becomes manifest. Bondage and its opposite (*mokṣa,* liberation) occur from Him.

Bondage is associated with the body:

देहयोगाद्वा सोऽपि ॥

BrSū III.2.6

Bondage comes about on account of association with the body.

Śaṅkarācārya's commentary on **Brahma-Sūtra** (III.2.5) says that *bandha* (bondage) comes about due to ignorance on the part of →*jīva* and →*mokṣa* is attained through the knowledge of →*Īśvara.* He quotes here the following passage of **Śvetāśvatara Upaniṣad**:

ज्ञात्वा देवं सर्वपाशापहानिः क्षीणैः क्लेशैर्जन्ममृत्युप्रहाणिः ।
तस्याभिध्यानात् तृतीयं देहभेदे विश्वैश्वर्यं केवल आप्तकामः ॥

ŚvUp I.11

The knowledge of the Divine leads to destruction of all *pāśas* (lit. snares). Upon the decay of *kleśas,* birth and death are destroyed. On account of contemplation of Him, when the body falls, one becomes *āptakāma* (all fulfilled), having forsaken the third world, i.e. *svargaloka* and all powers.

Here *kleśas* have been identified as *pāśas* (snares) or *bandhas* and the five-fold *avidyā* has to be uprooted for the sake of liberation. *Kleśas* are born of the *rajas* aspect of *avidyā* and that is the cause of *bandha.*

कामः क्रोधो लोभदम्भाद्यसूयाऽहंकारेर्ष्या-मत्सराद्यास्तु घोराः ।
धर्मा एते राजसाः पुंप्रवृत्तिर्यस्मादेषा तद् रजो बन्धहेतुः ॥

Vicū 112

Desire, anger, greed, hypocrisy, etc. envy, pride, jealousy, selfishness, etc. – these terrible qualities pertain to *rajas.* The *puruṣa* is activated by this *rajas* and that is the cause of *bandha* (bondage).

The identification of the body as →*ātman* is a characteristic of bondage.

एताभ्यामेव शक्तिभ्यां बन्धः पुंसः समागतः ।
याभ्यां विमोहितो देहं मत्वाऽऽत्मानं भ्रमत्ययम् ॥

Vicū 144

The *puruṣa* gets bound through these two potencies (of *māyā,* viz. *āvaraṇa,* i.e. veiling and *vikṣepa,* i.e. distracting). Being infatuated by these two, he accepts the body as the *ātman* and wanders in the world.

Vikṣepa or distraction is the product of *rajas* and *āvaraṇa* or veiling is that of *tamas*; the latter has been added to *rajas* in the above passage and that completes the picture of bondage.

बीजं संसृतिभूमिजस्य तु तमो देहात्मधीरङ्कुरो
रागः पल्लवमम्बु कर्म तु वपुः स्कन्धोऽसवःशाखिकाः ।
अग्राणीन्द्रियसंहतिश्च विषयाः पुष्पाणि दुःखं फलं
नानाकर्मसमुद्भवं बहुविधं भोक्ताऽत्र जीवः खगः ॥

Vicū 145

The seed of the tree of *saṃsāra* is *tamas,* its sprout is the identification of the body with *ātman,* its leaves are in the form of *rāga, karman* waters it, its trunk is the body, its branches are *prāṇa,* the tips of the branches are *indriyas,* its buds are the objects of enjoyment and its fruit is suffering. The *jīva* in the form of a bird enjoys this fruit that comes into being on account of his various *karman.*

Rāmānujācārya commenting on the **Brahma-Sūtra** (III.2.5) referred to above (in Advaita Vedānta) says that beginningless *karman* of the *jīva* (individuated soul) are the basic cause of *bandha* and the *saṅkalpa* (will) of Īśvara is the stimulating cause.

पराभिध्यानात् परमपुरुषसंकल्पादस्य जीवस्य स्वाभाविकं रूपं तिरोहितम्, अनादिकर्मपरम्परया कृतापराधस्य ह्यस्य स्वाभाविकं कल्याणरूपं परमपुरुषस्तिरोधापयति । ततस्तत्संकल्पादेव ह्यस्य बन्धमोक्षौ श्रुतौ ॥

ŚrīBh III.2.4

On account of the *abhidhyāna* or *saṅkalpa* of *paramātman,* the real nature or *svarūpa* of *jīva* gets concealed. Through the chain of beginningless *karmans,* the blessed nature of the *jīva* who has committed offence is concealed by the *parama puruṣa.* Hence, the bondage and liberation of the *jīva* are known to come about through His *saṅkalpa* (will).

In Vallabhācārya's Śuddhādvaita, *bandha* has been explained in various ways in different contexts. Here *jīva* is accepted to be the *vyuccarita* (scattered) *aṃśa* (part) of Brahman. Many dimensions of *bandha* are discernible in the writings of Vallabhācārya as follows:

a. In the **Tattvadīpikā** commentary on the **Bhagavad-Gītā** (V.3), *bandha* is explained as the fruit of *karmans.*

b. In the **Aṇubhāṣya** (III.2.5), the cause of *bandha* has been said to be the *tirobhāva* or concealment of the six *guṇas* of Bhagavān, viz. *aiśvarya, vīrya, yaśa, śrī, jñāna* and *vairāgya.* When *jīva* gets scattered, these *guṇas* get concealed and the result is as follows – the concealment of *aiśvarya* (power) results in *dainya* (miserableness); of *vīrya* (prowess) in tolerance of suffering, of *yaśa* (glory) in inferiority, of *śrī* (majesty, grace) in becoming the object of all afflictions, of *jñāna* (knowledge) in identification of the body and the like with *ātman* and all types of false perceptions, of *vairāgya* to attachment to all objects of enjoyment.

Bandha results from the concealment of the first four →*guṇas* and *viparyaya* or false knowledge from the concealment of the last two.

In the Acintyabhedābheda-vedānta doctrine of Gauḍīya Vaisnavism, *karma* is basically accepted as *bandha. Jīvas* are said to be equal in respect of *caitanya* (intelligence), *aṇutva* (atomic nature) and *jñātṛtva* (state of being the knower) but they are unequal on account of their *karmans.*

The Vaiśeṣika system accepts the ignorance of Reality (→*tattva*) as *bandha.*

धर्मविशेषप्रसूताद् द्रव्यगुणकर्मसामान्यविशेषसमवायानां पदार्थानां साधर्म्यवैधर्म्याभ्यां तत्त्वज्ञानान्निःश्रेयसम् ॥

VaiśSū I.1.4

Niḥśreyas (ultimate good) is attained through the knowledge of Reality that comes about from the understanding of *sādharmya* (similarity of attributes) and *vaidharmya* (dissimilarity of attributes) of *padārthas* (categories of objects) which are the *samavāya* (concourse) of the *guṇas* (attributes), *karmans* (acts), *dravyas* (substances), *sāmānya* (general) and *viśeṣa* (special).

Thus, the knowledge of Reality leads to *niḥśreyas* or ultimate good or *mokṣa.* The false knowledge or *viparyaya* (transposition) of categories is born of *adharma* (violation of *dharma* or true nature). Hence, *bandha* which is opposite to *mokṣa* has two components, viz. *adharma* and *viparyaya* (transposition born of *adharma*). *Viparyaya* has been said to come about in six ways:

त्रयीदर्शनविपरीतेषु शाक्यादिदर्शनेषु इदं श्रेय इति मिथ्याप्रत्ययः विपर्ययः, शरीरेन्द्रियमनःसु आत्माभिमानः, कृतकेषु नित्यत्वदर्शनम्, कारणवैकल्ये कार्योत्पत्तिज्ञानम्, हितमुपदिशत्सु अहितमिति ज्ञानम्, अहितमुपदिशत्सु हितमिति ज्ञानम् ॥

VaiśSūBh sec. on Viparyaya in Guṇa (p. 429)

(i) The false understanding that the systems of philosophies like the one propagated by Buddha, that are opposed to the Vedas are repositories of *śreyas* (good), (ii) acceptance of the body, *indriyas* (sensory and motor organs) and mind as the *ātman,* (iii) seeing eternity in unreal objects, (iv) knowledge of the effect without the cause; (v) seeing the advice of *hita* (good) as *ahita* (bad), and (vi) seeing the advice of *ahita* as *hita.*

In the Nyāya system of philosophy *mithyājñāna* (false knowledge) is the cause of *bandha.* The attainment of *mokṣa* is explained in this system as follows:

दुःख-जन्म-प्रवृत्ति-दोष-मिथ्याज्ञानानामुत्तरोत्तरापाये तदनन्तरापायादपवर्गः ॥

NySū I.1.2

Apavarga or *mokṣa* comes about when *duḥkha* (suffering), *janma* (birth), *pravṛtti* (activity), *doṣa* (defects), *mithyājñāna* (false knowledge) – these get eradicated one after the other.

In Sāṃkhya philosophy, the *puruṣa* is *apariṇāmī,* i.e. devoid of transformation or change and hence there is no question of its being bound or liberated. It has been said:

> तस्मान्न बध्यते नापि मुच्यते नैव संसरति कश्चित् ।
> संसरति बध्यते मुच्यते च नानाश्रया प्रकृतिः ॥
>
> SāṃKā 62
>
> *Bandha* (bondage), *mokṣa* (liberation) and *saṃsāra* (passing through a succession of states) pertain to *prakṛti* and not to *puruṣa.*

→*Prakṛti* binds itself with the creation of →*bhāvas* or special states and liberates itself through knowledge.

> रूपैः सप्तभिरेव तु बध्नात्यात्मानमात्मना प्रकृतिः ।
> सैव च पुरुषार्थं प्रति विमोचयत्येकरूपेण ॥
>
> SāṃKā 63
>
> *Prakṛti* binds itself with seven forms (of *bhāvasarga* or creation of special states, viz. *rāga* or attachment, *vairāgya* or detachment, *dharma* or righteousness, *adharma* or non-righteousness, *aiśvarya* or power, *anaiśvarya* or lack of power and *ajñāna* or ignorance) and liberates itself through one form (viz. knowledge) towards *puruṣārtha* or *mokṣa.*

In Yoga, *viparyaya* (inverted perception) is identified with *kleśa.* That which is opposed to *kaivalya* is *bandha.*

Īśvara is said to be untouched by *bandha.*

> क्लेशकर्मविपाकाशयैरपरामृष्टः पुरुषविशेष ईश्वरः ॥
>
> YSū I.24
>
> *Puruṣa* is untouched by the five *kleśas* beginning with *avidyā* (the others being *asmitā, rāga, dveṣa* and *abhiniveśa,* the fruits of the maturity of good and bad deeds, in the form of pleasure and pain and their *āśayās* in the form of *vāsanās* (residual impressions). That *puruṣa* is known as Īśvara.

Bandha has been said to be of three types, viz. *prākṛta, vaikṛta* and *dākṣiṇa.*

In the Kashmir Śaiva Pratyabhijñā system, Śiva is the only →*tattva* or Reality but due to *śakti-saṅkoca,* i.e. the contraction of potencies, plurality is accepted. →*Māyā* is the name of the contracted potency of Paramaśiva which is in itself in the form of *kañcuka* (sheath) and gives birth to five *kañcukas.*

मायाशक्त्या विभोः सैव भिन्नसंवेद्यगोचरा ।
कथिता ज्ञानसङ्कल्पाध्यवसायादिनामभिः ॥
ĪPraKā I.5.18

Through the *māyāśakti*, the *jñānaśakti* of Paramaśiva that becomes known through different objects of perception, is given names as *jñāna* (manifested in *citta*), *saṅkalpa* (manifested in *manas*) and *adhyavasāya* (manifested in *buddhi*).

Thus, the contracted *jñānaśakti* itself is *bandha*.

The →*ātman* in its *baddha* (bound) state is said to be *aṇu* and is said to perceive duality.

अन्तः सुखादि-संवेद्य-व्यवसायादिवृत्तिमत् ॥
बहिस्तद्योग्य-नीलादि-देहादि-विषयोन्मुखम् ।
भेदाभासात्मकं चास्य ज्ञानं बन्धोऽणुरूपिणः ॥
तत्पाशितत्वादेवासावणुः संसरति ध्रुवम् ॥
ŚSūVā III.8–10

This (*ātman*) wanders (in the cycle of birth and death) as *aṇu* (atom) in the state of being bound by the *pāśa* (snare). In that state the knowledge is of the nature of *bhedābhāsa* (having the *ābhāsa* of duality); internally it is composed of the feeling of pleasure and the like and externally its objects are the body, blue (colour) and the like.

Thus, the atomic nature of →*jīva* known as *āṇavamala* in this system is said to be *pāśa* or *bandha*.

अज्ञानमिति तत्राद्यं चैतन्यस्फाररूपिणि ।
आत्मन्यनात्मताज्ञानं ज्ञानं पुनरनात्मनि ॥
देहादावात्ममानित्वं द्वयमप्येतदाणवम् ।
मलं स्वकल्पितं स्वस्मिन् बन्धः स्वेच्छाविभावितः ॥
ŚSūVā I.15–16

The first manifestation of *ajñāna* (ignorance) is the perception of non-*ātman* in *ātman* which is the effulgence of *caitanya* and the acceptance of *ātman* in the body and the like which is non-*ātman*. These two constitute *āṇavamala* which is created by the *ātman* in itself, of its own will.

There are two other *malas* besides *āṇavamala*, viz. *māyīyamala* and *kārmamala*. These two are also known as *bandha*. In this way, *bandha* or *pāśa* is three-fold.

In Śākta philosophy, *bandha* is said to be false.

यथा मनोरथे बद्धः केनचिच्छत्रुणा स्वयम् ।
ताड्यमानस्तर्ज्यमानो यावत् संकल्पवर्जनम् ॥
कुर्यात् तावत् ताडनं वा तर्जनं वापि लीयते ।
किं तत्र शिष्यते बन्धस्तथाऽत्रापि विभावय ॥

TRa jk XVIII.121–122

Just as one's imagination of being tortured and reprimanded by an enemy begets suffering until it is abandoned, *bandha* should be similarly understood. No remainder is left when the imagination of *bandha* is abandoned.

Bandha is not beginningless or eternal:

अनादिकालाद् नामात्र बन्धो नास्त्येव कस्यचित् ।
जडात्मभ्रान्तिमुत्सृज्य कोऽयं बन्धो विचारय ॥

TRa jk XVIII.123

There is no *bandha* for anybody since beginningless time. Just think what is *bandha* except the illusion of *ātman* in *jaḍa* and *vice-versa.*

Bandha is conceived here as an illusion:

एष एव महाबन्धो बन्धसत्यत्वनिश्चयः ।
मृषा भीतस्य बालस्य यक्षग्रह इव स्थितः ॥

TRa jk XVIII.124

This great *bandha* appears as true just as a child is frightened by a hallucination and it appears as if it has been possessed by a *yakṣa* or *piśāca* (evil spirit).

Bandha is considered to be impossible in unblemished *ātman.*

कोऽयं बन्धः कथं वा स्यान्निर्मलस्य चिदात्मनः ।
प्रतिबिम्बात्मकैः स्वात्मादर्शान्तः प्रविभावितैः ॥
बन्धो यदि तदादर्शप्रतिबिम्बाग्निरादहेत् ।

TRa jk XVIII.126–127ab

What is this *bandha* and how can it be possible for the unblemished *cidātman*? If *bandha* is accepted to be like a *pratibimba* or reflection, then it is ineffective just as the reflection of fire does not burn anything.

In this system, Tripurāśakti is *vidyārūpā*, hence *bandha* cannot be conceived as real.

In Jainism, *bandha* is counted under *āsrava* which is one of the seven *tattvas.* According to the **Bhagavatī-Sūtra** (XVIII.3), the description of *bandha* can be summarised in the following tree:

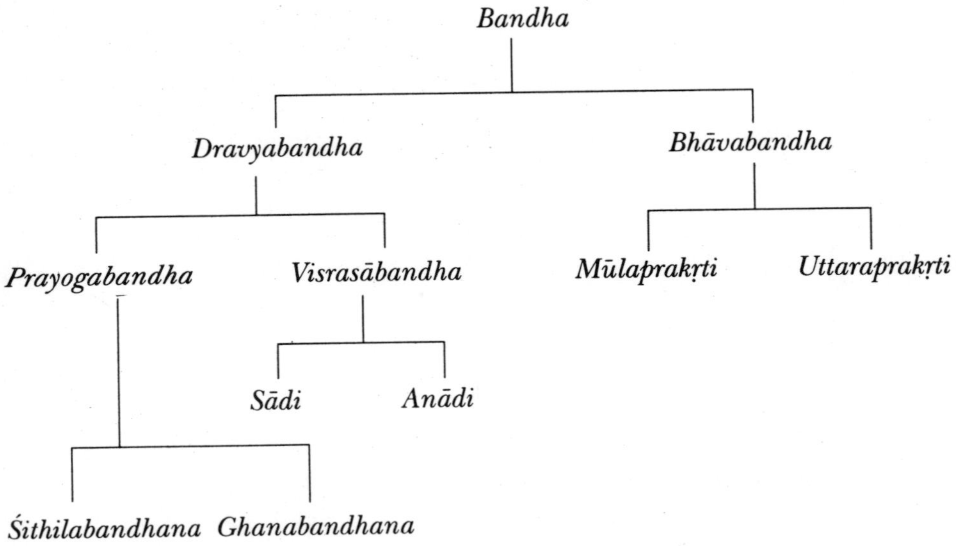

The *bandha* of the *jīva* through *mithyātva* (falsehood) and the like is known as *bhāvabandha.* It has been said to be two-fold on the basis of →*rāga* or love and *dveṣa* or animosity. In the **Bhagavatī-Sūtra** (VIII.7), *bandha* has been said to be three-fold according to a different classification – *jīvaprayogabandha, anantarabandha* and *paramparābandha. Prayogabandha* is the name of the →*karman* that takes place through activities of the mind and the like and of the configuration of *pudgalas* (roughly atoms). *Anantarabandha* is the unbroken stream of *prayogabandha* and many repetitions of the latter is called *paramparābandha.*

According to the **Samavāyāṅga-Sūtra**, *bandha* is of four types, viz. *prakṛtibandha, sthitibandha, anubhāgabandha* and *pradeśabandha. Sthitibandha* is the cluster of *karmans* and the co-existence of *pudgalas*; the acceptance of particular *pradeśa* is *pradeśabandha,* the auspicious or inauspicious result of the nature of *rasa* of *karmans* and *pudgalas* is *rasabandha* or *anubhāgabandha* and a group of all the above is *prakṛtibandha. Samudāya* or group is known as →*prakṛti,* the position of a particular time is known as *sthiti,* the *anubhāga* (part) of *karmans* and configuration of *pudgalas* is →*rasa* and piling up in groups is known as *pradeśa.* The above types can be seen in the following chart:

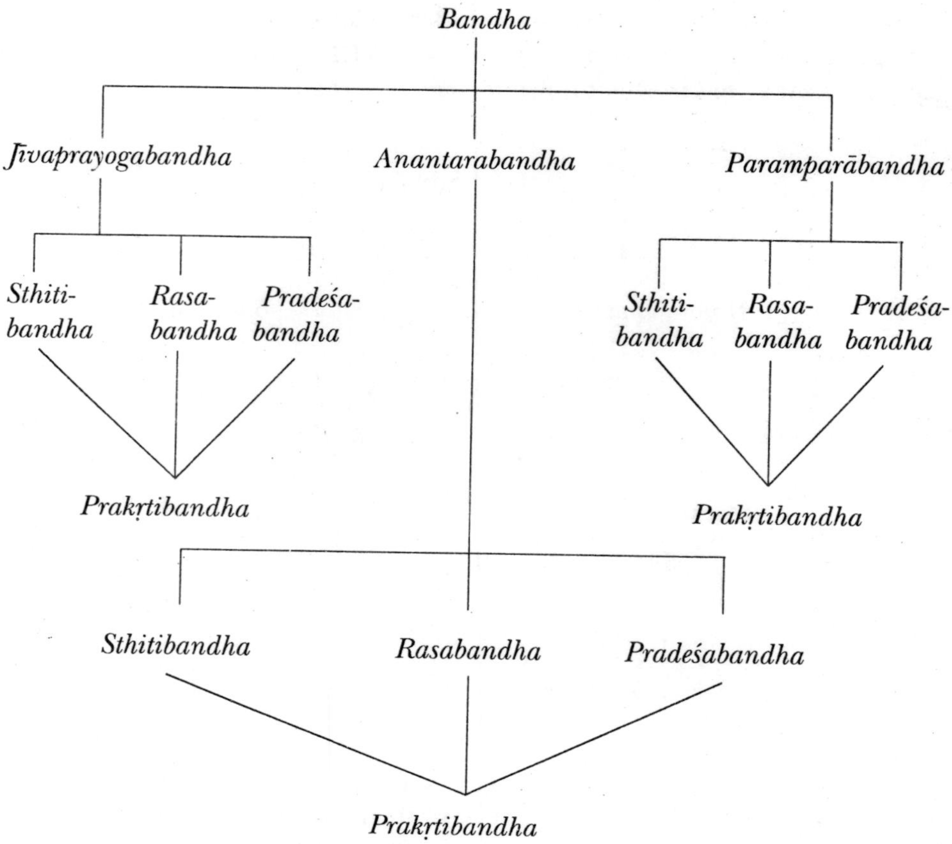

In one stream of Jaina philosophy, the seven *tattvas* are enumerated as: *jīva, ajīva, āsrava, bandha, saṃvara, nirjara* and →*mokṣa*. Ācārya Gṛddhapiccha has defined *bandha* as:

> आत्मकर्मणोरन्योऽन्यप्रदेशानुप्रवेशात्मको बन्धः ।
>
> SaSi I.4.18
>
> The mutual entry of *ātman* and *karman* in one *pradeśa* is known as *bandha*.

Bhaṭṭa Akalaṅkadeva has given the etymology of *bandha* as follows:

> बध्यतेऽनेन बन्धनमात्रं वा बन्धः । बध्यते येन
> अस्वतन्त्रीक्रियते अस्वतन्त्रीकरणमात्रं वा बन्धः ।
>
> TaVā I.4.10
>
> That which binds or bondage itself is *bandha*. That which binds, i.e. brings about dependence or the act of making dependent itself is *bandha*.

Thus, the loss of independence or its cause is known as *bandha.*

Bandha is two-fold in relation to *prayoga* and *visrasā* known as *prāyogika* and *vaisrasika bandhas.*

आद्यो द्वेधा आदिमदनादिविकल्पात् ।

TaVā V.24.7

The *vaisrasika bandha* is again two-fold, viz. *sādi* (with beginning) and *anādi* (without beginning).

The former, viz. *sādi* type of *vaisrasika bandha* is seen in lightning, thunder-bolt, water-stream, fire, rainbow, etc. through the qualities of *snigdhatā* and *rūkṣatā* (roughly unctuousness and dryness). The *anādi* (beginningless) *vaisrasika bandha* is of nine kinds – *dharmāstikāyabandha, dharmāstikāyadeśabandha, dharmāstikāyapradeśabandha, adharamāstikāyabandha, adharamāstikāyadeśabandha, adharmāstikāyapradeśabandha, ākāśāstikāyabandha, ākāśāstikāyadeśabandha* and *ākāśāstikāyapradeśabandha.* The whole is known as *astikāya,* its half as *deśa* and its quarter as *pradeśa.*

Bhaṭṭa Akalaṅkadeva(TaVā V.24.7) has compiled more information about *anādi bandha* as follows:

i) the *bandha* of *kāla-paramāṇus* is *vaisrasika anādi* on account of the lack of their mutual separation,

ii) *dharma, adharma, ākāśa* and *kāla* do not get separated from one another, hence these four are tied together with *anādi vaisrasika bandha,*

iii) the tying together of various *jīvas* with other *dravyas* is *anādi bandha.*

Prayoga is the name for the combination of the *śarīra, vāk* and *manas* of *puruṣa* and the *bandha* that comes into being for that purpose is known as *prāyogika.*

The above detailed description of *prāyogika* and *vaisrasika bandhas* treats '*bandha*' as a structural entity rather than in the negative sense of bondage. Further, varieties of *anādi vaisrasika bandha* have been enumerated and described by Bhaṭṭa Akalaṅkadeva but they have not been reproduced here in the interest of brevity.

Other systems of philosophy have treated *bandha* only in the context of the *jīva.* The description of *bandha* in Jainism also treats *bandha* in this context under *karmabandha.* The *jīva* with *kaṣāya* (stain or impurity) accepts the *pudgalas* useful for *karman* and this is *bandha.* The acceptance of *pudgalas* by the →*jīva* is dictated by the compulsion of beginningless →*karman* and the demands of future *karman.* The combination of *pudgalas* is *bandha. Karmabandha* is again dealt with great details of varieties and sub-varieties.

In the Buddhist texts, *bandha* is mentioned in the meaning of bondage. The following passages are pertinent:

को सुज्झति मुच्चति बज्झति च । केनऽत्तना गच्छति ब्रह्मलोकम् ?
अजानतो मे मुनि ब्रूहि पुट्ठो । भगवा हि मे सक्खि बह्मज्ज दिट्ठो ।
तुवं हि नो ब्रह्मसमोऽति सच्चम् । कथं उपज्जति ब्रह्मलोकं (जुती मा) ॥

SutNip 508

Who is purified, (who) is released, (and who) is bound? With what self does one go to the Brahma-world? Being asked, sage, tell me who does not know. For the Blessed one is my witness that Brahmā has been seen today, for it is true that you are equal to Brahmā for us. How is one reborn in Brahma-world, brilliant one? (Tr. K.R. Norman)

यस्सऽस्सु लुतानि बन्धनानि । अज्झत्तं बहिद्धा च सब्बमूलम् ।
(सब्ब) संगमूलबंधना पमुत्तो । आजानियो तादि पवुच्चते तथत्ताऽति ॥

SutNip 532

Of whom the bonds (may) have been cut, inside and outside, the root of attachment, (such a one is rightly called) 'thoroughbred'. (Tr. K.R. Norman)

बन्धनानि कतमानि । त्रीणि बन्धनानि । रागो बन्धनं सर्वः, द्वेषो बन्धनं सर्वः, मोहो बन्धनं सर्वः ।
कस्मादेतदेव त्रयं बन्धनमुक्तं भगवता ।

विद्वशाद् बन्धनत्रयम् ॥

त्रिवेदनावशात् त्रीणि बन्धनानि । सुखायां हि वेदनायां रागोऽनुशेते आलम्बन-संप्रयोगाभ्याम् ।
दुःखायां द्वेषः । अदुःखासुखायां मोहो न तथा रागद्वेषौ । स्वासान्तनिकालम्बनतो वा नियमः ।

AbhidhKoBh V.45d

How many *bandhanas* or bonds are there? Three, namely all lust, all hatred, and all ignorance. Why are only these three called bonds?

There are three bonds by reason of sensation.

There are three bonds by reasons of the three sensations. Lust creates *anuśayana,* that is, 'becomes lodged in and grows' in agreeable sensation, both by taking it as its object and by association; hatred in disagreeable sensation; and ignorance, but not in the same manner - lust and hatred, in the sensation of indifference. Or rather the preceding rule refers to the sensation of personality. (Tr. L.M. Pruden)

In Haṭhayoga, *bandhas* are included in ten →*mudrās,* that are static poses comparable to *sthānakas* in dance. Movement and static state are, really speaking, inseparable, one invariably follows the other or subsists in the other. All the same, for the sake of analysis, they are dealt with separately. The ten *mudrās* in which the *bandhas* are included, are as follows:

> महामुद्रा महाबन्धो महावेधश्च खेचरी ।
> उड्यानं मूलबन्धश्च बन्धो जालन्धराभिधः ॥
> करणी विपरीताख्या वज्रोली शक्तिचालनम् ।
> इदं हि मुद्रादशकं जरामरणनाशनम् ॥
>
> HyPrad III.6–7
>
> *Mahāmudrā, mahābandha, mahā-vedha, khecharī, uḍyāna, mūlabandha, jālandhara-bandha* and *viparītakaraṇī, vajrolī* and *śakti-cālana* (activising the energy) – these are ten *mudrās* that overpower old age and death.

The act of 'binding' is mentioned with reference to the restraint of breath, i.e. it is said for *kumbhaka* that when it is 'bound' and when the *siddha āsana* is mastered three '*bandhas*' or specific postures of the body become possible without effort.

> किमन्यैर्बहुभिः पीठैः सिद्धे सिद्धासने सति ।
> प्राणानिले सावधाने बद्धे केवलकुम्भके ॥
> उत्पद्यते निरायासात्स्वयमेवोन्मनी कला ।
> तथैकस्मिन्नेव दृढे सिद्धे सिद्धासने सति ।
> बन्धत्रयमनायासात् स्वयमेवोपजायते ॥
>
> HyPrad I.43–44
>
> What is the use of many other *pīṭhas* (*āsanas*), when the *siddha āsana* has been accomplished, and vital air is restrained in '*kevala-kumbhaka*' and attention is fixed on it. The *unmanī kalā* is born of itself, without any effort, and when only one *siddhāsana* is accomplished firmly, the three *bandhas* (*mūla, uḍḍīyāna* and *jālandhara*) are manifested by themselves, without any effort.

The above three *bandhas* (postures) are described in the following verses, but another one called *mahābandha* is added in the beginning of this description, as is the case in the enumeration of the ten →*mudrās* cited above:

(i) *Mahābandha*:

> पार्ष्णिं वामस्य पादस्य योनिस्थाने नियोजयेत् ।

वामोरूपरि संस्थाप्य दक्षिणं चरणं तथा ॥
पूरयित्वा ततो वायुं हृदये चुबुकं दृढम् ।
निष्पीड्य वायुमाकुञ्च्य मनोमध्ये नियोजयेत् ॥
धारयित्वा यथाशक्ति रेचयेदनिलं शनैः ।
सव्याङ्गे तु समभ्यस्य दक्षाङ्गे पुनरभ्यसेत् ॥
अयं तु सर्वनाडीनामूर्ध्वं गतिनिरोधकः ।
अयं खलु महाबन्धो महासिद्धिप्रदायकः ॥

HyPrad III.19–21, 23

The heel of the left foot should be placed on the 'origin' (the joining point between the anus and the organ of generation), the right foot should be placed on the left thigh; having filled the air and having firmly pressed the chin on the chest, having contracted the air, one should fix the mind inside. Having retained the air as far as possible, one should exhale it slowly. Having practised in this way from the left side one should again practise from the right side. This stops the upward motion of all the *nāḍīs*. Verily this *mahābandha* is the bestower of great *siddhi*.

(ii) *Uḍḍīyāna bandha*:

बद्धो येन सुषुम्नायां प्राणस्तूड्डीयते यतः ।
तस्मादुड्डीयनाख्योऽयं योगिभिः समुदाहृतः ॥
उड्डीनं कुरुते यस्मादविश्रान्तं महाखगः ।
उड्डीयानं तदेव स्यात् तत्र बन्धोऽभिधीयते ॥
उदरे पश्चिमं तानं नाभेरूर्ध्वं च कारयेत् ।
उड्डीयानो ह्यसौ बन्धो मृत्युमातङ्गकेसरी ॥
सर्वेषामेव बन्धानामुत्तमो ह्युड्डियानकः ।
उड्डियाने दृढे बन्धे मुक्तिः स्वाभाविकी भवेत् ॥

HyPrad III.54–56, 59

This *bandha* is called *uḍḍīyāna* by the yogins because the *prāṇa* bound with *suṣumṇā* flies with this *bandha*. That *bandha* is known as *uḍḍīyāna* where the *prāṇa* flies as a big bird, without rest. Backward pulling is to be done above and below the navel. This is *uḍḍīyāna bandha*, a lion for the elephant of death. *Uḍḍīyāna* is the best among all the *bandhas*. When this *bandha* becomes fire, liberation comes about naturally.

(iii) *Mūlabandha*:

पार्ष्णिभागेन संपीड्य योनिमाकुञ्चयेद् गुदम् ।
अपानमूर्ध्वमाकृष्य मूलबन्धोऽभिधीयते ॥
अधोगतिमपानं वा ऊर्ध्वगं कुरुते बलात् ।
आकुञ्चनेन तं प्राहुर्मूलबन्धं हि योगिनः ॥

HyPrad III.60–61

Pressing the *yoni* (origin), one should contract the anus, drawing the *apāna* air upwards. Then it is called *mūla-bandha*. Yogins call it *mūla-bandha* when *apāna* air is drawn upwards or pushed downwards with force, with contraction.

(iv) *Jālandhara bandha*:

कण्ठमाकुञ्च्य हृदये स्थापयेच्चिबुकं दृढम् ।
बन्धो जालन्धराख्योऽयं जरामृत्युविनाशकः ॥
बध्नाति हि शिराजालमधोगामि नभोजलम् ।
ततो जालन्धरो बन्धः कण्ठदुःखौघनाशनः ॥
जालन्धरे कृते बन्धे कण्ठसङ्कोचलक्षणे ।
न पीयूषं पतत्यग्नौ न च वायुः प्रकुप्यति ॥

HyPrad III.69–71

Having contracted the neck, one should place the chin on the chest. This *bandha* is called *jālandhara* and is the destroyer of old age and death. This is *jālandhara bandha* that destroys the suffering of the throat. It binds the net of nerves and dams the water (nectar) dripping from the sky (the cerebral cavity). When the *jālandhara bandha* which has contraction of the throat as its characteristic, is accomplished, then nectar does not fall into fire (of the abdomen) and air does not get aggravated.

Manifestation in the Arts

Bandha is the name given to various compositional patterns of poetry that follow pictorial designs. They are also known as *citra-bandhas*. A brief history of these *bandhas* as found in the *lakṣaṇa* texts of poetry is presented below:

Bharata's **Nāṭya-Śāstra** speaks of ten types of *yamaka* which stands for repetition of a syllable, word or part of a word. These names are: (i) *kāñci-yamaka*, where the beginning and end of a foot in a verse are identical, (ii) *cakravāla-yamaka*, where the ending of a foot and the beginning of the succeeding foot are identical, and (iii) *mālā-yamaka*, where one and the same consonant is repeated in combination with various vowels. The *cakravāla-yamaka* was represented as *cakra-bandha* in later literature.

In the **Agni Purāṇa**, eight types of *citra-bandha* are mentioned, viz. *gomūtrikā* (the flow of bull's urine), *ardhabhramaṇa* (half-cycle), *sarvatobhadra* (a square, right on all sides), *ambuja* (lotus), →*cakra* (disc or wheel), *cakrābja* (disc and lotus combined), *daṇḍa* (rod) and *muraja* (drum).

The **Kāvyādarśa** of Daṇḍin describes three *citra-bandhas*, viz. *gomūtrikā*, *ardhabhrāmaka* (half-cycle) and *sarvatobhadra*.

The **Kāvyālaṅkāra** of Rudraṭa describes many new *citra-bandhas* like *khaḍga* (sword), *mūsala* (pounding rod), *dhanu* (bow), *śara* (arrow), *śūla* (spear), →*śakti* (arrows on both ends of a rod), *hala* (plough), →*ratha* (chariot). etc.

कर्णिकायां न्यसेदेकं द्वे द्वे दिक्षु विदिक्षु च ।
प्रवेशनिर्गमौ दिक्षु कुर्यादष्टदलाम्बुजे ॥

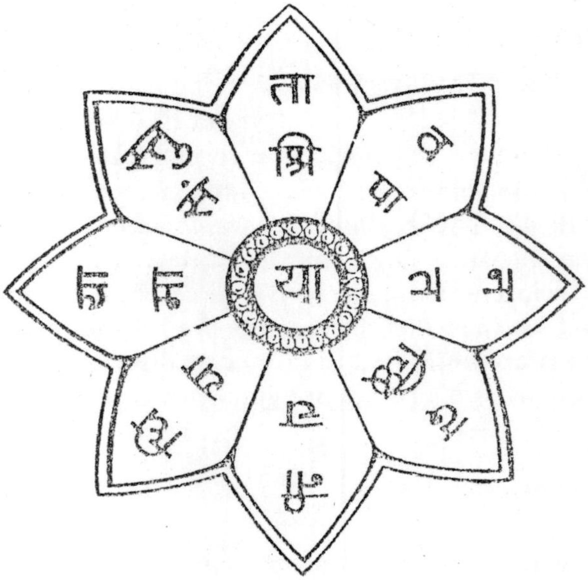

या श्रिता पावनतया यातनच्छिदनीचया ।
याचनीया धिया माया यामाया संस्तुता श्रिया ॥

Figure 18: *Aṣṭadalapadma-bandha* or eight-petalled lotus (II.284)

The **Sarasvatīkaṇṭhābharaṇa** of Bhoja gives the most elaborate treatment of *citra-bandhas* with illustrations. Three illustrations are reproduced below from the text:

1. *aṣṭadalapadma-bandha* or eight-petalled louts (II.284),
2. *vyoma-bandha* (space or sky) (II.319),
3. *muraja-bandha* (in the form of drum) (II.320).

अष्टादशशिखरचरीं गोमुत्रिकया चतुष्पदीं पश्येत् ।
यत्राद्यन्तैर्दृष्टां स ज्ञेयो व्योमबन्ध इति ॥

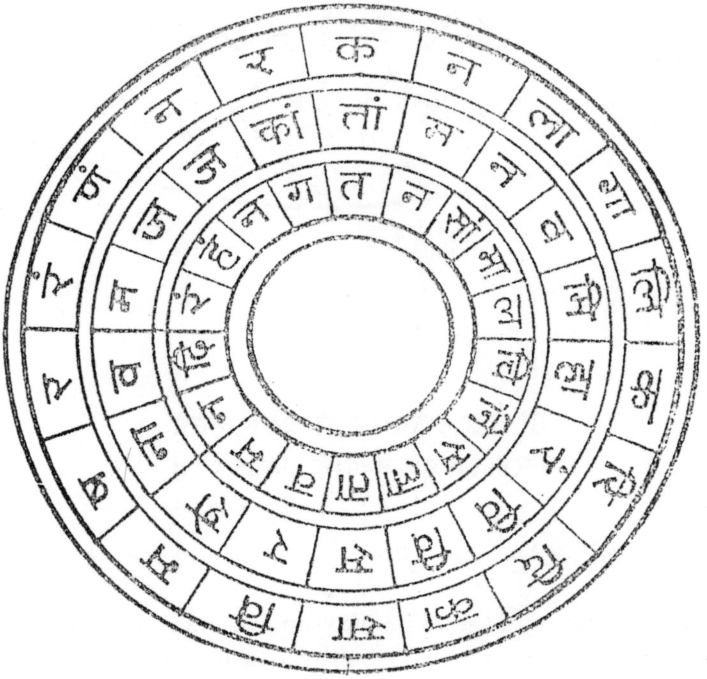

कमलावलिहारिविकासविशेषवहञ्जनकाङ्क ।
ननगामिकरन्दिविसारमनारमणञ्जरतान्न ॥
तमसां बलहानिविलासवशेन वरञ्जनकान्त ।
न नमामि चिरं सवितारमनादिमहञ्जगतान्न ॥

Figure 19: *Vyoma-bandha* (space or sky) (II.319)

अत्र पादचतुष्केऽपि क्रमशः परिलेखिते ।
श्लोकपादक्रमेण स्याद्रेखासु मुरजत्रयी ॥

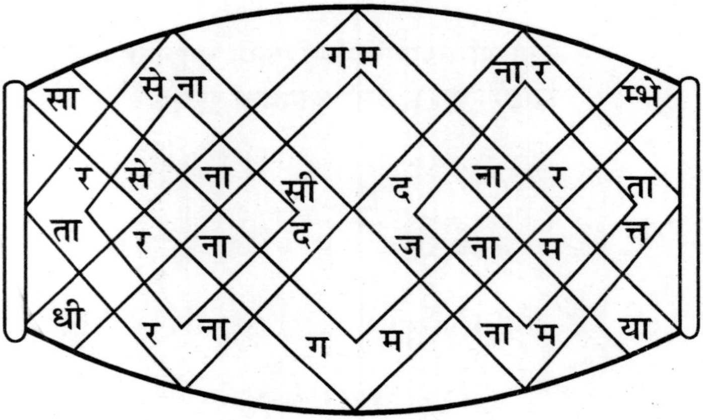

सा सेना गमनारम्भे रसेनासीदनारता ।
तारनादजना मत्तधीरंनागमनामया ॥

Figure 20: *Muraja-bandha* (in the form of drum) (II.320)

The **Kāvya Prakāśa** of Mammaṭa, **Kāvyānuśāsana** of Hemacandra, **Alaṅkāra-Kaustubha** of Kavi Karṇapūra and **Sāhitya-Darpaṇa** of Viśvanātha also mention some *citra-bandhas*.

It is notable that the **Kāśikā** commentary on Pāṇini's **Aṣṭādhyāyī** (III.4.42 and VI.3.13) mentions names of several *citra-bandhas*. The word '*bandha*' occurs in the latter *sūtra* mentioned above. It could, therefore, be surmised that poetic *citra-bandhas* were known to Pāṇini.

Bhāravi is the first poet to have devoted one whole *sarga* or canto (fifteenth) of his epic, **Kirātārjunīya** to *citra-bandhas*. He has composed there twelve verses in *gomūtrikā-bandha*, twenty-five in *sarvatobhadra* and twenty-seven in *ardhabhrāmaka*.

Māgha has also composed fourteen types of *citra-bandhas* in the nineteenth canto of his **Śiśupālavadha**.

Citra-bandhas have been composed in Sanskrit epics mostly in the description of battles where different formations of the army are involved.

Some poets have written exclusive compositions in *citra-bandha*. Some notable names are the **Citra-Ratnākara** of Citrakavi, **Citra-bandha-Rāmāyaṇa** of Veṅkaṭeśvara, **Rāghavapāṇḍavīya** of Kavirājasūrī, **Pārvatīrukmiṇīya** of Vidyāmādhava, **Kaṅkaṇa-Rāmāyaṇa** of Kṛṣṇamūrti, etc.

Citra-bandhas have a special place in Stotra literature. The importance of *yantra* (roughly geometrical design) in *upāsanā* is well-known. The forms depicted in *citra-bandhas* bear similarity to *yantras*. Hence, the preference for *citra-bandhas* in Stotra literature could be ascribed to this similarity. Some illustrations are – the **Devīśataka** of Ānandavardhana, **Īśvaraśataka** of Avatārakavi, **Lakṣmīsahasra** of Veṅkaṭādhvari, etc.

Citra-bandhas were profusely composed in Jain Stotra literature. Some notable names are – the **Jinnaśatakastutividyā** of Sāmantabhadrasvāmī, **Caturdhārāvali-citrastava** of Jaitilakasūra. Jain poets have made a significant contribution towards devising new forms of *citra-bandhas*.

Some contemporary poets who have composed *citra-bandhas* are – Dukhabhañjanakavi who has composed a work on prosody known as **Vāgvallabha**; Raghuvīra Miśra, the composer of **Śrīlakṣmīśvaropāyana**; Dāmodara Miśra Śāstrī of Magadha and Rāmarūpa Pāṭhak of Varanasi whose compositions were published under the name **Citra-kāvya-Kautukam** (edited by Prem Lata Sharma).

Citra-bandhas have been composed also in Prakrit, Apabhraṃśa to some extent. In Hindi, this poetic form found special favour from the sixteenth to eighteenth centuries. Names of some notable poets are Keśavadāsa, Bhikhārīdāsa, Lālakavi, Gokulanātha, Dīnadayālagiri, etc. Similarly, Gujarati, Marathi, Oriya, Kannada, Bengali, etc. have numerous compositions of this type.

Prabandha in literature is the contradistinct of *muktaka*, the former standing for a composition that has several units (known as *sargas* in Mahākāvyas) connected with one another, i.e. where there is a sequence of narration or treatment of events, e.g. Mahākāvya (epic).

The **Kāvyādarśa** of Daṇḍin classifies *kāvya* as *gadya* (prose), *padya* (verse) and *miśra* (mixed). *Padya* has four feet and is twofold, viz. *vṛtta* (*vārṇika* metres composed of long and short syllables) and *jāti* (*mātrika* metres composed of *mātrā* units). This is the classification based on verbal organization, metrical or otherwise. There is another classification based on the organizations of small or big units. Here four types are spoken of, viz. *muktaka, kulaka, kośa* and *saṅghāta*. The first two being described in the **Agni Purāṇa** as follows:

मुक्तकं श्लोक एकैकश्चमत्कारक्षमः सताम् ॥
श्लोकैरनेकैः कुलकं .... ॥

AgPur CCCXXXVII.36

Kulaka is formed with more than one *śloka*. *Muktaka* is that where each *śloka* is capable of bestowing *camatkāra* (lit. wonder, here aesthetic delight) on the cultured.

The latter two, viz. *kośa* and *saṅghāta* have been described in anonymous citations given in V. Narayan Ayar's commentary on the **Kāvyādarśa** as:

कोषः श्लोकसमूहस्तु स्यादन्योऽन्यानपेक्षकः । ..... यत्र कविरेकमर्थं वृत्तेनैकेन वर्णयति काव्ये सङ्घातः स निगदितः । यथा– वृन्दावनमेघदूतादिः ॥

Comm. on Kāvyād I.13

Koṣa is that group of verses where each one is independent of the other. ... Where the poet describes one subject in one verse (and there are many such verses that are loosely inter-connected), that is known as *saṅghāta*, e.g. Vṛndāvana Campu, Meghadūta and the like.

Mahākāvya is defined as *sargabandha* in the **Kāvyādarśa** (I.14), i.e. composed in cantos. Other details are not relevant here.

It is interesting to note that the word '*prabandha*' does not occur in the classification of the types of poetry in Daṇḍin's **Kāvyādarśa**. It does occur very prominently in the **Dhvanyāloka** (ca 9th century A.D.), the text that established the *dhvani* theory, where this form of composition is highly extolled.

In the **Dhvanyāloka**, *prabandha* is mentioned as a contradistinct of *muktaka*:

मुक्तकेषु प्रबन्धेष्विव रसबन्धाभिनिवेशिनः कवयो दृश्यन्ते । यथा ह्यमरुकस्य कवेर्मुक्तकाः शृङ्गाररसस्यन्दिनः प्रबन्धायमानाः प्रसिद्धा एव ।

DhvĀl III.7

There are poets to be seen, who are devoted to *rasa-bandha* (the delineation of *rasa*) in *muktaka* compositions in the same way as is done in *prabandha*, e.g. the *muktaka*s of Amaruka Kavi ooze out *śṛṅgāra rasa* and are well-known for taking the position of *prabandha*s.

Thus, *muktaka* has been extolled here to occupy the position of *prabandha* and *prabandha* is an umbrella term which covers all types of poetic and musical compositions that have interconnecting units, be it prose or verse, epic or drama.

The compound *rasa-bandha* occurs in the third chapter of **Dhvanyāloka** repeatedly. It stands for the poet's effort to delineate →*rasa* through his composition.

The word '*prabandha*' occurs for the first time in Saṅgīta-Śāstra in Mataṅga's **Bṛhaddeśī** (ca 6th century A.D.). It stands there for the compositional form, forming part of *deśī* music independent of drama. It is a vocal composition that has several textual components like →*pada* (verbal unit), *tena* or *tenaka* (formations of non-lexical syllables like *tenna, tenna*), *pāṭa* (syllables identified with instrumental strokes, specially those of drums), *biruda* (eulogic epithets), *svara* (solfa syllables), and →*tāla* being the sixth component. In the **Saṅgīta-Ratnākara** (chapter IV), it is described in greater detail and the number of *prabandhas* that are described is much more; they are also classified under three categories, viz. *sūḍa, ālikrama* and *viprakīrṇa*. It also speaks of *prabandha* as a →*puruṣa*. The components of *prabandha* are called *dhātus* on the model of the *dhātus* of the human body, conceived in Āyurveda as *aṅgas* or limbs (→*dhātu*). The number of *dhātus* is four or five and that of *aṅgas* is six. The *dhātus* are sections of the *prabandha* that are melodic-cum-textual-cum-rhythmic units. *Aṅgas* are textual components. Six →*aṅgas* of the human organism have been conceived in Āyurveda, similarly six *aṅgas* representing textual-cum-rhythmic units of the *prabandha-puruṣa* have been described.

प्रबन्धावयवो धातुः स चतुर्धा निरूपितः ।
उद्ग्राहः प्रथमस्तत्र ततो मेलापकध्रुवौ ।
आभोगश्चेति तेषां च क्रमाल्लक्ष्माभिदध्महे ॥

SR IV.7

Dhātu is the structural element of *prabandha* and is shown to be four-fold, viz. the first is *udgrāha,* then (follows) *melāpaka, dhruva* and *ābhoga*. These will now be defined seriatim.

Prabandha is divided, as a general rule, into four sections, viz. *udgrāha* (the starter), *melāpaka* (the joiner), *dhruva* (the invariable) and *ābhoga* (the concluding section). In certain cases, a section called *antarā* (the intermediary) is also introduced in addition to these four in-between *dhruva* and *ābhoga*. There is no rule appertaining to the introduction of *antarā* as such, but it is mentioned as a fact of observed phenomenon of musical practice.

Every *prabandha* need not have as many as four sections. Some times *melāpaka* is eliminated, and some times *melāpaka* and *ābhoga* both are eliminated. It has already been noticed that the three names for the structured melody, viz. *prabandha, vastu* and *rūpaka* are associated by some with the number of sections and integral parts that go to constitute it.

In modern Hindustani music, the *khyāls* generally have two parts called *sthāyī* and *antarā*, and *dhrupads* have four, viz. *sthāyī, antarā, sañcārī* and *ābhoga.* In the latter case, however, the last two sections are hardly distinguished from each other since they are not marked by the re-introduction of the first line of *sthāyī* in-between them. The two can, in terms of the division of *prabandha* into four sections, in fact be considered as one.

Prabandha is threefold, viz. as constituted of two, three or four *dhātus*; it has six *aṅgas* (integral parts), viz. *svara, biruda, pada, tena, pāṭa* and *tāla*; like the parts of the body they are the integral parts of the configuration of *prabandha.* Of these six *aṅgas, tena* and *pada* reflecting auspiciousness and meaning respectively are its two eyes, *pāṭa* and *biruda* are the two hands, because they are produced by the hand, the cause being figuratively taken for the effect; and →*tāla* and →*svara* are considered to be the two feet as they are the cause of movement in *prabandha.*

Thus, *prabandha* in music is a form in which textual, melodic and rhythmic components are knit together. It has no alignment with drama.

Nibaddha and *anibaddha* are two cognate terms that have a longer history than *prabandha.* In the **Nāṭya-Śāstra**, these two terms occur for describing three aspects of *pada* (verbal or syllabic structure), viz. the presence or absence of (i) metre, (ii) *tāla,* (iii) meaning. The presence of these three collectively or individually signifies the term *nibaddha* and similarly, their absence is associated with *anibaddha.*

> यत् स्यादक्षरसम्बद्धं तत्सर्वं पदसंज्ञितम् ।
> निबद्धश्चानिबद्धश्च येन तेन द्विधा स्मृतम् ॥
> अतालश्च सतालश्च द्विप्रकारं तदुच्यते ।
>
> NŚ XXXII.28–29ab
>
> All that which is structured with syllables, is called *pada.* It is known to be two-fold because it is *nibaddha* and *anibaddha.* It is (also) said to be with *tāla* and without *tāla.*

In the **Bṛhaddeśī**, of the two forms of *deśī* music, *nibaddha* is the one that is structured and has provision or scope for *ālāpa* (melodic elaboration) and *anibaddha* is relatively unstructured and does not consequently have scope for *ālāpa.*

निबद्धश्चानिबद्धश्च मार्गोऽयं द्विविधो मतः ।
आलापादिनिबद्धो यः स च मार्गः प्रकीर्तितः ॥
[आलापादिविहीनस्तु स च देशी प्रकीर्तितः ।]

BṛD I.15–16ab

This *mārga* (course) (of *deśī*) is known to be two-fold, viz. that which is *nibaddha* structured (lit. bound) and that which is *anibaddha* (lit. unbound, relatively less structured). That which is structured through *ālāpa* (melodic elaboration) etc. is called *mārga* (lit. path), but the one devoid of *ālāpa* etc. is called *deśī.*

In the **Saṅgīta-Ratnākara**, these two words stand for the two types of →*gāna* which is the contradistinct of *gāndharva.*

निबद्धमनिबद्धं तद् द्वेधा निगदितं बुधैः ॥
बद्धं धातुभिरङ्गैश्च निबद्धमभिधीयते ।
आलप्तिर्बन्धहीनत्वादनिबद्धमितीरिता ॥
सा चास्माभिः पुरा प्रोक्ता निबद्धं त्वधुनोच्यते ।
संज्ञात्रयं निबद्धस्य प्रबन्धो वस्तु रूपकम् ॥

SR IV.4cd–6

The sages have declared it to be two-fold, viz. *nibaddha* (composed) and *anibaddha* (improvised). That which is composed of *dhātus* (sections) and *aṅgas* (integral parts) is called *nibaddha. Ālapti* being free from such structural limitations is known as *anibaddha,* and that has already been dealt with by us. *Nibaddha* is now being expounded. *Nibaddha* has three names, viz. *prabandha, vastu* and *rūpaka.* (Tr. R.K. Shringy and P.L. Sharma)

Here *nibaddha* stands for pre-composed or pre-determined and *anibaddha* for that which is not pre-composed or pre-determined. *Prabandha* is one of the three names given to *nibaddha.* The **Saṅgīta-Ratnākara** does not explain the distinction of these three names – *prabandha, vastu* and *rūpaka* but the **Saṅgītarāja** gives this distinction.

विभज्य लक्ष्यते सम्यङ् निबद्धमधुना मया ॥
प्रबन्धो रूपकं वस्तु तस्य संज्ञात्रयं विदुः ।
एषामभेदेऽपि भिदा लक्ष्मतःस्यात् कियन्त्यपि ॥
अङ्गैःषड्भिश्चतुर्भिश्च धातुभिर्बध्यते यतः ।
ततः प्रबन्ध इत्युक्तो गजबन्धनचञ्चुना ॥
आरोप्यते गुणग्रामोपाधिकं यत्र नायके ।
रामादित्वं महीभर्त्रा तद्रूपकमुदीरितम् ॥

यस्मिन् वसन्ति नियतं धातवोऽङ्गानि कानिचित् ।
सद्वस्तुध्वनिमुख्येन तद्वस्तु परिकीर्त्तितम् ॥

SRāj II.4.2.2cd–6

Now I shall properly define *nibaddha* with its divisions. *Prabandha, rūpaka* and *vastu* are the three names known for it. Although they are *abheda* (non-differentiated), there is a slight distinction. *Prabandha* has been said to be so on account of being 'bound' (structured) with six *aṅgas* and four *dhātus* (described above), by one who is adept in controlling elephants. Where there is a state of being Rāma and the like, characterised by a cluster of qualities, by the king, that is known as *rūpaka.* Where some of the *aṅgas* and all the *dhātus* subsist, that is said to be *vastu* by one who prominently suggests Reality.

Thus, the presence of all the *dhātus* and *aṅgas* justifies the name '*prabandha*'. The dramatic quality of the basically non-dramatic music composition signifies the name '*rūpaka*' and the freedom to omit some of the *aṅgas* qualifies the name '*vastu*'. Basically the word, '*prabandha*', has been the most popular. Its current equivalent is '*bandhish*' and the equivalent of →*vastu* in current parlance is '*cheez*'. *Ālāpa* with all its varieties bears the name '*anibaddha*'.

Vādya-prabandha is the name given to compositions of drum syllables meant for being played on drums. They are described in the **Saṅgīta-Ratnākara** (VI).

In sculpture, *bandha* stands for a frieze or a row of figures. This row, as though, binds the temple and hence the name *bandha.* Two texts, viz. the **Śilparatnakośa** and **Śilpa Prakāśa** written in Orissa mention *nārībandha* and *rājabandha* and a few others that are described in the following terms:

नारीबन्धः सदा रम्यः शिखरे च विशेषतः ।
एतेन विधिना कार्यं गवाक्षादि मनोरमम् ॥

ŚiPrak I.480

Nārībandha or the row of female figures is always beautiful, specially in the *śikhara.* In this manner, elegant *gavākṣa* (window) and the like should be made.

तत्स्थानं नारीजाङ्घाख्यं जाङ्घमिति मनोहरम् ।
यदुच्चनारीबन्धश्च मध्ये गृहस्थले तथा ॥
तद्बन्धः तलपीठाङ्गं त्रिमोडगुण्डिकावृतम् ।

ŚiRaKo 130–131ab

This portion is called the *nārījāṅgha* and it is most pleasing to the mind.

The niches within (the *vimānikāgṛha*) are of the same height as the *nārībandha* (row of female figures).

This *bandha* and the pedestal beneath it are framed by *guṇḍikā* ornamentation in all the three segments. (Tr. B. Bäumer)

In the context of the *nāgastambha,* the *dhāraṇībandha* is spoken of as follows:

तदूर्ध्वे धारणीबन्धः ऊर्ध्वगः कमलाकृतिः ।

ŚiRaKo 156ab

Above this is the *dhāraṇībandha* which has the shape of an upward facing lotus (this is the third part). (Tr. B. Bäumer)

A few more compounds with the word *bandha* occur in the **Śilparatnakośa** (V). Their names are *jharābandha, pheṇibandha, puṣpabandha, sakhībandha* and *yugmabandha.* They are different forms of pieces of sculpture at specific points in the temple structure. Their function is to support or bind in an ornamented way.

रथहस्तितुरङ्गाणां चतुरङ्गबलादयः ।
नानाकारे कृते रम्ये राजबन्ध इति श्रुतः ॥

ŚiPrak I.509

The *caturaṅga* or four-winged army of riders on chariots, elephants, horses and the infantry, when carved in various beautiful forms is known as *rājabandha.*

Bandha as a structure in building is described as under:

लाक्षागुलमधुच्छिष्टगुग्गुलूनां समांशकाः ॥
एतेषां द्विगुणं भागं ग्राह्यं सर्जरसं तदा ।
गैरिकाचूर्णकं तस्मादर्धं तु घनचूर्णकम् ।
सर्वेषामर्धतस्तैलं निक्षिपेल्लोहभाजने ।
लोहदर्व्या चलं कुर्यात् पाचयेन्मृदुवह्निना ।
अष्टबन्धमिति प्रोक्तमश्मवद् दृढबन्धनम् ॥

Mayam XXXIV.64ab–66

Equal parts of wax, molasses, bees wax and bdellium are taken and a quantity of *sarja* resin is added, equal to or double (the total of the first four commodities), as well as pounded brick; all this is put into a metal receptacle with a quantity of oil equal to that of all (the other ingredients put together). Everything is mixed together with a metal spoon and cooked slowly. This is how eight ingredient mortar (*aṣṭabandha*) is obtained such as makes joins rock-hard. (Tr. B. Dagens)

In dance, *bandha* stands for acrobatic postures in the Odissi tradition. Some names are – Gaṅgāvataraṇa, Cīrā and Gaḍiyā, etc.

The compound *piṇḍī-bandha* is a compound mentioned in the **Nāṭya-Śāstra** (IV), its four varieties are:

पिण्डी शृङ्खलिका चैव लताबन्धोऽथ भेद्यकः ।
पिण्डीबन्धस्तु पिण्डत्वाद् गुल्मः शृङ्खलिका भवेत् ॥
जालोपनद्धा च लता सनृत्तो भेद्यकः स्मृतः ।

NŚ IV.288–289ab

Piṇḍī is four-fold, viz. *piṇḍī, śṛṅkhalikā, latābandha,* and *bhedyaka. Piṇḍī* is known as *piṇḍī-bandha* on account of *piṇḍatva,* i.e. being of the nature of *piṇḍa* (lump). *Śṛṅkhalikā* (chain) is similar to *gulma* (bower), *latābandha* (creeper-like formation) is composed with *jāla* (net). *Bhedyaka* (where the components are distinctly recognizable) is a combination of the preceding three *nṛttas.*

Thus, *piṇḍī-bandha* is the general name of these four types and it is also the name of the first variety. Abhinavagupta in his commentary on the above verses says that *piṇḍī* is to be performed by one dancer, *śṛṅkhalikā* by two, →*latā* by three and *bhedyaka* by four. The metaphorical names are suggestive of the nature of the formations.

In painting, *bandha* is a specific formation with numerous human bodies or various animals. *Nārīkuñjara-bandha* is an example of the former, where several *gopīs* are depicted to have made a formation resembling an elephant and Kṛṣṇa riding the same. The same collection has another illustration in the form of a horse put together with various animals. The idea of putting together various bodies to create a specific formation is evident here.

Conclusion

Thus, we have seen that *bandha* stands for specific forms in literature; compounds like *citra-bandha, sarga-bandha* are well-known there. In Haṭhayoga and dance, it stands for specific postures of the body, the compound *piṇḍī-bandha* signifying specific group formations in dance. In philosophy, *bandha* stands for bondage and different systems speak of the nature, and cause of bondage and they also deal with the question as to who is bound. Although bondage has a negative connotation here, it endows the →*jīva* with the capacity

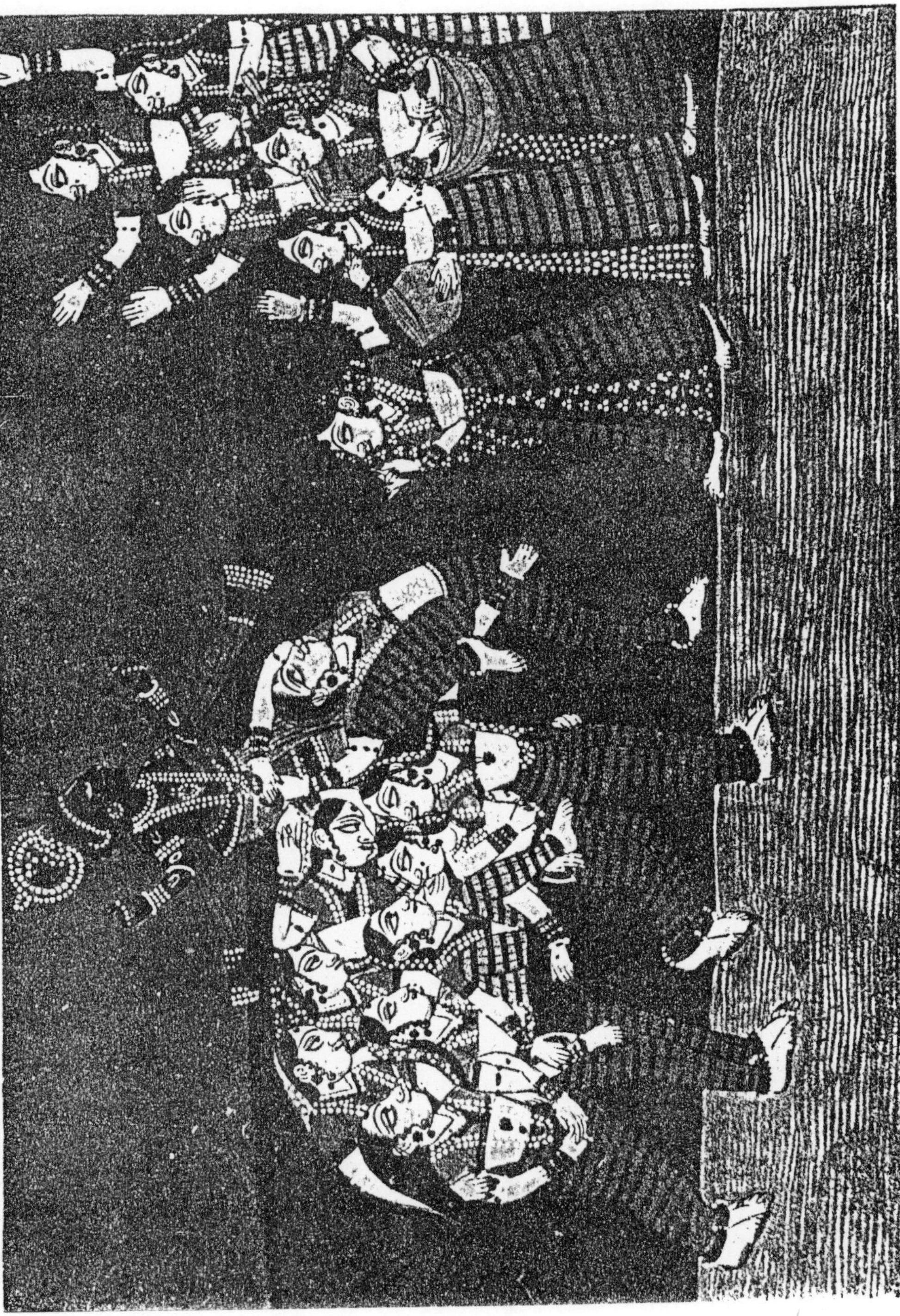

Figure 21: *Nārīkuñjara-bandha* (Bharat Kala Bhavan, BHU, Acc. No. 146p)

to function as doer and enjoyer. *Prabandha* is a more specific form in literature and music. The underlying idea of both these words is the act of 'binding' and 'limiting' which operates in time and space and bestows specificity of form which in turn is associated with function and manifestation of essence.

Prem Lata Sharma

Select Bibliography

Acharya, P.K.: A Dictionary of Hindu Iconography, Manasara Series No. I, Delhi: Low Price Publications, 1997.

Sharma, P.L. (Ed.): Citrakāvya Kautukam, Delhi: Motilal Banarsidass, 1965.

Solomon, E.A.: "The Spirit of Indian Thought, in Bulletin of Chunilal Gandhi Vidyabhavan, Vol. 18, 1974, pp. 58–76.

PRĀSĀDA

Overview

Prāsāda derived from the Indo-European root *sad-* to settle or sit, stands in its earliest occurrence for the Vedic altar, erected in the prescribed form by piling up bricks to the recitation of →*mantras,* to invoke the chosen god. The sacrifice is carried to the god by →*agni,* which in turn bestows benefit to the *yajamāna.*

When the soul of the individual leaves the mortal coil, the dead body is returned to the elements either by burial in the earth or consignment to the fire, an act also recognised as →*yajña.* The tumulus erected over the site as a memorial by heaping up earth is →*caitya* or *stūpa* and is verily a sacred place or *prāsāda.*

Prāsāda is a temple of god, given a relative permanence so that the offerings continue in perpetuity even after the demise of the *yajamāna.*

The cosmic tree, which is the support of the universe as the *axis mundi,* with its spreading branches and deep roots, a symbol of growth and eternity, together with its enclosure, is *prāsāda.*

Prāsāda is also the name of a *mantra,* the nature of light and bliss, light because it brightens knowledge, and bliss because it keeps one satisfied.

Prāsāda is popularly defined as the source of happiness, '*prasīdati asmin iti prāsādaḥ*'.

Residing in the built up space, the royal *yajamāna,* derives happiness by the grandeur of his palace. This is *prāsāda* since it gladdens both the king and his subjects.

The word *prāsāda* in essence is identical with supreme knowledge, the *upaniṣad,* revealing the identity of the individual soul with the cosmic entity, the *para-brahman.*

Etymology and Related Words

The word '*prāsāda*' is derived from the root *sad,* meaning to sit down, settle, rest, live, reside or dwell. An Indo-European root *sad-* appears as *sidere, sedere* in Latin; *seate, sedate* in Lithuanian; *sesti* in Slavonian; *sitam* in Anglosaxon and sit in English. The prefix *pra* is added generally in the sense of 'source', 'perfectness', 'purity', or 'prominence'. Appearing as *pāsāda* in Pali and *pāsāya* in Prakrit, *prāsāda* stands for a lofty seat or platform, a dwelling, home, abode, a seat in a conspicuous place, the top storey of palatial mansion, a palace, a sacrificial hall or a temple. It is traditionally derived from *sad-*, i.e. support or seat (*ādhāra*) with the prefix *pra* denoting the best or the highest, and ending with suffix, *ghañ* which lengthens the medial vowel '*a*' in '*pra*'.

The term *prāsāda* applies equally to a high seat, a sacrificial platform, a palace, a temple, a funerary or memorial monument or a →*mantra* in accordance with varying context. In its verbal form one gets from the root *sad-sadati*, or *sīdati* and in its causal form *sādayati.*

A number of words in Sanskrit like *sadman, sadana, sadas, sattram, sadaḥ,* and *upasadanam* are derived from the same root *sad-* and appear as synonyms. *Sadas-gṛha* is an assembly house, the court of a prince, council chamber. *Sādana* is a text recited when anything is being set down. The word *pra-sad* denotes an ordered tranquility. It also stands for 'to be pleased, gracious and propitious' – significantly extended to the word *prasāda,* meaning kindness, cleanliness, brightness, tranquility, purity and grace.

Upasadanam, i.e. sitting at the feet of the teacher, becoming a pupil and be of service, is also a Vedic word from the root *ṣad-*. Ādi Śaṅkara, derives the word *upaniṣad* from the same root *sad-*. *Sad-*, says Śaṅkara, means 'to destroy or to know', and holds Upaniṣad as *Brahmavidyā.*

More than 30 synonyms of the word *prāsāda* are found in different texts, such as *vimāna, bhavana,* →*āyatana, mandira,* →*caitya, citi, stūpa, harmya, ālaya, kīrtana-gṛha, sthāna, koil* (Tamil), *guṭi* (Kannada) and *ambalam* (Malayalam). The grammatical derivation of some of the words, indicate that they are 'the supports-affording protection' or 'the abode of protection'.

Vimāna is derived from the root *mā-* 'to measure', proportionate measurement (*pramāṇa*) is essential to the temple (*vimāna*) and to the image (→*pratimā*) alike. *Vimāna* is the name of the temple built according to tradition by the application of various proportionate measurements. *Vimāna* denotes the chariot of the gods as well.

Harmya is derived from the root *hṛ-* 'to captivate'. It denotes an edifice, an upper room, a turret, an apartment, building in general, a palace and a temple.

Mandira is from the root *mand-* to rejoice, to be glad. *Ālaya* is rooted in *lī-* to dissolve, implying concentration or absorption of mind.

Koil and *taḷi* are the two words commonly used in the Tamil country to denote the temple. *Koil,* most popular one, denotes both a royal palace and a temple and is the exact Tamil equivalent of the Sanskrit word *prāsāda.* The Tamil word *il* stands for a residence, abode, dwelling (its origin is not clear). Probably, it is connected with the Sanskrit root *lī-* from which *layana,* i.e. a house or dwelling, is derived. *Ko* (Sanskrit word *go*) is king or god. Thus *koil* means the abode of king or god. The other term *taḷi* is the Prakrit form of the word *sthala* in Sanskrit, a sacred or sanctified place. The word *kirtana* or *kīrti* stands for the rock-cut temple, same as *leṇa* or *layana* as recorded in the inscription in Kailāsa temple of Elora.

Ambalam (*ambaram* in Sanskrit) is commonly employed in Kerala for temple, though it is also used in Tamilnadu as in the famous temple of Lord Naṭarāja – Chidambaram. *Ambaram* stands for →*ākāśa* – the sky, ether or atmosphere. *Ākāśa* is of the nature of sound - the carrier of sound. *Ambara* or *ākāśa* is the divine or abode of the divine.

In Karnataka region, the term *guṭi* (*kuṭi* in Sanskrit) is employed to denote temple. *Kuṭi* stands for body, a hut, or a cottage. Similarly, the *basadi* (*vasati* in Sanskrit) stands for temple in the Jaina context in Karnataka.

The most extensively used word in Hindu, Buddhist and Jaina contexts to denote the place of worship is →*caitya* derived differently from two words: (a) *ciñ-* a Vedic root meaning 'to collect or to pile up', or (b) *caityaḥ-tyam* from *cayanam,* i.e. a pile of stone or a monument.

Stūpa is another synonym of *prāsāda,* derived differently either from the root *stu-* 'to praise', 'extol', 'glorify' and 'worship by hymn', or from the root *stup-* 'to heap up', 'pile', 'accumulate', 'collect'.

Layers of Meaning

Prāsāda may be considered at two distinct levels – the purely mundane level of physical existence, and the highly significant level of metaphysics. At the mundane level again it is considered under two broad categories: (a) as a dwelling of man and (b) as an abode of God. However, from the very beginning, the *prāsāda* is associated with a structure erected as a seat of God with all its association of sanctity and purity and the man invariably associated with it by being seated near it. At the physical level, both the categories are evolved as inter related phenomenon which continues throughout Indian thought. The first category as the 'abode of God, is the *deva prāsāda* and as the dwelling of human beings, especially of kings and nobles, it is *nṛpa prāsāda.* However, in both the instances, a conscious integration, of the cosmological principles, and their distribution in space and form, precedes the construction of both the temple of God and the Royal palace. In the process of visualisation, the Vedic and upanisadic concepts that have pervaded the entire Indian horizon, have played the pivotal role. Neither the temples, nor the royal palaces are mere structures. They project in space and volume the basic texts of Vedic ideas, as an intermediate seat, in the path of human progress towards the divine goal. It is this metaphysical formula, that brings into existence the *prāsāda*, sustains it during its relative existence, and in the inner vision of the whole withdraws it into itself.

Development of the Concept

Prāsāda in its micro-macro cosmic revelations is fully enshrined in the Ṛgvedic root *sad-* to settle. *Pra-sad-* to grow clear and bright, to become tranquil (and *sada*, i.e. cleanness and purity) of the Vedic period contains the seed for the later extensions of *prāsāda* in all its meanings. *Prasad* (PāDhā XX.24 and XXVIII.33) occurs in the **Ṛgveda, Vājasaneyi Saṃhitā, Atharvaveda**, and **Śatapatha Brāhmaṇa** in the meaning of 'to sit down'. 'It denotes settling down, and a seat made of that which has settled down and acquired concrete form, the form of a dwelling, a residence, the seat of God' (Kramrisch – *Hindu Temple*, Vol. I, pp. 135–136). *Sadanam* used in the **Ṛgveda** also occurs in the sense of 'abode, dwelling house' 'Place of sacrifice' and 'temple'. A similar word is *upasadanam* from the same root, for 'sitting at the feet of the teacher, becoming a pupil and be of service'. Related to *prasada* and *upasadana* and arising from the same root *sad-* is the great word *upaniṣad* which according to Max Müller meant originally, 'the act of sitting down near a teacher and submissively listening to him.' Deussen held that it meant 'secret instructions'. But according to Śaṅkara, the Advaita exponent, it means 'the knowledge that destroys the inborn ignorance and leads to salvation'. Śaṅkara reflects the true inner meaning of the word *upaniṣad* in all its aspect by holding it as →*vidyā*. The **Vājasaneyi Saṃhitā** (XII.53) names the hymn which effects the settling, setting or steadying bricks of the fire altar, *sādana mantra* (root *sad-*).

The word *prāsāda* as such is used in the **Śāṅkhāyana Śrauta-Sūtra** (XVI.18.13) in the meaning of a raised platform implying a seat: "During the midday, they erect *prāsādas* on all sides of the *āhavanīya* fire". The *Vedic Index of Names and Subjects* (II.44) understands *prāsāda* as a platform on a mound. The construction of the *prāsāda* is made by *sādana mantra*. To sit down near the *pra-sad*, the seat made of the bricks piled up, brightens the knowledge of the individual, gladdens his heart and reveals his nature, like the *upasadana*, sitting near the feet of *guru* who removes his ignorance through *brahma-vidyā* (*upaniṣad*). "*Prāsādas* please (*prasīdanti*) by their beauty the minds of gods and men" (Quoted by S. Kramrisch, *Hindu Temple*, Vol. I, p. 134, f.n. 17). Kramrisch further adds: "This they do, in virtue of their meaning and form. The temple is seen and comprehended by the look of knowledge" (*op. cit.*, Vol. I, p. 134, f.n. 17).

Prāsādas of Dhanapati, Rāma and Keśava are referred to by Patañjali in his **Mahābhāṣya** (II.2.34). *Prāsāda*, in the sense of palace occurs for the first time in the **Adbhuta Brāhmaṇa** (quoted in *A Dictionary of Hindu Architecture*, p. 419) as: *harmya prāsāda saṃkula.*

According to P.K. Acharya the term "*prāsāda* implies both religious and residential buildings. It denotes the gorgeous temples as well as small pavilions (→*maṇḍapa*) where a deity or the emblematical phallus of Śiva is installed. It includes magnificent palaces and smaller residences. It also implies a succession of storeys and a tower, a lofty seat or platform for spectators, a building erected on high foundations and approached by means of steps, a building consecrated to a deity, or inhabited by a prince, a temple, a palace and the assembly room and confessional hall of the Buddhist priesthood" (*Dictionary of Hindu Architecture*, Vol.I, p. 430).

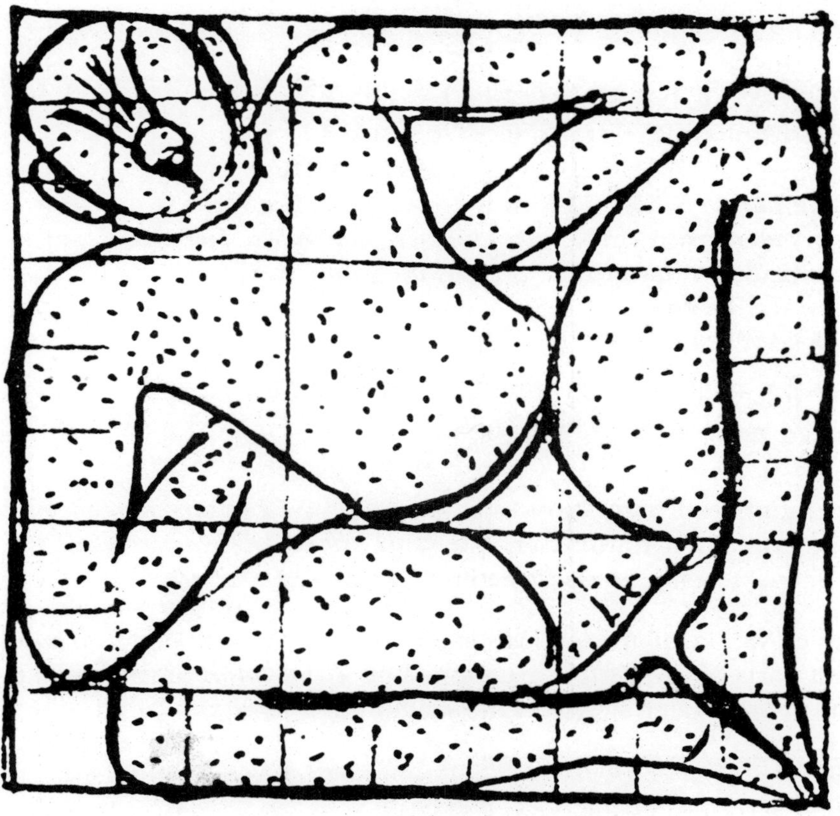

Figure 22: *Vāstupuruṣamaṇḍala*

For building both the temple and the royal palace the structures are built related to and over the magical diagram, the *vāstupuruṣamaṇḍala* (→ *puruṣa*). The palace, the treasury, the hall of justice, the wall of protection, etc. are related to the total →*vāstu* layout. The temporal power manifests through the king as well as his abode to bestow benediction to the subjects, hence the term *prāsāda*.

The temple as *prāsāda*, considered the →*deha* and the main deity in the sanctum considered the →*ātmā* of the temple, are identical with the Cosmic →*Puruṣa*, the →*brahman*. God resides in the temple and is identical with it. The twofold nature of the temple as God and his abode is also derived from the Vedic thought:

> द्वे वाव ब्रह्मणो रूपे । मूर्तं चैवामूर्तं च ।
>
> BṛUp II.3.1
>
> The Supreme Brahman has two forms of existence, the formless and with form.

Puruṣa is the cosmos:

> स वा एष पुरुषः पञ्चधा पञ्चात्मा येन सर्वमिदं प्रोतं पृथिवी चान्तरिक्षं च द्यौश्च दिशश्चावान्तरदिशाश्च सर्वैः सर्वमिदं जगत् .... ।
>
> MNUp XXIII.1
>
> The *puruṣa* is fivefold with five souls, by whom all this universe is pervaded; earth, midspace, heaven, the space directions and intermediate quarters. He is verily the whole world.

Puruṣa is identical with body castle:

> ऊर्ध्वो नु सृष्टास्तिर्यङ् नुसृष्टाः सर्वा दिशः पुरुष आ बभूवाँ ।
> पुरं यो ब्रह्मणो वेद यस्याः पुरुष उच्यते ॥
>
> AV X.2.28
>
> Stationed on high, *puruṣa* has pervaded all regions, spread aloft and stretched transversely. He who knows Brahma's castle, yea, the fort whence *puruṣa* is named. (Tr. R.T.H. Griffith)

The elevation of the *prāsāda* is also likened to the body of *puruṣa* and different parts of the temple are named after the limbs of the body, the soul being the consecrated image in the sanctum (→ *puruṣa*).

> पुरं प्रधानमित्युक्तं प्रपञ्चानेकसंकुलम् ।
> तत्पुरं पोषयेद्यस्मात् तस्माद्वै पुरुषः स्मृतः ॥
>
> SvT XI.101

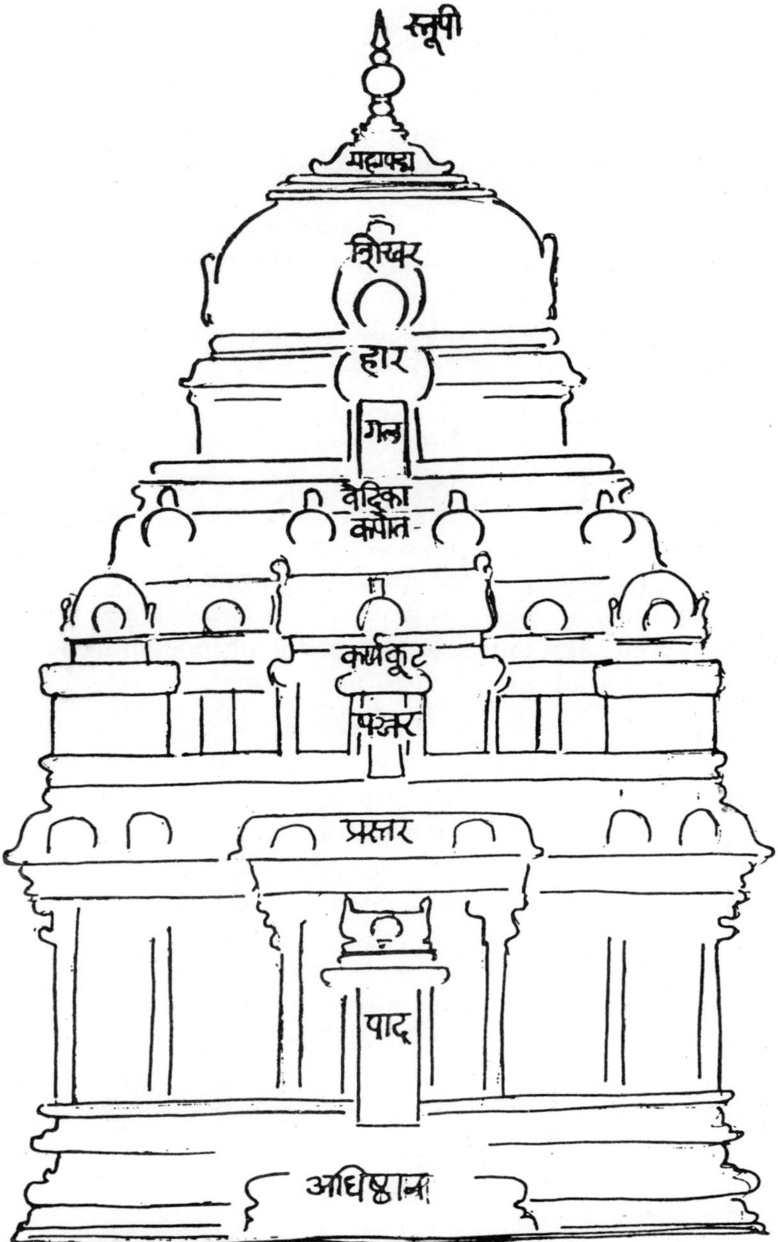

पाद अधिष्ठान

Figure 23: Temple as *prāsāda*

Pura is the *pradhāna,* which is possessed of multifarious manifestations. As it nourishes this form of *pura* (abode), it is called *puruṣa.*

पञ्चीकृतभूतकार्यसमष्टिस्थूलशरीरोपहितो विराट् पुरुष इति ।

SiddhSaṅg P. 97

Puruṣa is the supreme person or God. It is the Supreme, all pervasive Being, confined to the gross physical body.

Just as the moon has 16 digits, the *puruṣa* is also conceived as having 16 parts, *ṣoḍaśa kala puruṣa* (→ *puruṣa*). The relationship between the body and the main deity in the sanctum is like that of *śarīra* and *ātmā.* In music, *ātmā* and →*śarīra* are so intertwined that the two have not been referred to separately (→*ātman*).

"Not only the cult object (be it an image or symbol) is an abode for the luminous power for which the temple is built; after its presence is ensured by consecration rites, the entire cosmos is next invoked to come down and pervade the physical body of the temple". The cosmos may be looked upon as a single phenomenon. In a physical sense the universe; in a spiritual sense Supreme Being pervading in but also beyond matter, space and time. "The enormity of the material cosmos makes it inestimable, the profundity of its spiritual cosmos makes it imponderable and hence incomprehensible. It must then be reckoned through its parts and through its aspects" (M.A. Dhaky "*Prāsāda as Cosmos*", *The Adyar Library Bulletin,* Vol. XXXV, Pts 3–4, 1971, p. 212).

The **Parameśvara Saṃhitā** (X.3.19) sums up in a significant way the process of invoking the cosmos in the various limbs of the temple structure. It represents the seven spheres of existence (*loka*), the six paths (*adhva*), the five basic elements (*bhūta tattva*), the five rudimentary elements of cognition (*pañcatanmātra*), five instruments of cognition (*jñānendriya*), five organs of action (*karmendriya*) the →*prakṛti, puruṣa* and *para* constituting the 36 *tattvas.* For example, from the base to the foot (beginning of *adhiṣṭhāna*) represents *bhūloka*: the *adhiṣṭhāna* represents *bhuvarloka*: the end of the wall the *svarloka*: the *prastara* to the base of the *śikhara* – *maharloka*: the →*vedī* of *śikhara* – *janaloka,* the *śikhara* – *tapoloka,* and the *stūpī* culminates in *satyaloka.*

By this process the full import of the term *prāsāda* to settle down, and acquire concrete form, as the seat of God, is realised.

"The image of Śiva with five faces and ten hands or as an alternate shape with four hands is to be meditated upon as seated on a white lotus. The image corresponds to *prāsāda mantra*" (Kramrisch, *Hindu Temple,* Vol. I, p. 136. f.n. 21). The **Agni Purāṇa** holds the temple as the image of God.

प्रासादं वासुदेवस्य मूर्त्तिभेदं ... ॥

AgPur LXI.19cd

The temple is the image of Vāsudeva.

The world which is essentially of the nature of name (*nāma*) and form (→*rūpa*) is perceived through verbal form and visible colour. Both these are expressed through the word →*varṇa*, which at once stands for syllabic sound and colour. From the static form of existence, →*bindu*, the initial vibration causes the ripples of sound *nāda*, which passing through intermediate stages reach the audible stage, emanating as *oṃkāra* and splits itself into different *akṣaras*. The combination of *akṣaras* constitutes words (→*pada*), sentences (→*vākya*) and their meanings. If the *nāda* is not activated and the words constituted, the whole world will remain beyond comprehension, immersed in unfathomable darkness. The name (*nāma*) enables us to distinguish and perceive forms (*rūpa*), *akṣaras* serving as the illuminating source.

In the physical frame of the temple structure the *akṣaras*, the *padas* and *mantras* are visualised in the *adhiṣṭhāna* part. All the accumulated knowledge in the form of Āgamas, Purāṇas, Itihāsa, Darśanas and the Vedas are invoked gradually in various parts of the *prāsāda*, the *summumbonum* or Supreme Knowledge.

However, the outstanding visualisation comes from the **Chidambarakṣetra-Sarvasva** on the worship of Lord Naṭarāja, the cosmic dancer, in the temple of Chidambaram. The whole temple of Naṭarāja called *sabhā* and traditionally the centre of the universe, is graphically portrayed. Lord Naṭarāja is the culmination of Śaiva philosophy and combines in himself the essence of Vedas, Vedāṅgas, Yoga, Āgamas, Purāṇas, – the whole body of knowledge that has evolved in India through the centuries.

In the Buddhist context also the →*stūpa* or the *caitya* is said to represent Buddha himself in the *rūpakāya*.

The builder of the *prāsāda* (temple) is the *yajamāna* (sacrificer) on whose behalf the architect, guided by the priest builds the temple. Sthapati, in the **Āpastamba Śrauta-Sūtra** is designated the *yajamāna*, the sacrificer, who is to be consecrated as a priest. Throughout the history, building of and worship in a temple was likened to a Vedic sacrifice. The science of architecture is considered a part of Veda, Vāstū-Śāstra Veda. "Vāstu-Śāstra in its fullest exposition belongs to Tantra which is the applied knowledge of the **Atharvaveda**. As a ritual, architecture is moreover doubly linked with the primordial knowledge, the Veda, and is included in two of the six Vedāṅgas. These are appendices which are auxiliary to the Veda. The fifth Vedāṅga astronomy-astrology, Jyotiṣa, and the sixth Vedāṅga Kalpa, in which are laid down the rules of the sacrificial acts, the ritual are both, in parts, essential constituents of the science of Indian architecture. The Śulva-Sūtras contained in the Kalpa-Sūtras, represent the rules and give proportionate measurement for laying out and piling up the Vedic altar. On them basically rests the building of the Hindu temple" (Kramrisch, *Hindu Temple*, Vol. I, p. 11). Tantra, which includes Vāstu-Śāstra, is an *upaveda* attached to the **Atharvaveda**. The **Bṛhat Saṃhitā** (LV.2) referring to the object of building a temple states "Let him who wishes to enter the worlds that are reached by sacrificial offerings and the performance of religious obligations (*iṣṭāpūrta*) build a temple to the gods, by doing which he attains both the results of sacrifice and the performance of religious obligations. .... The sacrificial offerings secure for the sacrificer a place in heaven (*svarga*) according to the merit of his sacrifice. The *yajamāna*, the sacrificer is the donor of temple" (*Hindu Temple*, Vol. I, p. 139).

Bhṛgu speaks of three kinds of worship, *mānasapūjā, homapūjā* and *berapūjā*, i.e. mental worship, fire worship and image worship respectively.

मानसी होमपूजा च बेरपूजेति सा त्रिधा ॥
हृदये हृदयेशानं जगदीशं परात्परम् ।
ध्यात्वा तु हृदयान्तस्थं हेमवर्णमजं विभुम् ॥
तद्गतेनैव मनसा नैरन्तर्येण चिन्तयेत् ।
ध्यात्वैवं चिन्तयेद् देवं सा पूजा मानसी स्मृता ॥
अग्नीनाधाय विधिवदध्वरेषु द्विजादिभिः ।
इज्यते यज्ञपुरुषः सर्वदेवमयो हरिः ॥
यो यज्ञरूपी तस्यार्चा होमपूजेति कथ्यते ।
कृत्वा यत्प्रतिमां विष्णोः यथालक्षणमादरात् ॥
संस्थाप्य तान्तु विधिना देवागारे तु वेश्मनि ।
नित्ये आराधनं भक्त्या सा पूजा बेरपूजनम् ॥

BhṛSam I.16cd–21

The Supreme, the Lord of the universe, the omnipresent, omnipotent Lord, golden in colour should be meditated in the heart. He should be ever meditated with single-pointed devotion and with the mind always fixed on him. Such a worship is called *mānasa pūjā*.

Bringing the fire duly and offering sacrifice by the *dvijas* to Hari, the embodiment of all gods, as enjoined in the texts, and adoring him as the *yajñapuruṣa* is called *homapūjā*.

Making an image of Viṣṇu with all details and measurements and consecrating it duly in temple and worshipping it daily with devotion is called *berapūjā* or image worship.

तदाराधनं द्विविधममूर्तं समूर्तमिति । अग्नौ हुतममूर्तं प्रतिमाराधनं समूर्तं तच्छ्रेष्ठम् । यजमानाभावे अविच्छिन्नं भवति । तद्विमानार्चनं सर्वक्रतुफलप्रदं सर्वकामप्रदं च इति ब्रह्मा च आशंसत् ।

MarSam 1, p. 5

Worship is of two forms, formless worship and worship of form. Worship to fire is formless; and worship of an image is image worship. The latter is superior for even in the absence of the *yajamāna*, it is in perpetual continuity. It bestows the benefits of all the sacrifices and fulfils all desires.

That the Vāstu texts are called Vedas, and the Āgamas are divided into four parts as *caryā*, →*kriyā*, →*yoga* and →*vidyā* on the analogy of the four Vedas and that the worship in temples is held identical with Vedic sacrifices, tend to show that the concept of temple and its worship is only a linear extension of the Vedic cult of sacrifice. It is against this background that the terminology *jagatī*, *vedikā* and *stūpikā* employed as the names of temple parts and the terms *prāsāda*, *sadma*, *harmya*, etc. denote both the Vedic altar and the temple.

One type of the Vedic altar is prescribed to be made of rhythms only (*chandaściti*) and not of bricks which are their representative. In the case of *chandaściti* only →*mantras* are recited but the bricks are not actually laid. The *agnicit*, builder of fire altar, draws *agni* on the ground in the prescribed shape. He then goes through the whole prescribed process of construction imagining all the while that he is placing every brick in its proper place. The imagery created by the hymnal invocation is called the *mantramūrti* or *mantrarūpa* or *mantratanu*. In temple worship, in addition to the worship of various limbs of the physical temple, like *adhiṣṭhāna*, →*vedī*, etc. the philosophical import of each and every limb is also invoked daily during the *pūjā* through hymns, which is considered the *vidyādeha*, i.e. the body of knowledge. It thus leads one from physical to metaphysical level of the *prāsāda*, a knowledge of which is absolutely essential for the worshipper.

One of the important rites of the *prāsāda-pūjana* is to bring into manifestation, i.e. '*āvāhana*' of the supreme image. According to Āgamas, the term *āvāhana* is employed in the sense of establishing a relationship of worship between the devotee and the cosmic self. The *āvāhana* is done either by the process of creation – *sṛṣṭikrama*, or the process of dissolution *saṃhārakrama*. The process of creation *sṛṣṭikrama* begins from the *stūpī* and descends gradually to the *adhiṣṭhāna* while the process of dissolution, moves upwards from the *adhiṣṭhāna* to *stūpī*. Temple worship has the physical and metaphysical process, the latter is essentially based on the *yoga* system of Patañjali. It consists of raising the primordial energy, from its stationery seat (the *mūlādhāra*) to the *sahasrāra*, the thousand petalled lotus *mahāpadma* to unite with the cosmic existence. The number thousand stands for the unlimited circle. The *mahāpadma* on top of the *śikhara*, stands for *parabindu* identical with *śivatattva*. It is the supreme →*śakti*. The *mahāpadma* pours down immortality (*amṛtadhārā*).

In the Śaiva tradition the temple as *prāsāda* is classified into two categories: gross and subtle, i.e. the *sthūla* and *sūkṣma*. The entire temple (*prāsāda*) from the base to the *stūpī* is conceived as the very →*liṅga*–form of Śiva. At one level *prāsāda* is the *sthūla liṅga* and the *liṅga* inside the sanctum is considered the subtle *liṅga* identical with Sadāśiva. In this process, the visualisation proceeds from the external gross form to the subtle form enshrined in the innermost sanctum. Conversely, the innermost *liṅga* at another level is considered Śiva form expanding to the *vimāna prāsāda*, where it manifests as the Supreme Sadāśiva.

A different classification at three levels is provided in the case of *prāsāda mantra*. The *prāsāda mantra*, which in essence is *nāda*, manifests as →*sthūla*, *sūkṣma* and *para*, with three forms as *hrasva* (short), *dīrgha* (long) and *pluta* (prolated). The short destroys the sins, the long gives *mokṣa* and the prolated *sthūla* is called →*śabda*. Unmanifest but arising in consciousness state, the sound (the *cintāmaya*) is subtle, while the sound in its subtlest form, beyond the thinking process, is called *para*. One who does not understand this *prāsāda mantra*, cannot comprehend the nature of Śiva, who comprises the thirty six →*kalās*.

In the Kashmir Śaiva tradition *prāsāda* is a technical term. "It is the name of the *mantra* '*sauḥ*'. It contains within itself the entire panorama of manifestation. This *mantra* is formed by *s+au+ḥ*. The first letter '*s*' represents *sat* or existence from the earth up to *māyā* (the 31 *tattvas* of the Śaiva philosophy).... *Au* represents *Śuddhavidyā*, *Īśvara* and *Sadāśiva* who are full of →*jñāna* and *kriyā*. Now remains *visarga* (:). The upper dot of the *visarga* represents Śiva and the lower dot represents Śakti. Thus '*sauḥ*' represents all the 36 →*tattvas*. It refers to Paramaśiva who is the *fons et origo* of the entire world process. This *mantra* is known as *hṛdaya bīja* – the heart seed of Śiva. He who can enter into the spirit of this *mantra* will be identified with the supreme 'I' consciousness and will be liberated" (Jaideva Singh, *Śiva Sūtras*, 1982, pp. 84–85).

In the Śākta tradition, the →*yantra*, the mystic diagram is the equivalent of *prāsāda* in all its aspects. The meaning of the term *yantra* has been expanded to refer to religious enterprises and has acquired a special theological significance. "Mystic *yantras* are aids to and the chief instruments of meditative discipline. The *yantras* are an amalgam of three principles. *Ākṛti rūpa* – the form principle; the *kriyā rūpa* – the function principle; and the *śakti rūpa* - - the power principle. *Ākṛti rūpa* refers to inner or hidden form of structures.

The *kriyā rūpa* functions as revelatory symbol of cosmic truths and as instructional chart of the spiritual aspect of human experience. The *yantra*, by constant ritual worship, is said to move beyond form and function, and emerges as a power diagram, to transform a mundane experience into a psychic one. Every →*yantra* is a sacred enclosure, a dwelling or receptacle of Iṣṭadevatā" (Madhu Khanna *Yantra*: *The Tantric Symbol of Cosmic Unity*, London, 1979, pp. 11–12). The *yantra* is a significant abstraction, enshrining in itself all concepts and functions of a *prāsāda*. "The relationship of *yantra* and architecture is especially close in monuments which may be called →*maṇḍalas* in stone. A striking example is the Buddhist Barabadur →*stūpa* (8th century) in Indone-

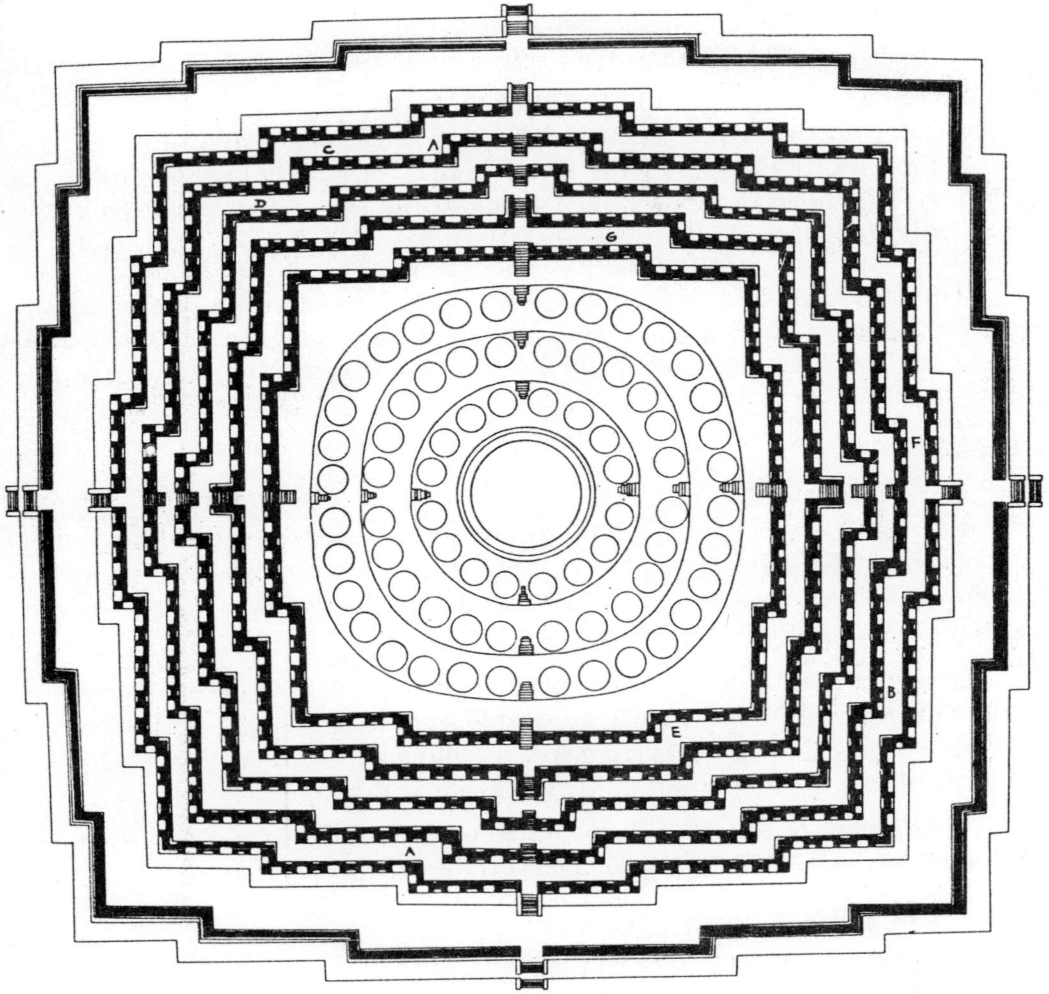

Figure 24: Buddhist Barabadur *stūpa*

sia, which rises like a terraced mountain with nine levels corresponding to the nine circuits of the *śrī yantra*" (*Yantra* – 148). The *yantra* is inherent in the *prāsāda*, in the *vāstu-puruṣa-maṇḍala*. The diagram as a planned site of the *prāsāda* precedes its erection. The *prāsāda* is directly related to and proportionate to the structure that arises. It is like the →*vedī*, sacred ground measured out for the sacrifices (*yajña*) (ṚV VIII.19.18).

एतद् यन्त्रानुसारेण कुर्यात्प्रासादमुत्तमम् ।

ŚiPrak II.73ab

The best temple has to be built in accordance with the form of this *yantra*. (Tr. A. Boner)

तन्त्रपीठे यन्त्रगर्भा प्रासाद सुमनो महत् ।
कल्पान्तयुगपर्यन्तं ध्रुवं कीर्तिः स्थिरा भवेत् ॥

ŚiPrak II.706

The Tantric temple (*tantra-pīṭha*) with a *garbha* made according to the (appropriate) *yantra* is always grand. Such a monument will certainly stand unmoved till the end of the last *yuga* of the *kalpa*. (Tr. A. Boner)

The Śākta tradition of identification of the devotee's body as the →*pīṭha* or the abode of the supreme, corresponds to the *antaryāga* of the Āgamas and is an invariable concomitant of the *prāsāda-pūjana* of all Indian systems.

Classification

The *devaprāsādas* – temples are differently classified, based on their plan, elevation, shape, size, architectural embellishment, proportionate measurements, material, consecrated deities, manifestation of deities and also the benefit they confer on the devotees.

From the square, which is the fundamental form of Indian architecture and which is considered the shape of the *vāstu* for gods, are derived other forms like circular, apsidal, rectangular, elliptical, hexagonal or octagonal that constitute the first criterion of classification of temples.

Accordingly, most of the South Indian texts classify the *prāsādas* into three fundamental categories as *nāgara, drāviḍa* and *vesara*. The **Mānasāra** states:

वेदाश्रं नागरं प्रोक्तं वस्वश्रं द्राविडं भवेत् ।
सुवृत्तं वेसरं प्रोक्तं चान्ध्रं स्यात्तु षडश्रकम् ॥

MāSā XLIII, 124–125

The square chariots are called *nāgara*, the octagonal ones *drāviḍa*, the circular ones *vesara*, and the hexagonal ones *āndhra*.
(Tr. P.K. Acharya)

The **Mānasāra** names *prāsāda*, square or rectangle from base to the *śikhara* as *nāgara*, the octagonal from the base or from above the neck as *drāviḍa* and that which is circular from the neck as *vesara*. Other texts like the **Tantrasamuccaya** and **Marīci Saṃhitā** mention only the square form of *harmya*, which is treated as a synonym of *prāsāda*, as *nāgara*, circular as *vesara* and the octagonal as *drāviḍa*.

The **Kāmikāgama** assigns the *nāgara* temple to the country from the Himalayas to the Vindhyas, *vesara* from the Vindhyas to the river Krishna and *drāviḍa* from the Krishna to Kanyakumari, thus indicating a geographical distribution. This division is only a convenient device to understand the forms and are neither strictly applicable nor exclusive to any regions, as all forms are noticed in all the regions.

Five basic shapes, viz. square, circular, octagonal, rectangular and elliptical are the plans of the *vimānas* on which the gods travel in the air. Brahmā travels in the *vimāna* called the *virāja*, square in shape; Śiva travels in Kailāśa, circular in shape. Puṣpaka is a rectangular *vimāna*, on which Kubera travels. Varuṇa travels on the Maṇika (elliptical) and Indra on Triviṣṭapa, which is octagonal in shape. From these five *vimāna* shapes, a number of sub-varieties of temples have evolved, different texts giving differing lists. For example, the **Samarāṅgaṇa-Sūtradhāra** mentions twenty four varieties of temple structures evolved from *vairāja vimāna* (square) and ten each from Kailāśa, Puṣpaka, Maṇika and Triviṣṭapa listing sixty four varieties. The **Garuḍa** and **Agni Purāṇas** list nine varieties under each *vimāna* shape, making a total of forty five.

A different classification based on the plan or shape of the *vimāna* refers to the square shape as masculine (*puruṣa*), and the rectangular as feminine (*strī*). Though this classification as →*puruṣa* and *strī* is based essentially on the shape of the buildings, some texts state that male gods should be installed in *puruṣa* temples and female gods enshrined in the *strī* type temples. However, all deities could be installed in *strī* type temples according to the same source.

The next important factor taken into account for classifying *prāsādas* is the measurement – the variations in measuring rods and the proportionate measurements. The proportionate measurements are based on the relation of the height of the *prāsāda* to the length or breadth of its base. It is relevant to mention the *sthānaka, āsīna* and *śayāna* types of temples, so called from the units of measure. If the height of the temple is taken as the unit of measure for building the structure it is called the *sthānaka prāsāda* (standing); when the length of the base is the unit of measure it is called the *āsīna* (seated) type and if based on its breadth it is called *śayāna* type (reclining). The terms *sthānaka, āsīna* and *śayāna* according to some schools, are also given to the buildings depending upon the posture of the idol installed – standing, seated and reclining. The *sthānaka, āsīna* and *śayāna* types of structures, according to the **Mānasāra** are also called *asañcita, sañcita* and *apasañcita* respectively.

The other factor that determines the classification is the variant *adhiṣṭhāna* – base. Different types of *adhiṣṭhāna*s are mentioned in different texts. The **Marīci Saṃhitā**, for example speaks of eight kinds of *adhiṣṭhāna*s of which *pādabandha, padmabandha, pratibandha* and *kapotabandha* are the most common. The **Mayamata** gives fourteen types of *adhiṣṭhāna*s. The **Śaivāgama-**

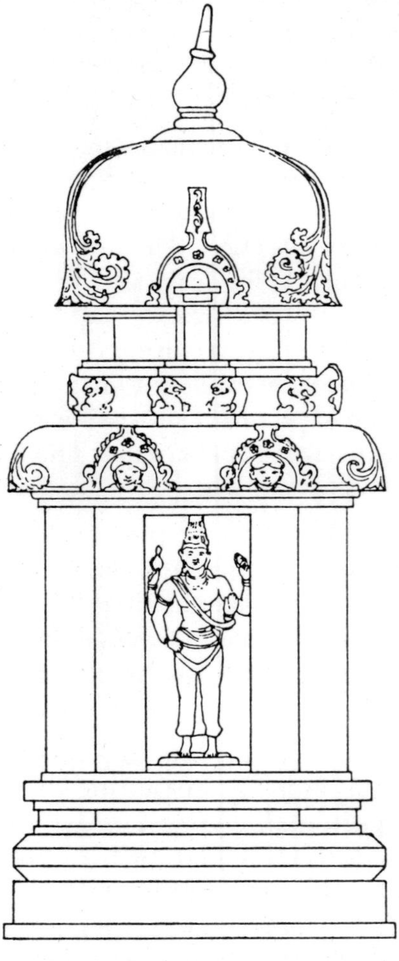

Figure 25: Cave temples, Mamallapuram

Paribhāṣā Mañjarī relates the standing, seated or reclining types of *prāsādas* to varying forms of *adhiṣṭhānas*.

The piled up structure over the sanctum resembling mountain, has attracted the names of the lofty mountains, Meru, Kailāsa and Mandāra, venerated for centuries. "Meru, Mandāra and Kailāsa are the first three names amongst the twenty types of temples described in the early texts, the **Bṛhat Saṃhitā** and the **Matsya Purāṇa**; all three are the names of the Mountain, which is the axis of the world; that is Meru, the pole of this earth; Mandāra as churning rod, planted on Viṣṇu, the tortoise, during the Satya Yuga, the first world age after the great commotion; and Kailāsa, as seat of Śiva, in the Himalaya. In these names, rises the temple, the image, aim and destination of this world edifice. To serve this image, various architectural forms such as the curvilinear Tabernacle having paraboloid lateral surfaces, the pyramid, dome and roof shapes, are employed. Their possibilities are exploited and yield a monumental unit. Their forms are developed logically; they are, moreover combined and indefinitely varied" (Kramrisch, *Hindu Temple*, Vol. I, p. 161).

Inscriptions extol eloquently the temple of Sūrya built in 437–438 A.D.; its lofty spires resembling a mountain. The Gaṅgādhara stone inscription of Viśvavarman, speaks of a temple of Viṣṇu (*viṣṇu-sthāna*) resembling the lofty peak of Kailāsa which is Śiva's mountain but in this instance represents the world mountain. The Pallava ruler Rājasiṃha equates one of the excavated cave temples at Mamallapuram to Kailāsa and Mandāra on account of its sanctity. The Bṛhadīśvara temple (Tanjore), the biggest temple ever to be built in South India by Rājarāja Chola (ca 1000 A.D.) is called by the builder in his inscriptions as *dakṣiṇa meru* (the Southern Meru).

The measurements and the number of storeys for each type of this class vary from text to text. The **Matsya Purāṇa** describing the architectural details of this *prāsāda* states that the *meru* type will have hundred *śṛṅgas* (cupolas), sixteen storeys and should be fifty cubits broad. Interestingly, the Tanjore temple has sixteen storeys. The *mandāra* type will have twelve storeys and Kailāsa nine storeys. The **Bhaviṣya Purāṇa**, on the other hand, stipulates twelve storeys for *meru*, ten for *mandāra* and eight storeys for Kailāsa.

The number of storeys, the distribution of the various architectural elements, and the shape of the *śikhara* also govern the class and nomenclature of the *prāsādas*.

The 5th *adhyāya* of the **Viśvakarmā Prakāśa**, cited in the **Śabdakalpadruma** mentions twenty different varieties of *vimānas* based on their elevation. About the *meru prāsāda* the following reference is pertinent:

शतशृङ्गश्चतुर्द्वारो भूमिकाषोडशोच्छ्रितः ।

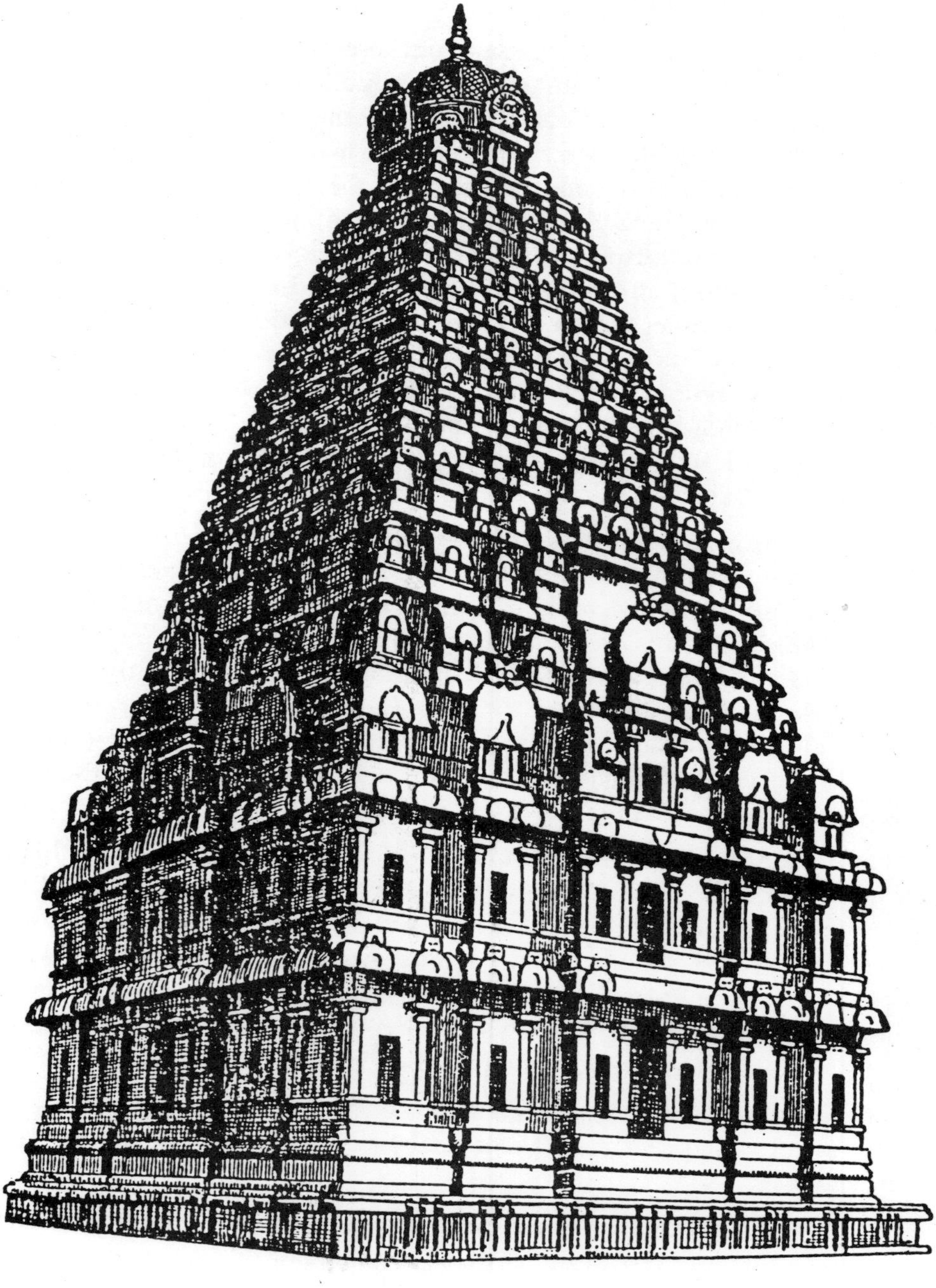

Figure 26: Bṛhadīśvara temple, Tanjore

नानाविचित्रशिखरो मेरुप्रासाद उच्यते ॥

ŚaKal part III, p. 366

(A temple) with four doors, hundred *śṛṅgas*, multiple extraordinary *śikharas*, sixteen storeys high, is called *meru prāsāda.*

The **Mānasāra** mentions hundred varieties of temples based on the number of storeys – from one to twelve. In each temple storey, a number of subvarieties are recognized. The **Marīci Saṃhitā** lists ninety six types of *vimānas.* An interesting 8th century Sanskrit text **Avantisundarī Kathā** speaks of an architect well versed in ninety six types of *prāsādas.*

वास्तुविस्तार-षण्णवति-प्रासाद-विधि-विशारदः ।

AvK p. 9

He (Lalitālaya the *sthapati* who repaired the Viṣṇu Temple at Māmallapuram) was an expert in erecting ninety six types of expansive *prāsādas.*

Another factor taken into consideration for classifying *prāsādas* is the material with which the building is erected. Stone, brick, mud, metal and wood are the materials prescribed for construction. When one material is made use of throughout the building, it is called the *śuddha prāsāda* (also *asañcita*); when two materials are used, it is called *miśra* (also *sañcita*) and more than two materials give the building the name *saṅkīrṇa* (also *upasañcita*).

Other technical terms used to denote different categories of *prāsāda* are:

i) *arpita* and *anarpita* – the former without verandahs or passages in the storeys, and the latter with built up verandahs,

ii) *sāndhāra* or *nirandhāra* – the former denoting a temple, whose sanctum enclosure is built of two walls with an intervening space (ambulatory), and the latter without an ambulatory,

iii) small temple as *alpa prāsādas* and magnificent temples as *mahā prāsādas.*

Realising the infinite varieties of *prāsādas*, that could be built and on the basis of various factors mentioned above, a number of texts state that it is impossible to give an exhaustive list but only a few varieties are mentioned and discussed by them.

Prāsāda in Architecture

The *prāsāda* generally consists in the Southern tradition of six limbs called *ṣaḍaṅgas*, represented by *adhiṣṭhāna* (base), *bhitti* (wall), *prastāra* (entablature), *grīvā* (neck), *śikhara* (crowning roof), and *stūpī* (final). Some temples of the *alpa prāsāda* varieties have only four main limbs and are called *caturaṅga vimānas*. The Vaisanavite texts like the **Marīci Saṃhitā** add another variety-namely *aṣṭāṅgavimāna* with eight *aṅgas*, including two additional sanctums over the main or the ground floor. The three-storeyed *vimāna*, having a sanctum in each storey, is designated *aṣṭāṅgavimāna.*

The different names given to each element of the *aṅgas* are tailed in Vāstu texts. The *adhiṣṭhāna* consists of the *khura, jagatī* and *kumuda* in the Southern tradition. The uppermost moulding varies and is called *paṭṭikā, prati* or *kapota.* The *adhiṣṭhāna* is the platform over which the temple rises. Occasionally, a sub-base called *upapīṭha* is introduced to raise the height of the temple with a view to add majesty and beauty. *Adhiṣṭhāna* is classified under various denominations on the basis of difference in the dimensions of its mouldings, or the presence or absence of one or the other of its mouldings.

The names given to various mouldings of the *adhiṣṭhāna* differ between North and South India. The *adhiṣṭhāna* is the seat or altar from which the superstructure of the temple, equivalent to the fire emanating from the Vedic altar, rises. In the North, the *vedībandha* or the *adhiṣṭhāna* consists normally of *khura – kumbha, kalaśa* and *kapota* mouldings, and is generally more ornate than in the South.

Over the *adhiṣṭhāna* rises the main wall of the *garbhagṛha* called →*stambha* or *bhitti.* It begins in the South with the part called *vedikā,* equal to the →*vedī* of the Vedic altar. The sanctum, the enclosed space in the *garbhagṛha,* is the womb of the higher self wherein is enshrined the Supreme Divinity. It is the innermost chamber, the *guhā,* the special abode of the deity, likened to the heart. Though the entire *prāsāda* is the body of the Supreme Divinity, the *garbhagṛha* is the centre of manifestation.

The walls of the *prāsāda* are usually divided on the vertical axis by pilasters and pilaster-framed niches, housing images of deities. The vertical lines break the horizontality of the *adhiṣṭhāna* and the plain surface of the walls. This vertical surge is continued in the curvilinear *śikhara,* up to the *āmalasāraka* resulting in the soaring height of the North Indian *śikhara.* In the South, the *prastāra* over the *bhitti,* converts the upward movement into horizontality to yield as the base for pyramidal superstructure for which the South had a fascination.

"The upper portion of the massive pile of the superstructure; above it (*vedī*) are the *āmalaka* or the High Temple and the finial above these. The Vedic altar survives in the structure of the body of the temple in its lowest and its highest part" (Kramrisch, *Hindu Temple,* Vol. I, p. 147).

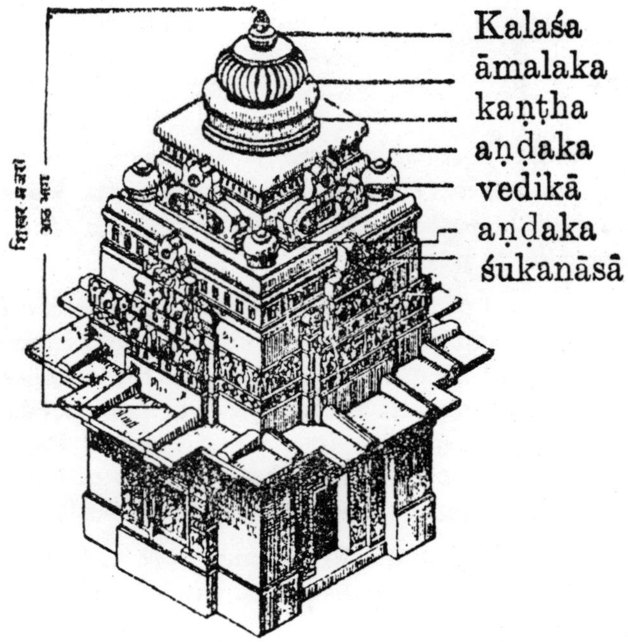

Figure 27: *Śikhara*, Deogarh

Prastāra is essentially the spread over the wall and denotes the joist, the cornice and a row of carved stones, virtually acting as the seat for the *vimāna*, to rise. →*Prastāra* means a couch of leaves or flowers, a bunch of *darbha* grass or flat surface on top. In the *prāsāda*, the architectural element above the wall is called *prastāra*, as it (a) tops the wall, (b) acts as a seat like the spread of *darbha* grass in Vedic sacrifices.

Above the *prastāra* rises the *śikhara* like the peak of the mountain. The superstructure is called *vimāna* in some texts, while other traditions hold the entire superstructure from *adhiṣṭhāna* to *stūpī* as *vimāna*.

In the North Indian tradition the entire superstructure is called *śikhara* whereas in the South, the part above the *grīvā* goes by that name. The shape of the *śikhara* governs the classification of the *prāsāda* in the South. In the North the *śikhara* is crowned by *āmalasāraka* in the shape of a cogged wheel. In the South the *śikhara* is topped by *mahāpadma*, the great lotus. The *stūpī* consisting of a →*kalaśa*, capped by a pointed bud, is the final element all over India.

The *stūpī* is the *pūrṇakalaśa*, the symbol of eternity and represents the overflowing immortality. The nectar overflowing from the *stūpī* falls on the thousand-petalled *mahā-padma* and trickles down the whole body of the temple structure and reaches the spectator-devotee.

Prāsāda as Stūpa

In Vedic literature, →*stūpa* represents 'the raised lock of hair', or 'the forepart of the head'. In the **Ṛgveda, Taittirīya Saṃhitā, Vājasaneyi Saṃhitā, Atharvaveda** and the **Śatapatha Brāhmaṇa**, the word *stūpa* occurs in the above sense (*Vedic Index*, Vol. II, p. 483).

Two types of disposal of the dead that were known to the Ṛgvedic people are the burial and cremation. Raising a mound over the burial, and also at the site where cremation used to take place were the established customs in the Vedic period. The **Śatapatha Brāhmaṇa** even distinguishes two forms of such mounds, the square for the *devatās* and circular for the *asuras*. The **Atharvaveda** frequently mentions the memorial erected for the dead– "Let these *gṛhāsaḥ* be a refuge for him for ever" (AV XVIII.3.51).

By the time of the **Śatapatha Brāhmaṇa**, *stūpa* came to be erected, to commemorate the place of a *mahāpuruṣa* as a memorial after his death. The commemorative function of the *stūpa* had been adopted by the Buddhists as seen from the **Stūpāvadāna, Mahāvadāna** and **Avadānaśataka.**

> चातुमहापथे रञ्ञो चक्कवत्तिस्स थूपं करोन्ति । एवं खो, आनन्द, रञ्ञो चक्कवत्तिस्स सरीरे पटिपज्जन्ति । यथा खो, आनन्द, रञ्ञो चक्कवत्तिस्स सरीरे पटिपज्जन्ति, एवं तथागतस्स सरीरे पटिपज्जितब्बं । चातुमहापथे तथागतस्स थूपो कातब्बो । तत्थ ये मालं वा गन्धं वा चुण्णकं वा आरोपेस्सन्ति वा अभिवादेस्सन्ति वा चित्तं वा पसादेस्सन्ति तेसं तं भविस्सति दीघरत्तं हिताय सुखाय ।
>
> DīghNik II.142 (P.T.S.)
>
> At the meeting of four ways a *stūpa* is raised for the universal monarch. So is it done, Ānanda, with the body of a universal monarch. And even, Ānanda, as with body of a universal monarch, so should it be done with the body of the Tathāgatas and at the meeting of four ways also a *stūpa* should be raised for the Tathāgata. And whosoever shall bring to that place garlands or incense or sandal (paste), or pay reverence, and whose mind becomes calm there to his weal and happiness will it be, for a long time. (Tr. Sister Vajira)

In the Buddhist sculptures of Sanchi the king, nobles and the common men are seen offering worship to *stūpa*. There were many *stūpas* which were

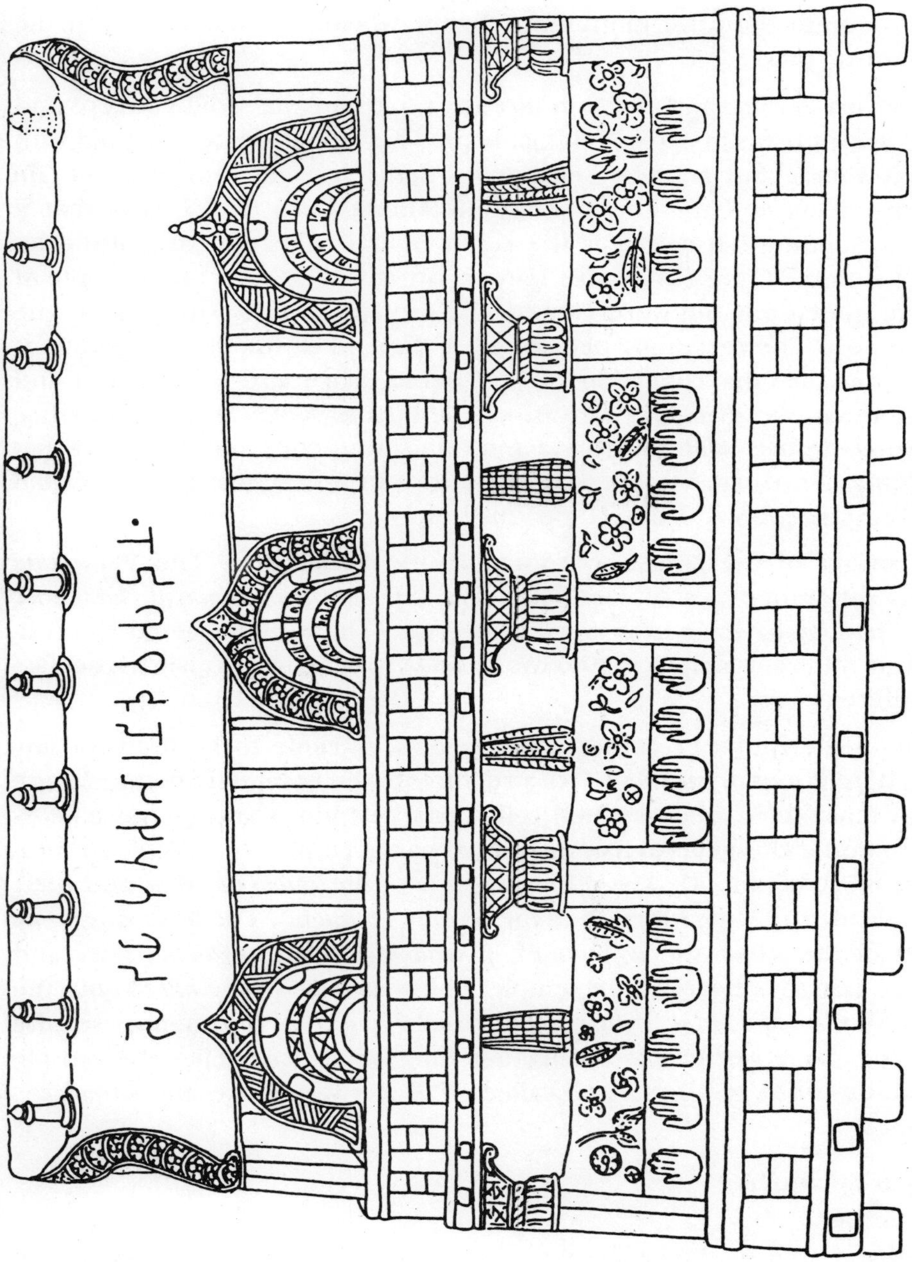

Figure 28: *Prāsāda* as *stūpa*

erected not only over the remains of the dead, but also as dedicatory structures to the celestial or the historical Buddha. That, even the Jainas held the *stūpa* as a commemorative monument, fit for worship, is mentioned in the **Rāyapasenīya-Sutta**.

The terms →*stūpa* and *caitya* in essence represent the same concept and are used as synonyms in early Buddhist texts. They are also interchanged with the words *harmya* and *prāsāda*. The word *caitya* is derived from the root '*cin̄ cayane*' to collect and the commentary on **Amara Kośa** (II.2.7) says that it denotes a building because it is the result of the collection or putting together of stones. "*Cīyate pāṣāṇādīna caityam.* But it will be seen that in some of the above quotations the word is used in close connection with →*yūpa*, the sacrificial post. The ceremony performed at the end of the great sacrifices is called *cayana*, i.e. the collection of the sacred ashes and other relics and grouping them into form of a tortoise or the bird *garudmat* as in the sacrifice called *garuḍacayana*; *cita* being the sacred things thus collected it appears that the building constructed to preserve them for purpose of worship was called *caitya*" (Burgess, *J.A.S.B.*, Vol. VII, pp. 20–21).

The origin of the *prāsāda* is rooted in the Vedic altar. The **Yajurveda** mentions different types of sacrificial *citis*, viz. *caturasra śyenaciti, kaṅkaciti, alagaciti, praugaciti, rathacakraciti, droṇaciti,* etc. These altars could be constructed in different shapes. Baudhāyana and Āpastamba furnish particulars about different *citis*.

Later in the Buddhist context, the term *caitya* came to be used for any building of religious monument. "All structures of the nature of sanctuaries are *caityas* so that sacred trees, statues, religious inscriptions and sacred palaces come also under this general name" (P.K. Acharya, *Dictionary of Hindu Architecture*, Vol. VI, p. 68, f.n. 4). The different parts of the *caitya* or *stūpa* and their names indicate the same function as the temple (*prāsāda*). The following basic elements of the *stūpa*, the *adhovedikā, jaṅghāvedī, aṇḍa,* →*garbha, grīvā* and *harmya* are akin to the parts of the temple. The *adho-vedikā* is the *adhiṣṭhāna*; the *jaṅghāvedī* is the *vedībandha* from which the wall (*jaṅghā*) of the temple rises, the *aṇḍa* is the main *garbha-gṛha* enshrining the *dhātugarbha*. Like the temple (*prāsāda*), the *stūpa*, too, has a part called *grīvā* over which rises the *harmikā*.

Prāsāda in Epigraphs

Prāsāda is used in the epigraphs in the sense of both royal mansion and temple. Other terms employed in epigraphs for a temple are →*āyatana, devāyatana, sahasrāyatana, bhavana, ālaya, āvāsa, harmya, guhā, mandira, mandiragṛha, devakula,* →*vāstu, vimāna* and *jātivimāna*.

Below are mentioned a few epigraphs which use *prāsāda* in the sense of temple:

1. A Bharhut Inscription refers to the *prāsāda* of Indra designated as *vaijayanta vejanto pasade* (*Indian Antiquary*, Vol. XXI, p. 233).

2. एष भगवतो वराहमूर्त्तेर्जगत्पारायणस्य-नारायणस्य
शिला-प्रासादः स्वविषयेऽस्मिन् ऐरिकिणे कारितः ।
Eraṇ Stone Ins of Toramāṇa (Corpus Inscriptimum Indicarum, Vol. III, F.G.I. No. 36, p. 160)
This stone temple of the divine Nārāyaṇa who has the form of a Boar (and) is devoted to the welfare of the universe, has been caused to be made in this his own *viṣaya* of Airikiṇa.

3. नानाधातुविचित्रे गोपाह्वयनाम्नि भूधरे रम्ये कारितवान्
शैलमयं भानोः प्रासादवरमुख्यम् ।
Gwalior Stone Ins of Mihirakula, *op. cit.*
Has caused to be made, on the delightful hill, which is feckled with various metals and has the appellation of Gopa, a stone temple, the chief among the finest temples of the Sun.

4. ते नोच्चैर्बोधिमण्डे शशिकरधवलः सर्व्वतो मण्डपेन ।
कान्तः प्रासाद एष स्मरबलजयिनः कारितो लोकशास्तुः ॥
Bodhgaya Ins of Mahānāman, dated A.D. 587 (C.I.I. Vol. III, F.G.I No. 71, pp. 276ff.)
By him this beautiful mansion of the Teacher of mankind, who overcame the power of Smara (god of love), dazzling white as the rays of the moon, with an open pavilion on all sides, has been caused to be made at the exalted Bodhimaṇḍa.

5. प्रासादः सुमहानयं भगवतः शौद्धोदनेः अद्भुतः ।
कैलासाभिभवेच्छयेव धवलो मन्ये समुत्थापितः ॥
Nalanda Ins of King Yaśovarman of Kanauj (A.D. 725–53) (Ep Ind, XX, pp. 37–46)
This great and wonderful temple excelling in purity and whiteness of the Kailāsa, was erected for the Buddha.

6. स प्रासादमचीकरद्दिविसदो केदारदेवस्य च ।
Gaya Ins of King Yakṣapāla (ca A.D. 1075-1085) (Ind. Ant., Vol. XVI, p. 64)
He caused to be built a temple of the inhabitants of heaven and of the god Kedāra.

7. अद्भुतः सिंहपानीय-नगरे येन कारितः ।
कीर्त्तिस्तम्भइवाभाति प्रासादः पार्व्वतीपतेः ॥

Sasbāhu Temple Ins of King Mahīpāla, Ind. Ant., Vol. XV, p. 37

In the town of Siṃhapānīya he caused to be built a wonderful temple of Śiva which shines like a column of fame.

Prāsāda in Literature

Like epigraphs, literature employs *prāsāda* more commonly in the sense of a palace or mansion than a temple.

One of the oldest examples of *prāsāda* as temple is, however, provided by the **Mahābhāṣya**:

प्रासादे धनपतिरामकेशवानाम् ।

Mahābh on Pā II.2.34

In the temple of Dhanapati (Kubera), Balarāma and Vāsudeva.

In the **Rāmāyaṇa**, *prāsāda* is used in the sense of royal palace:

अयोध्यां मन्थरा तस्मात् प्रासादादन्ववैक्षत ॥

Rām II.7.2cd

Mantharā looked at Ayodhyā from the *prāsāda.*

कैलासशिखराकारात् प्रासादादवरोहत ॥

Rām II.7.12cd

They got down from the *prāsāda,* resembling the peak of Kailāsa mountain.

At another place, **Rāmāyaṇa** considers *harmya* as part of *prāsāda.*

ततः प्रासादहर्म्याणि विमानशिखराणि च ।
अभिरुह्य जनः श्रीमानुदासीनो व्यलोकयत् ॥

Rām II.33.3

Ascending (the roofs of) temples and mansions and the tops of seven-storeyed buildings wealthy people gazed despondently on them.

Various types of *prāsādas* found in Ayodhyā, are also mentioned in the **Rāmāyaṇa** (II.100.42). The **Rāmāyaṇa** seems to indicate that a number of buildings in the royal palace complex were known by the name *prāsāda.*

भवनं राक्षसेन्द्रस्य बहुप्रासादसंकुलम् ॥

Rām V.9.2cd

The palace of Rākṣasendra – Rāvaṇa, consisted of a number of *prāsādas*.

The **Mahābhārata** alludes to lofty palaces as *prāsādas*:

ततोऽभ्रघनसंकाशं गिरिकूटमिवोच्छ्रितम् ।
श्रिया ज्वलन्तं प्रासादमारुरोह महायशाः ॥

MBh V.89.3

Then the great famed one, ascended the *prāsāda* nearing the clouds in the sky, high as the peak of a mountain, and resplendent with wealth.

The various parts and the furnishings of the palace are described graphically in the **Mahābhārata**.

सर्वतः संवृतैः शुभ्रैः प्रासादैः सुकृतोच्छ्रयैः ॥
सुवर्णजालसंवीतैर्मणिकुट्टिमभूषितैः ।
सुखारोहणसोपानैर्महासनपरिच्छदैः ॥
असंबाधशतद्वारैः शयनासनशोभितैः ।
बहुधातुपिनद्धाङ्गैः हिमवच्छिखरैरिव ॥

MBh I.176.19cd–20, 22

Surrounded all over by clean and white *prāsādas* with well articulated and embellished facades, built with golden windows, paved with jewelled floorings, provided with steps comfortable to climb and descend, and furnished with great seats, with hundred open doors, and beautified with cots, bonded with several metal plates and resembling the lofty peaks of Himalayas.

The **Mahābhārata** also distinguishes *prāsāda* and *harmya* at some instances:

अनेकविधप्रासाद-हर्म्य-वलभी-निर्यूह-शतसंकुलम् ... ।

MBh I.3.133

There were varieties of palaces (*prāsāda*) and mansions (*harmya*) comprising pinnacles (*valabhī*) and hundreds of gates (*niryūha*). (Tr. P. Ghosal)

The **Pañcatantra** refers to a seven-storeyed *prāsāda*. Kālidāsa refers to *prāsāda*, as high as reaching the sky, in the **Meghadūta** and the **Raghuvaṃśa**. The **Mṛcchakaṭika** refers to the *vedikā* of the *ārāma prāsāda* (P.K. Acharya, *A Dictionary of Hindu Architecture*, p. 423).

Prāsādikā in Music and Dance

One of the six Śravya Śabdālaṅkāras as applied to dance drama by Bhoja in his works is *dhruvā*. There are five *dhruvās*, viz. *prāveśikī, naiṣkramikī, antarā, prāsādikā* and *ākṣiptikī* and they are respectively sung at the entrance and exit of characters, and during their stay on stage. *Dhruvās* are for the purpose of informing the audience of the scene, situation and character, the mood of the character, and to provide the connecting link, etc.

In fact Bhoja derives his authority from Bharata who in his **Nāṭya-Śāstra** speaks of five kinds of singing, of what he calls *dhruvā*. They are *prāveśikī, ākṣepikā, naiṣkramikā, prāsādikī* and *antarā*. Among them *prāsādikī* is relevant to the present context.

Describing what is *prāsādikī*, Bharata says:

> या च रसान्तरमुपगतमाक्षेपवशात् कृतं प्रसादयति ।
> रागप्रसादजननीं विद्यात् प्रासादिकीं तां तु ॥
>
> NŚ XXXII.314
>
> That temperament delecting *dhruvā* (*rāga prasādajananī*) should be designated as *prāsādikī* which pleases the taste of audience (in regard to their feeling) with the aid of intervening a different *rasa*. (Tr. P. Ghosal)

Since it makes the main →*rasa* pleasant, or easily delectable (*prasādayati*), it is called *prāsādikī*.

Both Bharata and Abhinavagupta coin the word *prāsādikā* as it pleases the spectator – *prasādayati iti prāsādikī*. Bharata says that *prāsādikā* should be employed in happy moods, prayers, amorous situations and adventure.

> हर्षेऽथ प्रार्थने चैव शृङ्गाराद्भुतदर्शने ।
> ध्रुवा प्रासादिकी कार्या तज्ज्ञैर्मध्यलयाश्रया ॥
>
> NŚ XXXII.325
>
> *Prāsādikī dhruvā* should be employed by the experts in medium tempo (*madhyalayāśrayā*), in order to express ecstasy of joy, request, amorous situation or on seeing something peculiar.
> (Tr. P. Ghosal)

Conclusion

Prāsāda stands for both palace and temple, it also means a sacrificial altar (→*caitya*) and *stūpa*.

As a sacred structure, *prāsāda* has innumerable shapes, dimensions and varieties as stated in the Śilpa and Vāstu-Śāstras.

Prāsāda represents the Cosmic Puruṣa, the Cosmic Tree and the *axis mundi*.

Prāsāda enshrines →*mantra, tantra,* →*yoga* and →*jñāna* and is visulalised not only as an abode of godhood, but as the manifestation of God.

Prāsāda, in the ultimate analysis, is identical with supreme knowledge, the Upaniṣad, symbolizing identity of the individual soul with the universal soul, the Brahman.

R. Nagaswamy

Krishna Deva

Select Bibliography

Acharya, P.K.: A Dictionary of Hindu Architecture, New Delhi: Oriental Book Reprints Corporation, 1981.

Dhaky, M.A.: 'Prāsāda as Cosmos', in The Adyar Library Bulletin, Vol. XXXV, Pts 3–4, Adyar, 1971.

Khanna, Madhu: Yantra: The Tantric Symbol of Cosmic Unity, London: Thames & Hudson, 1979.

Kramrisch, Stella: The Hindu Temple, 2 Vols, Calcutta: University of Calcutta, 1946.

BIBLIOGRAPHY

A

Abhidhānacintāmaṇi Kośa of Hemacandra: ed. by H.K. Javeri, M.M. Chokasi. Surat: Jain Pustakoddhara Samstha, 1946.

Abhidharma Kośa of Vasubandhu: ed. by Swami Dvarikadas Sastri. Varanasi: Bauddha-Bharati, 1987.

— tr. into Eng. by Subhadra Jha. Patna: Kashi Prasad Jayaswal Research Institute, 1983.

Abhidharma Kośa Bhāṣya: by Louis de lavallee Poussin, tr. into Eng. by L.M. Pruden. Berkeley: Asian Humanities Press, 1988, 4 Vols.

Abhidharma Samuccaya: ed. by Prahlada Pradhan. Santiniketan: Visva Bharati, 1950.

— Le Compendium de la Super-Doctrine (Philosophie) (Abhidharmasamuccaya) d'Asaṅga, traduit et annoté par Walpola-Rahula. Paris: Ecole Française D'Extrême Orient, 1971.

Abhijñānaśākuntalam of Kālidāsa: with the Comm. Arthadyotanikā of Rāghava Bhaṭṭa, ed. by N.B. Godbole; Revised by W.L. Shastri Panasikar. Bombay: Tukaram Jawaji, Nirnayasagar Press, 6th edn, 1913.

— ed. and tr. into Eng. by M.R. Kale. Delhi: Motilal Banarsidass, 1987.

Abhilaṣitārthacintāmaṇi of Someśvara Deva: ed. by R. Samasastry. Mysore: University of Mysore, 1926.

Abhinaya Darpaṇa of Nandikeśvara: tr. into Eng. by A.K. Coomaraswamy & G.K. Duggirala. Cambridge: Harvard University press, 1917.

Adhyayanasūtra: ed.by Muni Puṇyavijaya. Jainagama Granthamala-15. Bombay: Sri Mahavir Jain Mahavidyalaya, 1977.

Āgamaprāmāṇya of Yāmunācārya: ed. by R.N. Narasimhacharya. Baroda: Baroda Oriental Institute, 1976.

Aghoraśivācāryapaddhati (Kriyākramadyotikā): with Prabhā Comm. of Nirmalamani, ed. by K. Krishna Sastri and P. Rama Sastri. Tamilnadu, 1927.

Agni Purāṇa: Ananda Ashram Sanskrit Granthavali-41. Poona: Ananda Ashram, 1957.

Āgniveśya Gṛhya Sūtra: ed. by L.A. Ravi Varma. Trivendrum Sanskrit Series-44, Trivendrum, 1940.

Ahirbudhnya Saṃhitā: ed. by M.D. Rāmānujācārya. Madras: Adyar Library, 1966.

Aitareya Āraṇyakam: with the Comm. of Sāyaṇācārya, ed. by Kashinatha Sastri. Ananda Ashram Sanskrit Granthavali-32. Poona: Ananda Ashram, 1979, 2 Vols.

— ed. and tr. into Eng. by A.B. Keith. Oxford: Oxford University, 1909.

Aitareya Brāhmaṇa of the Rigveda: ed. and tr. into Eng. by Martin Haug. London: Trubner and Co., 1863, 2 Vols.

— Rigveda Brāhmaṇa: The Aitareya and Kauṣītaki Brāhmaṇas of the Rigveda: tr. into Eng. by A.B. Keith. Harvard Oriental Series-25. Delhi: Motilal Banarsidass, 1981, Reprint.

Ajitāgama: ed. by N.R. Bhatt. Pondicherry: Institut Français d'Indologie, 1964, 1967, 2 Vols.

Amarakośa of Amarasiṃha: with Comm. of Ācārya Kṛṣṇamitra, ed. by Satyadeva Misra. Patna: Indira Prakashan, 1972.

Amṛtodaya of Gokulanātha: ed. by M.M. Sivadatta. Bombay: Nirnayasagar Press, 1897.

Anekārthasaṃgraha of Hemachandra: ed. by S.P. Jagannath Shastri Hoshing. Varanasi: Chowkhamba Sanskrit Series, 1969.

Aparājitapṛcchā of Bhuvana Deva: ed. by Popatbhai Ambashankar Mankad. Baroda: Baroda Oriental Institute, 1950.

Āpastamba Dharmasūtra: ed. by G. Bühler. Bombay Sanskrit Series-44, 50. Bombay: The Department of Public Construction, 3rd edn, 1932.

Āpastamba Gṛhyasūtra: ed. by A. Chinnaswami Sastri, and U.C. Pandey. Kashi Sanskrit Series-59. Varanasi: Chowkhamba, 1971.

Āpastamba Śrautasūtra: ed. by T.T. Srinivasagopalachary. Oriental Research Institute Publications Sanskrit Series-98. Mysore: University of Mysore, 1953, Vol. II.

— ed. by A. Srinivasaraghavacharya. Oriental Research Institute Publications Sanskrit Series-104. Mysore: University of Mysore, 1960, Vol. III.

Āpastamba Śulbasūtra: ed. by Satya Prakash and R.S. Sharma. Ratna Kumari Pub. Series-5. Delhi: Mahalakshmi Pub. House, 1968.

Arthaśāstra of Kauṭilya: ed. and tr. into Eng. by R.P. Kangle. Delhi: Motilal Banarsidass, 1986, 3 Vols.

Arthaviniścayasūtra: Patna: K.P. Jayaswal Research Institute, 1971.

Āryabhaṭīya of Āryabhaṭṭa: ed. by Kripa Shankar Shukla. New Delhi: The Indian National Science Academy, 1976.

Āryamañjuśrīmūlakalpa: ed. by M.M.T. Ganapati Sastri. Sri Satguru Publications. Delhi: Indian Books Centre, 2nd edn, 1989, 3 Vols.

Āścaryacūḍāmaṇi of Śaktibhadra: with an Introduction by S.Kuppuswami Sastri. Shri Balamanorama Series-9. Madras: Sri Balamanorama Press, 1926.

Aṣṭādhyāyī of Pāṇini: tr. into Eng. by S.M. Katre. Delhi: Motilal Banarsidass, 1987.

— ed. & tr into Eng. by S.C. Basu. Varanasi: Motilal Banarsidass, 1988.

Aṣṭaprakaraṇa: ed. by V.V. Dwivedi. Varanasi: Sampurnananda Sanskrit University, 1988.

Aṣṭasāhasrikā Prajñā Pāramitā: ed. by Rajendralal Mitra. Bibliotheca Indica, A Collection of Oriental Works. Calcutta: The Asiatic Society, 1888.

— tr. by Edward Conze. Bibliotheca Indica, A Collection of Oriental Works No.284. Calcutta: The Asiatic Society, 1970.

— Prajñāpāramitā and Related Systems: ed. by Lewis. Buddhist Studies Series. Lancaster, Berkeley, 1977.

Āśvalāyana Gṛhyasūtra: ed. and tr. into Eng. by N.N. Sharma. Delhi: Eastern Book Linkers, 1976.

Āśvalāyana Śrautasūtra: tr. into Eng. and ed. by H.G. Ranade. Ranade Publication Series-2, 4. Poona, 1981, 1986, 2 Vols.

Atharvaveda Pariśiṣṭa: ed. by J.M. Balling and J.V. Negelein, with Hindi Notes by Ram Kumar Rai. Varanasi: Chaukhamba Orientalia, 1976.

Atharvaveda Saṃhitā: ed. by Sripada Damodar Satvalekar. Paradi: Svadhyaya Mandala, 1985, 4 Vols.

— The Hymns of the Atharvaveda: tr. into Eng. by R.T.H. Griffith. The Chowkhamba Sanskrit Studies-66. Varanasi: Chowkhamba Publication, 1968, 2 Vols.

— Paippalāda Saṃhitā of the Atharvaveda: ed. by Durgamohan Bhattacharya. Calcutta: Sanskrit College, 1970.

Aṭṭhasālinī (on Dhammasaṅgaṇi): ed. by P.V. Bapat and R.D. Vadekar. Poona: Bhandarkar Oriental Research Institute, 1942.

— The Expositor: tr. into Eng. by Pe Maung Tin, ed. by Mrs. R. Davids. London: Luzac and Co. Ltd., 1958.

Aucityavicāracarcā of Kṣemendra: ed. by R.S. Tripathi. Chowkhamba Sanskrit Series. Varanasi, 1982.

Avadāna Śataka: ed. by P.L. Vaidya. Darbhanga: Mithila Institute, 1958.

Āvaśyaka Niryukti: Bhavanagar: Yasovijaya Granthamālā, w.d.

B

Baudhāyana Dharmasūtra: ed. by A. Chinnaswami Shastri. Kashi Sanskrit Series-104. Varanasi: Chowkhamba Sanskrit Sansthan, 1972.

Baudhāyana Gṛhyasūtra: ed. by R. Shamasastry. New Delhi: Meharchand Lachhmandas, 1982.

Baudhāyana Śrautasūtra: ed. by W. Caland. New Delhi: Munshiram Manoharlal, 1982, 3 Vols.

Baudhāyana Śulbasūtra: with Sanskrit Comm. by Dwarka Nath Yajvan, Eng. tr. by G. Thibaut, ed. by Satya Prakash and Ram Swarup Sharma. New Delhi: The Research Institute of Ancient Scientific Studies, 1968.

— Śulba Sūtras of Baudhāyana, Āpastamba, Kātyāyana and Mānava: ed. and tr. by S.N. Sen and A.K. Bag. New Delhi: Indian National Science Academy, 1983.

Bhagavadgītā: with Śāṅkarabhāṣya. Gorakhpur: Gita Press, 1967.

— with Commentaries ed. by W.L.S. Panasikar. Varanasi: Indological Book House, 1984.

— with Sarvatobhadra Comm. of Rājānaka Rāmakaṇṭha. Kashmir Series of Texts and Studies-64. Srinagar: Research Department, Jammu and Kashmir State, 1943.

— tr. into Eng. by R.C. Zaehner. London: Oxford University Press, 1981.

— tr. into Eng. by Swami Gambhirananda. Calcutta: Advaita Ashrama, 2nd edn, 1991.

— tr. into Eng. by A.M. Sastry. Madras: Samata Books, 1995, Reprint.

Bhāgavata-Purāṇa of Kṛṣṇa Dvaipāyana Vyāsa: ed. and tr. by A.C. Bhaktivedanta Swami Prabhupada. Manila: Bhaktivedanta Book Trust, 1982.

Bhaktirasāmṛtasindhu of Rūpagosvāmin: with 'Durgāsaṅgamanī' Comm. of Jīvagosvāmin and "Bhaktisārapradarśinī" Comm. of Visvanatha Chakravarti, ed. by Shyamdas. Vrindavan, 1981.

—— tr. into Hindi. P.L. Sharma. Delhi: Indira Gandhi National Centre for the Arts and Motilal Banarsidass, 1998.

Bhaktirasāyana of Madhusūdana Sarasvatī: ed. by Janardana Shastri Pandey. Varanasi, 1976.

Bhāradvāja Gṛhyasūtra: ed. by H.J.W. Salomons. New Delhi: Meharchand Lachhmandas, 1981.

Bharata-Bhāṣya of Nānyadeva: ed. by Chaitanya P. Desai. Khairagarh: Indira Kala Sangita Visvavidyalaya, 1961, 1976, 2 parts.

Bhāsanāṭakacakram: ed. by C.R. Devadhara. Delhi: Motilal Banarsidass, 1987.

Bhāṣāpariccheda: Swami Madhavananda. Calcutta: Advaita Ashrama, 2nd edn, 1954.

Bhāskarīya – Bījagaṇita: with the Comm. Navāṅkurā of Kṛṣṇa Daivajña, ed. by V.G. Apte. Ananda Ashram Sanskrit Series-90. Poona, 1930.

Bhāṭṭacintāmaṇi of Gāgā Bhaṭṭa: Varanasi: Chowkhamba, 1933.

Bhāvanākramaḥ of Acarya Kamalaśīla: ed. by Acarya Gyaltsen Namdol. Sarnath: Central Institute of Higher Tibetan Studies, 1985.

Bhāvaprakāśana of Śāradātanaya: ed. by Yatiraja Swami and K.S. Ramaswami Sastri. Baroda: Baroda Oriental Institute, 1986, Reprint.

Bhoja Prabandha: with the Comm. on Kedarnath Sharma. Varanasi: Chowkhamba Vidyabhawan, 3rd edn, 1970.

Bodhicaryāvatāra of Śāntideva: ed. by P.L. Vaidya. Darbhanga: The Mithila Institute, 1960.

— tr. into Eng. by Paramananda Sharma. New Delhi: Aditya Prakashan, 1990, 2 Vols.

Brahma Mahā Purāṇam: ed. by Pt. Nagasharan Singh. Delhi: Nag Publishers, 1985.

Brāhmasphuṭasiddhānta of Brahmagupta: ed. by Ram Swarup Sharma. New Delhi: The Indian Institute of Astronomical and Sanskrit Research, 1966, 4 Vols.

Brahmasūtra: with Śāṅkarabhāṣya. Bombay: Nirnayasagar Press, 1948.

— with Śāṅkarabhāṣya. Delhi: Motilal Banarsidass, 1985.

— tr. into Eng. by G. Thibaut. Sacred Books of the East Series-34,38. Delhi: Motilal Banarsidass, 1890, 1896, 2 Vols.

— ed. and tr. into Eng. by Swami Gambhirananda. Calcutta: Advaita Ashrama, 1983.

— Brahmasūtra-Śrībhāṣya of Rāmānuja: ed. by Uttamur Vira Raghavacharya. Ubhaya Vedant Granthamala. Madras, 1963.

— Vedāntasūtra of Bādarāyaṇa: with the Comm. of Baladeva, tr. into Eng. by Srisa Chandra Vasu. Delhi: Oriental Books Reprint Corporation, 1979.

— Vedāntasūtra: with the Comm. of Rāmānujācārya, tr. into Eng. by G. Thibaut. Sacred Books of the East Series-48. Delhi: Motilal Banarsidass, 1984.

Bṛhaddeśī of Mataṅga Muni: ed. by K. Sāmbaśiva Śāstrī. Trivandrum Sanskrit Series-94. Trivandrum, 1928.

— ed. and tr. into Eng. by Prem Lata Sharma. Kalāmūlaśāstra. Series – 8 and 10. Delhi: Indira Gandhi National Centre for the Arts and Motilal Banarsidass, 1992–1994, 2 Vols.

Bṛhaddevatā of Śaunaka: A Summary of the details and myths of the Ṛgveda, ed. by A.A. Macdonell. Delhi: Motilal Banarsidass, 1965, 2 Vols.

Bṛhat Jātaka of Varāhamihira: ed. by B.V. Raman and tr. into Eng. by B.S. Rao. Delhi: Motilal Banarsidass Publishers, 1998, Reprint.

Bṛhat Saṃhitā of Varāhamihira: ed. and tr. into Eng. by M. Ramakrishna Bhat. Delhi: Motilal Banarsidass, 1981, 1982, 2 Vols.

Buddhacarita of Aśvaghoṣa: ed. and tr. into Hindi by Suryanarayana Chaudhuri. Bihar: Samskrta Bhavana, 1948.

— tr. into Eng. by E.H. Johnston. Delhi: Motilal Banarsidass, 1992.

Buddha-Pratimā Lakṣaṇa: ed. by Haridas Mitra. Benaras, 1993.

C

Campūbhāratam (Bharatacampū) of Ananta: with the Comm. of Ramachandrabudhendra, ed. by Kashinath Pandurang Parab. Bombay: Nirnayasagar Press, 1930.

Campūrāmāyaṇa (Rāmāyaṇa Campū) of Bhoja: with the Comm. of Rāmacandrabudhendra, ed. by K.P. Parab. Bombay: Nirnayasagar Press, 1898.

Carakasaṃhitā: tr. into Eng. by P.V. Sharma. Varanasi: Chaukhamba Orientalia, 1981, 1983, 1985, 3 Vols.

— with the "Āyurveda Dīpikā" Comm. of Cakrapāṇidatta, ed. by Jadavji Trikamji Acarya. Delhi: Munshiram Manoharlal, 4th edn, 1981.

Chandas Śāstram: Śrī Piṅgalācārya with Comm. Mṛtasañjīvanī, by Śrī Halāyudha Bhaṭṭa: ed. by Pt. Kedaranatha, M.M. Pt. Durgaprasada and Wasudeva Laxmana Shastri Panashikara. Varanasi: Chaukhamba Orientalia, 1986, Reprint.

Chandomañjarī of Gaṅgādāsa: ed. with Sanskrit and Hindi Commentaries by Brahmananda Tripathi. Varanasi: Chaukhamba Surabharati Prakashan, 1997.

Citralakṣaṇa: ed. & tr. into Eng. by Asok K. Bhattacharya. Calcutta: Saraswat Library, 1974.

D

Daśabhūmikasūtra: ed. by P.L. Vaidya: Buddhist Sanskrit Text Series-7. Darbhanga: Mithila Institute of Post-Graduate Studies and Research, 1967.

Daśarūpaka of Dhanañjaya: with Comm. of Dhanika, ed. and tr. into Hindi by Bholasankara Vyasa. Varanasi: Chaukhamba Vidyabhavan, 4th edn, 1973.

Daśavaikālika Sūtra: tr. into Eng. by K.C. Lalwani. Delhi: Motilal Banarsidass, 1973.

Dattilam of Dattila: ed. by Sambasiva Sastri. Trivandrum Sanskrit Series-102. Trivandrum, 1930.

— ed. and tr. into Eng. by Mukund Lath. Delhi: Indira Gandhi National Centre for the Arts and Motilal Banarsidass, 1988.

Devatāmūrtiprakaraṇa of Sūtradhāra Maṇḍana: ed. by U.M. Sankhyatirtha. Calcutta Sanskrit Series – 12. Calcutta, 1936.

Devī Bhāgavatam: ed. by Maunalal Abhimanyu. Varanasi: Sanskrit Pustakalaya, 1955.

— tr. into Eng. Swami Vijnanananda. New Delhi: Munshiram Manoharlal Pvt. Ltd., 1921, 4th edn, 1992.

Dhammapada: Pali text, Eng. tr. and notes, ed. by S. Radhakrishnan. Delhi: Oxford University Press, 1950, 8th edn, 1984.

— tr. into Eng. by C. Kunhan Raja. Adyar: Theosophical Publishing House, 1956.

Dhammasaṅgaṇi: ed. by P.V. Bapat & R.D. Vadekar. Poona: Bhandarkar Oriental Research Institute, 1940.

– tr. into Eng. by C.A.F. Rhys Davids. London: The Pali Text Society, 3rd edn, 1974.

Dhvanyāloka of Ānandavardhana: ed. by Pattabhirama Sastri. Varanasi: Chaukhamba Sanskrit Series Office, 1940.

— Dhvanyāloka or Theory of Suggestion in Poetry: tr. into Eng. by K. Krishnamoorthy. Poona Oriental Series-92. Poona: Oriental Book Agency, 1955.

Dīgha Nikāya Pāli: ed. & tr. into Hindi by Swami Dwarikadas Shastri. Varanasi: Bauddha Bharati, 1996, 3 Vols.

Dravya Saṃgraha: Nemichandra Siddhanta Chakravartti, ed. by S.C. Ghoshal. Delhi: Motilal Banarsidass, 1989, Reprint.

G

Gāthā Saptaśatī of King Hāla: ed. and tr. into Eng. by Radhagovinda Basak. Calcutta: The Asiatic Society, 1971.

— The Gāhākośa of Hāla (Sātavāhana): Part II, ed. by M.V. Patwardhan. Delhi: Bhogilal Leherchand Institute of Indology, 1988.

Gaṇaratnamahodadhi of Vasubandhu: ed. by J. Eggeling. Delhi: Motilal Banarsidass, 1968, Reprint.

Gobhila Gṛhyasūtra: with Bhaṭṭanārāyaṇa's Comm., ed. by Chintamani Bhattacharya. Delhi: Munshiram Manoharlal, 2nd edn, 1982.

Gommaṭasāra Jīva-Kāṇḍa of Nemichandra Siddhanta Chakravartti: ed. with tr. into Eng. and Comm. by J.L. Jaini. New Delhi: Today and Tomorrow's Printers & Publishers, 1990, Reprint.

Gopatha Brāhmaṇam: ed. by Vijayapala Vidyavaridhi. Calcutta: Savitri Devi Bagadia Trust, 1980.

Gṛhya Sūtras: tr. into Eng. by H. Oldenberg and F. Max Müller. Sacred Books of the East-29–30. Delhi: Motilal Banarsidass, 1981, 1989, 2 Vols, Reprint.

Guhyasamāja Tantra: ed. by B. Bhattacharya. Baroda: Baroda Oriental Institute, 1967, Reprint.

H

Halāyudhakośa: ed. by Jaya Shankar Joshi. Lucknow: Uttar Pradesh Hindi Samsthan, 3rd edn, 1993.

Haṭhayogapradīpikā: with Jyotsnā Comm. of Brahmānanda, ed. and tr. into Eng. by Srinivasa Iyangar. Madras: Adyar Library, 1975, Reprint.

Hevajra Tantra: A Critical Study, with Yogaratnamālā Comm. of Kanhapada, ed. by D.L. Snellgrove. London: Oxford University Press, 1980, 2 Vols, Reprint.

I

Īśānaśivagurudevapaddhati: ed. by T. Ganapati Sastri. Delhi: Bharatiya Vidya Prakashan, 1988, 4 Vols.

Īśvarapratyabhijñā Kārikā of Utpaladeva: with Vimarśinī by Abhinavagupta, ed. by M.S. Kaul. Kashmir Series of Texts and Studies. Srinagar: Research Department, Jammu and Kashmir State, 1918, 1921, 2 Vols.

Īśvarapratyabhijñāvimarśinī of Abhinavagupta: with the Comm. Bhāskarī, ed. by K.A. Subramaniya Iyer and K.C. Pandey and tr. into Eng. by K.C. Pandey. Delhi: Motilal Banarsidass, 1986, 3 Vols.

J

Jaiminīya Brāhmaṇa: ed. by Raghu Vira and Lokesh Chandra. Delhi: Motilal Banarsidass, 2nd rev. edn, 1986.

Jātaka: ed. by V. Fausboll. Pali Text Society. London: Messrs Luzac & Company Ltd., 1962–1964, 7 Vols, Reprint.

Jātakamālā: ed. & tr. into Hindi by S.N. Chaudhari. Delhi: Motilal Banarsidass, 1991, Reprint.

— tr. into Eng. by J.S. Speyer. Delhi: Motilal Banarsidass, 1971.

Jayākhya Saṃhitā of Pāñcarātra Āgama: ed. by Embar Krishnamacharya. Baroda: Baroda Oriental Institute, 1967.

Jñānārṇava of Śrī Śubhachandāchārya: Published by Śrī Paramaśruta Prabhāvaka Maṇḍala, Śrīmad Rājachandra Āshram, Beriya, Gujarat, 5th edn, 1981.

K

Kalpadrukośa of Keśava: Baroda: Baroda Oriental Institute, 1932.

Kāmakalāvilāsa: with the Comm. of Naṭānandanātha, tr. into Eng. by Arthur Avalon. Madras: Ganesh and Comp. Ltd., 1953.

Kāmasūtra of Vātsyāyana: ed. by Gosvami Damodar Shastri. Banaras:

Chowkhamba Sanskrit Series Office, 1929.

Kapiṣṭhala-Kaṭha Saṃhitā: A Text of the Black Yajurveda, ed. by Raghuvira. Delhi: Meharchand Lachhmandas, 1968.

— Kāṭhaka Die Saṃhitā der Kaṭha Śākhā: ed. by Leopold von Schroeder. Wiesbaden: Franz Steiner Verlag, 1970, 2 Vols.

— Yajurvedīya Kāṭhaka Saṃhitā: ed. by Sripada Damodara Satvalekar. Paradi: Svadhyaya Mandala, 1985.

Kātyāyana Śrautasūtra: tr. into Eng. by H.G. Ranade, Ranade Publication Series. Pune: 1978.

— The Śrautasūtra of Kātyāyana: with extracts from the Comm. of Karka and Yājñikadeva, ed. by Albrecht Weber. Chowkhamba Sanskrit Series. Varanasi: 1972.

Kātyāyana Śulbasūtra: ed. and tr. into Eng. by S.D. Khadilakar. Poona: Vaidika Samsodhana Mandala, 1974.

Kauṣītaki Brāhmaṇa: ed. by E.R. Sree Krishna Sarma. Wiesbaden: Franz Steiner Verlag, 1968, 3 Vols.

Kāvyādarśa of Daṇḍin: with Comm. of Jīvānanda Vidyāsāgara Bhaṭṭācārya, tr. into Eng. by V. Narayana Iyer. Madras, 1952.

Kāvyālaṅkāra of Bhāmaha: ed. and tr. into Eng. by P.V. Naganatha Sastri. Delhi: Motilal Banarsidass, 1991.

Kāvyālaṅkārasūtra of Vāmana: ed. by Narayana Ram Acharya. Varanasi: Motilal Banarsidass, 1983.

Kāvyamīmāṃsā of Rājaśekhara: ed. by S.D. Dalal and R.A. Sastry. Gaekwad's Oriental Series-1. Baroda: Baroda Oriental Institute, 1934.

— with Comm. "Prakāśa", ed. and tr. into Eng. by Ganga Sagar Roy. Varanasi: Chaukhamba Vidyabhavan, 1964.

Kāvyaprakāśa of Mammaṭa: tr. into Eng. by Ganganatha Jha. Varanasi: Bharatiya Vidya Prakashan, 1967.

— with Comm. of Vaman Jhalakikar. Pune: Bhandarkar Oriental Research Institute, 1921.

— with Comm. "Saṅketa". Pune: Ananda Ashrama, 1921.

Khādiragṛhya Sūtra (or Drāhyāyaṇa Gṛhya Sūtra): ed. with Hindi Comm. by Thakur U.N. Singh. Delhi: Chaukhamba Sanskrit Pratisthan, 1991, Reprint.

Kiraṇāvalī of Udayanācārya: ed. and tr. into Bengali by Gaurinath Shastri,

Vol. 2, Calcutta, 1990.

Kulārṇava Tantra: ed. by Tārānātha Vidyāratna with Introduction of Arthur Avalon and Readings of M.P. Pandit. Delhi: Motilal Banarsidass, 1984, Reprint.

Kumārasambhava of Kālidāsa: with Comm. of Mallinātha on 1-8 Cantos, and Comm. of Sitaram on 8-17 Cantos, ed. by Wasudev Laxman Shastri Panasikar. Bombay: Nirnayasagar Press, 1961.

— ed. by M.R. Kale. Delhi: Motilal Banarsidass, 1986.

L

Laghu Yogavāsiṣṭha of Abhinanda: with "Vasiṣṭha Candrikā" Comm., ed. by Wasudeva Laxman Shastri Panasikar. Delhi: Motilal Banarsidass, 1985, Reprint.

Lakṣmī Tantra: Pāñcarātra Āgama, ed. by V. Krishnamacarya. Adyar Library Series-87. Madras: Adyar Library and Research Centre, 1975, Reprint.

Lakṣmī Tantra: A Pāñcarātra Text, tr. into Eng. with notes by Sanjukta Gupta. Leiden: E.J. Brill, 1972.

Lalitavistara: ed. by P.L. Vaidya. Darbhanga: Mithila Institute, 1985.

Laṅkāvatāra Sūtra: ed. by P.L. Vaidya. Darbhanga: Mithila Institute, w.d.

— Tr. into Eng. by D.T. Suzuki. London: Routledge & Kegan Paul Ltd., 1956, Reprint.

Liṅga Purāṇa: ed. by J.L. Shastri. Delhi: Motilal Banarsidass, 1985, Reprint.

M

Mādhavīyā Dhātuvṛtti: by Sāyaṇācārya; ed. by Swami Dwarikadas Shastri. Varanasi: Tara Book Agency, 1983.

Madhyamaka Śāstra of Nāgārjuna: with the Comm. Prasannapadā by Candrakirti; ed. by P.L. Vaidya. Darbhanga: Mithila Institute, 1960.

Mahābhārata: ed. by V.S. Sukhthankar. Poona: Bhandarkar Oriental Research Institute, 1971, 1974, 19 Vols.

— tr. into Eng. by M.N. Dutt. Delhi: Parimal Publications, 1988, 7 Vols.

— tr. into Eng. and ed. by J.A.B. Van Buitenen. Chicago: The University of Chicago Press, 1980, 1981, 1978, 3 Vols.

— tr. into Bengali and ed. by Haridas Siddhantavagisha with the Comm. of "Bhāratabhāvadīpa" and "Bhārata Kaumudī". Calcutta: Vishvavani Prakashani, 1976–93, 43 Vols.

Mahābhāṣya of Patañjali: ed. by F. Kielhorn, revised by K.U. Abhyankar. Poona: Bhandarkar Oriental Research Institute, 1985, 1965, 1972, 3 Vols.

— Paspaśāhnika: tr. into Eng. by K.C. Chatterji. Calcutta, 1957.

La Mahā Nārāyaṇa Upaniṣad: ed. critique, tr. Française... en annexe La Prāṇāgnihotra Upaniṣad per Jean Varenne. Paris: De Boccard, 2nd edn, 1986.

Mahāpurāṇe Ādipurāṇa of Acharya Jinasena: ed. and tr. into Eng. by Pt. Pannalal Jain. New Delhi: Bharatiya Jnanapith Publication, Part I and II, Part I, 4th edn, 1993 and Part II, 3rd edn, 1988.

Mahāpurāṇe Uttarapurāṇa of Acharya Guṇabhadra: ed. and tr. into Eng. by Pt. Pannalal Jain. New Delhi: Bharatiya Jnanapith Publication, 4th edn, 1993.

Mahārthamañjarī of Maheśvarānanda: with the Comm. Parimala, ed. by V.V. Dvivedi. Varanasi: Varanaseya Sanskrit Visvavidyalaya, 1972.

Mahāsubhāṣita Saṅgraha of Ludwig Sternbach: ed. by S. Bhaskaran Nair. Vishveshvarananda Indological Series-71 (New revised edn, 1986 ff.). Hoshiarpur: V.V.R.I., 1977, 5 Vols.

Mahāvīracarita of Bhavabhūti: with Vīrarāghava Comm., ed. by T.R. Ratnam Iyar, S. Rangachariar and K.P. Parab. Bombay: Nirnayasagar Press, 1901.

Mahāyānasūtrālaṅkāra of Ārya Asaṅga: ed. by Swami Dwarikadas Shastri. Varanasi: Bauddha Bharati, 1985.

Mahāyānaviṃśaka of Nāgārjuna: ed. with tr. into Eng. by Pt. Vidhushekhara Bhattacharya. Vishva Bharati Studies-1. Calcutta: Vishvabharati, 1931.

Maitrāyaṇī Saṃhitā: ed. by Sripada Damodar Satavalekar. Paradi: Svadhyaya Mandala, 1942.

— Die Saṃhitā der Maitrāyaṇīya Śākhā, Herausgegeben von Leopold von Schroeder. Wiesbaden: Franz Steiner Verlag GMBH, 1970, 3 Vols.

Majjhima Nikāya: ed. by Rahula Sankrityayana, Vol. II. Nalanda: Bihar Pali Publication Board, 1958.

– ed. & tr. into Hindi by Swami Dwarika Das Shastri. Varanasi: Bauddha Bharati, 1989–1993, 5 Vols.

Mālatīmādhava of Bhavabhūti: with Comm. of Jagaddhara, ed. and Eng. tr. by M.R. Kale. Delhi: Motilal Banarsidass, 3rd edn, 1967.

Mālavikāgnimitram of Kālidāsa: with Comm. of Kāṭayavema, ed. by K.P. Parab. Bombay: Nirnayasagar Press, 5th edn, 1918.

Mālinīvijayottara Tantra: ed. by Madhusūdana Kaul Shastri. Kashmir Series of Texts and Studies-37. Bombay: Research Department, Jammu and Kashmir State, 1922.

Mānameyodaya of Nārāyaṇa: ed. with tr. into Eng. by C. Kunhan Raja and S.S. Suryanarayana Shastri. Madras: Theosophical Publishing House, Adyar, 1933.

— tr. in Hindi by Swami Yogindrananda. Varanasi: Chaukhamba Vidya Bhawan, 2nd edn, 1996.

Mānasāra: tr. into Eng. by P.K. Acharya. Allahabad: Oxford University Press, 1933.

Mānasollāsa of Someśvara: ed. by G.K. Shirgondekar. Gaekwad's Oriental Series. Baroda: Baroda Oriental Institute, 1967, 1939, 1961, 3 Vols.

Manusmṛti of Manu: ed. by J.L. Shastri. Delhi: Motilal Banarsidass, 1983.

— The Laws of Manu: tr. into Eng.by G. Bühler. Sacred Books of the East Series-25. Delhi: Motilal Banarsidass, 1964, Reprint.

Mataṅga Pārameśvarāgama: with Comm. of Bhaṭṭa Rāmakaṇṭha, ed. by N.R. Bhatt. Pondicherry: Institut Français d'Indologie, 1982.

Matsya Purāṇa of Vyāsa: Bombay: Laksmi Venkatesvara Press, 1980.

— ed. by Nag Sharan Singh. Delhi: Nag Publishers, 1983, 2 Vols.

Mayamata: critically ed. and tr. into French by Bruno Dagens. Pondicherry: Institut Français d'Indologie, 1976.

— tr. into Eng. by B. Dagens. Delhi: Indira Gandhi National Centre for the Arts and Motilal Banarsidass, 1994, 1985, 2 Vols.

Meghadūta of Kālidāsa: with Comm. of Mallinātha, ed. and tr. into Eng.by M.R. Kale. Delhi: Motilal Banarsidass, 1987.

Medinīkośa of Medinikara: ed. by J.S. Hoshing. Varanasi: Chowkhamba Sanskrit Series Office, 1968.

Milindapañha Pāli: ed. and Hindi tr. by Swami Dwarikadas Shastri. Varanasi: Bauddha Bharati, 1990.

Mīmāṃsāsūtra of Jaimini: with Śābara Bhāṣya, ed. by Ratna Gopal Bhatta. Varanasi: Chaukhamba Publications, 1910.

— ed. by Ganesh Shastri Joshi. Poona: Ananda Ashram Sanskrit Granthavali – 97. Ananda Ashram, 1981, 6 Vols.

Mṛcchakaṭika of Śūdraka: with the Comm. of Pṛthvīdhara, ed. and tr. into Eng. by M.R. Kale. Bombay: Booksellers Publishing Co., 1962.

Mṛgendrāgama (Kriyāpāda and Caryāpāda): with the Comm. by Bhaṭṭa Nārāyaṇa Kaṇṭha, ed. by N.R. Bhatt. Pondicherry: Institut Français d'Indologie, 1962.

— (Vidyāpāda and Yogapāda): ed. by Madhusudan Kaul Sastri. Kashmir Series of Texts and Studies-50. Srinagar: Research Department, Jammu and Kashmir State, 1930.

Mudrārākṣasa of Viśākhadatta: critically ed. and Eng. tr. by K.H. Dhruva. Poona: Oriental Book Agency, 2nd edn, 1923.

Mūlācāra of Ācārya Vaṭṭakera: with Ācāra Vṛtti – Sanskrit Comm. of Vasunandi Siddhanta Chakravarty, ed. by Pt. Kailashchandra Sastri, Pt. Jaganmohanlal Sastri and Pt. (Dr.) Pannalal Jain., Part - I, 1st edn, 1984, Part - II, 2nd edn, New Delhi: Bharatiya Jnanapitha Publication, 1992.

N

Nāgānanda of Harṣa: ed. by J.M. Ashar. Bhavanagar: Students Publishing Co., w.d.

— tr. into Eng. by Bak Kun Bae. Delhi: Motilal Banarsidass, 1st Indian edn, 1992.

Ṇāṇasāra of Śrī Padmasingh Munirāj: ed. by Pt. T. Jain. Surat: Mulchand Kisandas Kapadiya, Digambara Jaina Pustakalaya, Vira Samvat 2470.

Nārada Bhaktisūtra: ed. and tr. into Eng. by Swami Chinmayananda. Bombay: Chinmaya Mission Trust, 1982.

Nāradīya Śikṣā: with the Comm. of Bhaṭṭa Śobhākar, ed. and tr. into Eng. by Usha R. Bhise. Poona: Bhandarkar Oriental Research Institute, 1986.

Nartananirṇaya of Paṇḍarīka Viṭṭhala: ed. and tr. into Eng. by R. Sathyanarayana. Kalāmūlaśāstra Series-17. Delhi: Indira Gandhi National Centre for the Arts and Motilal Banarsidass, 1994–1998, 3 Vols.

Nāṭyaśāstra of Bharata: with Abhinava Bhāratī Comm., ed. by M. Ramakrishna Kavi and J.S. Pade. Gaekwad's Oriental Series-36, 68, 104-105. Baroda: Baroda Oriental Institute, 4 Vols (Vol. I-Chapts 1-7, 1956; II-Chapts 8-18, 1934; III-Chapts 19-27, 1954; IV-Chapts 28-37, 1964).

Netra Tantra: with the Comm. by Kṣemarāja, ed. by Madhusudana Kaul Shastri.

Kashmir Series of Texts and Studies. Bombay: Research Department Jammu and Kashmir State, 1926, 1936, 2 Vols.

Nighaṇṭu and the Nirukta of Yāska: ed. and tr. into Eng. by Lakshman Sarup. Delhi: Motilal Banarsidass, 1984, Reprint.

— Niruktam (in Bengali): Yāska's Nirukta, ed. by Amareswara Thakur. Calcutta: University of Calcutta, 1955, 1960, 1963, 1970, 4 Vols.

Niṣpannayogāvalī of Abhayākargupta: ed. by B. Bhattacharya. Baroda: Baroda Oriental Institute, 2nd edn, 1972.

Nīti and Vairāgya Śatakas of Bhartṛhari: ed. and tr. into Eng. by M.R. Kale. Delhi: Motilal Banarsidass, 1971.

Nyāya Kusumāñjali of Udayanācārya: ed. & tr. into Eng. by E.B. Cowell. Delhi: Caxston Publishers, 1983, Reprint.

Nyāya Sūtra of Gautama: with Bhāṣya of Vātsyāyana, tr. into Eng. by Ganganatha Jha. Delhi: Motilal Banarsidass, 1984, Reprint.

— tr. into Eng. by Mrinalkanti Gangopadhyaya. Calcutta: Indian Studies, 1982.

P

Padmānanda MahāKāvya of Amarachandra Kavi: ed. by H.R. Kapadia. Baroda: Baroda Oriental Institute, 1932.

Pañcadaśī: tr. into Eng. by Swami Svahananda. Madras: Sri Rama Krishna Math, 4th imp., 1967.

Pañcāstikāyasāra of A. Chakravartinayanar: ed. by A.N. Upadhye. New Delhi: Bharatiya Jnanapith Publication, 1st edn, 1975.

Pāṇinīyaśikṣā: ed. by Man Mohan Ghosh. Delhi: Asian Humanities Press, 1986.

Parānanda Sūtra: ed. by Swami Trivikrama Tirtha. Baroda: Baroda Oriental Institute, 1931.

Parātrīśikā Vivaraṇa of Abhinavagupta: ed. by M.S. Kaul Shastri. Kashmir Series of Texts and Studies-18. Srinagar: Research Department, Jammu and Kashmir State, w.d.

— ed. by B. Bäumer, tr. into Eng. by Jaideva Singh. Delhi: Motilal Banarsidass, 1988.

Pauṣkara Saṃhitā: ed. by P.P Apte. Tirupati: Rashtriya Sanskrit Vidyapeetha,

1st edn, 1991.

Prabodha Candrodaya of Kṛṣṇamiśrayati: with the Nāṭakābharaṇa of Govindāmṛta, ed. by K. Sambasiva Sastri. Trivandrum Sanskrit Series-22. Trivandrum, 1936.

Prakaraṇa Pañcikā of Śālikanātha Miśra: ed. by A. Subramaniyam Shastri. Darśana Series-4. Varanasi: Banaras Hindu University, 1961.

Prapañcasāra Tantra of Śaṅkarācārya: revised by A. Avalon, ed. by Atalananda Sarasvati. Tantric Text Series-19. Delhi: Motilal Banarsidass, 2 parts in one Vol., 1989, Reprint.

Prāsāda Maṇḍana: ed. & tr. into Hindi by Bhagawan Das Jaina. Jayapur: B.S. Sharma, 1963.

Praśamaratiprakaraṇa of Umāsvāti: ed. by Rajkumar. Bombay: Sri Paramasrutaprabhavakamandala, 1950.

Prasthāna Ratnākara of Puruṣottama Gosvāmin: Varanasi: Vidyavilasa Press, 1909.

Pratimālakṣaṇa of Viṣṇudharmottara: ed. & tr. into Eng. by D.C. Bhattacharya. New Delhi: Harman Publishing House, 1991.

Pratimānāṭakam of Bhāsa: with Eng. tr. by M.R. Kale. Bombay: Motilal Banarsidass, 1930, New Delhi: 1991, Reprint.

Pratiṣṭhālakṣaṇa-Sāra-Samuccaya: ed. by Damodara Sharma. Nepal: Rajakiya Pustakalaya, 1st edn, 2023–2025 V.S., 2 Vols.

Pratyabhijñā Hṛdayam of Kṣemarāja: ed. and tr. into Eng. by Jaideva Singh. Delhi: Motilal Banarsidass, 1973.

Priyadarśikā of Śrīharṣa: ed. by R.V. Krishnamachariar. Sri Vani Vilas Sanskrit Series-3. Madras, 1906.

Puggalapaññati: ed. by Bhikkhu J. Kasyap. Nalanda Devanagari Pali Series. Nalanda: Pali Publication Board, Bihar Government, 1960.

— Designation of Human Types (Puggalapaññati): tr. by Bimala Candra Law. London: Messrs Luzac and Company Ltd., 1969.

R

Raghuvaṃśa of Kālidāsa: with Mallinātha Comm., ed. and Eng. tr. by G.R. Nandargikar. Delhi: Motilal Banarsidass, 1982.

Rājataraṅgiṇī of Kalhaṇa: tr. into Eng. and ed. by M.A. Stein. Delhi: Motilal

Banarsidass, 1979, 3 Vols.

Rājavārtika (Tattvārthavārtika) of Shri Akalaṅka Deva: ed. by Prof. Mahendra Kumar Jain. Varanasi: Bharatiya Jnanapitha Kashi, Part I, 1953; Part II, 1957.

Rāmāyaṇa of Vālmīki: with the Tilaka Comm. of Rama, ed. by Wasudev Lakshman Shastri Panasikar. Delhi: Indological Book House, 1983, 2 Vols.

— tr. into Eng. by M.N. Dutt. Patna: Eastern Book House, 1987, 4 Vols, Reprint.

– tr. into Hindi by Dwarka Prasad Sharma. Allahabad: Ram Narayan Lal, 1950.

Rasagaṅgādhara of Jagannātha: with the Comm. of Nāgeśa Bhaṭṭa, ed. by Mathuranatha Sastri. Kāvyamālā Series-12. Bombay: Nirnayasagar Press, 6th edn, 1947.

Ratnāvalī of Śrīharṣa: ed. and Eng. tr. by M.R. Kale. Bombay: Booksellers Publishing Company, 3rd edn, 1964.

Rauravāgama: ed. by N.R. Bhatt. Pondicherry: Institut Français d'Indologie, 1961, 1972, 2 Vols.

Ṛgveda Saṃhitā: ed. by Sripada Damodara Satavalekara. Paradi: Svadhyaya Mandala, 1985, 4 Vols.

— The Hymns of the Rigveda: tr. into Eng. with Comm. by R.T.H. Griffith. Varanasi: Chaukhamba Sanskrit Series Office, 1971, 2 Vols.

Ṛtusaṃhāra of Kālidāsa: with "Haripriyā" Comm., ed. by Laksmiprapannacharya. Varanasi: Chaukhamba Amarabharati Prakashan, 1977.

Rūpamaṇḍana: ed. & tr. into Hindi by Balaram Srivastav. Varanasi: Motilal Banarsidass, 1992, Reprint.

S

Saddharmapuṇḍarīka: ed. with Hindi tr. by Ram Mohan Das. Patna: Bihar Rastrabhasha Parishad, 1966.

– ed. by P.L. Vaidya. Darbhanga: Mithila Institute, 1960.

— The Lotus of the True Law: tr. into Eng. by H. Kern. Sacred Book of the East Series-21, 1884. Delhi: Motilal Banarsidass, 1986, Reprint.

Sāhitya Darpaṇa of Viśvanātha: with Kusumapratibhā Comm., ed. by Haridas

Bhattacharya. Calcutta: Hemacandra Bhattacharya, 1945.

Sakalādhikāra: ed. by V. Gopal Iyengar. T.S.M.S. No. – 141. Tanjavur, 1973.

Samarāṅgaṇa Sūtradhāra of Bhoja: ed. by V.S. Agrawala. Gaekwad's Oriental Series-25. Baroda: Baroda Oriental Institute, 1966.

Sāmaveda: ed. and tr. into Eng. by Devi Chand. Delhi: Munshiram Manoharlal, 1980.

Sāṃkhya Kārikā of Īśvarakṛṣṇa: with Yuktidīpikā Comm., ed. by Ram Chandra Pandeya. Delhi: Motilal Banarsidass, 1967.

Sāṃkhya Sūtra: with Pravacanabhāṣya of Vijñāna Bhikṣu, ed. by R.S. Bhattacharya. Varanasi: Bharatiya Vidya Prakasana, 1977.

— The Sāṃkhya Philosophy: containing Sāṃkhya Pravacana Sūtram, with the Vṛtti of Aniruddha, and the Bhāṣya of Vijñāna Bhikṣu and extracts from the Vṛttisāra of Mahādeva Vedāntin; Tattva Samāsa; Sāṃkhya Kārikā; Pañcaśikha Sūtram, tr. into Eng. by Nandlal Sinha. Delhi: Oriental Books Reprint Corporation, 1979, Reprint.

Samūrtārcanādhikaraṇa: ed. by V. Raghunatha Chakravarti Bhattacharya. Tirupati: Sri Venkatesvara Sanskrit Kala Shala, 1943.

Saṅgītaratnākara of Śārṅgadeva: with Comm. of Siṃhabhūpāla and Kallinātha, ed. by S. Subramanya Sastri. Madras: Adyar Library and Research Centre, 4 Vols, Vol. I. Chapt. I, 1943; II Chapts II-IV, 1944; III Chapts V, VI, 1986; IV Chapt. VII, 1953.

— ed. and Eng. tr. by R.K. Shringy and Prem Lata Sharma. Delhi: Motilal Banarsidass, 1978, Vol. I.

— ed. and Eng. tr. by R.K. Shringy. Delhi: Munshiram Manoharlal Pub. Pvt. Ltd., 1989, Vol. II. and forthcoming Vol. III.

Saṅkalpa Sūryodaya of Veṅkaṭanātha (Vedānta Deśika): with Sanskrit Comm., ed. and Tamil tr. by T. Viraraghavacharya. Madras: India Printing Works, w.d.

Śāṅkhāyana Āraṇyaka: ed. by Sridhar Pathak. Poona: Anand Ashrama, 1987.

— tr. into Eng. by A.B. Keith. London: The Royal Asiatic Society, 1908.

Śāṅkhāyana Brāhmaṇa: ed. by Gulabrao Vajesankara Ojha. Poona: Anand Ashrama, 1977.

Śāṅkhāyana Śrautasūtra: with Comm. of Varadattasutra Ānartīya and Govinda, ed. by A. Hillebrandt. Delhi: Meharchand Lacchmandas, 1981, 4 Vols.

— tr. into Eng. by W. Caland and ed. by Lokesh Chandra. Delhi: Motilal Banarsidass, 1980, Reprint.

Śāradā Tilaka of Lakṣmaṇa Deśikendra: ed. by Arthur Avalon. Varanasi: Motilal Banarsidass, 1933.

Sarasvatīkaṇṭhābharaṇa: ed. by B. Bhattacharya. Varanasi: Banaras Hindu University, 1979.

— ed. by Anundoram Barooah. Assam Publication Board, 1969, Reprint.

Sarvadarśana Saṅgraha of Sāyaṇa – Mādhava: ed. by T.G. Mainkar. Poona: Bhandarkar Oriental Research Institute, 1978.

– tr. into Hindi by Uma Shankar Sharma. Varanasi: Chowkhamba Vidya Bhawan, 1984.

– tr. into Eng. by E.B. Cowell & A.E. Gough. Delhi: Motilal Banarsidass, 1996.

Sarvārthasiddhi of Pūjyapāda: ed. and tr. by Pt. Phoolchandra Shastri. New Delhi: Bharatiya Jnanapith Publication, 5th edn, 1991.

Śatapatha Brāhmaṇa of the White Yajurveda in the Mādhyandina Recension: ed. by A. Chinnaswami Sastri, Pattabhirama Sastri and Ramanatha Diksita. Varanasi: Chaukhamba Sanskrit Sansthan, 1984.

— according to the Mādhyandina recension with the Vedārthaprakāśa Bhāṣya of Sāyaṇācārya, supplemented by the Comm. of Harisvami. Delhi: Gian Publishing House, 1987, 5 Vols.

— according to the text of Mādhyandina recension, tr. into Eng. by Julius Eggeling. Sacred Books of the East Series-12, 26, 41, 43, 44. Delhi: Motilal Banarsidass, 1986, Reprint.

Ṣaṭcakranirūpaṇam: ed. by Tārānātha Vidyāratna and tr. into Eng. by A. Avalon (The Serpent Power), Madras: Ganesh & Co., 3rd rev. edn, 1931.

Ṣaṭkhaṇḍāgama of Puṣpadanta and Bhūtabali: with the Comm. Dhavalā of Vīrasena, Vol. IV, Kṣetra-Sparśana-Kālānugama, ed. by Hiralal Jain. Amraoti, Berar: Published by Shrimanta Seth Shitabrai Laxmichandra, Jaina Sāhitya Uddhāraka Fund Kāryālaya, 1942.

Ṣaṭtriṃśattattva-Sandoha: ed. & tr. into Eng. by D. B. Sensharma. Kurukshetra: B. N. Chakraborty University, 1977.

Sātvata Saṃhitā: ed. by V.V. Dvivedi. Varanasi: Sampurnananda Sanskrit University, 1982.

Saundarananda of Aśvaghoṣa: ed. and tr. into Eng. by E.H. Johnston. Delhi: Motilal Banarsidass, 1975.

Saundaryalaharī of Śaṅkarācārya: ed. and tr. into Eng. by W. Norman Brown. Cambridge: Harvard University Press, 1958.

Siddhāntaleśa Saṅgraha of Sri Appaya Dīkṣita: ed. with the comm. by Jivananda Vidyasagar. Varanasi: Chowkhamba Vidyabhawan, 1992, Reprint.

Siddhāntaśekhara of Śrīpati: with the Comm. of Makki Bhaṭṭa and Babuaji Misra, ed. by Babuaji Misra, Calcutta: University of Calcutta, 1947, 2 Parts.

Śilpa Prakāśa of Rāmacandra Kaulācāra: ed. and tr. into Eng. by Alice Boner and Sadasiva Rath Sarma. Leiden: E.J. Brill, 1966.

Śilparatna of Śrīkumāra: Part II, ed. by K. Sambasiva Sastri. Trivandrum: Deptt. of Publication, Govt. of Travancore, 1929.

Śilparatnakośa of Sthāpaka Nirañjana Mahāpātra: ed. and tr. into Eng. by B. Bäumer and R.P. Das. Kalāmūlaśāstra Series-16. Delhi: Indira Gandhi National Centre for the Arts and Motilal Banarsidass, 1994.

Śiśupālavadha of Māgha: with Comm. of Vallabhadeva, ed. by Ram Chandra Kak and Harabhatta Shastri. Delhi: Bharatiya Book Corporation, 1990.

Śivadṛṣṭi of Śrī Somānandanātha: with the Vṛtti by Utpaladeva, ed. by M.S. Kaul Shastri. Kashmir Series of Texts and Studies-54. Srinagar: Research Department Jammu and Kashmir State, 1934.

Śivamahimnastotra of Puṣpadanta: with the Comm. of Jagannātha Chakravarty, ed. and tr. into Eng. by Arthur Avalon. Madras: Ganesh and Co., 3rd edn, 1953.

Śiva Purāṇa: ed. by Ramtej Pandey. Varanasi: Chowkhamba Vidyabhavana, 1986.

— tr. into Eng. by J.L. Śhastri. Ancient Indian Tradition and Mythology Series-1-4. Varanasi: Motilal Banarsidass, 1981-1988, 4 Vols, Reprint.

Śivastotrāvalī of Utpaladeva: tr. into Eng. by N.K. Kotru. Delhi: Motilal Banarsidass, 1985.

Śiva Sūtras: The Yoga of Supreme Identity, ed. and tr. into Eng. by Jaideva Singh. Delhi: Motilal Banarsidass, 1979.

Śivasūtravimarśinī of Kṣemarāja: ed. by J.C. Chatterjee. Kashmir Series of Texts and Studies-1. Srinagar: Research Department of Jammu and Kashmir State, 1911.

Śivatattvaratnākara of Basavarāja of Keladi: ed. by R. Rama Shastry. Mysore Series – 108 & 112, Mysore: Oriental Research Institute, 1964, 1969, 2 Vols.

Skanda Purāṇa: Calcutta: Manasukharai Mor Prakashan, Vol. I, 1965.

Ślokavārttika of Kumārila Bhaṭṭa: with Comm. "Kāśikā" of Sucarita Misra and

Nyāya Ratnākara of Parthasarathi Mishra, ed. and Eng. tr. by Ganganatha Jha. Delhi: Satguru Publications, 1979.

— ed. and tr. into Eng. by Durgadhar Jha. Darbhanga: Kameshvar Singh Darbhanga Sanskrit Visvavidyalaya Prakashan, 1979.

Smṛtitattva of Raghunandana Bhattacharya: ed. by Jivananda Vidya Sagar Bhattacharya. Calcutta, 2nd edn, 1895, 2 Vols.

Somaśambhupaddhati: ed. and tr. into French by Helene Brunner Lachaux. Pondicherry: Institut Français d'Indologie, 1963.

Spandakārikā: The Divine Creative Pulsation, The Kārikās and the Spanda Nirṇaya of Kṣemarāja, ed. and tr. into Eng. by Jaideva Singh. Delhi: Motilal Banarsidass, 1980.

Śrautakośa: ed. by R.N. Dandekar. Pune: Vaidika Saṃśodhana Maṇḍala, Vol. I, Part I and II, Vol. II, Part I and II, 1962.

Śrītattvacintāmaṇi of Pūrṇānanda: ed. with Comm. and by Bhuvanamohan Sankhyatirtha and Chintamani Bhattacharya. Calcutta: Metropolitan Printing and Publishing House Ltd., 1936.

Śṛṅgāramañjarī Kathā of Bhoja: ed. by Kalpalata Munshi. Singhi Jaina Series -- 30. Bombay: Bharatiya Vidya Bhawana, 1959.

Śṛṅgāra Prakāśa of Bhoja: ed. by G.R. Josyer. Mysore: International Academy of Sanskrit Research, 1955, 1963,1969, 1977, 4 Vols.

Stavamālā: ed. by Bhavadatta Sastri and Sivadatta. Bombay: Nirnayasagar Press, 1903.

Śukranītisāra: tr. by Jagadishvarananda Saraswati. Sonipat: Rishidevi Rupalal Kapur Dharmartha Trust, 1983.

Sūryasiddhānta: ed. by Phanindralal Gangooly. Delhi: Motilal Banarsidass, 1989.

Suśruta Saṃhitā: with "Nibandhasaṅgraha" Comm. of Śrī Ḍalhaṇācārya and Nyāyacandrikā Pañjikā of Gayadāsācārya on Nidānasthāna, ed. by Jadavji Trikamji Acharya. Varanasi: Chaukhamba Orientalia, 1980, Reprint.

— ed. with Eng. tr. by K.L. Bhishagratna. Varanasi: Chowkhamba Sanskrit Series Office, 3rd edn, 1981, 3 Vols.

Suttanipāta: ed. by P.V. Bapat. Delhi: Sri Satguru Publications, 2nd edn, 1990.

Suvarṇa Prabhāsa sūtra: ed. by S. Bagchi. Darbhanga: The Mithila Institute of Post-Graduate Studies & Research in sanskrit Learning, 1967.

Svacchanda Tantra: with the Comm. of Kṣemarāja, ed. by Madhusudana Kaul Sastri. Kashmir Series of Texts and Studies-31, 38, 44, 48, 51, 53, 56. Srinagar: Research Department, Jammu and Kashmir State, 1921-35, 7 Vols.

T

Taittirīya Āraṇyaka: with the Comm. of Bhaṭṭa Bhāskara Miśra, ed. by A. Mahadeva Sastri and K. Rangacarya. Delhi: Motilal Banarsidass, 1985.

Taittirīya Brāhmaṇa: with the Comm. of Sāyaṇācārya, ed. by Narayanasastri Godbole. Sanskrit Granthavali-37. Poona: Ananda Ashram, 3 Vols.

— with the Comm. of Bhaṭṭa Bhāskara Miśra. Delhi: Motilal Banarsidass, 1985, 4 Vols.

Taittirīya Prātiśākhya: with the Comm. Tribhāṣyaratna, ed. by W.D. Whitney. Delhi: Motilal Banarsidass, 1973.

— ed. by R. Samasastri and K. Rangacarya. Delhi: Motilal Banarsidass, 1985.

Taittirīya Saṃhitā of the Black Yajurveda: with the Comm. of Bhaṭṭa Bhāskara Miśra, ed. by A. Mahadevasastri and K. Rangacarya. Delhi: Motilal Banarsidass, 1986, 10 Vols.

— Kṛṣṇayajurvedīya Taittirīya Saṃhitā: ed. by Sripada Damodar Satavalekar. Paradi: Svadhyaya Mandala, 4th edn, 1958.

— Veda of the Black Yajus School entitled Taittirīya Saṃhitā: tr. into Eng. by A.B. Keith. Harvard Oriental Series-18–19. Delhi: Motilal Banarsidass, 1967, 2 Vols.

Tāṇḍyamahābrāhmaṇa: with the Comm. of Sāyaṇācārya, ed. by A. Chinnaswami Sastri. Kashi Sanskrit Granthamala-105. Varanasi: Chaukhamba Sanskrit Series Office, 2nd edn, 1987, 2 Vols.

Tantrāloka of Abhinavagupta: with the Comm. "Viveka" by Rājānaka Jayaratha; ed. by M.R. Sastri and M.S. Kaul. Kashmir Series of Texts and Studies. Srinagar: Research Department, Jammu and Kashmir State, 12 Vols, Vol. I, 1981; II, III, IV, 1921; V, VI, 1922; VII 1924; VIII 1926; IX 1933;X 1936; XI and XII 1938.

— with the Comm. "Viveka" by Rājānaka Jayaratha, ed. by R.C. Dwivedi and Navajivana Rastogi. Delhi: Motilal Banarsidass, 1987, 8 Vols, Reprint.

Tantrasaṅgraha: ed. by M.M. Gopinath Kaviraj. Varanasi: Varanaseya Sanskrit Visvavidyalaya, 1970, 2 Vols.

Tantrasāra of Abhinavagupta: ed. by M.S. Kaul. Kashmir Series of Texts and Studies-17. Srinagar: Research Department, Jammu and Kashmir State, 1981.

Tantravārttika: tr. into Eng. by M.M.G.N. Jha, Delhi: Sri Satguru Publications, 2nd edn, 1983.

Tarkasaṅgraha of Annambhaṭṭa: tr. into Eng. by M.R. Bodas. Bombay Sanskrit Series-45. Bombay: The Department of Public Instruction, 1930.

Tattvacintāmaṇi of Gaṅgeśa Upādhyāya: with Comm. "Prakāśa". Darbhanga: Mithila Vidyapith, 1957.

Tattvārthādhigama Sūtra of Umāsvātivācakācārya: ed. by Pt. Motilal Ladhaji. Pune, Vira Samvat 2453.

Tattvasaṅgraha of Śāntarakṣita: with the Comm. of Kamalaśīla, ed. by Embar Krishnamacharya. Baroda: Baroda Central Library, 1926, 2 Vols.

— tr. into Eng. by Ganganatha Jha. Baroda: Baroda Oriental Institute, 1937, 1939, 2 Vols.

Tilakamañjarī of Dhanapala: Kāvyamala No. 85. Bombay: Nirnaya Sagar Press, 1938.

Tiloya Paṇṇattī: ed. by A.N. Upadhye & Hiralal Jain. Sholapur: Solapuriyo Jaina-Samskriti Samraksaka Samgha, 1956, 2 Vols.

Trikaṇḍaśeṣa Kośa: ed. by R.S. Bhattacharya, Varanasi: Ratna Publications, 1995.

U

Ubhayābhisārikā of Vararuci: ed. by V.S. Agrawala and Moti Chandra. Bombay: Hindi Grantha Ratnakara Karyalay, 1959.

Udāna: ed. by Paul Steinthal. London: Oxford University Press, 1948, Reprint.

Udayasundarī Kathā: ed. by C. D. Dalal & E. Krishnamacharya. Baroda: Baroda Oriental Institute, 1920.

Ujjvalanīlamaṇi of Rūpa Gosvāmin: Delhi: Chaukhamba Sanskrit Pratisthan, 1984.

Upaniṣads:

— Upaniṣatsaṅgraha: ed. by J.L. Shastri. Delhi: Motilal Banarsidass, 1970.

— Eighteen Principal Upaniṣads (Aṣṭādaśa Upaniṣadaḥ): ed. by V.P. Limaye and R.D. Vadekar. Poona: Vaidika Saṃśodhana Maṇḍala, 1958.

— Thirteen Principal Upanishads: tr. into Eng. by R.E. Hume. Delhi: Oxford University Press, 1983, Reprint.

Uttararāmacarita of Bhavabhūti: with the Comm. of Ghanaśyāma, ed. by P.V. Kane and C.N. Joshi. Delhi: Motilal Banarsidass, 1962.

— With the Comm. of Vīrarāghava, ed. and tr. into Eng. by M.R. Kale. Delhi: Motilal Banarsidass, 1993, Reprint.

Uvāsagadasāo: ed. by N.A. Gore. Poona, 1953.

V

Vaijayantīkośa of Śrī Yādavaprakāśācārya: ed. by Pt. Haragovinda Shastri Mishra. Varanasi: Chowkhamba Sanskrit Series Office, 1971.

Vaiśeṣika Sūtra Bhāṣya: tr. into Eng. by M.M.G.N. Jha, 1915. Benares: Chowkhamba Orientalia, 1982, Reprint.

Vaiśeṣika Sūtra of Kaṇāda: with Bhāṣya of Praśastapāda and Comm. 'Upaskāra', ed. by Dhundhiraja Sastri. Varanasi: Chaukhamba, 1923.

Vaitānasūtra: The Ritual of the Atharvaveda, ed. by R. Garbe. New Delhi: Mahalaksmi Publication House, 1982.

Vakroktijīvita of Rājānaka Kuntaka: ed. by Sushil Kumar De. Calcutta: Firma K.L. Mukhopadhyay, 3rd edn, 1961.

Vākyapadīya of Bhartṛhari: with the Comm. of Puṇyarāja and Vṛtti, ed. by K.A. Subramania Iyer. Delhi: Motilal Banarsidass, 1966.

Vāmana Mahāpurāṇam: ed. by Pt. Nagasharan Singh. Delhi: Nag Publishers, 1983.

Vāstusūtra Upaniṣad: The Essence of Form in Sacred Art, ed. and tr. into Eng. by Alice Boner, Bettina Bäumer and Sadasiva Rath Sharma. Delhi: Motilal Banarsidass, 1982.

Vedānta Paribhāṣā: tr. into Eng. by Swami Madhavananda. Howrah: Ramakrishna Mission Sharada Pitha, Belur Math, 1963.

Vedānta Sāra: ed. by Nikhilananda Swami. Calcutta: Advaita Ashrama, 1974.

Veṇīsaṃhāra of Bhaṭṭa Nārāyaṇa: ed. and tr. into Eng. by R.S. Venkatarama Sastri. Madras: Malati Trades, 1943.

Vibhaṅga Pāli: ed. by Bhikkhu J. Kashyap. Nalanda: Pali Publication Board, Bihar Government, 1960.

— The Book of Analysis: ed. and tr. into Eng. by P.A. Thiṭṭila. London: Luzac and Company Limited, 1969.

Vijñānabhairava: ed. and Eng. tr. by Jaideva Singh. Delhi: Motilal Banarsidass, 1979.

— with the Comm. of Kṣemarāja and Śivopādhyāya, ed. by M.R. Shastri. Kashmir Series of Texts and Studies-8. Srinagar: Research Department, Jammu and Kashmir, 1918.

Vijñaptimātratāsiddhi: ed. and tr. into Eng. by K.N. Chatterjee. Varanasi: Kishor Vidya Niketana, 1980.

Vikramorvaśīyam of Kālidāsa: ed. by Surendra Nath Shastri. Bombay: Nirnayasagar Press, 1942.

Vimalaprabhā of Kalki Śrī Puṇḍarīka: A Comm. on Śrī Laghukālacakratantrarāja of Śrī Mañjuśrīyaśa, Vol. I, ed. by Jagannatha Upadhyaya. Bibliotheca Indo-Tibetica Series 11, Vol. II–III, ed. by V. Dwivedi and S.S. Bahulkar, Rare Buddhist Text Series 12–13. Varanasi: C.I.H.T.S., 1986, 1994.

Vinaya Piṭaka: ed. by J. Takakusu and Makoto Nagai. London: Pali Text Society, 1947.

Viṣṇudharmottara Purāṇa: ed. by Priyabala Shah. Gaekwad's Oriental Series. Baroda: Baroda Oriental Institute, 1958, 1961, 2 Vols.

Viṣṇu Purāṇa: Gorakhpur: Gita Press, 1961.

— tr. into Eng. by H.H. Wilson. London: Trubner and Co., 1864, 4 Vols.

Viṣṇusmṛti with Keśavavaijayantī Ṭīkā: ed. by Pt. V. Krishnamacharya. Adyar Library Series-93-94. Madras: Adyar Library and Research Centre, 1964, 2 Vols.

Visuddhimagga: ed. by Dharmananda Kosambi. Bombay: Bharatiya Vidya Bhawan, 1940, 2 Vols.

— ed. by Revatdhamma. Varanasi: Varanaseya Sanskrit University, 1962.

— The Path of Purification: tr. into Eng. by Bhikkhu Ñyāṇamoli. Srilanka: Buddhist Publication Society, 1979, 2 Vols. Reprint.

Viśvāmitra Saṃhitā: ed. by U.S. Bhatta. Tirupati: Rashtriya Sanskrit Vidyapeetha, 2nd edn, 1991.

Vṛttaratnākara: ed. by Aryendra Sharma. Hyderabad: Sanskrit Academy, Osmania University, 1969.

Vyaktiviveka of Rājānakamahimabhaṭṭa: with the Comm. of Rājānaka Ruyyaka, ed. by Madhusudana Mishra. Haridas Sanskrit Granthamala-121. Benaras: Chowkhamba Sanskrit Series, 1936.

Y

Yājñavalkya Śikṣā: with the Comm. "Śikṣāvallī", ed. by Amaranath Sastri. Kashi: Padmanabha Sharma Diksit, 1937.

Yājñavalkyasmṛti of Yājñavalkya: with Mitākṣarā Comm. of Vijñāneśvara, ed. by Umesh Chandra Pandey. Varanasi: Chowkhamba Sanskrit Sansthana, 1983, 2 Vols.

— with Mitākṣarā Comm., tr. by Srisa Chandra Vidyarnava. Allahabad: Panini Office, 1918, Book I.

Yajurveda Saṃhitā: ed. by S.D. Satavalekara. Paradi: Svadhyaya Mandala, 1957.

— The Text of the White Yajurveda, tr. into Eng. with Comm. by R.T.H. Griffith. Banaras: E.J. Lazarus and Co., 1957.

Yogasārasaṅgraha of Vijñānabhikṣu: tr. into Eng. by Ganganatha Jha. New Delhi: Akay Book Corporation, 1986.

Yogasūtra of Patañjali: with the Comm. of Vyāsa and Gloss of Vācaspatimiśra, tr. into Eng. by Rama Prasada. Allahabad: Panini Office, 1924.

— tr. into Eng. by J.H. Woods. Delhi: Motilal Banarsidass, 1988, Reprint.

— with the Vyāsa Bhāṣya, tr. into Eng. by Bangali Baba. Delhi: Motilal Banarsidass, 1982, Reprint.

Yoginī Hṛdaya: with "Dīpikā" Comm. of Amṛtānanda and "Setubandha" of Bhāskarācārya, ed. by M.M. Gopinath Kaviraj. Banaras: Govt. Sanskrit Library, Saraswati Bhavan, 1923.

— ed. by Vrajavallabha Dwivedi. Varanasi: Motilal Banarsidass, 1988.

Reference Works

Bharatakośa: A dictionary of technical terms with definitions collected from the work on Music and Dramaturgy by Bharata and others, ed. by M. Ramakrishna Kavi. Delhi: Munshiram Manoharlal, 1983.

Bhāratīya Vyāvahāra Kośa: ed. by V.D. Narawane. Pune: Meheta Publishing House, 3rd edn, 1993.

Buddhist Hybrid Sanskrit Grammar and Dictionary: ed. F. Edgerton. New Haven, U.S.A.: 1953.

Concordance to the Principal Upanishads and Bhagavadgītā: ed. by G.A. Jacob. Delhi: Motilal Banarsidass, 1985.

A Dictionary of Hinduism: Its Mythology, Folklore and Development 1500 B.C.–A.D. 1500, ed. by Margaret and James Stutley. London: Routledge & Kegan Paul, 1985, Reprint.

Dictionary of Indology: complied by A.K. Roy and N.N. Gidwani. Delhi: Oxford & IBH Comm., 1983, 4 Vols.

Encyclopaedia Indica – Hindi Viśvakośa: ed. by Nagendra Nath Vasu. Delhi: B.R. Publishing, 1986, 25 Vols., Reprint.

Encyclopaedia of Indian Literature: Chief editor Amaresh Datta. New Delhi: Sahitya Akademi, 1987, 1988, 1989, 3 Vols.

Encyclopaedia of Indian Philosophies: Gen. ed. Karl H. Potter. Delhi: Motilal Banarsidass, 1970–1999, 8 Vols.

Encyclopedia of Indian Temple Architecture, South India: ed. by M.A. Dhaky, Vol.I, Part 3. New Delhi: AIIS and IGNCA, 1996.

Encyclopaedia of Puranic Beliefs and Practices: ed. by Sadashiv Ambadas Dange. 3 Vols; Vol. I-A-C. 1986; Vol. II-D-G. 1987; Vol. III-H-N., 1987. Delhi: Navarang.

Encyclopaedia of Religion: ed. by Mircea Eliade. New York: MacMillan Publication Company, 1987, 16 Vols.

Encyclopaedia of Religion and Ethics: ed. by James Hastings. Edinburgh: T & T Clark, 1979, 12 Vols.

Encyclopaedia of the Upaniṣads: ed. by N.S. Subrahmanin. Delhi: Sterling Publishers, 1985.

An Encyclopaedic Dictionary of Sanskrit on Historical Principles: Gen. editors A.M. Ghatage & S.D. Joshi. Poona: Deccan College Postgraduate and Research Institute, 1976–1995, 5 Vols.

A Glossary of Indian Figures of Speech: ed. by Edwin Gerow. Paris: Mouton, 1971.

Hindi Viśvakośa: ed. by Nagari Pracharini Sabha. Varanasi: 1986, 12 Vols.

Hindu World: An Encyclopaedic Survey of Hinduism: ed. by Benjamin Walker. Delhi: Munshiram Manoharlal, 1983, 2 Vols.

A History of Indian Literature: ed. by J. Gonda (Chief editor). Wiesbaden: Otto Harassowitz, Several Vols.

Iconographic Dictionary of the Indian Religions – Hinduism – Buddhism – Jainism: ed. by Gösta Lievert. Delhi: Sri Satguru Publications, 1986.

The Illustrated Dictionary of Hindu Iconography: ed. by Margaret Stutley. London: Routledge & Kegan Paul, 1985.

Jainendra Siddhānta Kośa of Jinendra Varni: New Delhi: Bharatiya Jnanapith Publication, 4 Vols, Vol. I. 4th edn, 1993, Vol. II. 3rd edn, 1992, Vol. III. 2nd edn, 1987, Vol. IV. 2nd edn, 1988.

Kalātattvakośa: Gen. ed. Kapila Vatsyayan. New Delhi: Indira Gandhi National Centre for the Arts and Motilal Banarsidass Publishers Pvt. Ltd., 1988, 1992, 1996, 1999, 4 Vols.

Kurzgefasstes Etymololgiches Wörterbuch des Altindischen: A Concise Etymological Sanskrit Dictionary: ed. by Manfred Mayrhofer. Heidelberg: Universitätsverlag, 1956, 4 Vols (New revised edn, 1987 ff.).

Pali-English Dictionary: ed. by T.W. Rhys Davids and William Stede. New Delhi: Munshiram Manoharlal Publishers Pvt. Ltd., 1989, Reprint.

Pauranic Kośa: ed. by Rana Prasad Sharma. Varanasi: Jñāna Maṇḍala, 1950.

Puranic Encyclopaedia: ed. by Vettam Mani. Harvard Oriental Series-10. Delhi: Motilal Banarsidass, 1964, Reprint.

The Practical Sanskrit-English Dictionary: V.S. Apte. Delhi: Motilal Banarsidass, 1992, Reprint.

The Sanskrit-English Dictionary: M. Monier-Williams. Oxford University Press, 1986, Reprint.

Sanskrit-Wörterbuch: O. Böhtlingk, & R. Roth. 7 Vols (1855–1875).Delhi: Motilal Banarsidass, 1990, Reprint.

Vedic Experience: Mantramañjarī: An Anthology of the Vedas for Modern Man and Contemporary Celebration: ed. by R. Panikkar. Delhi: Motilal Banarsidass, 1983.

Vedic Index of Names and Subjects: ed. by A.A. Macdonell & A.B. Keith. Delhi: Motilal Banarsidass, 1982, 2 Vols.

Wörterbuch zum Rig-Veda: H. Grassmann. Wiesbaden: Otto Harrassowitz, 5th edn, 1976.

INDEX

A

B

C

D

E

F

H

I

J

K

L

M

N

O

P

Q

R

S

T

U

V

W

Y

Z

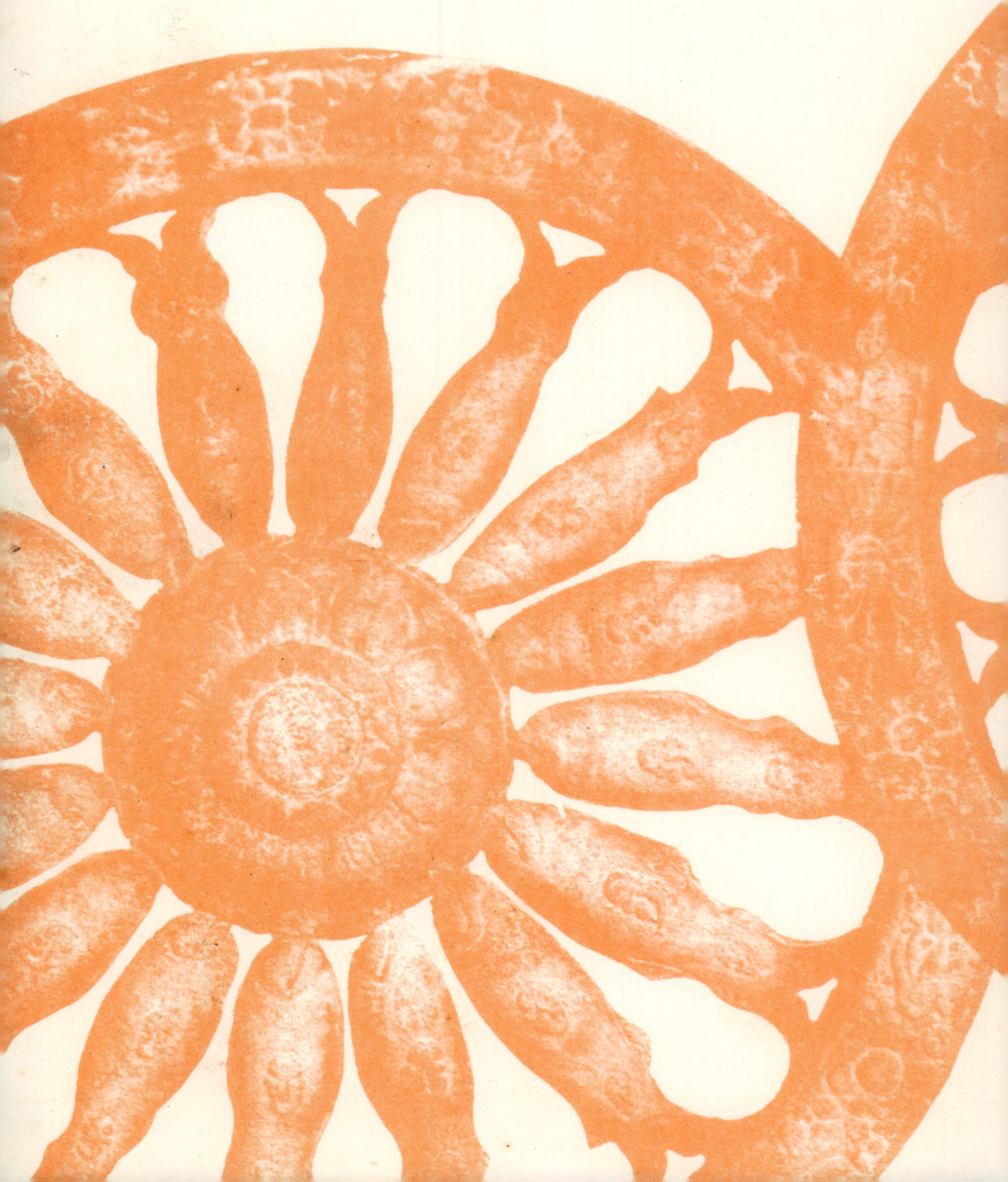